D1563585

Public life and late capitalism

Public life and late capitalism

Toward a socialist theory of democracy

JOHN KEANE

The Polytechnic of Central London

CAMBRIDGE UNIVERSITY PRESS

Cambridge

London   New York   New Rochelle

Melbourne   Sydney

Published by the Press Syndicate of the University of Cambridge
The Pitt Building, Trumpington Street, Cambridge CB2 1RP
32 East 57th Street, New York, NY 10022, USA
296 Beaconsfield Parade, Middle Park, Melbourne 3206, Australia

First published 1984

Printed in the United States of America

Library of Congress Cataloging in Publication Data
Keane, John, 1949–
Public life and late capitalism.
Includes bibliographical references and index.
1. Democracy – Addresses, essays, lectures.
2. Bureaucracy – Addresses, essays, lectures. 3. Socialism –
Addresses, essays, lectures. I. Title.
JC423.K36 1984 321.8 83-10584
ISBN 0 521 25543 0

Contents

Acknowledgments

I should like to express my thanks to Susan Allen-Mills of Cambridge University Press for her insightful and helpful editorial advice. I am also indebted to a number of friends, to whose suggestions and criticisms of earlier drafts of these essays I tried hard to respond: Andrew Arato, David Beetham, William Carey, Anthony Giddens, Michael Ignatieff, Ernesto Laclau, Dieter Misgeld, Chantal Mouffe, James O'Connor, Claus Offe; Carole Pateman, Paul Piccone, David Wolfe, and Irving Zeitlin. For their constant encouragement and support, I should especially like to thank David Held, Paul Mier, and my best critic, Nancy Wood. Finally, I wish to acknowledge that these essays were written originally under the guidance of C. B. Macpherson, whose quiet helpfulness and always discerning criticisms forced me to think more freely about the subjects of socialism and democracy. With respect and gratitude, these essays are dedicated to him.

J.K.
London, August 1983

Introduction

Within the late capitalist world the prospects for democratic socialism have been seriously weakened during the past four decades by the dogmatic assumption that socialism and democracy were destined to advance *pari passu*. Social democracy has been the most influential version of this dogma, which has served to justify new forms of bureaucratic domination while at the same time impeding the renewal of theories of democratic autonomy. According to the theory of social democracy, the defense of democracy is virtually equivalent to the struggle to win control over bureaucratic state institutions; to utilize their directive capacity in economic, social, and foreign policy matters; and thereby to weaken or negate the power of private capital and the inequalities and unfreedoms for which it is responsible. No doubt, some tendencies within social democracy envisaged the "withering away" of state and capitalist institutions as an ultimate socialist goal. For the time being, however, political power was considered to be an indispensable condition of political and social change. State power was necessary to consolidate already existing socialist achievements, and to protect these accomplishments and future changes against the sabotage and retaliatory actions of "antisocialist" elements. In opposition to these elements of resistance, the bureaucratic state would become the temporary caretaker of existence. Ingraining itself into social life by pursuing redistributive strategies that secured capital investment, the reduction of unemployment, and the expansion of social security provision, it would make possible the securing of justice and equality between individuals and groups. An age of democratic "sociability," of unrestricted production and generous welfare services, would thereupon begin.

This forecast presumed a more "democratic" order to be both a necessary condition and a consequence of the path to socialism. The democratic qualities of social democracy were said to consist not only in its anticapitalist policies of redistribution. The state's socialization of property relations in the name of democracy would be reinforced by its commitment to the "equilibrium model" of democracy (Macpherson), that is, its acceptance of the conventional mechanisms of choosing and authorizing governments – mechanisms, such as periodic elections, the rule of law, and the sovereignty of legislatures, that ensured competition between political party elites. Convinced of the necessity of this cluster of mechanisms, social democracy further assumed that social groups would not engage in autonomous political judgments; cast in the role of passive citizens,

1

the populations of late capitalist countries would rather choose political elites, which in turn would acquire the power to decide by means of a competitive struggle for the votes of their constituents. This *dirigiste* model of equilibrium democracy was regarded as self-evidently emancipatory; in the confident view of social democracy, the cooperative and democratic society could be achieved by installments through the gradual extension of networks of bureaucratic state power.

What is striking about this presumption concerning the necessary relationship between democracy and socialism is the degree of truncation of the concept of democracy itself. If by democracy we mean, very loosely speaking, a differentiated and pluralistic system of power, wherein decisions of interest to whole collectivities are made autonomously by all their members, then from a normative point of view, postwar social democracy can be seen to have effected a decisive (and regressive) shift in the meaning of this concept. Through some ill-explained hermeneutic, democracy becomes equivalent to the transmission of decisions from the governors to the governed. Formerly recognized as the main procedure for limiting the abuse of authoritarian power, democracy becomes the ally of heteronomy, and democratic socialism becomes virtually synonymous with the bureaucratization of existence within the domains of state and society.

The various assumptions of social democracy are described here in an admittedly abbreviated manner. There can however be little doubt about their considerable influence upon the social organization and political life of late capitalist countries. From the circles of its own party-political organizations to the state institutions it has occupied and expanded, this social democracy has greatly accelerated the bureaucratization of contemporary life. It has contributed to the further apportionment of everyday life, the labeling and confining of individuals and groups, and the strengthening of a whole system of institutions that regulate and program life through bureaucratic-professional techniques. Social democracy is not, however, without its dilemmas and self-contradictions, and indeed there is growing evidence that it is rapidly ceasing to be a viable and legitimate political option under late capitalist conditions. Especially under pressure from slowdowns and transformations within the world economy and controversies about state bureaucracy, it has become evident that the social democratic goal of securing an age of democratic "sociability" through administrative means is much more difficult to achieve than its advocates have until now assumed.

This at least is the point of departure of the theoretical essays assembled here. Structured in the form of an immanent critique of the bureaucratizing tendencies to which social democracy has strongly contributed, these essays are guided by the conviction that the radical reform of late capitalist societies depends crucially upon the weakening of the power of corporate and state bureaucracies through the establishment and strengthening of spheres of autonomous public life. In the perspective of these essays, a public sphere is brought into being whenever two or more individuals, who previously acted singularly, assemble to interrogate both their own interactions and the wider relations of social and political power within which they are always and already embedded. Through this autonomous association, members of public spheres consider what they are doing, settle how they will live together, and determine, within the estimated limits of the means available to them, how they might collectively act within the foreseeable future. From the point of view of democratic socialism, the permanent elimination of public spheres in this sense would be as disastrous today as the loss of the common land was to the peasantry of the Middle Ages. The arguments offered in support of this conviction draw extensively from traditions of twentieth-century German political thought, especially the contributions of Max Weber, Jürgen Habermas, and Claus Offe, and are in turn bound together by three interconnected theses. These theses are very briefly summarized here. Considered together, they may be seen as a contribution to the renewal of socialist theories of democracy and, more precisely, as a preliminary effort to rethink and clarify what it means to speak of the democratic road to socialism.

According to the first thesis presented here, late capitalist societies live under the continuously lengthening shadow of professionally staffed, bureaucratic organizations. Everywhere in the late capitalist world, and especially in its North Atlantic heartlands – countries such as the United States of America, the Federal Republic of Germany, France, and Great Britain – bureaucratic rationality tends to become a way of life. Within these countries, the nineteenth-century hope that the governance of persons would give way to the administration of things is being realized, albeit in a highly inverted and debased form. Not only things but also persons themselves are becoming drawn into multiple and extensive forms of bureaucratic administration and control. This "rationalization" of daily life is not restricted to the dynamics of the labor–capital relationship within the factory. As Max Weber first convincingly argued, the orthodox Marxian critique of capitalist domination at the point of production is misleading, precisely because of its incompleteness; the control of the wage laborer by capital is but one instance of a more extensive and highly complex process of bureaucratization. The evident converse of this point is that relations of bureaucratic power are not restricted to the sphere of state administration, upon whose mode of operation the apparatuses of capitalist production and consumption have come increasingly to depend. The various references to bureaucracy as rule by political officials first developed by Christian Kraus, Johan Görres, J. S. Mill, and others must now be modified; the term *bureaucracy* can no longer be deployed to characterize only the processes of state policy making and administration.

Admittedly, to speak in the terms of this first thesis is to risk minimizing the distinction between late capitalist and bureaucratic socialist regimes, to stress rather their continuity. These essays do not intend this error, for they emphasize that the powerful networks of bureaucratic organization that penetrate and organize late capitalist life do not entirely obliterate the distinction between society and the state – a feature that crucially distinguishes late capitalist orders from bureaucratic socialist regimes. In the latter, state bureaucracies strive to define, pacify, and sometimes terrorize life from the household to the factory, from the cradle to the grave. The basic economic, political, and cultural means are monopolized by a hierarchically organized, bureaucratic apparatus – the Party-supervised command state – which aims to make impossible the growth of centers of power external to it. Legitimated by claims concerning the sovereignty of the party form, political bureaucracy has a global, even if crisis-ridden, character: It rules over the whole of society, and it is premised upon the disappearance and repression of autonomous spheres of public action.*

Under late capitalist conditions by contrast, the elimination of the distinction between social and political life is not yet a reality; by virtue of the systematic antagonisms between capitalist and state bureaucracies, for example, late capitalist systems do not converge toward bureaucratic socialist systems. Social and state institutions are nevertheless becoming more and more interdependent. As Hilferding and others long ago pointed out, late capitalist orders are not composed of "naturally" free individuals and autonomous social organizations that check and restrain the bureaucratic collectivism of state power. Bureaucratic relations of command and obedience are on the advance within *all* spheres of contemporary life—from the fields of incarceration, communications, and health to those of production, education, law, and public policy formation. Guided by this thesis, these essays draw attention to the ways in which the most modern and advanced factories and offices come to resemble schools, hospitals, and prisons, in which managerial and professional groups strive to define, monitor, and control life, health, and death. Within the sphere of mass communications, it is observed that the directors of radio, film, television, and news agencies seek to prescribe the exact type and amount of culture to be digested by their publics. The monitoring, disciplining influence of professionally staffed, bureaucratic organization is seen as extending even to the most intimate spheres of household life.

Correctly understood, then, bureaucratization processes are on the advance within the realms of state *and* society, in both public and private spheres of late capitalist life. Within both of these spheres the traditional means of coercion and control are gradually being downgraded or phased out; the exercise of manipulative power tends increasingly to rely upon techniques of supervision, professionalism, and science and technology. As a consequence, bureaucracies are forming themselves into an all-encompassing circle, from which it seems no one is permitted to escape.

This process of encirclement is of course conditional upon the propensity of bureaucratic organizations for securing the regularized discipline of their members and clients. The bureaucratic will to administer the populations of late capitalist countries forms the second thesis of these essays. It is argued that all

* This is one crucial reason why the establishment of autonomous public spheres is a qualitatively more dangerous project within bureaucratic socialist regimes than under late capitalist conditions. This point is movingly expressed in the exhortation of György Konrád: "Freedom can be practiced wherever you are. Talk to others and don't dissemble; go public. You are surrounded by secretive section chiefs, department heads, assistant heads. The lowliest official is proud of his secrets, even kindergarteners learn to watch what they say. In our region a revolutionary is one who shuns secrets. So go public, be naïve, and catch your friends at their naïve best....Whether you are free or not will always be decided in the very next minute. You could be on a street corner waiting for a bus, in your room waiting for a telephone call, in bed waiting for a dream" ("Letter from Budapest," *New York Review of Books*, 5 November 1981, p. 49).

bureaucratic organizations tend to institute highly differentiated arrangements of privileges, tasks, and responsibilities, one of whose fundamental organizing principles is depoliticization. This thesis cuts across the grain of a long tradition of liberal theory, which supposes that the antagonistic relationship between bureaucracy and democracy derives simply from the tendency of state officials to defeat the aims and methods of equilibrium democracy. This supposition is misleading, inasmuch as bureaucracies nowadays thrive upon dependent and unquestioning subjects who accept the normalcy and necessity of bureaucratic relations of command and obedience. Feeding upon the depoliticization they themselves tend to produce, both private and public bureaucracies consequently strive to plunge their roots deeply into all social and political relations. Under late capitalist conditions, bureaucratic organizations tend to become institutions of everyday routine. Daily life comes under the generalized influence of networks of hierarchical organizations, each managed by directors, professionals, and expert advisers, each employing legal advisers, security staff, and publicity agents, each out to transform unorganized populations into reliable instruments for the achievement of the goals of the organization. This means, from the point of view of this second thesis, that ruling bureaucratic minorities seek to institute decisions in the absence of discussion and control from below. Questions pertaining to the organizational form and its goals tend to be decided through authoritarian and formally rational means. Everywhere bureaucratic organizations feed not only upon cults of prestige and authority – a feature of all oligarchy, of which bureaucracies are only one form – but also, and more important, upon the will to master and administer spheres of life professionally, to constitute them as depoliticized objects of possible technical control.

Theoretical justifications of this process of bureaucratic subordination have of course enjoyed a certain notoriety during recent decades. Together, these justifications of depoliticization may be seen to have produced something like a "metaphysical pathos" (Gouldner), that is, a reinforcement of the fatalistic belief that there is no escape from the imperatives of bureaucracy. Numerous examples of this pathos are critically examined through the course of these essays: the "equilibrium model" of democracy and the security state proposed by social democracy; the "refeudalization" of the concept of public life; official concern with the "government" of populations; the degradation of the classical concept of politics and early liberal theories of legitimate power; and, finally, the rise of various forms of scientific-technical discourse.

Most of these "ideologies" of depoliticization are in one way or another heavily indebted to Max Weber, whose penetrating analyses of bureaucracy are considered here (Essays 2, 4, and 7) to constitute a profound obstacle to a socialist theory of public life. Of course, to implicate Weber within the metaphysical pathos surrounding bureaucratic domination seems at first sight harsh and misleading, for he was concerned to challenge the unquestioning idolization of bureaucracy. Not all events and things, he insisted, can be defined and controlled through bureaucratic means; abstract and calculating bureaucratic organizations stifle particular needs and events, and systematically produce a loss of sense of political purpose. The technical superiority of these organizations nevertheless ensures their continuous expansion, an advance that Weber for the most part defended as indispensable. Under contemporary conditions, he concluded, the renunciation of the struggle for democratic public life becomes imperative; only "passive democratization" is possible.

In the view of these essays, this conclusion is highly unconvincing. Weber's defense of the necessity of bureaucracy is seen as marked by several decisive weaknesses. Two of these can be briefly mentioned here, because together they force the conclusion that Weber conspicuously failed to demonstrate the impossibility of defending autonomous public life against the "forward progress" of bureaucratic domination. In the first place, he overestimated the technical and administrative proficiency of bureaucratic organizations; he thereby understated the persistent tendency of these organizations to subvert their own claims to discharge business efficiently and in accordance with professional, formally rational rules. The second weakness is linked with this first deficiency: Weber failed to analyze the ways in which the bureaucratic will to define, administer, and depoliticize all reality systematically prevents bureaucracies from securing the discipline of those under their tutelage. Weber too readily assumed that always and everywhere politics is for most people naturally an avocation; he therefore seriously misjudged the degree to which bureaucracies would catalyze power struggles in defense of the principle of autonomous democratic discussion.

These charges against Weber foreground the third thesis guiding these essays. Under late capitalist conditions, it is argued that the "lifeless machinery" of bureaucratic administration continually generates *demands* for autonomous public action. In the contemporary period it is of course true that democratic, public freedoms are everywhere caught in the scissors grip of state and corporate bureaucracy; falling into the arms of bureaucratic servitude, the populations of late capitalist systems are expected to adore cheerfully or curse quietly those into whose hands are being concentrated the means of production, administration, communications, and war. It is nevertheless also evident that there can be no harmony within or between state and corporate bureaucracies; the hegemony of these organizations cannot naturally prevail but, rather, depends on continuous administrative maneuverings and readjustments to autonomous resistances. The commonplace laments about the widespread turning away from public life are in this respect premature and overdrawn, for bureaucratic administration everywhere tends to be the subject not only of "class struggles" (as Lukács first insisted against Weber), but of various struggles outside the office and factory. These struggles effect continuous readjustments within bureaucratic organizations and also enhance the conditions of growth of autonomous public spheres. These resistances directly contradict the *dirigiste* model of socialism favored by social democracy. In opposition to that model, they may also be said to foster a novel need or expectation that late capitalist orders cannot readily satisfy: the need for spheres of autonomous public activity within the realms of society and the state.

Through the course of these essays, two closely interrelated reasons are adduced in defense of this third thesis that state-regulated capitalist systems are

6

subject to disorganizing and politicizing crisis tendencies. First, certain bottle-necks, planning failures, and other disequilibriums are generated by the inability of public and private organizations to coordinate their relations with each other bureaucratically. Under continuous pressure to act with or against *other* bureaucracies, as Offe and Habermas convincingly argue (see Essay 3), bureaucratic elites are typically forced to abandon their own principled rejection of doing business on an informal basis. These elites' will to administer their environments through impersonal and technically proficient rules of operation is contradicted by efforts to *entreat* the cooperation of other bureaucracies and oppositional movements – through, for example, corporatist mechanisms of policy making and informal bargaining. This form of horizontal limit upon bureaucratic attempts to secure the depoliticization of populations tends to be reinforced, secondly, by analogous difficulties *within* bureaucratic organizations. The attempt of these organizations to discharge their business quietly and "without regard for particular persons and situations" (Weber) is contradicted by their obligation to invite the participation of their own members. This solicitation process is necessary, and not only because "the organization" is at all times dependent upon at least a minimum of initiative from its members. Of greater significance is the fact that the depersonalized mode of operation of bureaucracies continually alienates their members and generates their active resistance. These self-contradictory dynamics within and between bureaucratic organizations constantly disrupt their tendency to become institutions of everyday routine. Bureaucratic relations of power must be understood as the always fragile medium *and* outcome of struggles over the credibility and distribution of power. Structured by a self-contradictory principle of organization – depoliticization – bureaucratic institutions are continually obliged to solicit the active participation of their members and clients, whose initiative and autonomy these institutions at the same time forbid. Public spheres, in which assembled subjects speak, interact, and autonomously decide on courses of action, are a continuous, if unintended, effect of the processes of pseudomutual recognition inscribed within bureaucratic forms of power. Certainly, state and corporate organizations constantly promote the reduction of their members and clients to mere objects of administrative control. They also typically stimulate demands for autonomous public life, by feigning acceptance of the principle of mediating conflicting interests through controversy, open discussion, compromise, and consensus. The fundamental source of trouble within and between corporate and state bureaucratic organizations is that they must secure a steady and continuous flow of active support from their members and clients – without at the same time promoting their steady and continuous interference.

Various instances of this dialectic of discipline and participation are analyzed in these essays: welfare state attempts to respond to various social claims through depoliticized strategies of "problem definition and control" (Essay 1), the incitement and regulation of public opinion by communications media (Essays 3 and 5), the capitalist rationalization of the labor process through techniques of participation (Essay 6), and so on. These examples serve to vindicate the third thesis presented here, namely, that bureaucratic organizations both repress and incite the growth of autonomous publics and, by implication, enhance the *possibility* of subjecting both state and corporate organizations to scrutiny, transformation, and supervision from below.

This democratic potential of course provokes reflection upon new questions and old doubts, several clusters of which are explored further in these essays. Questions are raised in Essay 4 about the limitations of attempts (by the young Habermas, Arendt, and others) to criticize bureaucratic rationality through the retrieval of the old Aristotelian distinction between *technē* and *praxis*. The excessively formal character of several theoretical attempts since the time of the Bolshevik Revolution to defend the principle of "free and systematic communication" is critically scrutinized in Essay 5, where certain substantive properties of autonomous public action – disobedience, merrymaking, and rhetoric, for instance – are also seen as themes necessary to any plausible socialist theory of public life. A reinterpretation of the well-known controversy between Herbert Marcuse and Jürgen Habermas serves in Essay 6 to focus some considerations on the antagonistic relationship between autonomous public life and contemporary forms of scientific-technical development. Finally, two essays (1 and 7) emphasize the need for further theoretical reflection upon the institutional forms capable of realizing autonomous public spheres. While their conclusions are admittedly prefatory, these latter essays argue that the struggle to defend public life is not synonymous with the will to institute spontaneous agreement, as if democratic socialism could somehow escape the weight of controversy, resistance, and unforeseen consequence common to all polities. From a strategic point of view, indeed, it is implied that the democratic "road to socialism" can be envisaged only as a difficult and extended process of decentralization of decision-making power to a plurality of public spheres. The achievement of democratic socialism in this sense would become possible only insofar as *political* institutions could defend autonomous public spheres, realize their demands, and mediate their conflicts and antagonisms. Conversely, a multiplicity of public spheres (for example, workers' councils, independent health centers, housing cooperatives, and communications media) within the sphere of "civil society" would retain the effective power to check and control their political representatives; these political authorities would in turn be strictly accountable to the sovereign publics for their administrative activities.

It should be emphasized that the three theses guiding these essays – the claim that late capitalist societies are bureaucratic orders whose disorganizing and depoliticizing effects continually incite the growth of oppositional public spheres – are marked by an ideal-typical and highly unfinished character. They evidently raise many questions, not all of whose terms and implications have been sufficiently explicated or worked through. Precisely because of these lacunae, a choice was made to present these theses in the form of a series of connected essays. Their fragmented, discontinuous form serves as a reminder that these contributions to a socialist theory of public life can make no claim to have provided certain and unambiguous knowledge. The theses presented here admit of the limitations of bureaucratic theory; they reject theories of socialism that attempt to grasp the "truth" of the present so as to constitute its constituents and their "real interests" as objects of possible technical control. The theses developed here rather assume the posture of the advocate: Their provisional claims should be understood as provocations, as calls to further argument about developments that presently threaten the democratic potential of our times.

1

Bureaucracy and its discontents: crisis tendencies of the welfare state

> Envisaging public life – of which we know very well there is all too little – requires an almost childlike feeling of omnipotence.
>
> Alexander Kluge

Public life and crisis

Some years ago, Oskar Negt and Alexander Kluge proposed the thesis that autonomous public spheres typically develop and flourish within crisis-ridden historical phases marked by war, surrender, revolution, and counterrevolution.[1] In view of the fact that all bureaucratically organized, late capitalist systems are nowadays pressured by a series of novel quandaries, this thesis takes on a renewed and pressing significance. Rather obviously, these quandaries have generated new dilemmas, political arguments, and social struggles. These controversies and conflicts have in turn facilitated, on an unprecedented scale, the proliferation of images of crisis. A chorus of commentators swears by it, all the empirical indicators are seen to prove it: Welfare state capitalism, it is said, has definitely entered a crisis phase.[2] Not without confusion, *crisis* comes to signify (and falsely unify) a thousand apparently random events. Crises are seen to appear in every field of social and political life: from the arenas of international affairs and race relations, through the economy, to the most intimate spheres of the lives of individuals. *Crisis* has become front-page material – a key word in the vocabulary of official and everyday speech.

This proliferation of images of crisis cannot be dismissed as the product of the deception and trickery of ruling groups.[3] Certainly, careless references to the certainty of crisis can easily become valuable material in the hands of corporate and state administrators – but this is no different from almost any other aspect of common sense and popular fantasy. The widespread talk of crisis, it must be emphasized, also has a potentially liberating or utopian dimension. This talk is ideological, to invoke the old metaphor: The unthinking deployment of images of crisis both hinders critical, explanatory accounts of "objective," institutionalized social life processes *and* is suggestive of (perhaps formerly obscured) contradictions and breakdowns within those processes – ruptures that expand the possibilities for refusal and subjective intervention against the old order. So

10

to speak, discussions of crisis operate as one complex of narrations through which late capitalist systems hide from themselves and reveal themselves. In turn, these narrations function as a material force, acting upon these systems they express and declare. The proliferation of images of tension, conflict, and catastrophe, in short, currently serves to rupture the simpleminded, happy belief that welfare state capitalist systems are rational, even "natural." Talk of crisis is necessarily expressive of social and political formations whose quandaries tend to produce fears and disillusions – and hopes and struggles for a different, perhaps better, world.

In the wake of such developments, Negt and Kluge's suggestion that questions concerning public life and crisis are intimately related must be examined more thoroughly. At the outset, indeed, their suggestion can be rendered plausible only through a careful reconsideration of the meanings of the more classical concept of crisis.[4] In definite contrast to the uninhibited references to crisis in the present period, this classical concept sustained itself upon two interrelated and very precise themes. A theory of autonomous public life cannot afford to ignore these. First, a crisis-ridden process, according to the classical concepts, signifies a fateful phase in its life history, a turning point during which its reproductive capacities are severely reduced. The point tends to be reached where even the routine subjectivity of the agents of this process is imperiled. Seemingly taking on a life of its own, the crisis process unfolds ruthlessly and "objectively" behind the backs of its constituents. Their taken-for-granted or natural attitudes tend to be subverted, their normal powers of judgment and action paralyzed, at least temporarily.

This syndrome was spelled out clearly in the original medical meanings of the concept. For example, Goethe's famous question, "All transitions are crises; and is a crisis not a sickness?"[5] merely retrieved a theme common among the classical Greek physicians. According to the Hippocratic insight, a crisis occurs in diseases whenever they increase in intensity, change into other diseases, or end altogether. This understanding, which enjoyed a wide influence, is quite evident in the writings of Thucydides. Both his analysis of the Corcyraean revolution and, above all, his well-known characterization of the crisis of the fateful plague of Athens during its seventh or eighth days referred to an objective, seemingly contagious process that generates symptoms within the afflicted, whose identities are disturbed and whose normal, active powers are robbed.[6] In the twentieth century, this meaning reappears in Gramsci's reflections on Italy in the 1920s: "The crisis consists precisely in the fact that the old is dying and the new cannot be born; in this interregnum a great variety of morbid symptoms appears."[7]

Moments of crisis are not exclusively fateful, morbid, "objective" processes, however. Lukács's reaction to the First World War and (to mention a second example) Kuhn's analysis of the rupturing and transformation of scientific discourse both correctly emphasize that the concept of crisis signifies a process of destruction *and* construction, of unsettling anomaly *and* intervention against the old normality.[8] The classical concepts of crisis connoted a second meaning, which was implicit in their medical usage: Crisis tendencies, disruptions of the hitherto-existing, familiar continuity of a process, are *Dämmerung* (dusk, dawn). They

11

signal the end of a phase of reproduction and the possibility of its renewal, or of breakthrough to the novel and unfamiliar. With reference to crisis-ridden social processes, this means that the disintegration of the natural attitudes of those who have become objects of system paralysis facilitates both an expanded awareness of this objective paralysis and active attempts to overcome it. The dialectical, discontinuous quality of a crisis tends to produce its own "otherness" and, hence, a condition of its resolution – speaking and acting subjects. The tradition of tragic theater, in which the perilous moment of crisis is central, exemplifies this sense of crises as moments that present rich possibilities for the renewal of free subjectivity against the apparent power of Fate. So understood, a crisis (*kpísis*, from *kpínein*, "to decide," "to sort through") is therefore a moment during which it becomes possible, even necessary, to decide upon and carry through different courses of action.

In the modern world, this meaning was powerfully regathered by Rousseau. His conviction that the rulers of Europe were blindly working in concert to hasten the fateful coming of revolution was also the ground of his hope that modern society could be remade through political intervention.

> You reckon on the present order of society, without considering that this order is itself subject to inscrutable changes...Does fate strike so seldom that you can count on immunity from her blows? The crisis is approaching, and we are on the edge of a revolution. Who can answer for your fate? What man has made, man may destroy. Nature's characters alone are ineffaceable, and nature makes neither the prince, the rich man, nor the nobleman.[9]

The universal triumph of exchange relations that molded (potential) citizens into commodities, things, "tools to be used," had reached its limit, according to Rousseau. The coming crisis would threaten the voluntary servitude of civil society and its state, thereby raising the possibility that citizens could remake themselves politically in the image of their true selves.

Inasmuch as crises are understood as moments of discontinuity wherein momentarily trapped agents can envisage and reassert their subjectivity, the overcoming of crisis is inescapably a normative process. Rousseau's insistence that theoretical analysis is inescapably partisan in this process still stands. As the following essays demonstrate, there can be no value-neutral crisis interpretation in the cruder positivist sense. To analyze crisis tendencies is to adopt the role of advocate, to speculate on the likelihood and desirability of their successful overcoming or avoidance. Technobureaucratic versions of crisis analysis – such as Wiener and Kahn's *Crisis and Arms Control*[10] – are quite in accord with this maxim. Crises are here said to be turning points in an unfolding sequence of events and actions, whose uncertainties precipitate a reduction of control over these events and their effects. It is assumed that these heightened uncertainties can be overcome only through the reorganization of society and its state from the top down. An emancipatory, political theory of crisis tendencies is diametrically opposed to the repressive intentions of such technocratic formulations. Offering critical accounts of those objective, structural antagonisms which presently block the political emancipation of speaking, laboring, and acting subjects, it seeks to foster the growth of historically new and anti-authoritarian struggles.

These two interrelated meanings of the classical notion of crisis (as moments of paralysis and potential renewal through struggle) are strongly evident in the mid-nineteenth-century Marxian theory of crises (of tendential decline of the average rate of profit, underconsumption, disproportionality). Karl Korsch's efforts to periodize the writings of Marx in accordance with the rise and fall of the prospects for European revolution are helpful in interpreting this theory of crisis.[11] Prior to the failure of the 1848 revolutions, Korsch argues, the Marxian formulations expressed the real possibility that the emerging proletariat would subjectively intervene to revolutionize European capitalism in accordance with the communist vision. The theoretical apogee of this phase is the well-known *Manifesto* thesis: "The history of all hitherto existing society is the history of class struggles."[12] History is subjectivity, a process of the continuous transformation of humanity and nature through the struggles of living labor power.

Beyond this first phase, and commencing with *Wage Labour and Capital*, the theoretical emphases within Marx's writings shift to the logic of objective historical processes. The critique of political economy protests against the domination of things over the weakened proletariat. It probes the institutional preconditions of self-conscious, proletarian intervention. Revolution is now seen as possible only through ruptures of the objective, institutional framework of capitalist society – through crisis tendencies whose certainty is no less than the coming revolution itself. The warning of the 1859 *Critique* becomes the ensign of this phase and its objectivist account of the past and present. The history of society is understood as the history of material production and the contradiction between the material forces and relations of production.[13] It is as if the present phase of capitalist society were a natural process. Its "sum-total of social relations" seems to develop according to definite laws. Those who produce under liberal capitalist conditions become personifications of reified economic categories, created objects of those laws of motion which operate under the sign of "iron necessity" and the imminence of communist revolution. According to the last issue of the *Neue Rheinische Zeitung*, the subjectivist formulations of the *Manifesto* must be reworked and supplemented: "In view of the general prosperity which now prevails...there can be no question of any real revolution. A new revolution will be made possible only as the result of a new crisis, but it is just as certain as the coming crisis itself."[14]

The disruption of the welfare state

This Marxian crisis theorem (and its conviction that the greatest hindrance to production in capitalist society is capital itself) of course continued to exercise considerable influence throughout the period of the Second and Third Internationals.[15] Whether this theorem continues to be plausible, however, is very much an open question. Indeed, attempts to recover this theorem in an abstract and formal manner (see Nicos Poulantzas's early "A propos du concept de crise")[16] or even more literally (as in some contributions to the German *Staatsableitung* debate)[17] are outwitted by a pressing and novel political development, whose consideration is of great importance to a theory of autonomous public life. The

13

trajectory of this development, which has caught many by surprise, is becoming more or less familiar: the disruption of the welfare state and the widespread electoral defeat of its party-political defenders. There is increasing evidence that the project of converting the depressed, conflict-ridden political economies of the 1930s into the bureaucratic welfare state prosperity of the postwar world has reached an impasse. As Hegel might have remarked, the political victories of the welfare state have transformed themselves into definite losses. The welfare state produces more problems and unintended consequences than it is presently able to solve through administrative-bureaucratic means. The conditions for profitable economic growth have been at least temporarily disrupted; the welfare state itself has been subjected to a growing chorus of criticism – and surprisingly soon after the serious structural problems of the world political economy of the 1930s and 1940s. A hiatus in the history of the welfare state has evidently been reached. When, in the mid-1970s, the British Labour Party adopted the language of belt tightening and formulated an austerity program of cuts in state expenditure, and when, after forty-four years in office, the Swedish Socialdemokratiska Arbetarparti was defeated at the polls, it seemed as if an entire era had come to a close.

The present controversies occasioned by welfare state capitalist systems can be contrasted with the marked self-assurance and optimistic consensus of the immediate post–World War II period. At that time, within ruling circles at least, the permanent victory of the welfare state–social democratic project seemed inevitable. It was as if the manifold struggles of the past century in favor of what Bismarck had called "the positive advancement of the welfare of the working classes" had at last come to fruition. Progress under welfare state conditions definitely seemed to be part of the natural tendencies of the day. This once self-assured project – its formal recognition of collective political rights and the power of trades unions, and its official commitment to such policies as economic growth, less unemployment, more social security provision[18] – displayed at least *five* crucially interrelated themes. It is important to reexamine these themes in the current historical conjuncture, inasmuch as they indicate certain immanent weaknesses of the welfare state project – and, hence, the endogenous sources of its present quandaries.

In opposition to the revolutionary socialist and classical liberal opposition, first, advocates of the welfare state insisted upon the primacy of the principle of social pacification through state supervision. This principle was most often articulated through the language of greater equality of opportunity through state entitlement. Inequality deriving from unearned economic privilege was represented as the great blot upon contemporary society. In opposition to such privilege, the welfare state was to become the caretaker of existence, ingraining itself into social life and thereby making possible the realization of the ultimate goal of a classless, fraternal, and cooperative mode of life. In pursuit of this (often poorly specified) goal, the welfare state would strive to redistribute rewards and privileges so as to minimize social resentment, to secure justice between individuals and groups, and to equalize opportunities. This social pacification and redistributive strategy was represented as subversive of existing relations of power and production. Equality of opportunity for all persons was to be encouraged by socially provided and state-sponsored egalitarian measures, to whose benefits some or all would be entitled. A just and equitable distribution of property, power, and status, in this view, required that there be equal rewards for equal performances. The distribution of these resources, according to this performance principle, would justly be dependent upon individuals' and groups' performance and skills. This proposal admitted of the possibility of *inequality* of outcome of performances. Nevertheless, it was observed that individuals and groups would from here on be separated from each other less sharply by variations in wealth and origin than perhaps by differences of "character." In accordance with the principle of bureaucratically guaranteed equality of opportunity, the highest rewards (of wealth, power, and status) would legitimately accrue to those whose rendered skills or services contributed most to "progress" and "national prosperity."

The reassertion of social control and equality of opportunity against class privilege, secondly, was viewed as contingent upon the fostering of privately steered capitalist accumulation. Textbook descriptions of the welfare state as the protector of minimum standards of income, nutrition, health, housing, and education for every individual are misleading with respect to this point. It is true that the degree of reliance upon bureaucratic corporate activity was always (and remains) a controversial issue among defenders of the welfare state. It is equally clear, however, that defense, nuclear, and aerospace industries; corporate agribusiness; the industrial users of government-guaranteed foreign loans; and publicly financed scientific research and development together consumed from the outset a disproportionate (indeed, overwhelming) share of welfare state funds.[19] Various justifications were offered for this "corporate bias." In addition to the (highly misleading) claim that the stimulation of domestic capitalist growth would indirectly assist development of the peripheral capitalist countries, guardians of the welfare state insisted (1) that among the population there existed a settled expectation of a permanently rising discretionary purchasing power and standard of living and that inasmuch as this population was quite determined on the "television-set-refrigerator civilisation" (Crosland) through the full employment of labor and capital, governments must accordingly attend to their wishes; (2) that the financing of redistribution and welfare programs – the relief of hardship and stress – and social capital schemes (hospitals, mental homes, schools) depended, at least in the short run, on the taxation revenues generated by such capitalist growth; and (3) that the abolition of class domination was no longer synonymous with the revolutionary socialization of the means of production. According to most social democrats, for example, the liberal capitalist ruling class had lost its commanding social position because of several more recent developments. These included the general expansion of state activity and nationalized industry, the increased bargaining power of organized labor under conditions of full employment, the growing divorce of ownership and control of property, and the heightened power of scientific-technical expertise consequent upon the growing scale and technical complexity of the corporation. These developments signaled an end to the age when profit assumed the form of

15

surplus value, which in turn accumulated in the personal hands of the rich bourgeoisie. According to many proponents of the welfare state, profit generated within the private capitalist sector tended now to be productively reinvested. Profit had become a source of collective capital accumulation. Conversely, the stimulation of profitable capitalist production was a necessary, even desirable, condition of a more equal and more just distribution of property and income. Wigforss's advice became an axiom of all postwar advocates of the welfare state: "One must produce before one has something to distribute."[20]

Thirdly, privately steered, capitalist accumulation was to be fostered and directed through bureaucratic state action. In partial opposition to the strategy of commodification (market competition) as the desirable medium of production, exchange, and consumption, defenders of the welfare state project insisted that the power of the bureaucratic state could restrict the crisis-ridden and socially undesirable efforts of this capitalistic mechanism. Through its allocative and productive policies, the state could transform capitalists into private contributors to the public's welfare without altering the juridical status of private property itself. Here the lead of Keynes's critique of laissez-faire and its "passive state" was followed.[21] The good society, the welfarists claimed, was not one in which self-interested individuals possessed and willfully exercised their natural liberties in the domains of economy, polity, and family life. That form of arrangement had until this point been dominant. Yet it by no means had produced harmony between private individuals and the public at large. Nor was the former reliance upon self-interest necessarily enlightened.

Welfarists thus recommended that the agenda of the state would have to be modified and enlarged. The "active, responsible," and bureaucratic state was from here on to exercise its "directive intelligence" (Keynes) over social life. At the same time, private initiative and enterprise would be left unhindered. Guided by the steady, helping hand of government, particular groups, classes, regions, and individuals would contribute more fully to a genuinely public interest, in which the old impediment of individual greed and self-interest and its attendant irrationalities would be modified, perhaps even fully eradicated. It was assumed that the state could willfully subject a wide and strategically decisive segment of social decisions to deliberate administrative control. The era of "value in exchange," of aggressive and unfettered market relations, would thereby come to an end, or at least be counterbalanced by the statist principle of "welfare value."[22] Progress in the eradication of inequalities of wealth and power would become possible – through numerous state strategies designed both to redirect and to enhance capitalist economic growth. These strategies were to include the maintenance of stable prices, a surplus on the balance of payments, and full employment of labor and capital, mainly through fiscal policy directed at determining within broad limits the division of total output among consumption, investment, exports, and social expenditures; heavy taxation of the unearned income of the very rich (through death duties, capital gains, and corporate taxation); the expansion of pace-setting public enterprise; and the proliferation of forms of "decommodified," collective consumption (such as standardized education, public health, and housing) to reduce the qualitative gap between public and private

16

provision. Through these (and other) bureaucratically crafted policies, defenders of the welfare state forecasted that cakes for some before bread for all would become a thing of the past. The age of "sociability," of full employment, generous welfare services, and generalized harmony, could begin.

Fourthly, the bureaucratic welfare state project positioned itself squarely within the tradition of quiet reformism. Reacting against earlier social democrats' ambivalence about the efficacy and legitimacy of formal democratic procedures,[23] advocates of the welfare state became deeply persuaded that they could achieve their goals by installments. Elections could be won, and their winning would obtain for the welfare state project the support of an overwhelming electoral majority. Precisely because it seemed as if History were on their side, welfarists urged that the goal of affirmative action, of a more welfare-oriented socialist society, was to be achieved through peaceful and realistic reforms. Consistent with their *dirigisme*, such reforms were to be initiated by social democratic administrations and supported especially by the rank and file of the organized labor movement. Progress toward a more egalitarian society was to be a pragmatic, gradual, and level-headed process. Much remained to be done, insisted the champions of the welfare state: Social injustice and collective manifestations of discontent persisted, social inefficiency and waste of talent remained. Nevertheless, peaceful reforms within the boundaries of the rule of law and periodic elections had so far procured a more just and humane society. These already impressive and irreversible achievements had softened the once bitter reactions to soup kitchens, dole queues, and hunger marches and muffled the angry clamor of past strikes and lockouts. Further progress toward social pacification through state-secured equality of opportunity was a matter of time, patience, and popular willingness to reelect pro-welfare state administrations.

Finally, a more "democratic" order of society was viewed as a necessary condition and consequence of the welfare state. Notwithstanding the widespread (and justified) suspicion of their *dirigisme*, champions of the welfare state passionately espoused their belief in the mechanisms of formal democracy. These mechanisms – whose democratic qualities were almost always poorly specified – were often regarded as self-evidently emancipatory. These were typically said to include the improvement of the privilege and power of the manual worker through full employment policies, the extension of more enlightened mechanisms of joint consultation between management and trade unions (so-called high-level industrial democracy), and collective productivity bonus schemes; more genuinely universal access to higher educational facilities; the "corporatist" devolution of certain powers of decision making onto private and quasi-state bodies; the retention of legislatures, the political party system, and the rule of formal law; the preservation of cherished political traditions and "national character"; the benevolent provision of "progressive" social legislation (more funds for the arts, less restrictive liquor laws, reform of censorship and sexual legislation, and so on). That the welfare state project would necessarily extend a net of state and parastate bureaucracy over the daily lives of its citizens seemed unproblematic. In cooperation with capitalist enterprise, the welfare state was to be the parent of democratization, freedom, and social tranquility. Combining the provision of

17

material security and mechanisms of social surveillance and control, it was to be welcomed as "the climax of a long process, in the course of which capitalism has been civilised and, to a large extent, reconciled with the principles of democracy."[24]

In the present historical conjuncture, this confident scenario has begun to appear strange and unfamiliar. The factors contributing to the decay of the welfare state project are, of course, manifold and complex, and cannot be identified easily through the classical Marxian theorems. Moreover, the intensity with which these factors are experienced by individuals, groups, regions, and nations varies considerably. Finally, some of these factors are no doubt unique to particular countries or regions. The severe deindustrialization of the British economy, the decisive and growing dependence of the American political economy upon the production of weapons systems, and the early struggles over nuclear power in Sweden are examples of this specificity.

Nevertheless, at least two sets of unresolved dilemmas and deep-seated tensions are common to all late capitalist systems. Each of these quandaries presently functions as a source of disruption of the welfare state project. In the first place, the massive postwar wave of capital investment and accumulation has clearly given way to (admittedly uneven) stagnation. This postwar boom was induced by (among other factors) war, political demands (especially from labor movements) for improved social conditions, the American accession to world dominance, and welfare state countercyclical stabilization and growth policies. The new economic situation, by contrast, has placed enormous pressure upon the welfare state project. The international economic situation is now marked by at least three internal difficulties. The first of these is uneven threats to the rate of profit, which are in large measure traceable to organized labor's struggle for higher wages and oligopoly capital's attempt at recouping these gains through its price-making powers. These threats have had obvious investment-disturbing consequences, which in turn have become synonymous with increases in rates of inflation, structural unemployment, trade imbalances, instabilities within financial markets, and numerous (and self-contradictory) attempts by states to restore conditions of profitability (stimulation of growth, wage indexing, social contracts, control of the money supply, and so on). Second is the failure, until now, to satisfy the need that has been created for a "global Keynesianism," that is, for something like state coordination of corporate investment on a global scale. This need is simultaneously fostered and blocked by an increasingly interdependent and rationalized world economy still mediated through the anachronistic policies of competing nation-states. This failure is deepened by the fact that the welfare state project and the capitalist world economy now seem less able than before to rely on the central coordinating role of the United States. The destabilization process is symbolized by the end of the convertibility of the U.S. dollar into gold, the aggressive saber rattling in American foreign policy, and new patterns of international military tension. The third problem in the international economic system is the widespread evasion of state controls by transnational corporations, whose investment and marketing policies definitely exacerbate the two difficulties just mentioned. There is evidence, indeed, that profound changes in the international division of labor are forcing corporations to reorganize their production on a global scale. Indexes of this transformation include the accelerated relocation of export-oriented production to new industrial sites, especially in the peripheral capitalist countries, and the consequent acceleration of rationalization policies (sometimes in the face of bitter opposition from organized labor) within traditional sites and forms of industrial production.[25]

The entanglement of welfare state policies in this first set of difficulties within the capitalist world economy is linked with a second set: an accentuation of muddled patterns of state decision making. During the course of this century, it is evident that all states within the centers of the capitalist world became heavily interwoven with economic and social life processes. Any discussion of these welfare states as "superstructural" (compare the classical Marxian crisis theorem) obfuscates questions about the mode of operation of these states, their novel crisis tendencies, and their drastically expanded role in the reproduction of new forms of domination. Indeed, the continuing theoretical tendency to derive accounts of the welfare state from the external, capital–labor struggles generated by the late capitalist mode of production ignores the fact that these (and other) struggles are not simply fought out at the level of the state, but are already mediated and modified by this state. Consequent upon the welfare state project, the accumulation process and social life in general have tended to become functions of organized political struggle *and* bureaucratic forms of state crisis management.

This expansion of bureaucratic state power encouraged by advocates of the welfare state is by no means without opposition, however. Especially under pressure from a slowdown of economic growth, it becomes clear that a complementary relationship between the state and civil society is much more difficult to achieve than defenders of the welfare state had supposed. The welfare state cannot serve as the uncontested parent of social tranquility. As we have seen, welfare statists had assumed that higher standards of living, a wider diffusion of power, and improved labor relations and rates of employment would not be conditional upon large-scale alterations of existing patterns of ownership and control of industrial and financial capital. Production for social use and commodified production for profitable exchange were now deemed to coincide broadly. Remaining discrepancies could be corrected through the political willpower of welfare state administrations, whose "political solvency"[26] would in turn be ensured by revenues generated by capitalist economic growth.

Under the new conditions of languid investment, it becomes evident that the welfare state cannot redistribute wealth without adversely affecting incentives to labor, save, innovate, and take risks. Conversely, it becomes clear that the structural pressures generated by the late capitalist economy confound and confuse the welfare state. Talk of "fiscal crisis," "ungovernability," and "overload" correctly suggests that an equilibrium between the state's "legitimation" and "accumulation" functions (O'Connor) is not presently attainable.[27] Historically novel disruptive tendencies and patterns of conflict appear within the manifold institutions of the political system. In particular, as many contemporary elections evidence, a new conflict in the implicit and declared goals of state policy tends to break out into the open. This conflict situation has always been implicit within

19

the welfare state project, but it now openly assumes the following form. On the one hand, governments are supposed to perform all their legitimate tasks (of ensuring stable economic growth, providing various forms of collective consumption, maintaining social control) without subverting the accumulation process in general, and capitalist profit considerations and "business confidence" (Kalecki) in particular. On the other hand, it is upon these accumulation processes that these same governments continue to depend (for their sources of revenue, employment policy, planning information, legitimacy, and so on). State policies are forced at the same time to promote the productive power of private capital and to weaken and counteract its effects. Under pressure from the disruptions within the international economic system, this inner conflict within state policies is called into question from at least three different standpoints. These are considered below in some detail. Some (supporters of the new liberal movement) criticize the welfare state for its hindrance and neglect of free, private enterprise; others (advocates of corporatism) censure this state as highly inefficient and therefore in need of restructuring; yet others (those who participate in the new social movements) criticize the welfare state for not in fact living up to its democratic promises and welfare responsibilities.

The following essays on the theme of public life and bureaucratic domination seek to engage this controversy critically. Their initial thesis is that each of these sets of criticisms – symptoms of the present internal difficulties of the welfare state, of its failure to operate in accordance with its promises – has decisively provoked a reconsideration of the bureaucratic character of late capitalist societies. The symptoms of this controversy about the virtues and limitations of bureaucratic organization and planning are many-sided, and can only be sketched here. They include, for example, concern over the erosion of democratic government; the popularity of "overload" and "ungovernability" theorems; criticisms of the authoritarian regulation of everyday life by professionally directed agencies of social policy; and the widespread calls for cutbacks, for free markets, and for the rolling back of bureaucratic state power. This diffuse controversy over bureaucracy indicates that, contrary to the claims of its protagonists, the bureaucratic welfare state project is no stable finality. Precisely because of the controversy and political and social conflict it has unwittingly generated, it must be seen as a highly unstable formation in transition, a crisis-ridden complex of relations of power whose future shape remains at this point undecided. To retrieve the terms of crisis analysis: The contemporary welfare state project has reached something like a fateful turning point, a moment of discontinuity in which its reproductive capacities have at least temporarily declined. This disruption of the welfare state project *also* coincides with active attempts to resolve and overcome that disruption with interventions against the old normality.

The new liberalism

In the present conjuncture, to repeat, at least three contradictory modes of intervention are in evidence. For the time being, these have seized the initiative against the welfare state project, rendering problematic – to a highly variable degree, admittedly – its bureaucratic character. According to the very influential new liberal movement,[28] the bureaucratic welfare state definitely hinders and restricts free, private enterprise. In spite of their best intentions, welfarists are alleged to have built a system of state coercion around individuals – a system of bureaucracy wherein "one man's actions are made to serve another man's will, not for his own but for the other's purpose."[29]

In apparent opposition to this generalized statism, the new liberalism posits itself as the defender of what is taken as the primary (and self-evident) goal of any political arrangement: the freedom of the abstract, calculating (but not always rational) individual. Within the field of economic production and exchange – a field concerned with the "basic problem" (Friedman) of any social order – this freedom is best attained in and through relations of capitalist commodification. Unlike the schemes of centralized, bureaucratic direction organized by welfare states or trade unions, the price and profit mechanisms of commodified relations ensure competition, risk taking, disciplined work, innovativeness, and, above all, the self-reliance and "freedom" of anonymous collaboration. Competitive exchange processes are represented as genuinely voluntary arrangements. Within these processes, private individuals or firms are said to be the ultimate contracting parties, who can always exercise their freedom *not* to enter into any *particular* contract or exchange. (Of course, the new liberal schema deems unjustified the freedom *not* to enter into commodified exchange at all. It equally neglects cases in which some – from temporarily unemployed labor power to the permanently marginalized – are forcibly excluded from "free competition" by manifold institutional pressures. Finally, the politically privileged position of oligopolistic fractions of capital is excused.) This freedom within the field of production and consumption constitutes a necessary condition of political freedom, that is, freedom of individuals from arbitrary state power. Competitive capitalism is said to promote political freedom precisely because it separates and counterbalances economic and political power.[30] Through this allegation, the new liberalism seeks to "denaturalize" the welfarist belief in the absolute necessity and desirability of bureaucratic state action. It urges that the welfare state project has hastened the arrival of an age of bureaucratic serfdom. Hardly any aspect of daily life, from the domain of the household to those of work and leisure, is now exempt from the attempted "conscious control"[31] of state administrators and planners. The welfare state "has given birth to a large bureaucracy that shows tendencies of growing by what it feeds on, of extending its scope from one area of our life to another."[32]

In (partial) opposition to this statism, the new liberalism insists that both economic and political freedom can be achieved through the reassertion of the boundaries of a commodified civil society against the encroachments of the state. Free enterprise, private health care, fee-paying education, the selective "recommodification" of collective services are crucial conditions of genuine equality of opportunity and individual freedom. This argument *accurately* emphasizes that welfare state policies never unequivocally served the needs of private capitalist accumulation. This unintended development (which also explains the very raison d'être of the new liberalism) is clearly evidenced in certain incongruities between the planning activities of welfare state and corporate bureaucracies. The diagnosis of the new liberalism is not altogether misleading. By virtue of its growing monopoly of social policy provision and its increasing switch from the manipulation of aggregate demands (for example, through "Rehn model" policies of full employment, the reducing of labor bottlenecks, the squeezing out of inefficient firms) to more specific, direct interventions within the commodification process, the welfare state *has* interrupted or distorted the price and profit mechanism as the primary medium of allocation of demand and supply of commodities. In defiance of this medium, the state generates both a permanent budget deficit and new demands that it has in a sense sanctioned by its affirmative actions. Especially within the current conjuncture, these deficits and demands tend to undermine the welfare state goal of social control. Political and social divisions are exacerbated. The state becomes the object of new needs and social grievances (concerning nuclear power, unemployment, and so on) that have been unwittingly generated by its formal recognition of the powers of trade unions and by its affirmation of the principles of state supervision and collective rights.

In opposition to these principles, the new liberalism insists that, from here on, governments are to be allowed to monopolize and supervise only those matters which cannot be directed (or which can be directed only at great cost) through voluntary commodity production and exchange. Principally, the state is to serve as a strong (and not necessarily minimum) means of rule making, adjudication, and enforcement for a free market of contractors who engage in "spontaneous collaboration."[33] This supervision is to be supplemented, the new liberalism typically adds, with authoritative norms (such as those associated with patriarchy), which are the "unintended outcome of custom, accepted unthinkingly";[34] with certain social policy institutions designed to manage the mentally handicapped; and with voluntary associations such as the patriarchal family, school, and church. Anticipating a renaissance of liberty through a strong, disciplinary state and a free market, the new liberalism designates its enemies: bureaucracy, welfare abuse, confiscatory taxation burdens, public enterprise, and all those – immigrants, trade unionists, welfare chiselers, students, feminists – who are seen to constitute a threat to "public order."

A new corporatism?

Unlike the new liberal defense of oligopolistic and competitive capitalism, the arguments of those who defend neocorporatist solutions to the present difficulties of the welfare state tend to concentrate upon the bureaucratic state and its unintended consequences.[35] Their questions concern not *whether* late capitalist social life must be governed by a bureaucratic state, but *how* the restabilization of this state and its policies is possible. It is stressed that the system of "organized welfare state capitalism" is now subject to definite centrifugal tendencies, and is therefore in urgent need of internal renovation or reorganization. This centrifugalism is often contrasted with the happy and sweet (and surely mythical) tranquility of times past.[36] Customarily, it is noted that the range of matters for which governments are held responsible has rapidly increased during the era of the welfare state. This state has become a "corporatist" state, the bearer of social order and control. Through its provision of various social policy and productive measures and the enactment of schemes of bargaining between key interest groups (principally, oligopoly capital and organized labor), the state is more and more regarded by electorates as an unlimited-liability insurance company, providing coverage against all conceivable risks.

This is the alleged source of the present crisis tendencies of the welfare state. For the accelerated growth of social demands on this state coincides, in the view of the neocorporatists, with a decline of its capacity to respond. The "sharing-out function of government" (de Jouvenel) – its allocation and redistribution of resources through its taxing, spending, and policing policies, together with its direct interventions in the commodification process – is excessively burdened. The advocates of neocorporatism here *accurately* draw attention to the fact that the state is not a unified subject tied *a priori* to the needs of capitalist accumulation. On the contrary, like the proverbial sorcerer who became the victim of his own powers, the welfare state *has* engendered misunderstandings and technical failures (of local and regional government reform, incomes policies, educational planning, and so on) and *is* besieged by an overload of demands and by movements who refuse their cooperation.

The neocorporatists offer their own explanations for these failures: scarcity of resources; noncompliance and/or indifference of citizens (a crucial point, for which further explanations are rarely provided); the fiscal problems produced by the "inertia commitments" of states (that is, aging public policy programs that survive as if in mortmain); and, above all, the increased complexity of the expanding web of relations of power and responsibility within which state bureaucracies are ensnared – and made more vulnerable. According to the neocorporatists, there is a trend not only toward larger but also toward less effective organization, a marked clumsiness of bureaucratic planning, contradictions between policy programs, and so on. Indeed, the growth of government can be expected to reduce efficiency, because of the multiplying need to coordinate a larger and more heterogeneous number of bureaucratic organizations. Efforts at coordination, it is often said, have thus far been unable to rely on a common denominator (such as money), through which the inputs and outputs of single administrative programs could be monitored.[37]

Stern warnings of the possible consequences of these irrationalities are issued. Governments, it is argued, may be subjected to a "run on government," with the result that their social control function may be irreversibly disrupted by extrapolitical contenders for power. Inasmuch as the increasing complexity and interdependency of social and political life seem irreversible (compare the new liberal reassertion of the state–civil society duality), these irrationalities can be avoided only if governments act with less pusillanimity. They must reduce the range and quantity of social demands for which hitherto they have been deemed responsible. The language of the defenders of neocorporatist strategies is typically technobureaucratic. States, it is insisted, must redirect, control, and guide their own complex of institutions, in order successfully to convert resources into programs that from here on will produce outputs more in accord with planned policy commitments. "Avoiding the crisis of ungovernability means, above all, avoiding the disappointment, frustration and disaffection resulting from visible policy failures."[38] In the view of the neocorporatists, the dramatic proliferation of the welfare state assumption that citizenship rights extend from the legal to the social sphere has produced an exponential growth of state activity – to the point where the very size of "big government" prevents it from operating efficiently and authoritatively. The state not only fails to achieve its objectives; by democratizing equity claims it also creates new expectations that become just as many new problems to be solved bureaucratically. The welfare state has necessarily heightened popular aspirations that it is unable to satisfy. It therefore has deepened the sense of relative deprivation among its clientele.[39]

Against the welfare state project neocorporatists accordingly propose more explicitly beggar-thy-neighbor solutions. Proportional inequality is assumed to be both desirable and necessary. Thus some hitherto taken-for-granted functions of government (for example, "unnecessary" social welfare services) must be "unloaded" or removed from the purview of government. Principles such as competition between political parties and ministerial responsibility must be weakened (further eroding the already weak influence of legislatures in policy-making procedures). Moreover, other state functions ought to be transferred (at least in part) to non-government authorities (such as voluntary social service organizations, business, and, if possible, organized labor). Above all, the bureaucratic state must abandon its democratic pretensions and reduce expectations. The state must agitate on behalf of the principle of restraint: Marginal groups must learn to demand less from government, politicians must at times make unpopular decisions, trade union leaders must learn to avoid inflexible demands. Neocorporatist advocates typically insist that the growth of the state under democratic pressure has implicated it within more and more demands of clients, recognized interest groups, and the struggles of "marginalized" grass-roots movements. Though the institutionalized participation of these groups seems to increase the responsiveness and legitimacy of the state, the reverse is in fact the case. Institutionalized participants easily become veto groups and thereby limit the effectiveness of government. An "excess of democracy" directly promotes ever more complex bureaucratic mechanisms and "distemper" (Huntington) among their dissatisfied clients.

Neocorporatist discourse is necessarily silent about those actually existing (and glaring) inequalities of power perpetuated by the welfare state project. It is as if those already without access to state and corporate power (for example, those on welfare and pensions; aboriginal and immigrant peoples; sexual and racial minorities; people in economically depressed rural, urban, and national regions), will be left to fend for themselves – no doubt under the watchful, professional eye of the administrator, social worker, and policeman. Evidently, the maxim of neocorporatism is: To them that hath shall in future be given.

Autonomous public spheres

The maxim of neocorporatism provokes crucial questions. According to which principles or criteria are the proposed privileges of power, wealth, and authority (of state planners, trustworthy unions, and oligopolistic corporations) to be allocated? Why are the needs of some and not other groups and individuals to be screened out? Neocorporatism's proposals for a reorganized fusion of social power and state authority are notoriously embarrassed by such questions. This embarrassment constitutes a fundamental flaw in all neocorporatist theories of proportional equality – namely, that their *particular* schemata cannot provide compelling reasons for investing certain privileged groups with the authority to make what are in effect more general, *public* decisions. In the present phase of late capitalism, this decisive defect has been underscored by the radical demands of a multiplicity of autonomous, potentially democratic movements. In opposition to the new liberalism and neocorporatism, these movements criticize welfare state administrations for their inefficiency and wastefulness, their systematic dependence upon the power of capital, their consequent failure to enhance social welfare, and, finally, their restriction of popular democratic initiatives in various policy matters. There are signs, consequent upon the crisis tendencies of the welfare state project, that the old debate over questions of power and democracy is again resurfacing as a central theme within all late capitalist societies. Certainly, welfare state policies continue to be supported by numerous of their clients as beneficial, productive, and humane. The "governmentality" (Foucault) of the welfare state project, its self-representation as beneficial to life by virtue of its capacity to subject everything to precise controls and comprehensive regulations, has still not been effectively ruptured. In addition, and somewhat in opposition to this governmentality, the crisis tendencies of the welfare state have produced apathy and quiet disillusion, of which lack of involvement or subjective indifference to organized party politics is the most conspicuous feature. Especially when coupled with continuing allegations about the state's responsibility for alleviating the effects of all systemic problems, this apathy and disillusion often transform themselves into a renewal of autonomous, public initiatives – against depoliticized state planning.

Nowadays, the deep-seated, unresolved difficulties of contemporary welfare states – the above-mentioned decline of capital accumulation and the institutionalized anarchy within state policy making – are widely reinforced by *bürger-initiativen* in most fields of state planning. Some of the most important of these initiatives include the growth of urban autonomy groups, regional separatists, tenants' rights advocates, and others concerned with urban regional and housing policies; the civil libertarian focus upon the making, adjudication, and enforcement of law; actions by medical staff, students, teachers, feminists, and gay rights advocates within the fields of health, education, and sexual policy; the growth of alternative communications media; movements that challenge energy, weapons, and immigration programs; and, within the sphere of industrial relations, struggles over incomes policies, redundancy, and cutbacks. Few if any state (and, indeed, corporate and trade union) institutions are today immune from the practical criticism of ordinary citizens acting within autonomous public spheres. Welfare state attempts to eliminate social protest and permanently secure an age of "sociability" unwittingly provoke a process of "desubordination" (Miliband), a rise in the level of political activity, and radical democratic expectations.

25

One of the principle sources of this desubordination is the self-contradictory mode of operation of the bureaucratic welfare state. This state's self-proclaimed *political* task of responding to various social claims (that is, of responsive problem solving) contradicts its chronic reliance upon *depoliticized*, bureaucratic strategies (that is, upon problem definition and control mechanisms). This self-contradiction is not limited to welfare state strategies. It marks all bureaucratic organizations, including capitalist corporations. Inasmuch as they typically institute decisions about all matters in the absence of open discussion and control from below, bureaucratic organizations are antithetical to democratic, public life. Bureaucracies are systems of depoliticized activity; at all levels within these organizations, lower authorities tend to be monitored and controlled by higher authorities. These relations of command and obedience are characteristically structured by a range of anonymous, formal mechanisms. These range from differential salaries and career opportunities and specialized and fragmented functional tasks, through concern with expertise and efficient, means-calculating action, to the crafting and execution of particular decisions by means of reliance upon systems of general rules.

Notwithstanding the depoliticizing effects of these mechanisms, bureaucracies' will to control all activities of their constituents and clients is typically unsuccessful. The hierarchical discipline of bureaucratic organization is continually undermined by its own efforts at guaranteeing unity, maintaining continuity of action, and permanently controlling in every minor detail those constituents upon whose actions it chronically depends. Bureaucracy is everywhere marked by self-destructive tendencies. This is because its attempts to enhance its command through reliance upon administrative, abstract-general calculations tend to estrange its constituents, whose frequent resistance in turn obliges the bureaucratic organization to solicit their active participation. Ironically, bureaucratic organization must seek to resolve its problems of self-maintenance by acknowledging the necessity of its members' *not* acting in purposively rational ways. Thus, at all levels and within all fields, bureaucratic structures generate oppositional public spheres that continually tend to contradict and thereby reshape these structures' mode of operation.* Under late capitalist conditions, it becomes clear that there is no preordained or necessary harmony within or

---

* Generated by the self-contradictory mode of operation of bureaucratic organizations, autonomous public spheres are in this sense an expression of a *timeless* "condition of human existence" (Arendt, Pitkin), of an elementary articulation of the human condition in which subjects experience meaningfulness only because they communicate with each other. The theory of public life presented in these essays also rejects the prepolitical and apologetic implications of the "geographic" model of private and public proposed by Richard Sennett's *The Fall of Public Man* (New York, 1978). Oppositional public spheres are not equivalent to impersonal and formal spaces of life predominantly defined by a diffusely shared sense of "out there," which stand in contrast to the "in here," the private domain of intimate feeling. *Autonomous* publics should not be confused, thirdly, with the new liberal view of the public as equivalent to a domain constructed by bureaucratic state institutions (public authorities), whose function is to regulate and supervise public standards in accordance with which the public is supposed to live quietly and passively. (This view is evident in Thomas Nagel's account of the morality of

between bureaucratic organizations. It is therefore highly misleading to speak of an ultimate or final point of bureaucracy. Contemporary late capitalist societies tend to be more or less advanced in the process of bureaucratization, more or less marked by self-destructive tendencies. It is as if corporate, social, and state bureaucracies are allowed to exercise authoritative control only on the condition that, at the same time, they undermine their own authority.

Pressured by this more general contradiction, the welfare state project of generalized administrative intrusion into the spheres of commodification and everyday life directly presupposes a *control* of (potentially) democratic demands. From the point of view of this project, social and political life can be secured and enhanced only through comprehensive bureaucratic networks of surveillance, regulation, and control. Autonomous public spheres cannot be allowed to develop within the realms of either society or the state. The contemporary drift of all welfare states in the direction of heavily armed "nuclear states" (Negri) is not the only symptom of this authoritarianism. These states have always relied upon strategies that reinforce "non-decisions" (Bachrach and Baratz), and that thereby produce "marginality" at the very centers of state decision making. In other words, they have consistently adopted means of policy making that selectively co-opt, suffocate, or ignore demands for change in the existing allocation of benefits and privileges of property, status, and power.

This administrative restriction of the scope of potential social and political conflict is not only a self-protective device on the part of the state. It is also a necessary feature of a political system that must take note of the immense obstruction potential of other bureaucratic organizations (organized labor and, principally, oligopoly capital), upon whose cooperation this system structurally depends for its own legitimacy and effectiveness. These social groups (and especially fractions of capital) not only have privileged access to institutions of state policy making; they also tend to determine the form and content of what can be officially negotiated. This "corporate bias" predisposes welfare states to operate technocratically, in accordance with "the lowest common denominator of policies designed to avoid trouble."[40] Political decisions are taken not through adversary politics and widespread public discussion, but by way of an informally organized, often inaccessible, and arcane bargaining process between the state and leaders of these bureaucratic governing institutions. Under welfare state capitalist conditions, bureaucratic compromise and give-and-take consensus is supposed to be the mark of official politics. The attempted welfare state compromise necessarily assumes the form of a seemingly endless and aimless process of adaptation and control, of stabilizing always emerging risks, bottlenecks, and conflict situations.[41] This means also that the high aspirations and rosy promises

public actions in "Ruthlessness in Public Life," in Stuart Hampshire (ed.), *Public and Private Morality* [Cambridge, 1978], pp. 75–91). By virtue of their often carnival-like and conflict-ridden character, finally, public spheres are not necessarily synonymous with the formation of deception-free consensuses through rational speech, as Habermas and others imply (see Essays 5 and 7).

associated at an earlier historical phase with the welfare state project have tended to give way to the "stagnant mediocrity" (Middlemas) of compromise agreements.

The foregoing discussion of some difficulties within the welfare state project suggests that this compromise and mediocrity are short-lived tendencies. In addition to the authoritarian crusades of the new liberalism and neocorporatism, the welfare state project and its "interest group liberalism" have also become the object of criticism of numerous radical citizens' movements. Their containment has become a permanent problem for all late capitalist systems. For these (potentially) democratic movements signal the emerging fact that autonomous public discussion and action and the bureaucratic welfare state have now parted company. The "end of politics" promoted by this "security state"[42] gives rise to new modes of public action, whose protagonists address specific, concrete needs without delegation. These movements perceive that, in the absence of renewed subjectivity, the present crisis tendencies are a condition of the renovation and renewal of the existing order. These autonomous movements tacitly acknowledge the insight – forcefully emphasized in the nineteenth century by Marx, Burckhardt, and others – that crisis tendencies can have authoritarian consequences. These movements are therefore not necessarily analogous to the breezes of an approaching dawn; within their analyses, actions, and demands to push harder and further, there are often pessimistic undertones, reflections of uncertainty and the possibility of defeat. Many within the new movements accurately sense that crisis situations facilitate the authoritarian abolition of a host of democratic practices, practices from which it is officially declared that life has long since departed and that could not have been swept away so arbitrarily under "normal" conditions. These movements nevertheless correctly emphasize that the bureaucratically negotiated compromises of the welfare state necessarily suppress a wide gamut of political and social demands. In view of this repression, it is not surprising that in the present conjuncture these excluded demands continue to be articulated through the radicalization of existing welfare state–social democratic parties. Alternatively, and with at least equal frequency, these demands are reexpressed, as it were, in unofficial and highly unpredictable ways – through votes for candidates and parties outside the welfare state consensus, by electoral absenteeism and massive abstentions from formal political processes, and through situational protest.[43]

Inasmuch as it is unified by a suspicion of bureaucratic authoritarianism and by its demands for an overcoming of the "programmed society" (Touraine) through open-ended discussion and self-assumed consent and obligations, at least some of this resistance can already be understood as a nascent reassertion of democratic public life. Evidently, this resistance is a *systematic* effect of the self-contradictory, bureaucratic character of the welfare state project. This resistance nevertheless assumes the form of an eclectic mosaic. The new autonomous movements tend to be highly differentiated, fragmented, and localized, in part because of the structural differentiation of various sectors of the state and civil society; partly because they demonstrate a remarkable sensitivity to questions of power and therefore a capacity to deepen their self-criticism (as in the renaissance of feminism through its initial critiques of the patriarchalism of the student movement); and also in part because the bureaucratic state itself struggles to divide, suppress, and rule these movements, which it cannot allow to become an autonomous political force.

Under late capitalist conditions, then, it is clear that the bureaucratization process by no means effects its own destruction by raising against itself, so to speak, the mass of the dispossessed. This is one reason why all talk of old and new working classes, "humanity," "a public sphere," or "the people" must be given up. So, too, must the anticipation (Touraine's, for instance) of the emergence of a new social movement that tomorrow will take over the central role that the workers' movement yesterday played. In the present conjuncture, the scope and location of conflicts are many and varied; their heterogeneity does not necessarily tend to dissolve and converge toward a single revolutionary class or movement.[44] The autonomous movements institute a *plurality* of public spheres. Notwithstanding their dispersed and fragmented character (which may in fact serve to confound the classic state responses of co-optation and repression), these movements signal the emergence of a new political theme under late capitalist, welfare state conditions. This theme assumes the form of something approaching a generalized confrontation between, on the one hand, administrative-bureaucratic attempts (championed by the new liberalism and corporatism) to restructure the welfare state and social life for a new phase of capitalist accumulation and state power and, on the other hand, the autonomous movements' struggles to speak and be heard, to repoliticize their everyday lives, to establish qualitatively new forms of social and political relations in which public spheres of mutuality, discussion, and concern with concrete needs predominate.

2

The legacy of Max Weber

This passion for bureaucracy...is enough to drive one to despair.

Max Weber

Bureaucracy: the organizing principle of modern life

To speak about bureaucracy, as many nowadays love to do, is to engage the central concern of Max Weber. Preoccupied with understanding the distinctively individual or unique character of the present historical phase,[1] Weber was convinced that modern bourgeois reality is marked by an unprecedented "passion for bureaucracy." In no previous country or historical period has existence come to be so absolutely confined within calculating, rationalized forms of organization. Their scope and influence tend to become universal. Everywhere houses of bureaucratic serfdom are being constructed and finished; the advance of bureaucracy seems irreversible.[2]

Weber was of course aware that the bureaucratization of modern existence was not without precedent. Through a great variety of complex processes, all former civilizations successfully rationalized particular areas of daily life. The rational calculation of architectural stress and arching patterns, for example, was clearly evident in the medieval Gothic vault; rationalized forms of bookkeeping appeared in the ancient Mediterranean and Near East, as well as in India and China; Roman jurisprudence and legal practice were inscribed within rigorous and calculating schemata of argumentation; the beginnings of military discipline, with its prohibition of fighting out of line, were already displayed among the heavily armed Hellenic and Roman foot soldiers; the Renaissance elevation of the rationally calculated experiment to a key principle of scientific inquiry was preceded by the war technology and mathematized astronomy of Hellenic antiquity, the techniques of experimentation in Indian yoga, and the mining operations of the Middle Ages. Moreover, numerous social formations have in the past organized themselves through highly developed and quantitatively large bureaucratic organizations: Egypt during the period of the new Empire; the Roman Catholic Church, especially from the end of the thirteenth century; China from the time of Shi Hwangti; and so on.[3] In the face of these

30

well-known examples Weber nevertheless insisted that modern, occidental processes of bureaucratization are without precedent. Their fundamental novelty
lies in the fact that they tend to penetrate and capture *all* realms of life.[4] The
modern civilizing process is virtually identical with the development of calculating, bureaucratic organization. The whole of life falls under the sway of
"formal" or purposive rationality – goal-oriented conduct that is guided by the
spirit of calculation and abstract-general rules, and that therefore reduces its
fields of operation to objects of administration. Under conditions of total bureaucratization, voluntary associations and value-oriented relations of mutual
agreement are increasingly subverted and replaced by purposively rational organizations. These strive to realize their respective goals by way of the definition
and regulation of all situations as problems, which subsequently can be solved
through computation and reckoning. In short, the champions and defenders of
bureaucratization struggle to "disenchant" the world, to rid it of all inestimable,
mysterious forces. It is assumed that all events and things can be defined, monitored, and controlled through bureaucratic means and calculations.

Weber's account of the unique realities of modern life, it must be emphasized,
does not presume that the proliferation of bureaucratic conduct is *identical* with
the modernization process. He insists that his own discussion of the specificity
or individuality of modern bourgeois life tends to be one-sided.[5] Like all comparative inquiries, its emphases are selective, structured by judgments about the
significance of contemporary bureaucratic domination. These judgments positively determine the goals and methods of inquiry into bureaucratic forms. By
way of these judgments, bureaucratic organizations are estimated to be characteristic of the contemporary world, setting it apart from all previous sociohistorical formations. Conversely, these judgments exclude a rich infinity of
general and particular aspects of life under modern conditions. This point is of
great importance to the following essay. Simply, Weber's analysis does not pose
as an exhaustive description of the dynamics of the bureaucratization process.
It does not claim to depict or reproduce conceptually the "really real" content
and form of modern bureaucratic reality. Its concern to clarify and understand
this reality instead systematically relies upon ideal-typical categories. These one-
sidedly emphasize and scrutinize certain characteristic features of bureaucracy.
Weber continually emphasizes that there can be no presuppositionless representation of bureaucratic processes that somehow allow themselves to be fully
disclosed. These processes can be observed, analyzed, or criticized only through
methods of inquiry that depend upon a series of conceptual abstractions. His
account of bureaucratic rationality is thus avowedly selective, conditioned by the
mode of contemporary historical interest in understanding that rationality.

Guided by this premise, Weber analyzes at least four elements common to
modern bureaucratic institutions. These elements, to repeat, are by no means
expressed in their pure form anywhere within the landscape of modern life.
They nevertheless together constitute (in his view) the most highly significant
attributes peculiar to all contemporary public and private bureaucratic organizations. In the first place, bureaucracy can be analyzed as an ensemble of consistent, methodically prepared, and precisely executed relations of command

and obedience. Relations between "subjects" within the organizational hierarchy are ordered firmly, and in accordance with the necessary principle of appointment and supervision from above. These subjects are "unswervingly and exclusively set for carrying out the command."[6]

Bureaucracy constitutes an objective matrix of power, into which officials (and their clients) at all levels are slotted, by which their activity is structured, and according to which they are to be depoliticized and governed anonymously as beings who "need order and nothing but order."[7] Within all spheres of the organization, subordinates are expected to rely upon the initiative and problem-solving ability of their superiors. As a system of organized inequality, bureaucratic organization therefore thrives on the suspension of all personal criticism, passive obedience, faith in authority, and attention to directives among the subordinated. Nervous and helpless when severed from their organization, individuals become organization people, whose one ideal in life is to conform. They become single cogs who strive for bigger jobs within an ever-moving and more or less precisely functioning apparatus, whose course, in turn, can be altered only by those (bureaucrats) at the very top. Bureaucratic administration is therefore crucially premised upon the concentration of the means of production, war, and administration in the hands of those who govern. In turn, those who deploy and administer these means consider the world and all that is within it a mere object of their concern. Bureaucracy always subsists and expands through bureaucrats.

These relations of subordination, secondly, are subject to rigorous internal differentiation, that is, are structured in conformity with a usually complex division of tasks or offices. The rules specifying these tasks are typically calculated through empirical observation, guided by such considerations as the minimum of costs, and spelled out in written documents. The skillful, efficient operation of bureaucratic organizations such as the factory or the department store depends upon rational and continuous specialization. Within the bureaucratic apparatus, the activities of speaking, interacting, and laboring staff are subject to continuous administrative dissection from above. Each level and sphere of activity is compartmentalized, governed by particular rules of action. These rules specify the requisite qualifications and duties necessary for staff employed at each level or post within the organization: Those who occupy positions of command, for example, tend to be expertly trained; all are to obtain remuneration and material advantages in accordance with the degree of privilege of their condition of existence within the organization; and so on. Although these rules are to a greater or lesser extent subject to change, an office and its corresponding rules of operation tend to continue in existence beyond the life of its incumbent. The "bearers" and clients of bureaucratic organization are compelled to consider it their duty to act in conformity with these rules.

Bureaucratic forms of organization, thirdly, are marked with a definite impersonality. "Without regard for *particular* persons and situations" is a watchword of bureaucracy. Bureaucratic relations of power are systems of formal, depersonalized rationality. They are guided by abstract-general regulations, which are applied exhaustively and consistently to every case. All bureaucratic administration (whether of its internal staff or its external clients) is inscribed within a rule-bound matter-of-factness, a principled rejection of doing business on a case-by-case basis. According to Weber, this principled "impersonalism" implies that these organizations are unswervingly neutral, placing themselves at the disposal of any and every power that claims their businesslike service. Modern bureaucratic organizations tend to abolish the practice (typical in patrimonial institutions) of individuals' assignment of tributes, usufructs, and services to others in return for personal favors. Whereas, for example, ruling groups of the ancient Orient, European feudalism, and the Mongolian and Germanic empires of conquest all systematically depended upon personal trustees, court servants, and table companions, the commanders of modern bureaucratic structures typically discharge their business according to calculable, objective rules. They rule without regard for individual persons. Conversely, the governed objects of bureaucratic administration are not deemed to be the personal servants or property of those who rule.

The more actual bureaucracies approximate this mechanical, depersonalized form, the more their clients and staff are dehumanized, forced into a procrustean bed of general rules and regulations. Bureaucratic domination is the enemy of singularity and impetuousness. Routinized, bureaucratic discipline lays to rest all heroic ecstasy, cults of honor, and spirited and personalized loyalty to leaders: "Love, hatred, and all purely personal, irrational, and emotional elements" that cannot readily be calculated and administered through abstract-general rules tend to be eliminated.[8] In respect of their mechanical impersonality, modern bureaucracies ensure the submission of all ranks to their superiors, and much more effectively than ancient despotisms. Compared to the nonmodern attempts to organize the enslavement of bodies bureaucratically (for example, the strict, militaristic disciplining of slaves in the Roman latifundia, or the pharaoh-guided Egyptian state bureaucracy), modern bureaucracies effect submission through less personal and more subtle and reliable mechanisms – such as the payment of wages and salaries; the provision of tenure; superannuation; annual vacations; and appeals to objective regulations, careerism, job experience, and the senses of duty and conscientiousness.[9] In exchange for these material guarantees, functionaries and clients at all levels render service not to persons, but to objective and impersonal organizational goals.

Of very great importance, finally, is Weber's insistence that, under modern conditions, formal bureaucratic organizations tend to predominate by virtue of their *technical* superiority. It is precisely because of their technical competence that bureaucratic institutions can deal with this world's complexities.[10] Irrespective of the goals of ruling groups – goals such as the self-expansion of value or the defense of the nation-state through the deployment of standing armies under conditions of power politics – their reliance upon bureaucratic means is essential. In Egypt, the oldest country of bureaucratic domination, the state regulation of national waterways was unavoidable because of technical economic factors. Under modern state-guided capitalism, analogously, bureaucracy is indispensable because of its purely technical superiority.[11]

Weber persistently speaks of bureaucratic mechanisms through the metaphor

33

of the machine. The modern bourgeois world is a calculating, mechanized world. Its dominant, machinelike institutions depend for their functioning and coordination on strictly objective and technical expertise, itself more and more trained within bureaucratically organized scientific research institutes of the universities.[12] Compared with the achievement capacities of other forms of organization (such as patriarchal and patrimonial systems of administration), mechanized, expertly guided bureaucracy – especially in its monocratic form – is unsurpassed. It seeks, in principle, to calculate everything rationally. Typically depending upon specialized knowledge and concrete information relevant to its performance, bureaucracy is qualitatively more precise, unambiguous, flexible, smoothly operating, and cost-efficient than other forms. "Precision, speed, unambiguity, knowledge of the files, continuity, discretion, unity, strict subordination, reduction of friction and of material and personal costs....trained bureaucracy is superior on all these points."[13] Under modern conditions, and exactly because of these qualities, bureaucracy ensures its own relentless advance, just as the modern machine irreversibly guarantees its own triumph over various inferior forms of manual production. In comparison with other, less technically efficient forms of organization, bureaucracy is distinguished therefore by its much greater inescapability.

Modern capitalism

The subtle depth and exactness of Weber's discussion of bureaucratic rationality undergo something of a dissipation in the foregoing introduction. The claims of his discussion must be analyzed in considerably more detail, and with particular reference to the modern spheres of society and state. To begin with, it is only under modern conditions, Weber insists, that there have emerged highly specialized, bureaucratic capitalist enterprises that deploy fixed capital and "free" labor power. Large capitalist enterprises have become the historically unequaled model of the bureaucratic mode of organization. Interlocking networks of these organizations form an immense, and apparently unshakable, cosmos, an institutionally differentiated market economy in accordance with whose rules of action individuals are pressured to conform: In the struggle for the satisfaction of desires for "utilities," those who do not follow suit either go out of business or are flung into the ranks of the unemployed. Breaking down traditional habits of life, subjecting the whole world to its bureaucratic administration, the capitalist mode of production constitutes itself as "that force in modern life which has most influence on our destinies."[14]

Under these conditions dictated by the capitalist market economy, Weber stresses, the single corporation is compelled to discharge its official business continuously, precisely, unambiguously, and with as much speed and cost efficiency as possible. In respect of its permanently rationalizing tendencies, the capitalist mode of production is not synonymous with irrational speculation, with the reckless and unscrupulous pursuit of profit. Weber rejects the association (proposed by Simmel's *Philosophie des Geldes*, for example)[15] of acquisition through a money economy with capitalism. In the first place, from a technical point of view the reliance upon money entails the most rational *means* of orienting economic activity.[16] Moreover, the uncontrolled release of impulses greedy for gold may well be as old as the history of the species. Such daredevil acquisitiveness has often appeared, indeed, as the underside of strongly traditional societies: "The inner attitude of the adventurer, which laughs at all ethical limitations, has been universal."[17] At any rate, entrepreneurial adventurers have for ages and in all parts of the world operated as speculators and financiers in wars, piracy, and contracts of all kinds. Absolute unscrupulousness and avarice bear little resemblance to modern capitalism, and brigands, pirates, usurers, and large merchants bear still less to its spirit.

Under modern conditions, it is true, reckless avarice and speculation continue. Modern capitalism by no means eradicates what Weber calls "speculative" calculations – those oriented to possibilities whose realization is more or less fortuitous, and therefore in a certain sense incalculable.[18] Modern capitalist firms, for example, heedlessly consume natural resources, for which there are often no substitutes.[19] Those directing or sharing in the fortunes of profit-making enterprises also continue to be motivated by risk taking, ambition, and opportunities for large income from profitable undertakings. And the monopolistic struggle for economic gain through territorial annexations – imperialist capitalism – continues to play a crucial and destabilizing role in modern life.[20] As a consequence of all these factors, capitalist firms, monopolies, and trusts are necessarily institutions of limited duration. Weber was nevertheless convinced that modern capitalism tends to tame or moderate the backward irrationality of speculative ventures. Although the dangers of economic crisis have by no means disappeared, their relative importance has diminished, precisely because of continuing capitalist attempts to rationalize production, prices, turnover, and sources of credit.[21]

Inasmuch as its activities are bureaucratically organized on the basis of rigorous foresight and continuous calculation, the modern capitalist enterprise also overcomes the privileged traditionalism of the guild craftsman, the hand-to-mouth mode of life of the peasant, and the occasional capital accounting made by precapitalist traveling merchants (such as the *commenda*). Under capitalist economic conditions, Weber emphasizes, private enterprises are subject to the more generalized imperatives of bureaucratic rationalization. In order to avoid going under in the market struggle, corporations must avoid operating in accordance with the reckless and unmediated logic of profitability. Unlike the infamous Dutch sea captain who was prepared to scorch his sails in hell just for the sake of gain, capitalist entrepreneurs must rather conduct their operations in accordance with the greater foresight and caution associated with the bureaucratic, rationally calculated pursuit of profit.[22] Industrial capitalist enterprises *systematically* pursue profit through relations of exchange and by means of ongoing calculations that have monopolistic effects. Under contemporary conditions, the organizing principle of the social exchange with outer nature is "capital calculations" in monetary terms. These calculations are associated with corporate attempts to plan and administer nature, material goods, and labor power bureaucratically as means of profitable acquisition. The corporate orientation to capital accounting takes the form of continuous exante calculations of the probable risks and chances of profit, supplemented by continuous expost calculations to verify the actual resulting profit or loss.[23] The final (or periodically estimated) revenues generated by the capitalist firm are supposed to exceed its capital, that is, the estimated value of its fixed means of profit making (buildings, machinery, raw materials, products, reserves of cash, and so on).

This tendency for the limited-liability enterprise to adhere to the logic of continuous rational capital accounting – a rare and usually discontinuous achievement outside the modern Occident – is contingent upon the fulfillment of several crucial conditions. It is appropriate to mention at least four such conditions within this context. First, and most obviously, autonomous, share-granting capitalist enterprises tend to enhance their calculated expectations of profit by striving to exercise exclusive control over the utilized physical means of production.[24] Typically, capitalist enterprises' central organization of these means have entailed the spatial separation of households from the site of production or commerce. Although this development is not without precedent (Weber mentions the case of the oriental bazaar), this spatial concentration of the forces of production provides a radical contrast with the nonmodern situation. Formerly, commercial or productive enterprises were constituted as part of the wider *oikos*, or household, of the prince or landowner or town (as in the *ergasteria* of the Piraeus). Consequent upon the legal detachment of corporate from personal wealth, by contrast, the corporate monopoly and spatial segregation of productive capital has come to prevail completely in modern economic life.[25]

Weber insists, secondly, that this corporate monopoly and geographic concentration of the physical means of production depends upon a market system of formally free, but actually dominated, labor power. In contrast, say, to the feudal socage system or the slave plantations of antiquity, the modern bureaucratic corporation operates on the basis of the *selection* of its labor power.[26] This implies that the capitalist mode of production tends to minimize workers' appropriation of jobs and of opportunities for earning; conversely, this mode of production minimizes the legal appropriation of workers by owners. Through its powers of hiring and firing, and under pressure from competition with other employers, the modern capitalist enterprise seeks to organize free labor power in accordance with its rationally calculated pursuit of profit. "Exact calculation," Weber adds, "is only possible on a basis of free labor."[27] Under conditions in which entrepreneurs enjoy freedom to hire and fire workers, and in which workers are employed for wages and salaries, operational efficiency through capital accounting tends to be maximized. Under these conditions, capital investment in the labor force of the enterprise is relatively lessened (compared, say, with former practices of purchasing and maintaining slaves and their dependents).

Moreover, according to Weber, the institution of nominally free conditions of labor enhances the power of management to select its labor power according to labor's ability and willingness to work. As a consequence, strict capital accounting establishes a novel and less visible "system of domination [*Herrschaftsverhältniss*]." The bureaucratic enterprise strives to effect the permanent enslavement of workers individually and collectively to the machine by securing their peaceful and permanent separation from their tools of labor. Military discipline is the ideal model for the modern capitalist factory; like Cromwell's rationally disciplined Ironsides, modern workers become the objects of cunning capitalist strategies aimed at having "everyone regimented, ordered about, constructed."[28] Not only do all material means of production become fixed or working capital, but all workers are transformed into mere "hands." Weber typically argues that this expropriation of workers' (potential) control over the means of production by managerial capitalists is determined by purely technical factors. Only if the profit-making firm wrests exclusive control of the means of production can it function efficiently as an organized, internally differentiated, and continuously supervised workshop. Only through its monopoly over the means of production can it rationally exploit its sources of power, maximize control over the speed of work, standardize the quality of its products, and secure their consumption through aggressive marketing strategies that awaken and direct consumer wants.[29]

This corporate shutting out of labor power has the unintended effect – inadequately analyzed by Weber – of generating class struggles, especially between the big industrial entrepreneur and the free wage laborer.[30] This means that the profitability-accounting processes of firms must be continually oriented to expectations of estimated changes in costs and prices caused by competition with other corporate bureaucracies and the bargaining and struggles of labor.[31] According to Weber, such expectations are not necessarily undermined by a uniform trend to proletarianization and uncompromising class struggle.[32] Struggles against the lifeless machinery of capitalist industry are not synonymous with its inability to function efficiently. Indeed, bureaucratic control over the free labor power of the "negatively privileged classes" is facilitated by a range of conditions: the fact that laborers, in varying degrees, subjectively value their work as a mode of life; their recognition that they also run the permanent risk of going entirely without provisions for themselves and their dependents; the establishment (in the case of manual laborers, at least) of common working discipline that is spatially concentrated on the shop floor; continual managerial attempts to manage scientifically, "de-skill," and discipline living labor power through the uneven deployment of labor-saving machinery; and, perhaps most important, the institution of new strata of specialized and commercially or technically trained officials (such as clerks and administrators at all levels), whose sensed interests are by no means identical with those of the people trained to attend and handle machinery.[33]

This proliferation of strata of expertly trained, technical officials directly promotes modern corporations' fulfillment of a third condition of rational capital accounting – the reliance upon "mechanically rational technology."[34] The corporate drive to calculate and compare income with expenditure, Weber urges, tends to become more and more dependent upon forms of exact guesswork, reckoning, and prediction. Rationalized bookkeeping is only one example of this more general corporate dependence upon rational technical means that are mechanized to the greatest degree. Weber also stresses the growing merger of the capitalist enterprise, machine technology, and the "mathematically and ex-

37

perimentally exact natural sciences"[35] – a scientization process that, as it were, builds a decisive "meta-calculability" into an already calculating production and distribution process. These and other examples of mechanically rational technology indicate that, under modern conditions, technical progress has come to be largely oriented to the furtherance of bureaucratically calculated profit making. Conversely, these examples indicate that profit-making enterprises become progressively more reliant upon mechanized sources of power, machinery, and administration. From a technical point of view, Weber argues, this mechanization process is understandable. Rational technical means are highly productive. They also serve to discipline (and save on) labor power and, in general, to maximize the uniformity and calculability of performance of the bureaucratic organization.[36]

Weber proposes, finally, that the modern corporation's achievement of the highest possible degree of efficient capital accounting is dependent upon an ensemble of politico-legal conditions that, in principle, are estimable with at least some degree of certainty.[37] The problem of whether the modern bureaucratic state could – or even should – satisfy this certainty condition is of great concern to Weber.

The bureaucratic nation-state

Weber's well-known emphasis upon the modern state as a specific form of bureaucratic domination complements his general insistence that the bureaucratization of the modern world was not a simple *consequence* of capitalist activity. The emergence and triumph of rational capitalistic enterprises cannot be explained through economic reasoning alone. The processes of bureaucratization that now grip modern life by no means have a uniform, singular history or logic of development. Weber thus insists that modern forms of state cannot be analyzed as "superstructural" vis-à-vis the primary determinations of economic conduct. He radically rejects the view that state institutions are parasites engendered by internal contradictions of social power. State bureaucracy is not the result of the division of modern society into classes and class struggles. Nor is its function simply that of securing the formal acceptance of the rules of a configuration of social (that is, class) power. Nor, finally, would the abolition of the real historical agents – classes in struggle – signal its necessary disappearance.

Certainly, the modern bureaucratic state is compelled to engage in what Weber calls "economically oriented action."[38] And it is no less evident, especially in his political writings, that Weber insists on analyzing the conditions of social power and conflict within which contemporary states are always and already embedded.[39] Weber nevertheless reasons against the modern "over-estimation of the 'economic,' " which represents – falsely – the nation-state as a mere parasitic superstructure, as the political organization of the dominant classes.[40] The break with the tradition of classical Marxism is strongly evident at this point. Against Hegel, Bauer, and Ruge, for example, Marx had consistently defended the thesis that the modern state was bound to the unfettered logic and power of civil society. The modern bourgeois state was seen as without historical precedent, inasmuch as it was restricted to mere "formal" and "negative" activities. Its powers ceased where the depoliticized hustle and bustle of commodity production and exchange processes commenced. Emancipated from the yoke of politics, the capital-dominated civil society became the natural foundation upon which the modern state rested and to which it had to react. Precisely because the bourgeoisie was the leading source of revenues from taxation and loans, the liberal bourgeois state had become nothing more than the form of organization that this class adopted for the purposes of guaranteeing its property and interests. This state was an insurance pact of the bourgeoisie both against the proletariat and against itself, that is, against the persistent anarchy of individual capitalist interests. As the most famous (and, in Weber's time, still influential) 1848 formulation had it, this state was "but a committee for managing the common affairs of the whole bourgeoisie."[41]

According to Weber, this kind of singular emphasis upon the determining power of the economic is not without some justification. The strictly economic explanations proposed by historical materialism successfully produce insights into the unique importance of economic activity within those events that constitute modern life. Historical materialism's monist type of thinking, its attempt to provide one-sidedly economic explanations of the modern state, nevertheless produces a host of embarrassing difficulties. For example, historico-political events that cannot be explained through recourse to economic hypotheses are dismissed as accidental or insignificant; occasionally, the concept of "the economic" is defined so broadly that all questions of political organization and power are falsely subsumed under that definition; at other times, the magisterial primacy of the economic factor is falsely preserved through the claim that political institutions are creations (and also functional defenders of the interests) of identifiable class groupings.[42] These difficulties, Weber proposes, are generated by historical materialism's fetish of the economic, which results, in turn, from its failure to respect the self-imposed limits of ideal-typical analysis. Any empirical science of concrete reality (*Wirklichkeitswissenschaft*) must rely upon ideal-typical categories that aid the selection and meaningful analysis of an infinite multiplicity of ever-changing social and political phenomena that can never be known in toto. The confident will to totalized knowledge displayed among both the defenders and the critics of historical materialism disregards this decisive methodological point.[43] Conversely, the materialist conception of history forgets that its knowledge of the modern capitalist economy *constructs* this reality through definite and simplifying categorical forms: "The distinction between 'economic' and 'noneconomic' determinants of events is invariably a product of *conceptual* analysis."[44]

Consistent with this rejection of unreflexive and one-sidedly "economistic" accounts of modern life, Weber denies that capitalism somehow created *ex nihilo* a bureaucratic state system dominated by specialist officials, jurists, and politicians. The modern bureaucratic state is not a necessary effect of modern capitalism. The formation of this state, rather, has been compelled more by the need of emerging power blocs to create, within a context of power politics, standing armies disciplined and administered through law and funded by a regularized system of public finance.[45] Under nonmodern conditions, Weber proposes, the self-equipment and self-provisioning of those who fought (for example, the armed citizenry of ancient cities, the militias of the early medieval cities and feudalism) were typical. Under modern conditions, by contrast, the warfare generated by domestic disturbances and distant enemies has compelled the formation of permanent, centralized, and technically efficient magazines. In opposition to the nonmodern principle of self-equipped, privately managed armies, the commanders of the modern state concentrate the material means of violence in their own hands. This process was initiated (for example) in the Italian cities and seigniories, among the monarchies, and in the state of the Norman conquerors. In each case, modern standing armies came into being with the establishment of princely households. These households maneuvered to expropriate the tools of war from the hands of all those (self-providing and self-equipping soldiers, officers, and limited-share companies, such as the "Maonen" of the Middle Ages) who had hitherto managed warfare in private ways.

This expropriation of the means of violence by centralizing state elites was combined with similar developments in the realms of law and administration. Again, the decisive step in each case was taken by princes, who maneuvered to expropriate the legal and administrative powers of formerly autonomous groups: the clergy, the humanistically educated literati, trained jurists, the court nobility and gentry, and so on. Within the field of law, these expropriations effected an increasing dependence of the emerging modern state and its administration upon a legal system dominated by jurists with specialized training in rational, calculable law. This was a highly complex and heterogeneous process. The sources of this bureaucratized law, for example, extended as far back as Roman jurisprudence, itself uniquely implicated within a city-state structure that had developed into an imperial power. Roman legal practice, Weber argues, decisively placed the trial procedure under the jurisdiction of bureaucratically trained experts.[46] This early rationalization of legal procedure at the same time weakened modes of adjudication bound to sacred tradition; such modes had often been supplemented (with respect to single case disputes, as in the Athenian courts) by "charismatic" justice (for example, oracles, prophetic dicta) and various types of informal judgments. In place of this particularism of traditional justice, law became systematized and calculable. After the defeat of Rome, rationalized legal procedures were preserved by the medieval church. Its administration continued to rely upon fixed rules for the discipline of both its own members and the laity. Through the princely expropriation of this rationalized "legal" administration, the emerging modern state became increasingly dependent upon bureaucratized justice. The alliance between this state and formal, calculable jurisprudence was also indirectly favorable to the growth of capitalism. The new system in which capitalistic entrepreneurs engaged in the rationally calculated pursuit of profit was thoroughly incompatible with commercial claims and transactions decided by a competition in reciting formulas (as was the case in China, for example). In other words, bourgeois transactions thrived upon a technical, calculable body of legal rules, whose predictability was in principle no less than that of a machine.[47]

By the sixteenth century, this mechanization of justice was complemented by the bureaucratic reorganization of administration. The ascendancy of princely absolutism over the estates, or so Weber argues, definitely depended upon the simultaneous formation of an expert, bureaucratic officialdom comprising the administrator of finances, the military officer, the trained jurist. In this centralizing process, the officials of the feudal era, usually self-financing vassals invested with high judicial and administrative rank, were stripped of their former possession of the tools of administration. In their place, the princes appointed salaried officials, now fully separated from the the tools of their trade. This bureaucratization of administration, Weber points out, is directly analogous to the capitalist expropriation of independent forms of production. The modern state does not monopolize the means of production – this is the unique historical achievement of the differentiated capitalist corporation within the sphere of civil society. Rather, within a given territory the bureaucratic state comes to monopolize the material means of organization (violence, law, and administration). From the standpoint of state governors, all independent sites of violent, legal, and administrative power must be wiped out. In this unprecedented centralizing process, the bureaucratic nation-state necessarily separates its military, legal, and administrative workers from the material means of administrative organization. Waged and salaried state employees are proletarianized. They neither own nor personally control the state's means of violence, law, and administration. The state, Weber concludes, "has combined the material means of organization in the hands of its leaders, and it has expropriated all autonomous functionaries of estates who formerly controlled these means in their own right. The state has taken their positions and now stands in the top place."[48]

As a consequence of this expropriation process, the activity of politics becomes more and more synonymous with the organized and trained struggle for power within and between bureaucratic nation-state apparatuses. Under modern conditions, political action cannot be identified as the striving for a good ethical life: The meaning of *politics*, rather, tends to become identical with the struggle for control over the state, understood as a territorially delimited and compulsory system of continuously administered power.[49] Those who strive for mastery over this system seek to represent themselves as its legitimate bearers and, therefore, to monopolize wholly its special means of operation, particularly violence.[50] Especially in the contemporary period of formal democracy and the mass franchise, struggles for legitimate command over the state take place through strategies designed to woo, organize, and strictly discipline the masses. This bureaucratization of public life is facilitated by the growing interdependence of the capitalist press and the state,[51] and by the expansion of machine politics guided by professionally trained politicians and party officials. Formal democratic political life is increasingly structured by unprincipled bureaucratic parties, whose function (in addition to that of providing jobs for their own staff) is to direct the process of "vote grabbing" under the tutelage of party bosses and professional politicians.[52]

The growing influence of the bureaucratic political party – technically superior in its capacity to organize the apathy and "consent" of the legally enfranchised masses – also signals the decline of legislatures as the originating points of state policy making. With the exception of cabinet members and a few insurgents, members of legislatures become yes-people, who are expected to cast their votes without committing party treason. Professional party-political organizers outside the legislative arena begin to monopolize the policy-making powers once exercised by notables and parliamentary members.[53] In Weber's eyes, this decline of legislatures is hastened by the growing importance of specialist state officials in matters of public policy making. No doubt, the official is present within many nonmodern civilizations. Modern occidental nation-states, however, qualitatively expand the role and power of civil services staffed by commercially, technically, and legally informed and expert officialdom. These civil services, in collaboration with the military, courts of law, and bureaucratic political parties, come more and more to influence the daily existence of the whole population of modern capitalist countries. These populations become the generalized object of a constitutionally defined state guarded by its monopoly of the means of violence, a state that rationally formulates, administers, and adjudicates laws by means of highly trained specialist officials who obey strictly formulated rules. Modern democracies, Weber insists, are everywhere being transformed into highly ordered, bureaucratic state regimes. Under the sway of bureaucratic imperatives, the governance of the population by legal, military, administrative, and party-political experts and officials now appears to be inevitable.[54]

The merger of corporate and state bureaucracy

These political developments, to repeat, are not viewed by Weber as the simple consequences or effects of the capitalist accumulation process. Weber in fact proposes that in the contemporary period the rational capital accounting of the profit-seeking enterprise becomes increasingly dependent upon calculable and predictable state administration. Nowadays, if only for their mutual survival, the bureaucratic state and corporate capitalism have become interdependent in their patterns of reproduction and growth. "The significance of the state apparatus for the economy," Weber observes, "has been steadily rising, especially with increasing socialization, and its significance will be further augmented."[55]

There are several reasons for this development. From the viewpoint of the capitalist economy, so to speak, this growing interpenetration of state and economy is generated by the increasing dependence of the fixed-capital, rationally calculated capitalist enterprise upon a calculable monetary system and a strict and stable administrative, legal, and military framework. Contemporary capitalism thrives best under the guidance of formally rational systems of administration and law, conditions in which the mode of operation of state policy is to a great degree calculable.[56] The corporate dependence upon the state's military means is also decisive, especially in a world of intensifying economic competition; equally, the state's quest to secure itself militarily within a hostile nation-state system intensifies its dependence upon a permanently expansive and rational system of private capitalist production.[57] For these reasons, bureaucratic state administration more and more becomes a *sine qua non* of the orderly corporate pursuit of profit. This growing dependence of capital upon the state leads, conversely, to the increasing dependence of the state upon capital. This process of reciprocity derives from the fact that modern corporate capitalism (according to Weber) is the most dynamic and fecund system of production ever, and that it can therefore readily supply the requisite financial resources for a stable system of bureaucratic administration.[58] The modern bureaucratic state becomes a "taxation state," upon whose stability the whole political economy depends. It is increasingly dependent upon money contributions (that is, taxes) that are collected by its own staff and that are generated primarily from within the capitalist order. This growing importance of money taxation means that the state has become both the largest single receiver and the largest single maker of payments in contemporary capitalist society.[59] To be sure, the development of a money economy has not always been decisive for the secure expansion of bureaucratic state administration. The organized subsistence economies governed by the bureaucracies of the Roman Empire and the new Empire of Egypt are cases in point. Developed capitalist money economies nevertheless facilitate the predictable generation of revenues through taxation (of wages, salaries, and private profit). Weber contrasts the fiscal buoyancy of the modern state with its Roman counterpart. By virtue of the Roman state's attempt to organize large Continental areas politically by means of a salaried bureaucracy and professional armies, it incurred enormous expenditures. But as commerce, cities, and labor supplies declined, and as society relapsed into a natural economy, rural districts were less and less able to raise the constantly increasing sums of money demanded by the tax system.[60] By contrast, the capitalist economy indirectly promotes the formulation of regularized, systematic state budgets. It therefore also facilitates the overcoming of the uncertain, hand-to-mouth mode of operation typical of early states such as Rome, the intermittent payments in kind (fees, customs excises, and sales taxes) common throughout the Middle Ages, and the compulsory obligations to personal service (labor in mines, the maintenance of roads and bridges) typical of such corvée states as the New Kingdom of ancient Egypt.

Weber insists that the growing interdependence of society and state also derives from the fact that the successful and *precise* functioning of the modern bureaucratic state – and, correspondingly, of the modern corporation – is more and more conditional upon its centralized control of efficient systems of telecommunication and transportation. The collective form of these means of communication (such as the railway) has increased the need for their centralized state deployment.[61] In turn, their proliferation (and the corresponding rise in the rate and quantity of information transmission) has tended to improve the technical efficiency of state reactions toward various situations, including the field of capitalist accumulation.[62] This technological interdependence of state and economy is only accelerated by the fact that the precise tools of these communication systems are typically developed and marketed by dynamic capitalist corporations.[63]

Finally, Weber observes that the erosion of the boundaries of state and civil society is promoted by the growth of demands upon the state from the sphere of civil society itself. Unfortunately, Weber by no means analyzes this development and its implications in any depth. He merely notes, for example, that the state's social welfare policies have come to play a crucial role under contemporary capitalist conditions. These welfare strategies have been fostered by both the pressure of organized interests on the state and, in turn, the state's usurping of social policy formation to enhance its own power and legitimacy.[64]

These examples of the growing interpenetration of state and civil society are of immense significance, Weber argues, inasmuch as they reveal the growing convergence of the bureaucratic means of operation of the state and the modern corporation. Under contemporary conditions, the bureaucratic control of the wage laborer is contingent upon the same form of rational, calculable domination within the state sector. State organization, the specifically *political* form of modern bureaucratic domination, is more and more the indispensable medium of bureaucratic corporate domination. The separation of workers from their means of production is not restricted to the industrial capitalist factory or office. The separation of the worker

> from the material means of production, destruction, administration, academic research, and finance in general is the common basis of the modern state, in its political, cultural, and military sphere, and of the private capitalist economy. In both cases, the disposition of these means is in the hands of that power whom the bureaucratic apparatus . . . directly obeys or to whom it is available in case of need. This apparatus is nowadays equally typical of all those organizations; its existence and function are inseparably cause and effect of this concentration of means of operation – in fact, the apparatus is its very form.[65]

Everywhere, and in all spheres of conduct, from the factory to the university, the means of operation are concentrated in the hands of those who control machinelike bureaucracies. Marx's depiction of the complete separation of laborers from all ownership of the means by which they can realize their labor is but one instance of a more universal bureaucratization process.

The indispensability – and limits – of bureaucratic domination

It is precisely this bureaucratic concentration of the means of operation which makes the present phase of modern life so problematic for Weber. Consuming and replacing other forms of life, bourgeois rationalization processes tend to become an end in themselves. Under their monopolistic sway, contemporary capitalist societies knit themselves into a self-enslaving "iron cage" of bondage. All spheres of daily life tend to become chronically dependent upon disciplined hierarchy, rational specialization, and the continuous deployment of impersonal systems of abstract-general rules. Bureaucratic domination is the fate of the present, whose future is likely to be more of the same. A "polar night of icy darkness and hardness" is the specter that haunts the modern world.

It is worth emphasizing in this context that Weber does not mean to imply that the evolution toward a fully mechanized, predictable, and clocklike system of command is necessarily desirable. Though this bureaucratization process is fundamentally irreversible, Weber nevertheless remains concerned to emphasize – in explicit opposition to Schmoller, Wagner, and other defenders of bureaucracy within the *Verein für Sozialpolitik*[66] – that contemporary bureaucratic organizations systematically produce *irrational* effects. He is concerned to "challenge the unquestioning idolization of bureaucracy,"[67] to call into question the modern, bureaucratic presumption that all mysterious incalculable forces have been banished forever, that modern rulers can, in principle, master all situations by calculation and command. This arrogant presumption is in fact an unreal and unrealizable reverie. In opposition to this metaphysical reverie, Weber soberly insists that the irrational effects generated by organized capitalist societies are necessary, because symptomatic of a developing imbalance, under contemporary conditions at least, between the requirements of formal and those of substantive modes of rationality. This imbalance within the bureaucratization process is a key source at once of the unique achievements and of the *limitations* of modern civilization.

Weber discusses several instances of this disequilibrium; these are cited and analyzed further in the following three sections. At this point, it is necessary only to affirm his central thesis. Irrespective of the standards of value by which substantively rational action is judged, its requirements or conditions of realization, or so Weber wants to argue, are always in principle nonidentical with the exigencies of formal, bureaucratic rationality. The degree of formal rationality of any type of action, he recalls, consists in the degree to which it can be and actually is structured by a reliance upon quantitative calculation. Formally rational activity is goal-oriented, rational calculation guided by the most technically suitable methods at hand. By contrast, the substantive rationality of action does not refer to the degree to which it is structured by means based upon rational calculability. Rather, action and its outcomes are substantively rational inasmuch as they are oriented and judged by ultimate values that, in principle, are highly variable in content and number.[68]

Production, administration, and the suppression of particularity

Weber's first example of the disequilibrium between the requirements of formal and substantive rationality concerns the abstract-general mode of operation that is typical of all efficient bureaucratic organizations. With respect to particular individuals, cases, and events, Weber demonstrates, bureaucracies chronically produce definite obstacles to the coordinated discharge of their functions.[69] From the standpoint of substantively rational criteria (that is, various and competing conceptions of human needs), bureaucracies' fetishism of standardized and general calculation contradicts the plurality or particularity that typically attends the definition of those needs. This contradiction marks both private and public bureaucratic organizations. With respect to modern capitalist forms of production, for example, Weber comes very close to conceding the Marxian critique of capitalism as an abstract and calculating system of production for exchange, a system whose ability to satisfy a plurality of concrete human needs is erratic and, at most, unintentional. Typically, the bureaucratic mode of operation of capitalist corporations contradicts both the possibility of worker control over production and the simple interest of workers in the maintenance of their jobs. The substantive *irrationality* of the bourgeois mode of production derives from the fact that its compulsion to systematize and rationally perfect the calculating pursuit of profit is contingent upon the domination of workers by entrepreneurs.[70]

In Weber's eyes, the contemporary socialist movement's criticism of the "domination of things over humanity" under bourgeois conditions is not unfounded. This criticism accurately depicts the anonymous subjection of living labor power to the rationally calculated discipline of the bureaucratic factory and office. This contradiction between the corporation's formally rational calculation of profitability and particular substantive goals within the sphere of production is duplicated within the sphere of consumption. Profit-oriented capitalist production, Weber admits, can serve only those consumers who have sufficient income and therefore power to demand certain goods and not others *effectively*. The orientation of capitalist production to money prices and profits (and also to production opportunities provided by state power, as under colonialism) therefore means that certain expressed needs – those which are not backed by the means of consumption – may fail to be satisfied. "Profitability is indeed *formally* a rational category," Weber remarks, "but for that very reason it is indifferent with respect to *substantive* postulates unless these can make themselves felt in the market in the form of sufficient purchasing power."[71] This irrationality is further exacerbated by the power of capitalist corporations to determine the type, quantity, and degree of technical proficiency of production, a power that again derives from its control over the means of production. The corporate drive to profitability, that is, is not automatically or even necessarily identical with the optimum use of available productive resources for the satisfaction of a plurality of consumer needs.[72]

Within the sphere of state action, the bureaucratic rejection of doing business from case to case also directly presupposes the quashing or denial of the needs of particular individuals and groups. Weber was convinced that this suppression of particularity was already evident within modern state capitalist systems and would become especially problematic under conditions of state socialism. This conviction placed him at considerable odds with the naïve statism of many of his socialist contemporaries. In his view, their "camp following"[73] and simpleminded belief in historical progress through state planning was thoroughly misguided. The contemporary socialist movement too frequently believed that its victories were a matter of course, its defeats a symptom of backwardness, its failures a temporary rebellion against the judgment of history. This movement wrongly assumed that history, of whose knowledge Marxism was the privileged bearer, somehow expresses its animosity toward all complications and unintended effects that stand in its way.[74] As a consequence of its evolutionism, the contemporary socialist movement suppressed the point that there are no historical guarantees against the substantively irrational effects of bureaucratization. Peace, freedom, and the uncomplicated satisfaction of various needs do not necessarily lie hidden in the lap of a future guided by bureaucratic state planning.

This anti-evolutionist conviction stands behind Weber's bitter criticism of the Bolshevik (and Kautskyite) hopes of reconciling the goal of freedom from all forms of hierarchic domination with that of the abolition of the rule of private property through efficient, bureaucratically planned production for human needs.[75] Weber typically projects at least two complementary arguments in defense of his thesis that these hopes are radically at odds with themselves. In a more speculative vein, he proposes that a rationally planned, communist economy would in practice be impossible. This allegation follows largely from his presumption (derived in turn from arguments within the Second International) that the transition to communist society would entail the abolition of money, monetary accounting, and monetary categories – and therefore the possibility of rational capital accounting. Under communist conditions of production, regulation, and accounting in kind, the provision for mass demand would therefore be seriously impaired. At best, questions about the location, types, and quantities of production in postcapitalist economies would be soluble only in terms of very crude estimates; inevitably, there would be a reduction in the degree of formal, calculating rationality. At worst, decisions about production and consumption would be forced to fall back into a reliance upon either traditional rules or strategies of dictatorial regulation, which arbitrarily decreed patterns of production, consumption, and obedience.[76] The likelihood of dictatorial discipline would be increased, in Weber's estimation, because communist economies would exhaust that innovating, risk-taking, and "free struggle for economic existence" currently waged by capitalist entrepreneurs.[77] Hierarchical discipline would also result from the communist tendency to weaken the incentive to labor that derives (under capitalist conditions) from either opportunities for personal gain or the risk of going entirely without provisions.[78] Conversely, such discipline would likely entail limitations on the formal rationalization of production. This is because the free recruitment of labor power in conformity with its technical competence would be considerably restricted.[79]

By virtue of these probable inefficiencies, Weber considered it most likely that the attempt to realize communist ideals (universal material abundance and emancipation from domination) would necessitate an increased reliance upon bureaucratic administration. His second objection to the revolutionary hopes of his contemporaries took the form of a prediction: The socialist movement, he urged, would be forced to abandon its vision of general emancipation from hierarchical domination. In the here and now, it was clear to Weber that the communist movement was already being compelled to adopt efficient bureaucratic organizations in the struggle against "bourgeois" bureaucracies. Resembling the bureaucratic capitalist state to which it was avowedly opposed, the revolutionary movement had created an army of officials, hierarchies of offices, and a following interested in advancement.[80]

In addition, Weber considered that the efficient administration of production would be among the primary imperatives with which all future socialist governments would have to deal. Consequently, the management of socialist factories and offices would have to depend upon calculation, technical schooling, market research, and expert knowledge of demand. These factors alone would necessitate the expansion of a strata of highly specialized and lengthily trained administrators.[81] Their rational, calculating activities – Weber extrapolated from the example of the Prussian state-owned mines – would in turn rest upon the strict disciplining and control of the labor force.[82] Bureaucratically organized socialist economies, thus, would at the same time preserve the (capitalist) expropriation of all workers from control over the means of production and bring this expropriation process to completion, by substituting state officials for private capitalists. In sum, the struggle for socialism would *extend* the continuum of modern bureaucratic domination and its substantively irrational effects. Socialist society would assume the abstract-general form of bureaucratic, dictatorial socialism; it would appear as only a higher and more concentrated form of development of bourgeois society itself.

Weber was convinced from the beginning that the Bolshevik dictatorship of the proletariat provided evidence for these two arguments. Confidently armed with denunciations of the anarchy of capitalist production and proposals for the militarization of labor through standardized planning, the Bolsheviks, predictably enough, had already preserved or reintroduced practices formerly denounced as bourgeois: the secret police, the Taylor system, hierarchical discipline within the factory and military.[83] The Bolshevik struggle to abolish private capitalism, Weber anticipated, would weaken – indeed, destroy – the last remaining resistance to totalized bureaucratic command and its abstractionist effects. The lingering competition, under capitalist conditions, between private and public bureaucratic organizations – and the possibility of curbing the power of each through a process of "countervailing influence" – would be replaced by a centralizing state administration that controlled the whole of life without regard for particular needs.[84] Existence would come to be as stifling and servile as that of the New Kingdom of Egypt. Bureaucratic socialism would more effectively achieve precisely what the capitalist world was striving for – a bureaucratic dictatorship *over* the proletariat!

Nihilism: the fetishism of technique

The chronic incapacity of modern bureaucratic organizations to justify their raison d'être to themselves and others constitutes a second instance of the disequilibrium between the requirements of formal and those of substantive rationality under contemporary capitalist conditions. Modern bureaucratic life, Weber proposes, is marked by definite nihilistic tendencies. These must be viewed as the substantively irrational effect generated by the adoration of technical proficiency in all spheres of contemporary life. Precisely because of this fetishism of technical, that is, means-oriented considerations, the modern bureaucratic world is more and more often confronted with a loss of a sense of purpose. It unwittingly produces a bewildering and infinite morass of competing evaluative attitudes. Under these conditions of technical efficiency and ethical nihilism, Weber complains, value judgments tend everywhere to be made in a spontaneous and dangerously nonchalant way.[85]

This development is paradoxical, Weber explains, when it is considered that the formal rationalization of the early modern political economy was in part a consequence of a religious movement – Protestantism – marked by its fervent defense of substantive goals. The emergence of a capitalist culture, and with it the possibility of bureaucratic capitalism as an economic system, was not the product of mechanical financial transactions alone. The bureaucratization of the modern world was in part an effect of the prior rationalization of religious

48

conduct itself. Especially among the rising strata of the lower middle classes, according to Weber's still controversial thesis, Protestant asceticism stimulated the growth of an ethos that greatly facilitated that rational, bureaucratic organization of capital and labor which is peculiar to the modern bourgeois order.[86]

Weber stresses that the Reformation was not synonymous with the elimination of the church's control over daily life. Indeed, from the sixteenth through the eighteenth centuries, the new Protestant movements (Pietism, Methodism, Baptism, and, above all, Calvinism) effected new and more earnestly enforced modes of religious discipline, which penetrated deeply into their believers' personal and social lives.[87] These movements' *self-rationalizing* activities were guided by an unquestionably new substantive principle: the religious evaluation of the fulfillment of duty in worldly affairs as the highest form of ethical activity of which individuals could partake. According to the defenders of this principle, living acceptably to God was not to be equated with the suppression of worldly morality in monastic asceticism. From this point on, all individual Christians were to act like monks at all times and in the whole of life; they were duty bound to fulfill the obligations imposed upon them by their position in the world. It was precisely these obligations to serve the glory of God which constituted their "calling," the object of which was the world and all that is within it. Individuals were at all times obligated to prove themselves, to deepen their "inner isolation" even while they developed to the maximum their powers toward the external world.[88] Typically, the Protestant movements specified the content of these obligations through the appeal to labor as an approved calling. It was insisted that one does not work in order to live (that is, in accordance with what Weber calls the "natural relationship").[89] Rather, one was to live for the sake of one's work in the service of "impersonal" social utility. Restless, continuous, and systematic labor thereby became in itself the prime end of earthly life, the ascetic means of future salvation, the most certain sign of rebirth and genuine faith.

Upon this basis, and in opposition to what it described as the vanity and ostentatiousness of ruling feudal culture, Protestant asceticism sought to check and regulate the spontaneous enjoyment of possessions, especially luxury goods. Only the sober, calculating acquisition of goods was seen to be justified. The faithful Christian, it was urged, had to heed the divine call by taking advantage of the opportunities provided. The pursuit of wealth and profitable gain through labor was thus seen to be ethically dubious only if it served as a temptation to living carelessly. Otherwise, the ascetic compulsion to save and the strict performance of duties in a fixed and rationally planned calling were equally morally permissible and necessary, because commanded. Self-assured in its convictions, the new Protestantism also attacked the "sordid elegance" of aristocratic household life. In its place, the ascetics proselytized on behalf of the ideal of the clean, sober, and well-regulated middle-class home. Precisely because the spontaneous enjoyment of life was seen to lead away from both religion and work in a calling, Protestantism instituted new conceptions of time, new forms of patriarchal domination over women, and an unprecedented governance of the body.[90] The waste of time through idle talk, luxury, and sexual indulgence was to be ethically condemned. The calculating, shrewd, and properly self-disciplined men of Protestantism insisted that every hour squandered could have been an hour of labor to the glory of God. Equally, the frill and spontaneity of the ballroom and seigneurial sports event, the drunken laughter of commoners in the public house, became the enemies of rational asceticism. All idle temptations of the flesh were viewed as mere distractions from the hard, calculating pursuit of a righteous life.

Through the successful deployment of such claims, Weber argues, Protestantism made far-reaching contributions to the emergence of bureaucratic capitalism. Even before the emergence of the classical bourgeois ideologies of the eighteenth and early nineteenth centuries, the worldly asceticism of Protestantism functioned to legitimate the new (and highly unequal) patterns of distribution of wealth and power as the work of divine providence. It was said that both sexes of the propertyless classes could withstand the temptations (of idleness, the flesh, conspicuous consumption) that go hand in hand with wealth only by virtue of their generalized poverty. Obedience to God was contingent upon low wages, earthly frugality, and – if necessary – incarceration within the system of bureaucratic workhouses for the unemployed. Further, and to the extent that it penetrated into the lower ranks of society, religious asceticism also provided the emerging order with conscientious, punctual, sober, and highly industrious workers. These "self-rationalized" workers identified with their bureaucratized work life as if it had been willed by God.[91]

Weber's most far-reaching suggestion, however, is that the full economic effects of the Protestant movements generally appeared only after their ethical enthusiasm receded. Gradually, the intensity of the ascetic search for the kingdom of God eroded, giving way (among the rising propertied strata, at least) to comfortable and disciplined bourgeois lives, marked by a utilitarian worldliness supplemented only by a "good conscience."[92] The labors of the Protestant reformers produced unforeseen, and even unwished-for, effects. In this unintended development, there is a deep irony. Under pressure from the temptations of wealth – temptations that it had itself stimulated – Protestant asceticism succumbed increasingly to a secular consumerism and attempted self-renewals (such as the great revival of Methodism prior to the English Industrial Revolution). Under the "iron cage" conditions of contemporary capitalism, Weber argues, the spirit of religious asceticism has almost completely faded. The relentless pursuit of wealth through formal rationalization has become uncoupled from the old religious supports in whose name it once proceeded. Indeed, attempts of organized religion to influence the conduct of economic life are more and more deemed unjustified.

The upshot of this development is highly nihilistic. Immersing the whole of life in the icy waters of bureaucratic calculation, the fully developed capitalism of the present day continuously generates legitimacy problems. Money making, with its attendant bureaucratization, destroys its own meaningfulness. Whereas those formerly steeped in the Protestant ethic wanted, on ethical grounds, to work and engage in business, we are more and more *compelled* to do so: "The idea of duty in one's calling," Weber concludes, "prowls about in our lives like the ghost of dead religious beliefs."[93] Not only do the proponents of technical efficiency continuously challenge and enervate religion; having also undermined the legitimating power of magic and the norms of tradition, these "sensualists without heart" and "specialists without spirit" bracket questions concerning whether it makes sense to master life bureaucratically. The *value* of the capacity to master the whole of life through technical means and calculations remains thoroughly unclear. This is also why the advance of bureaucratization is synonymous with the irreversible growth of subjective and this-worldly forms of ethical reason. In bureaucratic societies, as it were, reality becomes confusing and heterogeneous. It is openly marked by an "infinite richness of events" and an inexhaustible "store of possible meanings."[94]

Weber is adamant that this is not altogether a regressive development. The advance of bureaucratization destroys, once and for all, the myth that it is possible for individuals to apprehend unambiguously the whole of reality. The disenchantment of the modern world contributes to the final erosion of claims upon universal knowledge of an objective totality. All spheres of conduct, especially those of scientific inquiry itself, have entered an unprecedented phase of specialization that, most likely, will forever continue.[95] Knowledge of reality therefore comes to be understood as fragmented, subjective knowledge constituted in accordance with knowers' one-sided, specialized points of view. It becomes evident that the populations of bureaucratic capitalist societies are fated to live without knowledge that can dispense sacred values and reveal the true meaning of the universe. Under conditions marked by bureaucratic efficiency and a this-worldly ethical nihilism, individuals are compelled to choose from among a bewildering array of competing cultural values; sensing the precariousness of the meaning of their existence, they must from here on select their own gods.

In defense of objectivity

Weber emphasizes that salvation from the ethical nihilism generated by processes of bureaucratization is not to be found through an uncritical reliance upon empirical-analytic science. He was constantly in opposition to scientistic, "realistic-empirical" (Menger) forms of thinking – and their defenders within the *Methodenstreit* of his time – and his metatheoretical writings must be interpreted as a crucial dimension of his more general concern with the limits of bureaucratic rationality. Their tortuous, often maundering quality is by no means an index of their insignificance to Weber's political project.[96] From the time of his earliest polemic against Roscher and Knies,[97] all of Weber's methodological and epistemological struggles can be seen as urgent, disciplined attempts at understanding the meaning of a form of social inquiry that refused the temptations of bureaucratic thinking. He was convinced that any further proliferation of scientistic discourses would only increase the likelihood that bureaucratic, capitalist societies would further lose their way in a twilight of normlessness.

This conviction forms the substance of his neo-Kantian arguments concerning the unique logic of the cultural sciences. Weber proposes – and not always self-consistently – that at least three arguments can be adduced against uncritical attempts at universalizing the methodology of the natural sciences. In the first

51

instance, the logics of the cultural and natural sciences are *in principle* distinct. Although, certainly, the concerns of both are grounded within historico-cultural processes,[98] the natural sciences seek *universally valid* knowledge. They analyze natural realities in terms of generalizing concepts, which guide the formulation of laws confirmed by empirical analysis and rational experimentation.[99] By contrast with this emphasis upon the quantitative, exact, and universal aspects of natural phenomena, the inquiries of the cultural sciences bear decisively upon the *qualitative* aspects of social life, that is, upon this life as it is manifested in all its particular or historically specific configurations. According to the young Max Weber at least, cultural-scientific analysis (of bureaucracy, for instance) avoids the explanatory subsumption of particular events as representative cases of general, that is, universally valid, processes; unlike the nomothetic natural sciences, the cultural sciences are preoccupied with the concrete individuality (or historicity) of phenomena. This means that the cultural sciences cannot attain knowledge of general laws. Their empirical knowledge is instead uniquely generated through the imputation of particular constellations of events (events that are reckoned to be of general significance for modern life) as the consequence of concrete causal relationships.[100]

Secondly, whereas outer nature is typically a domain of meaninglessness, Weber stresses that the cultural sciences are singularly concerned with psychological and intellectual (*geistig*) phenomena. These *understanding* of these phenomena presents problems specifically different from those encountered within the exact natural sciences, which are concerned with observing and explaining the laws of events. To be sure, social action chronically shares with natural events a certain dependence upon accidental disturbances and blind, nonrational prejudice. Unlike natural phenomena, cultural beings are nevertheless also endowed with the capacity to live in accordance with practical norms. Capable of representing themselves to themselves, they can therefore adopt a deliberative disposition toward themselves and their worlds. Typically, these beings subjectively ascribe "meaning [*Bedeutung*]" or "significance [*Sinn*]" to their own institutionally situated activities.[101] Methodologically speaking, this point is of considerable consequence for the sociocultural sciences. These sciences cannot systematically ignore the problem of understanding the meanings actors attribute to their own conduct. Within the cultural sciences, "realistic-empirical" inquiries ignore such meanings and are therefore bound to produce results that are conceptually and empirically misleading. Such realistic-empirical inquiries deceptively avoid a series of vital epistemological questions: Whose knowledge is under consideration here? Is it the ideas of investigators who, from the standpoint of various problematics, regard actors as objects of knowledge? Or is it the ideas of actors themselves?

Positivist efforts to assimilate the cultural and the natural sciences are criticized by Weber, thirdly, for their false claims to "value-freedom." This criticism is double-edged. In the first instance, efforts to cast cultural-scientific inquiries in the mold of the natural sciences are necessarily plagued by nihilistic outcomes. Ethical ideals can never be the final product or effect of the accumulation of lawlike empirical data. The days have finally passed, or so Weber contends, when the exact, quantifying sciences could be expected to discover the path to God by physically grasping his works. It has become evident that the natural sciences are both fundamentally irreligious and incapable of generating substitute ethical rules of conduct. Whether it makes sense to live within the modern bureaucratic world cannot be decided through reference to the empirical-analytic sciences. Weber quotes Tolstoi with strong approval: "Science is meaningless because it gives no answer to our question, the only question important to us: 'What shall we do and how shall we live?' "[102]

Furthermore, and secondly, Weber insists that efforts to exorcise ethical values from the cultural sciences are fraudulent, because impossible. "Human, all too human" ethical principles *always* guide the selection of data. He repeats the insight of Goethe: Theoretical principles are always involved in "the facts."[103] These principles or "evaluative ideas [*Wertideen*]" are not the products or conclusions of empirical investigations – as if the definition of the objects of cultural-scientific study could be separated from the evaluation of their significance. From the outset, these principles divine their empirical objects of investigation, investing them with a certain "value-relevance [*Wertbeziehung*]"; they serve as the presuppositions that render sociocultural reality an object of subjective theoretical inquiry. There is nothing within these objects themselves that sets them apart as deserving of recognition, attention, and analysis. A disposition of ethical indifference is thus by no means either appropriate or possible within the cultural sciences: Their problematics are always constituted (in the Kantian sense) by an ensemble of historically tainted practical questions. These questions serve as something like one-sided vantage points, from which – consciously or unconsciously, expressly or tacitly – social and natural reality is reckoned to be worthy of being classified, analyzed, understood, explained, and evaluated. Ideal-typical analysis, of which Weber's concern with modern bureaucratic domination and its irrationality is a key instance, is only an explicitly recognized form of these unavoidable processes of conceptual mediation. Confronted with an infinite reality of ever-changing events, Weber's ideal-typical inquiries seek to analyze a finite portion of this reality as important, as in certain respects significant and crucial to the fate of those who live within the present. With a certain (but never absolute) degree of exactitude, ideal-typical analyses bring about an ordering and clarification of the chaos immanent within the stream of contemporary life processes.

It is precisely through their capacity to analyze and clarify aspects of modern bureaucratic life that Weber's cultural-scientific analyses claim to achieve a form of objectivity.[104] Motivated by a concern with the problems attending bureaucratic domination within the spheres of state and society, Weber's inquiries, it is true, openly deny that their status is equivalent to value-free, objective knowledge in the positivist sense. Their "objectivity [*Sachlichkeit*]" is of a rather different, and very special form. Weber's inquiries self-reflexively acknowledge that their knowledge is constituted in and through categories that are marked by a definite subjectivity. Objective, *sachlich* knowledge of bureaucratic organization admits its dependence upon concepts and presuppositions, including the belief that this knowledge is indeed of value to those who live and act within the contemporary world.[105]

In respect of this admitted subjectivity, Weber repeats, the objectivity of his accounts of modern bureaucratic domination *cannot* transcend the latter's nihilistic tendencies. His insights are incapable of formulating ultimate – in the sense of unambiguous and incontrovertible – norms that could in turn crystallize and guarantee political obligations. Simply stated, his discussions of bureaucracy admit their own irrelevance to those for whom inquiries into bureaucracy have no value. Weber's inquiries thus cast themselves in the role of advocate. Their *belief* that objective knowledge of the bureaucratization process is worth attaining necessarily presents itself in the form of *recommendations*.[106]

Despite their acknowledged dependence upon the interest and concern of others, Weber considers his inquiries to be of great potential importance to the contemporary world. This potential derives from the capacity of these inquiries to clarify, for themselves and for others concerned, the significance of the processes of bureaucratization in accordance with which our actions are increasingly structured. It is Weber's conviction that the cultural-scientific task of clarifying the significance of bureaucratic rationality is made urgent by the growing fetish of technical calculation and the corresponding reliance upon common sense as the arbiter of ethical commitment. Contradicting this technicity and ethical ignorance, cultural-scientific inquiry serves as a "critique of concept formation and conceptual schemes."[107] Above all, it is concerned with the more ambitious task of educating judgment concerning bureaucracy and its irrational consequences. In an age confident of its capacity to administer all situations bureaucratically, cultural-scientific knowledge is concerned with generating "inconvenient insights."[108] Its strategy of clarification and defiance relies upon a fundamental analytic distinction, that between the categories "means" and "ends." Weber proposes that actors struggle either for goals that are valued for their own sakes or for goals that are desired as a means of achieving other, more highly valued goals.[109]

Under the influence of this categorical distinction, it is true that Weber's objective inquiries claim to eschew passing judgment upon those who pursue certain goals desired for their own sake. The choice and pursuit of such goals, Weber typically declares, is ultimately the responsibility of actors themselves.[110] Granting this caveat, the scientific analysis of modern bureaucracy can nevertheless clarify the appropriateness of bureaucratic means for the realization of various desired ends.[111] Weber's discussion of the substantively irrational consequences of bureaucratic domination are of course precise examples of this clarification process at work. As we have seen, these discussions propose informed estimates of the probability of successfully realizing various goals (communism, particular needs within capitalist society) given the (indispensable) reliance upon the presently available bureaucratic means. The utilized bureaucratic means, in other words, are judged to be appropriate or insufficient for the attainment of these goals. Conversely, such goals are themselves indirectly criticized or defended by Weber as capable of realization, that is, as practicable given the choice to utilize bureaucratic means. On scientific grounds, Weber's discussions disavow any capacity to indicate what actors *should* do. They are nevertheless capable of making explicit the ultimate axioms or value standards (for example, those of Protestant asceticism) for which actors strive. In addition, these analyses are capable of clarifying the likelihood that actors *can* or *cannot* achieve these value standards and, therefore, the degree to which these standards are internally consistent. Finally, and in accordance with these means–ends analyses, Weber's theses on bureaucracy speculate about the range of possible consequences (nihilism, abstractionism) attending the utilization of bureaucratic means. Those concerned are thus provided with greater objective insight into the desirable and undesirable outcomes that necessarily attend the decision to depend upon rational bureaucratic means.

The fate of democracy

Despite his anxiety about the substantively irrational consequences of bureaucracy, Weber is in general convinced of its indispensability. This conviction that bureaucracy is necessary forms one of the most striking features of his analyses. He is persuaded that, once established, bureaucratic domination cannot easily be shattered. By virtue of its indispensability as a technical means, "bureaucracy is among those social structures which are the hardest to destroy."[112] Weber does of course admit that the generalized substitution of democratic, decentralized, and less formally rational organization for bureaucracy is thinkable. Yet such a rupture with the continuum of modern bureaucratic domination would in his view assume the form of a *regression*: Within the spheres of state and society, it would result in a drastic reduction of technical efficiency and, therefore, of current levels of material prosperity, legal order, and administrative capacity. The renunciation of the visionary struggle for democratic public life therefore becomes imperative. The governed cannot nowadays dispense with bureaucratic apparatuses and their rational, calculating mode of operation. The reliance of the governed upon the strictly organized, virtuosolike mastery of complex problems and situations makes the revolutionary creation of entirely new and democratic forms of power impossible. "More and more," Weber maintains, "the material fate of the masses depends upon the steady and correct functioning of the increasingly bureaucratic organization of private capitalism. The idea of eliminating these organizations becomes more and more utopian."[113] Indeed, the hierarchical division of labor and power within both private and public bureaucracies is beyond reconstruction. Even for brief periods, Weber emphasizes, the industrial entrepreneur has come to be as little dispensable as the medical doctor.[114]

In view of this "iron necessity" of bureaucratic command, Weber recommends that its irrational effects be tempered or overcome through the expansion and principled deployment of nation-state power. In respect of this admonition, Löwith's claim that Weber offers only a resigned diagnosis of contemporary events is misleading.[115] Weber continually argues that an immense "labor of *political* education [*politische Erziehungsarbeit*]" is to be performed in the face of the present. Convinced of the necessity of impersonal, task-oriented bureaucratic organization, Weber urges that such organization is now in need of *direction* by the struggle to defend and enhance the sovereignty of the nation and its power.

The fundamental *political* problem posed by bureaucratic organization is how to subordinate, restrict, and harness its technical expertise and proficiency. Weber's response to this challenge is to advocate an ultimate and definite value: the power position of the nation in the world.[116] The primary and decisive voice within the affairs of state and society should be the interests of the nation-state, understood as a community of sentiments secured by military strength and economic interests. Especially in a world of nation-states bristling with arms, this is what political maturity means: the ability of state leadership to place existing social and political bureaucracies under the sign of the nation's power. This would make possible the preservation of the nation's external integrity; within the domestic sphere, such leadership would facilitate the protection, *embourgeoisement*, and acculturation of the laboring masses and the continuous expansion of efficient capitalist production. For Weber, the permanent diplomatic and economic (and military?) struggle of nation-states against one another is not only unavoidable; it also serves as a fundamental source of political vigor, of inspired governance. The mobilization of the nation through competent leadership might also weaken the problems of legitimation experienced within all modern capitalist societies. Within the context of the permanent struggle between "power states" and "outwardly small nations," the administrative redeployment of the language, customs, and political memories common to a group – leaders' appeal to the "honor" of the nation – can compensate for the loss of faith in religion and all objectively justified values.[117]

Weber's defense of the principle of national power politics is at the same time a justification of strong-willed, passionate political leadership.[118] Within the realm of corporate and state bureaucracy, Weber urges against Schmoller and others, "genuine officials" must not engage in politics but, rather, must restrict themselves to "impartial administration."[119] He is in principle opposed to *Beamtenherrschaft*, the dominating rule of senior civil servants without a calling, precisely because their authority, in his view, must (and can only) be limited to the conscientious execution of the orders of political leadership. The expertise of technically trained officials has no rightful place in politicians' ultimate decisions about political goals and strategies. For the same reasons, a "leaderless democracy" – the rule of civil servants supplemented with the rule of professional politicians without either a calling or charismatic qualities – is equally to be despised.[120]

Against the general encroachment of bureaucratic organization, what is now required is the securing of the primacy of politics over bureaucracy by way of genuine political leadership. Such leadership must demonstrate a highly developed and nontransferable sense of *personal* responsibility for the acts it performs: In an otherwise suffocating age of general and overwhelming bureaucratization, only a very few can realize the old Renaissance and classical bourgeois ideal of individuation. The ideal-typical leader, Weber recommends, must embody at least three decisive qualities.[121] First, genuine leadership necessitates a passionate devotion to a cause. The devotion to political leadership must be unconditional. The will to make history, to set new values for others, can only be born and nourished from feeling. Here Weber's ethical relativism resurfaces (and jeopardizes his insistence on the primacy of the goals of the nation-state): The inner strength necessary for the serving of a cause can only be based on faith. Though leaders may serve "national, humanitarian, social, ethical, cultural, worldly, or religious ends,"[122] they must choose and faithfully pursue one or more of these.

Nevertheless, secondly, passion must not succumb to "sterile excitation" (Weber invokes Simmel's expression). Authentic leaders must cultivate a sense of their objective responsibilities. Their goal-structured strivings for the means of power must avoid "self-intoxication," seeking in all matters, on the contrary, to further the cause responsibly. Their struggle for power must be synonymous with the servicing of a definite goal, for whose realization, effects, and unintended consequences they are personally accountable. Acting on their own convictions, leaders are to bear the sole responsibility for their actions; they are not the mandated representatives of their masters, the electors.[123]

In turn (and thirdly), this presupposes that leaders' actions must embody a "cool sense of proportion": the ability to grant due weight to realities, to take them soberly and calmly into account. Weber's recommendations display a quasi-positivist deference to realities. Genuine, passionate, and experienced leaders, he urges, must be relentless in "viewing the realities of life," and must have "the ability to face such realities and...measure up to them inwardly."[124] Effective leadership is synonymous with neither mere demagoguery nor the worship of power for its own sake. Passionate and responsible leaders will shun any uncompromising ethic of ultimate ends. Those who rely upon this ethic are blind to the chronic tensions between means and ends; such blindness, he notes sarcastically, "does rightly and leaves the results with the Lord."[125] Political infancy is in fact synonymous with the untrammeled pursuit of ultimate values; such infantilism forgets that, however the content of these concept pairs is understood, evil is not necessarily a product of evil alone, and that good does not follow only from good.[126] Prudent and mature leaders, by contrast, must be guided by an ethic of responsibility. Recognizing the average deficiencies of people, they must continually strive to take account of the foreseeable effects of particular actions that aim to realize particular goals through the reliance upon particular means. They must engage in action in which both means and ends are adjusted and coordinated responsibly in accordance with their possible outcomes and unintended consequences. Ethically responsible leaders must therefore incorporate into their actions an anguishing fact: in numerous situations, they must acknowledge that the attainment of good ends is dependent upon (and therefore jeopardized by) the use of ethically doubtful or (in the case of violence) even dangerous means.

According to Weber's last writings, the demand for ethically responsible leadership is no idle hope. Certainly, charismatic leadership has emerged in all places and in every historical epoch.[127] Under contemporary conditions, however, the possibility of mature leadership is systematically confirmed by the Caesarist, charismatic elements that more and more attend the increasing power of bureaucratic party-political organizations vis-á-vis legislatures. This development, which Weber thought to be most clearly evident under the U.S. presidential system, increases the likelihood that leaderless party machines will follow, even over the heads of legislatures, a charismatic leader. Party machines will submit to this leadership, in return for certain benefits. Amid electoral battles, for example, the competent leader (the "dictator of the battlefield of elections"[128] who fights with the spoken word) could actually enhance the legitimacy of the party and therefore the career prospects of individual party members.[129] In turn, the party machines would become the means facilitating leaders' seduction of the masses. Paradoxically, then, bureaucratization within the sphere of the state would facilitate the emergence of committed, responsible, and experienced individuals who could put their shoulders to the wheels of the present; plebiscitarian leader democracy would thereby in part compensate, or so Weber insisted, for the substantive irrationalism of bureaucratic domination. Even as Caesarist leadership would restrain and guide the routinizing forces of bureaucracy, efficient, technically rational bureaucratic organizations would moderate and rationalize the creative forces of individual leadership.

The forward progress of bureaucracy?

It is a commonplace among liberal scholars that one of the central difficulties of Weber's political theory is his failure to distinguish between two forms of leadership: the genuine charisma of responsible democratic leaders (such as Gladstone or Roosevelt) and the pernicious charismatic domination effected through the crafty and ruthless demagogues (such as Hitler, Mussolini, or Stalin) who rose to power after his death.[130] To be sure, Weber was aware that already in his time the political process within industrial capitalist countries increasingly resembled a "dictatorship resting on the exploitation of mass emotionality."[131] This administrative deployment of demagogic speech and action, he also recognized, differed from (for example) Cobden's intellectualist mode of discourse or Gladstone's consistent resort to "letting sober facts speak for themselves." Weber proposed, furthermore, that political orders could be evaluated according to the *type* of leadership that they generated.[132] He recognized, finally, that even authentic leaders could succumb to vanity. The genuine leader is "constantly in danger of becoming an actor as well as taking lightly the responsibility for the outcome of his actions and of being concerned merely with the 'impression' he makes."[133] In spite of these various observations, Weber is nevertheless charged with unwittingly holding to the naïve assumption that charismatic leadership in its various forms could resist these dangers and would always therefore be the repository of political understanding, maturity, and wisdom. It is alleged, not incorrectly, that he seriously conflated different types of charismatic leadership – the elected warlord, the great demagogue, the plebiscitarian ruler, the modern political party leader whose career is made in party bureaucracies.

This form of indictment of Weber is nevertheless highly incomplete, if only because it remains ensnared within the limited boundaries of the so-called elitist theory of equilibrium democracy.[134] Viewed from beyond these restrictive boundaries, Weber's legacy is in fact much more profound. It consists in a challenge to all dissident political thought in general and, in particular, a censure of the possibility of a democratic, socialist theory of bureaucratic domination.

This challenge is summarized by Weber in a well-known 1908 letter to Robert Michels: "Such concepts as 'will of the people', 'genuine will of the people'," he remarks, "have long since ceased to exist for me; they are fictitious. All ideas aiming at abolishing the dominance of humans over others are 'Utopian.' "[135]

It should be emphasized that to speak in this way of the *legacy* of Weber's challenge is to avoid a positivist critique of his theses. It has become almost customary, for example, to stress that Weber's account of bureaucracy is descriptively inaccurate, that it must be rejected – or at least amended – because it is out of tune with the actual realities of bureaucratic organization, and so on. Precisely because of their descriptivist assumptions, such allegations expose themselves to an obvious countercharge: Weber's account of modern bureaucratic organization and its irrational effects is ideal-typical. Weber persistently (and correctly) emphasized that descriptive analyses of the elements of modern bureaucratic reality can never be exhaustive. Everywhere and always the quantitative and qualitative influences upon the events that constitute this reality are infinite. Accordingly, attempts at capturing the concrete reality of bureaucratic organization exhaustively are disingenuous, because impossible. Definitive and exhaustive scientific knowledge of the "laws of motion" of bureaucratic processes is unachievable. All knowledge of the stream of historico-cultural events, Weber rightly insists, is knowledge from particular points of view. Such knowledge is conditioned by judgments about which aspects of these events are of general significance; in turn, these judgments or evaluative ideas are those which dominate or inform the historical period in which investigators conduct their inquiries.[136]

Weber's account of bureaucratic domination thus takes the form of avowedly one-sided or dogmatic accentuations of certain of its highly diffuse and discrete aspects by means of ideal-typical concepts. Inasmuch as they exclude an infinity of events that for the purposes of inquiry are deemed irrelevant, these concepts are not mere descriptions of a preexistent bureaucratic reality. They are not identical, true, and faithful reproductions of the empirical characteristics of bureaucracy. These concepts necessarily and explicitly exclude consideration of a rich variety of both particular and general aspects of bureaucratic organization. Weber's theorems on bureaucracy take the form of a series of conceptual reconstructions of aspects of modern life that, in ideal, pure form, are seldom, if ever, to be found within this historical reality. These reconstructions are derived from experience that is intensified and condensed through imaginative processes of thought, in order to facilitate further analyses of the empirical manifold.[137] These analyses, in short, never exhaust the objective meaning of bureaucracy; incompleteness is a logical property of the methodology of Weber's inquiries into bureaucracy. By virtue of the fact that concepts and objects of concepts are in a perpetual state of flux, these inquiries are necessarily provisional, "endowed with eternal youth."[138] They are continuously the objects of their own stated concern not to "make compromises nor cloak any 'nonsense.' "[139]

It is precisely in respect of their *admitted* failure to encircle their object – an admission typically overlooked by Weber's positivist critics – that Weber's ideal-typical descriptions can be analyzed and immanently criticized as utopian.[140] Unable to construct a closed and universally valid system of categories that would somehow express the essence of bureaucratic reality, Weber's ideal-typical discussion of bureaucracy leaves itself permanently open to further interrogation and supersession. This discussion unavoidably provokes novel questions (about other limitations of bureaucratic organization, for example) that it has failed to address or even anticipate.

Weber's lack of concern with such questions was again consistent with his thesis that only certain dimensions of any infinitely complex and changing reality are ever worth knowing – specifically, those to which is attributed "a general *cultural* significance."[141] This presupposition, however, provokes the standard retort: significance *for whom?* This retort suggests the presence of a self-destructive weakness within Weber's defense of the imperative of bureaucracy. When it is considered that the concept of rational bureaucracy was a solecism in the language of nineteenth-century theoretical discussion,[142] it is curious indeed that Weber took for granted that his account of bureaucracy was somehow expressive of the value interests of his time. This confident presumption, which suppressed a whole century's theoretical controversy and political and social struggle over bureaucracy, was arguably reinforced by his reliance upon an inverted evolutionism. The resulting comparisons of the present, ancient Egypt, and Rome in its decline; commentaries upon the "forward progress" of bureaucratic mechanization; exhortations to abandon false hopes – these and other claims provide hints that Weber's ideal-typical defense of bureaucracy sustained itself on prior, tacit, and pessimistic assumptions about the regressive character of the contemporary phase of the world historical process.[143]

These assumptions are contradicted, however, by Weber's other thesis that the points of view from which processes of bureaucratization become objects of inquiry cannot be fixed indefinitely. This indeterminacy thesis contains an important implication: so long as these processes of bureaucratization change, it must be admitted that new "facts," problematics, and interpretations concerning these processes will come to be deemed important. This admission is of decisive importance under late capitalist conditions, precisely because bureaucracy is widely criticized and opposed as undemocratic (see Essay 1). From the vantage point of such struggles for autonomous public life, it becomes evident, indeed, that Weber's theses are heavily committed to the defense of bureaucratic organization. Weber arrogantly presumed the redundancy of further questions about bureaucratic domination. He took it for granted, conversely, that the repression of autonomous public life was more and more necessary. These presumptions form the legacy of his account of bureaucracy, an account that functions to silence further discussion about the authoritarian, self-contradictory, and therefore contingent qualities of all bureaucracy.

There are at least three interrelated instances of this silencing effect. In the first place, and most obviously, Weber considerably overestimated the technical efficiency of both "public" and "private" bureaucratic organization. It will be recalled that he considered that the restless advance of bureaucratic organization was a consequence of its technical superiority. By virtue of its speed, precision, cost efficiency, unambiguity, and hierarchical unity, only bureaucracy is able to cope adequately and efficiently with the complexities of modern life. This ideal-typical valuation (as Essay 3 argues at length) fails to consider a number of chronically inefficient, that is, technically *ir*rational, aspects of the bureaucratic form. Two of these aspects can here be mentioned. First, Weber failed to analyze sufficiently the extent to which the horizontal or lateral relations among different bureaucratic organizations would continually generate turbulence within and between the spheres of civil society and the state. This is a curious oversight, inasmuch as one of his key defenses of modern capitalism concerns its capacity to secure the differentiation of social and political bureaucracies. He thus acknowledged that the logic of operation, means of financing, and goals of capitalist enterprises were by no means identical with those of state administration.[144] He noted, for example, that the substance of state policy may frequently be oriented to noneconomic ends, which thereby limit the capitalist, rational, calculating pursuit of profit. He also understood that modern capitalist processes of bureaucratization have consistently been marked by unevenness.[145]

These insights could never have been systematically developed by Weber, precisely because they would have seriously jeopardized his claims on behalf of the formally rational character of bureaucratic administration. It is in part because public and private bureaucracies cannot automatically or bureaucratically coordinate their relations with one another that their respective internal modes of operation are systematically prevented from achieving a machinelike technical competence. Under continuous pressure to act with or against other (corporate, church, trade union, state) bureaucracies within their often uncertain and always changing and conflict-ridden environments, bureaucratic administrations are typically forced to undermine their own principled rejection of doing business on a case-by-case basis by engaging in judgment calls, decisions made without the benefits of fixed, objective rules that can be applied with precision. In a continuously uncertain and often turbulent environment, the stable attainment of organizational objectives depends on continuous changes in the bureaucratic structure itself.[146] This means that under late capitalist conditions, "without regard for *particular* persons and situations" is an unrealizable watchword of all bureaucracies. They cannot self-consistently attain their respective goals through reliance upon abstract-general regulations, which are applied exhaustively and consistently to every case. Indeed, bureaucratic organizations that attempt to monitor and control all situations strictly through such formally rational regulations are continually subject to heterogeneous rivalries and struggles that, in turn, have internal disorganizing effects upon those organizations. Conversely, the persistence of such struggles and rivalries obstructs the formal rationalization of social and political life. Processes of bureaucratization display a definite unevenness or lack of uniformity. They are therefore also marked by continual efforts to readjust, reorganize, and redeploy their systems of command – through, for example, corporatist forms of policy making and bargaining between bureaucratic organizations. Bureaucracies do not necessarily display constant pressures toward caution and "playing it safe," a stifling and pedantic suspicion of experimentalism and departure from the wonted routine.[147] Under late capitalist conditions, everyday life is bureaucratized to different degrees and from incompatible and often contradictory points of view.

This kind of environmental restriction upon the formally rational mode of operation of public and private bureaucracies is typically reinforced, secondly, by analogous difficulties *within* those organizations. Certainly Weber was aware of numerous historical instances of the obstruction of formal rationality within bureaucratic institutions of production and administration.[148] This awareness is nevertheless not systematically extended into the present. Once again, Weber's account seriously exaggerates the degree to which bureaucratic organizations can and do conduct their operations in accordance with a key criterion of efficiency, that is, "without regard for persons" and in accordance with abstract-general rules. Within his political writings, and especially when he dealt with the political power of the Junkers, Weber occasionally recognized this point.[149] Nevertheless, his systematic underestimation of its significance prevented him from analyzing the dynamic and expansionist character of bureaucracies. The formal rationality of these organizations, it must be emphasized, is chronically obstructed by vested interests – a most important reason why bureaucracies have a tendency to perpetuate themselves in power and scope, if not to expand continuously. Within the upper echelons of bureaucratic organization particular individuals or groups typically appropriate and assign the resources of power in their own favor. As a consequence of their "hunting for higher positions" (Marx), bureaucratic elites usually fail to formulate and discharge their business cost-efficiently, anonymously, and without regard for particular persons.

As Norbert Elias first pointed out, what are officially called the imperatives and needs of bureaucratic organizations are always defined by the struggle for power and its monopolization.[150] The points associated with this observation are perhaps so familiar that they need once again to be spelled out. In spite of official proclamations, bureaucratic organization has not altogether eliminated the exploitation of officeholding for "rents and emoluments." Forms of nepotism, clientelism, and simple favoritism are not insignificant or exceptional characteristics of state and corporate organizations. The appointment and deployment of bureaucratic staff at all levels by no means always and everywhere proceed in accordance with unambiguous functional criteria, as if career opportunities and the rational allocation of tasks were unhindered by nods and winks, lobbying, incompetence, procrastination, threats, struggles between departments, pork-barreling, and duplication of effort. In the competition for power among and within public and private bureaucratic organizations, the directing authorities do not act entirely *sine ira ac studio*. They rather continually strive to appropriate the organization as their own private property, to increase their own superiority by multiplying services and positions, overseeing the proliferation of artificial controls and unproductive functions, providing those under their tutelage with opportunities for success, security of tenure, consumption and acquisition, and so on. "Bureaucracy loves bureaucrats," Lefort correctly notes, "as much as bureaucrats love bureaucracy."[151] Finally, bureaucratic authorities also typically seek to enhance their powers of command through claims upon knowledge and top secrets, and through the (initial) concealment of their plans and intentions. Especially among senior officials, privileged access to technical details and knowledge involves at the same time the accretion of power into their own hands.

Bureaucratic administration, as Marx already stressed (and as Weber sometimes recognized)[152] tends to be an administration of secret sessions. Bureaucratic hierarchy is a hierarchy of knowledge, information, and liaison behind closed doors. One of its supreme resources of power lies in its capacity to transform specialized and official knowledge into official secrets, classified material, and professional expertise.

No doubt, this list could be expanded considerably. These examples nevertheless suffice to illustrate the more general thesis: Bureaucracies, contrary to Weber's account, persistently undermine their own claims to competence in discharging their business economically and efficiently in accordance with formally rational rules. Bureaucratic organizations cannot be unfailingly neutral, as if they could place themselves at the disposal of every power that skillfully claims their precise service.

This thesis is of course well noted and widely sensed. It nevertheless is the carrier of a less frequently recognized *political* implication. Simply expressed, Weber's overestimation of the degree to which both public and private bureaucracies can and do operate in accordance with strict, formally rational rules directly jeopardizes his claim that the participation of citizens within autonomous forms of public life has become highly dysfunctional for efficient bureaucratic administration and must therefore be minimized. It is true, or so Weber argued, that the modern struggle for constitutional democratic government – for a political system that acknowledges the formal political equality of all citizens – has everywhere definitely fostered the growth of bureaucratic administration. Modern mass democracies typically take the form of bureaucratized democracies.[153] Such demands as equality before the law and equal rights of the governed accelerated the destruction of old forms of privilege, especially that based on birth.[154] These demands have nevertheless promoted, within the sphere of the state at least, the advance of bureaucratic administration against the localized rule of notables. The pacification of the governed through systems of bureaucratic organization – what Weber called "passive democratization" – is an unintended but nonetheless direct consequence of the popular struggle for mass, representative democracy.

Weber nevertheless proposed that this tacit alliance between bureaucracy and representative democracy is marked by unanticipated consequences. In spite of their former support for the bureaucratization process, demands for democracy more and more often turn against the rule of bureaucracy. In Weber's (not inaccurate) view, continuing struggles to realize the more substantive principles associated with formal, representative democracy are in definite contradiction to the rule of bureaucracy and its penchant for authoritarian command, secrecy, and the silencing of criticism. Demands for the universal accessibility to office and the popular election and recall of administrators and subordinate staff also directly endanger the precise functioning of the bureaucratic mechanism. Weber therefore concluded that the struggle for democratic, public life (whether in the sphere of the economy or in that of the state) would produce "technically irrational obstacles"[155] to the smooth formulation and deployment of bureaucratic commands. In his view, this antinomy between bureaucracy and autonomous public life could be attenuated through plebiscitarianism. Systems of plebiscitarian leader democracy, he proposed, would facilitate the emergence of genuine political leaders who could act as both free trustees of the masses and, at the same time, their virtually unrestrained masters. Weber's proposal appears highly implausible in view of his persistent overestimation of the technical competence of bureaucratic organizations. Indeed, given their substantively irrational effects (discussed by Weber) and their chronic technical incompetence under late capitalist conditions, his case against democratic, public life remains considerably weakened, even unwarranted.

This tentative conclusion is considerably strengthened by a second immanent weakness within Weber's ideal-typical account of bureaucracy. This second difficulty is not unrelated to the first, and might indeed be analyzed as its extension. Weber's account, it must be said, radically understated the capacity of the "lifeless machinery" of bureaucratic administration to catalyze new demands for public action. Hierarchically ordered relations of command and obedience are no doubt typical features of all contemporary bureaucratic organizations. These organizations plunge their roots deeply into all interpersonal relations; they have in common, as Weber suggested, the important characteristic of permanence. They tend to be institutions of everyday routine (*Alltagsgebilde*).[156] Within the bureaucratic apparatus, however, individuals and groups are rarely depoliticized cogs in a dynamic and precisely functioning mechanism. The helpless frustration of the dominated is not the inevitable and nightmarish effect of the impenetrable formalism and officiousness of bureaucratic command. Bureaucratic administration everywhere and at all times tends to be the subject not only of class struggles (as Lukács narrowly insisted against Weber)[157] but also of various power struggles outside the sphere of the factory and office. In addition to effecting the restructuring and redirection of the operation of these organizations, these struggles also produce conditions in which informal public spheres of argument, deliberation, and decision making tend to thrive.

Weber of course insisted that conflict could not be excluded from social and political life. The means, ends, and "bearers" of conflict may well be contingent, though conflict itself could never be permanently abolished.[158] Guided by this axiom, he was acutely aware that the modern process of bureaucratization was highly conflict-ridden. With respect to the past, to mention two examples noted by Weber, modernization provoked both the bloody resistance of the American planters' aristocracy to urban capital and, in Europe, the struggle of traditional, rurally based power blocs (such as the Roman Catholic and Lutheran churches) against the spread of urban rationalist culture.* In the here and now, Weber's participation in the *Verein für Sozialpolitik* survey of the industrial labor process

---

* From the viewpoint of the following argument, it is of great interest that such struggles are never analyzed in any depth or systematicness by Weber. His account of the bureaucratization process, it will be argued subsequently, seriously underestimates the constitutive role played by various collective protest movements in the modernization process – a role whose history has yet to be written. These collective protest movements formed part of a process by which modern, bureaucratic societies were created, challenged, and

alerted him to forms of worker resistance to bureaucratized work.[159] Concerning the future, Weber also speculated on the extent to which conflict would likely be an endemic feature of planned socialist economies administered dictatorially from above. This bureaucratic, state authoritarianism would probably effect a proliferation of (violent) power struggles, strikes over working conditions, boycotts, and the forcible dismissal of unpopular supervisors.[160]

Precisely as a consequence of his ideal-typical preference for analyzing bureaucracies as stable systems of command and obedience, Weber unfortunately never pursued these suggestions. Further reflection suggests that this preference was strongly reinforced by his confident presumption that, under contemporary capitalist conditions, bureaucratic organizations would induce among the governed a settled orientation for sticking unthinkingly to rules and regulations.[161] He took it for granted that very few are destined to live for politics as active, publicly involved citizens. It seemed obvious to Weber, the democratic elitist, that "a relatively small number of people are primarily interested in political life and hence interested in sharing political power."[162] Everywhere the law of the small number – the superior political maneuverability of small leading groups – determines political and social activity. Only a few strive to live off the state by making organized politics a permanent source of interest and income. Always and everywhere, politics is for most people naturally an avocation.

This conviction that the great mass of citizens can only be the objects of solicitation by bureaucratic ruling groups was supported by various – and highly conflicting – observations. On occasion (without further argument, and mostly with reference to the charisma of the ancient Judaic prophets), Weber assumed that officials and others submit easily to the appeals of demagogic leaders and their causes. This predisposition to voluntary servitude would be considerably encouraged by the capacity of charismatic leaders to create a willingness of others to follow them unconditionally: "Inwardly it is *per se* more satisfying to work for a leader."[163] Elsewhere (in language reminiscent of the ancients), he observed that efforts to institute the "old type" of direct, participatory democracy (such as that attempted in the Swiss cantons) always degenerate into aristocratic outcomes. Political involvement, he insisted, is always contingent upon a release

redirected. Such protest has sometimes taken the form of countercultures (e.g., Taborite millenarianism, the English Ranters, Romanticism, the communal movements), which reactively opposed the artificiality of bureaucratization with their own allegedly natural, spontaneous, and highly affective forms of life. At other times, this collective protest has been organized around political movements (e.g., those of Calvinists, radical liberals, workers, women, rural populists, anticolonialists, regional separatists) that sought a share of state or social power, or its decentralization. Throughout earlier phases of modernity, these countercultural and political movements were typically fragmented (i.e., at odds with themselves) and usually subject to wide geographic variation. As marginalized movements, they were unable fully to control, arrest, and redeploy the processes of bureaucratization. They were therefore subjected to violent suppression, integration, or processes of internal decay and self-destruction. Within the metropolitan capitalist countries at least, their synthesis into alliances of great scope and power of resistance to the "age of reason" was rare – the workers' movement of the nineteenth and early twentieth centuries being the last great instance.

from the everyday struggle for the satisfaction of economic necessities.[164] In at least one place, he even claimed that the contemporary division of the population into active and (mostly) passive elements is a product of genuinely voluntary choices. It follows from this "will to powerlessness" thesis that attempts at increasing the degree and quality of citizen involvement (for example, through the enactment of compulsory voting) are doomed to failure from the outset.[165] Finally, and most plausibly, Weber observed that the depoliticization of the masses under contemporary bureaucratic conditions is simply a *condition* of success of disciplined, plebiscitarian, and machinelike political processes. Under state capitalist conditions, it is not the politically passive citizenry that produces leaders, but the political leaders who seek to organize, recruit, and win followers through demagogy. This is the most reliable of Weber's attempted explanations, indicating why those who demand radical democratization are always in turn spitefully repudiated by him as "windbags," "street crowds," "mob-dictators," and believers in the "anti-political heroic ethos of brotherhood."[166]

This most honest of explanations is also the least implausible, for it accurately proposes that depoliticization is a fundamental organizing principle of bureaucratically organized relations of power within the realms of state and society. At the same time, however, Weber's explanation is self-limiting. It fails to grasp that, within all spheres of contemporary life, such depoliticization continually generates politicizing countertendencies, that is, demands for the autonomous discussion, reform, and reconstruction of bureaucratic organization. These autonomous demands and struggles are persistently generated by a fundamental disjunction or contradiction within the mode of operation of both public and private bureaucracies. All bureaucracies, it can be argued, are structured by principles of organization that negate their practical realization as such. Bureaucracies cannot regularly secure the discipline of their constituents and clients by relying on such impersonal mechanisms as the appeal to professional expertise, objective regulations, careerism, the payment of wages and salaries, and the sense of duty. As Weber correctly emphasized, bureaucratic organizations seek to discipline and depoliticize their constituents through the deployment of abstract, formally rational rules of command. Indeed, the greater the scope of any bureaucratic organization, the more its activities are diversified, specialized, and partitioned, the greater will be the scope of these mechanisms of administrative coordination and control.

Inasmuch as these disciplinary mechanisms continually estrange and provoke particular constituents at all levels, however, the commanders of bureaucratic organizations are continually forced to entreat or solicit the active, controlled involvement of these same dissident constituents whom the organization otherwise seeks to depoliticize as inactive, servile objects. The source of trouble in bureaucracies is that they must tacitly acknowledge that they are full of particular groups and individuals with initiative. Bureaucracies no doubt constantly tend to reduce their constituents and clients into pure and simple "executants." Given that this tendency cannot be fully realized – if only because of the active resistance generated, and because the typical dependence of the organization upon initiative at every level would be thoroughly thwarted – bureaucracies are obliged to invite the participation of their executants, who are then forbidden all initiative and control. Bureaucracies require that their members and clients be subjects and objects at the same time; absolute reification is impossible. The intense circulation of reports and memoranda, the multiplication of *paperasserie*, the proliferation of meetings, the trends toward corporatist mediation of conflict, the phenomena of "participation," decentralization, and joint consultations, the media campaigns – all these are expressive of the fact that bureaucratic organizations subsist and expand upon their involvement of subordinates, whose genuine autonomy they in turn deny.[167] All bureaucratic organizations depend upon processes of pseudomutual recognition. Ironically, they simultaneously *presuppose, deny,* and *anticipate* the regulative ideal of autonomous public association.

In respect of this ironic disjunction and its associated conflicts, the machinelike features of bureaucracy highlighted by Weber are typically contingent. Bureaucratic domination is the always fragile medium and outcome of (potentially) public, democratic struggles over the distribution and credibility of power. Weber's concern that the spread of formally rational organization to all domains of life might induce a new age of machinelike serfdom staffed by *êtres inanimés* is misleadingly overdrawn. Bureaucratic systems of command cannot permanently suffocate forms of politically secured individuality and value-oriented conduct. From the standpoint of this conduct, these systems are highly contradictory forms of organization. Even when judged according to their self-declared standards of calculating, technical rationality, bureaucracies must also be considered highly irrational processes. Weber's conviction that autonomous public spheres are not feasible under contemporary bureaucratic conditions is therefore also unfounded. Within all spheres of contemporary life, to conclude, bureaucratic processes repress *and* incite the growth of autonomous public spheres of discussion and decision making.

Still to be discussed, finally, is a third and unresolved difficulty within Weber's defense of bureaucratic domination guided by the principle of nationally conscious, plebiscitarian leadership. This unresolved difficulty derives from his failure to analyze further the conditions of possibility of his advocacy of *this* and not *another* principle. As we have seen, he consistently argued that judgments about the validity of value judgments are always a matter of faith. It is impossible, from the point of view of his decisionism, to establish and scientifically demonstrate fundamental ethical principles, in accordance with which solutions to political problems can be derived unambiguously. So-called ultimate ends, and even the apparently certain knowledge generated by mathematics and the natural sciences, are always debatable and therefore subject to variation and transformation through time and space. Inasmuch as the range of possible ultimate values is inexhaustible, their struggle can never be brought to a decisive and final conclusion. "Which of the warring gods should we serve?"[168] is a question permanently posed for a bureaucratic age that has virtually debunked the validity of metaphysical systems of absolute knowledge. This question becomes more pressing and serious by virtue of the fact that the daily existence of individuals is more and more divided, fragmented, and routinely organized; ensnared within complex, bureaucratic divisions of labor, they are, in the here and now at least, forced to sacrifice themselves first to this deity, then to that deity. Under modern conditions, then, the ancient plurality of gods reappears, but in a disenchanted and depersonalized form. These gods, Weber stresses, do not and cannot peace-fully coexist. They vie for potential believers, entering into an eternal struggle with one another.

Precisely because their most treasured, ultimate ideals are precarious and transitory, the inhabitants of the modern world can no longer credibly afford to let life run on as if it were an event in nature. Weber was adamant: The resolution of the struggle between gods is ultimately a matter of power and politics. The highest ideals of our polytheistic epoch are always crystallized in the struggle with each other. "Every meaningful *value-judgment* about someone else's *aspirations*," Weber urges, "must be a criticism from the standpoint of one's own *Weltanschauung*; it must be a struggle against *another's ideals from the standpoint of one's own*."[169]

Weber's advocacy of the antidemocratic goal of bureaucratic domination guided by nationally conscious, plebiscitarian leadership is no doubt in conformity with this polytheistic principle. It is curious, however, that he never systematically considered whether his opposition to democratic public life – his defense of the *necessity* of bureaucratic domination – was in turn compatible with this principle of polytheism, struggle, and contestation. Further reflection suggests that it is not. His disavowal of autonomous public life, on the contrary, logically contra-dicts his avowed value relativism. This self-contradiction is evidenced by his failure to reflect critically on the institutional grounds or conditions necessary for the realization of the polytheistic struggle. Clearly, the principle of polythe-ism, the presumption that individual personalities must choose the meaning and direction of their own existence, implies a range of conditions necessary for its political realization as such. For example, the maxim that ideals can and must be crystallized in struggle with other ideals tacitly presupposes an opposition to all claims and contexts that deny this maxim. In this respect, conversely, Weber's polytheism rests upon the claim that, in principle, a minimal agreement or consensus can and must be reached in order to facilitate the permanent con-testation of substantive principles. Actors must have already and always tacitly agreed to disagree.

Furthermore, this conditional agreement that every meaningful evaluation of another's ideals *must* involve a polemic against others' values from the standpoint of one's own presupposes institutional conditions in which this contestation can permanently and unrestrictedly take place. The private arbitrariness of sub-stantively rational decisions cannot ultimately rest upon prerational decisions or solipsistic acts of faith, as Weber supposed. The decision to follow and defend rules privately, as he understood it, must rather always depend upon intersub-jectively constituted, public spheres of discussion, argumentation, decision mak-ing, and disobedience. Only under conditions of unrestricted debate and a plurality of institutional mechanisms to ensure this debate could actors proficiently, com-petently, or even minimally defend their ideals. Weber's defense of bureaucracy becomes embroiled in a self-destructive paradox: The principle of polytheism (of which his polemic against substantive democracy is one instance) contains the imputation of democratic, public life. This principle presumes a special type of institutional form about whose validity actors must already have come to agreement – it presumes, in other words, the availability of actually existing forms of public life, to which speaking actors can have recourse, and only by means of which they can express their opposition to (or agreement with) others' ideals. Spheres of autonomous public life, in short, serve as a counterfactual, as a condition that must be established if value relativism of the type Weber defends is to obtain. This condition is not a substantial "ought," which takes the form of a heteronomous principle recommended to struggling actors. It is not just one condition among others, in the sense that actors struggling to realize their ideals could decide to satisfy the condition for a while, only later to reject it. On the contrary, it is not possible to renounce the counterfactually anticipated condition of democratic, public life without contradicting and wholly rejecting the polytheistic principle as such.

Especially granted the implausibility of his ideal-typical account of the technical superiority and disciplinary capacity of bureaucracy, Weber's failure to recognize this imputation strengthens the general charge proposed by this essay: Weber conspicuously *failed* to demonstrate the impossibility of defending autonomous public life against the "forward progress"[170] of bureaucratic domination. At the end of Max Weber's life, it remained for others to elaborate this charge.

3

A totally administered society? Developments in the theory of late capitalism

> The embarrassing secret of the welfare state is that, while its impact upon capitalist accumulation may well become destructive..., its abolition would be plainly disruptive.
>
> Claus Offe

Toward the totally administered society?

During the decades following the death of Max Weber, discussions of the organized or one-dimensional character of industrial capitalist societies enjoyed a certain notoriety. Numerous philosophical, political, and aesthetic writings warned of the advent of a brave new world of seamless, bureaucratic domination without opposition.[1] Within the German theoretical tradition, at least, the writings of Theodor Adorno serve as perhaps the most compelling and insightful illustration of this one-dimensionality thesis. Adorno's arguments are admittedly weakened by several defects and omissions. These difficulties no doubt hinder further consideration of the irrationalities that mark bureaucratization processes, irrationalities that have become readily apparent during the present phase of late capitalism. Adorno's account of the totalitarian tendencies of contemporary capitalism nonetheless remains of vital importance to any socialist political theory. The following analysis of the recent contributions to this theory by Claus Offe and Jürgen Habermas accordingly begins with a reconsideration of Adorno's theses, and for three reasons in particular. First, Adorno's arguments correctly emphasize that depoliticizing, bureaucratic forms of life continue to be a key organizing principle of late capitalist societies. These theses also provide, secondly, a more contemporary (that is, post-Weberian) framework of argumentation within which questions concerning the limitations of bureaucratic rationality and the possibility of autonomous public life can be considered anew. Connected with this point, finally, is that Adorno's theses bring into sharp relief the limitations of theories of late capitalism that draw heavily upon (classical Marxian) analyses of the commodity form. Adorno's claim that late capitalist societies tend to be ruled absolutely by bureaucratic commodification processes fails in particular to consider these processes' growing dependence upon *decommodifying* relations of state power. As we shall see, Adorno therefore underestimates the degree to which late capitalist systems continually generate disorganizing effects and autonomous social struggles against the commodity form.

Adorno's arguments are of course notoriously difficult and complex. His favorite motif is nonetheless clear: The current phase of the bourgeois modernization process, he insists, is synonymous with totalitarian administration. All late capitalist formations are in the grip of two false (and interconnected) principles of organization – those of expanding commodification and reification. Contemporary social and political life is structured, first, by rules of *equivalence*, in accordance with which all commodities are forcibly compared and calculated through the standardizing medium of money. Such rules of equivalence are reinforced, secondly, by processes of *reification*, as a consequence of which the contingent and historically produced character of these commodities is concealed by their ossified and fetishized appearance. In conformity with these two principles, which will be discussed and analyzed herein, all late capitalist formations institutionalize and defend a "law of exchange." Adorno maintains that this law of exchange now fully "determines how the fatality of humankind unfolds itself."[2] Under the power of its bewitching spell, the populations of late capitalist societies are more and more fashioned by an enchanted, totalitarian apparatus. Mere agents of commodification, these populations blindly submit to reified exchange processes as if this submission were naturally ordained. As a consequence – and notwithstanding its seemingly progressive and dynamic character – the age of late capitalism regresses. It assumes the form of an archaic, myth-bound epoch fully closed in upon itself. Past indignant rage and protest against commodified exploitation, such as that typically analyzed within the Marxist political tradition, becomes just that: a thing of the past. "The total organization of society through big business and its all-pervasive technology has...taken complete possession of the world and imagination."[3]

It should be emphasized that Adorno's theses must not be crudely dismissed as pessimistic, as pathetically resigned assessments of the prospects for revolutionizing late capitalist society. Not only do such dismissals typically rest upon psychologistic premises; they also rely too heavily upon unsophisticated and literal interpretations of his texts. It is clear, for example, that Adorno's preoccupation with his own mode of textual composition already presumes the possibility of rupturing conventional philosophical discourse and (insofar as this philosophical discourse is expressive of existing social and political relations) the bureaucratic commodification and reification of everyday life. Precisely because the contemporary bourgeoisie glorifies the existing order as natural and demands that fellow "citizens" speak naturally, Adorno is convinced that the defiance of this society must (and can) include a defiance of its philosophic and ordinary language.[4]

Under these historical conditions, the language of familiarity and straightforwardness merely shrugs off the crucial task of arousing critical imagination. This is why Adorno's rejection of philosophical first principles and of claims to absolute knowledge leads him to boycott the pseudoclarity of narrative discourse. His opposition to late capitalist commodification and reification is at the same time an opposition to the (corresponding) philosophical conviction that static, fixed theoretical concepts – identitarian thought – can exhaustively encircle and then capture the dynamic objects to which they are addressed.[5] Crystal-clear, identitarian thinking must be countered with "negative-dialectical," antibureaucratic forms of argumentation. Through a kind of tacking procedure that avoids the pitfalls of reified, identitarian thinking, Adorno's negative-dialectical criticisms most often express themselves through constellations of theoretical concepts. These constellations seek to induce a "sense of nonidentity"[6] through the reciprocal criticism of late capitalist reality and its ideal representations. Inasmuch as it is forced into hibernation by the prevailing commodification and reification, Adorno insists that the criticism of late capitalist societies must draw upon counterbureaucratic compositional forms – upon the modest essay form or fragmentary notes and "prisms,"[7] for example. He further argues that such compositional forms can be reinforced by a whole series of narrative-critical techniques: repetition and inversion of clauses (chiasmus); the refusal to define terms; the appeal to irony; and the deployment of hyperbole, which draws caricatures of its adversaries so as effectively to debunk their apparent naturalness.

From the point of view of this essay, Adorno's reliance upon hyperbole is particularly crucial. It is best illustrated by his thesis of total administration. If indeed this thesis is understood as literally and factually true, then, logically, it would of course be unthinkable. Simply, if the pseudo-equivalence and reification of bureaucratically steered exchange processes had already attained complete command over the present, then no independent and critical awareness of their hegemony would be achievable. Adorno avoids this rather obvious antinomy. His thesis of total reification instead rhetorically draws attention to the menacing possibility of a fully administered world without political opposition. Conversely, it seeks to debunk the dogmatism of those myths and ideologies which induce a fatalistic, passive acquiescence in this tendency. In short, his negative-dialectical caricatures seek the "explosion of reification."[8]

In pursuing this aim, Adorno's theoretical project both extends and breaks with numerous post-Weberian efforts to rework the classical Marxian analyses of value and commodity fetishism into a viable critique of the bureaucratized culture and political economy of late capitalism.[9] Unlike the less orthodox arguments (developed by Marcuse, for example) concerning science and technology as novel forms of deception and domination, Adorno's critique of late capitalism depends to a surprising extent upon the Marxian schema.[10] According to this schema, it will be recalled, the bourgeois commodification process forcibly makes producers, their products, and nature homogenized objects whose magnitude can be compared in monetary terms. In the eyes of those who produce, potentially differentiated and incommensurable social labor and its useful products assume the form of a relationship between identical "things." The exchange value of these things in turn appears to derive naturally from their properties as commodities marked by phantasmagoric – shadowy, weirdly lifelike – qualities. The socially mediated interaction of producers with nature, that is to say, appears to be the interaction between comparable, measurable objects that have the power of command over their producers.[11]

Adorno appropriates this Marxian thesis very selectively indeed. For example, he fails to query Marx's presumption that the use value of objects has an unproblematic immediacy and transparency.[12] Of equal seriousness is Adorno's virtual ignoring of the fact that the Marxian concepts of abstract labor and commodity fetishism are linked dialectically with theories of surplus-value extraction, crisis tendencies, class formation, and the possibility of concrete social labor. Adorno retrieves the Marxian theory of commodification only to subvert its central contention: that, in modern capitalist societies, the whole of human servitude and its overcoming through processes of enlightened struggle are rooted in the dialectics of the production process. This hollowing out of the Marxian theory of revolution is not unjustified, as Weber himself had already suggested through somewhat different arguments. Nevertheless, the unintended consequence of Adorno's weakening of the Marxian theses on revolution is the bracketing of the practical or political intentions of critical theory. Adorno appropriates the Marxian theory of commodification as if it were a theory of critical cognition, a theory whose validation and practical realization no longer appears to depend upon those (potential political subjects) to whom it is addressed. Against its avowed intentions, in other words, his negative-dialectical criticism tends to reinstate itself as a more subtle form of philosophy of first principles. It unwittingly becomes (to invoke Adorno's own expression) a form of *"prima dialectica."*[13]

The Marxian theory of commodification is altered in yet another sense fundamental to our concern with bureaucratization. According to Adorno, the "twofold nature" of labor and exchange processes analyzed by Marx has collapsed into a false unity: "Exchange values are enjoyed in the absolute, for their own sake."[14] Adorno here broaches his key thesis of the totalitarian, all-pervasive control of human needs. According to this thesis, under late capitalist conditions, use values cease to be spontaneously self-evident because of the unchallenged hegemony of exchange values. In other words, the commercialized production, distribution, and consumption of objects endows the exchange process with a natural utility. In actual fact, however, the commodified, fetishized character of this process is not abolished but definitely amplified. "Exchange value . . . dominates human needs and replaces them; illusion dominates reality."[15] As a consequence of this development, or so Adorno argues, the classical Marxian theory of value ceases to provide critical insight into the logic of late capitalist social relations. This is because the contradiction between the forces and the relations of production becomes inactive. The taming of this dialectic, the appearance of the existing relations of production as absolutely necessary, signals the emergence of a reified bourgeois world without opposition: "The productive forces and the relations of production are today one and the same . . . Material production, distribution and consumption are controlled in common."[16] It follows that Marx and Engels's prognoses concerning the subdivision of bourgeois society into "two hostile and opposing" classes cannot be realized. While the objective grounds of class division and antagonism remain, their conflict potential is thoroughly neutralized.[17] Like Odysseus's deafened sailors who are oblivious to the call of utopia, the contemporary proletariat labors under the spellbinding powers of universal commodity production and its principles of equivalence and reification. The total bureaucratization of the world is synonymous with the anesthetization and depoliticization of the masses. Their suffering can no longer be subjectively experienced as suffering. Political conflicts wither or, at best, focus on marginal issues and problems. Revolution is seemingly postponed forever.

Absolute reification and commodification thus tend to absorb the mind and its critical faculties completely. "The fetish character of commodities is not a fact of consciousness," Adorno writes, "but dialectic in the eminent sense that it produces consciousness."[18] Consistent with bureaucratic capitalism's equalization and standardization of commodities through monetary values, quantitative equivalence becomes the sacred canon of this society and its forms of language and thought. That which is novel and dissimilar is made comparable by being abased to abstract quantities that can be calculated, manipulated, and administered at will. Relations among outer nature, social actors, and their products appear as the values of commensurable and identical things. Whatever does not conform to rules of utility and computation is assumed to be suspect. Adorno presses Weber's concern about the forward progress of bureaucratization: "The spread of the principle [of exchange] imposes on the whole world an obligation to become identical, to become total."[19] The conceptual representation of value as the naturelike property of measurable commodities and also the philosophical representation of concepts as equivalent to their objects – identity thinking – are for Adorno aspects of the same rationalization process. Identity thinking is bureaucratic thinking. It strives to represent unlike objects and processes as fundamentally commensurable, purports therefore to know them exhaustively in all their particularity, with the consequence that these objects and processes are, in turn, falsely reckoned to be identical with their concepts. The insight that "truth" can only be historical is suppressed. Bureaucratic, identitarian thought posits unchanging constants that appear to dwell outside the possibility of historical interruption and transformation.

In the view of Adorno, the rise of the mass communications and culture industries strengthens the hegemony of this bureaucratic consciousness. Patterned in accordance with the logic of capitalist production, these industries produce and deploy stereotypic, identitarian patterns of signs. While these signs remain in a certain sense mysterious, they also are made to appear (in accordance with their reified, phantasmagoric character) immediately intelligible. The products of the culture industry encourage individuals to think that they are up to date with things, that they know what is happening. The outpourings of industrialized news and entertainment simultaneously instruct, enchant, and stupefy their consumers.[20] Adorno therefore insists that the leveling of the differences between high and popular culture through their bureaucratic commodification leads not to democratic emancipation but, rather, to the "stylized barbarism" (Nietzsche) of the mass culture industry. Gravitating in the direction of mythology, commodified culture thoroughly affirms the status quo. Purporting to separate itself from the world of the bureaucratic factory and office, this manufactured culture presents its phantasmagoric claims and promises as immediately realizable by every consumer – without the need for a political transformation of the present.[21] Under the sway of this culture's fetishistic illusions or "chimerical deities," the producers and consumers of late capitalist society in no way (contra Weber) sense their everyday lives as meaningless or disenchanted.

Adorno is adamant that all of these developments conspire to "naturalize" late capitalism's relations of production. These relations are now marked with a thoroughgoing paradox. On the one hand, the arrival of large-scale organization and rationalized planning associated with the commodification process tends to eliminate many inefficient and anarchic mechanisms that plagued the liberal phase of capitalism. On the other hand, the possibility that these potentially less complex and mystified social relations could become more genuinely intelligible is blocked by their more illusory and enchanted character. Ensnared within these "pacified" and enchanting relations of production and consumption, the members of late capitalism become victims of this pseudotransparency, mere bearers or agents of commodified exchange and its forms of thought. Adorno therefore agrees with Weber that the instrumental, calculating individualism of the heyday of liberal capitalism now tends to be liquidated. The increasing heteronomy and unintelligibility (more correctly, pseudo-intelligibility) of late capitalist society signals the growing predominance of the abstract-general over the particular.[22] While noncommodified enclaves of social and political life persist,[23] a fully "oversocialized" society conquers and swindles its individual constituents. Their psychological substance (as Hegel would have termed it) wanes. A completely commodified and depoliticized age of "postindividual collectivism"[24] is at hand. Late capitalist society congeals as "second nature" around its living members.[25] The perverse irony of its attempts to subjugate outer nature rationally and efficiently in the name of enlightenment and progress is that it produces and perpetuates patterns of "blind nature-like development [*Naturwüchsigkeit*]." The historicity of its organizing principles is thereby concealed. Under late capitalist conditions, all social and political relations are structured as if they were just "a piece of nature." Everything appears as "fatefully structured, preordained," as if real life were still life, *nature morte*. Even the attempts of negative-dialectical criticism to expose these naturalizing effects as historically produced second nature tend to be drawn into the present petrified abyss.[26] The transition to a blind, fully administered world of bureaucratic unfreedom seems all but complete.

In a certain sense, Habermas and Offe appear to be in agreement with this prognosis. Developing the theory of late capitalism further, they emphasize the growing deployment of administrative strategies aimed at disciplining and controlling the whole of social and political life. Modern capitalist orders are seen as entering a new phase of administrative planning. The bureaucratic, rationalizing tendencies typical of all modern societies are further intensified and more and more come to depend upon sophisticated techniques of planned choice – upon empirical-analytic knowledge, professionalism, forecasting, and crisis-management and problem-solving strategies. Late capitalist systems become permanently mobilized against disruptive crisis tendencies. In a way reminiscent of Adorno's theses on the totally administered society, Habermas and Offe therefore sometimes speak of the metropolitan countries as systems of "authoritarian total administration" or "organized capitalism." This affinity with Adorno's theses is rather superficial, however. In part, this is because Habermas and Offe are out of sympathy with Adorno's substitution of "an empty exercise of self-reflection"[27] for a critical theory of late capitalist societies. In their view, his theses rely too heavily on abstract-general epigrams (such as "second nature" or "total administration"), whose rhetorical value nevertheless tends to obscure the concrete patterns of institutionalized power and political resistance within late capitalist systems. In explicit opposition to Adorno, furthermore, they insist that these systems cannot be conceived (even rhetorically) as totalities whose smooth, calculated domination is unshakable. Adorno is accused of having developed a left counterpart to the once popular theory of totalitarian domination. According to Offe, "*all* advanced capitalist societies . . . *create* endemic systemic problems and large-scale unmet needs." "To use the expression 'late capitalism,' " Habermas urges, "is to put forward the hypothesis that, even in state-regulated capitalism, social developments involve 'contradictions' or crises."[28]

It is the contention of the remaining sections of this essay that one of the most decisive themes in the writings of Habermas and Offe is this conviction that the conscious rationalization of social and political life under late capitalist conditions suffers from an unintended unconsciousness of its logic and limitations. This theme is of great importance to a theory of socialist public life. According to Habermas and Offe, the naturelike descent of bureaucratic, late capitalist societies upon their populations cannot be achieved. Organized, welfare state capitalist systems continually generate disorganizing effects. These orders are systematically marked by their failure to eliminate the cyclical dynamics of the capitalist commodification process, by discrepancies between state and corporate planning, by state planning that chronically fails to achieve its goals, and by threatening patterns of mass disloyalty and political protest. Such developments are by no means the residual or lag effects associated with a gradual, step-by-step ironing out of uncertainties and planning problems. Nor can they be dismissed as products of bureaucratic trickery, as forms of "artificial negativity" generated by late capitalism's omniscient ruling groups. Offe and Habermas correctly insist that late capitalist societies are presently incapable of fulfilling the institutional and mass loyalty conditions of bureaucratic domination. Contrary to the claims of Adorno and all theories of technological or (in their cruder formulations) postindustrial civilization,[29] late capitalist regimes cannot homogenize and unify social and political life in the direction of rationalized totalitarianism.

The rise and fall of liberal capitalism

In working through the logic, implications, and weaknesses of Habermas's and Offe's arguments, several important caveats should be briefly emphasized at the outset. First, the following reading of their texts makes no claim to exhaustiveness; this reading, more inclined to analyze their theses on the limits to late capitalist orders, also to a certain extent conflates the differences between their respective approaches. Secondly, Habermas's and Offe's theses, as they often stress against frequent attempts to interpret them literally, must be considered highly programmatic. These inquiries should not be discussed as if they were finished, conclusive, and empirical statements, for they can at most be seen as theoretical formulations that serve as a preliminary framework for further research and empirical enquiries. Of more immediate importance, thirdly, is the point that their theories of the contradictions of late capitalist societies are placed within the framework of a more general understanding of historical processes. Habermas in particular tries to ground his account of late capitalism within a general theory of social evolution.[30] With reference to the period of liberal, market capitalism, this theory can be sketched here, inasmuch as it helps to clarify both Habermas's and Offe's several objections to Adorno's theory of total administration.

Habermas's theory of liberal capitalism strongly parallels the classical interpretations of the early modern civilizing process provided by such thinkers as Franz Neumann, Karl Polanyi, and Sheldon Wolin.[31] He also draws heavily upon the Marxian account of nineteenth-century capitalism. According to Habermas, what was unique about liberal capitalism was the extent to which "free" market relations of exchange between wage labor and capital became hegemonic. He sees liberal capitalism as a process of social evolution within which a sphere of economic production and exchange became uncoupled from the formal constraints of kinship and state power relations. This development strongly contrasts with the patterns of life typical of archaic (*vorhochkulturelle*) and traditional social formations. In the remarkably ordered and stable archaic societies that predominated until the close of the Mesolithic era, the age and sex roles and rituals and taboos of the kinship system closely regulated the expansion of the productive forces. Production was mostly for the immediate consumption of the tribal members. With the emergence of state-dominated, traditional societies, by contrast, the kinship system began to surrender its productive and socialization powers. The distribution of the fruits of the production process became less a function of kinship relations and more dependent upon access to state institutions, themselves legitimated by the sacred canopy of patriarchal and religious world views. Within these traditional systems structured according to the principle of class domination in political form, depoliticized relations of exchange between city and country and within local urban markets were for the most part constrained. And insofar as technical innovations were rather haphazard, the exploitation of labor power proceeded either indirectly through politically enforced rent payments or through more direct strategies of enforced labor.

The modernization process, or so Habermas wants to argue, radically altered all this. Modernization everywhere came to be synonymous with the invasion of traditional patterns of everyday life by rationalizing forms of labor, trade, transport, and communications. Whether in the country or the city, a class- and state-directed urbanization of the form of daily life came to power. The bourgeoisie struggled to institutionalize and legitimate decentralized exchange relations between private and autonomous commodity owners. Supplemented by the patriarchal, bourgeois family form, daily life came to be defined and ordered through the purposive and instrumental rationality of market exchanges, whose wage labor–capital relations were represented by the dominant bourgeois ideology as ones of equivalence or reciprocity. Certainly, Habermas does not deny the importance of other mechanisms (patriarchal and religious traditions, brute force) of maintaining the subordination of members of the new urban and rural proletariat.[32] Nevertheless, the growing power of the ideology of the exchange of equivalents was synonymous with the loss of validity of traditional world views. From this point on, the "legitimation of domination . . . is no longer called down from the lofty heights of cultural tradition but instead summoned up from the base of social labor."[33] Market relations of exchange, through which both male private property owners and the propertyless exchanged commodities, appeared to be just because of their equivalence.

Consequent upon this development, the market-mediated domination of outer nature feigned the arrival of civil society, of a sphere of *social* relations emancipated from coercive, personal power. The relations of exchange of civil society tended to become the steering mechanism of the liberal capitalist system, the pacesetter for developments within the spheres of political power and family life. It should be stressed that Habermas strongly dissents from the conventional interpretation of early modern civil societies as thoroughly depoliticized, self-regulating spheres of reciprocal social relations – an interpretation associated with that historical school known as the "liberal capitalist perspective."[34] In opposition to this perspective, Habermas emphasizes that the patriarchal, bourgeois family form was a crucial dimension of the liberal capitalist domain of privacy. This patriarchal household form operated both as the typical locus of capital formation through savings and as the source of internalization of paternal authority and family tradition.[35]

Habermas also corrects the liberal capitalist perspective by repeating the Weberian argument that market relations of exchange were always functionally dependent upon the taxing, military and lawmaking activities of the modern bureaucratic state. He is emphatic that the forcible creation of abstract, market individuals succeeded only under the aegis of abstract, centralizing states, such as those of the absolute monarchies (for example, the Tudors and early Stuarts). The centralizing state pillaged the church, suppressed foreign enemies, and dared to establish domestic order under the shadow of the sword. By no means can the operations of this central administrative apparatus, which more and more seceded from the business of production, be explained only with reference to the needs or imperatives of the emerging civil society. Following Weber, Habermas insists that modern state institutions came to embody a form of power *sui generis*. Their logic of formation was directed by internal imperatives of privately managed capitalist accumulation *and* by the external necessities that drove these states to protect and expand their territory against foreign military invasion.[36] Against "economistic" accounts of the modern state, finally, Habermas proposes that the modernization process was marked by immanently *political* discourses that sought the justification and/or criticism of this state. At first, these discourses urged the overthrow of theological justifications of state power (such as that of Marsilius of Padua). Later, in opposition to the theories of princely sovereignty of Bodin and others, attempts were made (by Locke, for example) to specify and justify the essential liberties of the individual that needed to be guaranteed by systems of public and private law oriented to the growing differentiation and dynamism of market relations.[37]

It is within the boundaries of this account of the *differentia specifica* of modern societies that both Offe and Habermas try to show that the activities of the state in liberal capitalism were increasingly restricted to the general securing of the *harmonies économiques* of market relations of exchange. The state and its legal system tended to become "the complementary arrangement to self-regulative market commerce."[38] The state sought to guarantee the reproduction of strictly delimited social spheres beyond its authority. According to Offe, "the bourgeois state confirmed its class nature precisely through the material limits it imposed on its authority."[39] In accordance with these material limits, the liberal capitalist state harnessed tax, banking, and business law to the dynamics of the capital-accumulation process; protected bourgeois commerce and family life via the police and military; and administered justice through formal law. The property order thereby began to shed its political skin; liberal capitalism's institutional framework and its mode of legitimation tended to become immediately economic and only mediately political. It was as if this social order were subjected to partition: An ensemble of state institutions set itself the task of mediating and defending the familial intimacies and productive anarchy of the private realm, in which, freed from the old "pernicious regulations," patriarchal individuals were supposed to pursue their interests and exercise their natural rights of private judgment. Habermas and Offe, however, insist that this assertion of bourgeois society against the state by no means dissolved processes of class structuration. Liberal capitalism was synonymous with their depoliticization *as* social labor and exchange processes. During the phase of liberal capitalism, in other words, there were real signs of "a depoliticization of the class relationship and an anonymization of class domination."[40]

This depoliticization of marked relations, guided by the patriarchal family and the "strategic-utilitarian action orientations of market participants,"[41] certainly permitted a dramatic development of the productive forces. Liberal capitalism, with its Manchesterite state, became the first social formation in world history to institutionalize nearly self-sustaining growth of its productive forces. What was really novel about this system was its ability to shake off the traditional fetters upon the bureaucratic rationalization of agriculture, craft production, and technical innovation. Habermas and Offe nevertheless remind us that the bourgeois dream of depoliticized, universally acceptable class domination resulted in its shattering opposite: proletarian struggles against the form and content of this society. The localized revolts against the periodic famines and tax and military conscription demands of early modernization began to be replaced by the confrontation of social classes. Under the twin pressures of threats to the rate of profit and problems of capital realization, liberal capitalism was rocked to its very foundations by class struggles and disorienting economic crisis tendencies. Habermas remarks, for example, that no previous social formation had ever labored under such fear and excitement about the possibility of revolutionary change.[42] The crisis tendencies of liberal capitalist commodification began to contradict blatantly the idea of bourgeois society as a system in which coercive power and force had been neutralized. To the toiling masses, the stalled, boom–bust character of liberal capitalism served as a visual demonstration of the Marxian truth that everyday life within this rationalizing society was bound to be changed radically by the contradiction between its developed productive forces, on the one hand, and its class-fettered relations of social production, on the other. The ideology of the reciprocal and just relations between competing individuals – an ideology that had been permanently under theoretical attack from the time of Rousseau – began to collapse in practice. Seizing upon the disparity between bourgeois ideals and reality, the emerging workers' movement began to sense the need to make a revolutionary leap out of the social and political violence inherent within the liberal capitalist order.

The late capitalist economy

The displacement of these crisis tendencies since the last quarter of the nine-teenth century, and the consequent frustration of the political potential of the struggles of the labor movement, occupy a central place within Habermas's and Offe's theories of late capitalism. It is their contention that the militant class struggles that racked capitalist societies until the mid-1930s have since been deflected. In opposition to Adorno's conviction that class-structured patterns of commodification (as analyzed by Marx) remain intact, they urge that the weak-ening of class conflict has been synonymous with alterations of this order's re-lations of production. They point, for example, to the emergence of an oligopoly sector of the economy, and its differentiation from a relatively competitive sector. In the latter, production is more labor-intensive, productivity is weakened by its dependence on employment (and not technical) growth, and wage rates and conditions are poorer than in the oligopoly sector, where workers are better organized. By contrast, what is most evident about the oligopoly sector is its capacity to expand the productive forces continuously by means of the national and transnational rationalization of wages, commodity prices, profits, consump-tion, work tasks, and technical innovation.[43]

The rise of corporate price making in the context of negotiated money wage rates is particularly crucial, according to Habermas and Offe. Within the oli-gopoly sector, union-filtered demands for a greater share of surplus *can* be granted and passed on in the form of higher product prices consonant with the extent of state taxation and individual firms' price-setting powers. The general level of administered prices in money terms is primarily adjusted by the nego-tiated level of money wage rates, and not by blind, naturelike market forces: "The market relationship has become virtual rather than real to the owner of labour power."[44] While this system of price administration and bureaucratic negotiation of wage rates and conditions produces permanent inflationary tend-encies (to the disadvantage of unorganized wage earners and other marginal groups), it nevertheless also tends to promote the possibility of class compromise and investment planning by oligopoly capital. As organized labor and oligopoly capital become practitioners of value theory, class conflict tends to be transfigured into company–union negotiations, whose effects can in turn be externalized.[45]

80

Structures of wage determination become the planning nets into which organized labor is drawn. Such planning is often enhanced by union–corporate agreement on the desirability of some state- and/or corporate-financed projects that are deemed mutually beneficial.

This partial reorganization and segmentation of the old civil society complicates Marx's argument (which was itself founded on competitive market assumptions) that the rate of profit tends to decline under conditions of capitalist accumulations.[46] In addition, one of the key Marxian assumptions – that the rate of profit tends to uniformity – needs to be reexamined in light of Habermas's and Offe's suggestion. In their view, however, the transformation of competitive, liberal capitalism through oligopolistic production and consumption is synonymous with neither the overcoming of the class-structured character of late capitalism nor the complete abolition of its unplanned, anarchic character. Habermas, for instance, recalls Adorno's discussion of the blind, naturelike development of late capitalist societies. "The spread of oligopolistic market structures," he comments,

> certainly means the end of *competitive capitalism*. But however much companies broaden their temporal perspectives and expand control over their environments, the steering mechanism of the market remains in force as long as investment decisions are made according to criteria of company profits . . . no matter how much the scope of the private autonomous commerce of commodity owners is administratively restricted, political planning of the allocation of scarce resources does not occur as long as the priorities of the society as a whole develop in an unplanned, nature-like [*naturwüchsig*] manner – that is, as secondary effects of the strategies of private enterprise.[47]

Bureaucratically planned production, in other words, continues to be marked by a certain blindness, by irrationalities that result from the fact that capitalist production remains structured by rules of commodified exchange and profit maximization rather than publicly determined rules of use. The blind laws of capitalist accumulation, according to this thesis, have been only partially overcome by intensified bureaucratic planning. Offe thus refers to the "anarchic ups and downs" of the private accumulation of capital. Habermas also speaks of "the independent, cyclical dynamic of the economic process."[48]

Unfortunately, they are quite unexplicit about the logic of these self-paralyzing tendencies of capitalist commodification. That units of both labor and capital continue to be periodically ejected from, and not automatically integrated within, such processes of commodified exchange seems beyond doubt. But whether – to take some examples from debates about the contemporary economic crisis – these tendencies are a necessary consequence of monopoly capital's search for investment outlets on a global scale, the product of squeezes on the rate of profit owing to the improved bargaining power of organized labor, or the outcome of declining rates of productivity resulting from the exhaustion of the potentials of scientific-technical innovation remains a confused point in both Habermas's and Offe's analyses. Their provocative thesis that the blind laws of capitalist accumulation have not been fully overcome should certainly be taken seriously. To insist on this point without, however, making explicit the logic of these "cyclical dynamics" of capitalist accumulation creates unnecessary ambiguity, and perhaps deserved suspicion among more orthodox Marxian commentators.[49]

In spite of this lacuna in their argument, Habermas and Offe are insistent that these irrationalities and periodic slowdowns in the rate of accumulation are not expressed directly through open class struggle. They do *not* assert that there has been a complete *embourgeoisement* (of voting trends, patterns of consumption, and family life) of the old industrial working classes.[50] The young Habermas also adds (duplicating the difficulties of Adorno's earlier-cited argument) that, by virtue of its lack of actual control over the means of production, the mass of the population of late capitalist societies remains objectively proletarian.[51] Even so, both Offe and Habermas emphasize that the uneven rationalization and segmentation of the late capitalist economy has resulted in a subdivision of the work force and its capacity to organize to articulate and protect its needs. Neither Marx's theses on the tendency leading to the "centralization of the means of production" (the conversion of "the pigmy property of the many into the huge property of the few") nor its corollary, the objective "socialization of labour," has yet come to pass. Instead, late capitalist societies become marked by an uneven and highly skewed distribution of property and income; the bifurcation of the work force results in an at least "temporary redistribution of income to the disadvantage of unorganized workers and other marginal groups."[52] This process of subdivision tends to enhance popular support for reformist, social democratic, and even conservative parties, while at the same time facilitating the deflection of militant class struggle into organized competition between bureaucratic political parties.

The expanded role of state power

The qualitatively expanded role of bureaucratic state power is another basis of the displacement of crisis tendencies through intensified bureaucratic planning. According to Habermas and Offe, the growth of state power has been a universal trend within the metropolitan capitalist world of the past half century or so. State intervention *against* the market around and after World War I has been especially crucial, insofar as it has contributed greatly to the overcoming of the liberal phase of capitalism and its disintegrative tendencies. As is well known, this transformation took place against the late nineteenth-century backdrop of economic cartelization and labor and tariff disputes, and coincided with a number of other developments: the gradual affiliation of political parties with particular economic interest groups, the emergence of party machines bent on engineering popular consent, and the massive economic mobilization of World War I. The rescuing of liberal capitalism from crises became possible only through its recasting in a corporate direction. More and more, the state came to negotiate with fractions of capital and organized labor (or sanctioned pseudo-unions, as in Italy); by building capital and labor into its structures, the state fostered the dissolution of the old dualism of state and civil society. These developments were recognized early in the pioneering analyses of Hilferding, Naphtali, and others on organized capitalism, and in the writings of Korsch, Horkheimer, and

Marcuse, and were emphasized in the famous warning of Friedrich Pollock: "What is coming to an end is not capitalism, but its liberal phase."[53]

Habermas and Offe pursue this theme. According to them, the state in late capitalism has become interwoven with the accumulation process to the point where the latter becomes a function of bureaucratic state activity and organized political conflict. No longer can the relationship between state and society be described through the metaphor of superstructure and base. Capitalist relations of commodity production have been repoliticized. "The 'separation' of the state from society which is typical of the liberal phase of capitalist development has been superseded by a reciprocal interlocking of the two in the state of organized capitalism."[54] Whereas liberal capitalism's organizing principle was nonpolitical class domination, under late capitalist conditions this class domination persists, but only in bureaucratic, state form. The (potential) antagonism within socialized production for particular ends has reassumed a directly statist form. The realization of privately controlled capital accumulation ("the universalization of the commodity form," to invoke a favorite expression of Offe's) is now possible only on the basis of an all-encompassing political mediation. In late capitalism, "the state advances to become the bearer of social order."[55]

Elsewhere Habermas and Offe defend this thesis by delimiting at least two different forms of late capitalist state activity. These include (to speak temporarily in Habermas's terms) the functions of global planning and, secondly, market-replacement and compensation strategies.[56] Unlike the less precise concept of "state intervention," Habermas's typology of the functions of the bureaucratic state is based not on their extent or systematization; rather, his analysis relies on some hypotheses about the *type* of state activity required to reproduce the accumulation process and the *means* through which the state seeks to fulfill them.

In the first place, according to Habermas, state institutions attempt to constitute and secure the conditions of profitable capitalist accumulation within the domestic and international spheres. Examples of these global planning functions include currency stabilization, trade and tariff regulation, the attempted (military, police, judicial) suppression of the system's opponents at home and abroad, and the adaptation of the taxation and legal system (banking arrangements, company law) to the dynamics of the oligopoly and competitive accumulation processes. To be sure, certain of these global planning functions were central in the operations of the liberal capitalist state. Under late capitalist conditions, their scope is nevertheless broadened. They also tend to be pursued more systematically through calculated, quantified, and professionalized means. More recent examples of this expansion and systematization of global planning include the proliferation of heavily armed and tightly coordinated state military/diplomatic strategies (a development insufficiently discussed by either Habermas or Offe), and domestic fiscal and monetary planning that seeks to moderate the capitalist business cycle through a whole range of measures designed to manipulate aggregate levels of investment and demand – the fixation of interest rates, the subsidization of oligopolistic and competitive capital, the provision or withdrawal of government contracts to stimulate or retard rates of investment, and so on.

It is important to note, Habermas stresses, that the state's global planning activities remain essentially reactive in character. Insofar as "private disposition over the means of production continues to be the basis of the economic process,"[57] such planning can react only to the imperatives of privately steered capital formation that are, as it were, external to state policy making. In this respect, global planning policies should be distinguished from a second form of state activity that is unique to late capitalism.

Habermas and Offe emphasize that late capitalist states now also actively strive to restructure the formerly unpolitical relations of production of liberal capitalism. This contention cannot be described – contrary to the claims of Müller, Neussüss, Blanke, and other advocates of "state-derivation" theory – as a social democratic argument about the absolute separation or full autonomy of the late capitalist state from the logic of capitalist production.[58] After all, the above-mentioned global planning activities of the state remain chronically dependent upon the rationalizing private property order. The really novel significance of Habermas's and Offe's thesis is, rather, that it undermines the view of Müller, Neussüss, Blanke, Adorno, and others that market-exchange processes continue to operate as the dominant medium of power and control. The process of class domination no longer unfolds through the anonymity of laws of value. Notwithstanding the extension of the money form to previously uncommodified zones of social life (for example, into the family, as Adorno had tried to show), Habermas and Offe insist that the market-mediated production and appropriation of surplus value has been restricted and modified by relatively autonomous relations of state power. The bewitching spell of bourgeois commodification (outlined by Adorno) has been at least partially broken by the activities of the bureaucratic state. This state's attempts to maintain and universalize family life and the commodification process rely upon strategies and forms of organization that are themselves not directly subject to the commodity form. State institutions produce and distribute use values that are not always controlled and dominated by the logic of exchange values.[59] Decommodification within the late capitalist public sector establishes a socialized form of organization that at the same time promotes and, because of its capitalist orientation, thwarts the possibility of a set of political relations freed from the bureaucratic commodity form. This liberated base of (potentially) concrete labor oriented to the production of use values is in no way a residue of precapitalist forms of life. It signals a new and vital need that this social formation has created, upon which it depends, but which it cannot satisfy.

This decommodifying activity takes at least two major forms: compensation and market replacement.[60] The state's *compensatory* activities – its provision of health and housing facilities, for instance – aim at offsetting the protest-inducing consequences of bureaucratic rationalization. The origins of these welfare policies, Habermas and Offe suggest, are closely tied to the struggles and political demands of organized labor in the nineteenth and early twentieth centuries. On at least two counts, this claim about the novelty of late capitalist compensation policies is rather inaccurate. First, it underestimates the extent to which civil society in the liberal phase of capitalism was already the object of manifold policing activities enacted by both the state and private organizations of charity and voluntary aid. Indeed, the emergence of the bourgeoisie as the politically dominant class during the liberal phase of capitalism typically depended upon the development and generalization of mechanisms of surveillance and discipline affecting most spheres of social life. From the seventeenth century, networks of hospitals, penitentiaries, and workhouses were erected all over Europe. These were intended to define, hide, and confine those eccentrics, beggars, vagabonds, rejected wives, alcoholics, and lunatics who were both a consequence of and a threat to the civilizing process. During the eighteenth century, this administrative sequestration of unreason was increasingly supplemented by official concern with population management (campaigns on behalf of marriage, child nurturance, vaccinations, and so on), of which the "government" of households was a crucial aspect.[61] This ubiquity of compensatory mechanisms of discipline throws doubt upon Habermas's and Offe's claims about their novelty under late capitalist conditions. In addition, their implicit claim that the state is now the sole source of compensatory policies ignores the continuing power of private welfare, health, and education agencies, perhaps the most important of which is the bureaucratic, corporate disciplining of labor power through the construction of housing and recreation facilities and the provision of various fringe benefits.

These two objections aside, Habermas's and Offe's stress on the quantitative growth of state compensatory strategies since the nineteenth century is not altogether misleading. They accurately emphasize that, through its welfare or compensatory functions, state administration now plays a crucial role in absorbing the social costs of the late capitalist order, and that social life does indeed become less directly dependent upon the logic of this order's commodified relations of production. Habermas and Offe contrast these compensatory policies of the bureaucratic state with its *market-replacing* activities. They interpret these activities as reactions to the perceived weaknesses and crisis tendencies of the old market mechanisms. Such market-replacing strategies seek either the encouragement of capitalist investment or the alteration of the form of surplus-value production. Their novelty consists in their attempt to provide inputs of accumulation in anticipation of disturbances within the domain of privately controlled accumulation. The state strives to bolster sagging supplies of both variable and constant capital, where such capital either is not provided or is provided in inadequate supply by private market decisions. Market-replacement policies are, therefore, crisis-management strategies, through which the state responds to actual or perceived blockages within the accumulation process.

By way of such policies, the state *self-consciously* attempts to overcome the socially disintegrative consequences of liberal capitalism's anarchic pursuit of profit. It seeks to immunize the relations of production against the classical conflict between labor and capital. "Crisis avoidance is thematized."[62] One crucial example of this attempt to replace market power by crisis-management strategies is the production of "reflective labor power" through the provision of formal schooling and vocational retraining. Such reflective labor power – of industrial chemists, engineers, and teachers, for example – can be seen as labor applied to itself. Its purpose is the enhancement of the productivity of direct, first-order labor. In view of the expanded role of this second-order labor power, Habermas insists that the production of surplus value through the unskilled (simple) labor power of the immediate producers becomes relatively less important under late capitalist conditions.[63] Unlike the unplanned growth of technical innovations in traditional and even liberal capitalist social formations, this state planning of the production of reflective workers is unique to late capitalism. Insofar as it inaugurates a more elastic form of production of surplus value, this market-replacing activity of the state signals the obsolescence of Marx's assumption (in his thesis concerning the tendency of the rate of profit to fall) that the rate of surplus value tends to constancy.[64] This state administration of the labor process is only one example of its more general involvement in the planned provision of scientific-technological support for the capitalist accumulation process. The bureaucratically planned character of such state activity (and its frequent corroboration by university research for military ends) reveals the wrongheadedness of those who argue that contemporary scientific-technical progress is driven by its own logic, whose imperatives in turn command their own practical realization.[65] Habermas is emphatic: "The pace and *direction* of technical development today depends to a great extent on public investments."[66] The contrast with the phase of liberal capitalism is again evident, for scientific-technical development was at that time not yet industrialized through state-funded research and development for the military and oligopoly sectors. Thus Marx could regard science as a kind of natural resource, like water or air.[67] Indeed, the gradual "scientization" of the oligopolistic and military productive process dates only from the last quarter of the nineteenth century, when the generation of absolute surplus value (through the lengthening of the working day and the enforced labor of convicts, women, and children) began to give way to the extraction of relative surplus value through the rationalization of the forces of production.

The consequences of this fusion of science, technology, and industrial production have been staggering, in Habermas's view. Not only has this fusion process helped remove the destructive uncertainty from the patterns of technological innovation in the oligopoly sector, but, within that sector, it has also rendered direct labor power more productive and cheapened the fixed components of capital. It has thereby tended to raise the rate of surplus value. Although Habermas admits this is an empirical question, his hypothesis is that these developments have had directly political consequences, especially since there has emerged an ability to pay higher wages to organized labor within the oligopoly sector. Scientific and technological innovation through bureaucratic planning directly promotes class compromise within the oligopoly sector, within which, in turn, the planned rationalization of production is facilitated. Habermas's argument is compelling: This type of state crisis-avoidance strategy cannot be dismissed as unproductive, by way of dogmatic defenses of the original Marxian value analysis.[68]

Marginality and rationalization

Together, the market-replacing and compensatory functions of the late capitalist state are expressions of the qualitatively altered role of political power vis-à-vis the sphere of commodified production and exchange. According to both Offe and Habermas, the state–economy dualism of the liberal capitalist past begins to disappear. In its attempts to prevent accumulation crisis tendencies from again appearing in an immediately economic form, the state "simultaneously fills functional gaps in the market, intervenes in the process of accumulation, and compensates for its politically intolerable consequences."[69] Moreover, with the interweaving of the state and market realms, not only do state administrators assume certain functions in the sphere of social labor and commodity exchange, but "social powers" (principally, organized labor and oligopoly capital) also assume directly political tasks; the state undergoes a process of socialization. In particular, Habermas and Offe argue that the state apparatus discriminates selectively in favor of (and is, in turn, therefore dependent upon) those social groups whose compliance is crucial for the reproduction of the whole late capitalist system. Upon these groups (and especially fractions of capital) are conferred responsibilities and privileges that the state has an institutional self-interest in maintaining.

Relying upon this argument, Habermas and Offe move beyond the restricted boundaries of the class-power versus state-power debate.[70] For them, the late capitalist state can be analyzed as both a passive instrument of class forces and an active, productive, and autonomous subject that seeks to organize and reorganize a multiplicity of interest groups. Because both the success of the state's global planning, compensatory, and market-replacing policies and its general budgetary obligations are ultimately dependent on revenues generated within the economy, the state *must* pursue strategies that contradict themselves. At the same time, the state must both *react* to the imperatives of the private accumulation process (as a "capitalist state" performing global functions) and *intervene* selectively therein (as a market-compensating and replacing "state in capitalist society"). State intervention in the accumulation process, they emphasize, is conditioned "structurally"; it is not a simple consequence of the facts of personal ties, conspiracies, or common social origins of actors within state, industrial, and financial circles.

Offe and Habermas also argue that one important consequence of this general politicization of the accumulation process is that it further weakens the plausibility of the old Marxian thesis of "the two great hostile camps." Within late capitalist countries, there is a tendency for vertically opposed classes to be replaced by a "horizontal" system of disparities between zones of social and political life – a development missed by those who continue to utilize the theoretical categories of "labor," "capital," and "class struggle." These formulations, or so Offe and Habermas argue, faithfully assume what has not emerged factually under late capitalist conditions.[71] It is true that Offe in particular emphasizes that the state's assignment of decision-making privileges to oligopoly capital and organized labor strongly discriminates against the latter. He argues that the late capitalist state attempts to absorb the (potentially) obstructive political resistance of organized labor by granting it certain "voice" options. This delegation of aspects of state policy-making power nevertheless typically seeks to *deprive* organized labor of certain of its crucial "exit" options, in order to prevent it from utilizing its veto power on the policy decisions of private capital and the state. Through something like a two-sided *noblesse oblige* effect, organized labor becomes subject to a whole series of restrictive obligations – for example, the obligation to behave predictably and responsibly by relinquishing demands and tactics that radically contradict the depoliticization upon which bureaucratic policy-making procedures depend. Such restrictions upon organized labor's capacity to withdraw its fundamental resource (labor power) collectively are rarely matched by direct sanctions upon associations of oligopoly capital. Their individual members can continue to exercise their powers not to invest (and therefore to disrupt state policy) without being organized in employers' associations. The private power of capital remains unchallenged; this power instead serves as a condition of what can be realistically negotiated within corporatist arrangements. It is precisely this asymmetrical effect of state corporatist strategies that frequently generates new patterns of political conflict – concerning, for instance, the degree to which decisions reached through corporatist policy-making institutions are equally binding – among organized labor, the state, and capital.[72]

It is nevertheless clear that such conflict can hardly be described as a repetition of the liberal capitalist struggle between relatively homogeneous social classes. Both Habermas and Offe insist that the uneven rationalization of the sphere of social labor and the state's bestowal of structurally determined privileges upon organized labor are synonymous with the partition or subdivision of the proletariat *qua* proletariat. To speak in Marxian terms: The rate of exploitation (that is, the rate of surplus value, or the ratio between surplus value and wages) becomes extremely uneven. Many of those blue-collar production and maintenance workers, and the so-called middle class of male, white-collar, administrative, and technical workers within the unionized oligopoly and state sectors, tend to become a labor elite with relatively privileged access to late capitalism's productive forces. This is what Habermas intends by the somewhat cryptic observation that class antagonisms have not been abolished but have become latent.[73]

It should be stressed that Habermas and Offe are *not* here proposing a variation on the theme of total administration or *embourgeoisement*. They argue, on the contrary, that those within the peripheries, within strategically less vital areas (the inmates of institutions; those on welfare and pensions; aboriginal and immigrant peoples; economically depressed rural, urban, and national regions; the areas of public transportation, health, and housing; for example) are relatively neglected in this scenario. The more the late capitalist political economy is centralized and administered through state action, the more the needs and demands of whole groups are excluded or expelled from this system. It is as if the pauperism of the liberal capitalist proletariat begins to give way to the pauperism of what Habermas calls "structurally neglected" zones.[74] At any point the degree of this "marginalization" is directly contingent upon the extent to which the state's resources are required for more urgent projects – for policies, that is, that seek some adjusted balance among the needs to guarantee and promote private investment without price inflation, full employment, the avoidance (or provocation) of major military conflicts through armed diplomacy, reproduction of international trade, and the repression of domestic unrest.

Habermas and Offe therefore contend that the electoral, legislative, executive, administrative, repressive, and judicial branches of the late capitalist state operate as "filters" or "sorting processes" with a marked degree of selective bias. Independent of the professed intentions and promises of particular political parties, civil servants, and politicians, the very dependence of state institutions upon the accumulation process preconditions these institutions' definition of what is taken to be a political need. Bureaucratic state institutions systematically enforce "non-decisions."[75] This also means, however, that the potential conflicts that remain inherent in the private mode of capital utilization are at the same time the least likely to erupt. Paradoxically, the likelihood that other forms of social and political conflict will break out increases as their immediately dangerous consequences for the stability of the oligopoly sector of production are reduced. Potential class conflicts tend to recede behind the politically determined, neo-populist conflicts arising from within the structurally neglected zones. This strife, whose frequent opposition to administrative procedures no longer directly assumes the form of class struggle, evidences the fact that, under late capitalist conditions, "*market + administration* cannot satisfy a whole series of collective needs."[76]

Publicity and technobureaucratic planning

Through references to this privilege-granting selectivity of the late capitalist state, Offe and Habermas can point both to its repressive bias and to at least one reason why this apparatus nowadays tends to become more technobureaucratic in its mode of operation. They frequently remark that the conflict-ridden, principled politics of the liberal capitalist past is typically being replaced by the administrative silencing and processing of populations. More and more, decisions on key political issues are the consequence of an arcane and highly inaccessible process of negotiation among commanding elites within the spheres of state and society. As state-sanctioned policies draw closer and closer to the lives of ordinary citizens, political decision making moves beyond their immediate control. Habermas and Offe allude here to one of the contradictory rules of administered politics in the era of late capitalism: The more the constituents of this order are administered through state and corporate actions, the more they are expected to undergo depoliticization, to busy themselves within a political culture that promotes public deference and private orientation toward career, leisure, and consumption. The attenuation of truly participatory decision making under the conditions of late capitalism is not fortuitous. Habermas and Offe correctly note that the attempted maintenance of mass loyalty through depoliticization is an imperative of this order. From the point of view of state administrators, at least, one whole range of the state's priorities – those concerning the *private* appropriation of *socialized* production – must be withdrawn from genuine public discussion.[77]

In turn, state institutions' crisis-management strategies come to depend upon the creation of requisite volumes of mass loyalty. Unlike their liberal capitalist counterparts (which sought their legitimation through references to their non-interference with the workings of the invisible hand of the commodification process), the busy hands of the late capitalist state must somehow justify themselves as neutral or as promoters of lawful order, welfare, democracy, progress, and prosperity. Unlike the more concealed domination of the liberal capitalist market, "the official power embodied in political institutions finds itself forced to declare and justify itself as power."[78] This imperative is described by Offe as *the* structural problem of the late capitalist state. Under late capitalist conditions, mass loyalty to the state becomes a permanent problem precisely because this state must at the same time practice its class-biased character and keep it concealed. In Offe's words, "the state can only *function* as a capitalist state by appealing to symbols and sources of support that *conceal* its nature as a capitalist state; the *existence* of a capitalist state presupposes the systematic *denial* of its nature as a *capitalist* state."[79] Under pressure from this structural problem, state elites definitely discourage autonomous public life. This is because substantive democratization processes would overload this already pressured apparatus with demands that, in turn, might bring to popular consciousness the contradiction between the state's socialization of production and continuing dependence upon the private appropriation of surplus value. As a consequence of this structural problem, and compared with the adversary politics of the liberal capitalist past, "politics . . . more and more contracts into administration and the [official] procurement of acclamation."[80] Conversely, as Habermas points out in an early essay, the officially sanctioned relation of citizens to the state becomes "not one of political participation, but a general attitude of expectation, of anticipation of welfare, but not an attempt to actually determine decisions."[81]

This tendency to suppress a conflict-ridden politics in favor of rationalized administration and passive citizenship has been analyzed by Habermas in particular. Of special importance is his *Strukturwandel der Öffentlichkeit*, the work that was originally written as a *Habilitationsschrift* and that earned him a considerable reputation among German intellectual (and, later, student militant) circles. In this text, Habermas demonstrates how a vital (though self-contradictory) institution of liberal capitalism, the "bourgeois public sphere," is subject to rationalizing processes under late capitalist conditions. Habermas's genealogy of modern public life and its corresponding principles (freedom of speech and assembly, open court hearings, the legitimacy of public opinion vis-à-vis the state, and so on) links their emergence with the seventeenth- and eighteenth-century bourgeois assault upon the secretive dominion of the feudal and absolutist orders.[82] It seems clear that this thesis considerably underestimates the lasting reversals of power effected by the popular classes of this period. His excessive focus upon *one* historical form of the public sphere has the effect of making other (plebeian) forms seem mere repressed or insignificant variants of the bourgeois public sphere. As Foucault has indicated (in the case of eighteenth-century France, at least), this is highly misleading. The public torture and execution of those who had violated the sovereign's law frequently occasioned carnival-like gatherings, in which rules were inverted, authority was mocked, and wider social disturbances were generated.[83] Habermas nevertheless correctly emphasizes that, under pressure from the emerging bourgeois public, discursive argumentation was installed as an organizing principle of the new civilizing order. In respect of its defense of the principle of rational discussion, or so Habermas argues, the bourgeois public sphere can be interpreted as an innovative phase within a world evolutionary process that began with the classical Greek dissolution of the claims of myth through philosophy. This process of evolution can be seen to have gradually systematized and universalized discursive argumentation as a principle of decision making. In conformity with this evolutionary process, the bourgeois public sphere was marked by a flowering of literary salons, coffeehouses, scientific groups, and discussion circles, whose growth was in turn catalyzed by the emergence of local political newspapers that had ceased to be mere vendors of recent news. The bourgeois struggle for public life sought the establishment of a locale or space that mediated the state apparatus and the private affairs of individuals and patriarchal families in civil society.

This entailed (as Habermas's analysis of Goethe's *Wilhelm Meister* reveals)[84] a radical transformation of the meaning of the older medieval principle of sovereign, public power. According to this older principle, the lord of the High Middle Ages was the authoritative representative of an omnipresent, higher power, a figure who re-presented this power before his creation, the people. The sole public dimension of these subjects' lives was supposed to be obedient awe, the passive acceptance of benefits; public life was to be identical with the glorious governance of the sovereign. By contrast with this medieval principle, the emerging bourgeois public understood itself as gathering on a site from which it could organize *itself* as the bearer of "public opinion." According to the bourgeois public sphere principle, "access is guaranteed to all citizens. A portion of the public sphere comes into being in every conversation in which private individuals assemble to form a public body. . . . Citizens behave as a public body when they confer in an unrestricted fashion – that is, with the guarantee of freedom of assembly and association and the freedom to express and publish their opinions – about matters of general interest."[85] Public opinion was to be formed through the conjoining of a body of politically competent and socially equal citizens who insisted upon their rights to confer informally and formally (through elections) and thereby to subject ruling state institutions and their arcane policies to critical scrutiny.

This growth of public life, in Habermas's view, is well expressed in the eighteenth-century theories of publicity. In the case of the Physiocrats, within whose circles the concept of *opinion publique* was first analyzed precisely, the laws of the *ordre naturel* were to be guarded by the monarch, whose attempt to render this natural order of things positively was in turn to be guided by an enlightened public. While public opinion – the enlightened, shared understanding engendered through public discourse – was not seen as ruling, the despotic ruler was nevertheless deemed bound to its insights. Scottish moralism appropriated this doctrine of publicity as the specifically political dimension of its not uncritical defense of liberal capitalist society. Here the complex evolutionary transformation from rudeness to modern civilization was seen as entailing – indeed, guaranteeing – two developments that, according to Habermas, were mutually contradictory: the unfolding of the natural laws of class-dominated market exchange and the growth of a political public sphere that allegedly ensured civil rights and equality of social rank.[86]

Habermas is well aware that this eighteenth-century ideal of an emancipated public was not identical with the principle of universal democracy, understood as the equal and effective freedom of all citizens to engage in public acts of "discursive will-information [*diskursive Willensbildung*]." At first, and with few exceptions, the public signified only male property owners. With particular reference to J. S. Mill and de Tocqueville, Habermas is emphatic that this public concealed the class and gender exploitation that made a mockery of its supposed authenticity. He insists: "Genuinely bourgeois ideologies...allow no authentic political ethic."[87]

Notwithstanding this criticism, Habermas is at the same time concerned to stress that the public sphere principle should not be forgotten or summarily dismissed as bourgeois ideology. This is a somewhat perplexing argument, inasmuch as he seeks to retrieve and defend, against late capitalist depoliticization, the significance of an old bourgeois illusion, whose repressive *bourgeois* character, however, he seeks to criticize. Despite all its inauthenticity, this regulative ideal also presupposed a form of life fundamentally subversive of the purposive-rational, bureaucratic rationality of civil society and its state power. It presupposed a self-enlightened, reasoning public dedicated to reaching agreement through genuinely political activity. It is therefore not surprising, in Habermas's view, that the struggle to preserve liberal, bourgeois society through the establishment of public life and its "principle of supervision" easily turned into its opposite: the battle to check, confine, and dissolve various forms of authoritarian civil and state power through their subjection to the scrutiny of a self-governing public. The bourgeois public sphere foregrounded, as it were, its own class and gender specificity. This dialectic became readily evident amid the squalor and blatant inequalities of property and political power generated during the Industrial Revolution. Pressured by economic crisis tendencies and the growth of political revolts (such as English Chartism), the form and content of the male, bourgeois public sphere was stretched, forced to permit the entry of proletarian elements for the first time. Thereupon, public life was forced to become less socially exclusive, a court of appeal for the disinherited, a realm racked by revolt, agitation, and violent repression. The bourgeois principle of reasoning, tolerant citizens coherently transacting with each other began to disintegrate: "Laws which obviously come about under the 'pressure of the street' can hardly be considered as arising from the consensus of private individuals engaged in public discussion. They correspond more or less blatantly to the compromise of clashing private interests."[88]

Habermas contends that both this disintegration process and the emancipatory potential of the bourgeois public sphere have been suppressed in the transition to organized, state-managed capitalism. As large, bureaucratic organizations increasingly negotiate with one another within the framework of state power, numerous organized interests (including large corporations, organized labor, the cartelized political parties, incumbent governments, and the organized mass media) impose themselves upon the public – so as to achieve public prominence.

This transformation is no doubt deep-seated. It first began around the 1830s in Europe and North America and was, according to Habermas, the harbinger of the later "public relations work," the "transformation from a journalism of conviction to one of commerce," the rise of the "catch-all party," and the dramatic growth of extraparliamentary consensus formation and public opinion dealing.[89] The democratic potential of the liberal capitalist public sphere is repressed amid state and corporate attempts to create a world after their own image.[90]

In the era of late capitalism, a form of public life is thereby retained. This preservation of public life has its rationale, if only because the dramatic increase of bureaucratic state and corporate activity must be justified and explained to its constituents. The official power embodied in these institutions is forced to declare itself as power. "Publicity" (or what Habermas sometimes calls the "mediatization [*Mediatisierung*]" of the population) cannot be dismissed as simply a veil or sham. For, as is evident in the case of electoral and consumer advertising, it comes to be useful for those who plan and administer from the heights of bureaucratic organizations. Organized political activity and social life become encased within public opinion fabricated with great skill and cunning: "Often enough today the process of making public simply serves the arcane policies of special interests; in the form of 'publicity' it wins public prestige for people or affairs, thus making them worthy of acclamation in a climate of non-public opinion."[91] Everyday life is colonized with signs that are presented and repeated as "the way things are," as impenetrable common sense. Drawing explicitly upon strategies of wartime propaganda and consumer advertising, public opinion makers take on the task of ideology planning. They seek to create a deferential, follow-the-leader disposition among the state's clients through the systematic tapping of existing fantasies, prejudices, and unconscious motives. Networks of public meetings, inquiries, and select committees; the sensationalizing of political personalities and their (now undermined) private lives; and the fabrication of party conflict and other spectacles frequent the public realm. Public life is endowed with "an apparent display of openness [*demonstrative Publizität*]." Having fallen into the arms of bureaucratic servitude, the citizens no longer deliberate; they are expected to adore cheerfully or curse quietly.

This thesis concerning the engineering of public opinion and life, it is true, is weakened by its lack of specificity. As a result, the various twentieth-century forms of colonized public life (such as those discussed by Mills, for example)[92] remain unexamined. Furthermore, Habermas's puzzling call both to retrieve and to supersede the bourgeois public sphere ideal has produced much criticism from his opponents.[93] In some measure, this has been justified, because the argument of *Strukturwandel der Öffentlichkeit* never adequately considered the possible mediations and antinomies between the bourgeois public sphere and autonomous public spheres within a future socialist order.

This weakness is evidently linked with and reinforced by at least three other difficulties. First, Habermas seems to adhere too closely to the self-image of the liberal bourgeois public sphere, with the result that he tends to exaggerate its inner homogeneity and coherence. Secondly, his account of the "refeudalization" of the bourgeois public sphere draws rather too heavily on Adorno's theses on

93

the mass culture industry. As a consequence, as Oskar Negt has also argued, Habermas fails to analyze the ways in which present struggles to reassert autonomous public life can draw upon the blocked potential (if any) of late capitalist communications media. Finally, he has consistently displayed an unwillingness to envisage the prospects for alternative or counterpublic spheres, especially those whose historical novelty would consist in their encouragement of debate and decision making about needs and attempts to reconcile politically the concrete interests that arise not only within the formal political process but also from within the spheres of household life and capitalist production. These weaknesses, it can be argued, together produced within Habermas's argument a thoroughgoing ambivalence. In his early writings, at least, a certain nostalgia for the bourgeois public sphere ideal coexists uneasily with a deep pessimism about the possibility of constituting new forms of autonomous public life. In short, the promise of Habermas's pathbreaking study of the bourgeois public sphere is checked by its undisclosed dependence upon its very object of criticism.

Habermas's emphasis on the decline of the old bourgeois public sphere is nevertheless not entirely unjustified. Against his critics, he correctly warns that the power-critical function of the late capitalist public sphere is undergoing serious erosion. State and corporate planners seek to dissolve freely formed publics by manufacturing their own. Inasmuch as these oligarchic interests represent themselves as authoritative, this public sphere begins to undergo a form of refeudalization. The public becomes synonymous with that space or domain constructed and supervised by authoritarian state and corporate institutions. This public is supposed to live passively in accordance with public standards, with principles of public order and decency laid down by public authorities themselves.

In conformity with these standards and rules, late capitalism tends to become a system of depoliticization. The constituents of this order are systematically encouraged to become conformist subjects with limited rights to withhold acclaim for incumbent governments and politicians. There is a "drying-up of communicative zones of action," an "erosion of the genuinely public realm."[94] A whole continuum of issues and needs that might become of truly public concern is regulated bureaucratically, personalized, or labeled "deviant behavior," to be treated professionally as illness, crime, or madness. Under pressure from late bourgeois publicity and its cynical realism, the rosy liberal capitalist hopes for democracy wither. This refeudalization of public life is even expressed theoretically. There are moves to redefine and formalize the concept of democracy in accord with alleged administrative imperatives. *Democracy* comes to signify a rationalized means of maintaining system equilibrium. The self-developmental, public themes of earlier models of liberal democracy (such as that proposed by J. S. Mill, for example) tend to be forgotten or dismissed as "unrealistic."[95] Analogous to the ideological role played by the classical theories of political economy in the era of liberal capitalism, new discourses on the necessity of depoliticization serve to reinforce the historically produced depoliticization as second nature.

A totally administered society?

Bureaucratic planning triumphant?

This essay's discussion of Habermas's and Offe's contributions to the theory of late capitalism might briefly be recapitulated at this point. As we have seen, the end of the liberal phase of capitalism and the overcoming of its crisis tendencies are for them synonymous with the intensified but uneven rationalization of production and consumption, and the emergence of an at least temporary suspension of open struggle between oligopoly capital and organized labor. Despite continuing irrationalities within the accumulation process, and in spite of the marginalization of certain areas of social life, the rationalization of economic life is facilitated by the global planning, market-replacing, and compensatory activities of the bureaucratic state. The reorganization of the old civil society is possible only through state-administrative mediation and its crisis-management strategies. Finally, Habermas's theses on the refeudalization of public life indicate the flourishing attempts by organized interests (including the state itself) to seek their accreditation through the permanent management of opinion.

If these insights have a certain validity, if indeed these developments are suggestive of broader historical tendencies and not merely temporary aberrations from the type of liberal capitalist development analyzed by Marx, then the critique of modern bureaucratic rationality seems to remain dumbstruck. Critical consciousness must remain unhappy. Must not Habermas's and Offe's arguments lapse into melancholic despair? Are not these rationalizing trends suggestive of the Weberian specter of "the polar night of icy hardness and darkness," of an emerging society whose planned alienation would appear to be thoroughly natural? Habermas and Offe certainly acknowledge that the contemporary drift toward an authoritarian, bureaucratic, state-administering capitalism is real enough. For them, however, this is not the only noteworthy feature of the present. In response to their early critics (such as Abendroth),[96] and against the neo-Weberian thesis of total administration, they are convinced that all bureaucratic, late capitalist societies are self-contradictory systems that *create* political and social conflict. According to them, questions must be raised not only about whether capitalism has changed, or whether it is marked by totalitarian tendencies, but also about whether the bureaucratization of contemporary political and social life is subject to self-crippling tendencies. In short, they ask whether it is still plausible to speak (in the sense analyzed in the first essay) of crisis tendencies and therefore of emancipatory struggle under late capitalist conditions.

Habermas's and Offe's general view is that, under late capitalist conditions, bureaucratic planning processes tend to undermine their own quest for coherence and legitimacy. These processes tend to weaken the conditions of depoliticization upon which they depend for their continued reproduction. The reality of bureaucratic planning is that of unrealistic goals and modes of operation; late capitalist social formations systematically create unforeseen difficulties, problems, and challenges to their supremacy. Two aspects of these systematic failures of rationalization processes can be discussed in turn. First, under these systems of class domination in state form, the bureaucratically planned elimination of bottlenecks and irrationalities within and between the state-administrative and accumulation systems cannot be achieved. In Habermas's and Offe's view, indeed, the logics of state and corporate planning are systematically in conflict with each other. Second, and perhaps of greater importance for them, is the fact that these planning difficulties are interwoven with general and deep-seated patterns of symbolic disintegration, that is, tendencies that undermine mass loyalty to the existing relations of power. There are, to speak in Habermas's language, chronic deficits of legitimation and motivation resources. These deficits indicate that there is a highly unbalanced relationship between the political economy and the interpreted needs and legitimate expectations of many constituents of this society. Under late capitalist conditions, the ruling powers cannot necessarily or even easily secure mass loyalty.

Restrictions upon state planning

In the first place, Habermas and Offe point to the impossibility of the state's becoming an "ideal collective capitalist" (Engels), inasmuch as structural and political limits are continually placed upon its attempts at middle-range, bureaucratic planning for the privately controlled accumulation of capital. This thesis can be seen in part as an important confrontation with the Weberian argument that the decisive reason for the advance of impersonal, bureaucratic forms of state organization is their technical superiority over other means of goal attainment. To be sure, they admit that the ad hoc, reactive character of state activity, with its attendant bottlenecks and reversals of policy, may be a universal feature of all complex social formations. In Habermas's words, "not *every* incrementalism – that is, every type of planning limited to middle-range horizons and sensitive to external impulses – *eo ipso* reflects the rationality deficit of an overloaded administration."[97] Under the specific conditions of late capitalism, nevertheless, the attempts of the centralized, bureaucratic state to fine tune and coordinate the execution of global planning, market-replacing, and compensatory policies are typically marked by an excess of failures and unplanned outcomes. In part this is because such policy making continually meets with various forms of organized resistance. The sharpening of disputes over wages and conditions (especially within the state sector) owing to uneven sectoral rationalization, the continuing competition between capitalist enterprises, the outwitting of state planning by the internationalization of labor and capital, the competition of capital with other groups (environmentalists, peace movements, dissident labor unions, and so on) – all these different kinds of resistance tend to hinder or "privatize" the state's general planning activities. Social turbulence is continually internalized within the state apparatus. Contrary to Weber, Offe and Habermas propose that the frequent dependence of state policy production upon fixed *general* rules systematically prevents this bureaucratic state from responding flexibly and coherently to *specific, concrete* struggles and demands generated within the spheres of state and society. This limit upon inflexible technobureaucratic planning is compounded by the typical lack of coordination

96

among various state bureaucracies and by the considerable length of the production cycles of the state's market-replacing activities.

As a consequence of these factors, the bureaucratic state's activities are marked with a vacillating, active–reactive character; it is these inefficiencies which ensure, in turn, that certain organized, particular interests penetrate the administrative apparatus. On many occasions, the late capitalist state pursues a clumsy compromise course between proposed interventions and politically enforced renunciation of such intervention plans. This "muddling through" and the consequent reliance upon (often ineffective) indirect controls are further aggravated by the fact that one set of state priorities (the attempt to reproduce the privately steered accumulation process) is typically accommodated within other forms of policy planning and public administration. The state's dependence upon the logic of the commodification process systematically prevents it from opening itself up to modes of policy formation that rely upon extensive and detailed public debate. State policy makers who do actively encourage such public discussion (about, for example, the dangers of nuclear power or problems of pollution and urbanism) invite a surplus of controversies, whose possibilities of resolution are limited by the state's dependence upon the sphere of commodity production from which it is excluded. This is why protest against the undesirable consequences of capitalist growth is chronically met with state attempts to silence this protest and accelerate this growth. In Habermas's words: "The late capitalist limitation on [state] rationality consists in the structural inadmissibility of that type of planning which . . . could be designated as democratic incrementalism."[98]

These arguments concerning the systematic restrictions upon state planning under late capitalist conditions in a certain sense resurrect Marx's critique of Hegel's theory of the state. According to Offe and Habermas, both the obstruction potential and the structurally privileged access of organized labor and oligopoly capital to the state's decision-making processes unwittingly subordinate that administration to particular, private interests. State planners' (antidemocratic) dependence upon the information and cooperation of these organized blocs is a necessary feature of the late capitalist order. Consequently – and especially under the above-mentioned pressures emanating from a slowdown in the rate of capital investment and accumulation – a systematic conflict between state planning and corporate-controlled zones of social life tends to break out into the open. The rationalized planning of late capitalist society can only be partial, Offe and Habermas propose, since the guiding criterion of private control of production for profit cannot itself be easily subjected to state planning. The state is supposed to fulfill all its self-incurred tasks (of ensuring growth, satisfying needs for collective commodities, ameliorating existing patterns of social inequality, and so on) without violating the logic of the capitalist economy as a commodified system of self-expanding value. In other words, state planning is not supposed to intervene within the privately steered accumulation process, upon whose cyclical dynamics, however, this state's revenues and planning resources fundamentally continue to depend.[99]

Two additional and persistent consequences of this contradictory dynamic are readily identifiable. First, Habermas in particular remarks on the chronic incapacity of states to solve effectively the environmental problems more and more often generated by late capitalist production. In his view, the current overtaxing of outer nature – for instance, the growing possibility of abrupt climatic change consequent upon the overproduction of heat waste generated by the unprecedented levels and types of economic growth – may be endemic within all complex social formations (that is, within both late capitalist and state socialist systems). He nevertheless sees that the management of environmental problems by the state is specifically limited by the irrationalities of late capitalism's principle of organization. Late capitalist states cannot readily restrict the rate and type of economic growth without abandoning one of the crucial principles of organization of this order; a shift from semiplanned, state-secured capitalist growth to qualitative growth would require that production be planned in terms of publicly determined use values – a form of planning, of course, that openly violates the logic of this system of corporate and state bureaucracy.[100]

A second consequence of the contradictory relationship between state and corporate rationalization is the chronic fiscal difficulties that plague state planning itself. Habermas and Offe here argue that the state's attempts at administering the accumulation process tend to become more and more costly.[101] The self-expansion of capital (especially within the more highly profitable oligopoly sector) becomes increasingly contingent upon giant investment projects that entail huge capital outlays and growing social overhead costs. Within the phase of late capitalism, furthermore, there is a permanent underutilization of capital and lack of investment outlets. To the extent that the state seeks to overcome private capital's (periodic) preference for disinvestment by socializing its capital and social overhead costs, the likelihood of fiscal problems therefore grows. Moreover, as Offe demonstrates in a study of the West German construction industry,[102] state attempts to increase the level of revenues or cooperation from corporate sources run the risk of causing capital to disemploy itself.

This dilemma becomes particularly acute under conditions of bottlenecks and slowdowns in capitalist growth. As Habermas notes: "In order to guarantee the continuation of the accumulation process, the state must assume ever clearer planning functions. But these must not be recognizable as administrative performances for which the state is accountable, because it would otherwise be liable for compensations, which retard accumulation."[103] The fundamental source of these fiscal problems lies in the asymmetry between the growing socialization of capital and social overhead costs by the state, on the one hand, and the continuing private appropriation of profits on the other. It follows from Habermas's and Offe's thesis that, in the era of late capitalism, state expenditures (whose cost–benefit accounting is notoriously difficult) tend to outrun state revenues, to the point where it is in the state's self-interest to "cut back," to rationalize its own expenditure patterns. The presence of these fiscal problems, they suggest, may be of great political significance, for at least several of the measures aimed at their amelioration (for example, managed recession, the introduction of wage and price controls, monetarist strategies to "get the nation off the government payroll," and the like) serve only to exacerbate the marginalization process (already analyzed). These fiscal problems may even serve to undermine the basis of mass loyalty and depoliticization upon which late capitalism's bureaucratic strategies depend.

Even *if* state attempts at economizing and maintaining the employment of oligopolistic capital are successful, Offe emphasizes that this success can be achieved only at the risk of generating "surplus labour power."[104] Especially within the oligopoly sector of production, there is a constant tendency for the organic composition of capital to increase, that is, for capital–labor ratios to rise continually. Paradoxically, the decline in demand for labor power within this sector is the other side of the state's attempts at universalizing the commodity form. Within late capitalist societies, then, a certain stratum of unemployed labor is produced not only by economic recession, but also by prosperous times. This stratum is in no way a "reserve army of the unemployed" for other sectors of the political economy. More and more, this surplus labor, which may threaten fiscal austerity programs or (as evidenced by the student movement) conditions of depoliticization, lives within the urban and rural ghettos, on reserves, within military institutions, and in educational and training facilities that effectively extend the period of adolescence and unemployment.

Habermas and Offe insist that these various restrictions on state planning systematically inhibit the drive toward "total administration." The persistence of these planning problems at the same time throws real doubt on the validity of those theories (of "state-monopolistic capitalism," for instance) which represent contemporary reality through the image of a smoothly functioning, technocratic state capitalism. The late capitalist state cannot function as an unhindered planning organ that serves to organize the "collective monopoly capitalist will" self-consciously. Indeed, because of the necessarily disjointed, conflict-ridden relationship between state power and monopoly capital, contemporary state planning is fated to proceed in an ad hoc, reactive fashion. It is precisely this anarchy which facilitates the success of particular organized interests, whose privileged access to state power in turn hinders the formation of more genuinely democratic policies through public discussion. According to Habermas and Offe, the late capitalist state is a highly undemocratic state that is confronted continually with unanticipated problems (such as bankruptcy, unemployment, fiscal difficulties, environmental degradation) whose form and (im-)possibility of resolution are *specific to the system.* This state's processing and repression of the old system crisis tendencies cannot be successful. This state seeks to plan rationally that which cannot be planned bureaucratically – the private appropriation of socialized production. This for Habermas and Offe is the fundamental contradiction of late capitalist state activity: "The controlling principle of maximization of profit is not disposable."[105] Certainly, the state is not simply (as it tended to be in liberal capitalism) an unconscious executive organ. It does after all engage in deliberate attempts to avoid economic crises, to absorb social expenses, and so on. Habermas and Offe rightly insist (against Adorno) that state crisis-management policies tend to be structured according to the logic of bureaucratic compromise, bargaining, and struggle; this logic is not identical with the anonymous, unconscious, naturelike processes of exchange under market capitalism. By virtue of the fact that it is actually victimized by a system of accumulation that it seeks to regulate, however, the contemporary bureaucratic state and its planning operations now suffer from a more diffuse, "secondary unconsciousness."[106]

The return of mass loyalty problems

It should be emphasized that Offe and Habermas warn that this second-order unconsciousness, which marks state efforts to process and repress crisis tendencies intentionally, cannot be interpreted as immediately synonymous with new crisis tendencies of the late capitalist system. According to a number of recent commentators, for example, the erosion of mass loyalty to the system of late capitalism can be understood as a spontaneous effect of its planning difficulties. It is as if the antinomies between state and corporate planning are translated immediately into widespread awareness of these quandaries, into an automatic decay of old forms of thinking and acting.[107] Habermas and Offe oppose these objectivist versions of crisis theory. They correctly point out that an analysis of the limits to bureaucratic rationalization must entail a consideration of those resources of legitimation and motivation generated by late capitalism's sociocultural system. This consideration is essential, in their view, because such resources of mass loyalty *may* offset or compensate for the disorganization of everyday life by state and corporate activity. In other words, they insist that claims about the impossibility of a totally administered society are plausible only if it can be shown that there are shortages of available but nevertheless *indispensable* reserves of mass loyalty – above all, a shared sense of motivated enthusiasm and respect for existing social and political institutions.

It is precisely this line of inquiry to which they attach great importance in their respective analyses. They point both to operations of the political economy that cannot be adequately justified by existing "supplies" of legitimation and motivation and to disruptions within key sociocultural practices that result in this political economy's "denaturing." At least three specific arguments, which can be discussed in their turn, are adduced in support of this claim. Each argument reinforces their general contention (against Adorno) that the extent to which the late capitalist order can secure its relations of command and obedience as second nature is very limited indeed. First, they suggest that the "liveliness" or meaningfulness of old, premodern traditions and early bourgeois ideologies, which together helped crystallize liberal capitalist patterns of everyday life, now tends to be subverted. The fate of religion and the private institutions of family and civil life are two cases in point. Their demise is seen to be due in large part to the encroachment of state power upon domains of commodified exchange and tradition-bound areas of social life. Secondly, Habermas in particular points to the persistence and diffusion of cultural and artistic movements whose needs and expectations are dysfunctional for the continuing hegemony of bureaucratic power. Finally, Offe and Habermas reinforce these two claims with an argument that implies that the increased institutional need for mass loyalty resources seems difficult to satisfy, principally because of structural limits upon popular, democratic participation in bureaucratic decision-making processes.

100

A totally administered society?

The erosion of cultural traditions

Religion and disenchantment

In the first place, Habermas examines the fate of nonmodern, tradition-bound aspects of everyday life now under increasing pressure from bureaucratization processes. This concern with the decay of tradition is clearly indebted to Marx's account of the revolutionary character of the bourgeois era ("all that is solid melts into air, all that is holy is profaned," and so on) and also to Weber's discussion of the "disenchantment" of the modern world. In developing this Marx-Weber thesis, Habermas reaffirms the point that the modernization of everyday life and the formation of an industrial proletariat rested upon the forcible elimination of peasant and artisan culture. This sacking of tradition was by no means instantaneous; with the triumph of the liberal capitalist world, the hand of tradition by no means suffered an immediate death. "Capitalist societies...always...fed parasitically on the remains of tradition."[108] In the phase of late capitalism, however, these nonmodern remains have all but decomposed: "Things that were culturally taken for granted have been worn out and the traditional claims to validity have been undermined."[109] For Habermas, the most immediate example of this is the irreversible blow that has been dealt to fatalistic forms of Christianity by the tangible successes of scientific-technical growth. This outcome (as Weber also indicated) is ironic inasmuch as the modern natural sciences have religious roots. Calvinism's depiction of God as remote from the earthly world implied the susceptibility of this earth to investigation, calculation, and transformation – and the undermining of Calvinism itself. Nowadays, indeed, the former puissance of religious conviction has been debilitated by a mass atheism made credible by the productive wonders of the scientized, capital-deepened accumulation process.

Habermas suggests that this disenchantment process generates at least two unintended consequences. Among nonbelievers who can no longer recognize the godly in themselves and their world, firstly, the utopian (that is, antibureaucratic) elements of Christianity stand in danger of being abandoned. Religion tends to become at best a matter of mere subjective belief. The specter of widespread meaninglessness is a consequence, especially inasmuch as substitute bourgeois ideologies are dumbstruck when confronted with basic existential questions concerning sickness and death.[110]

Surprisingly, neither Offe nor the later Habermas take up the crucial question whether the thrust toward higher and more sophisticated forms of consumption is capable of warding off these nihilistic developments.[111] In any case, Habermas in particular remains convinced that the erosion of the motivating powers of religion is one reason why late capitalism tends to develop the mentality of the life insurance company. The ruling ethos of late capitalism tends to become scientific-technical, moral relativist, fact and efficiency hungry, materialistic. The contemporary period develops, in Habermas's words, a "glassy background ideology which idolizes and fetishizes science."[112] As might be observed in the scientization of the professions, or the bureaucratic planning (informed by experts) of everything from school curricula to consumption, moral-practical concerns are more and more liquidated by an obsession with purposive-rational calculations and mathematization, with an almost exclusive emphasis upon the *means* of attaining assumed or unchallenged ends such as "economic growth" or "stability." This scientization process has clear depoliticizing consequences, insofar as matters of power and questions of politics can be surreptitiously transferred to the counsel of experts and their talk of objective exigencies. Though Habermas denies that scientific-technical expertise begins to seize power as an emergent new class,[113] its more recent influence in both advising and *formulating* strategies of state and corporate policy is unmistakable, and represents a heightened phase of the same rationalized administration analyzed by Weber. As Habermas warns in his discussions of the bureaucratic reorganization of the old elitist and classically humanist West German universities, "scientism," the uncritical belief in that which is scientific, enters academia, even enveloping the self-understanding of philosophy and the sociohistorical sciences.[114] Within the social sciences, the triumph of forms of scientistic discourse intensifies both the quest for rigor and predictable certainty and the attempt to brand discussions of epistemology and the great political issues old hat. The logic of the attempt to generate the power of technical control over outer nature through scientific discourse is openly extended to the sphere of sociopolitical relations.

Habermas understands this to be a largely regressive development. This conviction underpins his discussion of the scientization of post-Hegelian social theory and is at the center of his provocative thesis that since Kant science has not been comprehended seriously by philosophy. The old Lockean hope that philosophy would be modestly employed as an underlaborer to remove the rubbish blocking the path to knowledge tends to be realized. "Scientism has sublated philosophy without realizing it."[115] Habermas is nevertheless convinced that the capacity of scientistic discourse to legitimate the rationalizing tendencies of late capitalism is more apparent than real. Whether in the classroom or the state planning office, Habermas wants to claim, scientistic discourse is a weak justification of bureaucratic power, precisely because it disavows critical self-reflection upon its own premises. It is unable to distinguish between its claims to authority and the truth grounds of those claims. It is this fundamental, immanent flaw of technocratic consciousness which fuels both the growth of meaninglessness in late capitalist society and the questioning of the truth basis of that consciousness. In Habermas's words, "scientism also sets standards by which it çan itself be criticized and convicted of residual dogmatism. Theories of technocracy and of elites, which assert the necessity of institutionalized civil privatism, are not immune to objections, because they too must claim to be theories."[116]

Habermas also mentions a second unintended consequence of the erosion of religious conviction under late capitalist conditions. In his view, disenchantment processes also have their impact upon the remaining bodies of organized Christianity, to which talk of a return to the divine and the renewed intellectual interest in Christian doctrine attest. Within these besieged circles (such as the charismatic movement), there are feverish attempts at reconstructing the meaning of stewardship and salvation. Sometimes, Habermas suggests, this reconstruction and renewal follow the path of democratic, political activism. Radical political theology, which "enjoins a destruction of the *Beyond* in favor of the social realization of the religious promise in *this* world,"[117] serves only to work against the depoliticization demanded by bureaucratic rationalization.

The disruption of the civic culture

Habermas and Offe analyze other examples of the undoing of previously taken-for-granted traditions. Habermas in particular discusses the decline of late capitalism's "civic culture." He draws upon Almond and Verba's classic study, which suggested that, among the American and British populations, at least, beliefs such as "Yes, citizens must watch out for their interests" are frequently tempered with references to the need for "not getting mixed up with politics."[118] The civic culture, in this view, comprises an eclectic mixture of meaningful beliefs in privacy, premodern deference, and the orientation to active political involvement. The "democratic citizen" is called on to pursue contradictory goals; he or she must be involved, yet not involved; active, yet passive; influential, but deferential. Habermas adds that this civic culture has typically been reinforced by widespread attachment to occupational norms and the values of patriarchal family life. Under late capitalist conditions, in his view, this civic culture tends to be irreversibly weakened by the spread of bureaucratic planning.

This argument (as has already been suggested) seriously underestimates the extent of institutionalized policing of the private domains of civil society during the so-called liberal phase of capitalism. It therefore exaggerates the novelty of the erosion of the civic culture. Habermas's thesis nevertheless retains a measure of plausibility. He correctly points to the fact that certain zones of everyday life once considered to be properly regulated by the private power of patriarchal family life are subsumed to an ever greater extent within both the commodity form and the welfare provisions of private and state agencies. In the case of household services, for example, the privacy of family life is increasingly infiltrated by a plethora of social policies and marketable services, from the provision of mass consumption goods, through compulsory schooling, to the supervision of the young, aged, and sick by the steady hand of the "helping professions." Even though the form of bourgeois family life may well survive these colonizing processes, its substantive content tends to suffer serious enervation. This growing dependence of households upon various outside agencies is evidenced by numerous developments: a considerable questioning of monogamous heterosexuality, a temporary rise in the level of intergenerational conflict, an ever-earlier attainment of puberty and sexual experience, concern over growing old, and so on.

According to Habermas, this dialectic associated with the erosion of bourgeois family life is above all catalyzed by intrusive state planning. Nowadays, mechanisms of bureaucratic state power invade and overwhelm the most intimate (and formerly taken-for-granted) spheres of privacy. As an ironic result of state guarantees of its status, the model bourgeois family form undergoes a considerable "de-privatization." It ceases to be the typical locus of private capital formation and of individuals' (patriarchal) disciplining and nurturance. Of greater political significance is the fact that this state intervention facilitates the exposure of the fictions of bourgeois family life as a voluntary "community of affection" that also protects and deploys property.[119] Under late capitalist conditions, sexual discrimination, poor quality (or dependency-inducing) health care, and the quality and scope of education can no longer be seen as having natural origins, whose irremediable consequences must be suffered privately or through religious practices. "State planning actually makes problematic matters that were formerly culturally taken for granted."[120] The current renewal of assaults upon patriarchal family life and feminist and homosexual attempts at generating new self-identities might be seen as important symptoms of this unintended weakening of the civic culture. Not only do such movements promote a wider awareness of the contingency of the contents of traditions; they even challenge the form of cultural life as itself contingent and alterable. The tendency of these movements to retrieve and reaffirm certain normative claims popular during the liberal phase of capitalism (notions concerning individuals' right to consent, for example) serves only to strengthen this challenge. In short, these movements launch demands for widespread public discussion that, as Habermas and Offe convincingly indicate, is anathema to the silence upon which the bureaucratic, class-structured system of late capitalism thrives.

Possessive individualism

Bureaucratic rationalization within the state and oligopoly sectors also contributes to the undermining of the institutional supports of certain key components of classical bourgeois ideology. Neither Habermas nor Offe analyzes this development adequately (see Essay 7). Their arguments focus almost exclusively (and rather too narrowly) on the fate of the ideology of possessive individualism or the "achievement principle." They argue that, throughout Europe and the New World, from the seventeenth century, this world view legitimated the spread of instrumental exchange relations mediated by a state-guaranteed system of formal law. The growing influence of possessive individualism by the nineteenth century marked a revolution in the official bourgeois understanding of ontology: The (male) individual's essence was viewed as that of an insatiable desirer and consumer of utilities. The everyday life of this (male) individual was seen as properly determined by the ethos of competitive achievement, the pressure of status seeking, and the unlimited accumulation of property guaranteed by law. In accordance with this ethos, the freedom of the (male) individual could be realized only through a state-guaranteed ensemble of competitive market relations, in which (male) individuals were to wield their labor power and property instrumentally, that is, without regard for the substantive goals of other competitors. In the achieving society, privately mediated exchange with outer nature was seen as the most desirable way to accumulate social wealth and happiness. "The ethos of the achieving society," Offe remarks, "is based on the general rule that the social status of an individual is supposed to depend upon his status in the sphere of work and production, while in turn his status within the hierarchical organizations of the production sphere is meant to depend on his individual performance."[121]

The principle of possessive individualism, Habermas and Offe propose, is much less subjectively convincing to the populations of late capitalism than it was to those who lived during the heyday of liberal capitalism. In part, this is because the institutional guarantees of the principle of free, market-allocated labor as the means of individual achievement are cast aside; in place of these guarantees, there emerge planned, union-mediated, increasingly automated labor processes relatively immune from the competitive threat of the reserve army of labor.[122] Secondly, the state's provision of transfer payments and compensatory subsidies (to the young, old, unemployed, or psychosomatically disabled) tends to rupture the allegedly direct relationship between the achievement orientations of individuals' activity and remuneration within the market for that activity. In many zones of social life, work and pay are less closely interrelated as individuals find themselves temporarily or permanently outside the sphere of the labor market. The former dependence on the vicissitudes of the commodified market is replaced by growing dependence on bureaucratic state compensation.[123] Finally, with the spread of zones of bureaucratic state activity, the rationale of the exchange processes of the old market is undermined.[124]

Offe in particular emphasizes that the expansion of state policies that attempt to reproduce the commodity form (that is, the exchange of labor and capital) through decommodified means definitely undermines both the institutionalized power and the legitimacy of commodification processes. The public sector's production and distribution of use values (transportation, postal systems, education, health, the provision of security against unemployment) for an economy that continues to be dominated by exchange values tends to call the latter into question. Having expanded its global planning and market-replacing policies of decommodification, the state makes itself the focus of political conflict over the ways in which social and political resources should be utilized. The quantitative costs and qualitative *aims* of social labor and technological development within these zones of "collective commodity production" readily become a subject of autonomous public criticism. The illegitimating effects of less than full employment perhaps afford no better example of what Habermas and Offe mean when they speak of the subversion of possessive individualism. Whereas in liberal capitalism unemployment was often depicted as a blind, periodic event in the economic cycle or seen as the fault of the lazy or incompetent individual, under late capitalist conditions administrative attempts at increasing unemployment (for example, through cutbacks in the state sector) lead directly to the popular interrogation of the motives of that administration. Unemployment becomes questionable and, indeed, is very often questioned as having been deliberately or politically inspired.

The critical potential of art

In support of the general contention that late capitalist society tends to be incapable of sufficiently justifying itself and motivating its constituents, Habermas raises a second major argument. This focuses upon certain aspects of modern cultural life whose dynamism, as it were, takes revenge on rationalization processes. The critical potential of art and aesthetic theory, their frequent defense of those needs which have been ostracized by the civilizing process, serve as one illustration of this thesis. At least some so-called bourgeois art, according to Habermas, has been characterized by its issuing of indictments against the world as it is, by its struggle to bring the bourgeois world to its senses. Frequently, for example, the art and philosophies of beauty of the liberal capitalist period underwent a radicalization. They became, so to speak, a refuge for the opponents of the bureaucratization process, preserving in artistic form dreamlike promises of spontaneous happiness, mutual recognition, and solidarity.

This radicalization process is evidenced in the appearance (during the eighteenth century) of an autonomous field of aesthetic theory. Previously, *art* had signified any skill of a higher kind (the medieval university, for example, designated rhetoric, grammar, and astronomy as arts). With Kant and Baumgarten, by contrast, aesthetics found itself in transition from a general concern with theories of the beautiful, including nature itself, to the philosophy of art, of "disinterested pleasurable experience." Bohemianism is for Habermas a classic nineteenth-century example of the transformation of this theory of the beautiful illusions of classical bourgeois art into protest against the mechanical unfreedom and sacrifices of liberal capitalism. The second generation *bohèmes* (Rimbaud, Corbière, and others) frequented beer halls, separated themselves from the order and conspicuous consumption of ruling-class life, and, having been raised in the homes of the bourgeoisie, became a circle of wandering, anarchic vagabonds and outlaws dedicated to the overthrow of their fathers' society. Similarly, *L'art pour l'art* mocked the illusions of bourgeois art and warned that art itself could become a victim of industrial capitalist bureaucratization.

These movements, or so Habermas wants to insist, indicate the truth "that in bourgeois society art expresses not the promise but the irretrievable sacrifice of bourgeois rationalization."[125] In support of this thesis, he suggests that the protest potential of "post-auratic" art and aesthetics in the late twentieth century needs to be reexamined. Here he engages, in rather too summary form (see Essay 5), the various controversies surrounding Benjamin's theses on the revolutionary implications of the collapse of the gap between art and daily life consequent upon technological innovation (the radio, microphone, cinema) and the proletarianization of artists and intellectuals. As is well known, certain writers (such as Ortega y Gasset and T. S. Eliot) dismissed this industrialization of art as the harbinger of mass vulgarity and the destruction of all genuine art. For Benjamin, on the contrary, the weakening of the "aura" of art by forces of industrialization served as the potentially new basis for a truly revolutionary and collective production and reception of art.[126] In turn, as we have seen, this thesis was countered by Adorno's emphasis upon the dangers attending the commodification of cultural life by culture industries. These industries' drive to administer the self-understanding of the late capitalist world fully feeds upon the crumbling aura of high art, only to reproduce it as manufactured stardom and programmed sensationalism and fantasy. This reification and commodification of art prompted Adorno to proselytize on behalf of negative, critical forms of art (for example, the works of Samuel Beckett and Arnold Schoenberg); the struggle for eman-

cipation must recognize that the rationalization of art under late capitalist conditions has precipitated a crisis in the beautiful itself.

Habermas's attitude toward these controversies is complex. Against Benjamin, he insists that the "desublimation" of art into everyday life and the corresponding dismantling of the old artistic auras had already been attempted, *before* the mechanical reproduction of art, by movements (such as surrealism) distinguished by their heightened awareness of the artistic medium as such.[127] And in opposition to Adorno's secret nostalgia for classical bourgeois art, he points out that the liberation of art from its former obligations to traditional and absolutist structures of power – its defense of bourgeois public life – from the outset coincided with its commodification. Paradoxically, art became "autonomous" (that is, became independent of those prebourgeois powers who sought its strategic employment in contexts external to its production) only inasmuch as it at the same time became a commodified object of consumption for the coffeehouses, theaters, and exhibition halls of the bourgeois public sphere.[128] With Adorno, Habermas nevertheless acknowledges the appropriation and imprisonment of formally autonomous art within the rationalized commodity form. In his view, this development certainly spells out the possibility of art's surrendering its critical capacities because of its degeneration into manipulative, public propaganda. Nowadays all autonomous art tends to be bureaucratically liquidated. Thus avant-garde culture – an example might be the Pop Art movement – is easily industrialized and made the fetishized object of mass consumption and entertainment. This can equally be the fate of so-called political art and even of hitherto moribund art (such as that of Brueghel), whose planned commodification brings it back to commercial life only to subject it to a kind of "mummification [*Musealisierung*]."[129]

Despite these dangerous tendencies, Habermas remains convinced that the administrative production of culture is nowadays a contradictory process. The unintended consequence of the bureaucratic production and consumption of art is the heightened risk that it will lose its meaningfulness and motivating capacity for large numbers of people. The bureaucratization of culture increases the likelihood that the consumers of culture will find it difficult both to recognize themselves and to articulate and satisfy their sensed needs adequately. This argument, it must be emphasized, is not a repetition of the vulgar conservative belief in tradition *qua* tradition. Without necessary damage, Habermas proposes, cultural traditions can be reflexively or habitually appropriated by their heirs. Yet precisely because daily life is always articulated through meaningful codes of norms that serve to secure (or obstruct) the identity of individuals or groups, cultural traditions cannot be bureaucratically processed and manufactured *ad libitum*. Habermas defends a thesis familiar to these essays: The *instrumental* logic of bureaucratization is in fundamental contradiction with the *intersubjective* logic of development of processes of communication and socialization. In view of this antagonism, he correctly emphasizes, traditions cannot be administratively produced and distributed without becoming dead and without meaning for their recipients.[130] This is also why, in his view, the late capitalist culture industry unwittingly precipitates countercultures and unconventional forms of art, movements determined to subvert the bureaucratic rationality crystallized in the political economy and culture industry.

The limits upon bureaucratic domination

The emergence of countercultures and the erosion of religion, patriarchal family life, the civic culture, and the ideology of possessive individualism – these late capitalist developments strengthen Offe's and Habermas's general conviction that bureaucratic planning processes have their unintended, disorganizing consequences. Even though the likelihood of a general system crisis is diminished by strategies of state crisis management, the continuing anarchy within the sphere of capitalist production and the secondary unconsciousness of state planning itself constitute fundamental limits upon the possibility of a system of totalized, smooth bureaucratic domination. This society's search for rationality is elusive: Even from the point of view of its own standards of bureaucratic rationality, late capitalism systematically produces irrationalities. That bureaucratic rationalization may cast a veil of natural fate over its constituents also seems improbable. Traditions tend to be wholly razed, the credibility of old bourgeois ideology tends to be subverted, and the administrative production of substitute symbols runs the risk of being seen through. The mechanisms of cultural integration tend to be overloaded. " 'Meaning' is a scarce resource," Habermas insists, "and is becoming ever scarcer."[131] Finally, neopopulist political struggles break out on the peripheries of the most highly organized sectors of the political economy and culture. Whether these have the potential to disrupt the present depoliticization and thereby call the entire system of late capitalism into question depends at least in part on their ability to make coalitions with other movements, especially radical elements among organized labor.[132] In short, the persistent failures of state attempts at processing the imperatives of the private accumulation process are matched by systematic failures of this bureaucratic administration to legitimate itself and motivate its clients.

In a certain sense, the whole system of late capitalism is placed in an embarrassing double bind by these developments. Its self-declared intention of overcoming the widely perceived irrationalities and injustices of the old liberal capitalist order (compare the introductory discussion of the welfare state project) cannot be realized. Having raised widespread expectations about the competence of administrative planning to achieve prosperity, progress, and other goals, the late capitalist order definitely breaks down the natural fateful appearance of life as it is. This order tends to create new needs it cannot easily satisfy, novel expectations it must necessarily disappoint. Contrary to the claims of Adorno, this social and political order cannot make everything appear as "fatefully structured, preordained." In Habermas's words: "Because the economic crisis has been intercepted and transformed into a systematic overloading of the public household [fiscal difficulties, muddled decisionmaking, etc.], it has thrown off the cloak of a natural fate of society. If governmental crisis management fails, it lags behind programmatic demands *that it has placed on itself*. The penalty for this failure is withdrawal of legitimation."[133] Offe and Habermas propose, in addition, that the possible renewal of the authority of state (and corporate) institutions through unimpeded citizenship and public discussion is systematically hindered by their bureaucratic, authoritarian character. Late capitalism is correctly understood by them as a system of depoliticization. Because (1) the state in particular tends to be held accountable for its self-imposed promises and (2) it cannot readily mobilize through democratic means, mass loyalty in pursuing these goals, Offe and Habermas suggest that the deep-seated structural problems of this state cannot easily be expunged by the refeudalization of the public sphere. Indeed, the arguments, sloganeering, and public relations work of the refeudalized public sphere do not escape the disorganizing effects of unsuccessful bureaucratic planning: "The symbolic use of politics...becomes more and more susceptible to exercises in self-contradiction."[134]

To be sure, Habermas speaks of the dangerous possibility of automating the activity of (potential) subjects who presently live their everyday lives within (more or less) meaningful frameworks of communication.[135] The bureaucratic production of symbols in the public sphere, the available technology of psychotechnic manipulation for individual action, and the general tendency for scientific-technical planning to stand watchful, like a policeman, over everything are indexes of this authoritarian tendency. But Habermas's and Offe's analysis of the contradictions of bureaucratic planning and the undermining of mass loyalty provides trenchant reasons for their doubting the possibility of a brave new world of planned domination. Their fascination with the "postacquisitive" ethos among sectors of the new, urban middle classes, and with the socialization processes initiated among women, pacifists, environmentalists, and active and dropout youth during the past several decades, serves to reinforce their insistence that the limits to rationalization coincide with its denaturing.[136]

It is true that Habermas's and Offe's theses on late capitalism are marked by a number of ambiguities and limitations. At least four such difficulties have been discussed in this essay: the lack of clarity concerning the self-paralyzing tendencies of capitalist commodification; the inadequate treatment of both the policing of liberal capitalist populations and the continuing private provision of social policy under late capitalist conditions; the failure to consider the military and foreign policies of late capitalist states; and, finally, the several difficulties attending the theses on the refeudalization of the public sphere. These ambiguities and unresolved difficulties are further reinforced by Habermas's and Offe's proclivity for discussing the question of mass loyalty by way of abstract-general propositions. As a result, a detailed treatment of a series of theoretically pertinent and politically important questions about the persistence and recent flourishing of new (and potentially democratic) movements (for example, of women, environmentalists, regional separatists, homosexuals, and ethnic groups) is preempted. This lacuna tends to be reinforced by their serious underestimation of institutional counterstrategies calculated to quash protest movements that feed upon planning and mass loyalty difficulties. Especially crucial is their failure to consider and analyze *systematically* the extent to which, in periods of accelerated social and political disorganization, there emerges widespread nostalgia for decaying traditions and ideologies, a nostalgia that, as Franz Neumann long ago warned, can often be successfully manipulated by the ruling groups of dominant institutions.[137]

Despite these lacunae, the more general thesis proposed by Habermas and Offe must be acknowledged as extremely insightful: Late capitalism *is* a contradictory unity, whose naturalizing tendencies are counteracted by a falling rate of the production and reproduction of meaningful sociopolitical relations. Reinforced by the disorganizing and contradictory effects of bureaucratic planning, these mass loyalty problems reduce the capacity of ruling groups to motivate and discipline their dependents. This failure (as Offe and Habermas acknowledge) is exacerbated by the psychic stress induced by the mechanization and privatization of everyday life and by the motivational boredom attending the erosion of leisure and consumption as meaningful activities; it is further deepened by the weakening of nationalism as a resource that can be strategically mobilized against alleged enemies of the state and society.[138]

According to Offe and Habermas, these mass loyalty problems, together with the anomie induced by the resulting plurality of incompatible values, tend to trigger widespread searches for autonomous and meaningful political activity beyond the organized precincts of bureaucratic life. Their preference for the expression "*late* capitalism" follows from each of these hypotheses. To use this epithet in no way implies that this order automatically breaks down, that it is now fated to live out an inescapable and agonizing death.[139] To speak of *Spätkapitalismus* is not to anticipate an apocalyptic breakdown of contemporary capitalist societies in the not-too-distant future. To speak in this way is to indicate more modestly the difference between these later societies and their earlier liberal counterparts. It is also to indicate that amid the irrationalities and failures of bureaucratic planning, mass loyalty resources are in danger of being exhausted and cannot be readily renewed within the confines of the system. The expression "late capitalism," in short, calls attention to the fact that this system's survival in its present form is now crucially dependent upon mass loyalty assets – economic and state resources having already been used up, as it were, in the management of liberal capitalist crisis tendencies. Save for strategies of thermonuclear war, says Offe boldly, there "is no identifiable dimension in which *new* mechanisms for the self-perpetuation of the capitalist system...could be found and applied. All that remains is the variation and refinement of the usual triad of economic, political, cultural self-adaptive mechanisms, which at least to some degree have been applied in all advanced capitalist systems."[140]

No doubt, Habermas and Offe are aware that the administrative and cultural contradictions of late capitalism tend to foster authoritarian state responses and a certain paramilitary organization of society.[141] In opposition to these tendencies, a political theory of late capitalism must set itself the crucial task of extending the contributions of Habermas and Offe, of pursuing the thought that these contradictions might equally be seen as a condition of the affirmation of autonomous public spheres of decision making, against the hegemony of bureaucratic domination within the spheres of state and society.

4

Technē and praxis: the early Habermas's recovery of the concept of politics

What for me constitutes the idea of socialism . . . is the possibility of overcoming the capitalist simplification of the process of rationalization – simplification in the sense of the rise to dominance of cognitive-instrumental aspects, in consequence of which everything else is driven into the realm of apparent irrationality. With the overcoming of capitalism, these aspects would be put in their proper place, as it were.

Jürgen Habermas

The concept of rationality revisited

Irrespective of the goals by which they are guided, "substantively rational" forms of action, according to Max Weber's famous thesis, are always in principle in conflict with the requirements of formal, bureaucratic rationality. Actions can be deemed formally rational insofar as their explicitly stated goals are pursued and guided by the most technically suitable and proficient means available. Actions are substantively rational, by contrast, insofar as they are structured by ultimately irreconcilable standards of value, that is, by preferences that are highly variable in number and content.[1] It is this variability or contingency of substantively rational forms of action which ultimately precludes their systematic cultivation and cumulative development. Weber's account of the rationality of action is therefore marked by an unmistakable lopsidedness: Formal, purposively rational action is presented as the only type of action that is capable of "progress." Only formally rational, bureaucratic action is susceptible of rationalization.

A reconsideration of the *multiple* meanings Weber attached to the concept of rationalization generates the suspicion, however, that he did not always consistently hold fast to this strong thesis.[2] There is no doubt that he typically analyzed the growth of capitalism, the modern state, and its systems of law as rational institutions; from this point of view, the modern world undergoes rationalization insofar as it falls under the spell of multiple forms of calculating, bureaucratic thought and action (see Essay 2). On other occasions, it is nonetheless clear that Weber wields the concept of rationalization to signify a range of events in addition to that of strictly disciplined, bureaucratic organization. It is as if his concept of bureaucratic rationalization is overstretched and weakened by its own lack of precision and scope of deployment. With reference to patterns of religious belief or legal conduct, for

111

example, Weber speaks less rigorously of rationalization as a process in accordance with which the scope of activity becomes more precisely delimited and its rules of operation more explicitly defined through *reasoned* concepts and specialized knowledge. His well-known distinction among traditional, affectual, value-rational, and purposive-rational forms of action is tacitly framed by a concern with degrees of rationality in these latter senses.[3]

It can be argued that this ambiguity within Weber's account of rationalization unwittingly helped prepare the way for subsequent theoretical attempts to analyze forms of bureaucratic organization as only one type of action susceptible of rational development. Such efforts to subdivide, outflank, and thereby restrict the Weberian concept of rationality characterized the work of numerous thinkers under the immediate influence of Weber.[4] More recently, this early insistence that bureaucratic rationality is a *limited* measure of the degree to which actions are capable of cumulative rationalization has resurfaced, especially (in Germany at least) within the writings of Gadamer, Apel, Habermas, and others.[5] The following remarks are not concerned to analyze the broad and deep contours of these writings on the concept of rationalization; they are concerned, more narrowly, to indicate certain of the *political* implications of this work. As a consequence, the figure of Jürgen Habermas looms large in the narrative, for it is within his theoretical work that the political potential of the theory of rationality is most clearly developed. More than any other contributor to the current controversies over rationality, and from the time of his very earliest essays of the 1950s, Habermas has continually tried to question all attempts to privilege bureaucratic forms of rationality. In Habermas's eyes, what is distinctive and troubling about modern bourgeois societies is precisely their propensity to universalize the power of purposively rational bureaucracy. Modern capitalism and its constitutional state *illegitimately* seek to ensure "the *permanent* expansion of subsystems of purposive-rational action" by overturning all circumscriptions of this rationality by various traditional, symbolic and institutional practices.[6] As Habermas writes in a letter to Sontheimer, "modern societies were forced to pay the price of their unrivaled success in the development of the forces of production and the enforcement of legal domination: little by little they forced all domains of life into forms of economic and administrative rationality and stifled forms of practical rationality."[7]

Habermas is of course concerned to show that the bureaucratization of life under late capitalist conditions is a highly "irrational" process, even when judged immanently, that is, by the standards of its own restricted form of rationality (see Essay 3). It is precisely this irrationality which in his view weakens the plausibility of several earlier critiques of bureaucratic rationality. Under pressure from new and contradictory outcomes of late capitalist rationalization processes, arguments once conceived to expose the destructiveness and potential of bourgeois modernization – Marx's theses on the dialectic of the forces and relations of production; Weber's yearning for "freedom of movement" and statesmanship; Adorno's and Horkheimer's theses on instrumental reason[8] – prove to be inadequate. These arguments are outwitted by the fact that contemporary managerial attempts to produce a smooth-functioning, harmonious, and fully bureaucratic world tend to come unstuck. Weber's fear that the modern world would fall into a dreamless bureaucratic slumber is groundless, or at least exaggerated. Late capitalist processes of rationalization cannot drive all other forms of life into the realm of apparent irrationality. By way of this thesis, Habermas brings into play his fundamental distinction between the concepts of work and communication. This dualism, which serves as the decisive connecting thread in his early (that is, pre-1970) critiques of bureaucracy, has been a persistent feature of his writings during the past three decades. Contrary to the claim of Lepenies, the categorical separation of work and communication is by no means a recent theme in Habermas's work.[9] This dualism's rich and sometimes perplexing meanings, and the unintended and unsettling questions they pose for his critique of late capitalist society, can be understood only by turning to a classical formulation that at first sight seems far removed from Habermas's project: the Aristotelian distinction between *technē* and *praxis*. It is my argument that Habermas's early critical theory – upon which the following comments will focus exclusively – is premised upon a retrieval, reconstruction, and subsequent refinement of this distinction. As we shall see, this return to Aristotle leads Habermas to criticize the modern world's successive obliteration of the distinction between two forms of life and knowledge. This critique is directed at the apologetic defense of a bureaucratic, administrative politics by certain thinkers within the modern bourgeois tradition (especially Machiavelli and Hobbes) and also at Marx, whom Habermas sees as a carrier of bourgeois forms of rationality. Habermas reproaches Marx with an Aristotelian argument: The Marxian conviction that the self-constitution of the species unfolds through processes of social labor conflates the distinct logics or rationalities of mutual recognition and production. This dissatisfaction with Marx, in turn, becomes the foundation upon which the work–communication dualism is reconstructed, the outlines of a critique of late capitalism are projected, and a series of unanticipated theoretical questions and problems are provoked.

Making and doing: the return to Aristotle

The corpus of Habermas's early epistemological inquiries and political criticisms of late capitalism presupposes one major distinction already familiar to Aristotle: that between making and doing, means and ends, production (*poiēsis*) and action (*praxis*).[10] It will be recalled that, for Aristotle, the earthly world is a panorama of teleological processes, a world whose things (*ousiai*) are endowed with immanent powers to unfold their potentiality into actuality. Structured by final causes ("that for the sake of which"), everything is marked by an impulse or tendency (*hormē*) to realize its powers, to become the thing it can become. The "nature" of things is their potential destiny. The human species is itself immersed in this panorama of teleological processes. In Aristotle's view, the *telē* or goals of human life are threefold: (1) *theōria*, or the philosophical contemplation of the necessary, universal, and immutable things of the cosmos and their apprehension in scientific knowledge; (2) sensuous bodily activity that rightly tastes of pleasure, though slavishly so in cases of incontinence or lack of self-control; and

(3) the capacity to develop practical wisdom through public deliberation, speech, and action.[11]

For the sake of clarity, we can here disregard Aristotle's cautiousness about sensual pleasure and the primacy he attributes to scientific knowledge and the contemplative life. For our immediate purposes, what is most striking about this schema outlined in the *Ethica Nichomachea* is that which it excludes: the activity of production, understood by Aristotle to encompass the life of day laboring, farming, craftmanship, and, in the household proper, slavery and childbearing and nurturing. This exclusion is by no means trivial, for it directly discloses Aristotle's fundamental distinction between citizens, who are "integral parts" of the polis by virtue of their active contribution to its life of association, and those who are the "necessary conditions" of the state's existence.[12] Through their provision of housing, food, and services of many kinds, the latter always exist for the sake of the former. Aristotle is concerned to demonstrate that the "whole of life is...divided into two parts, business and leisure, war and peace, and of actions some aim at which is necessary and useful, and some at what is honorable."[13] Indeed, those engaged in providing citizens' necessaries are to be reckoned as prehuman, as permanent resident aliens within the city; their labors are means of attaining the loftier human goals of praxis and (what is but a more perfect form of praxis) the leisured life of cosmic contemplation.[14]

As Hannah Arendt has suggested, this division between the spheres of necessity and (potential) freedom was expressive of the destruction of archaic kinship systems and their replacement by the new institutional forms of the Greek polis.[15] Aristotle's distinction reminds us that, within this class-divided social formation of antiquity, there was not an altogether tranquil coexistence between these two different and hierarchically ordered forms of activity. The sphere of means is thus seen by Aristotle as structured by necessity (*anagke*) and as including, first, the bodily toil of women and slaves and, secondly, the artistic "making" of craftsmen and farmers. In the former case, the blind toil of slaves and women is structured by the aim of fulfilling the conditions necessary for the perpetuation of the species. Like tame and shamed beasts, men must labor to provide the material prerequisites of the lives of citizens, and women must necessarily bear the burdens of species reproduction and nurturing. Both slaves and women are therefore by nature living possessions of their masters, "instruments for the conduct of life." Ministering to the life of honor and leisure, bodily toil is also aided by the development of artistic skills and craftsmanlike productive knowledge. Those (like the craftsman) who make seek to apply general, artful knowledge in the fabrication of particular objects. The craftsman struggles to bring himself into mimetic correspondence with the nature of his materials so as to alter those materials manipulatively through the application of acquired technical knowledge.[16] Through this making knowingly guided by productive knowledge, the craftsman "by art [*apo technēs*]" realizes the potentiality in the matter upon which he works; in other words, art "partly completes what nature cannot bring to a finish, and partly imitates her."[17] Such productive skills are nevertheless not immediately or directly humanizing. Both the skilled making of the craftsman and the bodily labors of slaves and women remain at or near

114

the level of beastly life; hidden away in the private and shadowy corners of the *oikos*, both forms of activity are perforce mere means for the realization of doing or action.

Here a common misconception concerning Aristotle's theory of means must be discounted. The struggle to produce things useful and necessary in anticipation of the good life of public citizenship is not considered by Aristotle to be unfree on positivist grounds, that is, because it is presently executed by slaves, women, craftsmen, or foreigners. On the contrary, Aristotle explicitly opposes the subjugation and enslavement of others through force and conquest in war.[18] Not all those who are actually slaves, for example, are by nature slaves. What is more, the child of a slave by nature may not always be naturally destined for a life of slavery.[19] Finally, Aristotle even admits of the possibility of the obsolescence of the labors of slaves (though presumably not that of women, whose relationship with men is assumed by him to be ineluctably one of inferior to superior) through their replacement by mechanized techniques of production.[20]

The general point to be stressed concerning the Aristotelian theory of slavery is that a division of tasks between the toil and production of makers and the actions or doings of citizens is seen to be by nature inevitable because of the ubiquity of necessity: "No man can live well, or indeed live at all, unless he be provided with necessaries."[21] The very possibility of a sphere of political life founded upon a realm of necessity presupposes the subservience of the latter to the former. The just servitude of those who toil and are aided by instruments of production is in the nature of things: "There must be war for the sake of peace, business for the sake of leisure, things useful and necessary for the sake of things honorable."[22] The ubiquity of necessity renders the lives of some incapable of the higher, more fully human achievements of others. Undignified and merely useful, making is a species burden; the private realm of necessity is a space wherein capacities and powers ineluctably work themselves out blindly and must therefore be directed to higher ends by others. Burdened by the effort and pain arising from necessity, those who toil and make are fated to live their lives shrouded by muteness and idiocy; they are merely useful instruments for the actions of others.

The toil and unfreedom of labor as the precondition of moral wisdom and virtue, production and reproduction as the basis of action – this is the Aristotelian formula for the securing of the virtue, freedom, and "well-being [*eudaimonia*]" of the good life against the ubiquity of necessity. The transcendence of necessity through the exclusion of those who toil and work introduces the possibility of men as human, as *zōon politikon*. By nature political animals, men are capable of the good life, rather than mere life. For Aristotle, men have the capacity for partnership or mutual association within the polis. By contrast with the mere animal-like potential of the domain of necessity and toil, citizens can be reborn within and through the intersubjectivity of *bios politikos*. They can come to develop new "habits [*hexeis*]", acquired powers of acting politically, of ruling and being ruled in turn. The political is the domain in which the capacities for action (*praxis*) and speech (*lexis*) are mutually generated. It is the realm of truly public activity, in which speaking and acting individuals are seen and heard and take

115

one another seriously. Speaking is a form of praxis. Men are living beings capable of speech and deliberation; good, "political" men are ones who exercise these capacities *eu kai kalōs*, "well and beautifully." The exercise of this capacity precludes the desirability of instrumental relations between speaking and acting individuals, for articulate praxis relies upon nonviolence and persuasion through the force of good argument – violence is coercion, the arbitrary silencing of one by another, as if that individual were a solitary piece in a game of chess, to repeat Aristotle's metaphor. The life of speaking and acting citizens is therefore unlike that of those who either slavishly toil or rule others, for the latter are ensnared within relations of command and obedience, inequality and subjection; as Aristotle remarks, "there is nothing grand or noble in having the use of a slave, in so far as he is a slave; or in issuing commands about necessary things."[23]

Marked both by its emancipation from the exigencies of the reproduction and nurturing of life and by its presupposition of a fundamental equality between interacting subjects, this public space in which citizens live together and talk to each other is therefore also the realm of potential freedom. Through speaking and acting, men not only articulate and effect their commonality or interdependency (their language of communication, after all, is no private, solitary affair); by communicating as equals to equals (*homoioi*), they also come to individuate themselves, to speak and act *for themselves*. In and through political life, men's true individuality can be cultivated within an ensemble of responsibilities (sharing in tasks of deliberating and executing public decisions, and so on) that encourage them to see what is good for themselves and desirable for others in general. This is why to engage in political life means to choose deliberately between competing means and ends. To be political means to take the lead, to exercise initiative concerning what one should or should not do.[24] Inasmuch as actions are involuntary if they are due either to compulsion or to ignorance, Aristotle insists that it is only for voluntary, political actions that men can be praised or blamed. Praxis, therefore, introduces the possibility of moral virtue: "Moral virtue is a state of character concerned with choice, and choice is deliberate desire."[25] To struggle to be morally virtuous is to admit of the possibility of human affairs being other than they are, of men developing toward that of which they are capable among "equal and like" partners. This possibility is captured in Aristotle's well-known description of men as political animals: Men are beings who are capable of public association and whose nature is therefore positioned between that of the animals and that of the gods. Those who lead an apolitical, amoral, and solitary life must be either beasts or gods.

It is through the fundamental distinction between the realm of necessity and that of potential freedom that we can understand Aristotle's complementary distinction between two types of knowledge. Both forms of knowledge endow (potentially) human activity with *proairēsis*, with a certain foresight or clarity about its potentials and consequences. Whereas the provision of life's necessaries is appropriately guided by productive knowledge, practical wisdom (*phronēsis*) both is generated through and comes to inform properly the "moral deliberation [*boulēsis*]" of citizens in the public realm. The differing horizons of each form of knowledge need some explication, for the contrast between their essentially different logics is at least three-dimensional.[26] First, unlike artful knowledge, which is *applied* in the bringing into being or fabrication of particular material objects, the guiding principles concerning what men ought to do in the realm of praxis are not marked by their subsumption of instantial cases to universal rules. True, unlike scientific knowledge, which consists in judgment about necessary and universal things, both art and practical wisdom are concerned with processes that are mutable. Yet the principles of practical wisdom are variable in a special and unique sense, for they are always contingent, to a certain degree at least, upon the political conditions in which action unfolds. Against the Platonic equation of virtue (*aretē*) with exact knowledge of the Good, Aristotle urges that moral knowledge can by no means be possessed or even applied in the manner of artful knowledge. To be practically wise is not equivalent to knowing what is in general prudent. Citizens can acquire generalized practical wisdom only in the course of performing particular prudent acts. Practical wisdom can be developed and exercised only through deliberation and within the context of particular problems and action situations. "We are not investigating the nature of virtue in order to know what it is," says Aristotle, "but in order that we may *become* good."[27] Moral-practical knowledge therefore seeks at the same time to relate the particularity of given action situations in which citizens find themselves to the possible universal goal of becoming practically wise and good.

Secondly, the different rationalities of art and prudence do not turn on the fact that the *telos* of moral knowledge concerns human ends, whereas productive knowledge is concerned only with the correct means of attaining higher human ends. After all, as Aristotle again stresses against the Platonic idea of the Good, forms of moral knowledge are also immanently concerned with the means or strategies of reaching morally virtuous ends through processes of deliberation.[28] The prudent man is nevertheless not endowed with mere cleverness, the capacity to "do the things that tend towards the mark we have set before ourselves, and to hit it."[29] This is because moral knowledge is concerned with more than calculating expediency. It is additionally concerned with choosing acts for their own sakes: "Its end is what ought to be done or not to be done."[30] Whereas making always has an end other than itself (its *telos*, as it were, stands outside itself), good actions are structured by their own self-posited goals. Unlike productive knowledge, self-knowledge does not blindly lose itself within its limited concern with the means. In contrast to the informed doing of praxis, the prepolitical or private activity of making guided by artful knowledge has ends outside itself: "Every one who makes makes for an end, and that which is made is not an end in the unqualified sense (but only an end in a particular relation, and the end of a particular operation) – only that which is *done* is that; for good action is an end, and desire aims at this."[31] To speak and act wisely, to engage in good action, is to overcome the unfreedom and possible blindness of mere making through concern with both means and ends. Aristotle repeatedly maintains that citizens' activities can become good only through their self-knowledge of what is possible *and* desirable.

Finally, whereas the knowledgeable craftsman concerns himself with considering how his mute materials' potentiality may be brought into being, the citizen who seeks moral knowledge must at all times be mindful of the extent of his mutual dependence upon other persons; that is, he must modify his actions and self-knowledge by understanding himself in and through others.[32] As a consequence of their association with other political beings, men can come to acquire what Aristotle calls "self-knowledge," to learn what is good for themselves. Cleverness, the propensity of one speaking and acting subject to manipulate and devour another, is seen by Aristotle as having nothing in common with practical wisdom.[33]

The particular details of the Aristotelian schema of action and knowledge discussed here are perhaps not greatly important to our more immediate concern with the limits of bureaucratization processes in the modern world. It is nevertheless my contention that the young Habermas's critique of bureaucratic rationality cannot properly be grasped unless his key concepts of *work* and *communication* are seen, *mutatis mutandis*, as elaborations and reconstructions of this fundamental Aristotelian dualism between the differing rationalities of means and ends, technē and praxis, technical skill and moral-practical wisdom. This point has been missed by most discussions of Habermas's project – an oversight all the more surprising when it is considered that he himself explicitly acknowledges his indebtedness to Aristotle.[34] This indebtedness underpins his controversial thesis that the birth and maturation of the modern bourgeois world has been synonymous with the reckless erosion in theory and practice of the distinction between production and praxis, artful and moral-practical knowledge. Notwithstanding the influence of the Aristotelian conception of politics into the nineteenth century,[35] the establishment of the capitalist mode of production within the framework of a civilizing culture and the modern bureaucratic state strips this old distinction between two forms of life and knowledge of its former veracity and meaningfulness.

Habermas discusses a number of aspects of this obfuscation of the production–politics dualism. Science, which was once synonymous with contemplation, is in his view brought to earth, methodologically assimilated to the logic of calculating reason, and subsequently set to work within the production and social reproduction processes.[36] Modernity's overthrow of the primacy of the *vita contemplativa* by the *vita activa* also coincides with a dramatic depoliticization of this active life and its self-understanding. The classical goal of a political life guided by practical wisdom is more and more abandoned as an unworkable shibboleth. The reputation and scope of production and productive knowledge expands, to the detriment of political life and prudent knowledge. The ideal of practical wisdom succumbs to the rigor and utility of scientific-technical knowledge that informs political life, itself now increasingly understood as the strategic art of organizing civil society through direct, bureaucratic governance. In short, the concern of the classical doctrine of politics with establishing a free and wise life of citizenship through the overcoming of necessity is lost forever, a casualty of the calculating rationality of the bourgeois world. From the standpoint of the late twentieth century, the classical vision of political life appears to be passé, hopelessly old-fashioned. A victim of a successively bureaucratized society that is permanently mobilized against the past, this classical ideal has been forcibly forgotten. Habermas thinks that the apogee of this amnesia is reached under late capitalist conditions. Nowadays, under the sway of admittedly self-contradictory processes of bureaucratization, "humanity's consciousness of the dualism of work and interaction is eclipsed."[37]

The eclipse – and retrieval – of politics

Even granting Habermas's wish to write a critical and politically oriented history of the present and not a detailed history of the past, it should be recognized that his theses on the obfuscation of this production–politics distinction remain very schematic. The sketch offered is often perplexing by virtue of its overly skeletal character. One consequence of this brevity is that the inquiry into the quarrel between the ancients and the moderns and its mediation by the self-understanding and events from the emergence of Christian medievalism to the fall of the premodern *Ständestaat* is too highly attenuated. A further and equally serious lacuna is produced by Habermas's failure to acknowledge the extent to which bourgeois modernity's relations and forces of production (including productive knowledge and technical skills) are in certain crucial respects fundamentally different in their logic from the classical productive means discussed by, say, Aristotle. The case of productive knowledge and the fundamentally dissimilar notions of mastery to which it aspires provide one brief illustration of this point. Modern empirical-analytic knowledge seeks to apprehend everything under the sign of calculable quantity by converting it into a repeatable, replaceable process; by contrast, productive knowledge in Aristotle's sense seeks the realization or completion of the potentiality in the matter to which it is addressed. Habermas's conflation of this particular difference, as we shall see, is a consequence of his problematic assumption that the development of the productive means is historically cumulative (this theme is pursued further in Essay 6).

These preliminary difficulties can be left to one side, for Habermas's general thesis remains compelling and disturbing. It alleges that the administrative depoliticization of daily life under late capitalist conditions is not simply (as some might assert) confined to this phase. The eclipse of political life and the distinction between the realms of freedom and necessity are by no means consequences of (for example) the scientization and souring of bourgeois consciousness or of state interventionism, both of which mark the transition from the liberal to the late phase of modern capitalism. Following one of Rousseau's insights ("The politicians of the ancient world were always talking of morals and virtue; ours speak of nothing but commerce and money"),[38] Habermas insists that the obliteration of the dualism of production and politics and the suppression of the latter are fundamental features of bourgeois modernization processes. It should not be thought that Habermas views these processes as constituting a regression, a simple downfall from the grace of the classical era. Indeed, his mediated return to Aristotle in search of a critique of the particular rationality of the modernization process diverges considerably from the abstract rejection of the achievements of the modern world of such thinkers as Strauss and Voegelin. Voegelin's crusade against the "manifestations of Gnostic insanity in the practice of contemporary politics," for instance, proposes the renewal

119

of the classical philosophical quest for *prima principia* – in opposition to contemporary scientism, the modern murder of God, and the general elimination of the experience of transcendence. Strauss's rejection of all forms of positivism and historicism analogously rests upon a defense of the ancients and, in general, upon a denial of what is taken to be the disastrous modern denial of "*the* political truth" discovered by Aristotle.[39]

In opposition to such totalizing critiques, Habermas insists that the progressive, emancipatory moment of bourgeois modernization must not be overlooked. This is a revamped Marxian point: According to Habermas, the modern capitalist mode of production is more energetic, fecund, and recklessly efficient than any earlier system of transforming and humanizing nature (see Essay 6). Thanks to the accumulated, rationalized development of modern capitalism's productive *means*, the goal of universal emancipation from material necessity – a possibility about which Aristotle had only speculated – has for the first time in the history of the species become possible. This productive superiority of the modern world is at the same time, however, the source of its *limited* rationality. Modern life is marked by a deep-seated contradiction, for the rational elaboration and realization of political goals can never be synonymous with the rationalized improvement of productive means. Although hunger still holds sway over two thirds of the earth's population, Habermas remarks,

> the abolition of hunger is not a Utopia in the negative sense. But to unfetter the technical forces of production, including the construction of cybernetic and learning machines which can simulate the complete sphere of the functions of purposive-rational action far beyond the capacity of natural consciousness, and thus substitute for human effort, is not identical with the development of norms . . . in an interaction free of domination, on the basis of a reciprocity allowed to have its full and non-coercive scope. *Liberation from hunger and misery* does not necessarily converge with *liberation from servitude and degradation*, for there is no automatic developmental relation between labor and interaction.

Elsewhere this point is expressed more tersely: "The growth of the productive forces is not the same as the ultimate goal of the 'good life'. It can at best serve it."[40] This contention of course directly draws upon the language of Aristotle. Throughout the past three decades, indeed, Habermas has consistently agitated for the remembrance of the old Aristotelian dualism. This in turn has allowed him to distinguish two different forms of rationality, that is, to point to bureaucratic rationalization within the sphere of necessity and moral-practical, political development as two fundamentally different types of progress. This distinction between two modes of rational action is reinforced by an attempt to reassert the claim that there is a fundamental lack of identity between knowledge that is justifiably interwoven with productive activity and that which is appropriately enmeshed in (potentially) public or communicative life.

It is true that Habermas's retrieval and reconstruction of the Aristotelian dualism is at first very rudimentary indeed. In an early essay (first delivered as his inaugural lecture at Marburg in December 1961),[41] he traces the intellectual developments through which the collapse of the Aristotelian technē–praxis distinction was effected. Anticipated by the Thomist rendering of the Aristotelian concept of political life as more or less equivalent to the mediate, earthly goal of establishing an orderly *societas*, the history of philosophies of the social order from the time of the Renaissance is seen by Habermas as the history of the subversion of the vision of an integrated ethics, law, and politics culminating in the good life. He sees Machiavelli, the first great bourgeois political thinker, as the writer of recipes for modern political life. Machiavelli, he argues, generated a theory of politics that would have appeared to the ancients a strange contradiction in terms. This theory of *technical politics* was guided by the aim of administering humans within society. Habermas submits that

> Machiavelli reduces the practical knowledge of politics to a technical skill.... This art of governing people as we would say today, is also a technical skill in its way, but it has – and this was inconceivable for the Ancients – human behavior rather than nature on which it operates. The behavior and conduct of human beings themselves, especially their impulses toward self-assertion and subjection, are the materials which the princely artisan is to shape.[42]

Whereas Aristotle's central thesis is that citizens can exercise their political capacities by complying with the natural order of things, Machiavelli insists that the statesman can technically master the malevolent propensities of an immutable human nature. Concerned with the decay of tradition, the allegedly fickle and selfish desires of individuals, and the fragility of many European political systems under the pressure (in Florence especially) of an emergent mercantile bourgeois class, Machiavelli aims at securing human survival through the technical redesign of political institutions. It is precisely these seemingly ineradicable threats of life and death and struggle which lend the new concept of politics its meaning and raison d'être. Politics becomes the art of reinforcing the subordination of private citizens and insuring the sovereign prince and his state apparatus against their clamors. Under these conditions, the study of politics ceases to be an interrogation of the conditions of the good and exemplary life; it must from this point on focus upon the actual conditions of survival. The assertion of physical life, of elementary survival, becomes the fundamental political issue at hand.[43]

Habermas's assertion that Machiavelli advocates the wholesale divorce of ethics from the political actions of the prince is rather overdrawn.[44] This overstatement results at least in part from his close reliance upon Horkheimer, whose earliest work posited Machiavelli as an apologist for manipulative state control over the field of human affairs, itself conceived as a mere natural object of command.[45] It is perhaps more accurate to say that Machiavelli apologizes for the fact that politics and ethics have entered into a mutually antagonistic relationship. Under the new conditions of modernity, politics is no longer identical with the struggle for the good life of speech and action; from here on, it is insisted that the lionlike and foxlike princes must frequently *appear* to be merciful, faithful, humane, sincere, and religious.[46] Thus Machiavelli also advises that a prince should exterminate the families of rulers whose territory he desires to monopolize; that true generosity consists in liberality with what belongs to others and guardedness with one's own possessions; that maltreatment of enemies and benevolence toward friends should be hastened and prolonged, respectively, so as to maximize their effect; and so on. These and other Machiavellian maxims support Habermas's more general proposition: Politics now proceeds strategically and not pedagogically. In Machiavelli's hands, the category of politics undergoes a decisive transfiguration – it now signifies the skillful, pseudopolitical art of dominating *il populo* and *la plebe*, of regulating *fortuna* through the strategic organization and correct deployment of cunning, appearance, money, and men.

Hobbes's concern to scientize the understanding of "the matter, forme and power of a commonwealth"[47] considerably accelerates this undermining and forgetting of the old politics. His obsession with the problem of bourgeois society – the *bellum omnium contra omnes* – leads him to take up Machiavelli's concern for its pacification and neutralization through state action. In Habermas's view, Hobbes's theoretical project corresponded with two great processes sweeping the England of his time: the centralization and bureaucratization of political life into the shape of sovereign state power, and the sacking of older household forms of production through the expansion of capitalist commodity relations.[48] Under pressure from these processes, Hobbes is seen as making two really novel turns. First, the investigation of the means whereby these disruptive processes could be ordered draws directly upon the mechanized world picture of the natural sciences. Through its study of the laws of motion of civil life, the political science of Hobbes seeks the establishment of an enduring political order informed by apodictic propositions whose validity is independent of space and time. In contrast to Machiavelli, Hobbes appropriates the empirical-analytic self-understanding of Galilean science to found a scientifically informed, calculating politics. "It was Hobbes," Habermas points out, "who first studied the 'laws of civil life' with the explicit purpose of placing political action from now on on the incomparably more certain basis of that scientifically controlled technics which he had come to know in the mechanics of his time."[49] Abandoning the old vision of the good life and the assumptions of medieval natural law, Hobbes's argument for a sovereign Leviathan is derived objectivistically; he sees the valid concepts of political science as mimetically corresponding with their empirical object, namely, possessive, self-moving individuals who always tend to act instrumentally. Hobbes insists that sovereign state power is the only and necessary means of enforcing contracts between these desiring individuals; only the sovereign state can overcome the permanent danger of civil disorder.

Through these empiricist arguments, Hobbes's political science undermines the classical concept of politics and overturns the Aristotelian approbation of the *vita contemplativa* as a superior form of praxis. During Hobbes's time, the tradition of scientific, bureaucratic political thought was first established. The old dependence of political life upon the concrete rules of practical wisdom, upon a prudent and context-dependent understanding of what is to be done, gave way to a scientifically grounded politics. *Theōria*, the philosophic act of contemplating the eternal cosmic order, was brought to earth and transformed into useful, prognostic knowledge of what was scientifically and technically possible. In contrast to the contemplative character of Aristotelian *theōria*, the form and content of this scientific-technical knowledge were immanently designed for practical application. Machiavelli's political advice to princes had the character of "workmanlike-technical knowledge"[50] developed through long experience in the contemporary world of political affairs. Habermas agrees with Hannah Arendt's claim that the new science of politics, by contrast, seeks to produce, with scientific precision, regulative state institutions that can be compared in reliability with a watch that moves itself by springs and wheels.[51] This rationalization of political reason – whose influence, Habermas insists, is still felt in the phase of late capitalism – openly abandons the Aristotelian concern with practical wisdom, with "what ought to be done or not to be done." The new political science is guided by the entirely new concern with ways to avoid disastrous civil war amid the newly established relations of commodified exchange and bureaucratic, nation-state power. With Hobbes, political theory takes its first steps toward its goal of becoming a "physics of human nature"[52] founded upon empirically derived knowledge of causes and effects. Political science must from this time on instruct and serve power.

The second novelty in Hobbes's project is that it focuses, to a qualitatively greater degree than Machiavelli's, upon the increasingly problematic relationship between the supreme power of the sovereign and a bourgeois-directed, civil society in the process of emancipating itself from tradition and the old primacy of political life.[53] Habermas reminds us that, in Hobbes, society is posited as a sphere of contract-guaranteed exchanges freed from politics in both the Aristotelian and the Machiavellian senses. Hobbes's recognition and defense of society (a sphere wherein subjects ought rightly to exercise their "Liberty to buy, and sell, and otherwise contract with one another; to choose their own aboad, their own diet, their own trade of life, and institute their children as they themselves think fit")[54] presupposes that it is the mere object of depoliticized administration. Not only the classical meaning of politics but also its subject matter is altered by the new political science. The political goal "of virtuous conduct is changed into [that of] the regulation of social intercourse."[55]

In Habermas's view, Hobbes's insistence that the possible devouring of social intercourse by the state must be prevented through their mutual regulation by a system of formal law foreshadows several of the central axioms of the later liberal theory of the political.[56] Within this liberal tradition, the celebration of society against absolute political power that appears in personal form presupposes, in turn, that government and the state are instituted for the sake of peace and the general welfare. Within a legal system that declares a formal equality of rights and duties of citizens, the state seeks to guarantee to (patriarchal) individuals the quiet and free use and enjoyment of their property. The Aristotelian vision of a common life of involvements is declared null and void. According to the Hobbesian (and liberal) theory of the political, "welfare does not merely consist in the preservation of life as such, but in the most pleasant life possible. But this is not the fruit of virtue, as is the 'good life' of the classical tradition, but rather the fruit of the enjoyment of freely disposable property."[57] From here it is but two small steps to the Lockean conception of the property order of bourgeois society as the natural basis of state power established contractually and in accordance with the premises of natural law. A second step, equally dismissive of the substantive claims of the old politics, is taken by the arguments of the political economy tradition in the second half of the eighteenth century. Within this tradition, bourgeois natural law effectively undergoes a form of socialization. Amid the growing differentiation of a sphere of commodified exchange from the formerly supreme power of the state, such natural law is seen as the natural laws of motion governing the *société civile* itself. In Habermas's view, anarchistic liberalism (such as that of Paine) represents something like the apogee of this movement to depoliticize the world through the celebration of an unfettered society: Government is supposed to derive from our weaknesses, and society is said to be born spontaneously from our needs.[58]

It should not be forgotten, of course, that the complex processes through which the modern world ceased to recognize itself through the strict separation of the categories of praxis and production were by no means uncontested. As shall be argued subsequently, Habermas's account of several modern attempts to recover the classical justification of political life is an overly brief and perhaps too Germanic treatment (Rousseau, for instance, is hardly treated at all in this connection),[59] which needs only to be sketched at this point. Habermas correctly points out that Vico's critique of the moderns (from Galileo to Hobbes) concerns their attempts to "carry the method of scientific judgment over into the practice of prudence."[60] Though Vico does not recognize that the new science of politics *reveals* (that is, does not simply conceal) the historically novel emergence of civil society and its state, he nevertheless insists upon the illegitimacy of the abandonment of rhetoric and prudence in political life. According to Vico, this depoliticization of politics failed to recognize that the uncertainty and choices that encumber human affairs can be resolved only through prudence, and not through the measurements of the straight and sure ruler of mechanical science. In connection with this argument, Habermas also mentions the conservative revolt against the procrustean age of "sophisters, oeconomists, and calculators" and, in particular, Burke's defense of the classical doctrine of prudence in public affairs.[61] Finally, the emergence of the Enlightenment doctrine of the public sphere is seen by Habermas as heralding a brief but highly important challenge to the abolition of the classical vision of political life (see Essay 3). According to this public sphere principle radicalized by Rousseau and others, citizens are capable of assembling to form a public that mediates between the bureaucratic, constitutional state and the private needs of bourgeois society; moving from the private realms of production and family life, they enter a uniquely political space, which allows for the unshackling of the "spirit of free discussion" (Dugald Stewart).

This is the theoretical context within which Habermas reconsiders the challenge mounted by German Idealism against liberal bureaucratic politics and its instrumentalization of political reason. The young Hegel's critique of the Kant-Fichte tradition is seen by Habermas as especially decisive, inasmuch as it directly recovers and presupposes a distinction between making and doing.[62] It will be recalled that, for Kant, ego development consists in the formation of a self-conscious "I" that, abstracting from all possible objects in the world, knows itself by referring back to itself as its sole object. The free subjectivity of the "I" consists precisely in its capacity to know itself as self-constituting. This presupposition

124

of an autonomous ego underpins the theory of practical reason. This theory deems the ethical conduct of the rational, free, and solitary individual to be in harmony with (abstractly) universal laws, insofar as each individual supposes that its maxims are equally obligating maxims for other solitary individuals. Fichte's contention that the thing-in-itself is actually the thinking principle itself deepens, yet by no means breaks decisively with, this Kantian thesis of the synthetic achievements of the transcendental ego. According to Fichte, it is the sovereign, assertive, and objectifying ego whose practical freedom is manifested through its struggle to realize itself by creating the world and itself. The ego exists only inasmuch as it posits itself as a being-for-itself.

In opposition to Kant's and Fichte's understanding of the solitary "I" as a pure unity creating itself by reflecting upon itself and its objects, the young Hegel argues that self-consciousness emerges only as *intersubjectively developed* self-consciousness. In Habermas's eyes, this is the radical, even if idealistic, insight of the *Philosophie des Geistes*: The constitution of the self-conscious ego is seen as taking place not through its solitary reflection upon itself, but only through the complex mediation of definite stagelike, formative processes. The self-formative process of Spirit, according to the *Jenenser* system, unfolds through three discrete, but nonetheless dialectically interwoven, media: those of symbolic or linguistic representation and the distinct processes of labor and reciprocal interaction. The first medium, that of name giving, is in a fundamental sense the necessary mediating condition of both labor and interaction. Hegel speaks of the ability of human consciousness to employ symbols, to give names to things. Unlike the chaotic and enigmatic images in nightly dreams, the power of waking consciousness to represent objects symbolically is synonymous with its capacity to make distinctions and systematically recognize and remember that which it has distinguished. Through the employment of symbols, speaking consciousness experiences itself as subjective through its objectifications.

The development of an artful or cunning consciousness (which presupposes the capacity of consciousness to represent) signals the propensity of humans to distinguish themselves from nature by overcoming the immediacy of their bodily desires. According to Habermas's interpretation of Hegel, this is the second medium of the self-formative process of Spirit: artful consciousness. Through artful consciousness, labor, and the fabrication of tools, the cunning subject makes itself an object for itself by outwitting and overcoming the power of natural processes. Thirdly, and finally, through interaction with others (for example, in the family), the individual subject learns to recognize itself in and through the eyes of another subject or "I." Unlike his predecessors, Hegel urges that self-consciousness is not an original or primal experience that is fundamentally solitary. It is formed only through the intersubjectivity of Spirit, whereby the "I" develops not in relation to itself but, rather, in its communication with another "I," which also serves as its Other. According to the young Hegel, the exemplar of this process (which again presupposes consciousness' power of representation) is the ethical relationship established between lovers against the background of their previous conflicts. Love is here understood as concretely universal knowing that derives from, and sustains itself upon, the mutual recognition of each loving

125

partner. Love, in short, is *developed* through the nonviolent overcoming of a prior contempt and lack of identity, through a life-and-death struggle for reciprocal recognition.

Hegel soon abandons this idealist account of the self-formation of Spirit through symbolically mediated labor and the struggle for reciprocal recognition. From the time of the *Enzyklopädie*, or so Habermas argues, the more familiar categories of subject, object, and absolute Spirit predominate: The fundamental Aristotelian dualism is suppressed; theoretical and practical reason are immediately identified.[63] In existing for itself, Spirit is seen as positing a natural world, recognizing it as its own, self-created presupposition. Nature is conceived as the Other, the congealed product of a mind actively unfolding itself: The concept is both object and subject of the Idea.[64] As Habermas points out, the discussion of the master–slave dialectic (in the *Phenomenology of Mind*) is the last occasion where Hegel can be seen recalling and rendering the old *Jenenser* schema. The dialectic of labor, interaction, and Spirit is there resurrected: The one-sided, consciously *political* recognition of the lord by the bondsman is seen as overturned by the bondsman's ascendancy over nature, a conscious ascendancy one-sidedly acquired through *labor*.[65]

It is precisely this model of the dialectic of self-conscious labor and political recognition which was appropriated by the Young Hegelians and in turn radically transformed by Marx.[66] This dialectic is reinterpreted by Marx by way of a critical examination of the possibilities arising out of the liberal capitalist contradiction between the forces of production (in Hegelian terms, the power over nature accumulated through social labor) and the relations of production (the fateful struggle for reciprocal recognition). Through an explanation of history as the self-movement of active, sensuous labor, Marx seeks to demonstrate convincingly that the self-conscious struggle of proletarians to reappropriate their congealed and living powers of labor must be synonymous with their political struggle for recognition as a class opposed to all relations of capitalist commodification. The early Habermas finds the conceptual ambiguity of this Marxian thesis unacceptable. This disagreement brings us to the heart of Habermas's neo-Aristotelian censure of Marx. In Habermas's view, Marx does not properly explicate and analyze the fundamentally separate rationalities of interaction and labor; relying upon the diffuse concept of social praxis, he instead *reduces* the one to the other – namely, communicative action to instrumental action.[67] Despite his explicit defense of the project of revolutionary political action, Marx turns this project against itself; at the categorical level, at least, he attempts unsuccessfully to think against the bourgeois tradition by using its own concepts. His theses on the revolutionary possibilities attending the dialectic of the forces and relations of production thereby leave themselves open to productivist or economistic misinterpretations. According to Habermas, the critique of bureaucratic rationality must penetrate into the home territory of Marxist theory itself, for Marx does not separate himself sufficiently from the bourgeois tradition of administrative reason. Insofar as this is the controversial and still hotly contested charge upon which Habermas attempts to reconstruct the production–praxis dualism within a Marxian framework, his arguments need to be examined in some depth.[68]

126

The ambiguity of Marx

At least in its earliest formulations, Habermas's critique of Marx is an exercise in immanent criticism, in thinking with and against Marx, an attempt at understanding Marx better than he understood himself. It is important to stress that this immanent critique does not rely exclusively upon close analyses and "sympathetic" readings of the key Marxian texts. From the vantage point of late capitalism and his more encompassing concern with bureaucratic rationalization, Habermas insists that the Marxian discourse must *also* be interpreted as a pathbreaking theoretical accomplishment peculiar to the phase of liberal capitalism, to whose theoretical traditions nevertheless it is in several crucial senses unthinkingly indebted.[69] In Habermas's view, Marxism is historically specific, in the precise sense that its formulations are both victims and accomplices of the modern bourgeois obliteration of the classical work–politics distinction. Marx's insistence that limitations of consciousness correspond to definite historical stages of development of the material productive forces applies equally to the Marxian project itself. This claim, it should be noted, is not identical with the several arguments (analyzed in Essay 3) concerning the obsolescence of the classical Marxian theories of crisis under late capitalist conditions; for Habermas complements this line of empirical reasoning with a more epistemological claim: By virtue of its fetish of the concept of social labor, the Marxian theory of exploitation and emancipation is accused of unwittingly contributing to modernity's eclipse of the dualism of making and doing.

To be sure, Habermas acknowledges the *prima facie* plausibility of Marx's critique of political economy and its dependence upon the category of social labor. The concern of the Marxian project with production seems, correctly, to expose the logic and irrationality of a unique social form, whose class exploitation and conflicts were indeed no longer institutionalized through immediate political control and justified by cultural myth or tradition. By contrast with all earlier epochs, liberal capitalism was characterized by ruling-class attempts to stabilize such exploitation and conflict through the commodity form, itself guaranteed by a system of formal law and an ideology that served to camouflage the coercive, power-ridden character of this form by presenting the commodified exchange of equivalents as just.[70] It was precisely this natural unfolding of depoliticized class exploitation which Marx sought to denaturalize through critical inquiries into the capitalist value form. In Habermas's view, these inquiries revolve around the category of nature-transforming, value-producing labor, through which the daily confirmation of the species and its synthesis with nature is seen as being effected. Habermas recalls Marx's famous critique of the last chapter of the *Phenomenology of Mind*:

> The great thing in Hegel's *Phenomenology* and its final result – the dialectic of negativity as the moving and productive principle – is simply that Hegel grasps the self-development of humanity as a process, objectification as loss of the object, as alienation and transcendence of this alienation; that he thus grasps the nature of labor and comprehends objective humanity, authentic because actual, as the result of its own labor.[71]

Habermas explicates this Marxian critique in the following way. The world-constituting subject, he says, is no longer conceived as a consciousness actively externalizing itself but, rather, as a concrete, active human species producing its life under natural conditions. Such active production is the condition of all past, present, and future human existence. Through its capacity to produce its means of subsistence, humanity *becomes* humanity, overcoming its embeddedness in nature and distinguishing itself from the animals. Though nature is the presupposition or ground of this process, Marx does not see labor as a naturelike process. Through labor, a portion of nature (humanity) becomes subjective, for itself, consciously separating itself from outer nature, which therefore becomes objective nature *for* human natural beings. History is the synthesis of humanity and nature; through the labor process, outer nature is successively humanized, and humanity's needs are developed, transformed, and gratified within and through definite social relations.

It should be recognized that Habermas's account of the Marxian category of labor tends to be rather incomplete – indeed, one-dimensional. This truncation of the richness and subtlety of the Marxian category can merely be noted here; its undesirable consequences must be analyzed elsewhere (see Essay 6). The point is that to view social labor as synonymous with a "behavioral system of instrumental action [*Funktionskreis instrumentalen Handelns*]," as Habermas consistently does, is (from the point of view of Marx) to forget that labor in general has *become* precisely this under the conditions of liberal capitalist development. Curiously, Habermas forgets the richness of his own description (cited in Essay 3) of the liberal phase of capitalism as structured by the principle of the legally guaranteed, commodified relationship of wage labor and capital. He simultaneously recalls and represses Marx's central insight: Liberal capitalism is a quantifying, homogenizing system of social labor, whose abstract-general character obliterates the unique and subjective capacities of laborers by forcing them to conform to the complementary logics of the domination of nature and commodity. production. In repressing this insight, in adopting the "standpoint of capital," so to speak, Habermas also conceals the Marxian concern with liberal capitalism as a system of alienated and abstract labor, a system whose subjects are temporarily but systematically unable to unfetter their *self-transforming* powers of objectification. Evidently, the Marxian schema (unlike that of Weber, to whom Habermas is on this point very close) rests upon a dialectical model of the subject–object relationship: Through the medium of social labor, human natural beings create their objective world *and* themselves. Through its labors, humanity alters the external world of nature by at the same time transforming its own nature, developing its slumbering powers. Human labor produces both objects for the subject and subjects for the object.

It is precisely this visionary concept of concrete labor as the self-realization and objectification of the emancipated subject which is occluded in Habermas's rendition. He usually credits Marx with speaking only of what might be called the objective, Aristotelian moment of the labor process – its capacity to fabricate a world of need-satisfying objects by outwitting and dominating objective, natural processes. Habermas interprets labor as a means-oriented activity, insofar as its

128

immediate goal (compare Aristotle) is the satisfaction of the perpetual necessaries of life through the struggle to perfect the means of technical control over, and adaptation to, nature. Labor wrestles with the ubiquity of necessity; it is a calculating, rationalizing process whose aim is the efficient working up of a world of useful objects for human consumption. Correspondingly, the knowledge generated within the framework of such instrumental action is productive or technical knowledge "acquired through trial and error in the realm of feedback-controlled action."[72] Not surprisingly, it is this neo-Aristotelian truncation of the Marxian theory of labor which leads Habermas to celebrate the well-known *Grundrisse* passages on the displacement of variable by constant capital.[73] Here Marx suggests that the capitalist accumulation process is increasingly dependent upon scientific research. Invention becomes a business, as capital tends to give production a scientific character. The capitalist drive to dominate nature is accelerated, and to the extent that fixed capital guided by productive knowledge replaces direct, living labor power, the latter becomes of relatively lesser importance. Inasmuch as it strives to reduce labor time to a minimum while continuing to posit labor time as the sole measure and source of wealth, capital itself becomes the moving contradiction. It is as if the restless movement of capital heralded the reduction of socially necessary labor time, of unfree "material production proper" (as the third volume of *Capital* expresses it) that is determined by "necessity and mundane considerations."[74]

Habermas reinterprets Marx and pursues this point: "The self-generative act of the human species is complete as soon as the social subject has emancipated itself from necessary labour and, so to speak, takes its place alongside scientized production."[75] At precisely this point of liberation from necessity, Habermas explains, labor time and the quantity of labor expended also become obsolete as an index of the value of goods produced. The shadow formerly cast over the process of humanization by the shortage of available means and the compulsion to labor is thereby dispelled. Seen through Habermas's eyes, then, the *Grundrisse* passages anticipate the overcoming and permanent suspension of labor *qua* labor. The promise that the spell cast by "the Biblical curse of necessary labor"[76] will be broken is heralded. The forthcoming collapse of production based on exchange value signals the imminent possibility of realizing Aristotle's reverie. Marx is here said to envisage not the revolutionary supersession of abstract, alienated labor by concrete, differentiated labor but, rather, the transformation of the labor process into a scientifically rationalized process. This scientific-technical rationalization of labor would bring humanity's "material exchange" with nature under the control of a human species now fully and permanently emancipated from necessary labor. "In Aristotelian concepts," Habermas concludes, "Marx anticipates automation. He discerns that the development of the productive forces to this degree only commences once the sciences together with their technological applications become the primary productive force."[77]

Habermas correctly acknowledges Marx's conviction that the tendential displacement of variable capital by scientized, constant capital does not lead with any iron necessity to the emancipation of the associated producers.[78] The casting of producers as mere attendants of an automated process of production is not synonymous with their liberation. This is because the development of the forces of production (including living labor power itself) continues to be mediated, indeed fettered, by definite *social* relations of production guaranteed by the naturalizing power of bourgeois ideology. The emancipation of living labor power is therefore contingent upon the political transformation of symbolically mediated relations of power that, in Marx's opinion, have largely assumed an economic, class-structured form. A well-known thesis proposed in *The Eighteenth Brumaire of Louis Bonaparte* serves to illustrate this thought. Here Marx insists that the proletarian revolutions of the nineteenth century can succeed only when (potential) social individuals cast off the cloak of superstition and the fate that constricts their everyday life. The power of tradition and ideology within liberal capitalism is not simply immaterial, no mere phantom. Members of the dominated class must struggle against its naturalizing effects. Through their struggle for recognition, they must break the power of appearances, for the traditions of the past bear down forcefully on the brains of those proletarians living in the present.[79]

In principle (and even allowing for his reductive interpretation of the category of labor) Habermas concurs: "The growth of the productive forces is not the same as the ultimate goal of the 'good life.'"[80] In Habermas's view, however, the plausibility of the Marxian political conviction is decisively contradicted by the categories through which this conviction is entertained and justified. Habermas reproaches Marx with an Aristotelian insight: The Marxian contention that the self-constitution of the species unfolds through two interwoven processes – that in which humanity acts on nature and that in which it acts upon itself – misleadingly posits the primacy of the former over the latter. At the level of categories, the Marxian critique of political economy is marked by a thoroughly "productivist" or "economistic" logic. Productive activity and social relations of production are seen as merely different aspects of the same fundamental process – social labor. Just as the Fichtean ego comes to know itself only by asserting itself, so the self-positing activity of labor becomes conscious of itself only through its externalizing, objectifying accomplishments. Within the Marxian schema, the transcendental accomplishments of a world-constituting subject are seen as rooted in deep-seated structures of human labor. This is equally the contention of "The German Ideology," the first volume of *Capital*, and the "Notes on Adolph Wagner": "Conscious life activity" means neither "abstract, mental labor" (as for Hegel) nor politically generated consciousness and norms (compare Aristotle) but the historically grounded labor of a species-subject that produces itself and its self-interpretations. In Habermas's words: "The category of humanity as a tool-making animal signifies a schema both of action and of apprehending the world [*Weltauffassung*]."[81] In the view of Marx, humans' will to power over things and their fellows originally underpins their intellectual activity, so to speak. The Spirit is initially empty; the concepts formed by it are the effect of accumulated "practical-instrumental" experience.

It therefore follows, according to a strict interpretation of the Marxian schema, that the revolutionizing of liberal capitalist society is a consequence of the struggles generated by the dialectic of the level of development of the forces of material production and the restrictive productive relations in which those forces are embedded. The dissipation of ideology – the proletariat's critical reflection upon relations of dependence and exploitation – seems to be a mere feedback of this dialectic of production and its struggles. Because of this formulation, and notwithstanding his acute awareness of the propensity of the dominant classes for legitimating their own dominance, Marx does not adequately pose and analyze the question of proletarian consciousness raising. Frequently, the Marxian analysis remains vague, even tautological ("The existence of revolutionary ideas in a particular epoch presupposes the existence of a revolutionary class,"[82] and so on). Most often it presumes that practical action by workers in their revolutionary movement would automatically reshape their self-understanding, thereby cleansing them of the "muck" of ideological thought and traditional habits.[83]

The problem that Habermas has brilliantly and convincingly spotted in these formulations remains unsolved. Proletarian self-consciousness still appears to unfold in a manner similar to the Hegelian Idea, thus begging questions about the logics of those processes which mediate the formation of this self-consciousness. This point reconnects with Habermas's broader objection to Marx. In his view, the inexact, ill-defined concept of social labor or "praxis" unwittingly conflates two analytically separable moments of human activity: *labor*, or the subject–object relations inscribed within the metabolic exchange between humanity and nature; and *communication*, the intersubjective, normatively regulated relations between reflecting, speaking actors who exchange with and/or act against one another. Habermas consequently claims that there is an odd hiatus between Marx's empirical inquiries and their philosophical self-understanding. Marx's empirical analyses of the history of the species are mediated by the categories of material activity *and* the critical abolition of ideologies; by instrumental action (labor) *and* revolutionary praxis and critical reflection. Curiously, however, Marx squeezes his overall inquiries into the more restricted concept of the species' self-reflection through labor.[84]

And this is not the only difficulty. Because he identifies and conflates the nonidentical rationalities of symbolically conditioned mutual recognition and production in the single category of labor, Marx, like many of his bourgeois progenitors, is unable to distinguish scientific-technical information and practical, enlightened wisdom as fundamentally incommensurable forms of knowledge.[85] He unwittingly succumbs to the power of bureaucratic, rationalized thinking; the logical status of the empirical-analytic natural sciences and the criticism of ideology are not adequately distinguished. A context-dependent, critical understanding of "what ought to be done or not to be done" (to recall Aristotle's description of the *telos* of practical wisdom) is incarcerated within the categories of empirical knowledge of what is scientifically and technically possible. This failure to distinguish two theoretical projects – the interpretation of reality from a technical and from a practical point of view – means that, from the beginning, the Marxian theory was marked by a lack of clarity concerning its normative and political foundations.[86] It is therefore not surprising, in Habermas's view, that Marx (and later Marxist traditions) continually interpreted the critique of political economy as a natural-scientific project. Conversely, it is clearer why Marx never precisely examined the meaning of a "science of humanity" elaborated as a critique of ideology with political intentions, a science itself distinct from the instrumentalism of the empirical-analytic, natural sciences. Habermas summarizes these charges in definite Aristotelian language: "Marx equates the practical insight of a political public with successful technical control."[87]

In support of this thesis, Habermas adds that Marx's belief that "the material transformation of economic conditions of production . . . can be determined with the precision of natural science"[88] should be wholly unsurprising. This was, after all, a period whose intensifying faith in scientific progress marked it as the heir of the older, post-Machiavellian movement to instrumentalize political reason. Comte, for instance, approvingly heralded these times as the beginnings of a "positive age." He and others reckoned that a new era was dawning – an epoch in which the benefits of empirical-analytic science would penetrate into all aspects of social and political life, thereby bringing this life within the scope of calculated prediction and control. Adhering closely to the rules of observation, methodical certainty, and concern for precision, technically utilizable, positive knowledge was to become a tool of social transformation.[89]

In Habermas's view, Marx's break with the influence of this bureaucratizing "positive" age is indecisive. In search of a scientific grasp upon the economic laws of motion of bourgeois society, the Marxian critique of political economy assumes the form of a "philosophy of labour"[90] that represents its own logic as identical with that of the empirical-analytic sciences. Practical, critical reason – "the relentless criticism of all existing conditions, relentless in the sense that the criticism is not afraid of its findings and just as little afraid of the conflict with the powers that be," as the 1843 letter to Ruge expresses it so forcefully[91] – is unwittingly humiliated. Moral-practical knowledge is misconstrued as a species of technical knowledge. The Marxian critical theory of society thereby reinforces the tendency within post-Kantian philosophy, and within social and political life more generally, to abandon critical inquiries into the logic and *limits* of the empirical-analytic sciences. Ironically, Marx helps complete the positivist yoking of epistemological self-reflection to the blindly confident *methodological* inquiries of analytic philosophy of science.[92] By identifying *critical* reflection with natural science, Marx tacitly disavows this criticism and its epistemological and political tasks. Habermas is of course aware that certain currents of latter-day Marxism by no means escape the consequences of this scientistic tendency. The attempts of this Marxism to retain its credibility through recourse to arguments about its scientific status[93] risk absorbing the danger common to all scientism, namely, that of faithfully and uncritically believing itself to be universal knowledge that can be technically implemented. In short, this Marxism risks blindly handing itself over to the bureaucratic, calculating rationality of late capitalism.

I must not at this point leave the impression that Habermas's objections to Marx also take the form of a critique of the success and potentials of the empirical-analytic sciences. On the contrary, Habermas praises these sciences as a progressive achievement of the bourgeois world. He sees them as having greatly aided the species' attempts to bring external nature under control through social labor processes.[94] Effectively combining the rigor of mathematical form and the certainties of controlled experimentation, scientific-technical thinking, as Marx foresaw, has become a key ally in the struggle of the species to abolish scarcity permanently through the mastery of the natural world. Marx is, however, accused of failing to see that this project, to which the empirical-analytic sciences have greatly contributed, has regressive consequences insofar as its power and influence have tended to become all-pervasive in the modern world. This blindness with Marx's formulations is consistent with his conflation of the crucial Aristotelian distinction between productive knowledge, which can be legitimately applied within the sphere of necessary labor, and moral-practical knowledge, whose *telos* is the enlightened self-understanding of speaking and acting subjects. Marx thereby underestimates the point that, under modern conditions, productive knowledge and activity have been *misapplied*, illegitimately foisted upon realms of life and intellectual inquiry that properly stand, as it were, outside and beyond the sphere of necessary labor. Thus Habermas's caution: "Science as a productive force can work in a salutary way when it is suffused by science as an emancipatory force, to the same extent as it becomes disastrous as soon as it seeks to subject the domain of praxis, which is outside the sphere of technical disposition, to its exclusive control."[95] Technical reason and labor can come to their senses only by denying their absoluteness; they must, so to speak, be "relativized," put in their place by a more comprehensive understanding of rationality. This warning is analogous to that made some three decades earlier in the Frankfurt tradition by the young Horkheimer. If, to repeat Horkheimer's words, "the ideological reflex of bourgeois society" consists in this epoch's attempt to universalize falsely the calculating logic of the empirical-analytic sciences,[96] then, in Habermas's estimation, classical Marxian theory is a carrier of bourgeois ideology.

Knowledge and human interests: work versus communication

It has been the contention of this essay so far that Habermas's concern with the limits of bureaucratic rationality leads him to retrieve and interrogate the old Aristotelian distinction between production and praxis. In Habermas's view, modern bourgeois societies have, with several important exceptions, successively obliterated and forgotten this fundamental dualism. Even Marx does not break with this process of forgetting. Against the one-dimensionality of the Marxian philosophy of labor and its definite affinities with the modern bourgeois fetishism of bureaucratic, rationalized thinking and acting, Habermas repeatedly contends that, at the most general level, two forms of emancipation should be distinguished. Societies owe their emancipation from the external forces of nature to labor processes and technically exploitable knowledge; their self-emancipation from institutions based on violence, however, depends on their ability to construct and organize public spheres of life structured by the principle of "communication free from domination."[97]

Emancipation from necessity through labor versus nonviolent communication: Habermas's attempt to reinstate this fundamental distinction between two hierarchically ordered and incommensurable forms of conscious activity, it is true,

133

is at first rather rudimentary. A distinction between two forms of rationality is nevertheless already displayed within his earliest works of the 1950s. These writings evidence a familiar distinction between the realms of necessity and of freedom. Taking up a position within the perimeters of this dualism, Habermas's early essays speak of a goal whose possibility of realization, it is claimed, now haunts all organized capitalist societies: that of undisturbed freedom (*Musse*).[98] These societies are said to be marked by novel tendencies that serve to weaken and disrupt the general pauperization of producers and consumers by relations of leisure time burdened by the rationality of bureaucratized work.[99] Especially crucial for Habermas are those developments which facilitate a productive surplus and a reduction of socially necessary labor time. These tendencies, he proposed, furnish the populations of capitalist social formations with a new horizon of possibilities for minimizing necessary labor and establishing spaces of undisturbed freedom. Leisure time, until now burdened by the imperatives of a commodity-obsessed age bent on the production of an "excess of unreal needs,"[100] can be transformed into really free time.

According to the young Habermas, such genuinely free time is the precondition for universal cultural creativity. The thesis proposed has an explicitly classical thrust. "The Greek citizen," says Habermas,

> who was freed by the slave from work in its present-day meaning nevertheless had serious preoccupations. Otherwise, he would have produced neither the polis, nor its temples and statues and philosophy. Culture (*Kultur*), limited to such sublime creations of humanity is, of course, a product of abundance: it is not an outcome of free time, but a product of leisure [*Musse*]. The unskilled laborer of today has free time, perhaps even more free time at his "disposal"; yet he cannot produce the discipline which would make his "hobby" culturally creative for the first time.[101]

Only through the relaxed idleness (*entspannten Müssiggang*) and leisurely exertion (*mussevollen Anspannung*) afforded by authentically free leisure time could the populations of the advanced industrial countries exercise a "conscious participation in social activities."[102]

Habermas develops this theme by explicitly introducing the Aristotelian *technē–praxis* distinction for the first time in his writings of the early 1960s.[103] This distinction appears in the form of a theory of the "objective complex of underlying interests"[104] that structure cognitive processes and the logic of their deployment and application. In what was soon to be described as an "anthropological" turn, Habermas's indebtedness to Kant, Fichte, and Schelling is evident.[105] More immediately, this anthropological theory of interests can be seen as an early (and later-abandoned) attempt at radicalizing the old Aristotelian work–praxis dualism through a refinement of the well-known Weberian thesis: "Not ideas, but material and ideal interests, directly govern humanity's conduct."[106]

This refinement is most thoroughly elaborated in Habermas's major epistemological treatise of the 1960s, *Knowledge and Human Interests*. A rough draft of this work was outlined in his inaugural lecture delivered at the University of Frankfurt in June 1965.[107] In these two works, Habermas tries to synthesize Kant and Marx by demonstrating – to speak in their language – that the transcendental conditions of possible knowledge are constituted by the species' invariant patterns of "real," material life activity. Serving as a definite condition of all knowledge, these activities or interests are not to be understood psychologistically – for example, in the everyday sense in which it is said that all people should take an interest in politics. The concept of interests instead signifies anthropologically invariant vantage points from which the human species actively apprehends reality. Interests are knowledge-constitutive, that is, constitutive of the form of human learning processes. They must not be interpreted (as the illusory belief in "pure theory" would have it) as eradicable impediments that stand in the way of the production of objective knowledge. To the contrary, interests are the horizons that initially determine the logic according to which reality can become an object of rational knowledge. In Habermas's own vernacular, interests are "the system of basic terms (or the 'transcendental framework') within which we organize our experience *a priori* and prior to all science, and do so in such a manner that . . . the formation of the scientific object domains is also prejudiced by this."[108] In the eyes of the early Habermas, the knowledge generated within such transcendental frameworks contributes to more than the goal of the simple reproduction of the bodily needs of the species. Knowledge serves equally as an instrument of mere life and of the good life.[109] The human species learns not only in its necessary, life-preserving transactions with outer nature; in addition, it learns through its interactions with itself. The distinction between knowledge appropriate to necessity and that appropriate to freedom is once again recalled. Human knowledge is fatefully bound to the species' struggle to adapt to its embeddedness in nature through the metabolizing activity of labor. But knowledge also gives expression to the struggle through which humans have raised themselves *beyond* this nature through forms of symbolically mediated and normatively regulated communicative activity.

The meta-assumptions of this general schema – that knowledge is grounded in interests, which secure the species' adaptation to external nature and readaptation through symbolic culture – are elaborated by means of the insistence that there are two "basic" human interests: work (sometimes termed "labor," "social labor," or "purposive-rational action") and communication (sometimes called "communicative action," "interaction," or "symbolic interaction").[110] Through the activities of work and communication, history is seen by the early Habermas as a more or less evolutionary process through which outer nature is "humanized," brought under the species' conscious sway and domination, while at the same time "inner" or human nature is itself transformed, individuated, and emancipated through deliberation, speech, and interaction.

In preparation for some concluding remarks on the utility of this schema, these nonidentical forms of knowledge and interest can here be examined briefly and at the highest level of generality. *Work*, according to the early Habermas, is that knowledge-mediated activity prompted by the enduring need for the species to come to terms with outer nature. The immanent goal of labor is the expansion of an ensemble of objective productive forces and techniques that ensures the species' control over nature. Labor is properly the sphere of calculating, bureaucratic action: Through the cunning of work, things, events, and conditions (including the labor of others) are experienced as objective processes that in principle can be subjected to mathematical calculation, administrative manipulation, and transformation. To recall Aristotle's words, labor is a clever activity, the capacity to "do the things that tend towards the mark we have set before ourselves, and to hit it."[111]

Consistent also with Aristotle's rendering of production and toil as prehuman is the early Habermas's urging that work is by no means a distinctively human activity. This is true in both an anthropological and an evaluative sense. Ethological evidence since the time of Marx and Engels[112] indicates that calculation, toolmaking, and productive activity distinguish all *hominids* (including humanity itself) from the primate species. Predating *homo sapiens*, the early hominids (such as chimpanzees) also form hunting groups, develop weapons and tools, cooperate through a nascent division of labor, and even allocate their prey in accordance with certain rules of distribution. Habermas implies therefore that the (Marxian) concept of social labor is suitable only for distinguishing hominid forms of life from that of the primates; it does not per se capture what is specifically human in the reproduction of the species' life activity.[113] Work is also prehuman in an evaluative sense. Undignified, useful, and compulsory, work is a burden against which the species is condemned to struggle. It is not only that its successful execution presupposes the postponement of gratification of desires.[114] In Habermas's view, the ultimate, higher purpose of work – emancipated communication – is foreign to work itself; work is a *technical* interest, a means-dominated process saddled with the necessity of producing the material requirements of mere life. Unfettered partnership or communication cannot enter into the sphere of work: In principle, work is solitary and silent, a private realm of dumb necessity. Work is skilled, purposive-rational action.

Here the early Habermas draws directly from Weber, for whom purposive-rational action is "determined by expectations as to the behavior of objects in the environment and of other human beings; these expectations are used as 'conditions' or 'means' for the attainment of the actor's own rationally pursued and calculated ends."[115] In Habermas's rendition of this thesis, purposive-rational action is concerned with the realization of defined goals (broadly, human liberation from material necessity through the mastery of nature) under given conditions of knowledge of natural and labor processes, organizational efficiency, and available resources.[116] Concerned with the successful attainment of goals through the organization of appropriate means, such action can in principle be guided by theories of empirical-analytic science, with which work has a special – indeed, inner – affinity. Purposive-rational activity can also be informed by empirically derived technical and strategic rules that function to operationalize choice. These rules include scientific knowledge of empirical regularities, the calculation of technical possibilities, the reckoning of possible unintended consequences of certain adopted strategies, and so on.

Work as purposive-rational action can be analyzed (and not without some early confusion on Habermas's part, as Held and McCarthy have shown)[117] into two defining aspects or moments. First, Habermas proposes that work consists in means-calculating, *instrumental action* that manipulates natural objects, objects of congealed labor, and labor power conceived as an object according to criteria of efficient control. Work as instrumental action is structured by rules that have regard for the efficacy of means, for predictive capacity and technical appropriateness. It obeys technical rules based on empirical-analytic, prognostic knowledge. In this respect, instrumental action has a special affinity with the empirical-analytic inquiries of post-Galilean science. This science seeks to produce technically utilizable knowledge whose validity is determined pragmatically;[118] it aims at conditional predictions that both are dependent upon and foreshadow successful human control of objectified processes. That this predictive and pragmatic science has become the great ally of productive processes is abundantly clear under the conditions of late capitalism; the merger of experimental science and production, so to speak, reveals the interest of knowledge that guides this science. Just as artisans who worked on their materials were formerly guided by rules of experience that had been proved in the traditions of their trade, so the most advanced forms of capitalist production rely on scientific instruments, operations, and predictions. The function of the knowledge of modern empirical-analytic science must therefore be understood in connection with the system of social labor. This science "extends and rationalizes our power of technical control over the objects or – which comes to the same thing – objectified processes of nature and society."[119]

Habermas also speaks, secondly, of the strategic or rational choice aspects of work. Considered as *strategic action*, work is instrumental action supplemented by rules or decisions that select the most consistent and suitable means for the achievement of the goals of production.[120] Strategic action is concerned with maximizing the rationality of choice between potentially suitable means to the achievement of defined goals. To this end, strategic action can in principle be assisted by analytic knowledge (such as that provided by decision theory or administrative science) that facilitates the correct choice of means to ends. Strategic action thereby seeks to coordinate particular instrumental activities efficiently and also to analyze and evaluate their efficacy correctly in relation to a range of possible but competing objectives.

By way of the concept of strategic action, the early Habermas recalls the point that work as purposive-rational action is always structured by sets of rules that have been generated outside the realm of work, that is, within a framework of communicative interests.[121] Normative rules generated through communicative action specify the ultimate or higher purposes of work – for example, whether production should be for commodified exchange or for the use of a political community of transacting citizens. When the early Habermas speaks of communication as a distinctive interest, he means to refer to spheres of action – autonomous public spheres, for example – that are founded in ordinary language communications and guided by sanctions and norms.[122] In contrast to the *monologic*, cunning action of the sphere of work, in which processes of labor and nature are experienced as objective and capable of bureaucratic manipulation, communication takes the form of (potentially) intersubjective or dialogic relations between speaking and acting subjects. Communicative action presupposes the mutual identification of social and political actors, whose associations are structured by an at least minimal reciprocal awareness of the conventional rules of their interactions. These rules, and the mutual expectations and obligations they promote, are enforced through conventional sanctions. These rules and sanctions are of course subject to decay and transformation. Yet, whereas failures of purposive-rational activity are labeled inefficiencies or incompetence, such breakdowns of interaction are variously understood as misbehavior or deviance, as justified or unjustified insubordination, or as self-destructive, psychosomatic disturbances.[123]

Habermas by no means denies the importance of those processes through which communicative action assumes the form of *pseudo*mutuality. In his view (discussed in Essay 5), all hitherto existing social formations, including the present phase of late capitalism, have been marked by the institutionalized manipulation and processing of the species' unique *capacity* for reciprocal recognition through unconstrained speech and action. This capacity for speech and action is nevertheless what is specifically human about our being. In contradistinction to natural objects, the species are the producers and products of their language. Through language and communication, certainly, subjects *become* subjects by virtue of their acquisition of the capacity to engage in skillful, means–ends calculations; thereby they come to be equipped to act within the sphere of work. In Habermas's view, however, the development of subjectivity through ordinary language communication is potentially transcendent of mere skill and purposive-rational calculations. By virtue of their embeddedness within systems of language and communication, subjects come to be socialized, equipped with internalized norms or personality structures that furnish them with the capacity subsequently to accept or reject norms and to bring about interpersonal relations. Through the language system in which they grow, in sum, subjects can come to constitute and transform the meaning and form of their interactions with others.

As a consequence of this argument, whose substance and implications he will later develop more systematically, the young Habermas launches a series of novel and still controversial arguments whose Aristotelian flavor is unmistakable. According to him, within the realm of communication subjects learn to speak and act; no matter how poorly developed, this learning process anticipates a certain aptitude for public deliberation, practical wisdom, and the taking of moral-practical initiatives. The learning of language prefigures *Mündigkeit*;[124] to speak and act implies the will to engage competently in communicative acts with others. This communicative competence lurks, as it were, behind all acts of communication.[125] The possibility that speaking actors can become political beings who strive for mutual recognition and understanding is not mere fancy, for, as Habermas insists in one of his earliest and most intrepid formulations, "our first sentence expresses unequivocally the intention of universal and unconstrained consensus."[126] This thesis contains crucial epistemological and methodological implications for the sociocultural sciences. Inasmuch as communicative competence is signaled or anticipated within the realm of interaction, Habermas correctly warns against illusory theoretical attempts to apprehend the domain of communication through the objectifying, manipulative procedures of the empirical-analytic sciences. Whereas the latter suppose that the processes they objectify can in principle be bureaucratically controlled, the social or cultural sciences must seek to *understand* "objects" who are *also* speaking and acting subjects whose intentional utterances and life conditions are structured symbolically. As Weber argued earlier (see Essay 2), the cultural sciences must guard themselves against reducing intentional action to mere behavior. Processes of interaction "cannot be construed without reference to their guiding intentions; that is, they cannot be examined independently of something approximating to ideas."[127]

This is not the limit of the assignment of the cultural sciences, however. To the extent that structures of communication equip individuals with the potential for self-conscious speech and action, these sciences must also seek to explain the logic of the processes through which that potential comes to be blocked by a historical surplus of constraints. Conversely, in Habermas's view, the sociocultural sciences must concern themselves with the conditions under which this potential for communicative competence can be realized. These sciences must assume the form of a critical theory of society with political intent. Adopting the standpoint of "scenic,"[128] explanatory understanding, this critique seeks to publicize and denounce the manifold restrictions upon communicative competence. In its role as advocate, this theoretical discourse is marked by its struggle to recall, against the tremendous power and scope of modern bureaucratic organizations, the fundamentally nonidentical logics of the realms of necessity and freedom. The critical theory of society stands firm on this point: It maintains that the extension of bureaucratic forms of production and administration is not synonymous with the good life of political action. Against the modern bourgeois world, the early Habermas concludes that the rules of communicative action may well develop in response to changes in patterns of instrumental and strategic action; but in so doing, the rules of communicative action are guided by their own unique and autonomous logic.

Two concepts of rationality?

This concluding thesis allowed Habermas to reconstruct and restrict the Weberian concept of bureaucratic rationality. An earlier and remarkably parallel reformulation is evident in Mannheim's elaboration of the Weberian distinction between functional and substantial rationality. According to Mannheim, capitalist industrialization has undoubtedly introduced a measure of functional rationality into modern life, inasmuch as this industrialization has promoted the efficient organization of individuals for bureaucratically defined ends. This industrialization has not to the same extent fostered substantial rationality, namely, individual capacities for intelligent judgment and action.[129] This thesis is very close to Habermas's indeed. At the analytic level, Weber's notion of rationalization (and Marx's concept of labor) as increasing purposive and technical control over objectified processes is designated by Habermas as merely *one* form of rationalization. The bureaucratic development of the productive forces within the sphere of work must be understood as only the necessary precondition of the rationalization of communicative life through the development of unconstrained speech and action.[130] To speak of the rationalization of communicative action is to advocate the overcoming of systematically distorted communication, the extirpation of intrapsychic and interpersonal relations of force and domination that have become chronic impediments to the expansion of free, consensual action. In the view of Habermas's early writings, the successful, efficient growth of the productive forces must not be confused with political struggle for nonviolent intersubjectivity. Bureaucratic rationality is only *one* point of view from which actions can be rationalized. Not one but *two* fundamentally different forms of rationalization must be distinguished.

Drawing upon Aristotle and Marx, this conclusion no doubt considerably damaged the credibility of Max Weber's concept of rationalization and its one-sided defense of bureaucracy and leadership politics. It was also to generate new and unforeseen enigmas. Habermas's self-criticism of his major work of the late 1960s, *Knowledge and Human Interests*, provides a clue to some of these problems.[131] Still other difficulties persisted. These difficulties, which can be seen in some measure as an effect of the early theory of work and communication, continue to unsettle Habermas's more recent work, and may be expected to influence his future inquiries. From the point of view of a theory of autonomous public life, at least *three* constellations of these difficulties can be identified. They can, in anticipation of subsequent studies (see Essays 5–7), be briefly sketched in the following concluding remarks.

First, it is evident from this essay that the early Habermas's brief discussions of the emancipatory premises of all communicative action required considerable explication and refinement. Of course, the more recent theses on ego development, social evolution, and, especially, the theory of universal pragmatics have attempted to overcome precisely this weakness. Concerned to foreground and substantiate philosophically the political goal of "public, unrestricted discussion, free from domination," the theory of pragmatic universals in particular has tried to elaborate the unavoidable and universal rules that all adult speaking actors *must* presume when engaging in competent acts of communication. According to the research strategy of this theory, communication can be analyzed as a matter of performing speech acts that are constituted by systems of rules or validity claims. It is further reckoned that, within all unbroken or undisturbed communication at least, these rules together form something like a background consensus. Communication is said to presuppose an at least tacit agreement about what it means to communicate; all undisturbed communication rests on the counterfactual promise of communicative competence.

From the time of its earliest formulation in the late 1960s, the theory of universal pragmatics of course acknowledged that numerous mechanisms function to conceal and block this promise of communicative competence. It therefore recognized the need for an account of the mechanisms of systematically distorted or pseudocommunication and accepted, further, that it would have to address questions concerning those theoretical and political strategies most conducive to the defense of "communication free from domination." Not altogether successful in completing these assignments, the later theory of communication more and more came to suspend consideration of the problem of deformed communication. (For an elaboration of the following difficulties, see Essay 5.) It consequently came to theoretically privilege "consensual action," that is, forms of communication in which speaking actors already cooperate on the basis of a mutually recognized presumption that their interactions fulfill the conditions of authentic, domination-free communication. The competent subjects to whom the inquiries of the communication theory were later addressed would be *hypothetical* subjects; the actually existing forms of communication under late capitalist conditions were analyzed as if their participants were already communicatively competent subjects.

What is more, subsequent versions of the communication theory suspended consideration of certain aspects of communicative activity typically present within public, political life. From a theoretical point of view, Habermas's communicatively competent subjects were denuded of several important empirical and historical qualities. For instance, the later theory of communication tended to deemphasize the chronically embodied character of communication; its focus upon consensual forms of rational speech misleadingly represented rhetorical and aesthetic forms of communication as derivative of rational, consensual speech; the universal pragmatics' dependence upon the earlier (above-analyzed) distinction between the realms of necessity and of freedom, together with its special form upon consensual action, produced an uncanny theoretical silence about the proper role of controversy, disobedience, and other purposive-rational forms of action within public life; and so on. As a consequence of these several difficulties, it can be observed that the theory of communication has been forced to pursue its inquiries through highly abstract and general modes of argumentation. This abstract formalism has tended to contradict Habermas's earlier concern with retrieving and defending the classical ideal of public speech and interaction. Relinquishing its role as advocate, the theory of communication more and more came to rely upon the strategy of rationally reconstructing the competences of abstractly conceived, hypothetically competent subjects. The theories of communication and late capitalism have consequently become divorced from each other; the theory of communication is therefore unable to offer many insights into the substantive aspects of contemporary struggles for autonomous public life.

Habermas's early defense of *two* concepts of rationalization arguably generated an additional cluster of related difficulties. Bearing crucially on his project of retrieving and renewing the classical concept of politics, this second cluster of difficulties persists even within his most recent writings. These difficulties derive from his early – and continuing – conviction that modern scientific-technical progress has no necessary propensity for hindering the development of political autonomy. To be sure, Habermas's early distinction between work and communication helps explain why his praise of modern scientific-technical progress has been *limited*. He insisted (against the thesis of technological determinism, for instance) that the progressive mastery of outer nature through work should also be considered a political task. The struggle to deploy democratically the use values generated within the sphere of work must take the form of speech and action within public spheres of communication. Attempts to effect the *totalized* "penetration of areas of life by forms of economic and administrative rationality"[132] must be rejected. There is no continuum of rationality in the treatment of technical and political problems. Habermas has remained convinced, however, that bureaucratic rationalization within the sphere of work by no means renders impossible a good life of public speech and action; democratic, public life is not precluded by the patterns of progress that attend late capitalism's productive forces. In principle, the unprecedented power of technical control effected under modern capitalist conditions of production can be successfully deployed in support of public life.

It can be argued that this thesis has continually burdened Habermas's defense of public life (see Essay 6). His conviction that the growth of the modern productive forces is *equivalent* to technical rationalization implies, prematurely and falsely, that actually existing forms of strategic and instrumental action within the sphere of work are incapable of being transformed into nonbureaucratic, communicative institutions. To analyze bureaucracy through the concept of purposive rationality is unexceptionable. But to speak in turn of contemporary forms of work as the proper referent of *this* concept of rationality is inadmissible. The suspicion is provoked that Habermas's denunciation of the universal expansion of bureaucratic rationality under late capitalist conditions is at the same time a justification of that particular form of bureaucratic rationality. Curiously, his attempt to outflank and subdivide the Weberian concept of rationality resulted in a defense of bureaucratic rationality as one rightful form of rationality; he thereby seriously underestimated the historical contingency that marks contemporary forms of exchange with outer nature. These forms of exchange were elevated to the status of a point of absolute beginning, to a "nature" that precedes, guides, and outlines history. Directly generated by the early distinction between work and communication, this presumption tended to bracket questions about existing forms of science, technology, and labor (including housework and the nurturing of children). The legitimacy of attempted defenses of autonomous public life *within* the sphere of work was discounted. Here Habermas's formulations clearly owed (too) much to classical (and liberal bourgeois) conceptions of public life as spheres structured by rules and mechanisms that rightly exclude matters of private concern. Within the realm of work, it seemed that everything and everybody would have to fall silent.

The depoliticizing implications of Habermas's defense of work as a sphere of bureaucratic rationality tended to be reinforced by his account of the empirical-analytic, natural sciences. He analyzed these sciences as a cumulative learning process, whose aim is efficiency of successful prediction and control; for this type of science, which is inherently guided by the aim of establishing bureaucratic control over nature and objectified processes within the realm of work, there can be no other democratic substitute. This conclusion was not entirely plausible. He did not consider, for example, the possibility that the bureaucratic orientation of these sciences is expressive of the embeddedness of scientific research and development within historically specific relations of bureaucratic production and power. His discussion was also silent about the political implications of a certain form of empirical-analytic knowledge – that generated by the medical and biological sciences – which has typically attended the growth of mechanisms of surveillance of the populations of the modern world. Nor, finally, did he adequately consider the degree to which the scope of prediction and bureaucratic control generated by the progress of these sciences is highly uneven, in some cases even limited. The problem of whether outer nature is itself susceptible of successful, totalized bureaucratic control was passed over, for instance. In sum, Habermas's early identification of actually existing forms of work as the embodiment of a *necessary* bureaucratic rationality can be seen to have concealed a range of problems that in turn cast doubts on the validity of the work–communication dualism. A series of vital political questions was temporarily repressed: How justified is Habermas's (neo-Marxian) view that the modern capitalist mode of production has been more energetic, fecund, recklessly efficient, and *therefore* potentially emancipatory than any earlier system of transforming and humanizing nature? Does not the democratization of communication practically require the abolition of heteronomy within the sphere of work? Is not the realization of domination-free communication conditional upon a radical restructuring of late capitalism's forms of interchange with outer nature? Might it not even be said that the defense of autonomous public life within the spheres of communication and work nowadays implies political defenses of outer nature itself?

Finally, and again briefly, a third problem: The early Habermas's account of the erosion of the Aristotelian concept of politics, it can be argued, insufficiently discussed the ways in which the modernization process has continuously been checked and restricted by political traditions that persisted in the face of the advance of bureaucratic domination. (With reference to liberal contractarianism, this problem is treated at length in Essay 7.) The analysis of the eclipse of the dualism of work and communication too strongly rotated around the contraposition of a classical era and a modern society mobilized against the authority of the ancient past. With some important exceptions – his references to Vico, Burke, the young Hegel, and the classical bourgeois public sphere being the most important – the early Habermas interpreted the tradition of Aristotelian politics as the unfortunate victim, or the mere detritus, of the revolutionizing movement of modern society. Relying upon the parallel discussions of Arendt and Wolin,[133] he too readily concluded that modernity is synonymous with the displacement of the distinctly political by forms of depoliticized association.

There can be no doubt that bureaucratization processes have effected a substantial disintegration of nonmodern traditions. It is also true that late capitalist societies feed like predators on the remains of certain traditions. Residual traditions such as patriarchy have constantly aided the growth and legitimation of forms of bureaucratic power. It is nonetheless certain that *other* traditions have proved to be more stubborn enemies of the modernization process. Against all odds, the classical dead have continued to make their presence felt upon those living within the modern world. The power of resistance of the modern civic humanist tradition is a case in point. From the time of Machiavelli, as Pocock and Skinner have shown,[134] the civic humanist movement defended the utopian content of neoclassical republicanism. Civic humanism posed the problem of

143

how political action could receive recognition within the framework of a Christian time scheme that, in opposition to this humanism, denied the possibility of any secular fulfillment. Confronting its own sense of temporal finitude, civic humanism consciously strived to defend the principle of republicanism amid the endless stream of irrational events conceived as fundamentally destructive of all systems of secular stability.

This confrontation of corruption and fortune with virtue has had a continuing history through to the present. It has crystallized itself in traditions that are by no means functional for processes of capitalist and state bureaucratization. Within eighteenth-century England, France, and America, for example, social and political discourse was vitally concerned with the problem of civic virtue, public life, and government legitimated through contractarian principles. This civic humanist discourse was in fact prompted by the lasting reversals of power effected by the plebeian classes of this period. The bourgeois assault upon the secretive privileges of the feudal and absolutist orders, a theme Habermas himself has argued at considerable length in *Strukturwandel der Öffentlichkeit*, might also be seen as a development – indeed, a self-conscious radicalization – of this civic humanist tradition. Under pressure from the emerging bourgeois classes, a restricted form of public life was installed as an organizing principle of the new civilizing order. Public life was to be enhanced through the conjoining of bodies of politically competent and socially equal (male) citizens, who insisted upon their rights to confer informally and formally (through elections) and thereby to subject ruling state institutions and their arcane policies to critical scrutiny.

This power-scrutinizing tradition of citizenship has by no means been exhausted. Under late capitalist conditions, the autonomous democratic principles preserved by the civic humanist, plebeian, and bourgeois struggles continue to inform battles to check, confine, and dissolve various forms of bureaucratic power. A socialist theory of public life, such as that posed in the early writings of Habermas, can ignore these tradition-informed struggles only at the cost of excessively empty and abstract-general formulations. Precisely this difficulty is evidenced in the later Habermas's account of communicative rationality, an account whose grand abstractionism in part issued from his earlier disavowal of the category of tradition and, in particular, from his overdrawn conclusion that modern societies have stifled all forms of practical rationality by successively forcing every domain of life into the shackles of bureaucratic rationality.[135] A theory of public life that is sensitive to its embeddedness within historical forms of life must openly reject this conclusion. Proceeding "hermeneutically," this theory can supplement, enrich, and thereby overcome excessively formal explanations of the rationality of communicative action. This sensitivity to historical forms of power and politics is not synonymous with an uncritical nostalgia for tradition *qua* tradition. Drawing upon the theoretical strategy of immanent interrogations of lived traditions of protest, resistance, and solidarity, rather, a socialist theory of public life can more readily "find the new world through

144

criticism of the old." The theory of public life can more openly acknowledge the historically situated character of its political claims, while at the same time nourishing itself upon living traditions of moral-practical reason that have survived – and continue to defy – the advance of bureaucratic unreason.

5

Elements of a socialist theory of public life

Public opinion...deserves to be as much respected as despised.

G. W. F. Hegel

From the time of the Bolshevik Revolution, all emancipatory political thinking has been concerned with the subject of public life. Initiated by Rosa Luxemburg's critique of the earliest phase of that revolution,[1] this tradition of autonomous political thinking is of considerable relevance to any deepened understanding of the growth of public spheres under late capitalist conditions. At least, this is the argument of the following essay, which can also be read as a tentative and by no means exhaustive survey of this tradition's achievements and failures. It should be emphasized that the starting point of this survey is immanent. It seeks to avoid "mere moralizing" (to recall Hegel's expression) by thinking with and against several important twentieth-century contributors to a theory of autonomous public life.

The argument begins with Tönnies's pathbreaking critique of public opinion. The narrative then broadens into an examination of Dewey's attempt to retrieve and radicalize the old liberal bourgeois principle of publicity. Dewey's defense of the principle of "free and systematic communication" is seen as especially important, inasmuch as it foregrounds themes of vital importance to more recent critiques of late capitalism – especially those of Jürgen Habermas. During the past several decades, it is argued, Habermas has made the most interesting and ambitious contributions to a socialist theory of public life. These contributions are analyzed and evaluated in some detail. It is proposed that his recent preoccupation with a theory of universal pragmatics is less than fully consistent with itself. Weakened by several internal difficulties, and therefore unable to realize its guiding political intentions and implications, this theoretical project is marked by political retreats. Habermas's advocacy of new forms of public life, it is argued, is contradicted by the abstract and formal mode of reconstructive argumentation that has more and more come to guide his inquiries. The theoretical project of defending the principle of autonomous public life, the remaining third of the essay concludes, must accordingly move beyond the antinomies and formalisms of Habermas's otherwise important arguments. This project must seek to internalize a range of substantive theoretical and political questions, several of which are briefly analyzed.

Toward a critique of public opinion

At the outset, it is important to appreciate the background historical context associated with the rise of theoretical defenses of public life. Evidently, the resurgence of a dissident tradition of public, political thinking during the twentieth century has not been without motivation. It must be seen as an effect of the general advance of bureaucratization since the late nineteenth century and, in particular, as a critical response to the dramatic expansion of corporatist relations between bureaucratically organized institutions of social and state power (see Essay 3). As Hilferding and others first recognized,[2] this corporatist recasting of life was prompted by a number of decisive background developments. The most important of these included the cartelization of economic power within civil society; the emergence of organized capital and labor groupings; the formation of alliances between these interest groups and mass, bureaucratically structured political parties; and, finally, the tendency for bureaucratic states everywhere to claim new and expanded powers of organization, powers that were typically delegated to business, agricultural, and labor organizations. These corporatist tendencies were considerably reinforced by the economic and political mobilizations of World War I, by the heightened struggles between the extra-parliamentary left and right, and by the manifold attempts to accredit organized labor. Everywhere in the heartlands of the capitalist world, political stability was seen by the ruling groups as demanding more bureaucratic and centralized structures of bargaining and control that defied the previous distinction between private power and public authority.

This call for bureaucratic centralization necessarily accelerated the erosion of parliamentary influence and representative government. The locus of bargaining and policy making from this point on began to shift to executive authority, to unofficial party or coalition caucuses, and to networks of state ministries. The formation of political consensus became more and more captive to processes of bargaining among key, bureaucratically organized interests bent on the mobilization of public opinion. This bargaining and mobilization process, it should be emphasized, did not result in the simple *repression* of public life. During this period of transition to late capitalism, bureaucratic organizations increasingly struggled to mobilize and optimize public opinion for particular ends. The ruling corporate and state powers began to rely less upon old-fashioned, public-be-damned strategies; guided by techniques drawn from wartime propaganda and consumer advertising, with the assistance of "counsels on public relations,"[3] public life was to be normalized and put in order. The accumulation of capital, it seemed, more and more presupposed the accumulation of bureaucratic state power, of which the administrative accumulation of public opinion was to be a crucial aspect. Public opinion was to be neither simply obeyed nor evaded. With a high degree of scientific-technical accuracy, it could be expanded and directed, fashioned to suit given interests.

This early twentieth-century disciplining of public life by the forces of order was mediated by intellectual campaigns against what was anachronistically and misleadingly termed the "classical" theory of democracy and public opinion.[4] A growing body of welfare liberal and postliberal discourse[5] now openly questioned the empirical and ethical validity of earlier liberal defenses of the public, especially their presumption of the male, property-owning "omnicompetent citizen."[6] This questioning process typically sustained itself upon deep-seated beliefs in the fruitfulness of empirical-analytic inquiry. The motivational origins of public opinion, it was said, could be uncovered and analyzed. The effectiveness of public opinion management could in turn be measured. Pareto's insistence that public opinion must be seen as an instance of derivations – nonrational actions clothed in idealistic garb[7] – and Wallas's conviction that "the empirical art of politics consists largely in the creation of opinion by the deliberate exploitation of subconscious non-rational preferences"[8] provide two illustrations of a more general tendency during this period to analyze the unconscious forces hidden behind the formation and manipulation of public life. Political men, it was claimed, skillfully exploit privately motivated formulas and compulsive gestures in their efforts at getting results with crowds. Their emotional, erratic behavior is in turn easily incited through the process of imitation and collective suggestion. Motives arising from maladjustments to the environment were said to be susceptible to transference; they could be displaced upon public objects and rationalized in terms of a more universal, public interest.[9]

These kinds of discourses on the motivational points of origin of political action commonly merged with efforts at measuring public opinion.[10] Drawing explicitly on market consumer research,[11] the investigation of public opinion tacitly proposed an equivalence between the universe of consumption and that of politics. Publics, it was announced, could be probed and measured, even predicted. Proceeding from the assumptions, first, that individuals must necessarily hold opinions about all matters and, second, that these opinions could be statistically sampled, tabulated as results, and mathematically reconstructed, the investigations deemed "public opinion" synonymous with the automatic opinion of all and the considered opinion of none: It constituted the sum of empirically existing beliefs of individuals, whose formation within an ensemble of relations of power was accepted (in accordance with a nominalist epistemology) as quite unproblematic.

It is necessary to emphasize that these antidemocratic vindications of the measurement and manufacture of public opinion by no means went unchallenged. Tönnies's discussions of public opinion, best expressed perhaps in his pathbreaking work *Kritik der öffentlichen Meinung*,[12] constitute one of the earliest and most insightful contributions to this resistance. Tönnies's contributions to a critique of public opinion are complex, and can only be sketched here. It suffices here to note that they form part of his more general concern (shared with Weber) with clarifying the meaning of aspects of modern bourgeois society through the elaboration and inductive, empirical rendering of "pure," ideal-typical concepts. In contrast to Weber, however, Tönnies places the category of public opinion (*öffentlichen Meinung*) at the center of his project. According to his schema, the modern civilizing process – the triumph of *gesellschaftliche* formations over those marked by patterns of *Gemeinschaft* – distinctively transforms the predominant types of collective will.[13] Modes of life structured by rationally calculated contracts, state legislation, and public opinion come to predominate. Contracts take the place of familial concord (*Eintracht*); legislation (*Gesetzgebung*) replaces the rustic folkways and mores of custom (*Sitte*); and public opinion – here Tönnies advances beyond Weber – displaces religious faith. The latter have been, the former are becoming, the decisive elements in modern social and political life.[14] In Tönnies's view, modern forms of collective will are increasingly structured by convention or calculation (especially at the site of economic production and exchange), by state legislation that seeks to regulate action by way of the establishment of rational, legal order, and finally by public opinion, which orients itself primarily to the political or ethical aspects of life in the associational type of society.[15]

Tönnies is convinced that the rise of public opinion is coterminous with the disenchantment of modern bourgeois civilization: "In recent centuries, the Christian religion has lost what public opinion has gained."[16] Formerly detested and forcefully proscribed as detrimental to peace and respectability, public opinion more and more places this age under the spell of atheistic criticism and "divisive and disintegrating purposive thought."[17] Public life and public opinion come to be seen as the principal powers in the political cosmos, lighting the paths of governments like guiding stars. The public comes to be loved for the enemies it makes: unproductive tyrants who choke public opinion; malefactors who avoid the detection of judges; the cowardly, who criticize the general incapacity only in defense of their own. The past is confidently berated by the bearers of public opinion as an age of unreasonable darkness. To speak through Tönnies's categories, the form of modern collective will, of which public opinion is a crucial aspect, ceases to be an "essential will [*Wesenwille*]," one defined by its traditional, emotive, or absolutist qualities. The modern collective will instead becomes identical with an "arbitrary will [*Kürwille*]," with forms of thoughtful action structured by the calculation of means of attaining ends reached through deliberation.[18] In accordance with this tendency, the bearers of public opinion manifest their social and political power by way of their approval or disapproval of political events, by demanding that the state adopt certain practices and abolish certain abuses, by insisting upon administrative reforms and legislative measures – in brief, by exercising critical judgments, after the manner of a calculating judge, for the sake of an allegedly common interest.[19]

It should be noted in passing that Tönnies here opposes the tendency of his contemporaries to speak of public opinion as the sum total of vaguely articulated opinions on any matter. Public opinion is not synonymous with the *volonté de tous* (to recall Rousseau's categories). It does not consist in the mere sum of actually existing opinions of individuals; it is not the automatic opinion of all and the considered opinion of none.[20] For Tönnies, on the contrary, public opinion must be viewed as properly directed both to the scrutiny of existing relations of power and to the formation of correct and good actions. The growth of public opinion under modern conditions presupposes reasonable and deliberate subjects who act in accordance with their considered opinions. It presupposes that these competent subjects can define the boundaries and relations between individual, private opinions and the general opinion of a politically conscious public. Public opinion is "a common will which exercises critical judgment for the sake of a common interest and thereby affects private forms of conduct and action in either a restraining or furthering manner."[21]

With reference to contemporary bourgeois societies, Tönnies again and again remarks upon the growing and already tremendous influence of the belief in public opinion so conceived. This belief has become a question of habit, no longer a controversial matter. He advances the thesis that the belief that public opinion is strong and forceful has become a crucial, taken-for-granted aspect of public opinion itself.[22] Through the course of the civilizing process, the power of public opinion begins to resemble that of the various religious creeds that it has supplanted. Public opinion can be compared to a sacred and dominating faith, jealous of its own sovereignty and sure of its own self-vindicating truth. By contrast with its more tenuous status in earlier phases of modernity, public opinion becomes (to invoke Tönnies's physics-derived term) more "solid": To believe in the tenets of public opinion is established as a reasonable conviction – indeed, a universal obligation. Public opinion undergoes something like a deification, assuming the phantasmic appearance of a living body over and above those who are its agents. It is increasingly represented "as a thinking being, and it is frequently either adored or maligned as if it were a Supernatural, quasi-mystical being."[23]

It is precisely this deification of public opinion which provokes a measure of trepidation in Tönnies's analyses. The triumphant emergence of public opinion as a crucial aspect of modernity's collective will is a fundamentally ambiguous development. The persuasive strength of this public opinion, it is observed, is inversely proportional to its authenticity. Tönnies observes Hegel's warning (issued in the *Grundlinien der Philosophie des Rechts*) that public opinion deserves at once to be respected and to be despised. Of fundamental concern to Tönnies is the growing tendency for organized, private interests to transfigure public opinion. He pointedly emphasizes that, in the history of the modern bourgeois world, public opinion has most often been the opinion of the dominant, urban, propertied, and educated classes; "the public" has typically excluded the plebeian classes. He nevertheless insists that the novelty of the contemporary situation consists in its more subtle and transparent formation of (pseudo-)public opinion through administrative means. Nowadays, organized powers become intent on promoting both a favorable opinion of their particular operations and goals and a more generalized public opinion that is in accordance with their own perceived interests. Urged on by the imperative to struggle against, or collude with, perceived opponents who are also bent on opinion making, all organized interests must strive to transform a possible public disfavor into a favorable regard. Public opinion is worked on, manufactured: "Public opinion is belaboured, with the frequent result that *the* public opinion is *made* thereby."[24]

The influence of the organized press (then the leading medium of formal communication) is especially crucial.[25] The press more and more represents itself as the organized expression – indeed, as the reflection – of a public that is in reality an agglomeration of power-seeking, private interests. This commanding, opinion-shaping role of the media flows equally from its formal aspects (such as oligopolistic patterns of ownership and control for the layout of "news"), its selective (or biased) content (editorials, disguised advertising, intentional or un-intentional falsification of events), and its systematic links of dependency with other social power groupings. The symbiotic relationship between organized capital and the press is seen by Tönnies as particularly decisive, inasmuch as advertising, which is the main business of newspapers, is simultaneously a crucial tool in the organizational strategies of commercial and industrial capital.[26] Tönnies therefore concludes that the logic of the production, exchange, and consumption of "judgments and opinion" tends to assume that form common to all commodities: "In this form of communication, judgments and opinion are wrapped up like grocers' goods and offered for consumption in their objective reality. It is prepared and offered to our generation in the most perfect manner by the newspapapers, which make possible the quickest production, multiplication, and distribution of facts and thoughts, just as the hotel kitchen provides food and drink in every conceivable form and quantity."[27]

It was Tönnies's hope that the subordination crystallized within this planned commodification of public opinion would soon come to an end: "Public opinion does not yet risk accepting 'socialism,' but it does no longer dare reject it."[28] The expansion of mass education and reforms of the media, he hoped, would foster the public acceptance of the need to democratize the formation of its own opinions. Of course, his anticipation of a "public ennobling of humanity"[29] was not to be realized. Everywhere in the organized capitalist world, there emerged during his time a deep skepticism within higher circles about the competence of autonomous, politically active publics. This skepticism resembled the earlier conservative turn against Enlightenment. Democratic, public life was denounced as a false, fluctuating, and transitory illusion. Far from being the vital and necessary principle of states, it was reckoned to lead them along false paths, to expose them to continual disturbances. This denunciation at the same time served to justify the bureaucratic management of public opinion. In view of the imminent threats it posed to the stability of the present order, the authority-usurping and perhaps nonrational public was increasingly advised not to proceed beyond the point of a passive conformity. The depoliticization of all spheres of life was viewed as an indispensable condition of the restoration of democratic order. Public business was from this point on to be guided more safely and efficiently by expert administrators, checked only occasionally by a public said to be incapable of leading an autonomous existence. The abandonment of the unworkable fiction of the "omnicompetent citizen" was deemed imperative.[30] Weber's famous defense of a plebiscitarian leader democracy anticipates and summarizes these developments. Under conditions of mass democracy, he concluded, "public opinion is communal conduct, born of irrational 'sentiments'. Normally it is staged or directed by party leaders and the press." As a consequence of the expanded role of the state and the necessities of bureaucratic command, general depoliticization had become imperative: "In a democracy the people choose a leader whom they trust. Then the chosen man says, 'Now shut your mouths and obey me. The people and the parties are no longer free to interfere in the leader's business.' "[31]

Public life defended: Dewey on "free and systematic communication"

Such arguments for depoliticization were by no means uncontested. In addition to Tönnies, several other critics sought to expose the authoritarian potential of the administrative production of public life. So to speak, these critics tried to rescue and radicalize the old bourgeois principle of public life, to turn it against aging bourgeois society itself. These attempts – from Rosa Luxemburg's critique of Lenin and Trotsky to John Dewey's concern over the "eclipse" of public life – form something like a background tradition against which more recent theoretical defenses of autonomous public life can best be understood. Here the influential case of John Dewey's *The Public and Its Problems* (1927) can be briefly analyzed. Building on the criticisms of Tönnies, this work broaches the theme of the eclipse of public life through the insistence that the commonsense political philosophy of the times functions to vindicate the power of ruling officials. According to Dewey, this common sense draws upon false allusions to an already bewildered, no longer existing public. The bourgeois publics that effected parliamentary, representative forms of state have passed away. Whatever their former veracity, the old principles of civic life (such as those embodied in the early American self-governing communities) have become worn out. They serve merely as a litany monotonously recited by those who administer: "The Public seems to be lost; it is certainly bewildered. The government, officials and their activities, are plainly with us...Politics...tends to become just another 'business': the especial concern of bosses and the managers of the machine."[32]

The symptoms of this eclipse of public life are manifold, yet by no means related in an evidently simple way. Dewey mentions the declining participation in formal political events; the proliferation of opinion making by way of hired publicity agents; the privileged access of big business to the state and the media; the growth of centralized, machinelike political parties; the unprecedented increase in the number, variety, and cheapness of amusements that serve as powerful diversions from political concern; the growing authority and role of scientific-technical expertise in state planning; and so on.[33] He insists that this eclipse of public life has no parallel in earlier phases of modern life. This is because the formalization and centralization of political activity is expressive of the universal hold of bureaucratization upon everyday life. Mass production tends no longer to be confined to the factory.[34] Nowadays, many correctly sense that "they are caught in the sweep of forces too vast to understand or master. Thought is brought to a standstill and action paralyzed."[35]

These claims about the unprecedented weakening of public life should not be interpreted as laments for a golden past. In opposition to the positivist new liberal and postliberal discourses on publicity, Dewey defends a radicalized version of the old bourgeois theory of a critical, power-scrutinizing public. He speaks carefully: "The public" is not yet. To form themselves into a more genuine public, marginalized political forces or "publics" (unfortunately unspecified by Dewey) must agitate and organize to break existing forms of institutionalized power.[36] The panacea for an ailing democracy is more democratic, public life.

This would be possible only insofar as these forces or publics established themselves as a self-directing, heterogeneous public, guided its day-to-day functioning, and shared its effects. This recovery of public life would have as its necessary prerequisite a radical expansion of "free and systematic communication."[37] This proposal is striking, inasmuch as it foreshadows a central theme within later critiques of late capitalism. Dewey is certain: The possibility of public life depends upon a radical expansion of those conditions which promote discussion, debate, and the formation of genuine agreement between transacting citizens. Only through "communication and enlightenment" (the radical opposite of force)[38] can the "naturalizing," apolitical tendencies of the present be undone. Dewey supports this proposal through the invocation of a rudimentary philosophical anthropology. He distinguishes mere spontaneous, interconnected behavior (the universalization of which the present promotes, however incompletely) from genuine action.[39] The latter is equivalent to forms of activity "saturated and regulated by mutual interest in shared meanings." The capacity for action is peculiar to the species. This faculty is defined by our ability to produce signs, through which enduring collective experience can be transmitted, considered, and willfully ruptured and reconstructed. In accordance with this ontology, Dewey defends the possibility of a liberation of action through the defense of autonomous public life. So conceived, public life would presuppose "face-to-face relationships" and the developed capacity of citizens to individuate themselves through the give and take of argumentation. It would sustain itself upon the promotion of a "critical sense and methods of discriminating judgement" and, conversely, the shattering of "emotional habituations and intellectual habitudes."[40] Public opinion, for the first time, would thereby become synonymous with those critical judgments formed and entertained by those who actively constituted the public. There could be no democratic public life without full "publicity" in respect of all matters that concerned it. This is Dewey's maxim: Whatever obstructs and restricts communication also limits and distorts the formation of a democratic and many-sided public.

Through this thesis, Dewey effects a radical inversion of the conventional (Weberian) meaning of the concept of the political. No longer equivalent to the struggle for power over others or the legitimate territorial organization of the means of violence, politics must in future become synonymous, Dewey suggests, with those processes by which a public organizes itself. This self-government could be implemented through the public's own officials, who would be constituted to perform their functions of caring for those who have empowered them.[41] The state would thereby become identical with an ensemble of public institutions continually searched for, scrutinized, criticized. By virtue of the open-endedness of political life so defined, "*the* just state" would be a figment of the antipolitical imagination. With respect to questions concerning both form and content, there is no single state that can be said to be best, save that which itself maximizes autonomous public life – and therefore its continual self-transformation. The formation of states would of necessity be an experimental process, open to the contingencies of historical creation.

153

Habermas: from undisturbed freedom to publicity

Dewey's defense of the possibility of free and systematic communication need not at this point be analyzed further. The sketch of his theory of self-government, reinforced by the brief remarks on Tönnies, serves merely to foreground the contours of recent developments in the socialist theory of public life. During the past several decades, the single most decisive contribution to this development, within the German-speaking socialist tradition at least, has undoubtedly been that of Jürgen Habermas. Concerned to develop insights into a range of problems pertaining to communicative competence and systematically distorted communications, Habermas's theoretical project can properly be seen as guided by concerns that have directly political implications. These concerns, which parallel remarkably those of Tönnies and Dewey, are by no means marginal within either his earlier or his later writings. Habermas has consistently and provocatively emphasized that late capitalist societies are profoundly threatened by bureaucratic, antipolitical tendencies. From even before the time of his classic account (in *Strukturwandel der Öffentlichkeit* [1962]) of the "refeudalization" of the liberal capitalist public sphere, through to his more recent writings on communication, Habermas has remained preoccupied with problems of public life. Highly critical of the advance of bureaucratic organization in all spheres of activity, he has consistently written on behalf of the possibility of a postmodern socialist order, in which life would properly be organized around the principle of the maximum feasible sharing of responsibility and face-to-face involvement, participation, and democratic control.

Following Tönnies and Dewey, Habermas emphasizes that public life under late capitalist conditions becomes the object of bureaucratic administration. He too recognizes that the persuasive strength of public opinion is often enough inversely proportional to its authenticity, that authentic public opinion is therefore not the mere sum of actually existing opinions of individuals and groups. Habermas also denies that we are "by nature" apathetic, private, and apolitical beings. Current levels of disinterest in questions of power and politics and the widespread inability (or unwillingness) to deliberate, criticize, and effect decisions actively through common involvements within autonomous public spheres – all these well-known features of daily life under late capitalist conditions seem to him to be a temporary and highly contingent consequence of a bureaucratic, disciplinary, and very unequal society. Like Tönnies and Dewey before him, he therefore remains convinced of the need to argue on behalf of the counterbureaucratic goal of "public, unrestricted discussion, free from domination."[42]

Unfortunately, almost all English-speaking interpreters of Habermas's *oeuvre* have so far failed to acknowledge this point adequately.[43] Preoccupied with other, less political themes, they forget that Habermas's defense of forms of nonbureaucratic rationality is already displayed within his earliest works of the 1950s. These writings are evidently structured by the distinction between the sphere of necessity and realms in which the goal of undisturbed freedom (*Musse*) can be realized (see Essay 4). The later Habermas was to retain this distinction between the spheres of necessity and freedom, amending it with the more explicitly political themes prominent in the above-cited works of Tönnies, Dewey, and others writing during the 1920s. Although the distinction between the toil and unfreedom of work and an autonomous realm of freedom was to be preserved, the latter realm would be specified through considerably different arguments. This shift of perspective is evident in numerous works from the time of *Strukturwandel der Öffentlichkeit*. The textual evidence suggests that this political turn in Habermas's work developed under the immediate influence of both Jaspers's theory of "limitless communication" and, especially, the works of his student, Hannah Arendt.[44]

Through the distinction between the two types of progress founded on the work–communication dualism, Habermas launches a radical critique of late capitalist societies. This critique no longer focuses upon the problem of undisturbed freedom and the need for cultural creativity. He argues instead that the general advance of bureaucratic organization is systematically obliterating all authentic forms of communicative action. He indicts late capitalist bureaucratization processes for their radical monopolization of the whole of social and political life, for their crushing of free and systematic communication *outside* or *beyond* the realm of social labor. Recalling Aristotle, he insists that purposive-rational, bureaucratic activity can only be appropriate in a *limited* domain – that of work. Political life, by contrast, must develop outside the boundaries and imperatives of bureaucracy and its hierarchic, centralized relations of command and obedience. The democratic opposition to late capitalist social formations must reassert the classical goal of citizenship, pursue the vision of speakers and actors as competent *zōon politikon*. Within the realm of the political, or so Habermas urges, classless, postmodern societies would strive to abolish the categories of "above" and "below." In principle, all relations of power embedded within the realm of communication would at all times become the possible objects of discursive scrutiny by any or all speaking actors.

This thesis parallels remarkably that of Dewey in particular. Yet the novelty and decisive political importance of Habermas's theory of communication consist in its development of what remains merely a hint in Dewey's philosophical anthropology. It attempts to ground philosophically and thereby to substantiate the vision of democratic, public life. During the last decade or so,[45] this grounding has been attempted through the so-called theory of universal pragmatics, whose arguments seek to elaborate the universal rules in accordance with which all communicative action is produced and reproduced. In view of the trajectory of these arguments, it is somewhat surprising to hear frequent remarks (in private, at least) that the theory of universal pragmatics is of little political relevance. Such impatient and disillusioned allegations have to be handled with the greatest of care. Indeed, only partial sympathy is extended to these allegations in the reading of Habermas proposed here. Thinking with and against Habermas, the remainder of this essay accepts some of the force of these allegations without, however, rejecting in toto the significance of his contributions to a socialist theory of public life. His valuable advocacy of alternative forms of public life, it is proposed, is contradicted by the mode of reconstructive and abstract and formal argumentation that sustains his project, especially in its most recent phase. As a consequence of this contradiction, or so it shall be argued, this ambitious and brilliant project cannot follow up on its own aims and political implications.

Habermas's persistent ambivalence about the political status and implications of the theory of universal pragmatics can be seen as a key symptom of this contradiction. Especially in his more recent writings, for instance, he humbly warns against treating the preliminary results of this theory as an ideal to be practically realized. The claims of universal pragmatics, he believes, must be argued for *theoretically* and at the level of inquiries that are at the outset not committed to any particular political project. The theory of universal pragmatics is intended as an abstractly formal, universalist account of human competences. It is not a theory with immediately political intentions, and certainly it does not depict actual or possible forms of life. Habermas does not always consistently observe these caveats, however, and it is precisely this ambivalence within his inquiries – his simultaneous denial and acknowledgment of their substantive political implications – which serves as the starting point of the following im-manent criticism of his writings on communication. Commonly enough, for example, the theory of universal pragmatics is said to be concerned only with highly restricted, "clear case" forms of communication – with "consensual" forms of speaking and acting – the analysis of whose logic, he further claims, can nevertheless be cumulatively extended to cover other, derivative forms of action, including, presumably, public or political action itself.[46] Elsewhere, for instance in a reply to Apel,[47] Habermas's abstractly formal references to "the species" and its dependence on language are developed into the conclusion that we are fated to rely on the "non-deceptive use of language," whose rules can be recon-structed by way of a theory of universal pragmatics.

Such talk of a species competence that *can* be exercised by every adult speaker of a natural language understandably heightens the suspicion that Habermas's concerns are immanently political. This suspicion is again reinforced, finally, by his flexible, sometimes careless deployment of concepts associated with the theory of communication into his political recommendations, and vice versa. "Discursive will formation," "communication freed from domination," and "public, unre-stricted discussion" are just three of these migratory concepts; freely traveling to and fro across the boundaries of his theoretical and political writings, such concepts arouse the expectation that his theoretical project is guided by explicitly political concerns, concerns that are nevertheless firmly denied. Once more, or so I argue here, the theory of universal pragmatics is evidently marked by a self-paralyzing contradiction. Unable to realize the political promise of its own claims, the theory stimulates the need for its own transcendence – in the direction of a theory of autonomous public life.

Toward a general theory of communication

A critical rereading of the theory of universal pragmatics and its associated claims – concerning the ideal speech situation, communicative competence, the problem of ideology, and so on – must form the point of departure in this strategy of transcendence. Concerned to rescue the theory of universal pragmatics from lapsing into depoliticized and overly formalistic claims, this rereading feeds upon the expectations that the theory's claims have themselves generated. These political inferences are strongly evidenced in the theory's concern with analyzing the "universal validity basis of speech"[48] and, thereby, the general capacities necessary for the *competent* performance of public speech acts. In view of this goal, Habermas might be seen as the Kant of the theory of speech and action. His universal pragmatics aims at an elucidation of the fundamental dialogue-constitutive universals that underpin or "preconstruct" each and every speech act. Habermas denies that the logic of our speaking and acting is mysterious, merely conventional, or simply arbitrary. The theory of universal pragmatics instead attempts a summary of the unavoidable and universal presuppositions that all adult speakers, irrespective of their natural language or dialect or particular historical context, must master competently if they are to engage in intelligible communication at all.[49]

In attempting this summary, Habermas acknowledges the crucial importance of the stress placed upon the performative aspects of speech by the ordinary language philosophy tradition from the time of Wittgenstein. He nevertheless insists that the well-known descriptivism that plagued Wittgenstein's analysis of language games must be transcended. The analysis of the pragmatic dimensions of communicative action must no doubt encompass the dynamics of particular speech acts within particular contexts, but only by reconstructing the general, unavoidable, and therefore universal principles that structure *all* speech acts.[50]

In furthering this claim, Habermas makes a crucial assumption. Communication, he argues, is a matter of performing speech acts in accordance with binding systems of rules that, even if only implicitly or intuitively, we *already and always* follow. Such rules or presuppositions are at the same time assumed to generate and describe that intersubjectivity which makes possible mutuality of understanding between competent speakers. These "anonymous" presuppositions, to use Searle's expression, are "constitutive rules" in the strict sense that they do not merely regulate but also create or preconstruct all forms of communicative action.[51]

In respect of this assumption, and drawing upon the work of Apel, Habermas insists that all unbroken or undisturbed communicative activity, regardless of its superficially heterogeneous character, presupposes a cluster of interrelated rules or claims.[52] These so-called validity claims (*Geltungsansprüche*) together form a kind of background consensus (*Hintergrundkonsensus*) upon which all ordinary communication depends. This deep-rooted, rule-structured consensus establishes the conditions of communicative action among the species; it constitutes a "species competence."[53] All participants within "language games" always and already, that is, *involuntarily*, presume that their communicative actions are self-consciously in accord with this consensus and its general rules, whose existence can in turn be vindicated or made plausible through discursive argumentation. In brief, communication already presupposes (among the interlocutors concerned) a tacit agreement about what it means to communicate. Conversely, communicative action already presupposes some measure of awareness of the possibility of the breakdown of communication because of speaking actors' failure to fulfill the so-called validity claims.

Habermas asserts that four such primordial claims can be identified: first, that speakers' utterances can be understood by others; second, that the knowledge or propositions that speakers are attempting to communicate are "true"; third, that speakers are in agreement concerning the normative rules that they establish and within whose boundaries they speak and act; and, finally, that speakers are "authentic," that is, sincere in speaking and therefore trustworthy.[54] These claims to, respectively, intelligibility, truth, rightness, and veracity can here be analyzed more fully. In the first place, communication can be sustained or remain undisturbed only if speakers make both their relations with others (as expressed in such performative utterances as promising and announcing) and the meaning of the propositional content of their utterances *intelligible*. This comprehensibility clause is partly fulfilled (as Chomsky's theory of linguistic competence has stressed) when speakers utter sentences that are grammatically well formed. However, agreement through communication is also and always conditional upon the deployment of intersubjectively valid or meaningful symbols, that is, upon a shared, reciprocally recognized awareness of the significance of chains of signifiers. Only if these two aspects of the intelligibility claim are satisfied does it become possible, in Habermas's view, for speaking actors to recognize the meaning of symbols from their own standpoint and that of others at the same time. In the absence of this "interlacing of perspectives,"[55] speaking actors could only assume the position of mute animals, drowned within an unintelligible ensemble of private meanings and utterances.

In addition to this presumption of comprehensibility, communicating actors raise different validity claims. The second of these operates within the referential dimension of speech,[56] in accordance with which contexts are objectified and spoken about as "the" world. Inasmuch as speech acts purport to say something about someone or something else (that is, about the totality of existing affairs, or what Habermas sometimes calls "the external world"), all unbroken communication presupposes that speaking subjects mutually recognize the propositional truth of their exchanged speech acts. Certainly, Habermas opposes Austin's suggestion that all four validity claims concern propositional truth.[57] He nevertheless maintains that all standard speech actions always contain a "constative" or propositional component. All continuous communication presumes that interlocutors share and agree upon their knowledge through the deployment of propositional sentences that truthfully represent a really existing state of affairs.

Thirdly, undisturbed communication presumes that there already exists a genuine and mutually recognized accord between speakers. All uninterrupted communication presupposes that all parties *can* and *do* recognize the appropriateness or rightness (*Richtigkeit*) of the normative rules to which their speech acts contribute, and in accordance with which those acts (of recommending, promising, prohibiting, and so on) are structured as acceptable or legitimate. The ensemble of speech acts that make up communicative activity cannot therefore be understood as the achievement of isolated, purposive-rational actors. All successfully executed communicative action always infers that participants' actions are in conformity with certain normative expectations. Such action supposes that hearers accept and enter into the "offers" proposed by speakers, into what Habermas calls the "social world" of normatively regulated, interpersonal relations.

Fourthly, and finally, communicating actors always infer that their exchanged speech acts satisfy a condition of mutual trust. In addition to presumptions about the intelligibility, validity, and legitimacy of utterances, all uninterrupted interaction rests upon the presumption that speakers are authentic and sincere in expressing themselves (that is, in divulging what Habermas calls their "particular inner world") and are therefore worthy of the trust accorded to them by their hearers. Communication can continue undisturbed if, and only if, speakers suppose that they already act in accordance with a "sincerity rule."[58] All communicating actors infer, in short, that the truthfulness or veracity (*Wahrhaftigkeit*) of their utterances need not, indeed must not, be called into question.

One point should be noted immediately about this validity claims schema, a point that is of considerable relevance to a socialist theory of public life. The theory of validity claims launches perhaps the most novel insight in Habermas's recent writings: Within all undisturbed communicative action, he says, this cluster of interdependent validity claims serves as an immanent standard against which the authenticity of communication can be evaluated. These claims counterfactually anticipate what, under late capitalist conditions, has not yet come to pass: free, systematic communication. "In communicative action," Habermas insists, "participants presuppose that they know what mutual recognition of reciprocally raised validity claims means."[59] By way of this thesis, he acknowledges Gadamer's claim (drawn in turn from Heidegger) that a "deep common accord [*tiefes Einverständnis*]" is presupposed within all communicative interaction.[60] This fundamental insight is turned back on Gadamer's philosophic conservatism. For this deep-seated common understanding (in accordance with which speaking actors engage each other) cannot be described, as Gadamer wants to claim, in terms of an enduring, customary tradition that exercises a largely unquestionable power over its bearers. The supporting consensus that sustains all communicative action has, rather, a profoundly political or *public* character. Communicative action already and always presupposes the emancipatory, political goal of subjects' living together and reaching agreement through reciprocal understanding, shared knowledge, common accord, and mutual trust. Although they rarely in fact achieve this under late capitalist conditions, all communicating speakers and actors necessarily and unavoidably proceed as if their speech and action were competent and situated within a genuinely public arena. To invoke Habermas's expression, all unbroken or undisturbed communication both presupposes and prefigures an "ideal speech situation," wherein "communication is not only not hindered by external, contingent influences, but also not hindered by forces which result from the structure of communication itself."[61]

On communicative competence

Through the thesis of the ideal speech situation, Habermas strengthens his case for the recovery of the classical Aristotelian category of politics (as public speak-

159

ing and acting) against late capitalist bureaucratization. At least, the political implications of the theory of universal pragmatics become rather more explicit, for Habermas urges that the principle of the ideal speech situation – the conviction that social relations could be organized "according to the principle that the validity of every norm of political consequence be made dependent on a consensus arrived at in communication free from domination"[62] – is implicit within all communicative action. Entering into a communicative relationship implies an obligation to make one's utterances intelligible, to provide good grounds for one's assertions, as well as an obligation to justify one's values in a trustworthy way. This means that the capacity to engage freely and competently in rule-structured communication is continually present, as it were, behind the backs of all those who speak and act within a communicative setting. Contrary to Gouldner and others,[63] this communicative competence cannot therefore be spoken of as a "norm"; strictly speaking, communicative competence is already presupposed and anticipated even before attempts are made to reconstruct and defend it by way of a *theory* of communicative competence. Communicative competence therefore has (in Freud's sense) an *illusory* status. With the gentle but irresistible force of transcendental necessity, this competence is at all times anticipated within communicative action. To engage the speech and action of others unwittingly implies the will to engage in consensual speech and action emancipated from all forms of domination. "Our first sentence," Habermas says in one of his earliest and most daring formulations, "expresses unequivocally the intention of universal and unconstrained consensus."[64] This intention cannot be analyzed either as a moralizing, regulative principle (Kant) or as an extant empirical reality (an *existing* concept, in Hegel's sense). It must be understood, rather, as an "operationally effective fiction"[65] that communicating participants must reciprocally and unavoidably impute to one another. All communicative action supposes, in short, that this fiction should be given its due, that it has (here Habermas adopts the language of Lask)[66] a certain worthiness to be recognized or acknowledged (*Anerkennungswürdigkeit*).

As a consequence of its positing of the ideal speech principle, Habermas's universal pragmatics may be taken as *implying* or inferring a radically political vision: that of communicative competence, of *Mündigkeit*, of individuated and autonomous citizens learning to deliberate, speak, and act for themselves in autonomous public spheres. This inferred vision is particularly evident in both his earliest writings on communication and his more recent writings on ego development.[67] So envisaged, communicative competence would be conditional upon the fulfillment of three necessary conditions. In the first place, the attempt to foster communicative competence would depend upon the development of symmetrical, reciprocal relations between speaking actors. This reciprocity would facilitate "an unlimited interchangeability of dialogue roles,"[68] such that no one speaker (or group of speakers) could rightly monopolize the powers and means of assertion, disputation, and persuasion. Under conditions of authentic public life, the speech and action of individuals and groups could not legitimately be sacrificed before abstractly defined or allegedly imperative opinions and norms ("the national interest," the "dictatorship of the proletariat," and so on).[69] Genuinely *intersubjective* communication would be conditional upon the reciprocal self-representation of individual speaking subjects who acknowledged each other.

In respect of this mutuality, Habermas insists that communicative competence ought not be confused with Chomsky's notion of linguistic competence. For Chomsky, such competence consists in individuals' creative mastery of an abstract network of linguistic rules, with the aid of which they can correctly produce chains of utterances.[70] Habermas rightly objects: Chomsky misleadingly assumes that this system of "generative" linguistic rules is somehow innate. Individuals' production and reproduction of these rules is wrongly assumed to be a process that unfolds monologically, that is, according to an "informational model of communication."[71] It is as if each sender and receiver of utterances is already and always an entity for itself, a solitary entity already outfitted with certain preestablished language rules, in terms of whose universal applicability and meaning communication with other individuals becomes possible. Habermas is adamant that this formulation thoroughly depreciates the pragmatic and inter-subjective dimensions of competent speaking and acting. Public, communicative competence is, and will always be, conditional upon subjects' practical mastery of dialogue-constitutive rules, their performance of speech acts within a language-structured context of intersubjectivity. This capacity for intersubjectivity is already anticipated under conditions of undisturbed communication: "Utterances are never simply sentences. Even if they do not expressly make pragmatic relations their subject, they are integrated from the beginning into a form of intersubjectivity of mutual understanding owing to their illocutionary force [that is, to the fact of their "doing something in saying something" in relation to others]."[72]

The nonidentity or autonomy of individuals and groups would constitute a second necessary condition of democratic, public life. Conceived as the development of genuinely intersubjective communities of speaking actors, democratic public life would not be incompatible with processes of individuation. According to Habermas, individuation could only be developed in and through genuinely democratic processes of public life. Such individuation is by no means "onto-logically given," as Chomsky and others assume. While beginning in the early phases of psychosexual development, individuation could only be *accomplished politically* through the development of a subtle interplay of "nearness and distance" between public, speaking actors. Autonomous public life would be marked by the same paradox analyzed in Hegel's famous model of the quarreling lovers (see Essay 4): Individuals, Habermas implies, would assert themselves against nonidentical others by way of the recognition of themselves in others.[73] Individuation would therefore presuppose a growing capacity of subjects to distinguish (and insist upon the difference between) their inner, private and outer, public worlds.[74] In the course of their public activities, subjects would unavoidably express themselves and their inviolable distance from others, even as they depended upon and interacted with others, with whom they would already be conjoined in a subtle, language-mediated relationship of nearness. This dialectic of identity and nonidentity would also operate at the level of relations between different collectivities. A democratic, public society can be envisaged only as pluralistic, as maximizing individuation and group diversity within a community setting. Habermas's implied model of democratic, public life therefore recognizes no fantastic futures, in which existence would become free, easy, and rid of division. Future public life, he infers, would openly recognize, indeed encourage, a plurality of groups and political divisions.[75] Under socialist conditions, the real antagonist of democratic, public life would be not the presence of particularities – competing claims, political quarrels, and disputes – but, rather, the denial of their legitimacy.

The implication that reciprocity and individuation are two necessary conditions of public life infers a third: the unfettering of critical discussion. Liberated from any form of official evaluation from above, discussion under conditions of genuine public life would be unrestricted. No dogmatically fixed or majority opinion could permanently avoid being made the object of public debate and criticism. Political space would be created wherein the hitherto minority position of a fraction of the public could become, through sustained, unrestricted, and compelling argument, acceptable to broader sections of the political community. Obviously, such unfettering of communication would depend upon the equalization of speakers' access to the available means of communication. (It would no doubt also depend upon a radical reconstruction of the presently available means of communication, although Habermas does not directly discuss this problem.) Only thereby could participants "horizontally" initiate discussion about their needs, invoke hypotheses that shattered the ruling truth claims, and perpetuate such communication through further questions, answers, demands, recommendations, promises, and so on. This would imply, in (the likely) cases of breakdowns of agreement, citizens' capacity to suspend action temporarily, so as to move over into "discourse" (as Habermas calls it),[76] that is, into deliberation freed from the constraints of organization and action.

Through such discourse oriented to reaching agreement, public discussants could fully exploit the "double structure" of speech acts by communicating about states of affairs as well as about their communication as such.[77] Depending upon discursive argumentation, subjects' hitherto repressed or heteronomously constructed needs and principles could be mutually redefined and acted upon. The validity of social and political principles would cease to be dependent upon the already established authority of groups or persons holding these principles. Imposed norms would be distinguished from norms that were in principle capable of discursive justification; at this level of communicative competence, norms could be "normed."[78] Only under such conditions of uncensored discussion would it be justified to equate existing political agreements and compromises with genuine agreements and compromises reached without violence. Authentic public life would be structured by the principle of rational speech. In accordance with this principle, or so Habermas implies, the truth of judgments and observations about facts would be synonymous with a public consensus reached, guaranteed, yet always contestable through unlimited and permanently renewable communication. This formulation contradicts Arendt's classical thesis that truthtelling is antipolitical and that public life is therefore properly the sphere of opinionated agreement and consent.[79] Nietzsche's observation that truth must always be equivalent to the solidification of old metaphors is also emphatically rejected. Pitted against mere opinion and old metaphors, the so-called consensus theory of truth insists that the validity of utterances (and their claims to propositional truth, normative appropriateness, and veracity) cannot be decided without reference both to the competency of those who decide and to the conditions under which agreements are reached. The truth of any politically negotiated consensus, in short, could not be decided without reference to the (non-)fulfillment of the validity claims upon which all communication is grounded. Conversely, public opinion could be considered authentic only if it had been achieved (and was capable of further renewal) under these three conditions of autonomous public life – conditions that maximized critical and unforced argumentation between individuated, equal, and communicatively competent citizens.

Systematically distorted communication

From the time of his earliest formulations of the theory of universal pragmatics, Habermas was of course acutely aware that numerous mechanisms serve to repress and conceal these conditions of public, communicative competence. He never assumed that Socratic forms of communication are everywhere and instantly possible. Late capitalist patterns of communication, he recognized, are also the site of the exercise of pseudocompromise and violence; precisely because of this, they cannot be described as (genuine) communication at all. Indeed, no previous society has lived in conformity with the principle of rational speech.[80] The history of all hitherto-existing societies, including those in the modern world that have had universal, democratic pretensions, has been a history of systematically deformed communication and struggles to overcome that repression. Every known social formation has been marked by attempts to distort the universal capacity to speak and act politically, to check its conflict potential through skewed distributions of state and social power, property, and communicative ability.

Habermas's advocacy of free, systematic communication finds itelf in opposition to these authoritarian tendencies. In relation to the past, the theory of universal pragmatics implies the need for dissipating the naturelike grip of authoritarian traditions on the present. Their dogmatic truth claims must be criticized, their important insights preserved.[81] With direct reference to the conditions of late capitalism, the theory of universal pragmatics also commits itself to the distinction between an imposed, "actually achieved consensus" and a genuine or "rational consensus" without deception.[82] Thereby it concedes the substance of Tönnies's thesis that public opinion must frequently be doubted, that this opinion's persuasive strength is often inversely proportional to its authenticity. This fundamental distinction between a rational and an actual consensus is plausible, Habermas argues, because the promise of unfettered speech and action immanent within all communication itself serves as a measure of the degree to which every actually achieved consensus is false. To illustrate this thesis, Habermas invokes the metaphor of the trial. The ideal of communicative competence is said to serve as a "court of evaluation [*Bewertungsinstanz*]" within

163

which any existing consensus can be brought to trial and interrogated concerning its claims to be a warranted consensus. Genuine opinion is not necessarily equivalent to the sum of actually existing opinions; it is not identical with the automatic opinion of all and the considered opinion of none. Actually existing agreements between speaking actors have no ultimate finality, as has been claimed in recent theoretical discussions of power and interest.[83]

Granted this distinction between two forms of consensus, Habermas infers that false or inauthentic agreements can be induced by at least two interrelated processes: speakers' internalization of authoritarian power relations (through the familial supervision of their psychosexual development, for example) and the uneven distribution of dialogue possibilities among nations, classes, regions, social groups, and individuals. Under such conditions of induced misunderstanding and deception, Habermas insists that there can be no presumption in favor of a rational consensus on the prevailing distribution of power. Any falsely induced consensus finds its limits or "otherness" in the always implied logic of free and systematic communication. Free and systematic communication therefore names its foe: systematically deformed communication. Habermas explicitly invokes and defends Walter Benjamin's sarcastic warning: "Pessimism all along the line. Absolutely...but above all, mistrust, mistrust and again mistrust in all mutual understanding reached between classes, nations, individuals. And unlimited trust only in I. G. Farben and the peaceful perfection of the *Luftwaffe*."[84]

Guided by this warning, Habermas is led to speak of distorted communication as the mutilation or dumbfounding of potentially free speaking and acting subjects. Such destruction of the capacity for public, communicative competence may assume either of two generically interrelated forms. In cases of psychotic character deformation, the destruction of communicative action results from faults internal to the organization of speech acts themselves.[85] These psychotic deformations (analyzed by Freud, upon whom Habermas explicitly draws) are seen to have originated within the young child's experience of suffering, and its attempted repulsion through unconsciously motivated forgetting. Typically, deformed communication of this first type displays a distinct dissonance between actors' utterances and their actions and accompanying gestures. The relatively coherent structure of undisturbed communication disintegrates; utterances, actions, and bodily gestures become estranged from one another. In addition, psychotically deformed communications can be described in terms of their evident contravention of patterns of speech that are recognized as binding or conventional. The absence of grammatical sense or the utilization of opposite words (and, therefore, the peculiar mingling of conventionally incompatible meanings) might be taken as instances of this contravention. Finally, psychotically deformed communication displays a certain compulsive repetitiousness and rigidity. The chronically reflective action of undisturbed communication degenerates into recurrent, stereotyped behavior, whose emotiveness is often unexpectedly catalyzed by external stimuli. The daily life of psychotic actors is held captive by certain archaic "palaeosymbols," by the private "inner foreign territory" (Freud) of compulsive fantasies and emotion-charged images. Accordingly, psychotics cannot easily dissociate their private fixations upon archaic symbols from their publicly expressed utterances, actions, and bodily gestures.

Psychotically deformed communication should be analytically distinguished, in Habermas's view, from a second form of distorted communication – that of "pseudocommunication." In contradistinction to psychotic communication, pathological disturbances or blockages within patterns of pseudocommunication assume a transparent form. These disturbances are not recognized by speaking actors as destructive of their subjectivity as such. Communication is invisibly marked with "unrecognized dependencies." Laboring under the illusion that they have reached genuine agreement through communicatively competent negotiations, interlocutors perpetuate mutual misunderstanding and self-misunderstanding without interruption. The validity claims of speech are naïvely assumed, even though they remain in fact unfulfilled. Under such conditions of voluntary servitude, "participants do not recognize any communication disturbances. Pseudocommunication produces a system of reciprocal misunderstandings, which are not recognized as such, due to the pretence of pseudoconsensus."[86]

Political action as therapy?

The boundaries of this typology of distorted communication are obviously incomplete. The silent pseudoconsensus induced by the systematic deployment of force or terror, for instance, remains unanalyzed.[87] This stimulating typology nevertheless provokes a series of questions concerning its political and strategic implications. Which forms of political life and tactics, we are prompted to ask, are most appropriate to fostering the awareness that an imposed and a genuine consensus are not identical? Which political strategies and organizations are most conducive to the defense of autonomous public life? How, in short, can dominated subjects emancipate themselves from themselves? It is clear that Habermas, in response to such questions, firmly rejects all justifications of the legitimacy and efficacy of vanguardist strategies. This refusal – uncompromisingly directed at Lukács and, implicitly, a long and respected tradition of Western political thought from the time of Plato[88] – directly draws upon Aristotle's theory of moral-practical knowledge and prudent political action (see Essay 4). Authentic political action, in Habermas's view, must always be guided by a certain foresight and clarity about its potentials and possible consequences. Such knowledge of "what is to be done" nevertheless cannot be possessed or applied in the manner of artful, technical knowledge. To be politically competent is not identical with knowing what, at all times and under all circumstances, is good for all. Political action cannot totalize history, tie all problems together, and happily orient itself to a future that is already written in the present and in which all problems will be neatly solved. Political action cannot flatter itself on its capacity to grasp the whole directly, for it is risky action in the process of self-invention. "Attempts at emancipation," Habermas stresses,

> can, under certain circumstances, be rendered plausible as *practical* [in the Aristotelian sense] necessities, taking into consideration the conflicts generated by the

165

system (which have to be explained theoretically) and the avoidable repressions and suffering. But such attempts are also tests; they test the limits within which "human nature" can be changed and above all, the limits of the historically variable structure of motivation, limits about which we possess no theoretical knowledge and, in my view, cannot in principle possess. If in testing "practical hypotheses" of this kind, we, the subjects involved, are ourselves included in the design of the experiment, then no barrier between experimenter and subjects can be erected. Instead, all the participants must have the opportunity to know what they are doing – thus, they must form a common will discursively.[89]

According to this compelling view, autonomous public life is conditional upon speaking actors' *self-involvement* in particular political acts. Becoming political can only be a developmental process, a discretionary capacity exercised through discussion, risk taking, and action within particular power situations. Accordingly, any movement that seeks to defend public life through reliance upon purposive-rational, bureaucratic means contradicts itself. This self-contradiction, Habermas claims, is evident in Lukács's classic formulation of the party as the mediator of theory and praxis. Not only does this formulation artificially tailor theoretical discourse to the alleged imperatives of organized, strategic action ("pure theory" is seen as proof of "opportunism"); the process of enlightenment of the oppressed (namely, the proletariat, who Lukács insists must not suffer "a terrible internal ideological crisis")[90] is also to be subordinated to the cunning designs of the Party leadership. Habermas flatly rejects such formulas. The immunity of the political educators from political education by others cannot, without certain authoritarian, bureaucratic consequences, be posited as given, necessary, or desirable. In the struggle against distorted communication and pseudocommunication, he intimates, all decisions of consequence must be made to depend on the practical discussion of the participants concerned.

In his earlier discussions of the theory of communication, at least, this thesis was elaborated with reference to certain methodological insights of psychoanalysis. It is true that Habermas's very first interest in Freud concentrated upon the implications of Mitscherlich's theses on the contemporary decline of patriarchal bourgeois authority.[91] Later, Habermas came to follow Alfred Lorenzer: He interpreted the psychoanalytic therapy situation as a mode of analysis of distorted communication and, by implication, an exemplar of the strategy through which a revitalized, socialist public sphere might be achieved politically.[92] Psychoanalytic therapy was understood as a critical and emancipatory mode of explanatory understanding structured by the regulative principle of the ideal speech situation. To invoke Habermas's terms, it is a form of "scenic understanding," a "depth hermeneutic [*Tiefenhermeneutik*]" that aims to break the power of the past over the present through future-oriented memory.[93] Like the theory-mediated, political struggle for genuine intersubjectivity, psychoanalytic therapy seeks to criticize (and thereby to promote patients' liberation from) distorted communication; psychoanalysis seeks to realize this goal through the systematic reliance upon self-reflection "materialized" or grounded in discussion. Psychoanalysis is a form of language analysis oriented to the restriction of "unconsciously motivated action" and the expansion of domains of intersubjectivity within which subjects' self-interrogation and cross-examination can proceed freely and systematically.

The history and controversial substantive details of psychoanalysis are of minor interest in this context. Of crucial importance, according to the earlier Habermas, is that the relationship between analyst and patients is in principle directly analogous to the association between interlocutors that obtains in the political struggle for public life. The analyst, like the political actor, seeks to understand others' distorted reactions as meaningful (and perhaps even as resting on good reasons). At the same time, both the activist and the analyst are concerned to provoke a corresponding reorganization in others' self-interpreted speech acts. Habermas extends the analogy further. In the enlightenment process, both the critical theory of communication and psychoanalytic theory serve as advocates of the possibility of genuine, nondeceptive communication. Each seeks to interrogate its addressees critically, to induce their self-reflection on the validity of the theory's own claims *and* on their own captivity within relations of domination and power. Both theoretical discourses seek in other words to initiate processes of critical reflection, to catalyze subjects' *self-liberation* through free and systematic communication.

Two immediate objections can be raised against this invocation of psychoanalysis as an exemplar of the critique of distorted communication. Both objections, which Habermas now acknowledges, but to whose implications he has not satisfactorily responded, derive from the strong suspicion that his analogy between the psychoanalytic therapy situation and radical political activity was from the outset highly misleading. In the first place, Habermas's own critique of Freud's scientism already pointed out that the Freudian therapy situation is premised upon the professional authority and expertise of the analyst.[94] Granted, the Freudian schema insists that patients' initial deference to this authority is "voluntarily" willed. Moreover, the process of validation of the claims of psychoanalysis seems consistent with Habermas's proposed consensus theory of truth: in the final analysis, the objects of analysis are the authorities, and, accordingly, they must themselves confirm (or deny) the hypotheses of the analyst, perhaps even supplementing them with their own self-understandings.[95] Finally, the psychoanalyst must refrain from making proposals for patients' prospective actions. These must be decided by patients themselves.[96]

Despite these caveats, the enacted therapeutic dialogue is in another respect singularly monologic. At the outset, as Habermas has subsequently admitted,[97] the relationship of the partners in therapeutic discourse is by no means egalitarian. Nor are their positions interchangeable. Psychoanalytic discourse inserts the patient in a position of fundamental disadvantage vis-à-vis the analyst. The patient is presumed to be as yet incapable of entering a genuinely communicative relationship. Such capability is at best achieved only through a successful therapeutic process. The analyst accordingly *confers* enlightenment; patients can only seek enlightenment about themselves. The validity claims of the psychoanalyst must not be disputed by the analysands. These claims form, at the outset at least, the irrevocable and unquestionable terms of argumentation within which interactions proceed. The analyst is therefore the privileged bearer of true insight, of genuine natural-scientific hypotheses that can be validated as knowledge of acknowledged "laws." At most, this knowledge can be denied by patients – but only through a change of analysts or the severance of consultations altogether. This point has severe implications for Habermas's prudent, nonvanguardist proposals for political enlightenment. Their insistence that the political process that exposes and undoes systematic distortions of communication can be likened to the psychoanalytic dialogue unwittingly harbors a dogmatic elitism.

Habermas's use of psychotherapy as an exemplar of prudent political action conceals another difficulty. This problem was long ago raised by Geigel, Gadamer, and others. In their not unwarranted view, Habermas's psychoanalytically informed political proposals seriously underestimate the measures typically pursued by the wealthy, powerful, and prestigious in late capitalist societies to stifle, co-opt, or violently repress political dialogue.[98] The adaptation of the therapy model to the political task of communicatively dissolving false consensus thereby clings to the reformist illusion that the demonstrative force of argument alone will engage and convince the commanders of existing bureaucratic institutions. This presumption, it has been argued, stems directly from the misleading comparison of therapy and politics. This comparison is deceiving precisely because, under therapeutic conditions, patients' sense of malaise and desire for cure serve as the raison d'être of their engagement with the analyst. In political struggle, by contrast, no such prior orientation to reaching an understanding can be presumed. At best, communicative action *within* and *between* oppressed groups is possible. The relationship of those who rule and those who struggle for emancipation from professionally organized, bureaucratic domination is one of confrontation. Resistance, compromise, and dissembling on the part of the ruling groups (as Machiavelli expressed so clearly at the onset of the modern world) are the norm. Again, Habermas has been forced to imperil his own argument in acknowledging this crucial insight.[99] The singular objection remains: The problem of distorted communication and its dissolution through theory-guided, democratic and political struggle cannot adequately be analyzed through the model of psychoanalysis.

The problem of ideology

It can be argued that this internal limit upon Habermas's early attempts to secure psychoanalysis as a model for political struggle was then compounded by an additional difficulty. This second limitation derived from his rather brief and later-abandoned attempt to explicate a theory of the mechanisms of pseudo-communication. Drawing heavily upon the Marxian theory of ideology, this theory of pseudocommunication aimed to expose and criticize, without authoritarian consequences, those processes which veil or conceal the possibility of communicative competence and, conversely, the servile dependency of some speaking actors upon others. Ideologically distorted communication, Habermas proposed, functions to conceal institutionalized relations of domination and violence. Under the hegemony of pseudocompromises and mutually accepted beliefs (in, say, the benevolence of patriarchy or the efficacy of professional expertise), this domination tends to become insulated against interrogation by both the individual subject and the community at large. Metacommunication about the routinized or normalized communication of daily life is thereby blocked. The formation of authentic agreements and mutual obligations, whose possibility is hypothetically posited within all unbroken communicative action, is adjourned, even deemed unnecessary.

This is the sense in which ideological distortion of communication is highly paradoxical.[100] On the one hand, the ideologies that prevent free and systematic communication "make a fiction of the reciprocal imputation of accountability." Speaking actors' presumption that their communication is in accord with its validity claims (of intelligibility, truth, rightness, and veracity) is violated. On the other hand, it is precisely these ideological impediments to genuine communication which serve to repress questions about the nonfulfillment of the presupposed validity claims. Actually existing communication appears to its authors and participants as unproblematic or legitimate. Ideologies thereby "reinforce the belief in legitimacy which sustains the fiction [of the fulfillment of validity claims] and prevents its being exposed."[101] This paradox is strongly evident, Habermas argued, in the classical bourgeois ideologies of formal law, the commodified exchange of equivalents, and the public sphere.[102] These ideologies represented the emerging modern world system as an achievement of free and equal subjects and as therefore emancipated from relations of domination in personalized form. Typically criticizing the past in the name of their own scientific and universally valid claims,[103] bourgeois ideologies radically weakened the objective, authoritative power of systems of myth, metaphysics, and customary ritual. The subjectivism of these ideologies in turn greatly strengthened the capacity of the bourgeoisie to induce voluntary servitude among the exploited. Representing its own particular interests as universal or *pro bono publico*, the bourgeoisie sought to rule without appearing to rule.[104]

By presenting the problem of pseudocommunication in this way, Habermas's synthesis of the theories of communication and ideology seemed at first sight to be highly credible. The novelty and suggestiveness of this attempted synthesis also provided support for the view (of Adorno and others) that the theory and phenomenon of ideology belong to the movement of history.[105] Whether this synthesis was plausible, however, remained much less certain. This uncertainty was generated by a pressing question that remains largely unanswered in Habermas's more recent work, namely: Can the critical theory of universal pragmatics and the Marxian concept of ideology be effectively synthesized? This question is provoked by the presence of a number of ambiguities and confusions within Habermas's account of ideological communication that are suggestive of deeper difficulties within his attempt to sketch a theory of pseudocommunication. These weaknesses include, first, the often timid and highly oblique references to the category of ideology (as in the theses on the "glassy background ideology which idolizes and fetishizes science");[106] secondly, the occasional overburdening of the concept with anachronistic meanings (as in the discussion of the "ideologies" of traditional social formations, or in the more general claim that the evolution of "the dialectic of forces and relations of production takes place through ideologies");[107] and, thirdly, the virtual abandonment of the concept of ideology within more recent formulations of the theory of universal pragmatics. These ambiguities and weaknesses, it can be argued, are neither fortuitous nor uninteresting nor without political implications. They are in fact suggestive of two crucial and hitherto-unresolved antinomies between the theories of universal pragmatics and the classical Marxian project of ideology criticism. From the outset, it can be argued, these two antinomies strongly hindered Habermas's further elaboration of the problem of pseudocommunication and its subversion, a problem that nevertheless remains of great importance to a socialist theory of public life.

First, and more obviously, there exists an unambiguous contradiction between the epistemological status of the Marxian critique of ideology and Habermas's above-mentioned rejection of vanguardism. This antinomy was spotted by Habermas himself in an early essay, where it was warned that, on account of its scientistic premises, the Marxian critique of ideology would require reconstruction if its utility for critical social analysis was to be preserved.[108] This point was again repeated in his criticism of Marx's identification of his critique of liberal capitalism as a natural-scientific project: "Marx never explicitly discussed the precise meaning of a science of humanity elaborated as a critique of ideology and distinct from the instrumentalist meaning of natural science."[109]

Habermas's later discussion of the problem of pseudocommunication repressed this conclusion. It overlooked the point that the Marxian advocacy of a revolution in the existing material conditions of production, which it knows to be the real foundation upon which rise corresponding ideological forms, is logically tied to its self-misunderstanding as a form of natural science. Against its own resolve, thereby, the project of criticizing pseudocommunication formed something like a tacit alliance with scientism – a scientism, it should be added, that has constantly bedeviled Marxian critiques of ideology from the time of their first formulation through to more recent amendments, such as those of Althusser.[110]

This self-contradiction within the theory of pseudocommunication was reinforced by a second difficulty, which derived from the fact that the classical Marxian solution of the riddles of ideology presupposed the existence of a domain of material activity purged of symbolic representation. Notwithstanding its own scientism, the Althusserian project correctly called attention to this metaphysical presupposition within the early Marxian critique of ideology.[111] The scope of Althusser's insight can indeed be extended, for it is clear that the tradition of ideology criticism from the time of Bacon has constantly suffered from the weight of its own illusory belief in the existence of a positive reality freed from the symbolic. Within this tradition, ideology has been understood as a form of misrepresentation of a subterranean reality of material life processes. These processes are explained as the precommunicative point of origin of ideology, a point of origin that is also the point of truth that contradicts the false nothingness of ideology. Marx himself never satisfactorily broke with this reasoning, which is also evident in Bacon's conviction that words and discourse obstruct understanding and throw the species into confusion, through the *Idéo-*

logues' concern to lay bare the origins of all consciousness, to Geiger's more recent positivist denunciation of the ideological as pure mysticism that is readily refuted by techniques of empirical verification.[112]

Consistent with these usages, Marx's search for the origin of representations ends by embracing the myth of an origin external to symbolic communication. His appropriation of the Roman myth of Cacus is illustrative of this unflagging enthusiasm for identifying the material foundations of ideology through the model of the *camera obscura*.[113] According to this model, the bourgeoisie's false, inverted representation of itself as the source of all wealth can be likened to the trickery of Cacus, who seeks to conceal his cattle-rustling efforts by herding his prey into his den backward, so that it appears that they have already departed. In the early works, Marx and Engels similarly propose a rebellion against the rule of the symbolic. The "actual existing world" is contrasted with that which humanity says, imagines, or conceives, with "the phrases of this world." Building upon this distinction, the materialist conception of history "scientifically" accounts for the latter through recourse to the logic of the former. The formation and pseudo-independence of the symbolic are unveiled and explained with reference to the beyond, behind, and beneath: material practice itself. The illusions of the epoch are said to be sublimations of the "material life-process," in accordance with whose divisions of labor and class struggles the species produces its own means of need satisfaction and social and political relations.[114] Ideologies therefore have no history – in the precise sense that the logic of their birth, rise to dominance, and decay is always and everywhere burdened by the primordial determinations of the division of labor. Inverted representations of reality can therefore be traced to the inversions and self-contradictoriness of the actual life process of "real, active humanity." Conversely, the dissolution of the hold of the ruling phrases over the lips and minds of the dominated can be achieved only through revolution. Liberation is a practical, and not a mental or discursive, act.

Through its dependence upon this Marxian theory of ideology, Habermas's theory of pseudocommunication unwittingly burdened itself with the metaphysical presumption that ideology is the "mask" of a subterranean reality, a reality that can be purged of all treacherous symbolic density. On at least one occasion (namely, in his early comments on Gadamer), Habermas in fact explicitly embraced this presumption.[115] Granted, this critique of Gadamer's "idealism of linguisticality" correctly conceived of linguistic communication as a kind of "metainstitution." Communication was seen as an infrastructure upon which *all* economic, political, and cultural institutions are dependent. "Social action," Habermas insisted, "is constituted only in ordinary language communication."[116] Curiously, this formulation was at once undermined by a fairly conventional Marxian account of language as a limited circle of the movement of ideas, as a superstructure divorced from the everyday realities of production. According to Habermas, particular modes of linguistic communication not only harbor deceptions (*Täuschungen*); language itself oftentimes deceives. "Language is *also* ideological," by virtue of its capacity to mask or veil certain constraints of reality (*Realitätszwängen*) that operate from "behind the back" of language. These constraints (such as a change in the mode of production) also effect "from below"

171

revolutions in the symbolically transmitted and intersubjectively shared patterns of meaning within any social formation.[117]

Habermas's embrace of this revamped base–superstructure formulation prompts a singular objection: The Marxian account of the "concealment" function of ideology does not sufficiently acknowledge that cultures – including the forces of production in both their objective and their subjective aspects – are historically variable, more or less meaningful orders of subjects and objects structured through definite symbolic schema. The "material life-process" is by no means coterminous with the pragmatics of production, for neither escapes symbolic mediation. Conventional Marxian accounts of ideology are in this respect unacceptable, for actors' symbolically mediated experience of themselves in relation to other subjects and objects cannot be understood (to invoke the words of Schmidt) as a mere translation of the "objective logic of the human work-situation."[118] It must be denied that signs are necessarily cognate to the terms of the deed, that both have a common origin in material utility. A reconstructed critique of ideology – which Habermas's work promised, but has so far never achieved – must not only fully reject the scientist premises of Marxism, but also note that situated or "formed" subjects' production and transformation of symbolically mediated communicative relations cannot be conceived as either a level or a dimension of any social formation. This communication is coextensive with symbolically mediated activity as such. Every experience of the world of nature or society is articulated through the production, reproduction, and transformation of signs. There is (see Essay 6) no specifically communicative relationship – not even the labor process itself – that is constituted from an Archimedean point outside or below this symbolically organized, discursive realm.

The hypothetical, abstract subject

This essay's discussion of the political implications of Habermas's theory of universal pragmatics has so far proposed that it is weakened by two conceptual problems: first, its reliance upon an inappropriate analogy between psychoanalytic therapy and public, political action and, secondly, the incompatibility between the premises of the theory of universal pragmatics and the Marxian theses on ideology. These difficulties, which Habermas himself has sensed, are threatening enough to the political implications of his project, the more so considering that they have in the meantime been reinforced and deepened by two additional problems.

Under pressure from the difficulties just analyzed, first, the theory of universal pragmatics has come more and more to suspend consideration of the problem of deformed communication. Of course, Habermas would not deny the ubiquity of systematically distorted communication under late capitalist conditions. Neither is he unaware of the empirical importance of organized lying, open and concealed discord, and strategic action – the "gray areas," as he calls them, in actually existing patterns of communication.[119] Finally, he is not unaware of the fact that the ability to speak and act competently is in part the outcome of a stagelike, crisis-ridden, and extraordinarily dangerous process of ontogenesis, a learning process marked by the interplay of cognitive, linguistic, and sexually motivated elements.[120] Under the impact of the above-mentioned difficulties, nevertheless, the idea of a communicatively competent public, whose *possibility* of realization the communication theory initially aimed to justify, is installed as a *premise* of its concern with the general and unavoidable presuppositions of communicative action. Communicative action that is guided (implicitly or explicitly) by the common conviction that the various claims to validity are being honored is analyzed as if it were *the* fundamental form of communicative and strategic action.[121] The universal pragmatics now theoretically privileges *consensual* action, communication in which speaking actors already cooperate on the mutually acknowledged presupposition that their interactions are in accordance with the four validity claims. Habermas's explication of the logic of communicative action thereby presumes the existence of competently speaking and acting subjects who are (1) already in explicit agreement about the necessity of cooperatively reaching mutual understanding; (2) already capable of distinguishing between the performative (that is, illocutionary) and propositional aspects of their utterances; and (3) already sharing a tradition and, therefore, a common definition of their situation.[122]

It is true that Habermas regularly denies that this presumption reinstates the Kantian concept of the hypothetical, transcendental subject, a subject that is removed from all experience and that, upon that basis, accomplishes certain syntheses through its transcendental knowledge of concepts of objects in general. This denial is less than convincing. Contrary to its claims to having overcome the classical separation of formal, transcendental inquiry and empirical analysis,[123] the research program of the universal pragmatics evidently reasserts a misleading dualism: that between the *a priori* knowledge of hypothetically competent public speakers and the *a posteriori* knowledge that could only be generated through inquiries into actually existing speech and action, inquiries that would ask how the operations of the basic institutions of late capitalist society interfere with, or promote, autonomous speech and action. As a direct consequence of this dualism, hypothetically competent speaking and acting subjects are made to serve as a "postulate" (in Kant's sense) of the critical theory of universal pragmatics. A revised version of Kant's transcendental subject reappears in a new, though admittedly less individualistic, guise. The competent subjects who are the focus of Habermas's communication theory are merely *hypothetical* subjects. Actually existing communication is analyzed as if its participants were already communicatively competent. The objection (of Dewey and others) that communicative competence and autonomous public life do not yet exist is scotched; autonomous public life appears no longer to be conditional upon the self-organization and agitation of marginalized political forces, upon their will to break existing forms of power, privilege, and opinion formation.

This difficulty, which arguably restricts the political potential of the theory of universal pragmatics, is deepened, secondly, by the fact that Habermas's hypothetically competent subjects are devoid of many empirical and historical qualities. Theoretically speaking, these subjects are highly artificial beings. The theory of universal pragmatics brackets, or simply fails to consider, a number of properties of public, political experience. With the aim of helping to resuscitate the political implications of Habermas's work, the remaining sections of this essay will briefly sketch and analyze several of these dimensions. No claims are made for the exhaustiveness of the following discussion. It is argued only that each of these properties of autonomous public action must be seen as an element having a rightful place in a socialist theory of public life. The elements discussed here are four in number and include the "embodied" character of communicative action, rhetoric, the aesthetic dimensions of communication, and, finally, the purposive-rational aspects of consensual forms of action.

Body politics and public life

In the first place, it is evident that Habermas's communicatively competent subjects suffer from a definite analytic disembodiment. His account of communicative action misleadingly presumes that speaking actors are capable of raising themselves above and beyond their bodies. Bodily expressions and nonverbal actions are thought to play the role of silent, passive spectators in consensual action renewable through discussion oriented to reaching mutual agreement. It is forgotten that the capacity for genuine storytelling and convincing argumentation depends equally upon the expressive language of gestures. Public communication indeed always draws upon speaking actors' capacity to coordinate and interchange their speech acts and bodily gestures. Within autonomous public spheres, this capacity is often developed to a very high degree. Communication is strikingly and sensuously "embodied." Through a kind of metacommunication, eyes, arms, noses, shoulders, and fingers effectively serve as mutually activating signaling stations, which in turn supplement or contradict their associated utterances in a highly evocative and meaningful manner.[124]

It is true that Habermas occasionally acknowledges the universal pragmatics' failure to consider the bodily dimensions of communicative action.[125] What he does not admit, however, is that this obfuscation is an effect of the universal pragmatics' dependence upon the theory of speech acts, notably as it has been formulated by Austin, Searle, and Wunderlich. In its present formulations, speech act theory represses questions concerning the language of gesture. It does this by virtue of its almost exclusive focus upon the performative or illocutionary aspects of speech, that is, upon speech acts such as promising, which do something in saying something to others. Under the influence of such formulations, Habermas's more recent writings suppress his earlier discussions of the bodily aspects of communicative action. Recognition of the embodied character of communication was evident, for example, in his early criticism of Dilthey's unsuccessful attempts to distinguish the logics of the natural and cultural sciences. While objecting to Dilthey's "monadological view of hermeneutics,"[126] Habermas nevertheless concurred with his description of two primary and normally interwoven forms of communicative action. These forms were said to include, first, "immediate lived experience [*Erlebnis*]" oriented by norms and practical knowledge and, secondly, nonverbal, bodily action – "experiential expression" such as laughter or anger – that signifies unstated or otherwise unstatable intentions

174

that are more or less meaningful to their authors and addressees.[127] Both forms of language-mediated activity, Habermas insisted, are marked by their motivated, self-externalizing capacities. The intercourse of everyday life is therefore chronically dependent upon actors' learned abilities to make both their immediate lived experience and their bodily or experiential actions understandable to themselves and others.

In the case of relatively nonpathological communication at least, this intelligibility is enhanced by the fact that bodily actions are translatable into utterances, and utterances into bodily actions. Invoking the authority of the later Wittgenstein, Habermas argued that the language games of daily life cannot be analyzed as if they obeyed the formally rigorous rules of a syntax or grammar.[128] It is not only that intentional and gestural actions and utterances are mutually irreducible elements of all communicative action, that speech, for example, cannot be understood as a mere reflection of the life world of institutionalized action and expression. The more decisive point is that within all communicative action, gestures, actions, and utterances mutually interpret one another. Communication between speaking and acting subjects ordinarily moves, as it were, between the boundaries of monologue and the delicate silence of mime. This fact lends communicative action a self-reflexive quality. Speakers are able to incorporate within their utterances allusions to nonverbal life expressions, through which their speech can in turn be interpreted by others as meaningful. The language of gestures and actions can interpret utterances, Habermas correctly remarked, while speakers can "talk about actions and describe them. We can name expressions and even make language itself the medium of experiential expression, whether phonetically, by exploiting the expressiveness of intonation, or stylistically, by representing in language itself the relation of the subject to its linguistic objectivations."[129]

From the point of view of a theory of autonomous public life, it is regrettable that this early concern with the dialectic of body, utterance, and action has largely receded from the horizons of Habermas's more recent accounts of communicative action. As has been suggested here, the universal pragmatics gives itself over to a numbed or disembodied account of the free and systematic communication of autonomous public life. There is a converse to this point, namely, that the theory of universal pragmatics potentially misses the democratic potential of several social movements that have made the body, that is, its symbolic representation and implication within late capitalist relations of power, a theme of political action. Here mention can be made of (male) gay attempts at subverting patriarchal homophobia through the celebration of the male body as a love object and feminist movements' concern with women's bodies as objects of patriarchal socialization, adornment, surveillance, and rape. These "body-political" movements can be interpreted as important attempts to reverse the contemporary bureaucratic administration and interrogation of the body. During the course of the modern civilizing process, as Doerner and others have proposed, the bodies of the "unreasonable" ceased to be punished in public in the name of the Sovereign, as had been the case prior to the nineteenth century. This apparently humane reversal was achieved only insofar as bodies came to be policed by networks of social and political institutions guided by expert, professional knowledge.[130] In the phase of late capitalism, life itself has come to be mobilized and administered by professionally organized, bureaucratic means. The powers that be even pride themselves on their ability to put this life in order, that is, to normalize, sustain, and multiply it by means of archipelagos of "carceral" institutions consisting of prisons, factories, offices, asylums, schools, and hospitals, each tending to resemble a prison in its mode of operation.

Whatever the degree of plausibility of this thesis concerning the normalizing society, its implications are of fundamental importance to a theory of autonomous public life. In the classical past, it might be said, the species was conceived (by Aristotle, for example) as living beings endowed with the capacity to lead a political existence. The populations of late capitalist societies, by contrast, can be viewed as beings whose administered politics increasingly place their existence as living, embodied beings in question. The "progressive" effect of this interrogation and administration of bodies no doubt consists in its erosion of old assumptions about the body as a natural force external to influences of power and symbolically mediated communication. This administration process nevertheless also calls into question populations' capacities to exercise their powers of labor, speech, and bodily action freely and publicly. Autonomous public life is jeopardized by the fact that bodies tend to fall – though unevenly and certainly not without opposition – under the watchful eye of normalizing bureaucratic control mechanisms. A socialist theory of public life needs to render problematic this normalization of daily life through the policing of bodies. Habermas's disembodied account of communicative action unfortunately leads away from this task.

The problem of rational speech

Rhetoric

The restricted political potential of the theory of universal pragmatics is a consequence not only of its disembodiment of communication; the abstractness and formalism of this account is also reinforced by Habermas's strong tendency to presume that communicatively competent actors employ their utterances in no other mode than that of soberly reaching understanding through rational speech. Oriented to the achievement of a rational consensus, these competent actors seem to eschew rhetorical speech and, secondly, to appreciate (and produce) neither film nor theater nor literature nor music. These rhetorical and aesthetic forms of communication, Habermas seems to imply, together stand in a subordinate relationship with respect to consensual speech. The general significance of what he elsewhere calls "symbolic action" – nonpropositional, symbolically expressive modes of speaking and acting[131] – is seriously devalued. Symbolic action is understood as a derivative, parasitic form of consensual speech act; its presence within *all* forms of communication is thereby underestimated.

This point can be illustrated and defended with reference, first, to the rhetorical character of all communicative action. Habermas's devaluation of questions pertaining to rhetoric, it seems clear, is an effect of his inadequate explication of the *formal* aspects of ordinary language communication. It is true that he repeats Searle's conviction that accounts of the formal dimensions of language are not incompatible with the analysis of communication as a rule-governed ensemble of speech acts.[132] Habermas also sometimes hints that language has a reality *sui generis*, a reality that persistently makes its mark upon speech acts. His early work on language, for example, expressed this point through the metaphor of the spider's web. Systems of linguistic representation, it was correctly argued there, cannot be analyzed as if they were the transparent and neutral product of resourceful, spiderlike, monadic subjects. Language was viewed, rather, as "the web on whose threads the subjects hang and on which they first begin to make themselves into subjects."[133]

Habermas has more recently adopted the view that the formal, representational aspects of communication are always contingent upon their pragmatic employment in communication contexts. In his view, speaking actors *learn* the meaning of illocutionary speech acts through their role as participants within communicative action. They likewise *learn* the meaning of propositional sentences by adopting (again within an intersubjective context) the role of observers who report their experiences as propositions. Through this formula, Habermas questions the old Saussurean distinction between processes of speaking (*parole*) that are contingent upon language as structure (*langue*).[134] Habermas openly denies the validity of this distinction. In the first place, communicative interaction cannot be interpreted as mere *parole*, as always subordinated to the compulsory structuring effects of systems of anonymous, collective codes. In his view, subjects capable of speaking and acting can also deploy and transform the "formal-structural" properties of ordinary language in processes of communication. He insists, furthermore, that speech acts are not simply haphazard or contingent, as the *parole–langue* dualism presupposes. Their pragmatic aspects are rule structured and are therefore not beyond the grasp of rigorous, formal analysis. Although performed by particular speakers concerned with particular states of affairs, acts of communication are nonetheless always structured immanently by validity claims. These validity rules are constitutive rules: They always and everywhere exercise an objective influence over speech acts.

This convincing censure of the *langue–parole* dualism nevertheless results in a considerable deemphasis of the formal dimensions of language systems. The processes whereby meaningfully performed speech acts are systematically mediated or preconstructed by the formal relations between signifiers (images, sounds, utterances), processes that Saussure had sought to analyze through the category of *langue*, fall into obscurity. In the opinion of the theory of universal pragmatics, language is to be understood as a transparent and contingent system of signs. Language is a pellucid medium that facilitates speakers' attempts to effect a coherent, usually demarcated relationship among the external world of nature, their social worlds, and their own inner worlds. Language, in this view, is a *means* through which facts can be represented, normatively regulated communicative relations established, and the singularity of speakers' subjectivity expressed.[135] Language by no means displays a productivity of its own. Habermas follows Searle in assuming the primacy of the principle of expressibility. Whatever can be meant, it is said, can be uttered. It is therefore concluded that rule-governed, explicit speech acts are the fundamental units of communication. For any and every speech act that a speaker wants to produce, a suitable performative or propositional expression can be made available and, in turn, uttered meaningfully.[136]

This not altogether unconvincing principle at the same time loses sight of the linguistic preconstruction of all subjective acts of communication. The crucial objection that the objective form of symbolic language always structures that which is subjectively spoken about is passed over in silence. The theory of universal pragmatics thus falls into a certain subjectivism. Analyzing only the pragmatic aspects of communication, it embraces an intentionalist account of meaning. It thereby underemphasizes what might be called the semantic productivity of any language of communicative action. This productivity (which is expressed in the commonplace distinction between what speakers mean and what they say) derives from those generative devices or objective rules which preside over processes of symbolic representation and, therefore, over both the performance of speech acts and their reception by audiences.

The rhetorical qualities of speech acts serve as a politically important illustration of this productivity. Contrary to Habermas's distinction between "symbolic action" and the "rational speech" of properly communicative action, rhetorical speech is a constitutive feature of all communicative action. Rhetoric is not restricted to expressive forms of speaking and acting, such as poetry or highly emotive forms of political oratory. With varying degrees of intensity, to be sure, all communication is marked by rhetorical characteristics that are generated by the play or tension within the chains of signs and utterances employed by speaking actors. No doubt, rhetoric *is* produced by speaking, sign-deploying actors, and effects new meanings only through the interpretive capacities of its addressees. Habermas correctly emphasizes this point. The convincing power of rhetoric does not exist in itself, so to speak; a minimal hermeneutic must be exercised if rhetorical communication is to effect meanings for speaking and acting subjects successfully. The productivity of rhetorical speech, its capacity of making the probable more attractive, nevertheless also derives from the "design" or representational form of this speech itself. The more classical accounts of rhetoric are rather misleading on this point.[137] Contrary to Aristotle and others, rhetoric cannot be understood as "artificially stylized" or decorative speech that persuades (or repels) through its exaggerations and insincerities. Nor is the semantic productivity of rhetoric generated by the willful introduction into communication of substitute signifiers that serve to "adorn" that communication through the invocation of resemblances.

Rhetoric, on the contrary, is genuinely productive of new meanings for its interpreting audiences. This semantic productivity is generated by processes of "metaphorical twist" (Beardsley), by the bringing together of two or more formerly unrelated signifiers into a new relationship of identity. The rhetorical quality of speech acts flows precisely from this play of equivalence and difference, synonymity and antonymity, within its chains of uttered signifiers. The inventiveness of highly rhetorical speech acts is only a limit case of this play of identity and difference. Their capacity to persuade is greatly enhanced by their juxta-position of formerly incompatible signifiers, whose new resemblance not only appears credible but also produces novel, hitherto-unrecognized meanings. The potential "impertinence" of juxtaposing two or more signifiers (for example, "gay power" or "property is theft") is overcome, with the novel consequence that the routinized interpretations of normally functioning communication are rein-forced or ruptured. The "semantic dissonance" within the chains of signification of this rhetoric is effectively resolved.

The particular case of rhetoric discussed here serves to illustrate a point of more general interest to a socialist theory of public life. Contrary to Habermas, it must be reiterated that the formal effects of language can never be expunged from communicative action. Certainly, as Habermas pointed out against Dilthey, language always serves as a key medium of public, political action. Language can indeed be described as the intersubjective ground upon which all speaking actors tread as they intentionally articulate themselves in words, bodily expres-sions, and actions. Under conditions of autonomous public life, as Habermas also observes, this linguistic ground frequently comes to have a more distinct reality for its speaking and acting "authors." By virtue of its semantically pro-ductive or rhetorical qualities, however, this ground is better described as drifting terrain. Even within autonomous spheres of "public, unrestricted discussion, free from domination," speaking actors continue to move through chronically ambiguous and slippery linguistic terrains. The formal density of these terrains can never be reduced to zero, as Habermas's theoretical defense of "rational speech" implies. Democratic public life can never take the form of an ideal speech situation wherein competent intersubjective communication is liberated from the dangers of being overtaken by the unforeseen, and unhindered by the formal or objective structures of linguistic communication itself. Public actors can never self-consciously bind, gag, and rationally control their language of interaction. They are never able, in short, fully to achieve a transparent, rational consensus purged of ambiguity.

Aesthetics

The universal pragmatics' privileging of rational speech and the corresponding devaluation of symbolic action produce a third fetter upon its political potential, namely, its bracketing of questions concerning politics and the aesthetic dimen-sion of communicative action. It is not true that Habermas entirely ignores or neglects such questions. In his more recent writings, he speaks occasionally of "aesthetic forms of expression."[138] And especially in his reflections on Adorno's and Benjamin's theses on "post-auratic" art (see Essay 3), he rightly observes that the administrative production of culture under late capitalist conditions is continually marked with unintended consequences that may be rich in demo-cratic potential. The bureaucratic manufacture and distribution of commer-cialized art also produces threatening artistic countercultures. Their quest for meaningful or novel aesthetic experiences oftentimes provokes open criticism of the culture industry and its implications within the late capitalist political economy.

179

Whether these countercultures can facilitate the growth of radical movements and autonomous public spheres remains a rather obscure theme in Habermas's writings. This obscurity concerning the political potential of "post-auratic" art is not fortuitous, but is a consequence, rather, of the universal pragmatics' fetishism of rational, consensual speech. It can also be argued that this vagueness is an unforeseen consequence of the universal pragmatics' – admittedly justified – turn against Marcuse's quantitative model of repression and emancipation.[139] Marcuse, it will be recalled, typically contrasts the vision of sensuous tranquility with the aggressive efficiency of daily life under late capitalist conditions. In opposition to the performance principle of bureaucratic capitalism, Marcuse speaks of liberated human beings coming into their own through the expression of their passions.[140] He defends the possibility of democratic socialism with a biological foundation; he anticipates an individuated, pacified existence, a world freed from surplus, unfree labor and dominated only by peaceful Eros. In support of this possibility of a new "rationality of gratification"[141] in which reason and happiness merge, Marcuse insists that the poetic, erotic language of art has a privileged status. By defending (and preserving the memory of) desires that remain unfulfilled, the work of art flouts the immediacy of the existing reality principle. For both its producers and its appreciative publics, art is the privileged medium of the sublimation of libidinal fantasies. Art is the formal expression of the imagination, of the psychic content of unconscious drives and wishes. It openly expresses the language of libidinal negation. It is the vehicle of The Great Refusal.[142]

To be sure, Marcuse admits that much bourgeois art exercises an "affirmative," depoliticizing function. For example, literature's positing of the freedom and beauty of a soul frequently facilitates its readers' surrender to the misery and enslavement of a bureaucratic existence. The potentially rebellious beauty of art tends to become the comforting narcotic of a vulgar daily life; the *promesse de bonheur* of art can be experienced only as an inner freedom.[143] Marcuse nevertheless insists: Neither great bourgeois art (such as that of Schiller or Goethe) nor certain tendencies within the avant-garde (for example, surrealist art and literature of the two decades before World War II) can simply be indicted as apologies for established forms of existence. In spite of its ambivalent consequences, this kind of art remains a decisive moment in the struggle for the sensuous fulfillment of humanity and nature. The moment of truth of even so-called bourgeois art thus consists in its anticipation of a liberated future. The most important works of art and literature (Marcuse curiously ignores media such as film) promise a forthcoming era of instinctual gratification, whose possibility late capitalist society must either systematically suppress or "repressively desublimate." Collaborating with the subterranean longings and refusals of Eros, the aesthetic dimension is secretly committed to the emancipation of sensibility, imagination, and antibureaucratic reason.

This defense of the aesthetic dimension, Habermas correctly surmises, is quite compatible with Marcuse's concern to synthesize an anthropological perspective with Marxist theoretical categories. His theory of art and liberation consistently presupposes the existence of a species-instinctual foundation for peaceful solidarity among human beings. (This species-essence is specified by drawing initially upon Heidegger's existential ontology and, later, upon Freudian metapsychology.) Under late capitalist conditions, this foundation – an immanently rebellious, unconscious nature – is hidden away, repressed, or falsely sublimated. The primary task of radical politics, according to Marcuse, must therefore be the unfettering of sensuous nature, for this nature already strives for the pacification of existence. Living antagonistically on the margins of the present system of domination, and older than individual character structure and institutionalized relations of power, this nature is the enemy of the present and the ally of liberation.

Habermas meets this provocative formulation with an equally bold and politically relevant reply. Marcuse's ontological approach, he insists, contains potentially authoritarian and antipolitical implications. Certainly, these are not intended by Marcuse. Especially within his last works, there is great emphasis placed upon the importance of "political education" and "radical enlightenment."[144] Nevertheless, Marcuse's postulation of a biological foundation that serves as the Archimedean point from which radical politics can take its cue unwittingly leaves itself open to appropriation by self-appointed revolutionary vanguards, whose claims to knowledge of this foundation could in turn serve to justify action on behalf of others who are in the here and now evidently less enlightened about their instinctual endowments.[145] According to Habermas, the doctrine of instincts short-circuits the *theoretical* and *political* problem of generating widespread public reflection upon existing patterns of distorted communication. Marcuse's critical appropriation of Freud is burdened, at the theoretical level, by a "chiliastic trust in a revitalizing dynamic of instincts which works through history, finally breaks with history and leaves it behind as what then will appear as prehistory."[146] This rather naïve, chiliastic belief in a future marked by great happiness, universal prosperity, and harmonious self-government derives from Marcuse's advocacy of a world governed by an Eros that naturally seeks tranquility and delight divorced from all egoistic interest. Habermas correctly insists that this formulation obscures the political insight that the genuinely democratic determination of needs can proceed only through public argumentation oriented to reaching consensus.

Habermas proceeds from this insistence to a more fundamental theoretical point. Marcuse's presumption that libidinal energy is the avowed enemy of existing relations of domination – his claim that "eros and power may well be contraries"[147] – forgets that such presumptions and even energy drives themselves are *ab ovo* formed within a communicative context. Within Marcuse's theory of liberation (to paraphrase Wittgenstein) the problem of language and communication goes on holiday. In the view of Habermas's universal pragmatics, Marcuse's metatheory of instincts therefore cannot consistently account for its own possibility. Such an account could only be generated discursively, that is, within a communicative, language-structured framework.[148] This is a crucial point: Pleasure and desire have no objective reality "in themselves." Desire and pleasure cannot be intuitively apprehended, quantified empirically (as Marcuse's references to "basic" and "surplus" repression imply), or somehow known in all

181

their beautiful objectivity. The body and its drives assert themselves, perhaps, in setting limits, the ultimate of which is death. But these limits always and everywhere operate entirely through systems of communicative action. Habermas correctly withdraws his earlier claim against Gadamer: He insists that there is no knowable subterranean reality beyond the realm of communication and its systems of symbolic representation.

This critique of Marcuse's "naturalization" of political reason is unexceptionable. From the point of view of a socialist theory of public life, however, this critique does entail at least one serious unintended consequence. Simply, Marcuse's privileging of art as a medium of social and political criticism is displaced; questions concerning the relationship between autonomous public life and art fall into abeyance. Artistic movements' power to subvert the normalizing effects of daily life, their capacity to express erotically the vision of a political life of common involvements, is by implication declared null and void. A converse consequence is of equal seriousness: This bracketing of questions concerning the relationship between art and public life, it can be argued, also by implication draws our attention away from what can be called (following Walter Benjamin)[149] the "aestheticization" of politics under late capitalist conditions. Habermas's concentration upon consensual, rational communication, that is to say, seriously underestimates the "affirmative," depoliticizing effects of the planned merger between art and late capitalist daily life.

It is precisely this merger of art and life which prompts the need to think *simultaneously* about questions of emancipatory art and autonomous public spheres. This need was of course first recognized by Benjamin. Echoing Tönnies's and Dewey's concern with the growth of state and corporate production of public opinion, Benjamin proposed that the defeat of pacifism and its revolutionary potential had been considerably aided by the state's strategies of manufacturing and deploying supplies of glory and militaristic idealism. It was Benjamin's thesis that post–World War I attempts to forget the lost war and its total "storms of steel" continued this celebration, even though no real enemy existed. The novelty of this celebration lay in its reliance upon the administrative harnessing of the "symbolic depths" of existence itself. This "post-war war effort [*Nachkrieg*]" by no means sustained itself upon the old-fashioned and withering phrases of rational, calculating militarism. In place of old-fashioned militarism, the imperialist forces of emergent Nazism sought the administrative production and celebration of a more threatening heroism, one that claimed to express the vital inner impulses of solitary, responsible individuals.

In Benjamin's view, this heroism could only serve to legitimate aesthetically the monstrous senselessness of battles to come. Unless checked by revolution, strategies of war could permanently sustain themselves upon allegations about the colossal energies of life. War could be represented as sport, as record setting, as synonymous with taking a stance. German fascism, as Benjamin and others later stressed, did indeed develop this authoritarian merger of art and bureaucratic politics to the point of near technical perfection.[150] Fascist "public life" became the site of official orchestrations of "heroic festivity" (Thomas Mann). In accordance with the Führer principle, celebrations, artificially created customs and folklore, staged ceremonies, and party conventions formed a grandiosely erected stage, on the foundations of which the practice of systematic terror unfolded. The old Romantic dream about the unification of art and the state was fulfilled in nightmarish form: Political life became a permanent and all-embracing work of art.

Such administrative efforts to aestheticize political life continue right through to the present day. Certainly, the utilized means and the outcomes themselves are rather different. Under late capitalist conditions, nevertheless, it still cannot be admitted officially that politics has so few givens, so many dangerous possibilities, and so few perfect situations, that no single leader or group of leaders has knowledge, skill, and prudence sufficient for all situations. The heads of the body politic therefore continue to present themselves to their public as characters charged with remedying the complexities and imperatives of political decision making. Relying upon new technologies of reproduction and drawing upon the pioneering efforts of those who manufacture the "beautiful illusions" of capitalist production and consumption, political authority typically casts itself as spotlighted performers. Mounting an elaborately prepared stage, this authority seeks to transform politics into show business, the art of seducing a public audience of spectators supposedly dispossessed of their critical faculties and collective power to speak and act. The *dramatis personae* appear in many and varied costumes. Their makeup is always expertly applied. They are at all times surrounded by a cast of thousands. Their lines are carefully rehearsed to elicit maximum audience approval (with perhaps an encore). The "populist" performers are reputed to lead down-to-earth, simple lives, or are known publicly to associate privately with trend-setting media figures. Their more conservative counterparts present themselves as decent family men or as stern nurses concerned only for the long-term health of their patients. One or two are even lucky enough to hail directly from Hollywood.

These examples of the aestheticization of political life make it clear that nowadays the relationship between art and daily life is fundamentally a matter of politics. By contrast with earlier phases of the modern, bourgeois world, late capitalist systems integrate art and bureaucratic relations of power to an unprecedented degree. This development means that a theory of autonomous public life cannot simply bracket or ignore the importance of aesthetic modes of communication, as Habermas's universal pragmatics proposes. Nor can this theory sustain itself upon the old-fashioned demand to integrate or reunite art with everyday life. Forgetting that all late capitalist systems already effect this normalizing integration, this demand may in fact unwittingly serve the existing conditions of depoliticization. Accordingly, a theory of autonomous public life must acknowledge that "political art" cannot be conceived as the mere underling of struggles for public life. Under late capitalist conditions, this theory must recognize that emancipatory art has been forced into more complex and subtle strategies. The indispensable functions of this art have evidently become many-sided, and especially include the "denaturalization" of bureaucratic administration, the calling into question of the normalizing art with which this administration collaborates – "slapping the face of public taste" (Mayakovsky) – and even, finally, the criticism of autonomous public movements themselves.

Public life as consensual communication?

It can be observed, finally, that Habermas's almost exclusive concern with consensual forms of communication also reinforces the abstract and formal character of the theory of universal pragmatics. This theoretical privileging of consensual action produces a deep silence about the possible relations, in public or political life at least, between consensual action and forms of purposive-rational action (such as civil disobedience) that are oriented to the successful attainment of political goals through the skillful organization of appropriate means. This silence seems to be not entirely fortuitous. It evidently issues from three sources: the unsuccessful analogy Habermas attempted to draw between the psychoanalytic therapy situation and public speaking and acting, the critical theory's continuing dependence (discussed in Essay 4) upon the fundamental distinction between the realms of necessity (work as purposive-rational action) and potential freedom (communication as unconstrained mutual recognition), and, finally, the strong tendency within recent versions of the theory of universal pragmatics to assume, for the purposes of analysis, that controversy, conflict, and purposive-rational action must be granted an ancillary status, that the latter forms of activity can in general be analyzed as *derivative* of speech acts governed by a mutual will to reach consensus.[151]

As a consequence of these presumptions, the theory of universal pragmatics gives off the impression – certainly not directly intended by Habermas – that purposive-rational action is best represented as pre-political. To be sure, this impression operates for the most part at the analytic level. In his political writings, Habermas is acutely aware of the ubiquity of power struggles and the difficulties of institutionally securing action oriented to reaching mutual agreement. Under pressure from these three presumptions, however, the concept of "public, unrestricted discussion, free from domination," tends to become identical with consensual interaction. By virtue of its assumptions and silences, the universal pragmatics implicitly revives a dualism familiar from the time of Greek antiquity: that which contrasts the peace, deliberation, and persuasion of the *polis* with the extrapublic realm, wherein "the strong did what they could, and the weak suffered what they must" (Thucydides). Unrestricted public discussion and action, it is inferred, does not properly extend beyond the boundaries of unbroken, intersubjective communication. This misleading inference carries two further implications, which are sometimes explicitly developed in Habermas's writings: first, that spheres of life properly guided by purposive-rational action (that is, work) are to be permanently depoliticized (a strong prejudice of Habermas's early works, as argued in Essays 3 and 6); and, conversely, that purposive-rational action has little rightful place within autonomous public spheres. To live a genuinely public life, according to this latter inference, consists in deciding everything exclusively through good-natured argument and deliberation oriented to reaching understanding. Not the skill and cunning of strategic and instrumental action, but words and persuasion, are the distinguishing mark of public life.

Within his writings on ego development Habermas openly embraces this second inference.[152] Amending Kohlberg's theory of the stages of moral consciousness, he proposes that at the level of a universal ethics of speech (*Sprachethik*), a level of "complete reciprocity," competently speaking actors would realize "a good and just life." Having reached this highest stage of ego development, they could distinguish between heteronomy and autonomy, differentiate and choose between particular and general ethical principles and interpretations of needs, and, in general, respect the dignity of others as "individuated persons" – all through consensual practical discourse. From the standpoint of a socialist theory of public life, this *implied* eschatology of nonviolent, consensual forms of communication is most inadequate. This is because it brackets the insight that public action must also be centrally concerned, to employ Apel's term, with dialectical, strategic rationality.[153] Public, political action is properly concerned with the *strategies* of reaching morally virtuous ends through processes of deliberation and action. In order to speak and act prudently, to engage in "good action," public beings must concern themselves with both means and ends. Habermas is no doubt aware of this point; but his failure to analyze this old (Aristotelian) insight deepens the abstractness of his account of communication, and thereby leaves untreated two crucial political problems.

In the first place, it cannot be presumed that the coordinated "instrumentalization" of the opponents of autonomous public life – their constitution as objects to be controlled – is always inadmissible. As has been proposed earlier in this essay, the defense of autonomous public life cannot consistently cling to the illusion that the resistance of ruling groups to radical social movements can be overcome through speech acts oriented to reaching understanding. Especially in the face of existing violations of public life (by military and political elites who threaten total annihilation through war, for instance), this presumption leaves itself open to the charge of naïveté.

The emancipatory potential of the principle of modest reformism and restrained gradualism, it must be reaffirmed, cannot be assumed to apply everywhere and at all times. Socialist public life will not necessarily be the cumulative result of progressive evolution, of the peaceful "determinate negation" of late capitalist society and its institutionalized depoliticization. The historical appearance of democratic, public life cannot be represented as a largely consensual process. The struggle for public life, as many of its defenders already understand, is synonymous with the desire for a genuinely different political order; this struggle is in certain respects a demand for a radical (as distinct from a modestly determinate) negation of the present. Oppressed groups' choice to employ forms of instrumental and strategic action from below against their oppressors is bound up with this concern to jump out of the present stream of the historical continuum. These groups must no doubt acknowledge the truth of the Weberian insight that those who rely upon force and other means of purposive-rational action necessarily contract with diabolical powers.[154] They must also recognize the validity of Weber's supplementary maxim: "In numerous instances the at-

185

tainment of 'good' ends is bound to the fact that one must be willing to pay the price of using morally dubious means or at least dangerous ones – and facing the possibility or even the probability of evil ramifications."[155] From the vantage point of theoretical defenses of autonomous public life, it is indeed not always true that evil follows only from evil and good only from good. Under certain conditions, theoretically informed instrumental and strategic action *may* be vindicable, providing it prudently prepares the way for the realization of democratic forms of life committed to the overcoming of heteronomy.

This point highlights a second problem left untreated by the theory of universal pragmatics. Habermas's failure to analyze the relationship between purposive-rational action and consensual public life, it can be argued, suppresses the point that hybrid forms of purposive-rational action, especially political disobedience, are a necessary condition of autonomous public life. Under postmodern conditions, no doubt, the defenders of public life would seek to maximize friendly argumentation. This public life would presuppose, on a vastly expanded scale, that speaking and acting subjects collectively recognize political life as a process of construction of mutual agreements and self-imposed obligations. With such mutuality, public life would enhance the sheer joy of politicking. Public life can be a community-enhancing process, whose participants can experience a certain *joie de vivre* (and, of course, its opposite: tragedy). Mirth is not an embarrassing, diversionary path leading away from the main road of democratic politics. To act politically, as Arendt and Negt and Kluge emphasize, is not to adopt the posture of a *Schwindelfrei*.[156] Political beings are not those whose sober maturity and communicative competence free them from all intuition, spontaneity, eroticism, and giddiness. The often carnival-like experience of political action within autonomous public spheres cannot be described as a joyless sacrifice. Thriving upon myth and fantasy and the playfulness of argumentation, public life deepens the joys (and disappointments) of persuading and being persuaded, of acting together through words and deeds. Under postmodern conditions, in sum, the freedom of publics, who would be from all walks of life, would consist in their self-gratifying determination to speak and act, to listen and be heard. Assured of their capacity to share in public business and therefore to change or preserve the world through their own efforts, publics would develop a taste for this experience of freedom, and could not be subjectively happy without it.

It is nevertheless true that autonomous public life could never become identical with joyful speech and action oriented to reaching mutual understanding. As Habermas's consensus theory of truth itself implies, the democratic formation and administration of public policy presupposes that agreements among publics can always legitimately be reinterpreted, called into question, or unconditionally revoked. In respect of this negotiability condition, autonomous public life so to speak prepares itself against the semantic ambiguity (see the section of this essay on rhetoric) and unintended consequences chronically associated with actually existing agreements. These agreements must always be understood as open-ended, as re-negotiable. In cases of unsuccessful re-negotiation or simple disagreement, minorities might well temporarily agree to consent to majoritarian arguments (compare Kant: "Argue as much as you will, and about what you will, only obey!"). Yet minorities might also justly insist that their *refusal* to consent is a condition of the maintenance of public life itself. Especially under pressure from resistant and dogmatic majorities, their disobedient action might provide a legitimate challenge to long-standing agreements and institutions now deemed obsolete or restrictive upon public life. Such dissident action constitutes a mode of collective action that defies the distinction between consensual and purposive-rational forms of action. Issuing from a group's prior and mutual agreement about the need to change, restore, or preserve the *status quo*, nonviolent direct action can be seen as a form of voluntary association[157] that is in turn directed instrumentally against the action of others.

This purposive-rational moment of disobedience – participants' switching to strategic action or their attempt to break off communication with others totally – cannot be deemed marginal within a theory of public life. Contrary to much contemporary liberal democratic discourse,[158] disobedience can be analyzed neither as an unthreatening symbolic act addressed merely to the "sense of justice" (Rawls) of others nor as a militant, obstructive action that, by virtue of its threats to the polity, must always be punished. The theory and practice of disobedience, it must be stressed, remains crucial to any defense of public life. This is not merely or even primarily because skillfully organized campaigns of obstruction are capable of effectively securing changes in state and corporate policy. There is a more important, counterfactually deduced reason. A political life structured through the principle of negotiated consent *implies* disobedience. The right to disobey constitutes a necessary condition of any voluntary social and political association. Any deviation from this maxim (and, indeed, any disobedience in favor of its subversion) would otherwise generate the possibility of authoritarian restrictions upon public discussion and association. Dissidence would be relegated to the status of a merely hypothetical possibility or a virtual prerogative, to be exercised by particular social interests only on condition that their disobedient actions would result naturally and properly in their punishment.

Conclusion

To the foregoing discussion of several quandaries and silences within the theory of universal pragmatics can be added, finally, a few concluding remarks on its increasingly abstract and formal character. This formalism, which seriously thwarts the political potential of the theory, is sensed by a growing number of commentators.[159] These critics have nevertheless usually failed to grasp that such abstractness and formalism do not issue simply from Habermas's "insufficient" treatment of "concrete" political questions. As this essay has attempted to show in some detail, rather, the political impotence of the theory of universal pragmatics is a necessary effect of several difficulties internal to its priorities and strategies of argumentation: its initially misleading comparison of therapy and political enlightenment, its inability to explicate a theory of distorted communication, and its conceptual privileging of abstractly conceived, consensual action.

Consequent upon these difficulties, or so it can be argued, the theory of universal pragmatics has been compelled to rely increasingly upon the strategy

187

of "rational reconstruction."[160] Habermas explains that this strategy is identical with neither formal logic analysis nor empirical-analytic observation of the behavior of lawlike, natural events. By virtue of its self-reference to the domain of communication, rational reconstruction is a species of understanding. (Compare Habermas's fundamental distinction between observation and understanding, outlined in Essay 4.) To "rationally reconstruct" communicative action is to analyze and explicate its underlying presuppositions systematically. This involves defending the distinction between deep and surface structures of communication.[161] Guided by this distinction, reconstructive understanding seeks to penetrate the surface phenomena of communicative activity. It seeks to discover the rules that actually determine the production of these surface communicative phenomena. It therefore directs its inquiries toward the intuitive, patterned competencies of speaking and acting subjects. It seeks to describe mimetically and then explicate the deeper meaning and implications of the fact that speaking actors are always embedded within a rule-governed universe of symbolically mediated communications.

Of course, as this essay has proposed, a central difficulty within such reconstructive interrogation is that it tends to presume that actually existing forms of communication are synonymous with abstractly conceived, consensual action! It misleadingly supposes that it can articulate, in the form of "objective and explicit knowledge,"[162] that which *hypothetically competent* subjects are assumed already to know and do intuitively. As Apel has also pointed out, Habermas's version of communication theory seriously overlooks the possibility of subjects' *refusal* or *inability* to enter into action oriented to reaching understanding. In view of this oversight, it is not surprising that the communication theory's quest for knowledge of the "rule consciousness of competent speakers" assumes the position of a will-o'-the-wisp. It holds fast to the unconvincing belief that it can gradually and successively discover what it is about by first developing exact arguments only with reference to hypothetical "clear cases" of communicative action that are assumed to be typical of everyday life under late capitalist conditions. Misleadingly suspending consideration of all actually existing deviations from its "clear case" principles, it mistakenly believes these can later be cumulatively extended to so-called borderline cases.[163]

Under the strain of this illusory reconstructivism, the political potential of the theory of universal pragmatics is eroded seriously. Habermas's long-standing insistence that the ultimate goal of critical theory is the political enlightenment of its addressees – the analysis and clarification of their needs and the positions they occupy within the contradictory system of late capitalism – begins to languish. The advocacy role of his project is crippled. This is true in two interrelated senses. In the first place, the theories of universal pragmatics and late capitalism become disconnected from each other. This separation results in a suppression of Tönnies's and Dewey's earlier thesis that a critique of public life must be centrally concerned with the tendency for contemporary public life and opinion to be manufactured by organized powers bent on promoting their own particular interests. This disconnection of the theories of universal pragmatics and late capitalism also has the consequence of bracketing some earlier suggestive theses

188

(analyzed in Essay 3) concerning the political potential of the administrative and cultural contradictions of late capitalist systems. Caught up in its reconstructivism, the theory of universal pragmatics places such theses to one side. Questions about the extent to which the crisis tendencies of late capitalism serve as a precondition of the emergence of alternative public spheres fall into obscurity.

There is a second sense in which the reliance on rational reconstruction undermines Habermas's earlier advocacy of free and systematic communication. The theory of universal pragmatics, to speak plainly, tends more and more to express itself over the heads of its potential adherents. Problems pertinent to the struggle for autonomous public life are subjected to a request: *Exeunt omnes.* The theory of universal pragmatics offers few insights into questions of practical struggle. Its account of the concept of communicative competence is vague and ungrounded. There is little consideration of concrete strategies that might facilitate a synthesis of existing opposition movements' sensed needs with new forms of public institutions. There is not even a clear indication of the groups to which the critical theory of communication is addressed.[164]

All late capitalist societies, it is true, are currently marked by the absence of powerful, unified, and highly articulate opposition movements. These social formations nevertheless evidence – indeed, generate – an array of important autonomous movements. In its present reconstructivist form, Habermas's theory of universal pragmatics seems far removed from these movements' day-to-day concerns. This estrangement is only exacerbated by this theory's more recent penchant for analyzing three distinct levels of the relationship between theory and practice. These levels are said to include first, researchers' elaboration of ideology-critical truth claims through discursive argumentation guided by the strategy of rational reconstruction; second, efforts at extending the boundaries of this argumentation, so as to include additional oppositional groups; and third, attempts to institutionalize such discourse through prudent political struggle.[165]

This typology no doubt has a certain analytic plausibility and political value. Under the weight of the critical theory's reconstructivism and abstractly formal concerns, however, its distinctions also obscure – to speak in old-fashioned terms – the possible mediations between theory and practice. As a consequence, Habermas's political prescriptions frequently rely on unhelpful truisms. "The enlightenment which produces radical understanding," he typically observes, "is always political."[166] Under pressure from the critical theory's several internal difficulties, such prescriptions assume the status of a moralizing imperative. Their efforts to defend the principle of discussion free from domination as *possible* and *desirable* are considerably weakened.

It is true that the argumentation of the universal pragmatics turns our attention away from factually imposed pseudoconsensuses to the possibility of genuine political agreements. It correctly emphasizes that the authenticity of political agreements and compromises reached without violence depends upon both the competency of those who decide and the conditions under which their agreements and compromises are reached. The theory of universal pragmatics therefore heightens our awareness of the patterns of bureaucratic exploitation and pseudocommunication within the contemporary situation. It reminds us also that politics is not necessarily synonymous with struggles between partial and conflicting interests oriented only by the logic of ruthlessness and profit, partisanship and the lust for dominion. Like the earlier arguments of Tönnies and Dewey, it strengthens hopes for a qualitatively different and better political order. Negatively speaking, it prompts further reflection upon the possibility of challenging heteronomous forms of power preserved through monopolies of the means of assertion, disputation, and persuasion; more positively, it anticipates pluralistic and self-interrogating forms of life, through whose free and systematic communication speaking and acting subjects could enter into mutually binding commitments. Above all, its formulations serve to clarify and focus a range of difficult distinctions and problems pertaining to public life. The communication theory rightly emphasizes, for example, that discussions of autonomous public life must seek to develop a theory of those mechanisms of pseudocommunication which serve to induce the servile dependency of speaking actors upon each other.

Granted these achievements, it is nonetheless evident that the excessively abstract and general claims of the universal pragmatics are couched in the language of tragedy: They are beyond the reach of ordinary actors within the present. It is implied that these participants must act as if the conditions of autonomous public life had already been established. Those who struggle for public life seem no longer to be engaged in discretionary action, in processes of self-invention through discussion, risk-taking, and action within particular power situations. What is more, these actors are supposed to speak and interact in highly artificial ways: It is inferred that autonomous public spheres are properly devoid of body politics, art, rhetoric, festivity, and disobedience. In short, a range of substantive theoretical and political questions – from those concerning ideology and disobedience to those concerning art and rhetoric – remain undiscussed. It is to these kinds of central political questions that future discussions of the theory of public life must, and will no doubt, attend.

6

Capitalism and creative destruction

> The whole question of human emancipation has taken a new form.
> The insight that the impulse to obliteration, to the self-extinction
> of humanity, lies in the very foundations of our industrial civili-
> zation and pervades every structure of its economy, science and
> technology ... is today of such immediate importance that the so-
> cialist perspective takes second place, and in any case must be
> redefined.
>
> Rudolf Bahro

Capitalism and creative destruction

The ecological movements that have grown remarkably within all late capitalist
societies during the past several decades show no signs of dissipation. Feeding
upon diffuse, popularly felt concerns about scientific-technical development and
the degradation of natural living conditions, these movements have considerably
shaken the confident belief that the whole of life, including outer nature, is
amenable to bureaucratic programming and control.[1] Establishing autonomous
organizations of discussion and resistance, the new ecological movements have
stimulated independent debate about the decimation generated by the restless
growth of late capitalist – and bureaucratic socialist – forms of labor, consumption, and scientific-technical research and development. This debate is of course
not without precedent in the history of the capitalist modernization process.
Since the last quarter of the eighteenth century, indeed, descriptions of the
capitalist mode of production as a reckless and dynamic system of production
for the sake of production and exchange have more and more become a commonplace of its political opponents. This opposition has correctly underscored
the pulverizing and authoritarian dynamism of modern capitalist economies.
From their inception, or so the following essay proposes, these systems of production, considered analytically *as* modes of production, have been singularly
marked by a restless and destructive vigor that contravenes the conditions of
possibility of autonomous public life.

The scope of this contradictory relationship between autonomous public life
and modern forms of production, science, and technology can usefully be introduced with some general remarks on the dynamism of the capitalist mode of
production. This dynamism may be seen, at a high level of generality, at any

191

rate, to have four central aspects. First, under the impact of the capitalist accumulation process, external nature, for the first time in the history of the human species, has come to be methodically hunted and hounded. Nature idolatry has been replaced by bureaucratic strategies that aim at the systematic domination of nature. To be sure, production continues to be nature-mediated: In capitalist societies, as in all noncapitalist orders, outer nature remains a vital condition of the production of material wealth and the reproduction and transformation of social and political life. Under the impact of the modernization process, however, this nature has virtually ceased to be recognized as a power for itself. Nature has become merely an object of consumption and a means of production for the sake of further production and exchange.

This presumption that outer nature is only a commodity just like any other has been complemented, secondly, by the fact that capitalist accumulation tends constantly to revolutionize its technologies and scientifically guided techniques of production. The incessant dynamism of this scientific-technological progress has commonly given rise to the suggestion that technology is a power unto itself, a force that obeys certain immanent laws of development. In point of fact, living labor power continues to plan and produce these techniques of production. Under capitalist conditions of production scientific-technological progress nevertheless appears to be a law unto itself, in part because – and this is the third respect in which the capitalist mode of production is without precedent – living labor has been uncoupled and divorced from all ownership of the means by which it can realize its labor. Wrenched from the unity formerly shared with their conditions of labor, laborers have tended to become "free" wage laborers. Their living labor, in turn, has been subjected to bureaucratic surveillance and discipline, in order that it might become a guaranteed means to the further accumulation of labor. Finally, and in accordance with its rationalization of free labor power, scientific-technological vigor, and growing domination of outer nature, capitalism has become the first civilization bent on universalizing itself. Modern capitalist societies form part of a totalizing world system. Conquering all barriers of time and space, capitalist production has sought to penetrate to all corners of the globe, to fashion the whole world in its own "civilized" and pulverizing image.

It can be argued that these "progressive-revolutionary" features of capitalist systems of self-expanding value have also contributed to their distinctively paradoxical – because reckless, violent, and conflict-ridden – character. As Schumpeter observed, the modern civilizing process has been chronically marked by the permanent revolutionizing and transformation of nature, technology, and social and political life, by a process of creative destruction that typically combines increases of production with the systematic deployment of violence and the generalization of squalor and misery and novel forms of discipline and unfreedom.[2] The productive dynamism of capitalist systems, that is to say, has developed only by conquering and exploiting, by invading, tearing apart, and subduing. On the peripheries of the capitalist world system, the lives and resources of the colonized have continually been ransacked and redeployed through massive investments of capital and arms. Within the centers of this system (to take some early examples) whole strata of craftsmen were eliminated, peasants were forcibly deprived of their rich folk culture and herded from their land, and the men, women, and children who formed the new proletariat were forced to suffer and struggle against all the pauperization this age could seemingly invent.

Among the critics of this paradoxical "creative destruction" attending the modern capitalist mode of production, two broadly different interpretive stand-points can be discerned. First, there have been those who criticize the capitalist mode of production for its *failed capacity* to abolish material scarcity and relations of command and obedience. This position was articulated most forcefully per-haps in the well-known Marxian thesis concerning the "fettering" of the forces of production by the capitalist relations of production. This thesis later under-pinned the old communist belief in capitalist production as a potential basis for socialism (Fordism without Ford, in Trotsky's version) and today informs pro-posals, championed by many European Communist Parties, to adopt nuclear technology "democratically." According to Marx, embittered talk of "dark Satanic mills" and acts of machine smashing among those who produce are without foundation – indeed, wholly self-destructive. It is not modern machinery and science per se that starve, overwork, and enslave their producers. Pauperization is rather the consequence of the mode of social and political relations of power within which the nonliving forces of production are (so to speak) "embedded." In the view of Marx, the potential of the already developed forces of production serves as a critical measure of the immaturity of the existing relations of pro-duction. In capitalist society, the forces of production – the accumulated products of past social labor – can plausibly be seen neither as neutral nor as immanently oppressive and dehumanizing. These scientific-technological forces constitute a historical triumph of the producing species over external nature. This triumph has been effected in spite of the fact that, under capitalist conditions, the de-ployment by capital of this science and technology definitely enslaves its pro-ducers to forces that assume the appearance of objective, natural powers. The existing stock of science, machinery, and techniques of production, in sum, contains the potential both to decrease the unfreedom of the working day rad-ically and to increase the associated producers' wealth and social and political freedom.[3]

It is precisely this kind of claim about the political innocence of the capitalist forces of production which has fueled the censures of modern scientific-tech-nological progress by a second political tradition. This tradition, whose origins date from at least the time of Rousseau, proposes the view that the creative destruction of the modern world is at least in part a consequence of its historically specific and *regressive* forces of production. This claim informs the arguments and struggles of the new ecological movements against contemporary forms of production and scientific-technical development. This claim also forms the object of the recent controversy between Marcuse and Habermas.[4] According to Mar-cuse – whose arguments will here serve to introduce Habermas's discussion of scientific-technical progress and, more generally, the limits of his understanding of the contradictory relationship between late capitalist forms of production and autonomous public life – modern scientific-technical development must be interpreted as a historically constructed, limited, and therefore *transformable* project. Under late capitalist conditions, Marcuse argues, the available forces of production are by no means indifferent toward political and social goals. These forces are particular, in the precise sense that they are expressive of the ruling powers' will to control both the underclasses and outer nature. By virtue of their own methods, contemporary science, technology, and techniques of production now secure a universe in which the organized struggle to dominate nature is both dependent upon and reinforced by systems of social and political heteronomy. The domination of nature and humanity is perpetuated and expanded not only *through* technology but also *as* technology, as bourgeois technical reason. *This* technical reason reproduces enslavement.

The consequences of this kind of argumentation are of course far-reaching, even dramatic. The emancipation of nature and society, Marcuse urges, is now contingent upon a complementary revolutionizing of late capitalism's labor processes and the science, technology, and techniques of production upon which they depend. There is even the suggestion – consistent with his less-than-convincing defense of socialism with a "biological foundation" (discussed in Essay 5) – that technics as such will be dissolved, giving way to a world permanently freed from the burdens of means-oriented action and surplus, unfree labor – a world, in short, governed solely by peaceful Eros.[5]

Habermas explictly rejects this kind of formulation. Under late capitalist conditions, in his view, the scientific-technical mastery of nature ought not be relinquished, because it has no necessary propensity for blocking the development of political autonomy. This project of mastering nature through the sphere of work does not render impossible a good life of public speech and action. On the contrary, Habermas is convinced that late capitalism's highly developed productive forces are destructive only insofar as their purposive rationality comes to reign supreme, that is, to assume hegemonic control over the whole of social and political life. The much-discussed problem of scientific-technological progress does not touch on questions about the need to reconstruct radically late capitalism's productive apparatus. The defense of autonomous public life is instead contingent upon the success of struggles that deemphasize and redeploy the existing productive apparatus, in *support* of a political project that aims at the qualitative expansion of public communication and citizenship. Habermas's theory of work thus stands within that tradition which criticizes only the hitherto-failed capacity of the capitalist mode of production to abolish heteronomy and material scarcity. In his view, the historical potential for public, democratic life is not precluded by the character of late capitalism's productive forces. This potential is hindered only by the (admittedly difficult and complex) problem of how to mediate the existing productive forces and institutionally secured forms of democratic speech and action. The heart of the problem of modern capitalist scientific-technical progress, in short, is that of harmonizing the relationship between work and communication, of bringing "the power of technical control...within the range of the consensus of acting and transacting citizens."[6]

Modern production as scientific-technical progress

From within the boundaries of this problematic, Habermas confidently opposes his arguments to recent wholesale criticisms of modern scientific-technical development.[7] Such criticisms are seen as ignoring two fundamentally progressive achievements of the gradual mechanization or bureaucratization of the modern bourgeois world. The first positive accomplishment – the profanation of religion and its legitimating powers – attended the emergence and diffusion of modern scientific discourses that sought to reveal the inner secrets of outer nature. Habermas's account of this confounding of religion by science can be usefully analyzed as a "materialist" version of the "cunning of reason" thesis (Hegel), according to which the avowed intentions and purposes ascribed by groups and individuals to their activity chronically produce self-contradictory and unforeseen consequences. These unintended consequences at the same time produce possibilities of different courses of action. The "cunning" of modern scientific reason in this sense was already evident during the nineteenth century. Habermas's thesis about the scientific disenchantment of the modern world appeared in many writings of that period: Saint-Simon's depiction of Physicism's expulsion of Deism from modern life[8] and Marx and Engels's famous description of the *embourgeoisement* process ("All that is solid melts into air, all that is holy is profaned") provide just two examples.

Perhaps the most compelling nineteenth-century rendition of this thesis was that of Nietzsche (whose arguments were of course later reconstructed by Max Weber). Contrary to the widespread expectation that modern science would provide an elaborate prop for Christianity's belief in the wisdom, goodness, and omnipotence of God,[9] Nietzsche proposed that the progress of this science in fact produces the very contrary of its intentions. Modern science subverts not only modern religion, but also classical metaphysics and archaic world views and myths. In traditional societies, for example, it was demons and gods who were seen as the mistresses and masters of the natural world. Under nonmodern conditions, external nature was "uncomprehended, terrible, mysterious Nature."[10] "When a man shoots with a bow," Nietzsche observed, "there is still always present an irrational hand and strength; if the wells suddenly dry up, men think first of subterranean doemons and their tricks."[11] Precisely because of its opposition to such beliefs, post-Galilean science was regarded by Nietzsche as critical and progressive in its thrust. Consequent upon the victories of modern science, "the doors leading to a religious life are closed to us once and for all."[12] At the expense of all previous forms of supernaturalism, this science legitimates the radically novel belief in *natural causality*. Steadying itself through reference to this notion, science confidently seeks hegemony over outer nature in the service of avowedly human ends. Modern science is therefore understood by Nietzsche as an activity that seeks to preserve and enhance human existence by imputing to outer nature ("Nature") notions of causality and law. It entails the "transformation of Nature into concepts for the purpose of governing Nature."[13] According to Nietzsche, the project of humanizing the natural world through

195

science directly reinforces humans' recognition of themselves as masters of the earth. Science becomes part of the rubric of *means*: It disposes of the confusion and flux of things natural and supernatural via control-oriented hypotheses that claim to explain everything.

Habermas's understanding of the delegitimating effects of modern scientific reasoning as a self-reflexive system of purposive-rational action closely parallels Nietzsche's account. Post-Galilean science, in Habermas's view, directly contributed to the subversion and secularization of the old religious shibboleths that had legitimated the feudal and early modern worlds. Faith, the assurance of things hoped for, the convictions about things unseen, was forced to yield before the earthward, action-oriented turn of the species' powers of scientific calculation. From the seventeenth century, he emphasizes, both society and nature were interpreted as aspects of the same mechanistic universe. Post-Galilean science not only inspired various philosophical attempts to reconstruct and modernize classical natural law in accordance with these mechanistic assumptions;[14] this science also inadvertently facilitated the emergence of a new anthropocentrism, which assumed that no longer God but the species itself would become the "masters and possessors of nature."[15] Within the context of the civilizing process, the diffusion of science accelerated the disenchantment of modern daily life by devaluing the sanctity of traditional world views. Their power *as* myth, *as* unquestionable tradition, *as* a justifying metaphysics, was thereby humiliated. The more thoroughly science claimed to have succeeded in revealing the formerly secret laws of nature, the more feeble the idea of the existence of a Creator and Preserver of the material universe became.

From the time of Galileo, according to Habermas, the intention of rigorous scientific research and experiment became less spiritual and more concerned with artificially reproducing the natural processes that God had made before; science became a rule-governed system of purposive-rational action that generates guiding principles for the accumulation of fresh information, itself to be revised when failures in anticipated results occur. Within this feedback-controlled process of experimentation and argumentation, nature itself appears to act as an impartial judge of the degree to which science has exposed its structure. Scientific statements are conditional predictions that are dependent upon, and foreshadow, successful human manipulation of natural objects. For Habermas, this is the revolutionary, sacrilegious accomplishment of a science whose very structure is designed for application. Stripped of its vitalism and divine characteristics, outer nature is now said to be knowable only insofar as it can be successfully manipulated and transformed by the species.[16]

Habermas considers the natural sciences' (unintended) assault on religious tradition to be only one aspect of the progressive character of the bureaucratization of the bourgeois world. Technical progress, the successive capitalist rationalization of the productive process, also reaches unprecedented levels. Habermas admits that material poverty remains a critical problem within the peripheral capitalist countries. Within the metropolitan countries, furthermore, the capitalist accumulation process has been chronically marked by disruptive crisis tendencies (as he stresses in his account of the liberal phase of capitalism).

Yet it is equally evident that "no other economic system has developed the forces of production as tremendously as capitalism."[17] The capitalist accumulation process has successfully rendered *permanent* the scope and expansion of the productive forces. Continuous growth of the means of production is an organizing principle of this epoch. Bourgeois modernization has been synonymous with the uncoupling and sustained expansion of the realm of work at the expense of all forms of communication reckoned to be obstructive. As if under the spell of their own momentum, the forces of production have been continually revolutionized: The division of labor becomes ever more complex, the deployment of machinery in the productive process is rendered almost permanent, and the size of units of production grows by leaps and bounds.[18]

As a consequence of state and corporate attempts to manage the crisis tendencies of liberal capitalism, this accumulation process has reached unprecedented levels, such that universal material abundance, at least within the late capitalist countries, definitely becomes possible. This possibility, according to Habermas, can in part be attributed to the direct (corporate and state) introduction of science into the productive process. Contrary to much received opinion – often generated by face-value accounts of the history of the natural sciences – Habermas correctly emphasizes that the planned and organized connection between science and the labor process was by no means intimate in the period prior to about the third quarter of the nineteenth century. To be sure, there is evidence that modern capitalist discourses were in part inspired directly by early innovations in machine technology and by the treatises of fifteenth-century craftsmen.[19] And it is furthermore true that there had often been a direct interest in science by manufacturers during the liberal phase of capitalism.[20] Habermas's thesis nevertheless remains plausible. Prior to the contemporary phase of capitalism, the chief influence of scientific discourses operated more diffusely, sharpening and clarifying approaches to problem solving, and radically heightening expectations and assumptions about the possibility of dominating nature and enhancing economic growth. This scientific legitimation of permanent technical progress is evident, for example, in the writings of Bacon, for whom the overcoming of "the inconveniences of man's estate" would from that point on be accomplished by scientifically "hounding," "subduing," and "vexing" outer nature.[21] Considered previously to be fickle, alive, and unpredictable, this "lawful" nature was from now on to be shaped "as on an anvil" through the integration of science and the organized system of social labor and machinery. Stable laws of a nature amenable to scientific explanation evidently went well with a civilizing process bent on stabilizing itself and achieving the goal of production for the sake of production and exchange.

By the last quarter of the nineteenth century, or so Habermas argues, the further extraction of absolute surplus value (through increasing the length of the working day, for example) had become politically unpopular. What is more, the technical developments associated with the first Industrial Revolution had been exhausted. It is precisely during this period that the earlier-signaled integration between science and the labor process tended to become a *fait accompli*. Scientific research work became bureaucratically organized and subjected to a division of labor appropriate to state institutions and capitalist industry. As a consequence of this "scientization of technology," research became oriented to the goal of producing technical knowledge that could be directly applied to the labor process.[22] Thus, whereas steam and coal had been the principal sources of power in the earlier phases of capitalist industrialization analyzed by Marx, electricity-powered and internal combustion, petroleum-fueled engines now became crucial. This period of the so-called second Industrial Revolution also saw the beginnings of the modern chemical industry. Moreover, cotton and coal were replaced increasingly by steel as the growth industry around which the more advanced capitalist economies revolved, so that the center of innovation diffusion in the industrialized world shifted from Britain to the United States.

By the end of the nineteenth century, or so Habermas wants to argue, such forms of technical innovation had become the official face of science,[23] thereby facilitating dramatic increases in labor productivity and cheapening the fixed components of capital. In earlier phases of modern capitalism, by contrast, technical innovations depended upon unpredictable and sporadic (even if impressive) patterns of invention. Under late capitalist conditions, this fortuitousness has been considerably reduced, as both technical development and the labor process tend to be drawn into a feedback relationship with scientific research. This is one reason why Habermas – correctly – tends to elide the conventional distinctions between science and technology and between pure and applied science. In his view, such distinctions forget that modern science has lost its former innocence. Science has become industrialized, a valuable commodity produced and deployed by the bureaucratic state and the oligopolistic corporations. Especially with the advent of state-funded research (a considerable proportion of which is initially for military purposes), science, technology, and industrial utilization have become fused into a single, and highly productive, system.

Scientific-technical progress as ideological

Interestingly, Habermas's defense of the progressive character of the modern capitalist forces of production also serves to illustrate his anxiety about their regressive effects under late capitalist conditions. His praise of modern scientific-technical progress, in other words, is limited. To the degree that scientific discourses have disenchanted the bourgeois world and have contributed to the impressive development of the productive forces, he argues that contemporary scientific-technical progress also turns against itself. The champions of this progress, he insists, fail to grasp the inherent limitations of this progress. Under late capitalist conditions, blind confidence in the project of bureaucratically dominating outer nature becomes apologetic about new forms of bureaucratic unfreedom.

This regressiveness of contemporary scientific-technical progess is evident in two interrelated senses. First, Habermas is highly critical of the widespread assumption – clearly evident in the "end of politics" school, for example[24] – that scientific-technical progress is the great and powerful panacea for most, if not all, contemporary sources of social misery and political unrest. Some recent writers (Habermas mentions Schelsky and Ellul, but his arguments apply with equal force to Carleton, Mesthene, Forbes, and the "futurologists")[25] have even elaborated a variant on this theme. This is the so-called thesis of technological determinism. The imperatives of modern technology, advocates of this thesis propose, are effecting a radical and (though here there are dissenters) *progressive* break with previous phases of human history. According to these advocates, the logic and fruits of technology now operate as a demiurge, which busily and efficiently works to create a tranquil and planned heaven on earth. Progress means little more than a *science- and technology-induced* drive to higher and higher summits of politically guided economic growth and the disciplining of subjects and consumers through the bureaucratic provision of social welfare. Within this scenario, there is neither time nor space for autonomous political discussion: Moral-practical progress becomes identical with technical progress. The logic of the productive forces appears to determine the development of the whole of social and political life. These forces seem to be the prime movers of history.[26]

In opposition to the assumptions and often rosy prognostications of this thesis of technological determinism, Habermas pits the fundamental distinction between work and communication. By distinguishing the logic of technical rationalization from that of the communicative or political framework within which it is always embedded, he insists that claims on behalf of a self-propelling and beneficent scientific-technical progress are profoundly illusory. Equally misguided are those concerned to develop techniques of technology assessment.[27] Advocates of such claims and concerns ignore the fact that the emancipatory potential of contemporary scientific-technical progress – its capacity to expand social and political freedom and equality on the basis of material abundance – cannot be realized so long as a critical consideration of its political, communicative context is bracketed.

This progress cannot per se bring its emancipatory potential to fruition. This is because the rationality of the part (that is, technobureaucratic rationalization within the sphere of work) can serve only as a condition of the rationality of the whole (that is, technical rationalization supplemented and steered by the rationalization of communicative activity through democratic, public life). The progressive mastery of outer nature through work ought also to be a political task; the struggle to develop and distribute the productive forces usefully must take the form of political speech and action within public spheres of communication. Under late capitalist conditions, conversely, allegations about the autonomy of scientific-technical development serve to conceal the prescientific decisions and preexisting class and state interests that *ab ovo* structure the pace and direction of that development.[28] It is precisely these private interests which also block the immanent potential of the productive forces at hand. This emancipatory potential is fettered because these productive forces are deployed through highly undemocratic, depoliticized modes of decision making. Within the spheres of state and society, particular ruling groups guide the development of scientific-technological progress and distribute its benefits and consequences according to their own private interests, over and against the (potentially) generalizable interests of a public *outside* the sphere of work.

Habermas seeks to strengthen this critical point by emphasizing a second flaw within contemporary scientific-technical progress. Despite its claims to being rational, democratic, efficient, professional, and life-enhancing, Habermas argues, the scientization of spheres of work and communication suffers from a serious unintended consequence. The spread of scientifically informed bureaucratization beyond the boundaries of work into the sphere of communication produces a pervasive meaninglessness. Attempts to plan and order communicative action scientifically (IQ testing in the formal education process, bureaucratic attempts to plan and number clients, and the like) are nihilistic. They are destructive of the possibility of meaningful communicative or political activity between subjects concerned to reach a consensus about moral-practical goals.[29]

This is a difficult argument, which can perhaps best be analyzed in this context with brief reference to Nietzsche's classical discussion of the unintended outcomes of post-Galilean science. In opposition to the (post-)Enlightenment fetishism and deployment of science within all realms of nature and society, Nietzsche insisted that the modern positivist sciences were necessarily unable to generate moral-practical meaning. This allegation was explicitly directed against the supposition (of Voltaire, for example) that scientific knowledge *qua* knowledge was good in itself, that is, had an inner connection with morality and happiness. Nietzsche also sought to repudiate another tradition of argument (which he traced to Spinoza), which had insisted that modern natural science, in contrast to the civilizing process and its unfettering of human hunger for power and dominion over others, was genuinely innocent, unselfish, and human.[30] Against these presumptions, Nietzsche proposed that the growing popularity of scientistic forms of thinking in the nineteenth century was identical with the dissemination of moral-practical ignorance. In part, this ignorance was the consequence of the diminution of the scope of morality by the deployment of the principle of scientific causality. Concerned only to grasp necessary effects and to conceive them as distinct from all chance possibilities and incidentals, modern science destroys numerous "imaginary causalities" (nature, God, and so on) that hitherto served as meaningful sources of authority. "As the sense of causality increases, so does the extent of the domain of morality decrease."[31]

More disturbingly, moral-practical ignorance is also a definite consequence of the fact that the sciences are capable only of generating information and technical recommendations. "Science traces the course of things," Nietzsche contends, "but points to no goal: what it does give consists of the fundamental facts upon which the new goal must be based."[32] The objectivist sciences' growing hold over both nature and social life directly annihilates morality; the information and techniques of these sciences have themselves no moral-practical meaning. Modern scientific-technical reason is itself subjected to a certain cunning: By unwittingly dissolving traditional myths and modern forms of religion, the pure light of science substitutes indifference and nihilism and lays the path to "sovereign ignorance."[33] Concerned with destroying imaginary causalities, science never creates values apart from the belief in science itself. Scientific knowledge *qua* knowledge is technical. Scientific discourse thrives on "numbering, calculating, weighing, seeing and handling" – essentially limited concerns that are incapable of providing meaning for human life. The growing influence of science therefore accelerates the emergence of a nihilistic world cluttered with piles of meaningless facts. "The development of science tends ever more to transform the known into the unknown."[34] Technobureaucratic presumptions about the desirability of the spread of science for its own sake must accordingly be rejected. "Science itself now *needs* a justification."[35]

The substantial parallels between these arguments and Habermas's concern to promote the development of public communication free from domination are unmistakable. Under late capitalist conditions, Habermas insists, the spread of scientifically rationalized patterns of life (in the direction of "an essentially mechanical world," in the words of Nietzsche)[36] tends to suppress awareness of the fundamentally unique logic of both the cultural, political sciences and communicative activity itself. The spread of scientistic discourses into the realm of communication, their self-misunderstanding as a type of knowledge and activity that cannot be surpassed, destroys those political processes according to which speaking and acting subjects could come to generate agreement freely on moral-practical ends. This is why the scientific-technical treatment of (potential) speakers and actors as though they were but mute objects runs the risk of weakening the processes through which the meanings of everyday life are intersubjectively produced. Conversely, the scientific preparation and bureaucratic deployment of substitute meanings become subject to the risk that these surrogate meanings will become alien and foreign to those for whom they have been prepared.

The scientization of contemporary social and political life is therefore no harbinger of happy and meaningful tranquility amid material abundance. To the contrary, moral-practical ignorance spreads; meaning tends to become a scarce resource; and struggles to revitalize autonomous communication proliferate. The scientific rationalization of daily life produces serious legitimacy and motivation problems – or, in the terms of Nietzsche's chilling aphorism, the arrival of the madman, lantern in hand, calling to the crowds of unbelievers gathered in the marketplace:

> Where is God gone? . . . *We have killed him,* – you and I! We are all his murderers! . . . Is there still an above and below? Do we not stray as through infinite nothingness? Does not empty space breathe upon us? Has it not become colder? Does not night come on continually, darker and darker? . . . God is dead! . . . And we have killed him! . . . Shall we not ourselves have to become Gods, merely to seem worthy of it?[37]

For Nietzsche, of course, the depreciation of the superior by the banal was both an indication of barbarous decadence and a first sign of regeneration, of the possibility of the self-surmounting of nihilism by *der Übermensch.* Under these conditions, the human species therefore resembles a rope stretched between the animals and a future political elite, a rope stretched across a contemporary abyss of absurdity.[38] According to a parallel argument with radically different, democratic goals, Habermas urges that the contemporary scarcity of meaning facilitates mass loyalty problems. These problems, which can also be interpreted as a condition of emancipation from the repressive aspects of scientific-technical

201

progress, can be genuinely alleviated only through the expansion of democratic politics. The problems of meaninglessness attending late capitalist scientific-technical progress must be seen as a a challenge that cannot be met with scientific-technical strategies alone. The latter's potential, to repeat, must be harnessed and realized by processes of effective public discussion and decision making. The establishment of public life beyond the sphere of work, Habermas insists, is now conditional upon the defense of political processes that systematically doubt, criticize, and overturn forms of bureaucratic decision making legitimated by beliefs in empirical-analytic science as a universal form of knowledge. Only through such political resistance would speaking and acting publics be able to evaluate their own needs meaningfully and, in the light of what is scientifically and technically feasible, judge the direction and extent to which the productive forces should be further developed.[39]

This possibility of democratizing the technical potential of the productive forces is currently concealed by scientifically guided, bureaucratic attempts to manage, handle, and control spheres of communicative life. Venturing beyond their legitimate domain (of work), these strategies of scientific-technical administration exceed their competence. Their emancipatory potential – within the sphere of work – is repressed. Through the confusion of the fundamentally nonidentical logics of work and communication, the project of mastering outer nature bureaucratically becomes a fetter upon democratic, public life. "The substance of domination," Habermas concludes, "is not dissolved by the power of technical control. To the contrary, the former can simply hide behind the latter."[40]

Nonbureaucratic exchanges between society and nature?

Habermas's theses on the regressive consequences of modern scientific-technical progress appear to be unexceptionable to this point. He forcefully argues that progress in the subjugation of outer nature (that is, the disenchantment of the early bourgeois world, the dramatic raising of the level of the forces of production) becomes regressive insofar as its democratic potential is regarded abstractly, that is, considered in isolation from the totality of relations of (potential) communication within which it is embedded. This progress becomes regressive (to make the same point from a different perspective) insofar as attempts are made to administer realms of social and political life scientifically outside the realm of work, that is, to colonize with bureaucratic forms of rationality what is properly the domain of intersubjective communication. The substance of this (neo-Aristotelian) point lies at the heart of Habermas's critique of contemporary scientific-technical progress (compare Essay 4). The essentially nonidentical concepts of purposive-rational and communicative action must be distinguished, he insists, in order to avoid conflating what are indeed two radically different rationalization processes. He is emphatic: There is no continuum of rationality in the treatment of technical and political problems. "The rules of communicative action do develop in response to changes in the domain of instrumental and strategic action; in doing so, however, they develop in accordance with their own dynamics."[41]

During the past several decades this fundamental thesis has been specified by way of several, not always compatible, arguments. Habermas's earliest writings sustained themselves upon the theoretical distinction between the realm of necessary labor and that of undisturbed freedom. Later, for instance, in *Knowledge and Human Interests*, the distinction between technical and political problems came to depend upon a theory of cognitive interests. Most recently, the rules of communication and work (instrumental and strategic action) have been specified through the theories of communication, ego development, and social evolution, and by way of highly abstract and formal discussions of the concept of rationality. Despite the shifting arguments produced by this tacking procedure, Habermas has consistently defended the neo-Aristotelian point that there is a fundamental disjunction between the realms of necessity and freedom; the development of the productive forces must not be mistaken for the good life of public speech and action. It is exactly the conflation of these two realms of life that has crippled the democratic potential of bourgeois modernization processes. As Habermas insists repeatedly, the "unity of theoretical and practical reason . . . [becomes] the key problem for modern world interpretations."[42]

This thesis, or so the remaining arguments of this essay propose, can serve as one starting point from which Habermas's defense of scientific-technical progress can be immanently criticized.[43] For essential to his theory of production is an unresolved difficulty that bears directly on the question of autonomous public life. This unresolved problem derives from Habermas's conviction that the non-identical rationalities of work and communication prevent their reconciliation at either the categorical or the historical level. Under pressure from this conviction, Habermas's insistence upon the primacy of the communicative realm as "the pacemaker of social evolution"[44] provides only cold comfort. The neo-Aristotelian sources of Habermas's difficulty remain. In both his earlier and his later works, the impression is generated that work (instrumental and strategic action) and communication (public life) definitely face each other as alien and antagonistic forms of life. Work or toil is represented as private and mute in the Aristotelian sense, whereas communication is represented as a (potential) domain of public speech and action. Work is understood as a realm of trans-historical necessity ("mere life") whose inner purpose is simply "the development of the productive forces,"[45] whereas communication is analyzed as the realm of potential individuation and autonomy (the "good life"). The empirical-analytic sciences are said by Habermas to strive for bureaucratic control over objectified processes, whereas the explanatory understanding provided by the critical social sciences is oriented to the goal of political emancipation from that bureaucratic rationality; and so on. In consequence of these formulations, it seems as if the human species is threatened with a major "ontological" obstacle in its own struggle for social and political emancipation. According to Habermas, the project of subjugating outer nature through the bureaucratic rationality of work, technology, and empirical-analytic science (rationalization at the technical level) is fated to collide with the goal of politically emancipating inner nature, of rationalization at the moral-practical level.

This apparent impasse suggests an underlying problem within Habermas'

203

thinking, a difficulty that has frequently produced the oversimplified criticism (by Ferrarotti, for example)[46] that Habermas's political theory is an expression of liberal bourgeois resistance to late capitalism. This deep-seated problem consists in the fact that the sphere of strategic and instrumental action (the productive forces, including direct and reflexive labor) is defined *a priori* as immune from criticism and historical reconstruction. Qualitative transformations of this technical interest, it seems, can never be effected. Only different historical combinations of the two forms of life – for example, a diminution of the scope of work and an expansion of the realm of communication – can be achieved. Habermas proposes a historic balancing out and compromise, so to speak, between two interests that have been at war throughout the whole of bourgeois modernity.

Unconvinced of this compromise proposal, and concerned to analyze the problematic relationship between autonomous public life and modern bureaucratic forms of production, the remaining arguments in this essay rely on the thesis that Habermas's discussion of labor, science, and technology is insufficiently critical. His conception of the exchange between society and outer nature is seen here as positivistically bound to actually existing systems of bureaucratized work. This is the crucial sense in which it may be said that his denunciation of the spread of rationalization processes under late capitalist conditions turns into an apotheosis of their particular form of rationality, namely, *bureaucratic* rationality. The contingency that marks the form and content of late capitalism's exchange with outer nature is seriously underestimated. It must be emphasized that this criticism – unlike that of Marcuse, for example – does not propose the absurd and impossible, namely, the ultimate abolition of all means-oriented, administrative action. The point, rather, is that questions about the depoliticizing effects of the type of rationality crystallized in *our* labor processes; *our* science, technology, and techniques of production; and *our* collective (dis-)regard for outer nature are too readily dismissed by Habermas. Falling behind the insights of the new ecological movements, his writings introduce a new and subtle form of objectivism. Their frequently (and genuinely) expressed intention of speaking against appearances, of "mobilizing the power of radical self-reflection against every form of objectivism,"[47] turns against itself. His critique of bureaucratic rationality becomes apologetic, surrendering to the historically specific unfreedom within existing forms of scientific-technical development. Habermas therefore cannot develop categories that demonstrate their depoliticizing effects. Nor can he challenge the falsity of allegations about technological imperatives that press upon the peripheral capitalist countries.[48] In sum, a nonbureaucratic exchange with outer nature cannot be envisaged.

Work, technology, and public life

This lacuna within Habermas's account of late capitalist production has two aspects; each prematurely and unjustifiably throws doubt upon the legitimacy of attempts to defend autonomous public life within the sphere of work. In the first place, or so Habermas implies, the logic of work is identical with bureau-

cratic, purposive-rational action. Only through this form of action can the material prerequisites of the good life be secured on an effective and efficient basis.
The sphere of work is defined by problem solving, the acquisition of technical
skills, and the bureaucratic production and deployment of tools against nature.
This characterization of work, which presumably for Habermas also includes
the labor typically performed by women within the household, owes much to
classical and liberal bourgeois conceptions of public life, a characteristic weakness
of which was their justification of mechanisms of exclusion of allegedly private
concerns.* In the domain of work, in Habermas's view, everything and everybody
must fall silent. Work is that process through which those who labor are at most
instrumentum vocale, mere speaking tools fated to struggle to separate themselves
from outer nature. Within the sphere of work, the "species . . . is compelled to
reproduce its life through purposive-rational action."[49] Only through this necessary objectification and manipulation of outer nature do they (potentially)
become speaking and acting subjects. To invoke the descriptive terms of Arendt,
to whom Habermas is close on this point, work is the domain appropriate to the
(prehuman) *animal laborans* (producing its necessary means of subsistence through
the labor of its body) and to *homo faber* (fabricating an artificial world of objects
through the work of its hands). The problems raised within this domain are not

---

* Cf. O. Negt and A. Kluge, *Öffentlichkeit und Erfahrung: Zur Organisationsanalyse von
bürgerlicher und proletarischer Öffentlichkeit* (Frankfurt am Main, 1972), p. 10: "The predominant interpretations of the concept of the public sphere are remarkable inasmuch
as they try to comprise a variety of phenomena, and, yet, exclude the two most important
spheres of life: the entire industrial mechanism of the plant and the socialization in the
family. According to these interpretations, the public sphere draws its substance from
an intermediate domain that does not give expression to any particular social life context
in any particular way, although the function of representing the sum total of all social
life contexts is attributed to this public sphere." The following arguments, which draw
upon Negt and Kluge's thesis, concentrate only upon Habermas's depoliticized treatment
of industrial labor and scientific research and development. His account of work is also
vulnerable to recent feminist critiques of the classical liberal division between the private
and the public (see Essay 7). As Carole Pateman argues convincingly ("Feminist Critiques
of the Public–Private Dichotomy," in S. Benn and G. Gaus [eds.], *Conceptions of the Public
and Private in Social Life* [London, 1984]), the classical liberal division has been the object
of almost two centuries of feminist writing and political struggle, precisely because the
alleged separation and opposition of the public and private domains has been continually
represented as equivalent to the unequal opposition between men and women. Although
Pateman does not adequately distinguish the shifting historical meanings of the public–
private distinction, she convincingly argues that classical liberalism – whose influence
has by no means been exhausted – supposed the naturalness of "private" women's
subordination to "public" men. The private sphere of domesticity was seen as the proper
domain of the economically dependent wife; within this sphere, her functions of child
rearing and maintaining the household were deemed to be appropriate to her "closeness"
to nature. Women and the domestic sphere were thereby made to appear inferior to
the male public world of culture, achievement, property, power, reason, and freedom.
By virtue of its silences about these matters, Habermas's account of work sits comfortably
within this patriarchal liberal tradition. Not only does his account falsely represent social
labor as a sphere of private compulsion; it also suppresses the insight that those who
engage in social labor are daily dependent upon the tasks of shopping, washing, cleaning,
providing food, and caring for children performed (without pay) by women.

issues that could be settled by processes of decision, persuasion, and compromise; they are rather matters of administration, to be put in the hands of experts.[50] The realm of work is, in sum, a functional sphere populated by objects that, under the pressure of necessity, assume the form of moving bodies – things, events, and conditions that are in principle capable of being manipulated.[51] So long as the species must preserve itself through social labor aided by technological means that substitute for this labor, spheres of bureaucratic organization cannot be renounced under any historical conditions.

Through the concept of strategic rules, to be sure, Habermas can admit of the need for a transformation of the *goals* that orient the labor process under late capitalist conditions. According to his schema, the late capitalist emphasis upon state-secured, capitalist production for the sake of exchange could be replaced by production for publicly defined needs. The planned humanization of work conditions and selective policies of anti-industrialism might therefore be appropriate to a socialist society freed from "systematically distorted communication." Consonant with the publicly perceived need to reduce current levels and types of material consumption,[52] such counterindustrial policies might accelerate processes of automation and enhance the possibility of a radical shortening of the length of the working day. Under conditions of democratic socialism, nevertheless, bureaucratic forms of work would persist; it is unlikely that capitalist forms of labor could be replaced by, say, systems of self-managing council-based production. The subjective, creative moment of labor (that is, the autonomous development of producers' capacities) would always be subordinated to its objective aspects, namely, to the tasks of controlling nature through the fabrication of a world of artificial objects. The function of work would be to release time and energy for public activities outside the sphere of work.[53]

Work as a "sacrifice" (Adam Smith), a "trouble" (Kant), a realm of purposive rationality burdened by necessity and the imperatives of efficiency (Weber) – Habermas's formulation stands within a long-established theoretical tradition that derides labor as an activity proper only to the mute and obedient. These formulations accurately indicate the extent to which working skills and competences have been mutilated successively under modern, capitalist conditions, largely in accordance with the attempts by capital to constitute itself as a separate power, as the bearer of exclusive control over the means of production. Contrary to Habermas's description of work as the purposive development of skills,[54] it is clear that, under late capitalist conditions, work tends to become the antithesis of skill, if by skill we mean the autonomously developed ability to produce competently and imaginatively through the calculated organization of tools, labor, and materials and the *communicatively learned* ability to estimate and decide the final work's useful and aesthetic qualities. Understood in these terms, the modern bourgeois world has been marked by continuous attempts (on the part of capital) to train, educate, and upgrade – and bureaucratically degrade – (potentially) free, skilled laboring activity to the level of a depoliticized means of life. Considered as a whole, the history of capitalist work processes can be read as the history of attempts to discipline bureaucratically and disqualify the direct producers, to transform them into *Fachidioten*, "specialized imbeciles."

Work becomes synonymous with an activity done for another's benefit; in exchange for pay and promotion, work is structured according to rules, schedules, and goals that are heteronomously imposed.

In the early modern period, this bureaucratization of work was evidenced in the forcible destruction of the master-journeyman-apprentice guild relations of production and the successive introduction of the capitalist division of productive tasks. In at least three respects, this guild production (which encompassed the activity of weavers, spinners, millers, bakers, blacksmiths, glaziers, and others) was marked by its less hierarchic and rigid and more properly autonomous and communicative character. First, the master, like the journeyman and apprentice, was also a producer and not solely a manager, as in the later capitalist organization of production. Secondly, the master-journeyman-apprentice hierarchy was lineal, in that, frequently enough, real upward mobility took place: Eventually the apprentice could expect to become a journeyman and, likely, a master. Finally, this guild relationship facilitated members' active control over both their finished products and their laboring activity; the relationship of master-journeyman-apprentice to market relations of exchange was not regulated by an intermediary, as soon came to be the typical case in capitalist modes of work.

The successive introduction of more bureaucratic forms of the capitalist division of labor in manufacturing was synonymous with the forcible penetration of the developing forces of production (namely, the material infrastructure of production, including the work site and machine technology, and the organization of laboring activity itself) by capitalist relations of production and exchange. These two moments of the accumulation process by no means developed in relative isolation from one another, as was until recently assumed by many commentators, Marxist and non-Marxist alike.[55] The capitalist subdivision of work involved more than the exigencies of what Weber called "technical efficiency" – the need to harness the full potential of new and more productive sources of energy such as water and steam, for example.[56] Indeed, the early emergence of capitalist production – for example, the forcible introduction of a more complex division of labor (the system of "putting out") and, later, forms of centralized administration typical of the factory system – presupposed the primacy of the goal of bureaucratic, capitalist control over the laborers and their products, and not that of productive efficiency per se. Technology and the organization of work tasks developed as efficient strategies of disciplining and subjugating labor to an alien goal.

While the managerial struggle to destroy the putting-out and craft systems of labor was typically resisted well into the nineteenth century,[57] their eventual breakup signaled the growing elimination of workers' (potential) control over both product and work process. Within the context of the overall productive process, this destruction of autonomous forms of labor also ensured an essential and profitable place for the entrepreneur as manager of the depoliticized and divided activities of those who toiled. This outcome is powerfully described in Marx's account of the "barrack discipline" of the nineteenth-century factory system. Prior to the factory system, Marx observed, laborers directly made use

207

of their machines; under the new conditions, by contrast, it appears that machinery makes use of the laborers. Machines are deployed by capital with the aim of transforming laborers into "mere living appendages" of those machines. These laborers tend to become private soldiers within an industrial army; because they are helplessly dependent upon factory discipline in general, and the power of the capitalist in particular, their bodily and intellectual freedom is almost wholly confiscated.[58]

This bureaucratic definition and laceration of the work process certainly persists under late capitalist conditions. The existing means of production are not in general means to existing ends that nevertheless might be put to other, autonomous and public ends. They are for the most part means that predetermine which ends can be reached. These means proscribe more democratic forms of organization guided by autonomous public spheres of discussion and decision making.

In new, expanded, and more subtle forms, the will of bureaucratic domination continues to be written into the geographic location and organization of production, into the very types, range, and spatial location of machinery. The various twentieth-century corporate attempts to modernize work, technology, and techniques of production – not to mention the state forces of military destruction produced through the work process – are instances of this. The growing divorce between mental and manual labor, monopoly control of scientific research and development by professional elites, the growth of parasitic labor power (quality-control inspectors, supervisors, engineers, and so on) whose function is to coordinate and discipline labor power, the fragmentation and specialization of tasks, the gigantism and centralized power of units of production and distribution – little of this is a consequence of "objective necessities" attending efficient and effective production. Each of these strategies must rather be seen as an element within corporate attempts to systematically routinize, fragment, and bureaucratically control the work process. From the standpoint of those who manage, technology, science, and the organization of work must always assume the form of techniques for maintaining control over those who produce. In this new phase of expanded bureaucratization, laborers are regarded as just one more badly designed machine.

There can be no doubt that these strategies of control have considerably hindered the possibility of political challenges to the bureaucratic rationality of the workplace. The rationalization of work helped destroy the factory council movement and, especially within the oligopoly spheres of production, pushed the subdivision, measurement, timing, and standardized planning of production to extremes. As the social and territorial division of labor has become more and more bureaucratic, the function of centralized corporate (and state) planning and administration has become ever more crucial, and efforts to increase its powers have accordingly increased. The bureaucratic development of the productive forces for exchange rather than for publicly determined use does not, however, obliterate producers' "consciousness of injustice" and moral-practical struggle.[59] Especially when catalyzed by collective social movements, the more privatized forms of resistance to bureaucratized labor processes – "allergies to

208

work" such as absenteeism, alcoholism, daydreaming, sabotage, time wasting – frequently transform themselves into communicatively organized "work to rule" campaigns, into labor revolts, or, as can be observed in the tremendous importance of "resistance through rituals" among contemporary youth,[60] into opposition to industrialized work per se.

These daily resistances might be seen as the counterparts of the mass loyalty problems depicted by Habermas outside the realm of work. They do not confirm the validity of essentialist models of labor as creative self-realization. They rather provide evidence for the thesis, proposed in earlier essays, that bureaucratization can never be an unrestricted, linear process. The actions of the direct producers constitute forms of inversion and resistance that express – to be sure, often incoherently and indirectly – the extent to which bureaucratic supervision within the workplace chronically produces struggles for the questioning and abolition of bureaucracy. These moral-practical struggles against a labor process rationally planned and executed from above and outside embody an embryonic form of autonomous public life; although fragmented and often transitory, these struggles generate the need to "demultiply" the leadership of bureaucratic organizations (including trade unions) by expanding the rank and file's possibilities of initiative, self-expression, and debate. No doubt, as with all nascent public movements, these struggles are continually subject to counterstrategies of bureaucratic co-optation, divide-and-rule, and outright repression.[61]

Apropos of these struggles, it is the argument of Habermas and others that the self-management of complex and socially necessary labor processes is an illusory and unrealizable goal. According to this thesis (which owes much to Weber's denunciation of public life as the enemy of technical efficiency), it is no longer possible to reverse the evolution of manufacturing and administrative processes. Producers' generalized mastery of both their products and the conditions of production is impossible. The reduction of forms of production to a socially necessary minimum inevitably entails a normalization and standardization of tools, procedures, tasks, and technical knowledge.[62]

Such means-oriented questions, it is true, will not wither away, as was frequently assumed within the nineteenth-century radical democratic vision of a society of self-governing producers freed from all opacity and disagreement. These technical or means-oriented questions concerning tools, the design of work procedures, and so on nevertheless cannot be reduced to technical rules of decision making. If only because these rules do not reveal themselves spontaneously and transparently, the case against the introduction of public spheres of discussion and decision making within spheres of (socially necessary) production cannot be closed.[63] This case is enhanced by continuing worker demands for job enrichment and worker participation, and by struggles over industrial safety, redundancies, and the introduction of technical innovations. These demands and struggles preserve the possibility of the common ownership and restructuring of the means of production through the defense of spheres of social life defined by the democratic principle of the self-government of the producers. Arising from producers' autonomous organizational forms, such demands and struggles indicate that bureaucratic forms of work and technology radically contradict and subvert public spheres of discussion and decision making outside the sphere of work. Contradicting Habermas's defense of bureaucratic imperatives within this sphere, these resistances imply that the possibility of a socialist society freed from "systematically distorted communication" additionally requires that autonomous public communication enter the realm of the office, the factory, the department store, and the laboratory.

On the empirical-analytic sciences

Habermas's uncritical account of the empirical-analytic, natural sciences constitutes a second reason why his defense of the "progressive" character of late capitalism's productive forces prevents him from envisaging a nonbureaucratic exchange with outer nature. The critique of scientific-technical progress, Habermas typically insists, must not extend to the rationality of natural science itself. This science is immanently structured by the goal of dominating outer nature; for this type of science, which is indeed "alien to nature," and well suited to its bureaucratic mastery and control, there can be no more humane or less bureaucratic substitute.[64]

In a descriptive sense, this thesis seems plausible enough. Habermas accurately observes that the validity claims and selection principles of the modern natural sciences have indeed moved in the direction of instrumental control over their external environment. Post-Galilean science precipitated a search, that is, for quantifiable, lawlike relations of appearances in the world of outer nature; more and more, this nature was conceived not as written by God but as an external and alien object, without soul or purpose, as mere stuff capable of controlled manipulation. In opposition to the prevailing Aristotelian interpretations of nature, and against the resistances provided by the contemporary revival of hermetic and natural magic traditions,[65] defenders of the new mechanical, empirical-analytic sciences emphasized at least four central postulates. These postulates of the new science included the necessity of granting priority to the concept of quantity over that of quality; the primacy of the concept of relation over that of contingent, accidental substance; the need to replace the former (Aristotelian) understanding of local motion with accounts of inertial motion regulated by geometrical principles that could in turn be developed through analytical geometry (as in the Cartesian method of structuring scientific thinking mathematically through deduction from axioms guided by algebraic calculation); and, finally, the imperative of adopting a mechanistic view of nature as a devitalized object capable of controlled domination by human subjectivity.

With one or two important amendments, Habermas's own account of the empirical-analytic sciences is quite compatible with these formulations, especially the latter postulate concerning the reification of outer nature. To be sure, he persuasively argues against the commonplace objectivist self-understanding of these post-seventeenth-century sciences. In very summary form, this self-understanding of science and the natural world was something like the following. There exists an outer natural world that is in principle capable of being exhaustively described through scientific language. The scientist, as both language user and observer, can "encircle" and capture these external facts of nature through propositions that are true in the sense that they rather exactly correspond to these facts. Through experimentation and observation, these facts can be uncovered and described by way of scientific propositions, which successively reveal and explain mechanisms of the natural world that were formerly concealed. The history of science, in this view, demonstrates a continuously progressive, cumulative approach to truth, where truth consists in the correspondence among systems of observation sentences, theoretical statements, and the natural world. In this correspondence lies the secret of the capacity of the modern sciences to aid in the species' control of outer nature.

Habermas questions this form of naïve realism.* He insists on the need to

---

* In this respect, Habermas's critique of realism parallels two crucial themes within recent philosophy of science. Both of these themes have undermined the plausibility of the naïve realism of earlier positivist models of science and, it might be added, considerably weakened the capacity of this science to legitimate bureaucratic relations of command and obedience. First, Duhem, the early Quine, and others have pointed to the "underdetermination" of scientific theory by empirical data. The inference of theories from observations, it is emphasized, is not an unambiguous, logically conclusive process. In principle, there are an indefinite number of alternative theoretical descriptions that appear to fit, or correspond with, the "natural facts" in question. Scientific discourses, in short, can be neither singularly derived from nor conclusively refuted by statements of fact alone. Cf. P. Duhem, *The Aim and Structure of Physical Theory* (Princeton, N.J., 1954), p.2, chs. 6–7; and W. O. Quine, *Word and Object* (New York, 1960), chs. 1–2; elsewhere (*From a Logical Point of View* [Cambridge, Mass., 1953], p. 43), Quine insists that, in the face of *any* evidence, theoretical statements can be maintained as plausible: "Any statement can be held true come what may, if we make drastic enough adjustments elsewhere in the system...Conversely, by the same token, no statement is immune to revision."

Secondly, it has been emphasized by Apel and others that every observation statement generated by the natural sciences is always constructed theoretically. It is argued that the empiricist thesis that theoretical language in the natural sciences is parasitic upon their "observation language" (i.e., sets of terms designating observable things and events) is fundamentally mistaken. (Some examples of this "dual language" thesis include E. Nagel, *The Structure of Science* [London, 1961], ch. 5; and A. J. Ayer, *Language, Truth and Logic* [London, 1946], p. 11.) This is so because the natural world is not somehow given or apprehended through intuition. Theoretical terms are not simply derivative of observation terms. Propositions pertaining to empirical data are always theoretically informed, that is, discursively constructed. Inasmuch as these observation statements must minimally be expressed by a community of investigators in and through a learned, spoken, and written language, empirical data are inescapably subject to processes of theoretical classification and interpretation. Like all speech acts, observation and theoretical statements are deployed, organized, and understood and accepted, modified, or rejected within a symbolically mediated, communicative framework. References to "degrees of theory-ladenness" and "levels of more direct observation" are in this respect deceptive. No predicates, not even those expressed in the form of an observation language, sustain themselves on direct empirical associations alone. The capturing of empirical facts always and everywhere involves a commitment to definite theoretical interpretations. Indeed, even the conception of the natural world as a nomological order of factual things or events is dependent upon intersubjective processes of interpretation. Within the boundaries of these communicative processes, communities of investigators raise questions and pose them to nature in the form of hypotheses and experimental actions; cf. Karl-Otto Apel, "Types of Rationality Today: The Continuum of Reason between Science and Ethics," in Theodore F. Geraets (ed.), *Rationality Today* (Ottawa,

211

acknowledge the importance of those processes of discursive self-reflection which typically preside over scientific research and development. Rejecting both the objectivism of early positivist interpretations of science (described briefly earlier) and rationalist attempts to uncover outer nature's "ultimate foundations," Habermas points to the relevance (and limitations) of C. S. Peirce's post-Kantian philosophy of science.[66] In the view of Habermas, the Peircean understanding of science as a self-reflexive, instrumental process of discovery correctly breaks with both early and modern positivism. Peirce is opposed to the ontologizing of facts. As an object of possible experience, reality is constituted not by a transcendental consciousness (as Kant supposed) but, rather, by cumulative, self-monitoring processes of inquiry directed and sanctioned by communities of scientific investigators.

Drawing upon this Peircean thesis, Habermas interprets scientific reasoning as a self-reflexive system of bureaucratic, purposive-rational action. He is of course well aware of the communicatively structured anthropomorphism of scientific model building. Scientific researchers always reflect, analyze, and experiment within a framework of intersubjective communication; "paradigms containing theoretical approaches," he notes in the language of Kuhn, "originate in the primary experiences of everyday life."[67] He is nevertheless convinced that the purposive-rational activity typically predominating within the realm of scientific research – as in the sphere of work more generally – cannot be analyzed as a form of communicative action. Science can be analyzed only as a system of calculating action that is in principle solitary; researchers' deployment of representational signs (say, in the form of syllogistic reasoning) is typically monologic. This system of activity operates as a guiding framework within which fresh information can be accumulated and revised by the community of investigators should failures in anticipated outcomes and results occur.

The validity claims of science take the form of lawlike hypotheses about a natural environment constituted as an opponent of the species. These hypotheses are discursively arrived at; they are conditional predictions that are dependent upon and foreshadow successful manipulation of objectified processes. Scientific knowledge generated within the scientific and industrial communities therefore has a cash value: It seeks to guarantee the chances of success of instrumental action directed at an objectified outer nature. Natural scientific discourses do not simply correspond to the outer world of nature. According to Habermas, the naïve idea that scientific knowledge describes reality must be wholly rejected as a shibboleth. Science cannot be plausibly interpreted as the progressive discovery of the truth of a self-subsistent world of facts structured in a lawlike manner. Science must rather be understood as a discursively framed learning process, directed (to speak in Kantian terms) by the synthetic achievements of knowing subjects. These subjects' capacity to test, predict, and control is chronically dependent upon self-corrective feedback processes, and therefore upon the recognition of the failure and success of empirical predictions. It is, in short,

(1979), pp. 307–50; and Mary Hesse, *Revolutions and Reconstructions in the Philosophy of Science* (Brighton, 1980), chs. 3, 7.

a system of bureaucratic action, a more precise, reliable, and systematic type of work.[68]

The strengths and weaknesses of these points, together with their implications for a socialist theory of public life, can be spelled out more precisely by indicating their close affinity with Popper's model of "critical rationalism." This model, which is analyzed here only with reference to Habermas's account of the natural sciences, can in certain crucial respects be interpreted as an elaboration of the work of Peirce.[69] Critical rationalism, in Popper's eyes, means, first, the defense of critical argumentation in the development of natural scientific knowledge. In opposition to what is viewed as a major threat to the liberal societies of the twentieth century, namely, passionate irrationalism, critical rationalism deliberately fosters the inclination to solve as many problems as possible by an appeal to reason, that is, "to clear thought and experience," rather than by appeals to emotion and passions. It is a predisposition to learn from experience and to deploy and accept or reject critical arguments. "It is fundamentally an attitude of admitting that 'I may be wrong and you may be right, and by an effort, we may get nearer to the truth.' "[70] This process of forming consensus through argumentation, Popper complains, is systematically underemphasized within instrumentalist interpretations of science, according to which scientific theories are merely useful modes of organizing domains of objective phenomena. Habermas's attack on Mach's uncritical belief in positivist methodology closely follows this first Popperian thesis. Habermas insists that the status of "truth" cannot be conferred upon scientific statements by individual, privately inquiring subjects. Scientific truth can only assume a public form. Hypotheses can be deemed valid only inasmuch as they hold independently of personal hunches, clues, and idiosyncracies, that is, only insofar as they are affirmed intersubjectively in the face of indefinitely repeated doubt.

Both Habermas and Popper are also opposed, secondly, to recent attempts to retrieve and modify the classical objectivist models of science. According to latter-day forms of observationalism (that of Putnam, for example),[71] theoretical propositions are accepted or rejected as scientific according to the criterion of empirical verification. Scientific statements are approximately true descriptions of the real. Popper counters this observationalism by defending the principle of empirical falsification: "Using all the weapons of our logical, mathematical and technical armoury," he insists, "we try to prove that our anticipations were false – in order to put forward in their stead new unjustified and unjustifiable anticipations, new 'rash and premature prejudices.' "[72] Habermas corroborates this point. Every genuine test of a scientific theory, in his view, consists in its attempted falsification. Empirical-analytic learning is a self-correcting process. Its insights and concepts, like the well-known fate of phlogiston, are always subject to refutation or reconstruction in the face of subsequent experimentation. Theories are corroborated and admitted as knowledge only to the extent that they can withstand the community of investigators' attempts to negate them through the formation of new concepts and hypotheses, through the derivation of conditional predictions and their testing through experimental practice and the discussion of anomalies. Habermas plays on the language of Hegel: the "movement of the concept," he remarks, "is neither absolute nor self-sufficient. It acquires its meaning only from the system of reference of possible *feedback-controlled action*."[73]

Through this argument, Habermas opposes the relativism of many postempiricist critiques of scientific realism. Scientific statements, he agrees, are not privileged, if by that is meant that they are not permanently subject to radical conceptual transformation. Contrary to Feyerabend and others, he nevertheless urges that the truth of scientific discourse must not be deemed "truth within a system," as a set of beliefs reinforced by the habitual conventions of scientific communities. Scientific statements are not simply meaningful in virtue of their dependence upon the premises of an entrenched, intersubjectively agreed-upon "scientific system." Every empirical object of inquiry, to be sure, is mediated by scientific discourse. The nonidentity of empirical objects with scientific discourse nevertheless implies that the former can serve as something like a touchstone of correct or adequate discourse. Under the promptings of a nature conceived as a thing-in-itself, old and problematic scientific beliefs are capable of revision and transformation into fresh and more plausible accounts. These "independent original stimuli"[74] serve as a condition of deciding the degree to which scientific statements are warranted: "From a pragmatic viewpoint . . . failures, whereby causal hypotheses founder under experimental conditions, possess the character of refutations. The hypotheses refer to empirical regularities; they determine the horizon of expectation of feedback-monitored activity and consequently can be falsified by disappointed expectations of success."[75]

It follows from the foregoing two arguments, finally, that for Habermas and Popper the empirical-analytic sciences are marked by rational accumulations of highly probable knowledge. These sciences, it is true, do not converge upon some fundamental truth about nature. They cannot fall back, as it were, upon either ultimate facts or first principles. Science is incapable of exhaustively catching natural reality through detailed strategies of experimentation and unambiguously true observation statements.[76] In another and highly important respect, nonetheless, the empirical-analytic sciences stand outside the boundaries of historical relativity. They are *instrumentally progressive*, in the exact sense that their capacity for controlling outer nature becomes ever greater. This is so because, according to the argumentation and falsifiability theses, only those explanations triumph which have a greater degree of experimental universality.

The empirical-analytic sciences can in this sense be regarded as bureaucratically organized learning machines. By means of theory construction and detailed experimentation, these sciences vastly increase the pragmatic possibilities of predicting and controlling objectified, empirical events. The cumulative development of these sciences' will to control nature progressively erodes illusions about that nature, leaving in their place transferable deposits of pragmatic knowledge marked by a high degree of probable accuracy and intersubjective recognition. Popper confidently insists that a "theory which has been well corroborated can only be superseded by one of a higher level of universality; that is, by a theory which is better testable and which, in addition, contains the old well-corroborated theory."[77] Habermas is also adamant that natural science is a not-yet-fully-mature inquiry developing toward greater *technical* insight. Science is a cumulative learning process, whose *telos* is efficiency of successful prediction and control. Science seeks to eliminate technical uncertainties. Scientific propositions about reality are therefore valid inasmuch as, under given conditions and on the basis of conditional predictions, they can be successfully transformed into technical recommendations. This also means, conversely, that their validity is permanently subject to the doubt, controversy, and revision provoked by the "resistances of reality." "Modern science...," he concludes, "permits nomological explanations and practical justifications, with the help of revisable theories and constructions that are monitored against experience."[78]

Ecology and the natural sciences

In spite of its convincing and highly valuable antipositivist thrust, Habermas's account of the empirical-analytic sciences is not entirely plausible. Indeed, it is evidently unable to deal with at least four crucial problems. Of great importance to a theory of the limits of bureaucratic domination, these difficulties can be considered in turn.

In the first place, Habermas fails to consider whether the empirical-analytic sciences typically unravel theoretical puzzles and successfully widen their horizons of technical control only by suppressing anomalies and novelties that are fundamentally subversive of their basic commitments. By virtue of his defense of the analytic distinction between the empirical-analytic and the communicative sciences, Habermas is forced to bracket the objection (of the type raised by Dijksterhuis against classical mechanics, for example),[79] that the empirical-analytic sciences typically assume that which is communicatively generated and therefore cannot be confirmed through feedback-controlled action.[80]

It may be, of course, that proposals for the methodical, systematic doubting of the totality of statements that make up contemporary scientific discourse are abstract, and in any case impossible: abstract, because it is only within the boundaries of certain taken-for-granted or unquestioned convictions that particular assumptions and problems can be subjected to processes of critical inquiry; impossible, inasmuch as scientific discourse cannot jump out of the dimension of communicative processes of mediation. No matter how rigorously or exhaustively it seeks to retrace its inferences to its own deep-seated premises, it must remain caught within the boundaries of communication itself.

The point nevertheless remains that Habermas devalues the significance of attempts to analyze further the "coherence conditions"[81] crystallized within all scientific discourse. These coherence conditions, recent philosophy of science has emphasized, are by no means trivial in their effects. They in fact function in the manner of historical *a prioris*, as typically taken-for-granted regulative principles whose boundaries considerably influence what can be discussed and analyzed through critical argumentation. These principles can of course vary considerably from one scientific discourse to another, as Feyerabend, Kuhn, and others have indicated. Scientific discourses diverge not only in respect of what they assert and understand as postulates. In a more diffuse sense, their incommensurability is also displayed in deep-seated presumptions about what is to be counted as constituting the elements of a good theory: for example, in what is to serve as a cause, good inference, or explanation; in criteria of logic, truth, simplicity, and adequate approximation; in suppositions concerning such general categories as substance, causality, time, and space; and, indeed, in the very aims of scientific argumentation and inquiry themselves.[82]

Habermas considerably undervalues the importance of these diffuse presumptions, instead describing the discourse of empirical-analytic science as exact, literal, and capable of formalization.[83] Problems of misunderstanding (and therefore the need for further argumentation) arise only in the context of unanticipated results generated by feedback-controlled processes of experimentation and hypothesis formation. His proposed description not only denies the power of coherence conditions within the empirical-analytic sciences; it also overlooks a subversive implication of further inquiry into these conditions, namely, that the relationship between the empirical-analytic sciences and those concerned more directly with relations among communicating subjects (that is, the historical-cultural sciences) is typically *continuous* rather than dichotomous. This is so, if only because both sciences are irrevocably marked by a certain type of "coherence condition," namely, speaking actors' production of, and dependence upon, rhetorical signifying practices. The history of the modern sciences is replete with examples of such rhetorical redescriptions of natural objects. Mention can be made of Copernicus's inference that the sun must lie at the center of the planetary system because it resembles a king at the center of his court; Kepler's belief that the mathematical harmony of the cosmos is the analogue of God and the soul; moral and political objections to the theory of natural selection and to mechanical theories of the mind; references to "free" particles within the atom; the assumption that "men" are biologically superior and unique among living organisms; and so on.[84]

These examples illustrate the point (discussed already in Essay 5) that rhetoric is not simply an artificial device that decorates the sciences' otherwise clear, precise, and unambiguous ways of speaking. It follows from this point that the commonplace defense of two-tiered models of communication cannot be upheld. According to such models, the natural sciences (in contrast to, say, the ambiguous rhetorical discourses of political life) are best understood as the bearers of irreducibly pristine and literal meanings. These models are quite misleading because natural-scientific discourse, like all other forms of inquiry, chronically sustains itself upon forms of argumentation, interpretation, persuasion, and controversy. Contrary to Habermas, these communicative forms cannot be purged (or plausibly bracketed for analytic purposes) from the self-understanding of the empirical-analytic sciences. Nor do such forms of communication enter scientific discourse only at the point at which its insights are technically applied.[85] Rather, the natural sciences' capacity for effecting instrumental control over objectified processes is always and everywhere conditioned by public processes of hermeneutic, communicative action that are present throughout social and political life.

Second: It is true that Habermas recognizes the important trends toward the industrialization of the empirical-analytic sciences. He nevertheless fails to pursue the more disturbing implications of this recognition. Relying instead on highly idealized accounts of the scientific activities of "communities of investigators," he does not adequately discuss the process of "finalization"[86] through which basic scientific theory formation and research are strategically directed by specific social and political interests. There is consequently no acknowledgment of the degree to which contemporary patterns of scientific research and development are marked by definite forms of lopsidedness or bias. These processes of industrialization are becoming decisive in the science-based industries – the lucrative domain of the new biology and its strategic development of new vaccines, hormones, drugs, and crops serving as only the most recent instance.

This bureaucratic finalization of scientific research under late capitalist conditions has of course broken down the classical ideal of research free from politics and domination and has contributed in turn to its questioning by successive public movements of scientists.[87] These movements have correctly indicated that scientific research capable of being "capitalized" within state and corporate bureaucracies has typically developed much more rapidly and intensively than publicly useful types of scientific inquiry. Scientific research, which Habermas plausibly describes as a form of (reflexive) labor designed to produce and apply knowledge, is indeed structured indelibly, like other forms of labor, by the bureaucratic relations of production and control within which they are situated. The corollary of this insight is that socialist forms of social and political life would structure the finalization of scientific research and development in radically different ways. Countering the present-day military-industrial development of science into a destructive force that menaces the whole of natural and social life, socialist society would redirect and redeploy scientific inquiry and application in accordance with needs generated through autonomous public spheres of decision making.

Third: Habermas's account of the natural sciences is marked by an uncanny silence concerning the political implications of the medical sciences. Producing hybrid forms of empirical-analytic knowledge whose object of concern is the human body itself, the medical sciences both defy Habermas's dualistic typology of the sciences and possibly threaten his conviction that empirical-analytic science is appropriate to the sphere of work. A socialist theory of public life cannot avoid further analyzing and questioning the validity claims and power implications of these medical sciences. The need for this interrogation is prompted by the fact that the bureaucratic cultivation of the medical sciences has recently produced a measure of anxiety about their complicity with professional strategies of controlling life, health, and death.[88]

Evidently, more is involved in this potentially authoritarian process of "medicalizing" life than the recent institutional abuse of otherwise rational natural-scientific discourses. The problem is clearly more complex and deep-seated, inasmuch as the medical sciences attended the birth of mechanisms of surveillance of populations in the earliest periods of industrial capitalism. The replacement of eighteenth-century classificatory medicine by the clinical gaze of modern medicine during this time was in fact a decisive aspect of the constitution of the mass of the population as a medical object, as a field to be mapped out, admin-

217

istratively supervised, analyzed according to documentary and statistical forms of registration, and regulated according to certain norms of health and life.[89] Early modern medical knowledge was not formed through the disinterested discourse of communities of investigators; nor was it oriented to the manipulative control of natural objects. From its inception, medical knowledge was what Max Scheler termed *Herrschaftswissen* – knowledge for the sake of domination. This knowledge was engaged in ethical questions of judging individuals, making administrative decisions, and laying down the norms of modern social and political life. This active involvement of early modern medicine in matters of morality, power, and administration appears not to have been altogether fortuitous. Its logic of inquiry, which privileged the empirical gaze of the professional doctor, well matched the conviction of doctors, philanthropists, and statesmen that the daily habits of whole populations were in need of policing. In support of this goal, modern positivist medicine reminded the species of its own finitude, of the obstinate limit of death; at the same time, it defended the possibility of an exorcism of the void of death by professionally cadaverizing the body, so as to discover and enumerate its inner secrets.

The final difficulty that marks Habermas's account of the natural sciences takes the form of three interrelated silences concerning their alleged instrumentally progressive character. First, Habermas's account does not adequately consider the degree to which the *scope* of prediction and control generated by these cumulative sciences is highly uneven, even limited. There are several respects in which this is the case. Most obviously, there are certain fields of the empirical-analytic sciences (such as mathematical cosmology) that are not themselves directly oriented toward instrumental control of objectified processes. What is more, in the shadow of Kuhn's *The Structure of Scientific Revolutions*, it is clear that the cumulative and progressive character of the natural sciences does not consist in an unfolding of valid explanatory-theoretical discourses toward universal pragmatic control. Habermas's conviction that the empirical-analytic sciences are in principle capable of generating *ever greater* instrumental command over objectified processes is misleading in this regard. Precisely because (to invoke only one possible argument) the stream of past, present, and future events that make up the natural universe constitutes an infinity, the control capacities of the theoretical and predictive frameworks of analysis can never become total. The whole of the "data" can never be received (as if by divine intuition) and subsequently analyzed and processed in their entirety; revolutions in these sciences' interpretive frameworks therefore cannot be ended once and for all. This means, at best, that instrumental progress within the natural sciences takes place only in limited or localized domains of experience. The generation of probable lawlike hypotheses and the attainment of pragmatic success vis-à-vis objectified processes is always approximate and relative to particular, local phenomena.[90]

Habermas's defense of the empirical-analytic sciences as instrumentally progressive also fails to justify whether, and precisely in which sense(s), outer nature is itself amenable to successful bureaucratic control. The possibility that late capitalist systems have better learned to control their natural environment locally – but only by losing control over large-scale environmental systems – remains undiscussed. This second objection to Habermas's theses on the control capacities of the natural sciences is intimately linked with a third. His vindication of the empirical-analytic sciences, it can be argued, seriously undervalues the contemporary significance of such ecological sciences as botany, zoology, and the more classically oriented and interdisciplinary forms of biology. These natural sciences are distinguished by their concern to develop less anthropocentric discourses on the relations between the species and outer nature. Strictly speaking, Habermas's discussion of the empirical-analytic sciences cannot accommodate their novel logic, for these ecological sciences are in principle opposed to a single premise upon which the empirical-analytic sciences fundamentally stand: the postulate of active, calculating subjects who are assumed to be capable of manipulating and controlling an outer nature constituted as a purposeless, thinglike object. This antinomy between the ecological and empirical-analytic sciences is missed in Habermas's overly formal description of the specificity of the natural sciences. As a consequence, or so it can be argued, his account unwittingly contributes to the continuing legitimation of the principle of the domination of nature – a historically specific principle that both services the "aura" surrounding late capitalist economic growth[91] and therefore (from the point of view of a socialist theory of public life) contributes to the legitimation of depoliticized, bureaucratic forms of control.

This principle of the domination of outer nature and, by extension, its depoliticizing effects are now seriously questioned by two interrelated claims of the ecological sciences. Both claims are associated with recent scientific efforts to block the replacement of classical biology (which was concerned, for example, with describing and classifying totalities of living plants and animals) by devitalized, reductionist forms of inquiry oriented to the secrets of molecular life.[92] Though anathema to Habermas's interpretation, these claims of the new ecological sciences vindicate the thesis that valid characterizations of the relationship between society and nature must deny the credibility of subject-object dualisms.[93] While emphatically rejecting the unfounded (neo-Romantic) thesis that nature can be analyzed as a dialogic partner, these sciences raise crucial questions about the instrumentalist character of the mainstream empirical-analytic sciences. They further suggest, again in opposition to Habermas's interpretation, that the relationship between these sciences and their communicative, hermeneutic counterparts is not so much dichotomous as continuous. In other words, these ecological sciences advocate a reform or circumscription of the operationalist biases of the physical sciences. They propose, through forms of argumentation that avoid recourse to religious or metaphysical world views, that the necessary interdependence of society and nature implies the need for less bureaucratically repressive relations between society and nature.

These hypotheses can be sketched and analyzed more carefully, for they are especially pertinent to contemporary defenses of public life. First, the new ecological sciences emphasize that humans are also *natural* beings circumscribed by their participation within the natural world. Outer nature is represented, so to speak, as the inorganic body of the species. This nature is analyzed as a condition of the species' failures and achievements, a condition with which the species

219

must remain in perpetual transaction in order that it not perish. This scientifically elaborated claim concerning the interdependence of outer nature and the species was of course largely assumed in nonmodern science, technology, and cultural forms. Anthropological inquiries into archaic societies abound with examples of this insight: The members of tribal societies named themselves after this nature; women often cared for young animals; expiation and purification rituals were common after hunting; indeed, every mountain, brook, forest, cave, or sea was seen as alive, like the species itself.

Under late capitalist conditions, awareness of this relationship of interdependence has been considerably quashed. The recognition that the species is but one element within a complex ecosystem has fallen into disrepute: "Despite Copernicus, all the cosmos rotates around our little globe. Despite Darwin, we are *not*, in our hearts, part of the natural process. We are superior to nature, contemptuous of it, willing to use it for our slightest whim."[94] As a consequence, the organized reification of outer nature for the purposes of bringing it under permanent control tends to become synonymous with its bureaucratization. States plan and organize natural reserves for the enjoyment of "publics" who seek to escape their urban complexes; remnants of animal and plant species are organized, catalogued, and placed on display in zoo pens and museums; within the state-guided spheres of capitalist production and exchange, this nature is bought, sold, and "developed" as a mere commodity, whose only worth is its function of servicing the self-expansion of capital. Under conditions of consumer capitalism, the bureaucratic stimulation of needs and accelerated turnover of goods and services comes to predominate – and these strategies increasingly produce visible degradation of the natural environment.

Insofar as it opposes these tendencies, scientifically informed, ecological reflection upon the destructive and constructive forms of exchange between society and nature cannot simply be absorbed back into autonomous publics that are assumed to be competent to act as a collective scientist (as contemporary forms of Romanticism anticipate). Nor can scientifically informed, ecological inquiries be replaced by common sense or by a disengaged contemplative science, whose object of knowledge resembles the poet's beloved: something to be contemplated but not analyzed, something that is permitted to retain its mysteries.[95] To the contrary, under late capitalist conditions the discourses of the ecological sciences perform a crucial political role in preserving and fostering the recognition of the interdependence of outer nature and society. Correctly insisting that nature is no thing-in-itself external to the realm of communication – as Habermas's defense of the empirical-analytic sciences implies – these sciences remind us that "nature" is a category that is itself produced through historical forms of communication. This is not a repetition of the self-evident insight that communicatively generated norms – concerning, for example, the significance of cancer research or the absolute disutility of nuclear weapons – are involved in the practical application of empirical-analytic knowledge. The ecological sciences propose a more challenging thesis, namely, that whatever is held to be natural at any historical moment is always communicatively conditioned. In turn, this communicative representation of outer nature is seen as preconstructing the self-understanding of speaking, acting subjects themselves. It is argued that all social formations interpret themselves partly by means of their representations of nature.

Guided by these arguments, the ecological sciences therefore insist upon the historical specificity of the modern empirical-analytical sciences' conceptual and experimental rendering of outer nature as a mere object. These sciences are accused of representing outer nature in conformity with what modernity has *made* of nature: a thing, matter, raw material for the continuous expansion of bureaucratic control.[96] According to the ecological sciences, the original and continuing error of the empirical-analytic sciences is their anthropocentric presumption that the species is immediately a separate, positing subject no longer posited in turn by its naturalness. Through their striving for power over outer nature, these empirical-analytic sciences have forgotten that this nature is one of their own conditions of existence. These sciences have become *heimatlos*, uprooted from the natural environment. They seek to examine and manipulate that which they have designated *a priori* as a mute and separate thing; they abandon the recognition that they already dwell within this nature.[97] In short, these sciences suppress the truth that outer nature is a necessary condition of the present — and of possible future forms of socialist public life.

In their attempts to retrieve and develop aspects of the tradition of classical biology, the ecological sciences raise a second claim. This is the converse of the first: Against the contemporary domination of nature, it is argued that future forms of social and political life are contingent upon the preservation and fostering of this nature's "potential." According to the more classically informed ecological sciences, outer nature is neither a passive, dumb object nor a partner in communication. Devoid of immanently suprahuman purposes and incapable of participating in dialogue, this nature can be regarded neither as a genuine subject of knowledge and understanding nor as an object that waits for its potential to be realized by the labor power of cooperating human subjects. This nature exercises its rudimentary purposes. Strictly speaking, however, these are neither purposeful nor teleological: As Monod has forcefully argued, nature's purposes are at best poorly formulated, blind, foolish, chronically dependent upon chance.[98] This highly intradependent, chance-ridden nature may therefore be said to have needs — above all, those generated by its struggle for mere survival and reproduction.[99] This struggle takes the form of the reproduction, growth, and decay of living matter, the diversification or simplification of species through natural selection and mutation. These survival, growth, and decay processes are entirely governed by the operations of chance upon simpler primary material. These processes therefore cannot be analyzed through the metaphysical concept of animate nature as one integrated whole, whose different parts have prescribed vital functions only within this whole and for the sake of this whole.

The recognition of this muted, chance-dependent subjectivity of outer nature analyzed by the ecological sciences points to the fallacious self-understanding of those who would again embrace the principles of *Blut und Boden* and live according to Nature. Beliefs in the imperative of returning to Nature are illusory on several counts. For example, they suppress the point that outer nature is not an "in itself" that somehow appears without the mediating effects of the species' conceptual, symbolic representation of that nature. These beliefs also usually exaggerate the extent of harmony between the species and nature in earlier social formations;[100] conversely, they forget that nature has a history – a point more and more emphasized by disciplines such as geology, cosmology, thermodynamics, and Darwinism – and that this outer nature has itself been radically transformed by modern capitalism's forces of production even while it has, so to say, transformed itself. Above all else, romantic calls for a return to Nature are marked by a definite antipolitical trajectory. Guided by the identitarian assumption that an end to the disharmony between human beings entails an end to the disharmony between humans and nature, these calls are bound to resubmit themselves to naturalizing modes of life because, to speak in language not entirely strange to the perspectives of the ecological sciences, outer nature is blind, foolish, and suffering, a poor coordinator of its own affairs. To cling to life blindly and silently, without other aims – this is what it means to be an element within the complex ecosystem that makes up outer nature. This raw nature is, to recall Nietzsche's commentary upon Goethe,[101] only a stammerer on behalf of whom the human species itself can and must speak out.

Ecology and public life

These two interrelated claims defended by the ecological sciences can be seen to amount to the single hypothesis that, under any historical conditions, the relationship between society and nature defies the dualism of subject and object. Guided by this hypothesis, signs of which have appeared also in twentieth-century physics,[102] the ecological sciences come to the assistance of the democratic opposition to late capitalist systems. By implication, though often quite explicitly, these sciences correctly emphasize that the (future) possibility of informed, critical publics is contingent upon a qualitative reduction in the levels of bureaucratic domination of nature through the sphere of work. Laboring, speaking, and acting subjects are urged to *encounter* nature scientifically and technologically as a constitutive partner. Although this nature certainly cannot be regarded as an identical partner in dialogue, its struggle for survival and reproduction must nevertheless be encouraged, its "surplus domination" actively opposed.

Nourished by these highly plausible claims, the new ecological movements resist the general fouling of our earthly habitat in the name of scientific-technical progress and production for production's sake. Breaking with the technological optimism of nineteenth-century working-class traditions, these movements correctly warn that the absolute limits at which outer nature might suffer an irreversible deterioration are unknowable but not inconceivable. Through the establishment of public spheres of discussion and resistance, these movements therefore oppose the careless destruction of predatory animals; the chemical fouling of food, soil, and water supplies; the technological and military invasion of the stratosphere and beyond; the discharge of surplus heat and radioactivity into the ecosystem – to mention just a few examples. The ecological defense of public life also projects a range of positive demands, on behalf of the refores-

222

tation of hills and valleys; the rebeautification of landscapes; the complete removal of nuclear weapons; the protection of endangered animal, bird, and plant species; and the cleansing of the seas, lakes, and streams.

There is no doubt that these new ecological movements are continuously endangered by strategies of bureaucratic manipulation and control: The proliferation of "environmentally conscious" corporate advertising and state-supported "dialogues with citizens" provide two indexes of this threat of co-optation. And it is also evident that serious antinomies currently exist between their goals and strategies and those of the autonomous workers' movements that resist bureaucratic, capitalist techniques of production.[103] The coordinated defense of autonomous public spheres within these respective movements therefore by no means escapes Max Weber's insistence that politics is an intense, concentrated, and slow boring of hard boards. Inasmuch as their demands and resistances rupture the existing continuum of bureaucratic decision making within the spheres of capitalist production and state policy, however, the new ecological movements greatly facilitate the realization of spheres of public autonomy in opposition to the dominant social and political powers. Stimulating independent public debate about late capitalism's relations of production, they seek to ensure the survival and self-development of the species in the face of the real possibility that contemporary forms of bureaucratic, consumer existence will be undermined by a rapidly deteriorating outer nature. The resistances and demands of the ecological movements cannot be analyzed as appropriate only to the political sphere of communication. Their challenges also properly arise from within (or enter into) the realm of work, which, as a consequence, can no longer be considered a pre-political domain of naturalness. Questions are raised about the safety and medical hazards of bureaucratically controlled labor, about which kinds of needs, consumer goods, and existing technologies have destructive, nonconvivial effects; demands are launched for a reorientation of priorities in scientific research and development; and proposals are made for living politically – as producers, consumers, scientists, and citizens – in accordance with the principle of prudent cooperation between outer nature and the species.

These interventions confound Habermas's otherwise provocative account of contemporary scientific-technical progress. As we have seen, he can admit of the need for selective policies of anti-industrialism. He can also advocate a more fully communicative relationship between the science establishment and an informed, active citizenry. And, in accordance with his analytic distinctions between work and communication, he can conceive of aesthetic modes of interaction with outer nature – "nature loving" – *outside* the domain of work.[104] His insistence that the creative destruction of late capitalist systems of production has no necessary propensity for stifling public life cannot, however, acknowledge the need for further critical reflection upon – and active resistance to – the existing forms of science, technology, and labor. It becomes evident that his uncritical account of the rationality of work falls behind the political principle affirmed by the new ecological movements: that the defense of autonomous public life within the spheres of social and political life is now contingent upon the political defense of nature itself.

7

Liberalism under siege: power, legitimation, and the fate of modern contract theory

In many people it is already an impertinence to say "I."

Theodor Adorno

Introduction: Max Weber's concept of legitimacy reconsidered

Sharing the fate of much of our early modern political vocabulary, the concept of legitimacy has in recent decades suffered a considerable loss of meaning. Our political discourses seem to have all but forgotten its deep significance. This impoverishment of the concept of legitimacy dates at least from the eighteenth-century efforts to overthrow the concern of the modern social contract tradition with "legitimate government"; in particular, it derives from Hume's assertion that government is founded only upon opinion, especially the "sense" of general advantage that is reaped from government.[1] The recent surge of writings on the "legitimation problems" of late capitalism has by no means exposed and arrested this impoverishment of the early modern concept of legitimacy. Most of these writings remain under the immediate spell of Max Weber, whose classic discussion of the concept contributed greatly to its eclipse.

The Weberian theory of legitimate domination countered the early nineteenth-century understanding of "legitimism" as divinely sanctioned hereditary rule with a potentially conformist thesis: Widespread belief in a system of governing institutions, it was argued, contributes to the stability of its relationships of command obedience. Legitimacy denotes the positive valuation and acceptance enjoyed by a system of power and its bearers, who "voluntarily" accept their masters as valid and deserving and their own subordination as an obligatory fate. This concept of legitimacy was therefore linked with a theory of the structural problem of all heteronomous social formations. According to Weber, the survival of every system of social action structured by relations of command and obedience depends upon its capacity to establish and cultivate widespread belief in its meaningfulness; to the degree that any system guarantees its reproduction in this way, it can be said to be legitimate.

As is well known, Weber's analysis of various modes of consensus or legitimate authority – tradition, affect, value rationality, charisma, legality[2] – produced the conclusion that the modern bourgeois world tends to legitimate itself by fostering belief in the legality of enacted rules and the right of those elevated to authority

224

under such rules to command. Not only obedience but also internalized respect tends to be granted to the impersonal, legally founded social and political order, which is more and more organized in administrative, bureaucratic form. Compared with earlier modes of legitimacy, Weber proposed, the modern form becomes thoroughly formalistic: The basis of legitimacy shrivels to mere belief in the legality of procedure. Institutions of power are legitimate by virtue of their legality; populations nowadays display a readiness to conform with rules that have been developed and deployed according to *formally* correct and accepted procedures.[3]

In spite of continuing controversy over its substantive assumptions and implications,[4] the influence of the Weberian theory of legitimacy has been sustained throughout the twentieth century. MacIver's classic, *The Web of Government*, typically establishes the constitutionality or "accepted standards of legality" as the single most important index of a government's legitimacy; an incoming government is to be deemed legitimate when its succession to power is predetermined under fundamental legal rules that it does not make or break.[5] More recently Luhmann has pursued this idea: He argues that systems of power legitimately stabilize themselves inasmuch as they operate in accordance with definite, positively established legal rules. Insofar as these systems generate decisions within the boundaries of formal legal procedure, the contents of their decisions can also be considered legitimate. This process of legitimation through legal procedure no doubt rests upon shared values; but these "deceptions" (as Luhmann calls them) are not normally questioned, and in any case they must be considered functionally necessary from the point of view of legal procedures themselves.[6] This latter conviction of course cultivates a theme found within the Parsonian theory of legitimation. Drawing upon Weber, Parsons is concerned to analyze those "functionally imperative" social processes whereby certain value orientations come to be shared, internalized in the form of personality, and institutionalized within the social structure. The legitimation process, according to this thesis, is that through which members of a social system come to appraise and regulate their actions in accordance with these shared and internalized value commitments.[7] Lipset's investigation of the necessary conditions of equilibrium democracy similarly concerns itself with the capacity of a social system to engender and perpetuate the belief that the logic of its institutions is most appropriate, and therefore necessary. Legitimacy is understood as "the degree to which institutions are valued for themselves and considered right and proper."[8]

In each of these accounts (and in Weber's), questions about the principles in accordance with which a regime comes to be seen as legitimate are confounded: There can be no independent inquiry into the validity of the beliefs of the regime's dominated groups and the claims of their rulers and their procedures to authority. Each of these Weberian theories prematurely rules out the possibility of investigating the truth basis of existing beliefs. The suspicion that such beliefs have a deceptive or ideological status that suppresses awareness of a regime's historical contingency cannot be pursued. As a consequence, the processes through which a regime more or less successfully secures its relations of power through the planned production and deployment of mass loyalty resources ceases to be

225

an object of critical analysis. "Legitimacy" connotes mass consensus, and it is presumed to be the work of some ill-conceived, naturelike mechanism whose cunning is no longer visible to the analytic eye. Habermas's critique of Luhmann's concept of legitimation applies more generally to a whole tradition of thinking since the time of Max Weber: "If belief in legitimacy is conceived as an empirical phenomenon without an immanent relation to truth, the grounds upon which it is explicitly based have only psychological significance."[9]

Several radical theorists have of course – and correctly – suggested that if the legitimacy of a social and political order consists simply in its being interpreted by its constituents as authoritative, then late capitalist societies can be said to be increasingly subject to deep-seated legitimation problems. The chronic dependence of these accounts upon the Weberian schema has nevertheless prevented their insight into a more fundamental sense in which contemporary capitalist systems are subject to legitimacy deficits. Indeed, what is curious about these analyses of contemporary legitimation problems is that they remain largely unreflective about the meaning of the concept of legitimacy. Uncritically situating themselves on Weberian terrain, they speak of legitimacy as equivalent to mass loyalty. Wolfe's discussion of the "limits of legitimacy," for instance, deploys a Weberian concept of legitimation as if its meaning were largely unproblematic; O'Connor similarly understands the late capitalist state's "legitimation" function as synonymous with its problem of "winning mass loyalty"; Miliband's analysis of contemporary processes of legitimation, to take a third example, depends upon a weakened version of the Gramscian concept of hegemony and the Marxian insight that the ideas of the ruling class tend in every epoch to be the ruling ideas.[10]

These usages, or so this essay proposes, share a decisive weakness. They fail to recognize that the legitimation problems of late capitalist systems are *also* symptomatic of the subversion of the principles of legitimacy established at an earlier phase of the modern bourgeois world. This assertion ceases to be quizzical or paradoxical when it is considered that the Weberian understanding of the concept of legitimacy both departs fundamentally from and does violence to its earlier meanings. In one crucial sense, the theories of legitimate authority of the early modern, ancient, and medieval worlds shared an *evaluative*, even *critical*, thrust that now stands in danger of falling into obscurity. These theories were emphatic: Legitimacy was only one very particular form of established consensus about the distribution and operations of power. In the case of the nonmodern world, for example, the force or validity of claims to power was seen as resting upon neither the "natural attitude" of believers nor the arbitrary and mystifying claims of those who exercised power. Such claims, on the contrary, were seen as drawing their validity from an objective order that had a relative independence or "otherness." It was this independent order that served as the standard against which the established universe of power could be evaluated or criticized or by which it could lay claim upon the lives and duties of its subjects.

There were numerous examples of these standards of political obligation, several of which can be briefly mentioned here. The Platonic theory of justice and virtue, for example, sought to specify the Good through discursive attacks on mere opinion and the uncovering of the transcendental realm of Forms or Ideas, objective essences whose unquestionable validity was "the most exact measure of all things." The Aristotelian defense of the good life of citizenship rested upon the presupposition that everything within the cosmos was natural process, moving teleologically from potentiality to actuality. In Rome, where the concept *legitimus* first appeared, the exercise of power was justified only insofar as it conformed to the eternal yesterday, whose sacred legal procedures were seen as originating in the decisive act of foundation. St. Augustine granted the legitimacy of the worldly *civitas* only inasmuch as it (imperfectly) prepared its subjects for the perfect and eternal peace of the heavenly city of God; and so on. In each of these cited cases, the validity of rulers' claims upon legitimate authority was not measured by the degree of mass loyalty or conformism to existing relations of power. It was grounded, rather, in a hypothesized meta-standard or principle, whose objectivity was reckoned to be independent of the sphere of existing opinions and relations of command and obedience.

The seventeenth- and eighteenth-century contractarian concept of legitimacy, with whose origins and fate this essay will be exclusively concerned, must be distinguished from its objectivist predecessors. Although it also eschewed the unthinking association of legitimacy and mass consensus, its singular achievement was the defetishism of the old claims upon power.[11] It insisted that the entitlement of legitimacy of power must be brought to earth and grounded upon individual *subjects'* natural capacities for self-reflection, judgment, and action. Legitimate power, in this novel view, only *emerged* from the agreements made by contracting individuals. This theme of subjectively produced legitimacy guided the overturning of the past by the political struggles, reforms, and revolutions of the modern Anglo-European world. These struggles aimed to initiate a fundamentally new mode of social and political life, whose theory of legitimate authority tended to have an unmistakable essence: the individual.

Especially from the time of the Renaissance, various movements represented the emerging order as a skilled achievement of their own efforts. Struggling to make meaningful sense of their life activity through the collective representation of themselves as individuals, these movements insisted that individuals were from here on to be the measure of all things. Climbing onto the stage of history in humanistic or egoistic costumes, and confident of their ability to shift for themselves, these modern individuals freely imagined themselves as alone and inwardly self-sufficient, as thrown back on themselves. Their humanity was seen as consisting in their liberation from all social and political relations of bondage, their uncoupling from any relations with others, save those obligatory contracts for which they opted out of self-interest, self-protection, or self-realization. Under pressure from the forces of reform and revolution, and especially during the seventeenth and eighteenth centuries, the idea and even the practice of organic and hierarchic control began to surrender to that of individual initiative, self-assumed control, and obligation. In various regions of Europe and the New World, the past was characterized as repressive, dingy, illegitimate. By contrast, the future was seen as synonymous with individuation, with the sacking of all institutional forms that smothered the individual.

227

In the name of this contractarian individualism, fierce struggles were waged against the dominion of churches, feudal cliques, the despotic power of the absolutist state, and foreign political domination. The defense of individualism underpinned the assault on monarchical tyranny by Lilburne, the Levellers, and other English advocates of parliament. It informed the decision of the Puritan movements of New England to "freely covenant and combine" themselves into civil body politics. This individualism fueled the American struggle for independence and was enshrined in various declarations of rights and state constitutions. Eulogies of the individual also typically attended the best-known texts of early modern political discourse: Hobbes's *Leviathan*; Pufendorf's *De Iure Naturae et Gentium*, Rousseau's *Du Contrat Social*, Kant's *Was ist Aufklärung?* and Paine's *Common Sense*.

It should hardly be necessary to stress that the process of construction of this new individualistic self-understanding was accomplished under conditions neither wholly comprehended nor intended by many constituents of the emerging modern order. Warnings against overestimating the convincing power and scope of officially sanctioned forms of legitimacy apply equally to the early modern doctrines of contract.[12] The "unregenerate mass of unbelievers," the marginalized peasantry, the colonized, and women constituted a few of the social categories whose entry into the atomization process was at first explicitly forbidden or retarded. These groups' compliance with the exigencies of the new contractarianism was rarely a consequence of their belief in the validity of its claims. Their loyalty to the new order was more often dictated by a combination of religious fear, threats of violence, and incarceration; or else simple compliance was induced by a sense of powerlessness, lack of alternatives, or pragmatic opportunism. Even when the new individualism was accepted by groups and bodily individuals as meaningful, it was also characteristically preconstructed by relations of power. From the outset, indeed, the contractarian theory of legitimation had an undeniably deceptive moment; its fetishism of the newly emancipated individual obscured or even denied the extent to which, at the outset, relations of power and dependence structured individualistic forms of life. This might be called the paradoxical achievement of the new contractarian theory of legitimacy. Its remarkable influence and its ability to induce voluntary servitude flowed from its capacity to sustain widespread belief in its emancipatory claims through the systematic concealment of those internal and external impediments – such as psychic neuroses, or class, gender, and political inequalities – whose exposure would have revealed those claims to be self-contradictory.

The analysis of this paradox of course preoccupied the critics of modern liberal ideology from the time of Hume and Rousseau through to that of Nietzsche. This criticism is not pursued here for the single reason that the generalized arrest and reversal of processes of atomization since the late eighteenth century have themselves thrown this doctrine of individual consent to power into disarray – and much more effectively than its early critics ever did. The central thesis of this essay is that the continuous growth of bureaucratic organization since the heyday of early modern capitalism has taken its revenge on the processes through which contemporary societies represent themselves to themselves. Bureaucra-

228

tization lays bare old presumptions about individuals who are naturally perched outside relations of power. What is more, bureaucratization casts radical doubt upon whether existing relations of power can be seen on any scale as having been constituted and legitimated through voluntary acts of individual consent. The validity of the earlier contractarian insistence that the entitlement or legitimacy of power must be brought to earth and grounded upon individual subjects' natural capacities for self-reflection, judgment, and action becomes highly questionable. The advance of bureaucratic organization makes it evident, conversely, that the old standards of legitimate power become dysfunctional for late capitalist orders. These standards enter into an antagonistic relationship with the dominant institutions of these societies; it becomes apparent to many that the old contractarian discourses on power cannot be given expression within these orders.

These several dimensions of the "decline of the individual" – to appropriate loosely Adorno's misleading and exaggerated expression – together constitute a key aspect of the limits of legitimacy of late capitalist societies. Simply expressed, these societies are presently incapable of plausibly justifying one of the necessary conditions of their bureaucratic power: depoliticization. This legitimation problem, upon which many oppositional movements now feed, helps to explain why these societies tend to generate a felt need for autonomous discussion about power, obligation, and consent. It also suggests why mass loyalty – when it is forthcoming – nowadays tends to become a matter of sheer necessity, of timely expediency and ulterior motives, or of acquiescent habit reinforced by various forms of ideological discourse – consumerism, scientific-technical planning, patriarchy, nationalism – that obscure or even censor questions about the legitimate constitution of power. Finally, this legitimation problem suggests why the old liberal theory of legitimation today stands urgently in need of reconstruction. Contemporary bureaucratization processes have unwittingly compelled a socialist theory of public life to retrieve and analyze further the old bourgeois problem of how to construct institutional forms whose legitimacy can be continuously secured. Socialist theory, in short, is forced to reconsider the various legal, social, and political conditions for realizing forms of life in which individuals and groups could legitimately develop their identity through the assertion of their nonidentity.

On the birth of modern individualism

This introductory consideration of the concept of legitimacy can be foregrounded and developed by way of a brief, and admittedly ideal-typical, appraisal of the origins and scope of the modern contractarian doctrine of individualism, a doctrine that reached the apogee of its influence during the seventeenth and eighteenth centuries. At the outset, it is well to avoid repeating the one-sided allegation, nowadays typically associated with crude versions of historical materialism, that modern liberal contract theory is best understood as having been initiated by thinkers such as Hobbes, whose discourses on individualism were in turn an effect of the rapid seventeenth- and eighteenth-century growth of bourgeois-directed market relations of symbolic and material production. According to more recent versions of this view, first proposed and analyzed by Marx, new material conditions at this time were synonymous with the birth of new forces and relations of production and a new philosophy of liberal individualism, whose more or less intended function was the ideological justification of the new bourgeois world that had come into being.[13]

Latter-day defenders of this thesis of course frequently recognize that liberal contractarianism was marked by wide regional and temporal variations during the course of these centuries. These proponents usually fail to recognize, however, that their thesis is in need of some considerable restructuring, if only because the origins of the individualism later espoused and defended by the bourgeois contractarian movements and revolutions of the seventeenth and eighteenth centuries *predated* the growth of these bourgeoisies. To concede this point is also to recognize, conversely, that liberal individualism cannot wholly be dismissed as bourgeois ideology. The political and social theory of contractarian individualism sustained itself on nonbourgeois traditions; it cannot be analyzed as a form of misrepresentation and veiling of "real material conditions." The bourgeois realities of the seventeenth and eighteenth centuries were not the only determinants of contractarianism; these realities cannot be understood as the point of truth that evidently contradicted the falsity of that contractarianism.

Latter-day historical materialist accounts of contractarianism must acknowledge what is elsewhere well recognized: The initial subversion of the organicism of the medieval world can be traced, first, to the Renaissance movements of the Italian city-republics and, secondly, to the various sixteenth-century struggles of religious minorities against political tyranny. These movements directly contradicted the medieval system of class and gender domination in political form. This system of power had sought to institute the principle of organic collectivism, which required that the identity and activities of bodily individuals be wholly submerged within the existing order of power. As de Tocqueville remarked, these bodily individuals were "often disposed to forget themselves," and thereby encouraged to form "a chain of all the members of the community from the peasant to the King."[14]

While it clearly experienced permanent disintegrative tendencies, feudal society in this respect tended to become an abstractly corporatist order, assuming a marked degree of facticity vis-à-vis its collectively organized constituents. The ruling groups of this order justified their suzerainty by understanding themselves as supervisors of a highly complex and static matrix of exchanges beween estates or functional orders. Understood as legitimate organisms of Creation and tradition, and mediated by the obligations and entitlements induced by the fief system, these functional groupings were by no means restricted to one political class. Their influence tended to be universal. There were various orders of chivalry; estates of cupbearers, cooks, and bread masters at court; sacerdotal and monastic orders within the church; estates of the realm and the trades – each superimposed upon the obligations arising from kinship relations.[15] These orders and estates were bound together by ties of superiority and subordination in accordance with the divinely sanctioned principle of honor, the mutual acknowledgment of the strivings, excellence, and virtue of various ranks.[16] In this matrix of exchanges, the individuals of early European modernity did not exist:

Still infinitesimally small, the bodily individuals of the feudal order were seen, by those who commanded at least, as in need of divinely sanctioned ordering. This principle of divinely sanctioned corporate subjugation was crystallized, for example, in the practice of collective punishment: In accordance with the assumption that they had been allotted a particular and special function within a system of power that was whole and indivisible, bodily individuals were legitimately punished without widespread concern over the violation of their (potentially) unique dignity.

Already by the early fourteenth century, and especially in the Italian city-republics, this pattern of domination began to dissolve. As Burckhardt earlier insisted, the societies of the city-republics began to "swarm with individuality; the ban laid upon human personality was dissolved; and a thousand figures meet us each in its own special shape and dress."[17] This atomization process, which can only be sketched here at a high level of abstraction, was facilitated by a complex of historical developments: the emergence of traditions of political discourse, whose deployment – by rhetoricians such as Brunetto Latini – hastened the formal separation of church and state, the radical reversal of their relative powers and the popularization of the virtues of equal and active citizenship; the rise of despotic states, aided and abetted by secretaries, ministers, and poets who out of dangerous necessity were forced to come to know their private, inner resources; the continuing rebellions against particular despotic rulers, rebellions that in turn exposed their protagonists to a succession of different personalities; the emergence of enclaves of market relations of commerce and production, and their corollary, the symbolic display and rivalry of wealth, power, and status.

Under the influence of these and other developments, the Renaissance movements began to subvert the divinely sanctioned corporatism of medieval feudalism by opening up a decisively novel self-understanding of the relationship between humanity and God. In such realms as poetry, politics, material production, and the visual arts, the authority of the curse of original sin was banished. This was at least in part an endogenous development, and not simply a rebirth of antiquity.[18] Religious discourse among certain strata of the population was transformed radically through a process of autocriticism and inner subversion. The achievement of a reconciliation between humanity and the divine was no longer seen as exclusively dependent upon acts of heavenly grace. Such reconciliation was now reckoned to be possible through individualistic activity and the self-development of the human spirit within a republican order. There was no longer an absolute above and below in the cosmic order; each individual was now "immediate to God."[19]

This was an era which prepared itself against the stream of irrational secular events – "fortune" and "corruption" – conceived as potentially destructive of all secular stability and individualism. This era represented itself as confronting the degenerate ebb and flow of secular life through the exaltation of civic humanism, of virtuous subjectivity and self-consciousness. It attempted, in other words, to reconstruct inherited formulations of the relationship and character of universal and particular, objectivity and subjectivity. As is evident in the iconoclastic writings of Nicholas Cusanus, for instance, the established medieval veil of legitimacy was so shredded that a rendering of the secular order as an *objective* force, as an outer world, became possible. This presupposed, conversely, an elaboration of an inner world, a self-recognition of subjectivity and the capacity of human *virtù*. An elaborate sense of individual sovereignty came to question and assail all objective hindrances. Everyday life on earth was granted a new lease on life. The world came to appear as a kaleidoscope of virtuous individual personalities: *L'uomo universale*, the self-confident, aggressive individual who sensed its sovereign powers of subjectivity and its separateness from its objective world, began to extend its influence.

During the course of the sixteenth century, the subversive influence of this Renaissance individualism expanded considerably. Its subversion of medieval organicism can indeed be seen to have unwittingly prepared the conditions for the remarkable later growth of contractarian discourses. Especially during the latter half of the sixteenth century, and in the circumstances of French and Scottish religious minorities and the political crises touched off by the spread of the Reformation, contractarianism – some of it guided by radically individualistic postulates – steadily achieved recognition, becoming a commonplace of political controversy and struggle.[20] To be sure, the numerous writers who denounced tyranny in the name of the new contractarianism did not always or usually question monarchic forms of state; nor were these advocates always disposed to the more radical individualism of the later bourgeois movements. This early contractarianism nevertheless decisively contradicted the divine standards of legitimacy hitherto invoked by earthly monarchic powers.

By the end of the sixteenth century, the writings of the *Monarchomachi*, Protestant and Catholic, had in particular popularized the theory of a governmental contract, and even several of the individualist concepts of the origins of the state. According to these writings (of Boucher, Mariana, Buchanan, and others), subjects could legitimately resist a prince who infringed the law of God. The contract of government, unlike those which typically appeared in the Middle Ages, was no longer represented as a mere means of expressing the reciprocity of rights and duties between ruler and ruled; rather, it was represented as an actuality generated by men who were stated to be free by nature. In this later view, the institution of political power and authority was analyzed as a deliberate act: There may have been a people without a king, but never a king without a people. Before this act of institution, even though they were destined by nature *ad civilem societatem*, men were deemed to have wandered alone, without fixed abodes, law, or government. Pressured by the consequent dangers to all and the need of protecting the defenseless young and the resources and experience of their elders, men were seen as having thereby instituted kings, but on condition that the latter obeyed the *leges civiles*. The legitimacy of kings was seen from this point on as conditional upon their protection of their subjects and their observance of the law, which was to direct and moderate the king's propensities to fraud, force, and therefore tyranny.

By the early seventeenth century, perhaps beginning with Althusius's *Politics Methodically Set Forth*,[21] the contractarianism and individualism bequeathed by the Renaissance and religious dissident movements were subjected to a process of reinterpretation and *embourgeoisement*. Individualism was increasingly viewed as realizable only through market relations of exchange guaranteed by the patriarchal family and the constitutional bureaucratic state. In pursuit of political liberties and wealth, though often guided by a deep sense of conscience and spiritual self-scrutiny,[22] individuals of the new liberal movement armed themselves for the competitive struggle against others. These individuals were convinced of their vocations, of the need to stamp their powers upon a world that seemed to await their actions. During the period from the early seventeenth century to the French Revolution, this liberal individualism accordingly sought to realize the emancipation of property-owning individuals, private entrepreneurs in the literal and metaphoric senses. This liberalism was more and more guided by its defense of a goal whose central postulate is easily recognizable: the patriarchal individual's free ownership and control of his body, his property, his powers of instrumental and communicative reason. Beyond this historically particular meaning, and the limited circles upon whom the privileges of individualism were zealously conferred, "the individual" was always an abstraction, expendable before these circles' monopolistic claims to property rights, political freedoms, and patriarchal privilege. The classical bourgeois individual accordingly understood himself as the sole proprietor of his resources and capacities, over and against the politically guaranteed society, to which he was not necessarily indebted or obligated.

Although frustrated by various protest movements and the political implications of the nationalism surrounding its birth and maturation, seventeenth- and eighteenth-century liberalism struggled against the past to constitute new modes of life that guaranteed constitutional government, private property, and partriarchal households. This liberalism represented itself as the bearer of free and equal patriarchal individuals' rights to the unfettered accumulation "of Power, of Riches, of Knowledge, and of Honour."[23] No doubt, the civic humanist assumption that (some) men were naturally political animals had not ceased to be influential during this time.[24] By the early seventeenth century, strongly individualist and contractarian principles had nevertheless come to exercise a firm influence over much European political thought. It was commonly said that men were naturally free and equal and that they therefore could have formed a society and a polity only through their own volition. All legitimate government was seen as originating in the free consent of individuals.

Particularly between the English Civil War and the French Revolution, this contractarian individualism enjoyed enormous successes. There were growing liberal, bourgeois victories for ethical toleration and even skepticism in religious matters. Contracts between individuals began to replace corporate status as the juridical premise of social and political life. Compulsory, slave labor (though by no means its newly instrumentalized forms) began to be abolished as the exchange between capital and labor was represented as the skilled achievement of isolated and free individuals. During this time, it was the *honnête homme*, the banker, manufacturer, and trader, who came to signify the new patriarchal individualism. Replacing the ecclesiastic, landowner, and warrior as the pre-

233

dominant political and social "ideal-types," these individuals became the living embodiment of "the economic virtues" (Tawney), of the requisite civilized and refined manners in an everyday life freed from political tyranny. Bourgeois individualism even interested itself in art, in which its interests were soon expressed, sometimes championed directly. The conflicts between outer and inner life became more and more central to the aesthetic dimension. In a world whose norms were sensed to be in dissolution, the substance of art relinquished its former concern with the religious life in favor of the earthly passions and wits, the struggle between youth and age, secular vice and virtue, subjective pleasure and pain.

The new contractarianism: state, civil society, patriarchy

With reference to the question of legitimation, the growth of this liberal individualism can be analyzed more precisely. Through the course of the seventeenth and eighteenth centuries, the European middle classes can be understood to have been struggling to assert their power to institute, and insist upon the legitimacy of, at least three institutions crucial for the reproduction of their hegemony. These were the state, civil society, and the patriarchal family; they can be examined in turn.

Insofar as it sought to guarantee its broadly defined property rights politically and legally, the new individualism called for the reconstitution of inherited theories of legitimate political power and the placing of restrictions upon that power. It was increasingly argued that the centralizing, bureaucratic state, under whose shadow Renaissance and religious legitimacy first flowered, had to be transformed into the constitutional liberal state. Once this centralizing state had crushed all indigenous rivals, its manifold interventions in economic and family life began to be criticized as arbitrary, capricious, and inefficient, and as a cramp on individual effort. This criticism was accelerated by numerous developments: the alleged inefficiency of mercantilist administration (the state was increasingly unable to regulate uniformly smuggling, wage rates, the apprenticeship system, or the foundation of new business ventures); claims against the ineptitude of the monopolists; the decay of the old guild system; the growing bourgeois dislike of burdensome laws, such as those in support of the poor, who, unlike those virtuous individuals paving the road to universal prosperity, were said to be irregular, lazy, and idle, victims of their own wickedness.[25]

Buoyed by these developments, liberal constitutionalism struggled to reconstruct the rules according to which old forms of law and state power were deemed legitimate authority. This project of political reconstruction drew immediately upon the defense of popular sovereignty by the sixteenth-century Calvinist revolutionaries. From this point on, the legitimate functions of the liberal constitutional state – which was by no means represented as weak – were to be limited to maintaining international sovereignty, national order, the sanctity of the patriarchal family, and the conditions of market-steered accumulation. Unlike either the classical and medieval polity, which was associated with ethical concerns, or even the mercantilist state, which was concerned with "the commonwealth," this state was to serve as a means for the protection of free and equal individuals and their natural rights of life, liberty, and property from foreign invasion and domestic extralegal incursions. This constitutionalism sought to guarantee the bourgeois power to make and unmake governments. Locke's "Wherever Law ends Tyranny begins"[26] became a standard caveat: The law was henceforth to be king over all actors, including kings themselves. The defense of constitutionalism in turn sanctioned a broad continuum of new demands: for wide religious freedoms, habeas corpus, the abolition of state control of the press, limited-term parliaments, majority rule and minority rights, a judiciary independent of executive power, the subservience of military and financial powers to an elected legislature, and the formation of leagues of peace to terminate war. These and other proposals were more or less explicitly designed to ensure that, after their day of business, the banker, manufacturer, and trader could sleep in their beds unhindered, their liberties, lives, families, and estates fully secured.

The liberal political theories of the state of nature and rights and laws of nature formulated by Hobbes, Spinoza, Berckringer, Pufendorf, Locke, and others vividly illustrated this attempt to reconstruct prevailing accounts of the legitimacy of state power. The originality of this post-seventeenth-century contractarianism consisted in its formulation of what might be called a correspondence theory of the state. The state was depicted as that institutional arrangement of political power which must respond more or less directly to the given and largely invariant interests and motives of individuals. Political society was, or ought to be, an association of self-moving individuals, who concentrated some of their powers in the state for mutually self-interested ends. As Wolff has pointed out, a deep methodological individualism was operative in this argument.[27] The individual was presumed to be sovereign, in the sense that it was the ultimate repository of reason from which sprang the state's legitimate authority. The power and legitimacy of political society was supposed to be constituted (at least originally) through an agreement of self-moving autonomous individuals, whose egoism or "unsocial sociability" (Kant) this state was required to serve and restrain.

This constitution process was typically understood as having been enacted through at least two phases. In the beginning, the state was seen as the created object of the will of an aggregation of hitherto-dispersed individuals owing nothing to any earthly power. It was as if political society were at the outset a voluntary schema; legitimate political authority was self-produced, and political obligation was self-imposed. Within the English social contract theories of Hobbes and Locke, for example, patriarchal individuals existed independently of society and the state: They formed and entered the latter only so as to place their natural liberties under the guardianship of its laws. All legitimate government was supposed to emanate from individuals' express power and to have their express sanction. Strangely, Hobbes could insist (in contradiction with this voluntarism) that covenants entered into even under conditions of fear of death by violence were to be deemed "voluntary" and therefore obligatory. Individuals' capitulation to others, their obligation to authority, were interpreted as having been formed through a voluntary consensus. At the same time, Hobbes was nevertheless convinced that there was "no Obligation on any man, which ariseth not from some Act of his own; for all men equally, are by Nature Free."[28] According to Locke, individuals were naturally and equally at liberty to "order their Actions, and dispose of their Possessions, and Persons as they think fit." Their political obligations could only be mutually negotiated and self-imposed. Insofar as the natural liberty of individuals (endowed with reason given by God) was synonymous with their freedom from any *a priori* duties to earthly sovereigns, the "Liberty of Man, in Society, is to be under no other Legislative Power, but that established, by consent, in the Commonwealth."[29]

Not only was this prior and original, active consent the foundation of the political; such consent was also deemed to secure the legitimacy of political power permanently. In the second phase of the contractarian argument, there tended to be an insistence upon the principle of *caveat emptor*. The initial and subversive insight that free, equal, and independent individuals could not legitimately be commanded by others was enfeebled. Hereafter, even though some individuals were said to retain limited rights to withdraw their consent under certain conditions (for example, when the Sovereign was no longer capable of commanding, as Hobbes argued),[30] they were deemed to abdicate and surrender some of their natural powers of self-direction. Individuals could now be regarded as culpable according to the criteria instituted by whoever declared law and dispatched political sovereignty. According to Hobbes, the erection of a Common Power that guaranteed the social tranquility necessary for industrious individuals to "nourish themselves and live contentedly" presupposed their unconditional and universal obedience to this political power.[31]

For Locke, the formation of "Political Society" was synonymous with the establishment of a permanent "Umpire" that, "according to the Trust put in it" by propertied individuals, would guarantee the reproduction of "one Body Politick under one Supreme Government." Operating in conformity with laws of nature and convention that were to be applied equally and "indifferently," this state institution was legitimately to seek the preservation of life, liberty, and estate by invoking the tacitly granted consent of the members of civil society.[32] Individuals' obligations were seen as owed to the state and its representatives, who were themselves in turn also obligated to the original contract and its covenants. As in Weber's later formulation, consent was to be inferred from the fact of obedient submission to an autonomous system of formal law, to which each individual was supposed to be equally and uniformly subjected. In turn, constitutional government would "in trust" guarantee life, health, liberty, and possessions. Until the later eighteenth-century attempts to specify the conditions under which forms of disobedience might be justified (compare Jefferson's suggestion that the tree of individual liberty would have to be watered periodically with the blood of patriots and tyrants), to demonstrate that life, liberty, and property could best be protected and preserved through the mechanism of free, periodic, elections, and, finally, to insist upon the corresponding need for the democratization of consent through the defense of (theories of) public life,[33]

236

individuals were supposed to have freely lifted themselves into political life, only to agree to endure a contract that legitimated their permanent submission.

The new contractarian individualism not only called for the reconstruction of what was taken to be legitimate political power; in principle it more and more insisted on the need for *restrictions* upon the scope of that political power. Keenly aware that state power could be deployed to destroy, enslave, or impoverish them, the new middle classes endeavored to defend "society" by pillaging old cultural and political fetters upon individuals' alleged acquisitiveness; no longer hindered by these fetters, individuals could rightly exercise their capacities to acquire property for themselves by mixing the labor of their bodies and the works of their hands with some portion of external nature. Economic aims pursued within the realm of society became a unique and specialized object of the concentrated efforts of individuals.[34]

These purposive-rational economic activities were represented as measurable through the independent and authoritative criterion of money. In defense of its economic aims, the contractarian movement thus sought to replace the corporatist relations of the medieval world with that battleground of avarice and private interests known as civil society. It was argued that former restrictions upon competition and the number of trade customers should be lifted, that feast days were no longer to be compulsory. There were efforts to deregulate wages, hours, and conditions of social labor as well as prices and rates of interest, and speculations and commerce were no longer to be forbidden on religious grounds. The different forms of interdependence confronting bourgeois individuals in civil society were to be transfigured into mere means of their privately calculated goals. Representing their objective relations of existence as contingent, individuals began to understand themselves as freer than their predecessors living in the dingy, hierarchic past, a past that was in any case in the process of being subverted by an interest-governed world. Acting freely and with their eyes open, individuals were now assumed to carry their powers and relations with society in their moneybags and pockets. Intersubjective relations of production were increasingly understood as instrumental, market relations among individual elements of capital and labor.

This defense of legally constituted spheres of life in which private individuals were to enjoy life, liberty, and estate peacefully was of course one of the key aspects of the struggle for "negative liberty"[35] in the early modern world. So understood, the defense of liberty entailed the constitution of realms of privacy or spheres of social action into which the bureaucratic state could not legitimately intrude directly. In the contractarian view, civil society was the truly appropriate domain in and through which sovereign individuals endowed with natural rights could pursue their own paths to their own goals. Its pure, ideal-typical form was the (hypothetical) state of nature. Logically and historically prior to the advent of society and the state, this was posited as a phase (to cite Hobbes) during which independent individuals already endowed with powers of speech and reason appeared to have "sprung out of the earth, and suddenly, like mushrooms come to full maturity, without all kind of engagement to each other."[36]

Such contractarian speculations served as the object of Rousseau's rightful complaint: Apparently posited by nature and now circumscribed by its political order, the atomized or quasi-social individual of the contractarians was positivistically conceived as the starting point and culmination of history, rather than as its temporary product. This critique fell mostly on deaf ears. Building upon the contention of Locke, Pufendorf, Mandeville, and others that individuals' natural condition was peaceful and sociable, liberal theorists argued increasingly – especially toward the close of the eighteenth century – that civil society was best left unhindered.[37] The practice of getting ahead through leaving others behind, of each for himself and thus each against all, was to endow particular interests with a higher universality. When framed by systems of law and guided by polite manners induced through policing, the economic domain of civil society might transparently and beneficently effect a "natural identity of interests"[38] out of the competition among transacting private individuals. Whereas the legally constituted state was seen as the necessary outcome of individuals' wicked and dissimulating proclivities, society was understood as a spontaneous, harmonious, and legitimate consequence of their egoistic virtues. As naturally as matter gravitated to a center, this society came to assume the appearance of a second nature determined by its own laws.

Throughout the period under consideration, at least one striking anomaly in contractarian defenses of individualism was evident. The contractarian principle of legitimate authority, according to which power was to be authorized and restricted in the name of free and equal individuals, was by no means extended to the sphere of domestic reproduction. Indeed, during the seventeenth and eighteenth centuries, the contractarian presumption that women and children were "mere auxiliaries to the commonwealth"[39] served to express and sanction the subversion of (feudal) kinship structures. Especially among the ruling political and class groups, the nuclear family in more authoritarian, patriarchal form began to predominate. This reconstruction of household life was facilitated during this period by the forcible intrusion of exchange relations of production into everyday life, the consequent separation of household life and production, and, in general, the extraordinary geographical disruptions and mobility of the population. States, which increasingly assumed monopoly powers of punishment and justice, military protection, welfare, and even the regulation of property, also launched a vigorous campaign against the old kinship system to reinforce directly the patriarchal nuclear family as the "germ-cell" or the locus of civilized psychosexual formation. These economic and political changes were in turn aided by the Reformation movements' concern with serving the ethical norm of conjugal affection and, thereby, domesticating the Holy Spirit – in opposition to both the Catholic ideal of virtuous chastity and the consensual sexual unions unblessed by the church among the plebeian classes.

In consequence of these developments, or so Stone and others have argued,[40] it was the male head of middle-class households who strove to monopolize property, the mediation of its bequest, and the inheritance of the power and symbolic authority of the priest. This patriarchalism heightened fatherly concerns about the sinful rebelliousness of children. Among the seventeenth-century middle classes, there is widespread evidence of a fierce paternal determination to break

238

the will and desires of young children through corporal punishment and strict formal education. The middle-class family began to supervise a profound trans-formation of the character structure of children, whose internalization of pa-rental coercion ensured that many affective impulses could not be lived out as spontaneously as before.[41] The command to "Honor thy Father" was also directed against women, whose obedience was deemed the first necessity for a happy Christian marriage. During the eighteenth century, with state and philanthropic campaigns on behalf of motherhood and the further subversion of the produc-tive power of women through the capitalist overthrow of home industry and middle-class women's trades and professions, bourgeois family life tended to assume its classical form: a hierarchical division of power and labor governed by the father, who, as breadwinner and symbol of the powerful bourgeois in-dividual, assigned his wife the victim-and-shrew role of adorning and managing the private domestic sphere.[42]

Assumptions about the naturalness of this form of household life are clearly evident within seventeenth- and eighteenth-century contractarianism. Under-standing itself in opposition to contemporary patriarchal attempts to justify the power of fathers over sons through allegations about the natural foundations of the fathers' procreative powers,[43] liberal contract theory directly reaffirmed such allegations with respect to women and children. Contractarians typically argued that the obedience of women and children to patriarchal power both had its "Foundation in Nature"[44] and was the *sine qua non* of the emergence of individualism. It is true that Hobbes, unlike many contractarians, represents the patriarchal household form as wholly conventional, arguing that, in the original state of nature, there was neither government, nor property, nor "lawes of Matrimony."[45] In this natural condition, females apparently shared with men the status of self-moving individuals. Within this condition, furthermore, women who bore children were viewed as both mothers and lords over their children;[46] by virtue of their preservation and nurturance by female individuals, children were deemed to have "voluntarily" consented (that is, submitted) to the rule of their mothers. Hobbes subsequently contradicts this reasoning. In the founda-tional contract, the liberty that all individuals formerly and rightly wielded to preserve their own natures was differentially relinquished and transformed. United in one "Person Representative"[47] – the father – families under conditions of civil government were to be legitimately ordered and governed under the ultimate jurisdiction of sovereign power. Hobbes assumed that "for the most part" only male individuals were active parties to the original contract and that, as a consequence, only they must exercise "domestic command." As an effect of their governance of households, Hobbes reckoned, male individuals became "naturally fitter" to engage in labor and to endure danger by relying upon their greater wisdom and courage.[48]

Locke's argumentation concerning household authority is no less explicitly patriarchal. He typically insisted that the "naturally" stronger and abler male had exclusive conjugal rights over "the weaker sex" to "order the things of private Concernment in his Family, as Proprietor of the Goods and Land there, and to have his Will take place before that of his wife in all things of their common

Concernment."[49] Women's powers over their lives, liberties, and estates were to be directly and legitimately appropriated by their husbands. This government by fathers, Locke insisted, was already present within the original condition. The conventional social and political organizations established through contract were seen as preceded by natural households, whose patriarchal rulers – and not isolated and autonomous individuals – were parties to the contract. Women were not endowed with that original, free, equal, and individualistic status claimed by men. Women's consent to the power of their commanding husbands was therefore to be inferred by virtue of their own formal acceptance of their natural subjection. Through what Pufendorf had earlier called a *pacto tacito*,[50] the agreements of women (and children and servants) were seen to have been concluded for them by their husbands and masters, around whom the whole world subsequently appeared to rotate. As a consequence of the original contract, all women were without separate existences, possessing neither natural nor civil nor legal identities.

Contractarianism in decline

As is well known, the contract theory of legitimacy continued to influence the course of political life after its eighteenth-century heyday. The later struggles against patriarchy, slavery, and the wage labor–capital relationship, for example, crucially sustained themselves upon the demand that liberal contractarians at the same time had supported and denied: the demand for the formal recognition of free and equal individuals who were deemed to be capable of rightfully disposing of their persons, of entering property contracts and enjoying legal and civil rights. The contractarian scenario of legitimate relations among the patriarchal family, civil society, and the state nevertheless entered a period of profound crisis during the late eighteenth century. Shaken to their foundations by criticisms from all sides, the principles of contractarian discourse slowly began to lose their capacity to convince and secure confidence in the established relations of power. Already in the eighteenth century, critics such as Hume and Bentham pointed out the obvious and undeniable – that in actual historical fact states had not been deliberately established by contract.[51] Hume, for example, ridiculed the idea of a compact expressly formed for general submission as "far beyond the comprehension of savages," and as evidently contradicted by the fact that all present governments were originally founded on usurpation or conquest or both. According to Hume, the "political or civil duty of allegiance" was impelled both by natural instinct (gratitude, pity, parental love) and by the sense of obligation generated by the "interest and necessities of society."[52]

Some critics viewed contractarian individualism as the point of view of bourgeois property. Hegel, for instance, was convinced that contractarianism mistakenly transposed the assumptions of private property into a sphere of a quite different and higher nature (the state), thereby producing the greatest confusion in both constitutional law and public life.[53] Burke analogously asserted that obligations to society and the state were in fact determined by the ancient order into which we are born and that, conversely, reverence for the state was undermined if it was considered as "nothing better than a partnership agreement in a trade of pepper and coffee, calico or tobacco."[54] Still other critics – with alarm but not without accuracy – insisted that contractarianism was productive of conclusions dangerous to all established privilege. Contractarian individualism was seen as embarrassing the deliberations of legislatures, as producing doubt, as affording dangerous pretenses for disputing the authority of laws. The acceptance of the premises of contract discourse, Paley noted, was endangering "the stability of every political fabric in the world, and has in fact supplied the disaffected with a topic of seditious declamation."[55]

These attacks foreshadowed the first systematic critical discussions of *individualisme*.[56] In France, for instance, Saint-Simon and the counterrevolution (de Bonald, de Maistre) bitterly criticized classical liberal individualism as the advocate of a "critical" epoch bent on the destruction of all order. Unlike the "organic" periods of the past and the period of "order, religion, association and devotion" to come, contractarianism's glorification of the individual was seen as synonymous with a pernicious age that considered the individual to be the center of the whole world. Contract thinking was viewed as responsible for an age that preached egoism and therewith filled the whole world with anarchy, disorder, and atheism. According to Saint-Simon, the deification of the doctrine of individualism, the worship of its two "sad deities" – conscience and public opinion – had led inevitably to one disastrous political consequence: "opposition to any attempt at organization from a center of direction for the moral interests of mankind, to hatred of power."[57]

These counterrevolutionary attacks on contractarian individualism and its principles of legitimate consent and obligation no doubt came at a politically opportune moment. As if by some strange and unintended consequence, the loss of confidence suffered by the contract theory of legitimation corresponded almost exactly to the growing tendency for liberal societies to pursue objectives they were forbidden to reach. During the course of the nineteenth century, rather obviously, the ruling groups of civilizing liberal orders endeavored to realize their visions of constitutionally limited government, market-steered accumulation, and patriarchal family life through strategies that continually obstructed these same objectives. The particular details of these self-destructive tendencies of classical liberal orders are of no interest in this context (see Essay 3). What *is* of vital importance to questions concerning legitimation is that the strategies designed to block and displace these crisis tendencies since the late nineteenth century have inflicted severe damage upon the old liberal discourses on legitimate authority. From the vantage point of late capitalist conditions, it is evident that over the course of the last century these crisis-management strategies have considerably undermined these discourses' credibility.

The debunking of the classical liberal principles of legitimacy, or so the following sections of this essay propose, is in large part due to the accelerated growth of bureaucratic forms of organization within all spheres of life, from civil society, to the state, through to household life. Three interrelated rationalizing tendencies have been especially decisive in this delegitimation process: (1) the growing administrative organization of markets for such commodities as wage labor, capital, and all types of goods and services, including leisure activities; (2) increased bureaucratic state penetration of commodity markets and family life; and (3) the weakening of patriarchalism through the subversion of the power and authority of the bourgeois household, whose functions tend to be usurped by corporate and state bureaucracies.

These tendencies are analyzed here, at an admittedly simplified and rather schematic level. It is proposed that each of these trends can be seen as a contribution to a new phase of modern bureaucratization, a phase synonymous with an unprecedented concentration of the means of production, political regulation, and socialization. No doubt, this concentration process is marked by incoherence and unintended difficulties (see Essays 1 and 3).[58] The scope of the bureaucratic power to administer is not necessarily cumulative. Under late capitalist conditions, bureaucratic organization is always dependent upon the cooperation of, and possible rejection by, its constituents. Bureaucratization is in this sense a learning process, whose outcomes are not necessarily unified, controllable, or cumulative; every instance of rule-governed bureaucratic action is a test of these rules, an experiment subject to the indifference, acceptance, or rejection of those to whom it is directed.

This caveat aside, it is nonetheless certain that, since the late nineteenth century, the organic composition of social and political life has risen. The late capitalist world has fallen under the influence of new forms and unprecedented levels of bureaucratic action. In these societies, all natural and social reality is more and more instituted from the point of view of possible instrumental control. Bureaucratic organizations everywhere seek to institute and secure formally rational relations of power. These organizations, as Weber pointed out, preclude or at least frustrate substantively rational forms of action oriented to the particular needs of bodily individuals.[59] This is why they are directly implicated in the legitimation problems of late capitalist societies. With the obvious exceptions of their personalized leadership and their chronic dependence upon the compliance of their constituents, bureaucratic organizations tend to institute rule-governed systems of power, in which individual producers, consumers, clients, patients, and others see themselves – accurately – slotted and manipulated according to impersonal calculations. It becomes evident to many that one of the premises of this process of depersonalized command is ghostly, obedient individuals, who must forgo their individuality and submit to governance and manipulation from above. As a consequence of this new phase of bureaucratization, in other words, the confident self-understanding of the classical bourgeois individuals tends to undergo a certain dissolution. Bureaucratic organizations can be represented, and challenged, as bearers of abstractly sovereign prerogatives, as aloof from all personal authorizations of bodily individuals. It becomes plainly evident, as the following examples suggest, that "the individual" is no longer the initiator and guarantor of legitimate authority.

Toward the bureaucratic planning of production and consumption

Strategies to overcome the crises of the liberal phase of capitalism have evidently produced profound structural alterations of civil society. A three-sector model of the accumulation process becomes descriptively more accurate, at least within the United States.[60] This differentiation of civil society into oligopoly, competitive, and state sectors indicates the extent of contraction of laissez-faire market forces in the allocation of wages, commodity prices, and profits. Marshall's doctrine – that industries resemble forests in which the individual trees are nurtured, reach maturity, and wither and die – has become outdated. The institutional foundations of the doctrine of the private calculating entrepreneur are being whittled away. In late capitalism, the market relations of civil society contract and become more and more organized. This contraction process is evidenced, first, by the dramatic expansion of a public sector, which is designed to correct, organize, and *replace* market forces. This sector establishes realms of service provision (postal facilities, health services, and the like) and state-contracted production (for example, the aerospace and armaments industry and, especially in Europe, heavy manufacturing industry) in which investment decisions operate relatively independently of market forces. The organization and shrinking of civil society is also evident, secondly, within the oligopolized "Industrial System" (Galbraith) of giant, technologically innovative national and transnational corporations.[61] As Marx and Weber understood,[62] this oligopolization process is the necessary outcome of capital as self-expanding value. The corporate drive toward bureaucratic standardization is designed to make its field of operations safe, thereby incorporating an element of predictability within its patterns of capital outlay, or investment for profit. Objective uncertainty had after all been a constant and nagging feature of exchanges within the earlier civil society, and one precondition of their crisis-ridden character; that which nowadays parades under the rubric of "rationalization" and "industrial planning" is precisely a systematic corporate attempt to suspend uncertainty through strategic calculations.

This intensified corporate rationalization of civil society is evidenced by at least three specific developments. Each takes its revenge on the old contractarian theory of legitimacy, weakening its credibility. First, as the pioneering work of Robinson, Chamberlin, and Kalecki indicated, under the competitive conditions of earlier civil society the individual capitalist enterprise was a price taker. In the phase of imperfectly competitive capitalism, by contrast, the giant corporation tends to become a price maker, intent only on ensuring for itself a suitable rate of return consonant with its prime costs (capital outlays, wages bill, and so on). Vertical integration is a typical case of the corporation's substantial market power: Insofar as the corporate planning unit administers its outlets and/or supply sources, competitive bargaining over the respective price and quantity schedules withers. This facilitates investment planning, production scheduling, and the forecasting of demand.[63] It also promotes the withering of the old belief in the calculating, enterprising, autonomous, individual entrepreneur, a belief that formed the cornerstone of classical bourgeois individualism. Contemporary civil society can no longer easily be viewed as a product of the association of previously isolated and free and equal entrepreneurs.

Secondly (and greatly facilitating this price administration), the market for the corporation's commodities is more and more administered through advertising strategies. Under the influence of strategies planned within corporations earlier this century, strategies temporarily retarded by world depression and war, late capitalist orders begin to resemble the model of "the bureaucratic society of controlled consumption."[64] This descent of bureaucratically produced publicity upon consuming publics is facilitated by productivity increases, the (uneven) systemic ability to pay higher wages, the extension of credit facilities, and the planned obsolescence of commodities. It is as if, through the symbolic magnetism of advertising, supply now strives to create effective demand. In the "society of the spectacle," advertising endeavors to create and build individual consumers and their desires into its symbolic realities; mobilized against "puritanism in consumption," organized advertising both speaks to its consumers ("People like you are changing to...") and in turn encourages them to reproduce its discourse actively. This is why the classical liberal image of sovereign, rational individual consumers bent on maximizing the satisfaction of their needs within the marketplace becomes less convincing. Individuals' alleged natural capacities to exercise their "liberty of tastes and pursuits"[65] undergo a denaturing. Nowadays, it becomes evident to many that late capitalist economies deconstruct their consuming subjects so as to facilitate their reincorporation into systems of planned and manipulated consumption.

The demoralization of contractarianism by the advance of bureaucratic administration within the realms of investment and consumption is reinforced, thirdly, by corporate and union attempts to rationalize the conduct and organization of wages bargaining and labor processes. Notwithstanding widespread lingering belief in the principle of individual worker achievement, the rationalization of labor tends to subvert the foundations of the old liberal idea of competitive market labor, according to which the "free" individual laborer was literally responsible for his or her own fate. Through the fair and legitimate wage generated by the exchange of equivalents, this liberalism asserted, laborers were supposed to take pride in their work, exercise at least some measure of control over it, and perhaps even become their own entrepreneurs.

A number of powerful tendencies illegitimate this liberal achievement principle. Within the oligopoly and state sectors, for example, the phenomenon of organized labor indicates the extent to which the corporate administration of prices depends in turn upon the bureaucratically *negotiated* level of money wage rates. Wage bargaining processes become relatively immune from the competitive threat of a "reserve army of labor." Under certain conditions, these systems of "political wages"[66] tend directly to promote class negotiation and planned compromise. Such planning – and the erosion of the old doctrine of individualism – is further enhanced by the possibility of agreements between corporations and organized labor concerning the mutual desirability of certain state- and/or corporate-financed projects (agreements on productivity, labor qualification, health, and so on). Again, under certain conditions, these may be seen as having routinizing and rationalizing effects. In return for improved conditions, productivity-pegged wage rates, or even the preservation of jobs, unions may serve to maintain labor discipline (by inhibiting wildcatting, slowdowns, and so on); they may also thereby promote the possibility of production planning by oligopoly capital.

Finally, the individualistic achievement principle is also subverted by the growing twentieth-century subversion of autonomous, craft labor through the constant managerial, bureaucratic restructuring of the labor process itself. This tendency was heralded in the work of Taylor and the uneven deployment of systems of scientific management – against the often bitter opposition of the rank-and-file labor movement.[67] Under late capitalist conditions, rationalization of labor continues, effectively weakening the illusion of individual worker achievement. Work tasks become subdivided, measured, timed, and standardized, the location of tools and materials systematically planned. The self-conscious control formerly exercised by workers over their conditions of labor is threatened from all sides. As a consequence of the radical separation of the planning and execution of tasks, the power to plan and control the labor process centrally tends to be snatched by the hands of management.[68] Laboring activity and the overall comprehension of that activity – whose unification Marx portrayed as the basis of the emergence of proletarian consciousness and the possibility of concrete labor in communist society – begin to part company. Those who execute tasks lose consciousness of the totality of the production process. This promotes rank-and-file revolts, countered by bureaucratic attempts to renew the potency of the achievement principle through job enrichment, worker participation, and profit sharing. For many, however, the image of "the achieving society" becomes less credible. Work continues to retain a momentum of its own. "The job" is sensed to be monotonous, unrewarding, and often trivial, a cage from which it seems one is powerless to escape unscathed. Dreams and fantasies, time wasting and slapdash work, absenteeism and holidays, become poor substitutes for another alternative: individuation through free, creative labor.

The politicization of civil society, the civilization of the state

The qualitative expansion of attempts by the bureaucratic state to manage the crisis tendencies of the nineteenth and early twentieth centuries constitutes another reason for the decay of the contractarian theory of individualism.[69] Tending to become the bearer of social order, the bureaucratic capitalist state becomes entwined with civil society, whose own survival and reproduction in oligopolized form is now directly dependent upon drawing this state into the business of production.

This politicization of civil society and civilization of the state is promoted by the allocative, production, and disciplinary functions of this state. Briefly, the state attempts, first, to constitute and secure the commodified property order through techniques of currency stabilization, trade and tariff regulation, the attempted (military, policy, judicial) suppression of the system's opponents at home and abroad, the adaptation of the legal and taxation systems to the dynamics of the accumulation process, and so on. Through a second form of activity, the state socializes a portion of national capital costs by limiting and suspending the once competitive commodity form of civil society. Bureaucratic state production becomes a defining and unique attribute of late capitalist societies. Ironically enough, productive state intervention replaces zones of civil society so as to ensure their reproduction. These productive strategies seek to foster oligopolistic accumulation by providing a material infrastructure (through the production of key capital goods, for instance) and regulating the human infrastructure, by way of the funding of scientific research and development, the provision of formal education, and the retraining of labor power. Finally, the state pursues strategies that seek to compensate for the socially and politically disruptive consequences of the accumulation and intervention processes. The state attempts to discipline society, to plan for peace with prosperity. Pressured to rescue corporations or industries threatened with insolvency, to insure against unemployment, industrial accidents, sickness, old age, and so on, the state endeavors to reproduce social harmony by defining and covering this society's social expenses.[70]

Together, these allocative, productive, and disciplinary activities of the bureaucratic state subvert the foundations of the old state–civil society dualism. This weakening of the boundaries between society and the state has profoundly unsettling effects upon the classical liberal theory of legitimacy.

With respect to civil society, that realm represented by contractarian theory as consisting in "private men in the exercise of several Trades, and Callings,"[71] it is clear that state attempts to reproduce it effect a decisive alteration of its competitive logic and an undermining of its former autonomy. This politicization of civil society devastates the classical liberal belief that the end of government is to be confined to the realization of individuals' private, acquisitive interests within a sphere of social relations. To the extent that the state meddles with private property and even produces the needs of private individuals, the individualistic presuppositions accompanying the old civil society are thrown into disarray. Indeed, bureaucratic state attempts to facilitate the private exchange between organized/unorganized labor and oligopoly/competitive capital through various decommodified and bureaucratic strategies represent a deep-seated contradiction within the activities of this interventionist state. This state's increasing socialization of the capital and social costs generated within civil society casts radical doubt upon the contractarian doctrine, through which this civil society was at one time legitimated.

Four examples of this development can be cited here.[72] First, state employment policies and direct and indirect subsidies and transfer payments can be seen as a response to economic crisis tendencies, both of which in turn definitely weaken classical liberalism's assumption that market competition would naturally ensure that the form of exchange would always be that of equivalent for equivalent. Second, state employment policies also call into question the earlier liberal explanations of the origins and dynamics of unemployment. Whereas classical liberal accounts of unemployment often masked their class biases through reference to "incompetent" or "lazy" individuals who had squandered their natural rights, it is the state that now tends to be held responsible for fluctuations in the level of unemployment. Consequent upon organized labor's insistence on "the right to a job" and state guarantees of certain citizenship or collective rights, the growth in levels of unemployment is revealed as institutionally inspired, as deliberate and intentional. Thirdly, as a result of their employment policies, their provision of a range of assistance payments, and the consequent reduction of income advantages to the marginally employed, state policies undermine the contractarian presumption that there would be a direct relationship between individuals' achievements and the monetary remuneration for their rendered labor. For many people the relationship between work and pay can be seen as rather less a consequence of individual energy and labor market forces and more a result of the logic of state activity. Finally, it is evident that bureaucratic state planning also tends to weaken the idea of the sanctity of the autonomous, private entrepreneur. The direct and extensive intrusion of various tiers of government into the process of urban and regional development is a typical case in point: Through their planning and regulation functions (the development of industrial and commercial zones, housing initiatives, limitations on high rises, and so on), governments accelerate the decay of justifications of the private ownership and control of property. States themselves become accountable for the planned administration of a sphere that, according to the old bourgeois theory of legitimate authority, was to be regulated only by self-generated, private calculations in pursuit of profit.

The systematic expansion of the state's allocative, productive, and disciplinary activities also has a devastating impact, conversely, upon the credibility of the old individualist theory of legitimate *political* power. In view of the qualitative expansion of bureaucratic state organization that monopolizes the means of violence, administration, and discipline, and even a portion of the means of production, the original contractarian presumption that an original act of consent among formerly dispersed individuals had constituted the state becomes illusory. The state can no longer easily be represented as the result of freely combining individuals who, originally living in isolation, subsequently instituted political forms "for quietness' sake." The unresolved (Lockean) antinomy between "express" and "tacit" consent comes to trouble this state. That process through which individuals – by virtue of their residing, traveling, or lodging within a nation-state – are deemed to have legitimated the power of that state, even though (as Locke expressed it) there are "no expressions of...[active or express] consent at all,"[73] remains thoroughly mysterious under the statist conditions of late capitalism. Popular assumptions about "consent" may well survive. No doubt many state agencies continue to be seen as authorized or entrusted to act on behalf of the body politic. Yet the mechanisms through which these agencies draw their legitimacy from the tacit, implicit consent of individuals, over whom they in turn hold sway, have become more and more unclear. Questions concerning whether the state's subjects actually consent actively or even tacitly, how they understand this consent, and whether they can actively articulate their refusal to consent continue to be obfuscated.[74]

This lack of clarity concerning the role of the individual as guarantor of legitimate political power is by no means offset by the participation of these individuals in legally constituted, competitive elections. In the view of classical contract theory, the vote would both protect the interests of individuals and, at the same time, maximize the aggregate satisfaction of individuals' separate and conflicting interests. It would ensure an identity of the interests of each individual

247

with those of the political community. This presumption becomes less credible under late capitalist conditions. Despite several extensions of the franchise, the principle of "one vote, one value" exercised by allegedly free and equal individuals now tends to be emptied of its content by numerous developments: ritualized elections and permanent campaigns, reinforced by attempts by elected representatives and unelected officials to "defactualize" the political world;[75] the cartelization of bureaucratic political parties; the displacement and weakening of legislatures as sites of political decision making; an enlargement of security agencies and their surveillance capacities; the continuous growth of a public opinion industry, designed according to the principles of corporate advertising;[76] and so on.

The denaturalization of the doctrine of individual consent is further strengthened by claims that obedience to the late capitalist state is now the *duty* of most individual citizens insofar as they are recipients of this regime's available benefits.[77] The insistence that the late capitalist state is voluntarily legitimated by its delivery of benefits, for which citizens should be truly thankful, has little credibility. This is because express consent becomes synonymous with hypothetical consent, with claims about the necessary *duties* of politically obedient citizens. Political questions concerning the nature of benefits, their differential allocation, and the needs that they allegedly satisfy, are thereby foreclosed. Clearly, *noblesse oblige* theories of legitimate authority reinforce the tendency for political power to discontinue displaying itself as the product of individuals' free negotiation and consent; this power instead begins to pride itself on its ability to mobilize and administer life productively for abstractly defined ends such as welfare or progress.[78]

The credence of the theory of individually granted consent to political power is additionally subverted by proposals to supplement or replace it with the principle of corporatist representation. The popularity of these proposals of course dates from the time of the crisis tendencies of the latter half of the nineteenth century (see Essays 3 and 5). At that time, the organized cartelization of civil society, the affiliation of organized labor and capital with bureaucratized political parties, and the dramatic growth of new state functions propelled many capitalist societies in a corporatist direction. The anonymously and individualistically regulated operations of the old civil society and state, it was argued, could be deliberately transfigured into a social and political order structured by the negotiation and bargaining among bureaucratic organizations.[79]

The more recent tendency of late capitalist states and oligopoly capital to seek an adjustment and reorganization of their already organized relations with organized labor represents an intensified phase of this corporatist tendency.[80] As in the case of every other bureaucratizing trend discussed so far, an unintended irony becomes apparent. Attempts to justify new corporatist arrangements through the retrieval of the old contractarian doctrine of legitimacy forget that the functional representation of this corporatism is formally analogous to that criticized by the early modern contractarian movements. Alternative efforts to justify this bureaucratic "interest-group liberalism" symbolically through recourse to notions of "unity, order, nationalism and success"[81] again clash fundamentally with the original contractarian theories of legitimate consent. Whereas the classical social contract theories presupposed a *direct* engagement of the individual in the foundation of the state and social life, the premise of contemporary forms of social contract is bureaucratic representation on the basis of function in the division of labor. The individual as the ground of legitimacy is displaced and overthrown. As is increasingly – and correctly – observed in intellectual discourse and everyday life, state-supervised corporatist strategies become both remote from the influence of bodily individuals and selectively biased in favor of corporate organization, including the state itself.[82]

Moreover, and finally, the drift toward corporatist arrangements clearly humiliates the legal traditions defended by the early modern contractarian movements. The mode of operation of corporatist schemes subverts these movements' insistence upon the need to subsume and protect individuals' natural rights of life, liberty, and property within a relatively autonomous, uniformly applied system of formal law, whose validity was deemed to be independent of the conflicting choices and values of individuals. Under corporatist pressures, this old jurisprudence is increasingly replaced by purposive, policy-oriented, and success-conscious modes of legal reasoning. These forms of reasoning again presuppose the displacement of "the individual" as the arbiter of legitimate authority. This displacement is reinforced in practice by the declining importance of promise-based liabilities; the corresponding growth of benefit- and reliance-based liabilities; the rapid proliferation of open-ended indeterminate clauses in legislation, administration, and adjudication; and, finally, the growing entanglement of substantive and procedural forms of law within the actual procedures and outcomes of bargaining between bureaucratically organized interests.[83]

The decline of the bourgeois household

The erosion of contractarian individualism by the advance of bureaucratic administration in the corporate and state domains of late capitalist societies is reinforced by a considerable – and seemingly irreversible – weakening of old contractarian justifications of patriarchal family life. This is a consequence of the fact that the content and functions of the bourgeois household tend to be usurped by colonizing bureaucracies; although its form no doubt persists, the bourgeois "good family," with its cheap imitation of the aristocracy (family trees, coats of arms, and the like), is increasingly seen to give way to alternative household arrangements (to single-parent households, for example) and to the professional supervision of broken homes decorated with illusions of togetherness and conviviality.[84]

This process of decay of bourgeois patriarchal authority has a complex history, dating from the second half of the nineteenth century. During this time, the structural problem of this family form – its subjugation of women through the institution of a well-defined sexual division of labor – was first questioned by middle-class feminist defenses of divorce and techniques of birth control, calls for an end to the double standards of bourgeois monogamy, and demands for

249

the vote, property rights, and other means of self-fulfillment for women outside the home. Early feminism by no means fully overcame this structural problem, a matter to which the second wave of feminism attests. There is no doubt, however, that early feminism considerably eroded the legitimacy of the bourgeois model of family life. The movement also accelerated the colonization of this family life by corporate, philanthropic, and state agencies. This disciplining of the bourgeois household had been foreshadowed in earlier philanthropic and state campaigns against foundling homes, the practice of wet-nursing, and the "disorders" of working-class sexual life; during the course of the nineteenth century, ironically, this disciplining process was increasingly turned back upon middle-class life itself.

As a consequence of its colonization, bourgeois family life is no longer able to represent itself credibly as a relatively autonomous and private domain within civil society. The bourgeois patriarchal family evidently becomes more and more an *affaire d'état*, dependent upon networks of (para-)state-organized agencies and "helping professions." Subversive of the old family form, these agencies presume that private life and its disorders can be analyzed, corrected, and professionally controlled: The causes and not merely the symptoms of these pathologies and disorders (juvenile delinquency, neuroses, and so on) are viewed as discoverable and amenable to therapeutic treatment.

This expropriation of the bourgeois family's powers through strategies of investigation, reform, and control is evident in a number of developments. No doubt of great importance is compulsory schooling, with its usurping of functions of disciplinary instruction in sexual morals, manners, domestic crafts, and manual training. Similarly, the former power of the middle-class father over his children is weakened by their exposure to children's aid societies, the social worker, juvenile courts, and visits to and from the probation officer. Furthermore, bourgeois family life and its health are increasingly defined or "medicalized" by general practitioners and such professions as obstetrics and pediatrics. Finally, the middle classes strive to upgrade the quality of their married life through parent-effectiveness training, marriage counseling, and various psychotherapies. These and other examples indicate that the colonization of the bourgeois household feeds upon its own dynamism: The bureaucratic professions' endeavor to become both disciplinary father and therapeutic, nurturing mother seems justified by the very disruption of the logic of family life they accelerate. This disruption is only reinforced by the commodification of family life. On an increased scale, middle-class women enter into segmented labor markets; many household services also fall under the influence of the corporate commodity form. Under late capitalist conditions, the private life of the old middle-class family contributes to big business and in turn becomes big business; now burdened with two jobs, the women of this class are expected to bear and nurture children, work for their independence, and coordinate the distribution of marketable goods and services at home.

There can be no doubt that this general subversion of the content of the bourgeois household has directly encouraged the renewal of struggles against the old patriarchal authority. The contractarian presumption that women, in-

250

cluding those who freely consent to give up their powers of self-determination, are perpetually obligated to their husbands is thereby further undermined. What is more, it can be observed that the colonization of middle-class family life has equally subversive implications for the individualistic premises of the contractarian doctrine of legitimation. Especially insofar as crime and other disorders are more and more defined in accordance with state-coordinated therapeutic modes of intervention, the individualistic clause of contractarian jurisprudence is subject to erosion; represented as creatures of diminished responsibility, bodily individuals are less and less deemed to be accountable for their acts against established law. The professional, bureaucratic definition of juvenile delinquency is indicative of this tendency. The delinquent is no longer to be understood as a criminal who has knowingly and willfully violated the law. The adversary relationship between the individual and state law is weakened considerably as the offender is understood by the surrogate parents as a product of an unhealthy environment or a victim of circumstances, to be reformed or rehabilitated through counseling, psychiatric treatment, and moral advice from magistrates. The new educative jurisprudence of the courts and the helping agencies and professions implicates offenders in their own subjugation; relieved of their guilt, culpability, and capacity for critical judgment, bodily individuals are to cooperate with the professionals in search of their reform, rehabilitation, or cure.[85]

Finally, there is some evidence that the credibility of patriarchal individualism is also menaced by the emergence of narcissistic character symptoms among the middle classes. These symptoms appear to be a consequence of the bureaucratic disruption of the individuation process typically instituted by the old bourgeois patriarchal family form. According to one recent psychoanalytic interpretation, the classic processes of ego development no longer operate within the confines of the weakened and dependent bourgeois family.[86] It is claimed that the young child is increasingly unable to form a strong psychic identification with its parents. Despite continuing parental supervision of the child's early depth-psychic development, the sexual phase once dominated by the Oedipus complex – and the corresponding ambivalence typically generated by the structuring of the child's desires by parents, who were symbols of both love and power – begins to lapse. As love objects, middle-class parents tend to become remote and unpredictable; sometimes callous and often shallow, they are concerned primarily with directing their energies toward themselves, their careers, and their pastimes. Their perfunctory attention to the child, combined with the oscillation between suffocating attentiveness and emotional distance, only exacerbates this process of estrangement. In the view of this revised psychoanalytic account, the estrangement of parents and children encourages the child's unconscious creation of substitute or symbolic parents.[87] The typical absence of the father and attempts by the mother to compensate for his desertion lead the child to create a fantasized, substitute father, who is a strong, vindictive, and punitive figure. In certain cases of pathological secondary narcissism, especially those which involve a narcissistic mother who understands her child as her self-extension, the child may even fantasize its mother as castrating and supremely seductive; though in these cases the mother tends to become the dominant parent, she too is constituted as "absent," as seductively aloof and devouring.

In either case, the relative absence or remoteness of the parents frustrates the child's capacity to mitigate its unconscious fantasies through the process of reality testing. The middle-class child's fantasies tend to be unconstrained. This child's self-understanding is consequently haunted and driven by ego-destructive fantasies, which are in fact archaic projections of its own desires and rages. There even tends to be a loss of the boundaries of the ego, whose tenuous and fluctuating morale becomes victimized by the unsatisfiable demands of the exaggerated ideal of a harsh and punitive superego. This psychic process is somewhat analogous to that of mourning,[88] whereby the mourner becomes reconciled to the loss of the loved object through its symbolic internalization and consequent overpowering of the ego. According to this interpretation, then, the essence of pathological narcissism is not self-admiration but self-deprecation. Narcissistic individuals tend to be marked with a certain "narcissistic entitlement" – with a sense of inner anxiety or hypochondria combined periodically with grandiose self-illusions.

Under the sway of these processes induced by the colonization of bourgeois family life, or so it is claimed, the competitive, patriarchal, and guilted personality type of earlier modernity begins to lapse into a state of permanent mourning and anxiety. Living within the bell curves of rationalizing bureaucracy, the bodily individual of the middle classes can no longer cling to his old self-understanding. He is marked by a mostly depoliticized craving for fulfillment and sexual gratification, to which the programmed hedonism of the late capitalist culture industry is directed with a vengeance. The individual, no longer regularly sure of himself, is beset by a chronic form of purposelessness, mild depression, and melancholia; he becomes preoccupied with a never-ending and self-destructive task of producing and consuming his identity. As the old sense of "wild, lawless" individualism is eclipsed, the insecure narcissist becomes thoroughly dependent upon others for self-esteem. He begins to sense his impotence.

The theory of legitimation reconsidered – Rousseau and beyond

It is true that these examples of the bureaucratic suffocation of the old ethos of individualism are merely indicative of trends. The weight of belief in the individual of the heroic days of contractarian individualism continues to hang over the present. Old presumptions generated by past liberal movements continue to be taken for granted by many, who neglect to reflect critically on the vast distance the present has traveled away from the spirit and substance of those movements. There seems to be no end to the mention of Ayn Rand and Milton Friedman, "doing one's own thing," "free markets," and the virtues of "the free, liberal society."

In the contemporary period, in which the decay of the welfare state project accelerates, there is a good deal of lip service paid to individualism, much of it invoked as a justification of new and expanded forms of bureaucratization. The influence of the so-called new liberalism, to take the leading example, can in part be explained by its ability to sustain itself upon nostalgia for the rapidly decaying themes of the classical liberal theory of legitimacy.[89] Inspired by the assumptions of classical political economy,[90] the new liberal authoritarianism rallies against the market-suspending operations of welfare state *dirigisme* and organized labor; under the catchall banners of "free markets" and the rights of "individuals" against "big government," it parades in defense of the power of private capital and strong, pro-business states. The new liberalism is in no sense critical of illegitimate power and the champion of the autonomy of bodily individuals against the authoritarian command of bureaucratic institutions. This movement does not (and cannot) advocate a return to the classical world of contractarian individualism, competing productive units, constitutionally restricted states, and small-scale organization. This new liberal campaign is therefore marked by a deep irony: Its protest against contemporary bureaucratizing trends within the spheres of society and the state at the same time involves a defense of corporate and state organizations, whose planning operations strongly contribute to this general bureaucratization process.

Under late capitalist conditions, not all invocations of liberal contract doctrine take the form of cunning justifications for the further exhaustion of the capacities of the powerless. Potentially democratic appropriations of the contract tradition are clearly in evidence. Some of these appropriations have no doubt been wholly implausible. The abstractly subjectivist thesis of existentialism – that the individual has no legislator but itself, that the individual, thus abandoned, must decide for itself – is a case in point. Other movements for autonomy – among women, oppressed sexual and ethnic minorities, environmentalists, peace campaigners, and rank-and-file labor – constitute more promising attempts at radicalizing the utopian potential of the contractarian theory of legitimation. Experiencing the retrenchment of contractarianism as a loss, these movements against heteronomy typically insist upon the need for individual autonomy through self-assumed relations with others. They consequently deepen the evident contradiction between the early modern standards of legitimation and the new realities of bureaucratic power; they heighten the sense that any compromise between this power and the old norms of legitimacy cannot be achieved under late capitalist conditions.

In respect of their reaffirmation of claims to autonomous consent and mutual obligation, these movements feed upon what might be called the progressive, emancipatory moment of late capitalist bureaucratization: its subversion of contractarianism and its subsequent generation of new forms of autonomous struggle. As has been argued earlier in this essay, bureaucratic organizations are marked by a deep-seated contradiction. They strive to discipline and order their constituents through the institution of abstract and calculating relations of power. Insofar as these abstract relations of power estrange their constituents, however, bureaucratic organizations are continually obliged to solicit the active but *coordinated* participation of the very constituents whom they strive to dominate. This contradiction and the conflicts it generates forcefully dispel the illusion of the self-determining, property-owning, patriarchal individual as mere illusion. Under the pressure of this contradiction and conflict, the "natural rights" of in-

253

dividuals undergo a denaturalization. It becomes clear to many that, far from being natural, individualism is itself the product of long, and always tenuous, processes of historical construction. The inflated sense of individual autonomy and will in the old theory of legitimate authority is undermined. The constituents of late capitalist society begin to discover that they are not natural beings abstractly perched outside relations of power and signification. Thanks to the ever-expanding bureaucratization of the world, in short, the old contractarian ideology begins to yield to bodily individuals' more accurate self-understanding as "nobodies," as beings incapable of conceiving and realizing their goals without the assistance of others. Subjects are forced to become aware that, as much as they actively constitute their social and political relations, they are at the same time the constituted agents of these relations, which are independent of their wills and not easily transformed.

Under the sway of this development and its associated conflicts, a socialist theory of public life is pressured to reconsider the role of bodily individuals in the constitution of legitimate relations of power. This problematic was of course central in an earlier phase of the modern bourgeois world. In defiance of this world, efforts to criticize the contractarian principle of legitimacy immanently had a remarkable influence from the time of Rousseau's pathbreaking critique of liberalism. This ill-fated movement sought to retrieve some themes of Renaissance individualism and (as Simmel has shown)[91] to sustain and politicize the influence of Romanticism. Understanding itself in opposition to the contract tradition's naturalization of atomized, "quantitative" individuals, this movement envisaged the realization of qualitatively new forms of cooperative individualism. The desirability of an individualism of cooperation and uniqueness (*Einzigkeit*) compared with that of mere singleness (*Einzelheit*) was emphasized because, as Rousseau himself stressed, the genuinely political individual would be "too magnificent a being to simply serve as the tool for others."[92] According to Rousseau, individualism could no longer be seen as consisting in emancipation through mere competitive opposition to others; its authentic and legitimate form could be constituted only through the communicative, intersubjective enrichment of each bodily individual's qualities and achievements to the point of uniqueness and incomparability. Only through political life could the individual become this specific, irreplaceable individual "called" or destined to realize its own incomparable capacities.

Convinced that the liberal contract tradition had failed to justify obedience to established relations of coercive, and therefore tyrannical, power, Rousseau called for the renegotiation of a social contract (*contrat social*) guided in all matters by the principle of the common good or general will (*volonté générale*). Coming together through a genuinely voluntary contract with their fellows, politicized individuals – laboring, speaking, and interacting within a small, egalitarian community – were to replace that agglomeration of unfree, private interests (the particular wills of civil society) guaranteed by the patriarchal family and the bureaucratic state. Judgments guided by the general will would consequently seek to guarantee the peaceful reconciliation of particular and universal interests, the establishment of concretely universal laws. According to Rousseau, these judgments could be ministered by government, but they could never admit of alienation or even representation. Citizens were to become sovereign, and their inalienable freedom would take the form of self-imposed obligations that would always in principle be subject to renegotiation.

In this regard, Rousseau distinguished at least three forms of liberty: (1) the "natural" liberty of the state of nature, in which liberty consisted in the savage's total independence from other bodily individuals; (2) "civil" liberty, the ability of individuals to do that which mutually agreed-upon law does not preclude; and (3) "moral" or political liberty.[93] It is the latter on which Rousseau placed most emphasis, since it was to be realized through the securing of a new social contract. Entering the contract voluntarily under similar conditions and with similar capacities, all bodily individuals, in giving themselves continuously to the polity, would have little or no interest in making the outcomes of the contract burdensome for others. To offend against the public interest by violating the legitimate relations of mutual assistance would indeed be to work (irrationally) against one's self and to risk retaliation by others. The political emancipation of each individual thus presupposed discursively initiated and self-imposed obligations. Only through self-assumed obligation and consent could relations of power be judged legitimate. As Rousseau stressed in his "Lettres écrites de la Montagne":

> Many have been the attempts to confound independence and liberty: two things so essentially different, that they reciprocally exclude each other. When every one does what he pleases, he will, of course, often do things displeasing to others; and this is not properly called a free state. Liberty consists less in acting according to one's own pleasure, than in not being subject to the will and pleasure of other people. It consists also in our not subjecting the wills of other people to our own. Whoever is the master over others is not himself free, and even to reign is to obey.[94]

This crucial distinction between independence and political liberty foregrounds Rousseau's controversial and frequently misrepresented insistence that an individual's refusal to continue obeying the principle of the general will must be reconsidered by that individual, that through the power of argument, "*on le forcera d'être libre.*" Moral freedom – "well-regulated liberty," as Rousseau referred to it elsewhere[95] – was "obedience to a law which we prescribe to ourselves."[96] Through their free agreement to obligate themselves, citizens could become duty bound, happy, and free, no longer slaves to their artificial and selfish passions, to those instrumental relations of civil society and the state which estranged individuals from themselves and from one another. Sharing in autonomous public life, individual citizens could live genuinely for others; through living for themselves, they could come to "feel at home [*chez eux*]." Rousseau concluded, in short, that subjects who governed themselves well would have little or no need of being governed.

In the phase of late capitalism this old notion of publicly negotiated consent and obligation survives, even if greatly weakened. Somewhat out of season, the theory and practice of citizenship and self-assumed obligations to power are assaulted from all sides by modes of bureaucratic authoritarianism that seemingly

255

take their time to become all-pervasive and that often appear in unobtrusive and banal forms. The public opposition to late capitalist society can nevertheless take heart. Through their unintended subversion of contractarian justifications of obedience to authority, the corporate and state bureaucracies of the late capitalist world manufacture disillusionment among their subordinated constituents. The advance of bureaucratic power unwittingly generates a sensed need to reconsider those subversive questions about the legitimation of power first raised and then obfuscated by the early contractarian tradition.

This felt need to retrieve questions raised by liberal contractarianism is surely paradoxical. After all, the questions and formulations of contractarianism were originally mobilized to defend new hierarchies of patriarchal bourgeois power, and thereby to prevent that power from becoming unified, centralized, and monopolized by *others*. Furthermore, since the early nineteenth century the radical, postliberal traditions have typically judged these questions to be old-fashioned, irrelevant, and therefore redundant. Declaring the season of fiction to be over, these traditions confidently assigned problems of obedience, obligation, and legitimation to the museums of prehistory. In retrospect, this radical rejection of the old bourgeois concern with the legitimacy of power appears to be less worldly and less radical than those bourgeois formulations themselves. From the perspective of a socialist theory of public life, indeed, the radical wish for a perfectly substantive democracy unhindered by problems of legitimacy, power, obedience, and conflict must be rejected for what it is: an exaggerated, anti-political, and never-to-be-realized utopia.

Resembling the wish of the foolish dove who bemoaned the resistance of the air and dreamed only of flying faster in a vacuum – the fool of whom Kant spoke – this utopia suppressed too many vital political questions, questions that were central for the contractarian movement and that are now of great importance to the autonomous, public opposition to late capitalist society. Indeed, this opposition demonstrates a remarkable capacity to provoke reflection on old-fashioned, contractarian problems, quite a few of which concern the institutional forms necessary for the realization of autonomous public spheres. A range of these can be mentioned here: Are not the quiet loyalty and deference to existing relations of bureaucratic power insufficient conditions of their legitimacy? Upon which principles, alternatively, could obligations to social and political power be legitimately founded under conditions of democratic socialism? Granted that the legitimation of power would depend upon the practical discourse of autonomous publics, would not the "liberty...of communicating whatever we please to the public"[97] be a necessary condition of restrictions upon the arbitrary exercise of social and political power? Must it not be admitted that the tasks of redistributing resources and administering decisions generated by autonomous publics can never wither away, even after the abolition of class distinctions? Might it therefore be deduced (with Franz Neumann) that one of the eternal contributions of contractarian political thought was its observation that political and administrative power will always be to some degree alienated, and that even democratic socialist systems are therefore in need of safeguards against the abuse of that power?

Assuming the need for these mechanisms of supervision of necessary political power, must we not from here on speak of the "road to socialism" not as the abolition of the (contractarian) distinction between civil society and the state, as Marx would have it, but, rather, as the *deepening* of this distinction? In other words, should not democratic socialist movements be concerned to constitute or reinforce public spheres within regions of social power now presently in distress and seriously endangered by the activities of state and corporate bureaucracies? Is it not only through a plurality of public spheres within the domain of society that individuals and groups could autonomously defend themselves from arbitrary political power? Can we therefore speak of the need for a postliberal reconstruction of civil society – of a "socialist civil society" of nonpatriarchal public spheres that relate to state institutions only at the levels of criticism, negotiation, and compromise? Could the relations between autonomous public spheres within a socialist civil society come to resemble relations between federated and highly differentiated local communities, which temporarily surrender and entrust only such part of their powers as is necessary for the realization of their aims? So conceived, might not autonomous publics legitimately exercise rights to secede from this federation? Might autonomous publics with good reason redefine areas of life as private, as beyond the scope of legitimate state activity?

Granted that the task of administering publicly negotiated agreements will not wither away, through which organizational forms could autonomous publics best execute their decisions? By means of which procedures, conversely, could the power delegated to those who administer be subject to recovery by these same publics? Does not the defense of autonomous public life practically require the restriction of state power, a reorientation of its tasks and prerogatives, and, in general, the subjection of the remaining "service-oriented" political institutions to criticism and supervision from below? Would it not remain true under democratic, socialist conditions, that the powers of these service-oriented institutions could "never become large enough to execute every possible wish of their possessors" (Spinoza); that these political powers would consequently need to be divided and dispersed, entrusted only for a time, subjected to permanent supervision by autonomous publics? Given that this dispersed power would be legitimated through the discussion and consent of autonomous publics, must the decisions of majorities always expressly bind dissenting minorities, as if majority rule were a "right of nature" (Grotius)? Under which conditions, through which means, and with respect to which substantive issues could minority publics legitimately withdraw their consent? Are not separate judiciaries and relatively autonomous codes of formal and generally applied law indispensable conditions of this resistance to illegitimate power? Finally, how warranted is the old conviction of Rousseau and Kant that war is a permanent effect of the "wild, lawless freedom" of the nation-state system, a system to be tamed and overcome in the future only through contractually negotiated leagues of peace?

In retrieving and radicalizing these and other old liberal questions – questions about which our Western tradition of socialist political theory is remarkably ignorant – it is clear that Rousseau's pathbreaking critique of both the liberal and traditional theories of legitimacy is a central point of departure. It is equally evident that a simple embrace of his formulations cannot be justified. For one thing, his rejection of the premises of the liberal contract tradition was only partial, blindly preserving its misogynist prejudices.[98] For another, his contention that citizenship was conditional upon securing rights to private property – he was thinking mainly of agricultural land – distributed equitably according to the principle of personal or familial need, now appears strange and hopelessly anachronistic.[99] No less problematic was his insistence that, because sovereignty was essentially indivisible, minorities must always defer to the will of the majority. This omission of questions concerning justified disobedience issued from his own – dare we say bureaucratic – yearning for a fully transparent political order, one that was to be visible, legible, and understandable in each of its parts. No longer obstructed by dark misunderstanding, individuals were to be able to see the whole of the political order, their hearts would communicate, and the universal will would govern each, who would recognize it as its own. The maxims of the common good, Rousseau wrongly assumed, could become "clear and luminous," permanently freed from tangled contradiction, requiring "only good sense to be perceived."[100]

For these reasons alone, it can be concluded that the defense of public life is forced to retreat not to Rousseau's formulations, but to his *problem* of constructing legitimate forms of institutionalized power, that is, forms of social and political association through which groups and individuals autonomously developed their identity by becoming conscious of their nonidentity.

Notes

1. Bureaucracy and its discontents

1 Oskar Negt and Alexander Kluge, *Öffentlichkeit und Erfahrung: Zur Organisationsanalyse von bürgerlicher und proletarischer Öffentlichkeit* (Frankfurt am Main, 1972), p. 7.
2 See, for example, Ian Gough, *The Political Economy of the Welfare State* (London, 1979), ch. 7.
3 This dismissal is attempted by Alain Touraine, but only through a reliance upon an overly restrictive understanding of crisis as a ruling-class category, which falsely asserts that democratic social movements have no capacity to act; see "Crisis or Transformation?" in Norman Birnbaum (ed.), *Beyond the Crisis* (London, 1977), pp. 15–45.
4 See my earlier formulation of this point in "Crisis in the Industrial World?," *Canadian Journal of Political and Social Theory/Revue canadienne de théorie politique et sociale*, vol. 3, no. 2 (1979), pp. 183–8; its deficiencies are well criticized by James O'Connor, "The Meaning of Crisis," *International Journal of Urban and Regional Research*, no. 5 (September 1981), pp. 301–29.
5 Quoted in Randolph Starn, "Historians and 'Crisis,' " *Past and Present*, vol. 52 (August 1971), p. 7.
6 Thucydides, *History of the Peloponnesian War*, ed. M. I. Finley (Harmondsworth, 1974), bk. III, pp. 236–45, and bk. II, pp. 151–6.
7 *Prison Notebooks*, ed. Quinton Hoare and G. Nowell-Smith (New York, 1975), p. 276; cf. Touraine, "Crisis or Transformation?," p. 43: "Crisis...manifests the end of a civilization, the growing difficulty of finding a meaning for that which loses its unity."
8 György Lukács, "Art and Society – Preface," *New Hungarian Quarterly*, vol. 13, no. 47 (1972), pp. 46-77: "I saw the World War then as the crisis of the whole of European culture; I regarded the present – in the words of Fichte – as the period of perfect sinfulness"; cf. T. S. Kuhn, *The Structure of Scientific Revolutions* (Chicago, 1962), chs. 7–8.
9 *Emile*, trans. Barbara Foxley (London, 1972), p. 157; cf. J. Habermas, *Legitimation Crisis* (Boston, 1975), p. 3: "Only subjects can be involved in crises."
10 A. J. Wiener and Herman Kahn, *Crisis and Arms Control* (New York, 1962).
11 Karl Korsch, *Karl Marx* (London, 1938).
12 Karl Marx and Frederick Engels, "Manifesto of the Communist Party," in *Selected Works*, vol. 1 (Moscow, 1969), p. 108.
13 Karl Marx, *A Contribution to the Critique of Political Economy* (Moscow, 1970).
14 Quoted in Franz Mehring, *Karl Marx* (Ann Arbor, Mich., 1962), p. 208.

15 For accounts of controversies surrounding what Bernstein first called the breakdown theory (*Zusammenbruchstheorie*) see Russell Jacoby, "The Politics of the Crisis Theory," *Telos*, no. 23 (Spring 1975), pp. 3–52; Paul Sweezy, *The Theory of Capitalist Development* (New York, 1968), ch. 2; and Giacomo Marramao, "Zum Verhältnis von Politischer Oekonomie und Kritischer Theorie," *Aesthetik und Kommunikation*, April 1973, pp. 79–93.

16 This appeared as an editorial introduction to *La Crise de l'état* (Paris, 1976).

17 See, for example, Bernhard Blanke et al. (eds.), *Kritik der politishen Wissenschaft*, 2 vols. (Frankfurt am Main, 1975); and W. Müller and C. Neusüss, "The Illusion of State Socialism and the Contradiction between Wage Labour and Capital," *Telos*, no. 25 (Fall 1975), pp. 13–90.

18 Richard Titmuss, "The Welfare State: Images and Realities," in Charles I. Schottland (ed.), *The Welfare State* (New York, 1967), p. 103; Gunnar Myrdal, *Beyond the Welfare State* (London, 1958), p. 45.

19 Claus Offe, "Advanced Capitalism and the Welfare State," *Politics and Society*, vol. 2, no. 4 (1972), p. 482.

20 Quoted in Timothy A. Tilton, "A Swedish Road to Socialism: Ernst Wigforss and the Ideological Foundations of Swedish Social Democracy," *American Political Science Review*, vol. 73 (1979), p. 516.

21 John Maynard Keynes, *The End of Laissez-Faire* (London, 1926).

22 T. H. Marshall, "Value Problems of Welfare Capitalism," *Journal of Social Policy*, vol. 2 (1972), pp. 26–7.

23 This ambivalence (often generated by sympathies for direct action and the open use of physical violence) expressed by turn-of-the-century social democrats has been well described in Peter Gay's account of Eduard Bernstein (*The Dilemma of Democratic Socialism* [New York, 1970], p. 7): "Is democratic socialism, then, impossible? Or can it be achieved only if the party is willing to abandon the democratic method temporarily to attain power by violence in the hope that it may return to parliamentarism as soon as control is secure? Surely this second alternative contains tragic possibilities: a democratic movement that resorts to authoritarian methods to gain its objective may not remain a democratic movement for long. Still, the first alternative – to cling to democratic procedures under all circumstances – may doom the party to continual political impotence."

24 R. H. S. Crossman (ed.), *New Fabian Essays* (London, 1952), p. 6.

25 Cf. Folker Fröbel et al., *The New International Division of Labour* (Cambridge, 1980); and Fred Block, *The Origins of International Economic Disorder* (Berkeley, Calif., 1977).

26 Daniel Bell, "The Public Household: On Fiscal Sociology and the Liberal Society," *Public Interest* (1974).

27 James O'Connor, *The Fiscal Crisis of the State* (New York, 1973); cf. Wilhelm Hennis (ed.), *Regierbarkeit: Studien zu ihrer Problematisierung* (Stuttgart, 1977); and Claus Offe, "Some Contradictions of the Modern Welfare State," *Praxis International*, vol. 1, no. 3 (1981), pp. 219–29.

28 The theoretical arguments of the new liberalism are popularly summarized in Milton Friedman and Rose Friedman, *Free to Choose* (London, 1980); see also Milton Friedman, *Capitalism and Freedom* (Chicago, 1962); F. A. Hayek, *The Road to Serfdom* (London, 1944); F. A. Hayek, *Individualism and Economic Order* (London, 1949); F. A. Hayek, *The Constitution of Liberty* (London, 1960); and C. J. Friedrich, "The Political Ideas of Neo-Liberalism," *American Political Science Review*, vol. 49 (1955), pp. 509–25.

29 Hayek, *The Constitution of Liberty*, p. 133.

30 See Friedman, *Capitalism and Freedom*, p. 15: "By removing the organization of economic

activity from the control of political authority, the market eliminates this source of coercive power. It enables economic strength to be a check to political power rather than a reinforcement."

31 Hayek, *The Road to Serfdom*, p. 69.
32 Friedman, *Capitalism and Freedom*, p. 189.
33 Hayek, *Individualism and Economic Order*, p. 7; cf Aaron Wildavsky's defense of "spontaneous social interaction" against state planning in *The Art and Craft of Policy Analysis* (London, 1980).
34 Friedman, *Capitalism and Freedom*, p. 25.
35 Advocates of new corporatist arrangements include Anthony King, "Overload: Problems of Governing in the 1970's," *Political Studies*, vol. 23, nos. 2–3 (1975), pp. 162–74; S. Brittan, *The Economic Consequences of Democracy* (London, 1977); and Samuel P. Huntington, "The United States," in Michel Crozier et al. (eds.), *The Crisis of Democracy* (New York, 1975). These discussions should not of course be identified with more empirical and analytic studies of the mediation of interest groups by welfare state institutions. These studies include Suzanne Berger (ed.), *Organizing Interests in Western Europe* (Cambridge, 1981); Ulrich von Alemann and Rolf G. Heinze (eds.), *Verbände und Staat* (Opladen, 1979); Philippe C. Schmitter and Gerhard Lehmbruch (eds.), *Trends toward Corporatist Intermediation* (Beverly Hills, Calif., 1979); Hennis, *Regierbarkeit*; and C. Offe, " 'Unregierbarkeit': Zur Renaissance konservativer Krisentheorien," in J. Habermas (ed.), *Stichworte zur "Geistigen Situation der Zeit"* (Frankfurt am Main, 1979).
36 See King, "Overload," p. 162: "Britain was an unusually easy country to govern, its politicians wise, its parties responsible, its administration efficient, its people docile."
37 This observation converges often with those of the new liberalism; cf. Milton Friedman, "The Line We Dare Not Cross," *Encounter*, November 1976, pp. 8–14.
38 F. W. Scharpf, "Public Organization and the Waning of the Welfare State: A Research Perspective," *European Journal of Political Research*, vol. 5 (1977), p. 345.
39 Empirical evidence for this claim (which is also defended by the new liberalism) is suggested in the comparative observations on Sweden and Britain developed by Richard Scase, *Social Democracy in Capitalist Society* (London, 1977).
40 Keith Middlemas, *Politics in Industrial Society* (London, 1979), p. 429; cf. Charles Lindblom, *Politics and Markets* (New York, 1977), p. 175: "In the eyes of government officials...businessmen do not simply appear as the representatives of a special interest, as representatives of interest groups do. They appear as functionaries performing functions that government officials regard as indispensable."
41 This tendency is best expressed theoretically in Charles Lindblom's defense of strategies of "disjointed incrementalism"; see especially David Braybrooke and Charles E. Lindblom, *A Strategy of Decision: Policy Evaluation as a Social Process* (New York, 1963), ch. 5.
42 Joachim Hirsch, *Der Sicherheitstaat: Das "Modell Deutschland," seine Krise und die neuen sozialen Bewegung* (Frankfurt, 1980).
43 Cf. S. Berger, "Politics and Antipolitics in Western Europe in the Seventies," *Daedalus*, Winter 1979, pp. 27–50; Claus Offe, "Konkurrenzpartei und politische Identität," in R. Roth (ed.), *Parlamentarisches Ritual und politische Alternativen* (Frankfurt, 1980); Alain Touraine, *La Voix et le regard* (Paris, 1978); and Alain Touraine, *L'Après-Socialisme* (Paris, 1980).
44 Under late capitalist conditions, that is to say, there is no overlapping and reinforcing of the lines of division between leaders and led, between those who consume and are content and those who are consumed and frustrated by bureaucratic power. This point is obscured by Oskar Negt and Alexander Kluge. Their provocative discussions

of public life are overburdened by the concept of a "proletarian public sphere," by which is meant the form in which the *universal* interests of the producing class are the driving force, as a "block of real life" whose homogeneity is constituted by its opposition to the "profit-maximizing interest" as such (*Öffentlichkeit und Erfahrung*, pp. 163, 107. Kluge's more recent attempt to define a genuine, oppositional public sphere as a form of commonly shared experience that does not entail "exclusions" is equally misleading; see his discussions with Klaus Eder, published in Klaus Eder and Alexander Kluge, *Über Dramaturgien: Reibungsverluste* [Munich, 1980]). In view of the highly differentiated character of both those who are subordinated and those who resist, the belief that there exists a single revolutionary class or group that is presently enduring a trial of powerlessness so that it can later become capable of a generalized critique of *all* powerlessness must be given up as dogmatic prejudice. Any political or theoretical attempt to impute or articulate the autonomous movements' "universality" (say, as "citizens," "working class," or "humanity") is not only bound to privilege the claims and organizational power of one fragment of these movements at the expense of others; such imputation also typically generates the chiliastic (and potentially authoritarian) anticipation of a future world stripped of all ambiguity and social division, a universe that is structured only by nonantagonistic contradictions and peaceful relations between "people," "workers," "human beings," and so on. This prejudice, which jeopardizes the possibility of a *plurality* of autonomous public spheres, has been a constant feature of critiques of bureaucracy since Lenin's *The State and Revolution*. It continues to be evident in a surprising number of recent discussions of the new autonomous movements' resistance to bureaucratic domination; in addition to Negt and Kluge, see, for example, Toni Negri, "Capitalist Domination and Working Class Sabotage," in *Working Class Autonomy and the Crisis* (London, 1979); James O'Connor, "*The Fiscal Crisis of the State* Revisited: Economic Crisis and Reagan's Budget Policy," *Kapitalistate*, vol. 9 (1981), pp. 41–61; and Touraine, *La Voix et le regard*.

2. The legacy of Max Weber

1 Describing the aims of the *Archiv für Sozialwissenschaft und Sozialpolitik* after its editorship was transferred to Edgar Jaffé, Werner Sombart, and Max Weber, Weber himself stressed: "Our aim is the understanding of the characteristic uniqueness of the reality in which we move. We wish to understand on the one hand the relationships and the cultural significance of individual events in their contemporary manifestations and on the other the causes of their being historically *so* and not *otherwise*" (*The Methodology of the Social Sciences*, ed. Edward A. Shils and Henry A. Finch [New York, 1949], p. 72 [hereafter cited as *MSS*]).
2 Max Weber, *Gesammelte Politische Schriften* (Tübingen, 1958), p. 60 (hereafter cited as *GPS*); cf. *GPS*, pp. 60–1: "It is highly ludicrous to impute to modern high capitalism...any elective affinity with 'democracy' or even 'freedom' (in any meaning of the word)."
3 Max Weber, *The Protestant Ethic and the Spirit of Capitalism* (New York, 1958), p. 26 (hereafter cited as *PE*); cf. *From Max Weber: Essays in Sociology*, ed. H. H. Gerth and C. Wright Mills (London, 1970), p. 141 (hereafter cited as *FMW*).
4 *PE*, pp. 13, 16; cf. Max Weber, "Socialism," in J. E. T. Eldridge (ed.), *Max Weber: The Interpretation of Social Reality* (London, 1972), p. 197 (hereafter cited as "Socialism"); *FMW*, pp. 139 and 155: "The fate of our times is characterized by rationalization and intellectualization and, above all, by the 'disenchantment of the world'"; and Max Weber, *Gesammelte Aufsätze zur Wissenschaftslehre* (Tübingen, 1968), p. 470 (here-

after cited as *GAW*), where Weber discusses the replacement of *Gemeinschaftshandeln* by *Gesellschaftshandeln*: "On the basis of our knowledge of the whole of past history, we observe... a steady advance of instrumentally rational regulation of actions based on mutual agreement, and in particular a progressive turnover of (voluntary) associations into institutions organized on an instrumentally rational basis." On the distinctiveness of occidental rationalization, see also the discussions of Benjamin Nelson, "Dialogs across the Centuries: Weber, Marx, Hegel, Luther," in J. Weiss (ed.), *The Origins of Modern Consciousness* (Detroit, 1965), pp. 149–65; and G. Abramowski, *Das Geschichtsbild Max Webers Universalgeschichte am Leitfaden das oksidentalen Rationalisierungsprozesses* (Stuttgart, 1966).

5 *MSS*, pp. 71ff., 130, 136–7; cf. *GAW*, pp. 427ff.

6 Max Weber, *Economy and Society*, ed. Guenther Roth and Claus Wittich, 2 vols., (Berkeley, Calif., 1978), vol. 2, p. 1149 (hereafter cited as *ES*).

7 Max Weber, *Gesammelte Aufsätze zur Soziologie und Sozialpolitik* (Tübingen, 1924), p. 414 (hereafter cited as *GASS*).

8 *FMW*, p. 216; cf. *ES*, p. 1149.

9 *FMW*, pp. 207–8. The propensity of bureaucratic systems for emancipating themselves from the "motivational structure" of their members is a favorite theme of Niklas Luhmann; see his *The Differentiation of Society* (New York, 1982), ch. 3.

10 *FMW*, pp. 214, 228, 232–5. It must be noted that, especially in his discussions of political events in Germany and Russia, Weber tends to weaken this explanation of the advance of bureaucratization under modern conditions. Not only technical competence, but also the arrogant will to power of bureaucratic elites, is reckoned to be a fundamental source of their expanded control. See, for instance, *GPS*, pp. 82–3, 140–1, 276, and 31–2, note 1, where, speaking of the 1905 Russian events, Weber refers to the " 'enlightened' bureaucracy, which quite naturally looked down scornfully on the 'muddling through' and impractical 'stubbornness,' the 'private interests,' the 'stupidity' and egoism, the 'utopian dreams' of the intelligentsia, the self-governing bodies, the 'clichés' of the Press – from its point of view, all this continually impeded its promotion of the utilitarian happiness of the people, and thwarted the appropriate respect for authority required by 'reasons of state.' "

11 *FMW*, pp. 105, 225. Weber here discusses several other examples of these technical imperatives. The bureaucratization of legal procedures in later Rome, he argues, was necessary because of the increasing complexity of both practical legal cases and the increasingly rationalized economy. Similarly, he explains the emergence of machine politics in nineteenth-century England as an effect of the parties' need to win the masses through the technical efficiency of a "tremendous" bureaucratic apparatus that relied (after 1868) on the caucus system.

12 Ibid., pp. 223–4. Thus Weber sees the "irresistible demand" for certificates of education as linked with opportunities for high status and salaried positions within expanding bureaucracies, and not with some disinterested thirst for education or a desire for cultivation and good learning; see, for example, ibid., pp. 240–4, and *GPS*, pp. 235–6.

13 *FMW*, p. 214; cf. "Socialism," p. 199.

14 *PE*, p. 17 (translation altered); cf. *PE*, pp. 54–5, 181; *FMW*, p. 196; and Max Weber, *Gesammelte Aufsätze zur Sozial- und Wirtschafts- geschichte* (Tübingen, 1924), pp. 277–8 (hereafter cited as *GASW*).

15 This was first published in 1900, and translated as *The Philosophy of Money* (London, 1978); see the critique of Simmel in *PE*, p. 185, note 2. Weber also wielded this argument against Lujo Brentano's *Die Anfänge des modernen Kapitalismus*. According

to Weber (*PE*, p. 198, note 13), Brentano "has thrown every kind of struggle for gain, whether peaceful or warlike, into one pot, and has then set up as the specific criterion of capitalistic (as contrasted, for instance, with feudal) profit-seeking, its acquisitiveness of *money* (instead of land)."

16 *ES*, p. 86. Conversely (*ES*, pp. 100ff.), Weber insists that rational capital accounting of economic activity is impossible in principle if calculations are in kind.

17 *PE*, p. 58; cf. *PE*, p. 69.

18 *ES*, p. 159.

19 *FMW*, p. 366; *PE*, p. 181; *ES*, p. 140.

20 *ES*, pp. 913–21. On Weber's various and unsystematic remarks on imperialism, see Wolfgang J. Mommsen, *Max Weber und die deutsche Politik, 1890-1920* (Tübingen, 1959), pp. 76ff.

21 "Socialism," p. 208; *ES*, p. 140.

22 *PE*, pp. 17, 64.

23 *ES*, pp. 91ff., 154–5.

24 The capitalist monopoly of the physical means of production, Weber argues (*ES*, pp. 147–8), was the effect of the complex ensemble of modern developments, including the effective monopolization of money capital by entrepreneurs; the appropriation of product marketing rights (e.g., through the formation of monopoly guilds or through privileges granted by political authorities in return for periodic payments and loans); the subjective disciplining of putting-out system workers by means of entrepreneurial control of the supply of raw materials; and finally, the development of workshops marked by the appropriation of all means of production by capitalistic entrepreneurs.

25 *PE*, pp. 21–2; *FMW*, p. 372; *ES*, pp. 109, 134–5.

26 *ES*, p. 162; cf. "Socialism," p. 201: "A modern factory proprietor does not employ just any worker, just because he might work for a low wage. Rather he puts the man at the machine on piece-wages and says: 'All right, now work, I shall see how much you earn'; and if the man does not prove himself capable of earning a certain minimum wage he is told: 'We are sorry, you are not suited to this occupation, we cannot use you'. He is dismissed because the machine is not working to capacity unless the man in front of it knows how to utilise it fully."

27 *PE*, p. 22; cf. *ES*, p. 92.

28 *GASS*, p. 396; cf. the description of the modern factory (*GASS*, pp. 224–5), with its "hierarchic authority structure, its discipline, its chaining of the men to the machines, its spatial aggregation and yet isolation of the workers (in comparison with the spinning rooms of the past), its formidable accounting system that reaches down to the simplest hand movement of the worker."

29 *ES*, p. 137. In only a few passages (e.g., *ES*, pp. 92, 99–100) does Weber discuss the modern corporations' propensity for bureaucratically manufacturing opportunities for selling the goods they produce. (The consequences and limitations of this corporate, bureaucratic stimulation of wants later became of central concern to Adorno, whose theses are analyzed in Essay 3.)

30 *PE*, p. 23; "Socialism," p. 201; *GASS*, pp. 452–3.

31 *ES*, pp. 92, 108, and 93: "Capital accounting in its formally most rational shape...presupposes the *battle of man with man*."

32 "Socialism," pp. 210, 211.

33 *ES*, pp. 108, 110, 150–1; "Socialism," pp. 201–2, 209–11. Weber's emphasis on the last-mentioned condition is linked with his belief that it was "the dictatorship of the

official, not that of the worker which, for the present at any rate, is on the advance" (ibid., p. 209).

34 *ES*, p. 162.

35 *PE*, pp. 24; see also *PE*, p. 75; and *FMW*, p. 131.

36 *ES*, pp. 67, 121, 135, 162.

37 Ibid., p. 92.

38 Ibid., p. 64.

39 This point is well emphasized in David Beetham, *Max Weber and the Theory of Modern Politics* (London, 1974).

40 "The National State and Economic Policy (Freiburg Address)," *Economy and Society*, vol. 9, no. 4 (1980), p. 442 (hereafter cited as "Freiburg").

41 Karl Marx and Frederick Engels, "Manifesto of the Communist Party," in *Selected Works*, vol. 1 (Moscow, 1969), pp. 110–11. Cf. the later discussions of Carey, Bastiat, and the United States in Karl Marx, *Grundrisse* (Harmondsworth, 1973), pp. 884–9, and *Capital*, vol. 1 (Moscow, 1970), p. 703, where Marx notes that "the power of the State" is "the concentrated and organized force of society." His typical account of the bourgeois constitutional state as superstructural is analyzed more thoroughly in my "The Legacy of Political Economy: Thinking with and against Claus Offe," *Canadian Journal of Political and Social Theory / Revue canadienne de théorie politique et sociale*, vol. 2, no. 3 (1978), pp. 50–5. Of course, it should be added that Marx elsewhere pointed to aberrant cases (e.g., the Bonapartist state in France, Bismarck's Germany, the Asiatic mode of production), where the relatively greater independence of the state to organize the relations of production more actively was seen as resulting from (1) unique territorial and climatic conditions, reinforced by the general absence of private ownership and control of land; (2) the fact that feudal remnants continued to hinder the achievement of bourgeois hegemony; and (3) the failure of one particular class (or class fraction) to attain dominance over the others. These exceptions can be interpreted as anomalies with which classical Marxism never satisfactorily dealt.

42 *MSS*, pp. 70, 188.

43 See Weber's discussion of Stammler's incoherently "scientific" refutation of historical materialism, in *Critique of Stammler* (London, 1977) (hereafter cited as *Stammler*).

44 *Stammler*, p. 87.

45 *FMW*, p. 212; *ES*, pp. 1150–6.

46 *FMW*, p. 218.

47 Though the principle and practice of a "law without gaps" was (and still remains) hotly contested, Weber remarks (*FMW*, p. 219) that the early modern legal system more and more came to depend upon the modern judge, who resembles "an automaton into which the files and the costs are thrown in order that it may spill forth the verdict at the bottom along with the reasons, read mechanically from codified paragraphs."

48 *FMW*, p. 83; cf. "Socialism," pp. 198–9.

49 *FMW*, p. 77; cf. *ES*, p. 64, where Weber elaborates Franz Oppenheimer's distinction between "economic" and "political" means, the latter being understood as synonymous with the direct appropriation of goods by force and with the direct coercion of others by threats (or actual use) of force.

50 See *FMW*, p. 78, where Weber expresses one of his most famous theses: "The state is a relation of humans dominating humans, a relation supported by means of legitimate (i.e., considered to be legitimate) violence."

51 Ibid., pp. 97–8.

52 Ibid., p. 108; cf. *ES*, pp. 284–8; and *FMW*, pp. 109–10: "The typical boss is an

absolutely sober man. He does not seek social honor; the 'professional' is despised in 'respectable society.' He seeks power alone, power as a source of money, but also power for power's sake...the boss has no firm political 'principles'; he is completely unprincipled in attitude and asks merely: What will capture votes?"

53 *FMW*, pp. 102ff. Weber's criticism of legislatures as "banausic" assemblies incapable of generating political leadership is particularly evident in his last writings (see *GPS*, p. 488).

54 "Socialism," p. 197; *PE*, p. 16.

55 *FMW*, p. 88.

56 *ES*, p. 162.

57 *GPS*, p. 239; *ES*, p. 920; "Freiburg," passim.

58 In at least one place (*ES*, p. 199), Weber does, however, anticipate the possibility of fiscal problems of the modern state. In the event of such problems arising, Weber argued for a form of corporatist rearrangement of state policy making: "One might proceed...in the 'socialization' of the capitalistic enterprises of individual branches, by imposing compulsory cartels or combinations with obligations to pay large sums in taxes. Thus they could be made useful for fiscal purposes, while production would continue to be oriented rationally to the price situation."

59 *FMW*, p. 208; *ES*, p. 167.

60 Max Weber, *The Agrarian Sociology of Ancient Civilizations* (London, 1976), pp. 389–411 (hereafter cited as *Agrarian Sociology*).

61 *FMW*, p. 213; cf. "Socialism," p. 199, where Weber insists that bureaucratic concentration of tools within all spheres (the factory, the state administration, the army, university faculties) is due in part to the nature of modern tools.

62 *FMW*, p. 215.

63 *ES*, p. 223.

64 *FMW*, p. 213.

65 *ES*, p. 1394; cf. *FMW*, pp. 81, 131; and "Socialism," p. 199.

66 On the background to controversies between the conservative and liberal factions of the *Verein für Sozialpolitik* see Dieter Lindenlaub, *Richtungskämpfe im Verein für Sozialpolitik (1890-1814)*, 2 vols. (Wiesbaden, 1967); and Beetham, *Max Weber*, ch. 1 and pp. 63ff.

67 *GASS*, p. 415.

68 *ES*, pp. 85–6, 108.

69 *FMW*, p. 215.

70 *ES*, p. 138; "Socialism," p. 202.

71 *ES*, p. 94; cf. *ES*, pp. 105, 108, 141, 166.

72 Ibid., pp. 95, 105, 108; cf. Weber's "Marginal Utility Theory and 'The Fundamental Law of Psychophysics,'" *Social Science Quarterly*, vol. 56 (1975), pp. 31–2 (hereafter cited as "Marginal Utility Theory").

73 "Freiburg," p. 441.

74 Cf. Weber's early inversion of this evolutionist assumption: "Abandon hope all ye who enter here: these words are inscribed above the portals of the unknown future history of humanity" (ibid., p. 437).

75 See, for example, Karl Kautsky, *The Labour Revolution* (London, 1925); and Lenin's polemic – directed at "autonomism," "anarchism," and bourgeois intellectuals who "accept organizational relations platonically" – in support of the thesis that bureaucrácy is "the organizational principle of revolutionary Social Democracy" ("One Step Forward, Two Steps Back," in *Selected Works*, vol. 1 [Moscow, 1970], pp. 275–7, 403ff., 430–1).

76 *ES*, pp. 103–7, 110–11.

77 *GPS*, pp. 474 and 448: "The *Communist Manifesto* rightly emphasized the *economically* – not politically – *revolutionary* character of the project of the bourgeois capitalistic entrepreneurs. No trade union, even less a state socialist functionary, can replace these entrepreneurs and perform this role for us."

78 *ES*, pp. 110 and 151: "Other things being equal, positive motives for work are, in the absence of direct compulsion, not obstructed to the same extent as they are for unfree labour."

79 Ibid., p. 128.

80 *GASS*, pp. 407–12.

81 "Socialism," pp. 197, 214–15; *ES*, pp. 139 and 148, where Weber notes that, in the contemporary capitalist world, this expansion of an administrative strata was *already* evident in the restructuring of capitalist enterprises into associations of stockholders.

82 *GASS*, p. 414.

83 *FMW*, p. 100; "Socialism," pp. 215–16.

84 "Socialism," p. 204; *GPS*, p. 242. Weber considered that this tendency for state bureaucracy to weaken private economic power was already at work within the period of "high capitalism." Statism was also a decisive characteristic of Rome during its decline: "Bureaucracy stifled private enterprise in Antiquity. There is nothing unusual in this, nothing peculiar to Antiquity. Every bureaucracy tends to intervene in economic matters with the same result. This applies to the bureaucracy of modern Germany too" (*Agrarian Sociology*, p. 365).

85 "Freiburg," p. 440.

86 *PE*. For an account of the early polemics (between 1904 and 1910) concerning this thesis, see J. Winckelmann, *Max Weber: Die protestantische Ethik II: Kritiken und Anti-Kritiken* (Munich, 1968); more recent controversies are analyzed in Gordon Marshall, *In Search of the Spirit of Capitalism* (London, 1982).

87 *PE*, p. 36.

88 " 'Kirchen' und 'Sekten' in Nordamerika," in J. Winckelmann (ed.), *Soziologie, Universalgeschichtliche Analysen, Politik* (Stuttgart, 1973), p. 395.

89 *PE*, p. 53; cf. *PE*, p. 153. Weber elsewhere (*ES*, p. 100) speaks of a "natural economy [*Naturalwirtschaft*]" to designate forms of economic life from which money as a medium of exchange is absent, either because there is no exchange at all or because exchange is only by barter.

90 *PE*, pp. 171, 250, note 152, 263–4, note 22.

91 Ibid., p. 177. Weber is overly ambiguous about the degree and scope of this self-rationalization process. His comment that the "treatment of labor...as a calling became as characteristic of the modern worker as the corresponding attitude toward acquisition of the business man" (ibid., p. 179) seems rather exaggerated. Elsewhere, for example, he proposes (with reference to the squirearchy, the original bearers of "merrie old England") that the elements of an "unspoiled naïve joy of life" remain a crucial aspect of English national character (ibid., pp. 173, 279, note 91).

92 Ibid., p. 176.

93 Ibid., p. 182; cf. ibid., pp. 54, 70–2, 188, note 3.

94 *FMW*, p. 117; *MSS*, p. 144.

95 *MSS*, pp. 134–5, 139.

96 Friedrich Tenbruck, for example makes this claim in "Die Genesis der Methodologie Max Webers," *Kölner Zeitschrift für Soziologie und Sozialpsychologie*, vol. 2 (1959), p. 583. On the historical background to the *Methodenstreit*, see Fritz Ringer, *The Decline of the German Mandarins: The German Academic Community, 1890–1933* (Cambridge, Mass.,

1969); and the comments on Ringer by Jürgen Habermas in "The Intellectual and Social Background of the German University Crisis," *Minerva*, vol. 9, no. 3 (1971), pp. 422–8.

97 *Roscher and Knies: The Logical Problems of Historical Economics* (New York, 1975) (hereafter cited as *RK*).

98 *MSS*, pp. 176 and 55: "Even the knowledge of the most certain proposition of our theoretical sciences – e.g., the exact natural sciences or mathematics, is, like the cultivation and refinement of the conscience, a product of culture." Weber is not always consistent on this point. See, for example, *MSS*, p. 160, where it is denied that those natural sciences which take mechanics as their model are conditioned by subjective values.

99 Ibid., pp. 76, 77, 80, 85–6.

100 Ibid., pp. 74, 78–80, 159, 173, and 78: "We seek knowledge of an historical phenomenon, meaning by historical: significant in its individuality (*Eigenart*)." Particularly in his later writings, Weber modified this singularity postulate. While the ideal-typical quality of all cultural-scientific categories is still insisted upon, cultural-scientific analysis is seen to be concerned with concepts, analogies, and rules of cultural development that are general by virtue of their applicability to the history of not only our own but all civilizations (cf. *GAW*, p. 265; *ES*, pp. 19–22; and *PE*, p. 13).

101 *MSS*, pp. 74, 81, 125, 175; cf. *RK*, pp. 154, 157–8, 185–6, 217–18; *GAW*, p. 332; *Stammler*, pp. 74–5, 96, 110–11, 139, 148; and *ES*, pp. 3ff.

102 *FMW*, p. 143; cf. *FMW*, pp. 144, 147.

103 *MSS*, p. 173; cf. *MSS*, p. 150; *Stammler*, pp. 88–9, 112–15; "Freiburg," p. 440; and *FMW*, p. 132.

104 This special concept of objectivity is frequently misunderstood, usually from a positivistic standpoint, the classic example of which is Theodore Abel, "The Operation Called *Verstehen*," *American Journal of Sociology*, vol. 54 (1948), pp. 211–18.

105 *MSS*, pp. 110, 150; "Freiburg," p. 440; *FMW*, p. 132.

106 *MSS*, pp. 55, 61, 84, 110–11; cf. *FMW*, pp. 152 and 153: "No science is absolutely free from presuppositions, and no science can prove its fundamental value to the person who rejects these presuppositions."

107 *GAW*, pp. 206–7.

108 *FMW*, p. 147.

109 *MSS*, p. 52.

110 Ibid., pp. 53, 54; *FMW*, p. 152.

111 *MSS*, pp. 52ff.; *FMW*, pp. 151–2; "Freiburg," p. 440.

112 *FMW*, p. 228.

113 Ibid., p. 229; cf. *PE*, p. 180.

114 *FMW*, p. 85.

115 Karl Löwith, "Max Weber und Karl Marx," *Archiv für Sozialwissenschaft und Sozialpolitik*, no. 67 (1932), pp. 61–2.

116 *GASS*, p. 416; *GPS*, pp. 169–70 and 152: "I have always viewed not only foreign affairs but all politics solely from a national point of view." So many interpreters of Weber's project have missed the significance of this conviction, which owed much to Ranke's theory of history as a struggle between great powers. This omission is evident in Benjamin Nelson's account of Weber's introduction to the *Gesammelte Aufsätze zur Religionssoziologie* (*PE*, pp. 13–31) as a "master clue" to his larger intentions. Weber is intepreted as a "pioneer in the comparative historical differential sociology of sociocultural process and civilizational complexes" ("Max Weber's 'Author's Introduction' [1920]: A Master Clue to His Main Aims," *Sociological Inquiry*, vol. 44, no. 4

[1974], pp. 269–78). The affinity between this interpretation and Parson's later works is here clear. See, for example, Parsons's "Comparative Studies and Evolutionary Change," in I. Vallier (ed.), *Comparative Methods in Sociology* (Berkeley, Calif., 1971), pp. 97–139. Such interpretations seriously ignore the political context to which Weber addressed his scholarly *and* political texts – a context in which, among the German middle classes, a militant nationalism informed by Social Darwinist and racist assumptions became increasingly influential (cf. Fritz Stern, *The Politics of Cultural Despair* [New York, 1961]). These interpretations also ignore and therefore depoliticize Weber's explicit concern with the need to intervene politically against the threats posed by the general advance of bureaucracy under contemporary conditions. On his defense of the primacy of the principle of the nation-state, his "passionate championship of a German national imperialism," see Mommsen, *Max Weber und die Deutsche Politik*, pp. xvi, 40; Wolfgang J. Mommsen, *The Age of Bureaucracy* (Oxford, 1974), ch. 2; Anthony Giddens, *Politics and Sociology in the Thought of Max Weber* [London, 1972); and Ilse Dronberger, *The Political Thought of Max Weber* (New York, 1971), pp. 116ff.

117 Cf. *ES*, p. 920: "Every successful imperialist policy of coercing the outside normally – or at least at first – also strengthens the domestic prestige and therewith the power and influence of those classes, status groups, and parties, under whose leadership the success has been attained."

118 Weber's defense of the leadership principle is strongly evident in his later writings, particularly those concerning his campaign for a presidential system of government during and after the German winter elections of 1918–19. See, for example, *GPS*, pp. 472–5, 486–9. His concern with developing a theory of charismatic authority is also expressive of this defense of strong-willed, passionate leadership; see Wolfgang J. Mommsen, "Zum Begriff der 'plebiszitären Führerdemokratie' bei Max Weber," *Kölner Zeitschrift für Soziologie und Sozialpsychologie*, vol. 15 (1963), p. 295–322.

119 *FMW*, p. 95. This recommendation continuously informs Weber's critique of the conduct of German domestic and foreign policy prior to and during World War I. This is summarized in *GPS*, p. 198: "Germany...has the best and most honest officialdom in the world. The German performance in this war has shown what military discipline and bureaucratic efficiency is capable of. But the frightful failures of German policy have also demonstrated what *cannot* be achieved through this means." See also his comparison of the British and German states' treatment of striking workers under conditions of war in ibid., p. 286.

120 In his earliest writings on the 1905 Russian Revolution (*GPS*, pp. 76-8), Weber therefore criticized monarchic regimes for their incapacity to generate consistent and genuine leadership in the face of creeping bureaucratization.

121 *FMW*, pp. 115ff; see also the discussion of the theory of *Führerdemokratie* in Mommsen, "Zum Begriff der 'plebisziträren Führerdemokratie.' "

122 *FMW*, p. 117.

123 Max Weber, "Die drei reinen Typen der legitimen Herrschaft," in J. Winckelmann (ed.), *Staatssoziologie* (Berlin, 1956), p. 110.

124 *FMW*, p. 127.

125 Ibid., p. 120.

126 Ibid., p. 123.

127 Cf. Reinhard Bendix, *Max Weber: An Intellectual Portrait* (Garden City, N.Y., 1962), ch. 10.

128 *FMW*, p. 106.

129 Ibid., p. 103; see also ibid., pp. 104-6, where Weber argues this thesis with respect to the democratization of the franchise in England (and the ensuing bureaucratization

of party politics, which culminated in Gladstone's ascent to office). Here Weber followed Ostrogorski's description in *Democracy and the Organization of Political Parties* of the growth of the plebiscitarian form in Britain and the United States. It should be noted that on other occasions (e.g., *GPS*, p. 214; *ES*, pp. 1419-20), and especially prior to the revolutionary disturbances of 1918–19, Weber criticized "token Parliamentarism" and proposed (with the British parliamentary model in mind) the *strengthening* of legislative institutions, in order that they might function as a site of "positive politics," as an arena for the protection of civil rights and, above all, for the recruitment and training of genuine leaders.

130 See, for example, Carl Friedrich, "Political Leadership and the Problem of Charismatic Power," *Journal of Politics*, vol. 23 (1961), p. 16, note 24; cf. Mommsen, *The Age of Bureaucracy*, pp. 79–80, 91–3.

131 *FMW*, p. 107.

132 *MSS*, p. 27.

133 *FMW*, p. 116.

134 C. B. Macpherson, *The Life and Times of Liberal Democracy* (Oxford, 1977), ch. 4; Peter Bachrach, *The Theory of Democratic Elitism* (London, 1970).

135 Quoted in Mommsen, *Max Weber und die Deutsche Politik*, p. 392.

136 *MSS*, pp. 84, 130, 169–70.

137 Ibid., pp. 93, 107, 130, 135, 171, 185; cf. *PE*, pp. 47–8; *FMW*, p. 138; *Stammler*, p. 73; "Marginal Utility Theory," p. 34.

138 *GAW*, p. 206; cf. the misleading thesis of Niklas Luhmann (*The Differentiation of Society*, p. 23) that Weber's theory "with its impressive compactness, cannot be controverted within its own premises."

139 Letter to Carl Peterson (14 April 1920), reprinted in Bruce B. Frye, "A Letter from Max Weber," *Journal of Modern History*, vol. 39 (1967), p. 123.

140 *MSS*, p. 90; cf. *GAW*, p. 184: "The conceptual boundaries within which the social world can become an object of observation and scientific explanation are impermanent. The presuppositions of the sociocultural sciences remain variable into the indefinite future, at least as long as an Oriental petrification of thinking does not smother the capacity to raise novel questions about the inexhaustible nature of social life." In respect of their admitted contingency, Weber's ideal-typical analyses are, strictly speaking, not outside "historical time," as has been claimed by Mommsen, *The Age of Bureaucracy*, pp. 15, 74, and by J. G. March and Herbert Simon, *Organizations* (New York, 1958), p. 36.

141 *MSS*, p. 78; cf. *MSS*, pp. 82, 157, 159.

142 This point is correctly emphasized by Martin Albrow, *Bureaucracy* (London, 1970), pp. 31, 51.

143 Consider the following statement (*GASW*, p. 277): "According to all available knowledge, the bureaucratization of society will at some point triumph over capitalism, in our civilization just as in ancient civilizations. In our civilization, the 'anarchy of production' will eventually also be replaced by an economic and social system analogous to that typical of the late Roman Empire, and especially of the 'New Kingdom' in Egypt or of the rule of the Ptolemies." For a somewhat different view of Weber's assumptions about historical processes, see Wolfgang J. Mommsen, "Universalgeschichtliches und politisches Denken bei Max Weber," *Historische Zeitschrift*, vol. 201 (1965), pp. 557ff.; and (from the perspective of developmental history) Wolfgang Schluchter, *The Rise of Western Rationalism* (Berkeley, 1981).

144 *FMW*, p. 82; *ES*, pp. 194ff.

145 Cf. *PE*, pp. 77–78, where Weber notes (1) that eighteenth-century philosophical

rationalism was most highly developed in geographic regions (e.g., France) where capitalist accumulation processes were considerably retarded, and (2) that the greatest degree of economic rationalization in England took place under conditions in which the great legal corporations retarded the retrieval and deployment of the rationalized Roman law of late antiquity.

146 P. M. Blau, *The Dynamics of Bureaucracy* (Chicago, 1963), p. 201; Claus Offe, "Rationalitätskriterien und Funktionsprobleme politische-administrativen Handelns," *Leviathan*, vol. 3 (1974), pp. 333–45; Luhmann, *Differentiation of Society*, p. 43.

147 This claim was often made during the nineteenth century (for example, by J. S. Mill, *Considerations on Representative Government* [London, 1912], ch. 6), and was subsequently repeated by Harold J. Laski, "Bureaucracy," in *Encyclopaedia of the Social Sciences* (New York, 1930), p. 71, and Michel Crozier, *The Bureaucratic Phenomenon* (Chicago, 1964), pp. 186ff.

148 *ES*, pp. 140–1, 201. The restricted development of market capitalism because of the turning of public contributions into privately held benefices or fiefs (as in China and the Near East after the time of the caliphs) and the monopolistic diversion of rational capitalism (as in the royal monopolies and monopolistic concessions of early modern times and the more recent corporate pursuit of short-run, speculative profit) are two cases in point.

149 *GPS*, pp. 32–3, 82–3, 140–1, 276; *FMW*, pp. 232–5; *GASW*, p. 473.

150 Norbert Elias, *State Formation and Civilization* (Oxford, 1982), pp. 99–100, 104ff.

151 Claude Lefort, *Eléments d'une critique de la bureaucratie* (Paris, 1979), p. 292; cf. Crozier, *The Bureaucratic Phenomenon*, pp. 192–3.

152 *ES*, p. 1418: "Bureaucracy's supreme power instrument is the transformation of official information into classified material by means of the notorious concept of the 'service secret.' In the last analysis, this is merely a means of protecting the administration against supervision."

153 *FMW*, pp. 224, 226; *GASS*, p. 497; *GPS*, pp. 254, 277, 466.

154 *ES*, pp. 983–7; *GPS*, pp. 256, 279.

155 ES, p. 138; see also *FMW*, pp. 201, 217, 226, 231; and "Socialism," p. 194.

156 *ES*, p. 1111. This aspect of bureaucratic organization has been analyzed subsequently by many organizational theorists, including P. Selznick, "An Approach to a Theory of Bureaucracy," *American Sociological Review*, vol. 8 (1943), pp. 47–54; R. K. Merton et al. (eds.), *Reader in Bureaucracy* (New York, 1952), pp. 361–71; and Marshall E. Dimock, "Bureaucracy Self-Examined," *Public Administration Review*, vol. 4 (1944), pp. 197–207.

157 Georg Lukács, "Max Weber and German Sociology," *Economy and Society*, vol. 1 (1972), p. 395; cf. Lukács's later remarks on Weber in *The Destruction of Reason* (London, 1980), pp. 601–19.

158 *MSS*, p. 27: " 'Peace' is nothing more than a change in the form of conflict or in the antagonists or in the objects of conflict, or finally in the chances of selection."

159 *GASS*, pp. 155-8. In his capacity as chief disciplinary officer of the military field hospitals in the Heidelberg district during the years 1914–15, Weber also noted the resistance of convalescing soldiers to the tedium and routinization of hospital conditions (see his unofficial report in Marianne Weber, *Max Weber: A Biography*, ed. Harry Zohn [New York, 1975], pp. 537–50).

160 *ES*, pp. 202–03.

161 *GPS*, p. 61; *FMW*, p. 370.

162 *FMW*, p. 99; cf. *ES*, p. 952; and *GPS*, pp. 197, 227, and (on Bolshevism) 440.

163 *FMW*, p. 104; cf. *FMW*, p. 79. Conversely, Weber argued that the masses' proclivity

to irrational identification with leaders should be harnessed and ordered – through, for example, forms of "orderly democracy" (*ES*, p. 1451) or the discipline provided by trade unions (*GPS*, p. 293). On the charismatic prophets' harnessing of the devotion of their followers, see Weber's *Ancient Judaism* (New York, 1967).

164 "Socialism," p. 194; *GPS*, pp. 260 and 263: " 'Political character' is cheaper and more acceptable for the wealthy man; no moralizing can change that."
165 *FMW*, p. 99.
166 Cf. ibid., pp. 113, 125; and *ES*, p. 1428. It does not follow from this suggestion, of course, that windbagging, street crowding, mob dictatorship, and "brotherhood ethics" are or ought to be identical with socialist public life.
167 This point is suppressed in Hannah Arendt's one-sided and pessimistic conclusion that bureaucracy "is a form of government in which everybody is deprived of political freedom, of the power to act" (*On Violence* [New York, 1970], p. 81). Concerning the propensity of bureaucratic organizations to strive continually to incorporate and instrumentalize the opposition that it generates, see A. Gehlen, "Bürokratisierung," *Kölner Zeitschrift für Soziologie*, vol. 3 (1950–1), pp. 195–208; Philip Selznick, *TVA and the Grass Roots* (Berkeley, Calif., 1949), p. 9; Robert Michels, *Political Parties* (Glencoe, Ill., 1949), pp. 185–9; and Luhmann, *The Differentiation of Society*, pp. 33–5.
168 *FMW*, p. 153; cf. "Freiburg," p. 437; *GAW*, p. 605; and *MSS*, p. 55.
169 *MSS*, p. 60 (original emphasis); cf. *MSS*, p. 57.
170 *GASS*, p. 412.

3. A totally administered society?

1 For example: Karel Čapek, *R.U.R. (Rossum's Universal Robots)*, in Josef Čapek and Karel Čapek, *"R.U.R." and "The Insect Play"* (London, 1961); Eugene Zamiatin, *We* (New York, 1924); Aldous Huxley, *Brave New World* (London, 1932); Samuel Beckett, *Waiting for Godot* (New York, 1954); W. H. Auden, "The Unknown Citizen," in *The Collected Poetry of W. H. Auden* (New York, 1960); Siegfried Giedion, *Mechanization Takes Command* (London, 1948); Herbert Marcuse, *One Dimensional Man* (London, 1968).
2 "Sociology and Empirical Research," Theodor W. Adorno et al., *The Positivist Dispute in German Sociology* (London, 1976), p. 80.
3 Theodor W. Adorno, "Reflexionen zur Klassentheorie" (1942), in *Gesammelte Schriften*, vol. 8 (Frankfurt am Main, 1972), p. 376.
4 *Prisms* (London, 1967), p. 225. Gillian Rose has correctly stressed Adorno's concern with style as the relation between textual composition and ideas (*The Melancholy Science* [London, 1978], ch. 2); cf. Susan Buck-Morss, *The Origin of Negative Dialectics* (New York, 1977), pp. 96ff., where Adorno's essay style and mode of composition are seen as the antithesis of the commodity structure. This preoccupation with literary form (and Nietzsche's influence) are especially evident in such texts as *Minima Moralia* (London, 1974) and "Der Essay als Form," in *Noten zur Literatur*, vol. 1 (Berlin, 1958), pp. 9–33.
5 Adorno insisted (*Negative Dialectics* [New York, 1973], p. 11) that "no philosophy, not even extreme empiricism, can drag in the *facta bruta* and present them like cases in anatomy or experiments in physics; no philosophy can paste the particulars into the text as seductive paintings would hoodwink it into believing."
6 Ibid., p. 5.
7 *Minima Moralia*, p. 87; in "Der Essay als Form" (pp. 27, 30) Adorno contends that the mode of argumentation of the essay form is critical theory *par excellence*, a form

of presentation that enhances the "joy of freedom with regard to an issue, a freedom which yields more from that issue than would result if it were coldly compelled into a system of ideas."

8 "Musikpädagogische Musik," in Wolfgang Rogge (ed.), *Theodor W. Adorno und Ernst Krenek: Briefwechsel* (Frankfurt am Main, 1974), p. 220.

9 Foreshadowed by such writings as Georg Simmel's *Philosophie des Geldes* (Leipzig, 1900), the particularly seminal work in this post-Weberian project is undoubtedly Georg Lukács's "Reification and the Consciousness of the Proletariat," in Lukács's *History and Class Consciousness* (Cambridge, Mass., 1971), pp. 83–122. In search of a solution to the "riddle of the commodity structure," Lukács attempted to reformulate the Marxian critique of the capitalist mode of production in light of the Weberian theses on the rationalization of the modern world. Lukács accordingly posited the dominance of the reified commodity form as the key structural problem of capitalist society in both its objective and its subjective aspects. Within this framework of interpretation, the classical antinomies of bourgeois philosophy, such as idealism's dualistic separation of the object and the subject, were seen to be expressive of the inner logic of the commodification process, through which products assumed the appearance of separate objects apparently divorced from their equally reified producers. Expressive of this fetishism of commodities, bourgeois philosophy reifies its object as a fixed and immutable given. This philosophy thereby obfuscates the historical processes through which both production and consciousness come into being. Adorno acknowledges the crucial importance of the theory of reification in "Erpresste Versöhnung," in *Noten zur Literatur*, vol. 2 (Frankfurt am Main, 1961), p. 152.

10 This is apparent from the time of his critical analysis of Kierkegaard, first published as *Kierkegaard: Konstruktion des Aesthetischen* (Tübingen, 1933). Buck-Morss's *The Origin of Negative Dialectics* and David Held's *Introduction to Critical Theory* (London, 1980), ch. 7., incisively show that the conventional observation that the post-1938 work of the Frankfurt Institute broke decisively with the Marxist tradition ignores Adorno's continuing adherence to certain key Marxian themes, an adherence mediated by the problematics raised by Walter Benjamin.

11 Karl Marx, *Capital*, vol. 1 (Moscow, 1970), pt. 1.

12 According to Marx, only the actual *qualities* of things have use value (*Theories of Surplus Value*, vol. 3 [Moscow, 1971], p. 129). These properties or qualities in no way contribute to the phantasmic character of commodities: "The mystical character of commodities does not originate . . . in their use-value . . . the existence of the things *qua* commodities, and the value-relation between the products of labour which stamps them as commodities, have absolutely no connexion with their physical properties and with the material relations arising therefrom" (*Capital*, vol. 1, pp. 76–7). This formulation fails to consider those intersubjective, symbolically mediated processes through which objects (and, indeed, human labor power itself) come to be represented as useful in the first place; see Marshall Sahlins, *Culture and Practical Reason* (Chicago, 1976), esp. ch. 3.

13 *Negative Dialectics*, p. 154.

14 "Is Marx Obsolete?" *Diogenes*, vol. 64 (1969), p. 8 and passim.

15 Adorno, "Sociology and Empirical Research," p. 80.

16 Adorno, "Is Marx Obsolete?," p. 5; cf. Theodor W. Adorno, "Anmerkungen zum sozialen Konflikt heute" (1968), in *Gesammelte Schriften*, vol. 8, p. 188.

17 Adorno, *Minima Moralia*, pp. 113–15; cf. Adorno, "Reflexionen zur Klassentheorie," p. 379: "In the market economy the untruth of the class concept remained latent; under monopoly [conditions], it has become as transparent as its truth – the survival

of classes – has become opaque." With this argument, Adorno rejects Lukács's designation of the proletariat as the necessary and universal object of capitalist rationalization, an object whose (potential) self-knowledge (unlike the necessarily abstract, fragmented self-consciousness of particular capitals) is synonymous with its *total* opposition to bourgeois society. It should be pointed out here that Adorno's concept of class is strange and antinomical, and easily lends itself to idealist interpretations. Simply, if it is claimed that objective class relations remain intact, their reduced conflict potential can be explained only through alterations of consciousness. This is highly unsatisfactory because, unless social consciousness is understood as fully constitutive of objective social being (a position Adorno clearly rejects), the withering of class struggle must be grounded in an account of the alteration of the social relations of production which, it is claimed, continue to survive as relations of class domination.

18 Adorno to Walter Benjamin (7 August 1935), in *Über Walter Benjamin* (Frankfurt am Main, 1970), p. 112, quoted in Buck-Morss, *The Origin of Negative Dialectics*, p. 85.

19 *Negative Dialectics*, p. 146; cf. Adorno, *Minima Moralia*, p. 47: "Anything that is not reified, cannot be counted and measured, ceases to exist."

20 T. W. Adorno, "Politics and Economics in the Interview Material," in Adorno et al., *The Authoritarian Personality* (New York, 1950), p. 665.

21 See Adorno, "Cultural Criticism and Society," in *Prisms*, p. 25. Even music, which Adorno sees as potentially the least representational mode of aesthetic expression – music, in all its richly complex mediations, tends not to represent anything outside itself – is uprooted from its former contexts of use value and succumbs to the rationality of the commodification process. The new "functionalized" music is marked by the faddish worship of the old and the new, cults of instruments, stardom, and pseudo individuality; it is characterized by its neglect of problems of composition in favor of an over-concern with evocative techniques of arrangement and, finally, by its promotion of the general withering of its listeners' critical capacities; see Adorno's "On the Fetish-Character in Music and the Regression of Listening," in Andrew Arato and Eike Gebhardt (eds.), *The Essential Frankfurt School Reader* (New York, 1978); and his *Introduction to the Sociology of Music* (New York, 1976), ch. 3. Adorno's thesis of total reification softens later, as in "Culture Industry Reconsidered," *New German Critique*, no. 6 (Fall 1975), pp. 12–19. Here (pp. 14–15) Adorno distinguishes the culture industry (whose operations are structured according to the logic of commodification) from "composition," deliberate attempts (such as those of the first Vienna School of Schoenberg, Berg, and Webern) to subvert established modes of culture consumption and production.

22 Theodor W. Adorno, "Society," *Salmagundi*, no. 10–11 (1969–70), pp. 148–9.

23 Theodor W. Adorno, "On the Logic of the Social Sciences," in Adorno et al., *The Positivist Dispute in German Sociology*, p. 107.

24 Adorno, *Negative Dialectics*, p. 307. Adorno's concern with the "liquidation of the individual" (a theme pursued in Essay 7) underpins his attempted synthesis of psychoanalytic categories with the theory of commodification. In Adorno's hands, depth-psychological analysis seeks to illuminate the processes that lead to the modification of the individuation process, incorporate unconscious mechanisms of the personality system into a class-dominated system of commodification, and lead to the triumph of irrational movements (prototypically, those spawned by Nazism and the culture industry) over the rational interests of their members; cf. his "Sociology and Psychology," *New Left Review*, nos. 46–7 (1967–8), pp. 67–80, 79–90.

25 From the time of his early interest in Benjamin's theory of "natural history [*Naturgeschichte*]" in *The Origin of German Tragic Drama* (London 1977), pp. 120, 177, Adorno

deemed the concept of (second) nature crucially important; cf. his "Die Idee der Naturgeschichte," in *Gesammelte Schriften*, vol. 1 (1973), pp. 345–65.

26 Adorno, "Sociology and Empirical Research," p. 73; Adorno, "Die Idee der Naturgeschichte," p. 346; Adorno, *Negative Dialectics*, pp. 345–8; Adorno, *Prisms*, p. 34.

27 Jürgen Habermas, "Why More Philosophy?" *Social Research*, vol. 38, no. 4 (1971), p. 649; cf. Jürgen Habermas, *Philosophisch-politisch Profile* (Frankfurt am Main, 1971), pp. 176–84; Jürgen Habermas, *Communication and the Evolution of Society* (Boston, 1979), p. 72 (hereafter cited as *CES*); and Offe's analogous comments on Marcuse in "Technik und Eindimensionalität: eine Version der Technokratiethese?" in J. Habermas (ed.), *Antworten auf Herbert Marcuse* (Frankfurt am Main, 1968).

28 Claus Offe, "Advanced Capitalism and the Welfare State," *Politics and Society*, vol. 2, no. 4 (1972), p. 480; Jürgen Habermas, *Legitimation Crisis* (Boston, 1975), p. 1 (hereafter cited as *LC*); cf. Jürgen Habermas, *Theory and Practice* (Boston, 1973), pp. 6–7 (hereafter cited as *TP*).

29 Examples of the latter include Helmut Schelsky, *Der Mensch in der wissenschaftlichen Zivilisation* (Cologne-Opladen, 1961); Zbigniew Brzezinski, *Between Two Ages: America's Role in the Technetronic Era* (New York, 1970); Jacques Ellul, *The Technological Society* (New York, 1964); and Herman Kahn and Anthony J. Wiener, *The Year 2000* (New York, 1967).

30 Habermas here follows some early theses of Klaus Eder, "Komplexität, Evolution und Geschichte," in F. Maciejewski (ed.), *Supplement 1* to *Theorie der Gesellschaft oder Sozialtechnologie* (Frankfurt, 1973), pp. 9ff.

31 See Franz Neumann, "Economics and Politics in the Twentieth Century," in *The Democratic and the Authoritarian State*, ed. Herbert Marcuse (London, 1957), pp. 257–69. In his *The Great Transformation* (Boston, 1957), Karl Polanyi has argued that nineteenth-century European civilization rested on four institutions: the balance-of-power system of international relations, which facilitated a century of relative international order and stability; the noninterventionist liberal state; the international gold standard; and (determining these developments) the triumphant rise of the self-regulating market; see also his comment in George Dalton (ed.), *Primitive, Archaic and Modern Economics: Essays of Karl Polanyi* (Boston, 1971), p. 65: "Man's economy is, as a rule, submerged in his social relations. The change from this to a society which was, on the contrary, submerged in the economic system was an entirely novel development." According to Wolin's *Politics and Vision* (Boston, 1960), the crystallization of the liberal tradition was synonymous with the shrinking of the sphere of politics and the "glorification of society."

32 *LC*, p. 22.

33 Jürgen Habermas, *Toward a Rational Society: Student Protest, Science, and Politics* (London, 1971), p. 97 (hereafter cited as *TRS*); cf. *LC*, p. 21.

34 Donald Winch, *Adam Smith's Politics* (Cambridge, 1978), pp. 1–27.

35 Jürgen Habermas, *Strukturwandel der Öffentlichkeit: Untersuchungen zu einer Kategorie der bürgerlichen Gesellschaft* (Neuwied, 1975), pp. 60–9 (hereafter cited as *SO*).

36 *CES*, pp. 188–91; cf. *TRS*, p. 62; and *LC*, pp. 21, 50–1. Habermas's (Weberian) understanding of state institutions as embodying a form of power *sui generis* is evident in his account (influenced heavily by Klaus Eder) of the origins of state forms as the most important condition for the emergence of class structures in the Marxian sense (see *CES*, pp. 158–64) and in his understanding of the ancient empires, European feudalism, and early modernity as class societies constituted in an *immediately* political form (see ibid., pp. 188–93; and *LC*, pp. 18–20).

37 The connections between the bourgeois revolutions and modern natural law are

traced in *SO*, pp. 74–5, 105; *TP*, esp. pp. 82–109; *TRS*, p. 97; and his critique of Hannah Arendt's *On Revolution* in *Kultur and Kritik* (Frankfurt am Main, 1973), pp. 365–70 (hereafter cited as *KK*). More generally on the modern state, see *CES*, pp. 188–93. Though it is true that Habermas tends to understress the political effects of the various early modern religious struggles in defense of tolerance and freedom of conscience, his persistent concern with modern political discourses throws doubt on Carole Pateman's suggestion (*The Problem of Political Obligation* [Chichester, 1979], pp. 166–7) that he overlooks the specifically political justification of the authority of the liberal state.

38 *LC*, p. 21; cf. *KK*, p. 72.

39 "Political Authority and Class Structures – An Analysis of Late Capitalist Societies," *International Journal of Sociology*, vol. 2, no. 1 (1972), p. 80.

40 *LC*, p. 21.

41 Ibid.

42 *KK*, pp. 70–1; *LC*, pp. 25, 29.

43 On the bureaucratic reorganization of markets for goods, capital, and labor, see *LC*, pp. 33–34, 38, 83; *TRS*, p. 107; *TP*, pp. 196, 202; and *CES*, p. 196; cf. Claus Offe, "Structural Problems of the Capitalist State," *German Political Studies*, vol. 1 (1974), pp. 33–4; and Claus Offe, " 'Crises of Crisis Management': Elements of a Political Crisis Theory," *International Journal of Politics*, vol. 6, no. 3 (1976), pp. 39ff.

44 Offe, "Political Authority," p. 94; cf. *LC*, pp. 38 and 57: "In the monopolistic sector, by means of a coalition between business associations and unions, the price of the commodity known as labor power is quasi-politically negotiated." Rudolf Hilferding (in *Protokoll des SPD – Parteitages in Kiel* [Berlin, 1927]) first developed this argument about "political wages" to indicate the shift, under organized capitalist conditions, from market-determined to administratively conditioned wage structures dependent upon the strength of trade union organization. It should be noted, as a passing qualification to Habermas's and Offe's formulation, that by no means are the returns to labor distributed evenly throughout the organized oligopoly sector: Women, immigrants, and racial minorities tend to be little better off than their counterparts in the competitive sector.

45 Jürgen Habermas, "Die Bühne des Terrors," *Merkur*, vol. 353 (1977), p. 955. In addition to the above-mentioned case of inflation, a further example of the capacity of participants within this oligopoly sector to externalize their conflict might be the recent sharpening of wage and conditions disputes within the state sector. Herein public sector unions attempt to peg their wage rates and working conditions to corresponding rates and conditions within the oligopoly sector; this is mentioned as a possibility in *LC*, p. 38.

46 In defense of Habermas against the claims of Peter Laska on this point (see his "A Note on Habermas and the Labour Theory of Value," *New German Critique*, no. 3 [Fall 1974], pp. 154–62), I have sketched this point in "On Belaboring the Theory of Economic Crisis," *New German Critique*, no. 4 (Winter 1975), pp. 125–30. In certain respects, the maintenance of excess profit or even an adequate rate of profit through the mechanisms of price making and corporate bargaining with the state and organized labor can be seen as analogous to the "profit upon alienation" of the mercantilist era; cf. Ronald L. Meek, *Studies in the Labour Theory of Value* (London, 1973), ch. 7.

47 *LC*, pp. 33–34; cf. Jürgen Habermas, *Student und Politik* (Neuwied, 1969), pp. 22–3 (hereafter cited as *SP*); and Jürgen Habermas, "On Social Identity," *Telos*, no. 19 (Spring 1974), p. 97.

48 Claus Offe, "The Separation of Form and Content in Liberal Democratic Politics,"

Studies in Political Economy, no. 3 (Spring 1980), p. 11; *CES*, p. 196; see also Offe, " 'Crises of Crisis Management,' " p. 48; and Claus Offe, *Berufsbildungsreform – Eine Fallstudie über Reformpolitik* (Frankfurt, 1975).

49 See, for example, Julius Sensat, Jr., *Habermas and Marxism: An Appraisal* (Beverly Hills, Calif., 1979). It might be remarked that Gerhard Meyer's recollection of the uneasy relationship between the inner circle of the early Frankfurt Institute thinkers and its economic analysts, such as Meyer himself, Kurt Mandelbaum, and Richard Löwenthal (see Martin Jay, *The Dialectical Imagination* [Boston, 1973], p. 152), continued to apply at the Starnberg Max Planck Institute, of which Offe was a member and Habermas codirector. This uneasy relationship is evident in the rather divergent analyses (of the new international economic order, urbanization, agricultural policy, unemployment, etc.) presented by another group of Starnberg researchers in Gernot Müller et al., *Ökonomische Krisentendenzen im gegenwärtigen Kapitalismus* (Frankfurt am Main, 1978), and Margaret Fay et al., *Starnberger Studien 4: Strukturveränderungen in der kapitalistischen Weltwirtschaft* (Frankfurt am Main, 1980). However, Offe's more recent work cannot be criticized for its neglect of questions pertaining to the relationship among state policy, trade unions, capital, and labor markets. These themes, which are not closely analyzed in the present essay, are discussed especially in Claus Offe and Karl Hinrichs, "Sozialökonomie des Arbeitsmarktes und die lage 'benachteiligter' Gruppen von Arbeitnehmern," in Claus Offe (ed.), *Opfer des Arbeitsmarktes* (Neuwied, 1977), pp. 3–61; Claus Offe and Helmut Wiesenthal, "Two Logics of Collective Action: Theoretical Notes on Social Class and Organisational Form," *Political Power and Social Theory*, vol. 1 (1980), pp. 67–115; and Ulrike Berger and Claus Offe, "Das Rationalisierungsdilemma der Angestelltenarbeit," in Jürgen Kocka (ed.), *Angestellte im europäischen Vergleich* (Göttingen, 1981), pp. 39–58.

50 See *TRS*, p. 109.

51 *TRS*, p. 109; *TP*, p. 196. This early comment (which also appears in Offe's writings) duplicates the substance (and weaknesses) of Adorno's thesis on the persistence of class divisions under advanced capitalist conditions (see note 17 above).

52 *LC*, p. 38; cf. *LC*, p. 57.

53 "Bemerkungen zur Wirtschaftskrise," *Zeitschrift für Sozialforschung*, vol. 2 (1933), p. 350. Important overviews of this period are provided by Charles S. Maier, *Recasting Bourgeois Europe* (Princeton, N.J., 1975); Gabriel Kolko, *Main Currents in Modern American History* (New York, 1976); and Theda Skocpol, "Political Response to Capitalist Crisis: Neo-Marxist Theories of the State and the Case of the New Deal," *Politics and Society*, vol. 10, no. 2 (1980), pp. 155–202.

54 *TP*, p. 195; cf. *TRS*, p. 101. See also Offe's formulations in *Industry and Inequality* (London, 1976), pp. 14, 16–17; "The Theory of the Capitalist State and the Problem of Policy Formation," in L. Lindberg et al., *Stress and Contradiction in Modern Capitalism* (Lexington, Mass., 1975), p. 125; and "Political Authority," p. 78: "In an era of comprehensive state intervention, one can no longer reasonably speak of 'spheres free of state interference' that constitute the 'material base' of the 'political superstructure'; an all-pervasive state regulation of social and economic processes is certainly a better description of today's order."

55 *SP*, p. 35.

56 *LC*, pp. 34–5, 53–5. This typology closely parallels Offe's early distinction between the late capitalist state's allocative and productive policies. *Allocation* is that form of bureaucratic state activity which seeks to foster the conditions of private capital accumulation through the deployment of resources and powers (e.g., tracts of land; the police, courts, and military) that already belong to the state. The *productive* activities

of the late capitalist state also seek to restore accumulation or eliminate perceived threats to accumulation, but through reliance upon strategies that aim to produce supplies of both variable and constant capital. These strategies therefore have definite market-shearing effects. For more detailed discussion, see Offe, "The Theory of the Capitalist State," pp. 127-34; and Claus Offe, "Further Comments on Müller and Neussüss," *Telos*, no. 25 (Fall 1975), pp. 101, 105.

57 *SP*, p. 23; cf. *LC*, p. 35.

58 Wolfgang Müller and Christel Neussüss, "The Illusion of State Socialism and the Contradiction between Wage Labor and Capital," *Telos*, no. 25 (Fall 1975), pp. 13–90; Bernhard Blanke et al. (eds.), *Kritik der politischen Wissenschaft*, 2 vols. (Frankfurt am Main, 1975).

59 See, in particular, Claus Offe, *Strukturprobleme des Kapitalistischen Staates* [Frankfurt am Main, 1972), pp. 27–63; Offe, " 'Crises of Crisis Management,' " pp. 39, 42–4, 63; Offe, "Advanced Capitalism," pp. 481–2; Claus Offe and Volker Ronge, "Theses on the Theory of the State," *New German Critique*, no. 6 (Fall 1975), p. 145; Claus Offe, "Some Contradictions of the Modern Welfare State," *Praxis International*, vol. 1, no. 3 (1981), pp. 219–29; and Claus Offe, "Introduction to Part II," in Lindberg et al., *Stress and Contradiction*, p. 255. This fundamental argument is missed in Gillian Rose's critique of Habermas's abandonment of the analysis of the commodity form; in her misleading view, the "unique advantage" of a Marxian account of the present is its "derivation of political relations and of the state from an analysis of the productive and social relations of a specific kind of society" (*The Melancholy Science*, p. 141). Rose's criticism also misses another serious objection that can be raised in particular against Offe's theory of decommodification and its crypto-statist implication for socialist political strategy (viz., the desirability of maintaining and extending decommodified state activities). Offe's assumption that the state's decommodifying activities are correlated directly or indirectly with the satisfaction of social needs through concrete, differentiated labor begs a question – left unexplored by either Offe or Habermas – about the veracity of these use values: Are not the form and content of most state-provided utilities distorted by their object (capitalist accumulation) and by their factorylike, bureaucratic mode of production and distribution?

60 *LC*, pp. 35, 53–4. This division corresponds roughly to James O'Connor's discussion (*The Fiscal Crisis of the State* [New York, 1973) of the state's "social consumption" and "social investment" expenditures (in Marxian terms, to social variable capital and social constant capital).

61 See, for example Klaus Doerner, *Madmen and the Bourgeoisie* (Oxford, 1981); Michel Foucault, "Governmentality," *I and C*, vol. 6 (Autumn 1979), pp. 5–21; Jacques Donzelot, *The Policing of Families* (New York, 1979); Michael Ignatieff, *A Just Measure of Pain: The Penitentiary in the Industrial Revolution, 1750-1850* (London, 1978); and (with particular reference to Germany) Franz-Ludwig Knemeyer, "Polizei," in Otto Brunner et al. (eds.), *Geschichtliche Grundbegriffe* (Stuttgart, 1978), bk. IV, pp. 875–97.

62 *LC*, p. 64.

63 Ibid., p. 56; *TRS*, pp. 104–5; "Habermas Talking: An Interview," *Theory and Society*, vol. 1 (1974), p. 50; cf. Offe, "Advanced Capitalism," p. 483; and "Introduction to Part II," p. 253.

64 *LC*, p. 68. Cf. Marx's unexplored hint (*Capital*, vol. 1, p. 570): "Even with a given magnitude of functioning capital, the labour-power, the science, and the land (by which are to be understood, economically, all conditions of labour furnished by Nature independently of humans), embodied in it, form *elastic powers* of capital, allowing it,

within certain limits, a field of action independent of its own magnitude" (emphasis mine).

65 Cf. Habermas's treatment of the theses of Freyer and Schelsky in *TRS*, pp. 58–9.
66 Ibid., p. 59; cf. ibid., pp. 1–12, 76, 105; and *KK*, p. 74.
67 "Habermas Talking," p. 50; cf. *LC*, pp. 56–7.
68 This is what Habermas intended in his earlier (and often misunderstood) claim (*TP*, p. 232) that "value arises from an increase in productivity per se" such that "*within an expanding capitalist system* the surplus value nourished by a twofold source [i.e., direct and reflective labor] can, under certain conditions, be sufficient to assure an appropriate rate of profit *and*, at the same time, a rising level of real wages" (first emphasis mine). Cf. the common enough argument of David Yaffe ("The Marxian Theory of Crisis, Capital and the State," *Economy and Society*, vol. 2 [1973], pp. 139–60), for whom state expenditure is a self-defeating strategy since it is "unproductive" and thereby curtails the quality of surplus value available for private capital accumulation. According to Yaffe, state expenditure certainly "realizes" surplus value; but the products purchased by the state are acquired with already produced surplus value.
69 *LC*, p. 55.
70 Cf. the formulation of this debate in Nicos Poulantzas, *Political Power and Social Classes* (London, 1973), pp. 99–119; and the critique of the French Communist Party "stamocap" thesis in Poulantzas's *Classes in Contemporary Capitalism* (London, 1976), pp. 156–64.
71 The insistence that the contradiction between "capital" and "labor" continues to be fundamentally constitutive of welfare state capitalism is a common feature of certain orthodox Marxist theory. See, for example Ian Gough, "State Expenditure in Advanced Capitalism," *New Left Review*, vol. 92 (1975), p. 66; Ulf Himmelstrand et al., *Beyond Welfare Capitalism* (London, 1981); and Nicos Poulantzas, "The Capitalist State: A Reply to Miliband and Laclau," *New Left Review*, no. 95 (1976), p. 69.
72 Claus Offe, "Die Institutionalisierung des Verbandseinflusses – eine ordnungspolitische Zwickmühle," in Ulrich von Alemann and Rolf G. Heinze (eds.), *Verbände und Staat* (Opladen, 1979), pp. 72–91; Offe's introductory remarks to Rolf G. Heinze, *Verbändepolitik und "Neokorporatismus": Zur politischen Soziologie organisierter Interessen* (Opladen, 1981), pp. 7-9; Wolf-Dieter Narr and Claus Offe, "Was heisst hier Strukturpolitik? Neokorporativismus als Rettung aus der Krise?" *Technologie und Politik*, vol. 6 (1976), pp. 5–26; Claus Offe, "The Attribution of Public Status to Interest Groups: Observations on the West German Case," in Suzanne Berger (ed.), *Organizing Interests in Western Europe* (Cambridge, 1981), pp. 123–58; Claus Offe, "Notes on the Future of European Socialism and the State," *Kapitalistate*, no. 7 (1978), pp. 36–7; and Offe and Wiesenthal, "Two Logics of Collective Action."
73 Cf. *TRS*, p. 109.
74 Ibid., p. 37.
75 This is the category of P. Bachrach and M. Baratz, *Power and Poverty, Theory and Practice* (New York, 1970); cf. Offe's remarks on their work in his introduction to P. Bachrach and M. Baratz, *Macht und Armut: Eine theoretisch-empirische Untersuchung* (Frankfurt am Main, 1977); and also his "Structural Problems," pp. 36ff., where he elaborates three forms of selectivity operating at the structural, ideological, process, and repressive levels. Note that Niklas Luhmann's systems-theoretical argument (which is presented in his *Soziologische Aufklärung* [Köln-Opladen, 1970] and in Jürgen Habermas and Niklas Luhmann, *Theorie der Gesellschaft oder Sozialtechnologie – Was leistet die Systemforschung?* [Frankfurt am Main, 1975], esp. pp. 291-316) that all sociopolitical

organizations involve a selective "reduction of social complexity," i.e., a necessary protection against a chaotic multiplicity of possible events, is seen by Habermas and Offe to be incapable of assessing these organizations' degree of historically specific repressiveness.

76 Jürgen Habermas, "Conservatism and Capitalist Crisis," *New Left Review*, no. 115 (1979), p. 81.

77 *TP*, p. 5; *TRS*, pp. 102–4; *LC*, p. 36. Offe's assumption ("The Theory of the Capitalist State," pp. 140, 143) that "participation and unfiltered conflict tends to interfere with the institutional constraints under which state agencies have to operate, and, as could be demonstrated in the cases of participation-based welfare policies, urban policies, and education policies, lead to a highly unstable situation" needs to be modified with an account of the phenomenon of pseudoparticipation. Within the spheres of state and society, as these essays suggest, pseudoparticipation frequently provides useful information and levels of client motivation for bureaucratic planners. Such pseudoparticipation often increases the scope and feasibility of the bureaucratic planning process: So to speak, the squeaky wheels receive their grease.

78 Offe, "Structural Problems," p. 46. This is also Theodore Lowi's argument in *The End of Liberalism: Ideology, Policy, and the Crisis of Public Authority* (New York, 1969).

79 "The Theory of the Capitalist State," p. 127. This point requires some clarification, for it can be argued that the general *form* of this structural problem predates the period of late capitalism. It first emerged with the disintegration of the kinship basis of tribal societies and the emergence of class-structured societies (e.g., the early civilizations of Mesopotamia, Egypt, ancient China, and India) governed by a state. The reproduction of these states chronically depended upon the conversion of power into political authority via the sacred canopy of traditional customs and rituals. This insight is of course expressed in the Weberian definition of *any* state as "a relation of humans dominating humans, a relation supported by means of legitimate (that is considered to be legitimate) violence."

80 Habermas, "Die Bühne des Terrors," p. 957.

81 *SP*, p. 32.

82 *SO*, pp. 28–41.

83 M. Foucault, *Discipline and Punish: The Birth of the Prison* (London, 1977), ch. 2.

84 *SO*, pp. 25–8.

85 Jürgen Habermas, "The Public Sphere: An Encyclopaedia Article," *New German Critique*, no. 3 (Fall 1974), p. 49; cf. *SO*, pp. 42ff.

86 *TP*, pp. 77–8, 89–90, 100–1.

87 *LC*, p. 78; cf. *SO*, pp. 158–71 and 151–2, where Habermas speaks approvingly of Marx's argument that liberal capitalism is "a class society, in which the chances of social ascent from wage laborer to property owner become ever slimmer. What are obviously lacking are the social preconditions for equality of opportunity, such that everyone with ability and 'good luck' can assume the status of property owner and thereby qualify to become the private individual of public life. This public life, which Marx sees himself confronting, contradicts its own principle of universal accessibility."

88 Habermas, "The Public Sphere," p. 54.

89 Ibid., p. 53; cf. *SO*, esp. pp. 233–94.

90 Habermas's early discussion of this development through the category of commodification draws upon the language of Adorno: "When the laws of the market which govern the sphere of commodity exchange and social labor also penetrate the sphere reserved for private people as public, critical judgment [*Räsonnement*] transforms itself

tendentially into consumption, and the context of public communication breaks down into acts which are uniformly characterized by individualized reception" (*SO*, p. 194).

91 Habermas, "The Public Sphere," p. 55; cf. *TP*, p. 4.

92 C. Wright Mills, "Mass Media and Public Opinion," in Irving Louis Horowitz (ed.), *Power, Politics and People* (London, 1972), pp. 577–98. Habermas's failure to analyze different forms of public life, it might be argued, leaves his thesis open to apologetic rebuttals. For example, explicitly in relation to his critique of the reduction of political life to a ritualized governance of a public that does not yet exist, consider Dahrendorf's charge that "mourning the death of public commitment is, like bemoaning the levelled in middle-class society, an ideology of the loss of structure that overlooks the fact that old institutions are usually transformed rather than abolished. There is sufficient room for public virtues both at the places where men meet ['in the family, the class-room, in road traffic, on the sports ground, at work, in shops, in passing encounters with strangers'] and abstractly in the institutions in which the roles of men are bound. 'Democratization' in the sense of a spread of the rules that govern a functioning public in the older liberal sense becomes more complicated, but no less real, and certainly not less useful" (*Society and Democracy in Germany* [London, 1968], p. 310). Habermas briefly reviews this and other charges in *Philosophisch-politisch Profile*, pp. 234–9.

93 Habermas's more recent attempts to develop a political theory of communicative competence [see Essay 5] can be seen in part as a response to this criticism. Notwith-standing such efforts, the remarks of Ulf Milde "Burgerliche Öffentlichkeit' als Modell der Literaturentwicklung des 18. Jahrhunderts," in Gert Mattenklott and Klaus Scherpe (eds.), *Westberliner Projekt: Grundkurs 18. Jahrhundert* [Kronberg, 1974], p. 51) echo a common reaction to Habermas's theses on the public sphere: "Habermas reveals himself as a late bourgeois ideologue inasmuch as he is forced to falsify his memories of heroic bourgeois illusions in order to take from them what he wants." The criticisms summarized here draw upon W. Jäger's thesis that Habermas's idealized account of the liberal bourgeois public sphere exaggerates its actual empirical scope (see *Öffen-tlichkeit und Parlamentarismus: Eine Kritik an Jürgen Habermas* [Stuttgart, 1973]) and, above all, upon the important discussions of Oskar Negt, "Massenmedien: Herr-schaftsmittel oder Instrumente der Befreiung?" in Dieter Prokop (ed.), *Kritische Kom-munikationsforschung* (Munich, 1973), and Oskar Negt and Alexander Kluge (*Öffentlichkeit und Erfahrung: Zur Organisationsanalyse von burgerlicher und proletarischer Öffentlichkeit* (Frankfurt am Main, 1972).

94 *LC*, p. 79; Offe, *Industry and Inequality*, p. 11. See also Offe's discussion (with Volker Gransow) of *etatisme* in "Politische Kultur und Sozialdemokratische Regierungspoli-tik," *Das Argument*, vol. 23, no. 128 (1981), pp. 551–64; and "Ein biedermeierlicher Weg zum Sozialismus?" *Der Spiegel*, vol. 24 (February 24, 1975), where Offe and Habermas criticize the West German SPD for its habitual reliance upon "silent con-fidence work [*geräuschlose 'vertrauensarbeit'*]" in its policy-making procedures.

95 *SP*, pp. 13–17, 23.

96 See Wolfgang Abendroth, "Planning and the Classless Society," in Erich Fromm (ed.), *Socialist Humanism* (Garden City, N.Y., 1966), p. 363: "Even an author like Jürgen Habermas...seems to postulate first, that the present state of affairs is permanent, stable and unthreatened; and, second, that it has abolished the source of socio-psychological division."

97 *LC*, p. 65. Presumably this rider applies not only to bureaucratic socialist societies such as the Soviet Union but, equally, to Offe's and Habermas's own vision of a postmodern, democratic, and socialist society.

98 Ibid., p. 66; cf. Offe, *Berufsbildungsreform*, pp. 287–302; and Habermas and Offe's critique of the West German SPD's abandonment of reformist strategies in "Ein biedermeierlicher Weg zum Sozialismus?," p. 44. For the above-mentioned critique of Weber, see Claus Offe, "Rationalitätskriterien und Funktionsprobleme politische-administrativen Handelns," *Leviathan*, vol. 3 (1974), pp. 333–45; and Offe, "The Theory of the Capitalist State," pp. 136–42.

99 *CES*, pp. 194–5. Cf. Offe, *Strukturprobleme*, ch. 4, and Offe and Ronge, "Theses on the Theory of the State," pp. 144–5, where Offe points to the reasons why the taxing away of corporate profits is usually unpopular among sectors of capital. In *Berufs-bildungsreform* (esp. chs. 3 and 6) Offe discusses various structural limitations upon different forms of state planning with particular reference to unsuccessful SPD attempts to rationalize the provision of vocational training.

100 *LC*, pp. 41–3.

101 *LC*, pp. 61–2, 38; Offe, " 'Crises of Crisis Management,' " pp. 58–9; Offe, "The Theory of the Capitalist State," p. 139; Offe and Ronge, "Theses on the Theory of the State."

102 Claus Offe and Volker Ronge, "Fiskalische Krise, Bauindustrie und die Grenzen staatlicher Ausgabenrationalisierung," *Leviathan*, vol. 1 (1973), pp. 189–220.

103 *LC*, p. 65.

104 "Introduction to Part II," pp. 252–3; "Further Comments," pp. 107–8; *Industry and Inequality*, p. 19; "Advanced Capitalism," pp. 487–8.

105 *LC*, p. 63.

106 Ibid., pp. 61, 65, 93; cf. Offe's comments on the continuing "unplanned, nature-like" chararacter of late capitalist systems in his introduction (with W.–D. Narr) to *Wohl-fahrtstaat und Massenloyalität* (Köln, 1973).

107 Cf. the overly simplified links between problems of "accumulation" and "legitimization" assumed in the early work of James O'Connor, *The Fiscal Crisis of the State*, p. 6. This automatic theory of crisis is also reproduced in the view of bourgeois ideology as resembling a blanket that covers the sleeping working-class giant during quiet periods (cf. Ernest Mandel, *Late Capitalism* [London, 1975], p. 494).

108 *LC*, p. 76.

109 Habermas, "On Social Identity," p. 102.

110 *LC*, p. 78.

111 Habermas's earliest writings did, however, engage this problem. Several important essays from this period have been collected in Jürgen Habermas, *Arbeit, Freizeit, Konsum: Frühe Aufsätze* (The Hague, 1973). Cf. the more recent analyses of Fred Hirsch, *Social Limits to Growth* (London, 1977); and William Leiss, *The Limits to Satis-faction: An Essay on the Problem of Needs and Commodities* (Toronto, 1976).

112 *KK*, p. 79; cf. *TRS*, pp. 62–80, 111; *TP*, pp. 114–5; and Habermas's early essay "Wissenschaft und Politik," *Offene Welt*, no. 86 (1964), pp. 413–23. Note that his strong claim (derived from Marcuse and others) that late capitalism's leading productive force (scientific-technical progress) becomes a transparent, impenetrable ideology is considerably weakened in *LC*.

113 Cf. the stimulating but overdrawn theses of Alvin Gouldner, *The Future of Intellectuals and the Rise of the New Class* (New York, 1979). On this point Habermas's argument nevertheless remains very ambiguous in relation to a crucial question: Is the increasing influence and power of this scientific-technical intelligentsia to be attributed to its foot-servant role (Chomsky), its accomplished hegemony (Galbraith), or its possible emergence as a new class, as Gouldner suggests?

114 *TRS*, pp. 1–12; see also *TRS*, pp. 21ff.; Habermas's self-description as a "last Mohican"

concerned with preserving the integration of philosophy and social science, in *Kleine Politische Schriften I–IV* (Frankfurt am Main, 1981), p. 487; and his discussion of the meaning of the alleged autonomy of the university and the sciences in "Demokratisierung der Hochschule – Politisierung der Wissenschaft?," in *Theorie und Praxis* (Frankfurt am Main, 1974), pp. 376–85.

115 Jürgen Habermas, "The Place of Philosophy in Marxism," *Insurgent Sociologist*, vol. 5, no. 2 (1975), p. 46; see also Jürgen Habermas, *Knowledge and Human Interests* (London, 1972), passim.

116 *LC*, p. 84.

117 Habermas, "The Place of Philosophy in Marxism," p. 44; cf. the discussion of the topic of "political theology" with Dorothee Sölle and others, "Legitimationsprobleme der Religion," in Hans-Eckehard Bahr (ed.), *Religionsgespräche: Zur gesellschaftlichen Rolle der Religion* (Darmstadt, 1975), pp. 9-30.

118 See Gabriel A. Almond and Sidney Verba, *The Civic Culture* (Princeton, N.J., 1963); and the somewhat earlier research project (to which Habermas contributed) summarized in *SP*.

119 See Habermas, "Conservatism and Capitalist Crisis," p. 76; *SO*, pp. 184–93; and an early essay, "Illusionen auf dem Heiratsmarkt," *Merkur*, vol. 10 (1956), pp. 996–1004.

120 *LC*, p. 73; cf. *SO*, pp. 187ff.; and Jürgen Habermas, "What Does a Crisis Mean Today? Legitimation Problems in Late Capitalism," *Social Research*, vol. 40, no. 4 (1973) p. 658.

121 *Industry and Inequality*, p. 42; cf. Offe and Ronge, "Theses on the Theory of the State," pp. 146–7. Habermas's discussion of this ideology (and the ancillary principles of achievement and exchange value) appears in *LC*, pp. 81–4; see also the earlier analysis of the fate of bourgeois natural law in *TP*, pp. 114–17. Both are indebted to the classic work of C. B. Macpherson, *The Political Theory of Possessive Individualism* (Oxford, 1962).

122 *TRS*, p. 122; *LC*, pp. 81–2; Offe, *Industry and Inequality*, pp. 135–7.

123 *LC*, p. 54; Offe, *Industry and Inequality*, pp. 17–20.

124 Offe, *Industry and Inequality*, pp. 15–7; Offe, *Strukturprobleme*, pp. 27-63; C. Offe, " 'Unregierbarkeit': Zur Renaissance konservativer Krisentheorien," in J. Habermas (ed.), *Stichworte zur "Geistigen Situation der Zeit"* (Frankfurt am Main, 1979), p. 315; see also Offe's critical discussion of Daniel Bell's theory of postindustrialism in "Postindustrielle Gesellschaft – ein politisches Programm?" *Merkur*, vol. 30 (1976), pp. 878–84. That state encroachment upon the sphere of civil society might have unintended politicizing consequences that help subvert the principle of exchange is an early suggestion of Habermas's "The Public Sphere," p. 54, and *TP*, p. 114. Cf. also *TRS*, pp. 31–49, where institutions of formal education are analyzed by Habermas as sites whose use-value possibilities are thwarted by their subjection to the logic of the production of exchange value.

125 *LC*, p. 85.

126 Habermas discusses Benjamin's thesis ("The Work of Art in the Age of Mechanical Reproduction," in *Illuminations* [London, 1973]) in "Consciousness-Raising or Redemptive Criticism - The Contemporaneity of Walter Benjamin," *New German Critique*, no. 17 (Spring 1979), pp. 30–59.

127 Jürgen Habermas et al., *Gespräche mit Herbert Marcuse* (Frankfurt am Main, 1978), pp. 43–4; cf. *LC*, p. 85.

128 *SO*, esp. pp. 46–60; cf. Leo Lowenthal's analysis of Goethe and Schiller in *Literature, Popular Culture and Society* (Palo Alto, Calif., 1968), pp. 18–28; Raymond Williams's

discussion of the post-seventeenth-century growth of a reading public in *The Long Revolution* (Harmondsworth, 1980), pp. 177–236; and the account of the emergence of "the public" as a special region of aesthetic sociability in Richard Sennett, *The Fall of Public Man* (New York, 1978), pt. 2.

129 Jürgen Habermas, *Protestbewegung und Hochschulreform* (Frankfurt am Main, 1969), p. 25; *SO*, pp. 193–210; Habermas, "Consciousness-Raising or Redemptive Criticism," pp. 40–2.

130 *LC*, pp. 43–44, 70–1.

131 Ibid., p. 73.

132 *TRS*, p. 110; cf. Offe, "Attribution of Public Status to Interest Groups."

133 *LC*, p. 69.

134 *CES*, p. 197. Offe, especially in his more recent writings, as in his critique of Edelman and Mayntz in "Introduction to Part II," pp. 257–9, tends to deny the state's capacity to manage the production of symbols.

135 *LC*, pp. 89–90; cf. *TRS*, pp. 117–18.

136 Offe, "The Separation of Form and Content," pp. 12–15; cf. *TRS*, pp. 13–0, 122; and *LC*, pp. 90-2.

137 Franz Neumann, *Behemoth: The Structure and Practice of National Socialism* (Toronto, 1942), pp. 365–69. This problem remains one of the poorly analyzed themes of Habermas's discussion of the contemporary political situation in "Conservatism and Capitalist Crisis." Offe shows greater sensitivity to these dangers of reaction; see, for example, his critique of Wilhelm Hennis's *Organisierter Sozialismus* in "Neukonservative Klimakunde," *Merkur*, no. 323 (1978), pp. 209–25; his discussion of theories of ungovernability, " 'Unregierbarkeit,' " pp. 294–318; and his replies to Wieland Elfferding in " 'Am Staat vorbei' "? Interview mit Claus Offe," *Das Argument*, vol. 22, no. 124 (1980), pp. 809-21.

138 *TRS*, p. 33; Habermas, "Die Bühne des Terrors," p. 956; *CES*, pp. 192-3, 196-7. Whereas national identity, reinforced through a shared language, could be summoned in support of crisis-ridden liberal capitalist states, there are some indications, in Habermas's view, that this resource has been overdrawn. This tendency results both from the cynicism-producing, overstimulating effects of official appeals to national solidarity and from the effects of the transnational planning of communications, commodity production, and leisure time. Thus (ibid., p. 197) nowadays "it is no longer so easy to separate out internal and external enemies according to national characteristics."

139 Cf. the gratuitous accusation of Ralf Dahrendorf ("Effectiveness and Legitimacy: On the 'Governability' of Democracies," *Political Quarterly*, vol. 51, no. 4 [1980], p. 408) that Habermas likes us to think "that we are faced, if not with a proletarian revolution, then with some other great historical earthquake; and as a result he tends to introduce the notion of a 'crisis of legitimacy' first and then seek material to support it."

140 *Strukturprobleme*, p. 24.

141 Offe, "The Separation of Form and Content," p. 8; Offe, "Advanced Capitalism," pp. 486–7; Offe, "Structural Problems," p. 52; cf. Habermas's comments on the rightist campaign against terrorism in the Federal Republic in *Kleine Politische Schriften I–IV*, pp. 328–39, 364–406.

4. Technē and praxis

1 Max Weber, *Economy and Society*, ed. Guenther Roth and Claus Wittich, 2 vols. (Berkeley, Calif., 1978), vol. 1, pp. 86-8, 108.

2 J. Dieckmann, *Max Webers Begriff des "modernen okzidentalen Rationalismus"* (Düsseldorf, 1961); David Beetham, *Max Weber and the Theory of Modern Politics* (London, 1974), pp. 68–9.

3 *Economy and Society*, vol. 1, pp. 24–6.

4 See Alfred Schutz, "The Problem of Rationality in the Social World," in A. Brodersen (ed.), *Collected Papers* (The Hague, 1964), vol. 2, pp. 64–88; Max Scheler, *Formalism in Ethics and Non-Formal Ethics of Value* (Evanston, Ill., 1973), pp. 81–111; and Karl Mannheim, *Man and Society in an Age of Reconstruction* (London, 1940), pp. 49–75.

5 Several of these writings (by Gadamer, Habermas, and Apel) are presented and informally discussed in Theodore F. Geraets (ed.), *Rationality Today* (Ottawa, 1979). Herbert Marcuse (*Negations: Essays in Critical Theory* [Boston, 1968], pp. 225–6) neatly summarizes this dialectical turn against Weber: "It is difficult to see reason at all in the ever more solid 'shell of bondage' which is being constructed. Or is there perhaps already in Max Weber's concept of reason the irony that understands but disavows? Does he by any chance mean to say: And this you call 'reason'?"

6 Jürgen Habermas, *Toward a Rational Society: Student Protest, Science, and Politics* (London, 1971), p. 96 (hereafter cited as *TRS*).

7 *Kleine Politische Schriften I–IV* (Frankfurt am Main, 1981), p. 385; cf. *Kleine Politische Schriften I–IV*, p. 531.

8 This is the clear message of Habermas's "Technology and Science as 'Ideology' " (*TRS*, pp. 81-122), for example, where the Weberian category of rationalization is reconstructed, and Marx and Marcuse are criticized immanently; cf. Jürgen Habermas, "Praktische Folgen des wissenschaftlich-technischen Fortschritts," in *Theorie und Praxis* (Frankfurt am Main, 1974), pp. 336–58; Jürgen Habermas, "Aspects of the Rationality of Action," in Geraets, *Rationality Today*, p. 192; and Habermas, *Kleine Politische Schriften I–IV*, p. 33.

9 Cf. Wolf Lepenies, "Anthropology and Social Criticism: A View on the Controversy between Arnold Gehlen and Jürgen Habermas," *Human Context*, vol. 3, no. 2 (1971), p. 218.

10 Aristotle, *Ethica Nichomachea*, 1140a 2ff.; Aristotle, *Politica*, 1254a 4–5. I am here relying upon *The Basic Works of Aristotle*, ed. Richard McKeon (New York, 1968).

11 *Ethica Nichomachea*, 1095b 17ff.

12 *Politica*, 1278a 1ff.

13 Ibid., 1333a 29–32. Thus Nicholas Lobkowicz (*Theory and Practice: History of a Concept from Aristotle to Marx* [London, 1967], p. 10) renders Aristotle's fundamental distinction between the useful and the honorable as a division between making and doing: " 'Making' has not achieved its end until it has reached the point at which it may stop, while 'doing' only fulfills its end while it is being done."

14 On *theoria* as a more complete form of praxis, see Lobkowicz, *Theory and Practice*, esp. p. 24: "The argument of the philosophers consisted in saying that all positive aspects of politics – that it was an activity relatively free from fatigue, an activity entailing independence and leisure, and thus a free activity – were found in contemplation as well, and that they were found in contemplation in a significantly superior way."

15 Hannah Arendt, *The Human Condition* (Chicago, 1974), p. 24: "According to Greek thought, the human capacity for political organisation is not only different from but also stands in direct opposition to that natural association whose centre is the home (*oikia*) and the family... It was not just an opinion or theory of Aristotle but a simple historical fact that the foundation of the polis was preceded by the destruction of all organized units resting on kinship, such as the *phratria* and the *phylē*."

16 Aristotle distinguishes art from other forms of knowledge in *Metaphysica*, 1025b 18ff. and 1046b 3.
17 Aristotle, *Physica*, 199a, 17–18.
18 *Politica*, 1255a, 5ff.
19 Ibid., 1254b 15ff. and 1255b 1–6.
20 Ibid., 1253b 30–40. On Aristotle's presumptions about women as "naturally" fit for reproducing, "keeping and storing," see Susan Moller Okin, *Women in Western Political Thought* (London, 1980), ch. 4; and Jean Bethke Elshtain, *Public Man, Private Woman* (Princeton, N.J., 1981), ch. 1.
21 *Politica*, 1253b 24-5. Therefore ownership of property (such as slaves) is to be regarded as merely a means to higher purposes; slaves are deemed necessary not as a means of production but as a means of political life. Households are to be concerned with the use of property and not its acquisition. Production for the sake of exchange is judged by Aristotle to be strictly illegitimate. Cf., for example, *Ethica Nichomachea*, 1096a 507: "The life of money-making is one undertaken under compulsion, and wealth is evidently not the good we are seeking; for it is merely useful and for the sake of something else."
22 *Politica*, 1333a 36–37; cf. *Ethica Nichomachea*, 1177b 4ff.
23 *Politica*, 1325a 26-7.
24 Cf. *Ethica Nichomachea*, 1140a 25–32: "The mark of a man of practical wisdom [is] to be able to deliberate well about what is good and expedient for himself, not in some particular respect, e.g. about what sorts of things conduce to health or to strength, but about what sorts of things conduce to the good life in general. This is shown by the fact that we credit men with practical wisdom in some particular respect when they have calculated well with a view to some good end which is one of those that are not the object of any art. It follows that in the general sense also the man who is capable of deliberating has practical wisdom."
25 Ibid., 1139a 22–3; cf. ibid., 1113a 9–13.
26 Ibid., 1140a 1ff. The following discussion draws from Hans-Georg Gadamer, *Truth and Method* (New York, 1975), pp. 278–89. It should also be noted that this discussion of the concept of productive knowledge (which is seen by Aristotle to be appropriate to types of activities including rhetoric, poetics, and, on occasion, physics) restricts itself to the single example of craftsmanship and material production.
27 *Ethica Nichomachea*, 1103b 27–9 (emphasis mine).
28 Ibid., 1142b 22ff.
29 Ibid., 1144a 25ff.
30 Ibid., 1143a 8–9; cf. ibid., 1105a 17ff.
31 Ibid., 1139b 1–5; cf. ibid., 1140b 6–7: "For while making has an end other than itself, action cannot; for good action itself is its end."
32 Ibid., 1143a 25ff.
33 Ibid., 1144b 1ff.
34 *Theory and Practice* (Boston, 1973), p. 286, note 4 (hereafter cited as *TP*).
35 Habermas here relies upon the arguments of W. Hennis, *Politik und praktische Philosophie* (Neuwied, 1963).
36 Jürgen Habermas, *Zur Logik der Sozialwissenschaften: Materialen* (Frankfurt am Main, 1970), p. 276, note 211.
37 *TRS*, p. 105; cf. *TP*, p. 255: "We are no longer able to distinguish between practical and technical power"; and Thomas McCarthy, *The Critical Theory of Jürgen Habermas* (Cambridge, Mass., 1978), ch. 1.
38 Jean Jacques Rousseau, *The Social Contract and Discourses* (New York, 1967), p. 132.

39 Eric Voegelin, *The New Science of Politics* (Chicago, 1952), pp. 170–1; Leo Strauss, *The City and Man* (Chicago, 1964), p. 10; Leo Strauss, "Political Philosophy and the Crisis of Our Time," in George J. Graham, Jr. and George W. Casey (eds.), *The Post-Behavioral Era* (New York, 1972), p. 242; Leo Strauss, *What Is Political Philosophy?* (Glencoe, Ill., 1959), pp. 68–69.

40 *TP*, p. 169; *TRS*, p. 119.

41 "The Classical Doctrine of Politics in Relation to Social Philosophy," in *TP*, pp. 41–81.

42 Ibid., p. 59: cf. Machiavelli's *The Prince*, in *"The Prince" and "The Discourses,"* ed. Max Lerner (New York, 1950), pp. 56–7.

43 *TP* pp. 50–1.

44 Ibid., pp. 52, 54. These passages are surprisingly close to Leo Strauss's *Thoughts on Machiavelli* (Glencoe, Ill., 1958), where Machiavelli is interpreted as a teacher of evil, an exponent of the principle that the foundations of political greatness are necessarily laid in crime. For a more balanced, if uncritical, interpretation of Machiavelli's attempt to transcend the humanist tradition of classical republicanism, see Quentin Skinner, *Machiavelli* (Oxford, 1981).

45 Max Horkheimer, *Der Anfänge der bürgerlichen Geschichtsphilosophie* (Stuttgart, 1930).

46 Cf. Machiavelli, *The Prince*, p. 32: "It cannot be called virtue to kill one's fellow-citizens, betray one's friends, be without faith, without pity, and without religion; by these methods one may indeed gain power, but not glory." On the necessity of concealing power with apparent virtue, see *The Prince*, p. 65.

47 *Leviathan*, ed. C. B. Macpherson (Harmondsworth, 1972), p. 73.

48 *TP*, p. 62.

49 Ibid., p. 61; cf. ibid, p. 124. In support of this interpretation, consider Hobbes's comments in *De Corpore*, in *English Works*, ed. Sir William Molesworth (London, 1838), vol. 1, pt. 1, ch. 1, sec. 9–10 and in "The Introduction," *Leviathan*, pp. 81–3.

50 *TP*, p. 60.

51 Ibid., p. 61; cf. Arendt, *The Human Condition*, p. 299; and C. B. Macpherson's comments on Hobbes's presumption of obligation from fact in *The Political Theory of Possessive Individualism* (Oxford, 1962), pp. 78–87.

52 *TP*, p. 64.

53 Ibid., p. 57.

54 *Leviathan*, p. 264.

55 *TP*, p. 43; cf. the earlier, almost identical, interpretation of Hobbes in Sheldon Wolin, *Politics and Vision* (Boston, 1960), ch. 8.

56 *TP*, pp. 67ff.

57 Ibid., p. 67. Habermas here suspends his earlier consideration of bourgeois family life as a crucial aspect of civil society, as presented in *Strukturwandel der Öffentlichkeit: Untersuchungen zu einer Kategorie der bürgerlichen Gesellschaft* (Neuwied, 1975), pp. 54–61.

58 *TP*, pp. 76–7, 94–5, 108.

59 Habermas's brief comments on Rousseau are scattered throughout *TP*, esp. pp. 96–101, 104–6.

60 G. B. Vico, *On the Study Methods of Our Time* (Indianapolis, 1965), p. 35; see Habermas's discussion of Vico in *TP*, pp. 45–6, 73–4, 242–5.

61 This doctrine is analyzed briefly in *TP*, pp. 42, 126.

62 Ibid., pp. 142–69. Habermas's thesis that the conventional understanding of Hegel's Jena lectures (of 1803–4 and 1805–6) as mere preparations for the later *Phenomenology* underestimates their discontinuity is in part supported by the interpretations of Georg

Lukács, *The Young Hegel* (London, 1976), and Herbert Marcuse, *Reason and Revolution* (Boston, 1960), pt. 1, ch. 3.

63 This reversal, in Habermas's view, is already implicit within the formulations of the young Hegel. For both the Jena lectures and the later *Enzyklopädie* presuppose the absolute identity of Spirit with nature: Spirit finds its identity only in comprehending its own differentiation from nature, which is its Other. According to Hegel, nature is thereby revealed as the opponent or latent partner (*Gegenspieler*) of Spirit, with the crucial consequence that the process of formation of naming and cunning consciousness can now be interpreted as identical with that of reciprocal recognition. This conclusion, which fails to understand nature as a mere object (*Gegenstand*), is anathema to Habermas's reconstructed Aristotelianism—but this is to anticipate the following elaboration of the work–communication dualism.

64 G. W. F. Hegel, *Encyclopaedia of the Philosophical Sciences*, in *Hegel's Philosophy of Mind*, trans. W. Wallace (Oxford, 1894), paras. 381, 384.

65 G. W. F. Hegel, *The Phenomenology of Mind*, trans. J. B. Baillie (New York, 1967), pp. 228–40.

66 Cf. Karl Löwith, *From Hegel to Nietzsche* (Garden City, N.Y., 1967).

67 *TP*, pp. 168–9.

68 The critique of Marx has provoked more controversy than perhaps any other single theme in Habermas's work. For a sample, see Johann Arnason, "Zur Rekonstruktion des historischen Materialismus," *Telos*, no. 39 (Spring 1979), pp. 201–19; Richard J. Bernstein, *The Restructuring of Social and Political Theory* (New York, 1976), pp. 188–9; Renate Damus, "Habermas und der 'heimliche Positivismus' bei Marx," *Sozialistische Politik*, vol. 1, no. 4 (1969), pp. 22–46; Anthony Giddens, "Labour and Interaction," in John B. Thompson and David Held (eds.), *Habermas: Critical Debates* (London, 1982), pp. 149–61; Eric Hahn, "Die theoretischen Grundlagen der Soziologie von Jürgen Habermas," in Hahn, *Die "Frankfurter Schule" im Lichte des Marxismus* (Frankfurt, 1970), pp. 70ff.; H. J. Krahl, *Konstitution und Klassenkampf* (Berlin, 1971); György Markus, "Practical-Social Rationality in Marx: A Dialectical Critique," *Dialectical Anthropology*, vol. 4, no. 4 (1979), pp. 255–88, vol. 5, no. 1 (1980), pp. 1–32; John O'Neill, "On Theory and Criticism in Marx," in Paul Walton and Stuart Hall (eds.), *Situating Marx* (London, 1972), pp. 72–97; Trent Schroyer, "Marx and Habermas," *Continuum*, vol. 8, no. 1 (1970), pp. 52–64; Julius Sensat, Jr., *Habermas and Marxism: An Appraisal* (Beverly Hills, Calif., 1979); Göran Therborn, "Jürgen Habermas: A New Eclecticism," *New Left Review*, no. 67 (1971), pp. 69–83; Paul Thomas, "The Language of Real Life: Jürgen Habermas and the Distortion of Karl Marx," *Discourse*, vol. 1 (1979), pp. 59–84; and Albrecht Wellmer, *Critical Theory of Society* (New York, 1971), ch. 2.

69 *Kultur und Kritik* (Frankfurt am Main, 1973), pp. 70–86.

70 Cf. *TRS*, p. 97; Jürgen Habermas, *Knowledge and Human Interests* (London, 1972), pp. 59–60 (hereafter cited as *KHI*); and ibid., p. 52: "The distinctive feature of capitalism (in its classical phase) is that the class relation is *economically* defined through the free labour contract as a form of civil law."

71 "Economic and Philosophic Manuscripts (1844)," in *Writings of the Young Marx on Philosophy and Society*, ed. L. D. Easton and K. H. Guddat (New York, 1967); cf. Habermas's discussion of the Marxian critique of Hegel's *Phenomenology* in *KHI*, chs. 2–3, and *TP*, pp. 168–9.

72 *KHI*, p. 36.

73 Karl Marx, *Grundrisse* (Harmondsworth, 1973), pp. 690–711.

74 In this third volume of *Capital* (Moscow, 1970), pp. 820ff., Marx apparently follows Aristotle in contrasting the realms of freedom and necessity. Yet it is quite evident

that, in contrast to both Aristotle and Habermas, Marx speaks of the realm of necessity as properly that in which associated producers overcome their blind dependence upon nature, bringing it under their common control through a minimum of expended energy and under conditions favorable to, and worthy of, their free creative capacities. Cf. also Marx's immanent criticism (*Grundrisse*, pp. 610–16) of attempts to represent labor as sacrifice (Smith) and jolly amusement (Fourier), attempts that in his view equally deny the possibility of concrete labor as "self-realization, objectification of the subject, hence real freedom."

75 *KHI*, p. 48.
76 Ibid., p. 58.
77 Ibid., p. 326, note 9. Cf. also Habermas's response to the young Hegel's discussion of the impact of modern bureaucratization on cunning consciousness and labor. According to Hegel (*Jenenser Realphilosophie 1*, in *Sämtliche Werke*, vol. 19 [Leipzig, 1923], p. 237), humanity's growing capacity to deceive and outwit nature through the use of machinery coincides with nature's revenge on humanity: By setting a variety of machines to work upon and subjugate a nature no longer conceived of as living nature, the remaining labors of humanity are themselves subjugated or "lowered." The former living character of labor takes flight, becoming like the machines it supposedly directs with will and consciousness. Against this critique, which anticipates later Marxian themes remarkably, Habermas speaks of the possible obsolescence of alienated labor through the self-progression of rationalized production itself. The dialectic of cunning mechanization and alienation would, as it were, outwit and abolish the realm of necessity. In Habermas's words (*KHI*, p. 298, note 27), "technical progress has gone far beyond that primitive stage represented by the mechanical loom [of Hegel's time]; the stage which confronts us is characterized by the self-regulating control over systems of purposive-rational action; [consequently]...it is an open question whether the cunning consciousness of machines...will not one day be itself outwitted [presumably, through fully rationalized systems of cybernetic control, etc.]...the worker would then no longer...have to pay the price, which up to now has been paid in the currency of alienated labour, for the growing power of technical control, for then labour itself would become obsolete."
78 *KHI*, p. 51; cf. Marx, *Grundrisse*, pp. 692–5 and 802: "Machinery inserts itself to replace labour only where there is an overflow of labour powers. Only in the imaginations of economists does it leap to the aid of the individual worker."
79 In Karl Marx and Frederick Engels, *Selected Works*, vol. 1 (Moscow, 1969), p. 400.
80 *TRS*, p. 119; cf. *TP*, p. 169.
81 *KHI*, p. 28. This is close to Alfred Schmidt's earlier discussion of Marx's transformation of the formal Kantian epistemology (*The Concept of Nature in Marx* [London, 1973], pp. 107–113, esp. p. 111). On the Marxian account of the genealogy of conceptual thought, cf. the following: "Morality, religion, metaphysics, all the rest of ideology and their corresponding forms of consciousness...have no history, no development. Rather, humans who develop their material production and their material relationships alter their thinking and the products of their thinking along with their real existence. Consciousness does not determine life but life determines consciousness" ("The German Ideology," in *Writings of the Young Marx*, p. 415). In the first volume of *Capital* (p. 352, note 2), Marx speaks of his own project as analogous to that of Darwin. However, the nonidentity of human and natural history is seen as flowing from the fact that "the history of the productive organs of humanity, of organs that are the material basis of all social organisation" is itself humanly created. Thus "technology discloses humans' mode of dealing with Nature, the process of

production by which they sustain their life, and thereby also lays bare the mode of formation of their social relations, and of the mental conceptions that flow from them." And (from the "Randglossen zu Adolph Wagners Lehrbuch der politischen Ökonomie" [1879/80], quoted in Schmidt, *The Concept of Nature in Marx*, pp. 110–11) perhaps the single most explicit sketch of the origins and development of conceptual thought, here quoted nearly in full: "For the doctrinaire professor, the human's relation to nature is from the beginning not practical, i.e. based on action, but theoretical...Humanity stands in a relation with the objects of the external world as the means to satisfy its needs. But humanity does not begin by standing 'in this theoretical relation with the objects of the external world'. Like all animals they begin by eating, drinking, etc., i.e. they do not stand in any relation, but are engaged in activity, appropriate certain objects of the external world by means of their actions, and in this way satisfy their needs (i.e. they begin with production). As a result of the repetition of this process it is imprinted in their minds that objects are capable of 'satisfying' the 'needs' of humans. Humanity and animals also learn to distinguish 'theoretically' the external objects which serve to satisfy their needs from all other objects. At a certain level of later development, with the growth and multiplication of human needs and the types of action required to satisfy these needs, they gave names to whole classes of these objects, already distinguished from other objects on the basis of experience. That was a necessary process, since in the process of production, i.e. the process of the appropriation of objects, humans are in a continuous working relationship with each other and with individual objects, and also immediately become involved in conflict with other humans over these objects. Yet this denomination is only the conceptual expression of something which repeated action has converted into experience, namely the fact that for humans who already live in certain social bonds (this assumption follows necessarily from the existence of language), certain external objects serve to satisfy their needs."

82 "The German Ideology," p. 439; cf. Karl Marx and Frederick Engels, "Manifesto of the Communist Party," in *Selected Works*, vol.1, p. 125: "The dissolution of...old ideas keeps even pace with the dissolution of the old conditions of existence."

83 Marx defends this thesis in "The German Ideology," p. 431.

84 *KHI*, p. 42; cf. *KHI*, pp. 31, 52–5, 62, 242, 326–9, note 14; *TRS*, p. 58; and *TP*, pp. 168–9. Cf. also Wellmer's comment (*Critical Theory of Society*, p. 92): "Marx has to deduce the various forms of domination directly from the various forms of productive labor because the sole logic of history which can still be permitted in a materialistic reference-system which reduces the dialectics of morality to that of production is the logic of the progressive technological self-objectification of humanity. According to this logic, the forms of social intercourse can be apprehended, so to speak, only as secondary productive forces, whose function is to make possible the application and development of the primary forces."

85 *KHI*, esp. ch. 3.

86 This accusation is tempered somewhat by Habermas's more recent acknowledgment (*Communication and the Evolution of Society* [Boston, 1979], pp. 96–7) that the Marxian promise to "find the new world through criticism of the old" could still draw upon the available traditions of moral-practical reason (classical political economy and modern natural law, German Idealism, utopian socialism) that were in potential or actual opposition to bourgeois rationalization processes. Marx's failure to clarify the normative foundations of the materialist conception of history within the highly politicized context of liberal capitalism might therefore be excused. Yet under late capitalist conditions, where bourgeois ideals have, as it were, retired hurt, and consciousness

tends to become cynical, the legacy of Marx's failure becomes particularly acute. Under the new conditions, according to Habermas, Marxism has no option but to attempt a reconstruction of the basic presumptions – and political norms – immanent within all acts of communication.

87 *TRS*, p. 58.

88 Karl Marx, "Preface to a Contribution to the Critique of Political Economy," in *Selected Works*, vol. 1, p. 504.

89 Cf. Habermas's discussion of Comte in *KHI*, pp. 71–80. As a supplement to Habermas's claim, see also Z. A. Jordan's *The Evolution of Dialectical Materialism* (London, 1967) for some estimation of Marx's indebtedness to the nineteenth-century positivist tradition. Jordan's discussion can usefully be compared with Leszek Kolakowski, *Positivist Philosophy: From Hume to the Vienna Circle* (Harmondsworth, 1972), ch. 3, and with Marcuse, *Reason and Revolution*, pp. 340–60.

90 *KHI*, p. 44; cf. *KHI*, p. 63: "Marx did not develop [the]...idea of the science of humanity. By equating critique with natural science, he disavowed it." See also Wellmer (*Critical Theory of Society*, ch. 2), whose claims about the "latent positivism" of Marx are close to Habermas.

91 In *Writings of the Young Marx*, p. 212.

92 *KHI*, p. 5. That Marx in part succumbed to the categories of Comtean positivism is also seen by Habermas as due to his indebtedness to Hegel. This is the difficult and controversial claim of part 1 of *KHI*. Insofar as the disavowal of epistemological inquiry is synonymous with positivism, the mature Hegel (indirectly and unintentionally, to be sure) is seen as reinforcing the growing aura and influence of the nineteenth-century positivist movement. Habermas is by no means in disagreement with Hegel's brilliant criticisms of Kant. Yet this critique, in Habermas's view, represses the point that the knowing subject must ascertain the conditions under which valid knowledge can in principle be formed against the power of natural, habitual consciousness, that is, that the subject *qua* subject must engage in epistemological inquiry. Thus Hegel could assert the phenomenological self-reflection of mind on the basis of the *assumption* of absolute knowledge. True, Hegel unmasks the unacknowledged presuppositions of the Kantian philosophy by insisting that all epistemology is caught within an epistemological vicious circle: Epistemology is encumbered with the need to examine the cognitive faculty critically *before* knowing itself is possible. In Habermas's view, Hegel's argument at first appears to be an immanent critique of Kant. In actuality, it is an abstract negation, because Hegel denies the validity of epistemological inquiry as such. But this is a self-contradictory tack: Hegel's presumption that the phenomenological self-reflection of mind can ascertain knowledge of the Absolute is equally vulnerable to the question formerly directed against Kant: How can we know that the standpoint of absolute knowledge upon which Hegel's phenomenology is developed is valid? Both Marx and Hegel remain silent on this question. Habermas is therefore not surprised that "Marx never explicitly posed for himself the *epistemological* question concerning the conditions of the possibility of a philosophy of history with political intent" (*TP*, p. 242, emphasis mine).

93 Cf. the well-known interview with Louis Althusser in his *Lenin and Philosophy and Other Essays* (London, 1971), p. 18, where Marx is described as the Galileo and Thales of historical science.

94 *TP*, pp. 263–4.

95 Ibid., p. 281.

96 Max Horkheimer, "Zum Problem der Wahrheit," in *Kritische Theorie*, ed. Alfred Schmidt (Frankfurt am Main, 1968), vol. 1, pp. 259–60.

97 *KHI*, p. 53; cf. *TP*, pp. 168–9.

98 This is an old-fashioned German expression – of aristocratic genealogy – which connotes not idleness, or otiosity, but peaceful tranquility, unharried leisure, ease, or rest. The meaning of *müsigkeit* as productive idleness or leisure persists in the vernacular or colloquial sense in which one speaks, for example, of "taking one's time over one's work [*in aller Musse Arbeiten*]" or says, "For this kind of hobby you need to have plenty of time and be in a leisurely frame of mind [*Für dieses Hobby muss man Zeit und Musse haben*]."

99 Jürgen Habermas, "Soziologische Notizen zum Verhältnis von Arbeit und Freizeit," in G. Funke (ed.), *Konkrete Vernunft: Festschrift für E. Rothacker* (Bonn, 1958), pp. 230ff.; Jürgen Habermas, "Die Dialektik der Rationalisierung: Vom Pauperismus im Produktion und Konsum," *Merkur*, vol. 8 (1954), pp. 713ff.

100 Habermas, "Die Dialektik der Rationalisierung," p. 717.

101 Ibid., p. 720; see also Jürgen Habermas, "Notizen zum Missverhältnis von Kultur und Konsum," *Merkur*, vol. 10 (1956), pp. 212–28.

102 "Soziologische Notizen zum Verhältnis von Arbeit und Freizeit," pp. 228, 231.

103 See Jürgen Habermas, "Dogmatism, Reason and Decision" (1963), in *TP;* and Jürgen Habermas, "Rationalism Divided in Two" (1964), in Anthony Giddens (ed.), *Positivism and Sociology* (London, 1974), pp. 195–223.

104 *TP*, p. 280.

105 The debt owed to Kant is clear, for Habermas seemed to be retrieving (albeit in materialist form) Kant's argument (e.g., in the final section of *Foundations of the Metaphysics of Morals*) that practical reason has an interest in discovering moral laws and that this interest, in turn, implies the *will* to be morally reasonable. For Kant, an "interest" is that by which reason becomes practical; that is, it is a cause determining the will. The notion of a special and inherent interest in moral-practical reason reappears in Schelling's theses on reason as controlled insanity, and Fichte's dictum that the sort of philosophy one chooses depends on what sort of person one is. Habermas discusses Fichte's and Schelling's appropriation of the Kantian arguments concerning interests in *TP*, pp. 259–62, and *KHI*, pp. 37–40 and esp. ch. 9.

106 Max Weber, "The Social Psychology of the World Religions," in *From Max Weber: Essays in Sociology*, ed. H. H. Gerth and C. Wright Mills (London, 1970), p. 289.

107 This was first published as "Erkenntnis und Interesse" in *Merkur*, vol. 19 (1965), pp. 1139–53, and translated into English by Guttorm Floïstad in *Inquiry*, vol. 9 (1966), pp. 285–300. I am relying on the improved translation that appeared as the appendix to *KHI* (pp. 301–17) under the title "Knowledge and Human Interests: A General Perspective."

108 *TP*, pp. 7–8.

109 *KHI*, p. 313.

110 Reference to Habermas's early mention of a *third* interest, that of power, has been deliberately omitted here. This omission has its rationale, for Habermas elsewhere (e.g., in *KHI*, p. 196, and *TP*, pp. 21ff.) speaks of work and communication as "basic" interests. Furthermore, as I shall show shortly, whereas in the 1965 inaugural lecture the "interest in emancipation" is understood to have a separate and independent logic, Habermas later argues that the possibility of political emancipation is rooted *within* communicative action itself.

111 *Ethica Nichomachea*, 1144a 25ff.

112 Cf. Jane Lawick-Goodall, *In the Shadow of Man* (Boston, 1971).

113 This point is later developed in *Communication and the Evolution of Society*, p. 135.

114 *TRS*, p. 91; cf. the earlier discussion in "Soziologische Notizen zum Verhältnis von Arbeit und Freizeit."

115 *Economy and Society*, vol. 1, p. 24.

116 *TRS*, p. 92.

117 David Held, *Introduction to Critical Theory* (London, 1980), ch. 11; McCarthy, *The Critical Theory of Jürgen Habermas*, pp. 16–40.

118 Cf. *TP*, p. 61: "From the days of Galileo on, the intention of research itself is objectively to attain the skill of *'making'* the processes of nature oneself in the same way as they are produced by nature. Theory is measured by its capacity for artificially reproducing natural processes... Thereby theory gains a new criterion of its truth (aside from that of logical consistency) – the certainty of the technician: we *know* an object in so far as we can *make* it." Cf. also Jürgen Habermas, "Discussion on Value-freedom and Objectivity," in Otto Stammer (ed.), *Max Weber and Sociology Today* (Oxford, 1971), p. 62.

119 *TP*, pp. 263–4; cf. *TP*, p. 269: "From the outset rationalization is confined within the limits posed by the system of social labor."

120 *TRS*, p. 92; cf. the later formulation of this in *Communication and the Evolution of Society*, p. 132: "The instrumental actions of different individuals are coordinated in a purposive-rational way, that is, with a view to the goal of production. The *rules of strategic action*, in accord with which cooperation comes about, are a necessary component of the labor process."

121 *TP*, p. 158: "Instrumental action... as social labor, is also embedded within a network of interactions, and therefore dependent on the communicative boundary conditions that underlie every possible cooperation."

122 *TRS*, p. 92.

123 Ibid.; cf. Habermas, "Rationalism Divided in Two, " p. 220.

124 The conventional translation of *Mündigkeit* as "adult autonomy" (effected by John Viertel throughout *Theory and Practice*, for example) actually truncates the much richer and more classical (Aristotelian) meaning Habermas wishes to convey. Translated more loosely (*mündlich* signifies that which is oral or verbal, and *Mund* means "mouth"), *Mündigkeit* connotes "the coming of age" through the process of "speaking and acting for oneself " within political processes of *lexis* and *praxis*.

125 Cf. Jürgen Habermas, "Toward a Theory of Communicative Competence," in Hans Peter Dreitzel (ed.), *Recent Sociology*, no. 2 (London, 1970), p. 115.

126 *KHI*, p. 314; cf. *TP*, p. 17; and an earlier hint of this thesis in ibid., p. 281: "The interest in the progress of reflection toward adult autonomy (*Mündigkeit*)... is indestructibly at work in every rational discussion."

127 Habermas, *Zur Logik der Sozialwissenschaften*, p. 161; cf. *TP*, p. 8.

128 Habermas, "Toward a Theory of Communicative Competence," p. 120.

129 Mannheim, *Man and Society*, esp. pp. 49–75. It might be argued that this distinction between two forms of rationality draws upon the recurrent German separation of *Zivilisation* (civilization) and *Kultur* (culture); cf. the comments of Herbert Marcuse, "Remarks on a Redefinition of Culture," in Gerald Holton (ed.), *Science and Culture* (Cambridge, 1965).

130 *TRS*, p. 118; cf. Albrecht Wellmer's comments in "Communication and Emancipation: Reflections on the Linguistic Turn in Critical Theory," in John O'Neill (ed.), *On Critical Theory* (New York, 1976), pp. 231–63.

131 "A Postscript to *Knowledge and Human Interests*," *Philosophy of the Social Sciences*, vol. 3 (1973), p. 157–89. This self-criticism is further analyzed and evaluated in Christian Lenhardt, "Rise and Fall of Transcendental Anthropology," *Philosophy of the Social*

Sciences, vol. 2 (1972), pp. 231–46; and Henning Ottman, "Cognitive Interests and Self-Reflection," in Thompson and Held, *Habermas*, pp. 79–97.

132 J. Habermas (ed.), *Stichworte zur "Geistigen Situation der Zeit"* (Frankfurt am Main, 1979), p. 28.

133 Wolin, *Politics and Vision;* Arendt, *The Human Condition*.

134 J. G. A. Pocock, *The Machiavellian Moment* (Princeton, N.J., 1975); J. G. A. Pocock, "*The Machiavellian Moment* Revisited: A Study in History and Ideology," *Journal of Modern History*, vol. 53 (1981), pp. 49–72; Quentin Skinner, *The Foundations of Modern Political Thought* (Cambridge, 1978).

135 On Habermas's neglect of the concept of tradition, see Jack Mendelson, "The Habermas/Gadamer Debate," *New German Critique*, no. 18 (Fall 1979), pp. 44–74. Dieter Misgeld's forceful and interesting reply to Mendelson ("Science, Hermeneutics, and the Utopian Content of the Liberal Democratic Tradition," *New German Cirtique*, no. 22 [Winter 1981], pp. 123–44) defends the thesis that Habermas's entire recent work should be regarded as an articulation of the utopian content of the liberal democratic tradition. Misgeld consequently rejects the argument – proposed in this essay – that a socialist theory of public life must carefully consider its relationship with existing political traditions of democratic autonomy and struggle. He takes this proposal to mean little more than a recommendation to engage more directly in political action. This thesis is not fully convincing, and not only because the theory of public life has more choices than those of abstractly universal morality and actionism. Aside from its incorrect presumption that liberal democracy forms something like a homogeneous and self-consistent tradition, Misgeld's defense of the reconstructive elements of Habermas's communication theory also underestimates the degree to which the excessive abstractness and formalism of these elements (see Essay 5) derive from their considerable ignorance of historical reality, that is, from their failure to analyze already existing political traditions, public spheres, and oppositional social movements. Misgeld thereby fails to see the possible complementarity between the ethical formalism of the theory of universal pragmatics and the capacity of immanent critique – of "finding the new world through criticism of the old" – to defend the possibility of a historically situated, but nevertheless universal, morality. Habermas appears to acknowledge this complementarity in "A Reply to My Critics," in Thompson and Held, pp. 250ff.

5. Elements of a socialist theory of public life

1 *The Russian Revolution* (1918; Ann Arbor, 1961), esp. chs. 4–6. Other important defenses of democratic public life during this period include Antonio Gramsci's analysis of council communism and, later, of the modern Prince as proclaimer and organizer of a "national-popular collective will" (see *Selections from Political Writings: 1910–1920* [New York, 1977], pp. 34–5; and *Prison Notebooks*, ed. Quinton Hoare and G. Nowell-Smith [New York, 1975], pp. 132–3, 158); Karl Korsch, *Was ist Sozialisierung?* (Hannover, 1919); John Dewey, *The Public and Its Problems* (London, 1927); C. Wright Mills's discussion of the formation of primary publics in opposition to the mass communications industry (see esp. *Power, Politics and People: The Collected Essays of C. Wright Mills*, ed. I. L. Horowitz [London, 1963], pt. 4, ch. 10); and, more recently, Franz Neumann, *The Democratic and the Authoritarian State*, ed. Herbert Marcuse (London, 1957); Hannah Arendt, *The Human Condition* (Chicago, 1974); Sheldon Wolin, *Politics and Vision* (Boston, 1960); Carole Pateman, *The Problem of Political Obligation* (Chichester, 1979); and Oskar Negt and Alexander Kluge, *Öffentlichkeit und*

Erfahrung: Zur Organisationsanalyse von bürgerlicher und proletarischer Öffentlichkeit (Frankfurt am Main, 1972).

2 Rudolf Hilferding, *Finance Capital: A Study of the Latest Phase of Capitalist Development,* ed. Tom Bottomore (London, 1981), pt. 5. More recently, see Charles S. Maier, *Recasting Bourgeois Europe* (Princeton, N.J., 1975); Robert Wiebe, *The Search for Order, 1877–1920* (New York, 1967); David Abraham, *The Collapse of the Weimar Republic: Political Economy and Crisis* (Princeton, N.J., 1981); and Gabriel Kolko, *The Triumph of Conservatism: A Reinterpretation of American History, 1900–1916* (New York, 1963). For the case of Britain, see Keith Middlemas, *Politics in Industrial Society* (London, 1979), pt. 1.

3 E. L. Bernay, *Public Relations* (New York, 1952), p. 79; see also his earliest study, *Crystallizing Public Opinion* (Chicago, 1923).

4 This intellectual assault of course began much earlier. Amid the political and social struggles of the mid-nineteenth century, for example, the question of public opinion became a favored subject of political leaders, newspaper writers, and intellectuals. In retrospect, this concern with the public served as the precedent to its bureaucratic reordering. Some early treatises that point in this direction include William A. Mackinnon, *On the Rise, Progress and Present State of Public Opinion in Great Britain and Other Parts of the World* (London, 1828); Joseph Mosely, *Political Elements; or, The Progress of Modern Legislation* (London, 1852); David Urquhart, *Public Opinion and Its Organs* (London, 1855); and Franz von Holtzendorff, *Wesen und Wert der öffentlichen Meinung* (Munich, 1879).

5 See Michael Freeden, *The New Liberalism* (Oxford, 1978).

6 This concept was invoked by Walter Lippmann in his *Public Opinion* (1922; New York, 1965), p. 173. Cf. also the more recent interpretations of the emergence and limitations of the theory of equilibrium democracy in C. B. Macpherson, *The Life and Times of Liberal Democracy* (Oxford, 1977), ch. 4; and Peter Bachrach, *The Theory of Democratic Elitism* (London, 1970), ch. 2. As Carole Pateman has convincingly indicated (*Participation and Democratic Theory* [Cambridge, 1970], chs. 1, 6), this theoretical critique of the omnicompetent citizen sustained itself on fictions about a homogeneous classical tradition of democratic thinking.

7 Vilfredo Pareto, *The Mind and Society* (London, 1935).

8 Graham Wallas, *Human Nature in Politics,* 3rd ed. (London, 1920), pp. 118ff.; on the analysis of the unconscious dimensions of public opinion during this period, cf. Francis G. Wilson, *A Theory of Public Opinion* (Chicago, 1962), pt. 2.

9 Cf. Harold Lasswell, "The Measurement of Public Opinion," *American Political Science Review,* vol. 25 (1931), pp. 311–26. See also his *Propaganda Technique in the World War* (New York, 1927); and Friedrich Schönemann, *Die Kunst der Massenbeeinflussung in den Vereingten Staaten* (Berlin, 1924).

10 See, for example, the somewhat later and classic study of Stuart A. Rice, *Quantitative Methods in Politics* (New York, 1928, p. 57), which insists that the concept of "attitudes" must be preferred to that of "public opinion," since the latter concept connotes too much of a "rational and conscious element in the actual motivation."

11 See the pioneering works of C. F. Higham, *Looking Forward: Mass Education through Publicity* (London, 1920), and *Advertising: Its Use and Abuse* (London, 1925). On the theoretical links between market research and public opinion measurement, see Friedrich Pollock, "Empirical Research into Public Opinion," in Paul Connerton (ed.), *Critical Sociology* (Harmondsworth, 1976), pp. 225–36.

12 Published in the same year as Walter Lippmann's famous *Public Opinion,* Tönnies's *Kritik der öffentlichen Meinung* (Berlin, 1922) was for many years, at least prior to the

rise of Nazism, considered the classic European treatise on public opinion. Unfortunately, it remains relatively unknown in the English-speaking world. Tönnies had also planned a companion volume to the *Kritik* wherein he would deal with the genealogy of the concept of public opinion. Regrettably, only fragments were published. See, for example, "Necker über die öffentliche Meinung," *Zeitungswissenschaft*, vol. 2, no. 6 (1927), pp. 81–2; and the discussion of the eighteenth-century writings of Wieland and Garve in "Die öffentliche Meinung in unserer Klassik," *Archiv für Buch gewerve und Graphik*, vol. 65, no. 4 (1928), pp. 31–49. Also of relevance to the following discussion are his "Macht und Wert der öffentlichen Meinung," *Die Dioskuren, Jahrbuch für Geisteswissenschaften*, vol. 2 (1923), pp. 72–99 (partly translated as "The Power and Value of Public Opinion," in Ferdinand Tönnies, *On Sociology: Pure, Applied and Empirical*, ed. W. J. Cahnman and Rudolf Heberle [Chicago, 1971], pp. 251–65); his early discussion of public opinion and the role of the press in *Community and Society* (New York, 1963), pp. 220–2; and his critique of Wilhelm Bauer's *Die Öffentliche Meinung und Ihre Geschichtlichen Grundlagen* (1914) in "Zur Theorie der Öffentlichen Meinung," *Schmollers Jahrbuch für Gesetzgebung, Verwaltung und Volkswirtschaft im Deutschen Reich*, vol. 40 (1916), pp. 2001–30.

13 Tönnies, *Kritik*, p. 219; cf. Tönnies, *Community and Society*, pp. 231–2.

14 Tönnies, *Kritik*, p. 80.

15 Ibid., p. 228.

16 Ibid., p. 570; cf. ibid., pp. 228–57; and Tönnies, *Community and Society*, pp. 220–22.

17 Tönnies, *Kritik*, pp. 71, 207.

18 Cf. ibid., pp. 77–8: "Public opinion is the common way of thought, the corporate spirit of any group or association, insofar as these opinions are built upon thought and knowledge rather than on unproven imaginings, beliefs or authority."

19 Tönnies, "Power and Value of Public Opinion," pp. 253–4.

20 Walter Lippmann's definition of public opinion is an early expression of this tendency opposed by Tönnies: "Those features of the world outside which have to do with the behavior of other human beings, in so far as that behavior crosses ours, is dependent upon us, or is interesting to us, we call roughly public affairs. The pictures inside the heads of these human beings, the pictures of themselves, of others, of their needs, purposes, and relationships, are their public opinions" (*Public Opinion*, p. 18). Such formulations were marked by a deeply ironic, self-fulfilling prophecy, for their assumption that all must hold privately formulated opinions amounted to a justification of stereotypic analyses and instant, on-the-spot, opinion formation – a justification, it can be argued, that only accelerated the growing suspicion of the public as the arbiter of legitimate social and political authority.

21 Ferdinand Tönnies, "The Divisions of Sociology," in *On Sociology*, p. 137; cf. Tönnies, *Kritik*, pp. vi–viii. Relying upon this more precise meaning, one heavily indebted to the phase of Enlightenment, Tönnies was highly critical of Lippmann's all-encompassing, positivist concept of public opinion as mere popular sentiment and feeling; see Tönnies's review of *Public Opinion* in "Amerikanische Soziologie," *Weltwirtschaftliches Archiv*, vol. 26, no. 2 (1927), pp. 1–10.

22 "Power and Value of Public Opinion," p. 251.

23 Ibid., p. 252; cf. ibid., p. 257: " 'Public opinion' is considered to be like a strong fortress which must at all times be guarded and defended."

24 Ibid., p. 262. Others agreed with Tönnies's assessment. See, for example, the passing remark in R. M. MacIver's classic, *The Modern State* (London, 1926), p. 195: "So many agencies are enlisted in the task of persuasion, and so few are concerned with the

mere business of exploring the truth. The great endeavour is not to elicit public opinion but to make it, to control it, to use it."
25 Tönnies, "Power and Value of Public Opinion," p. 254.
26 Ibid., pp. 255–6.
27 Tönnies, *Community and Society*, p. 221.
28 Tönnies, *Kritik*, p. 572; cf. Tönnies, "Power and Value of Public Opinion," p. 264: "The more the masses move upward and the more they participate in the advance of education and political consciousness, the more will they make their voices count in the formation of public opinion."
29 Tönnies, *Kritik*, pp. 572–3; cf. Ferdinand Tönnies, "Historicism, Rationalism, and the Industrial System," in *On Sociology*, pp. 266–87.
30 Lippmann, *Public Opinion*, p. 251. This highly influential kind of argument was repeated in Lippmann's subsequent works. *The Phantom Public* (New York, 1925) insisted that the democratic public had no political functions, save that of mandating those capable of deciding. According to *The Public Philosophy* (New York, 1955), the slow decay of free Western democratic governments is a consequence of uninformed publics' overriding the judgments of informed responsible officials.
31 The latter point is emphasized in Weber's discussion with Ludendorff, as recalled by Marianne Weber in *Max Weber: A Biography*, ed. Harry Zohn (New York, 1975), p. 653; the first point appears in *From Max Weber: Essays in Sociology*, ed. H. H. Gerth and C.Wright Mills (London, 1970), p. 221.
32 Dewey, *The Public and Its Problems*, pp. 116–17, 138.
33 Ibid., ch. 4.
34 Ibid., pp. 116, 126.
35 Ibid., p. 135.
36 Ibid., pp. 31, 129.
37 Ibid., p. 167.
38 Ibid., p. 154.
39 Ibid., pp. 152–3; cf. p. 152: "Combined activity happens among human beings; but when nothing else happens it passes as inevitably into some other mode of interconnected activity as does the interplay of iron and the oxygen of water...Only when there exist *signs* or *symbols* of activities and of their outcome can the flux be viewed as from without, be arrested for consideration and esteem, and be regulated."
40 Ibid., pp. 154, 163, 167, 218.
41 Ibid., p. 33.
42 Jürgen Habermas, *Toward a Rational Society: Student Protest, Science and Politics* (London, 1971), p. 118 (hereafter cited as *TRS*).
43 Cf. the striking absence of discussion of Habermas's *political* concepts in Thomas McCarthy's otherwise excellent study of his writings (*The Critical Theory of Jürgen Habermas* [Cambridge, Mass., 1978]) and in Garbis Kortian's account of their metatheoretical dimensions (*Metacritique: The Philosophical Argument of Jürgen Habermas* [Cambridge, 1980]).
44 Habermas acknowledges the importance of Jaspers's philosophy of communication in "Die Gestalten der Wahrheit," in *Philosophisch-politisch Profile* (Frankfurt am Main, 1971), pp. 99–109, and in "Über das Verhältnis von Politik und Moral," in H. Kuhn and F. Wiedmann (eds.), *Das Problem der Ordnung* (Munich, 1960), p. 111; his dependence upon Hannah Arendt (and esp. her major work, *The Human Condition*) is made explicit in "On the German-Jewish Heritage," *Telos*, no. 44 (Summer 1980), pp. 127–31.
45 The concern with a general theory of language and communication was suggested

in his 1965 Frankfurt inaugural lecture (*Knowledge and Human Interests* [London, 1972], p. 314), pursued systematically in "Toward a Theory of Communicative Competence" (first delivered as lectures during a visit to England in the late 1960s; published in Hans Peter Dreitzel [ed.], *Recent Sociology*, no. 2 [London, 1970]; and hereafter cited as "TTCC"), and greatly extended in many works during the past decade. See esp. "Vorbereitende Bemerkungen," in Jürgen Habermas and Niklas Luhmann, *Theorie der Gesellschaft oder Sozialtechnologie – Was leistet die Systemforschung?* (Frankfurt am Main, 1975), pp. 101–41 (hereafter cited as *TGOS*); Summation and Response, *Continuum*, vol. 8, no. 1 (1970), pp. 123–33 (hereafter cited as "SR"); the unpublished Gauss lectures delivered at Princeton University in the spring of 1971, "Towards a Communication Theory of Society"; "Wahrheitstheorien," in Helmut Fahrenbach (ed.) *Wirklichkeit und Reflexion: Festschrift für Walter Schulz* (Pfullingen, 1973), pp. 211–65; *Legitimation Crisis* (Boston, 1975), pt. 3 (hereafter cited as *LC*); and "Some Distinctions in Universal Pragmatics: A Working Paper," *Theory and Society*, vol. 3 (1976), pp. 155–67, which is developed more fully in "Was heisst Universal-pragmatik?" in K-O. Apel (ed.), *Sprachpragmatik und Philosophie* (Frankfurt am Main, 1976), pp. 174–273, and translated as "What Is Universal Pragmatics?" in *Communication and the Evolution of Society* (Boston, 1979), pp. 1–68 (hereafter cited as *CES*). For further commentary on the theory of pragmatic universals, see my earlier "Communication, Ideology and the Problem of 'Voluntary Servitude,' " *Media, Culture and Society*, vol. 4 (1982), pp. 123–32; McCarthy, *The Critical Theory of Jürgen Habermas*, ch. 4; Anthony Giddens, "Habermas's Critique of Hermeneutics," in *Studies in Social and Political Theory* (London, 1977), pp. 135–64; and John B. Thompson, "Universal Pragmatics," in John B. Thompson and David Held (eds.), *Habermas: Critical Debates* (London, 1982), pp. 116–33.

46 Cf. Jürgen Habermas, "A Postscript to *Knowledge and Human Interests*," *Philosophy of the Social Sciences*, vol. 3 (1973), p. 185; and Jürgen Habermas, "A Reply to My Critics," in Thompson and Held, *Habermas*, pp. 256–7.

47 "Discussion," in Theodore F. Geraets (ed.), *Rationality Today* (Ottawa, 1979), p. 346.

48 *CES*, p. 5.

49 Habermas, "Some Distinctions in Universal Pragmatics," pp. 155–6; *CES*, p. 26.

50 Cf. *CES*, pp. 7–8 and p. 208, note 1: "Hitherto the term 'pragmatics' has been employed to refer to the analysis of particular contexts of language use and not to the reconstruction of universal features of using language (or of employing sentences in utterances)."

51 John R. Searle, *Speech Acts* (London, 1978), pp. 33ff. Habermas acknowledges the fundamental importance of Austin's and Searle's theories of speech acts to the arguments of his universal pragmatics (*CES*, pp. 25ff.). The most important of this post-Wittgenstein literature includes J. L. Austin, *How to Do Things with Words* (Oxford, 1962); J. L. Austin, "Performative-Constative," in C. E. Caton (ed.), *Philosophy and Ordinary Language* (Urbana, Ill., 1963), pp. 22–33; J. L. Austin, "Performative Utterances," in *Philosophical Papers* (Oxford, 1970), pp. 233–52; Searle, *Speech Acts*; John R. Searle, "What Is a Speech Act?" in M. Black (ed.), *Philosophy of America* (Ithaca, N.Y.: 1965), pp. 221–39; John R. Searle, "Austin on Locutionary and Illocutionary Acts," *Philosophical Review*, vol. 77 (1968), pp. 405–24; and John R. Searle, *Expression and Meaning: Studies in the Theory of Speech Acts* (Cambridge, 1979).

52 Cf. Karl-Otto Apel, "Sprechakttheorie und transzendentale Sprachpragmatik – zur Frage ethischer Normen," in Apel, *Sprachpragmatik und Philosophie*, pp. 10–173.

53 *CES*, p. 14. This thesis has old roots: The proposition that speech is that medium of communication which already presupposes a tacit agreement concerning what it means

to communicate appears in Socrates; see Plato, *"Phaedrus" and "The Seventh and Eighth Letters"* (Harmondsworth, 1973), pp. 19–103.

54 *CES*, pp. 1–5; *Wahrheitstheorien*, pp. 220–1; "Some Distinctions in Universal Pragmatics," pp. 157–9; "Zwei Bemerkungen zum praktischen Diskurs," in *Zur Rekonstruktion des Historischen Materialismus* (Frankfurt am Main, 1976), p. 339.

55 "TTCC," p. 141.

56 See G. Frege, "On Sense and Reference," in *Translations from the Philosophical Writings of Gottlob Frege*, ed. P. Geach and Max Black (Oxford, 1970), pp. 56–78.

57 Austin, "Performative Utterances," p. 251.

58 Searle, *Speech Acts*, pp. 63, 66–7.

59 *CES*, p. 4; cf. *TGOS*, p. 120; *LC*, p. 110; and Jürgen Habermas, "Einige Bemerkungen zum Problem der Begründung von Werturteilen," in *Verhandlungen des 9. Deutschen Kongress für Philosophie* (Meisenheim, 1972), pp. 89ff.

60 Cf. Hans-Georg Gadamer, "The Universality of the Hermeneutical Problem," in *Philosophical Hermeneutics*, ed. David E. Linge (Berkeley, Calif., 1977), pp. 7–8: "We all know that to say 'thou' to someone presupposes a deep common accord. Something enduring is already present when this word is spoken. When we try to reach agreement on a matter on which we have different opinions, this deeper factor always comes into play, even if we are seldom aware of it."

61 "SR," p. 131.

62 *KHI*, p. 284; cf. *CES*, pp. 63–5, 88; Habermas, "Wahrheitstheorien," p. 265, note 46; and "SR," p. 131: "We name a speaking situation ideal where the communication is not only not hindered by external, contingent influences, but also not hindered by forces which result from the structure of the communication itself. Only then does the peculiarly unforced compulsion of a better argument dominate."

63 A. W. Gouldner, "The Norm of Reciprocity," *American Sociological Review*, 1960, pp. 161–78.

64 *KHI*, p. 314; cf. "TTCC," p. 115.

65 Habermas, "Wahrheitstheorien," p. 258; cf. *CES*, p. 88; and the reference to "tu quoque" argumentation in *Zur Rekonstruktion des Historischen Materialismus*, pp. 339–400.

66 Emil Lask, "Zum System der Logik," in *Gesammelte Schriften*, vol. 3 (Tübingen, 1924), p. 92; *CES*, pp. 4–5.

67 For example, in "SR," p. 126, Habermas explicitly invokes the claim of G.H. Mead (*Mind, Self, Society* [Chicago, 1934], p. 327): "Universal discourse is the formal idea of communication. If communication can be carried through and made perfect, then there would exist the kind of democracy...in which each individual could carry just the response in himself that he knows he calls out in the community." See also *CES*, pp. 78ff.

68 "TTCC," p. 143; cf. "SR," p. 131.

69 This insistence reinforces one of Habermas's objections to the Parsonian conception of cultural values as somehow *given* universalistic norms that outline the desirable orientations for a social system considered as a totality. In Habermas's view (*Zur Logik der Sozialwissenschaften: Materialen* [Frankfurt am Main, 1970], pp. 176–7 [hereafter cited as *ZL*]), this formulation *a priori* excludes the possibility of the *political* formation of value orientations through "a universal and public discussion by the members of the society based on available information about the given conditions of reproduction of the system. Thereupon, a relative agreement could be effected on a value system which included the objective value orientations previously hidden from the knowledge and will of the citizenry. Through such communication, formerly acknowedged cul-

tural values could not function only as standards; cultural values would themselves be drawn into the discussion."

70 *Aspects of the Theory of Syntax* (Cambridge, Mass., 1965).

71 "TTCC," p. 131.

72 Ibid., p. 140. This argument underpins Habermas's criticism of the model of linguistic behaviorism (developed out of the semiotics of Charles Morris); Morris's account of communication as symbolically mediated, stimulus–response behavior equally misses the importance of the intersubjective negotiations of meaning as a *developed* competence of speaking and acting subjects. See *ZL*, pp. 150ff.; and *CES*, pp. 6–7, 20, 27–9; cf. "TTCC," pp. 140 and 138, where Habermas stresses that any structure of intersubjectivity "is generated by neither the monologically mastered system of linguistic rules nor by the language-external conditions of its performance. On the contrary, in order to participate in normal discourse, the speaker must have – in addition to his linguistic competence – basic qualifications of speech and of symbolic interaction (role-behaviour) at his disposal, which we may call communicative competence."

73 Cf. *KHI*, pp. 138, 157; *CES*, p. 90; and "TTCC," pp. 122–3, 143, and 141: "Every being, who says I to himself, asserts himself toward the Other as absolutely different. And yet at the same time he recognizes himself in the latter as another I and is conscious of the reciprocity of this relationship; every being is potentially his own Other."

74 "TTCC," p. 122.

75 Ibid., p. 123.

76 *LC*, pp. 107–8; *Theory and Practice* (Boston, 1973), pp. 18–19 (hereafter cited as *TP*).

77 *CES*, pp. 41–3, 53. This ability to distinguish and uncouple the so-called propositional and illocutionary dimensions of speech acts is said to be unique to the species (*CES*, p. 41, where Habermas draws upon the analysis of I. Dornbach, *Primatenkommunikation* [Frankfurt, 1975]). Presumably, this capacity could be realized fully only under conditions of authentic public life. Only then could speaking actors openly and freely communicate about both the facts and the dynamics of their relations with each other.

78 *CES*, p. 86; *LC*, pp. 111–17.

79 Hannah Arendt, "Truth and Politics," in Peter Laslett and W. G. Runciman (eds.), *Philosophy, Politics and Society*, 3rd ser. (Oxford, 1967), pp. 104–33.

80 Cf. Habermas, "Wahrheitstheorien," p. 259; "SR," p. 132; Habermas, "A Reply to My Critics," p. 221; and *TGOS*, pp. 140–1.

81 See the appraisal of the work of Gershom Scholem (Jürgen Habermas, "Die verkleidete Tora: Rede zum 80. Geburtstag von Gershom Scholem, *Merkur*, vol. 32 [1978], pp. 100–1), where Habermas insists that criticism's power to intervene in tradition and explode the continuity of that which is passed down warrants a distinction between (1) authoritarian tradition, i.e., the seemingly unchallengeable renewal of "truths" of fathers by their sons, and (2) the creative appropriation of tradition, according to which the authority of the past can be critically scrutinized and transcended. See also *LC*, p. 70; Jürgen Habermas, *Kultur und Kritik* (Frankfurt am Main, 1973), pp. 302–44 (hereafter cited as *KK*); and "SR," p. 128.

82 "SR," p. 127; cf. Habermas, "Wahrheitstheorien," p. 258; and Jürgen Habermas, "Der Universalitätsanspruch der Hermeneutik," in Karl-Otto Apel et al., *Hermeneutik und Ideologiekritik* (Frankfurt, 1971), p. 13. Habermas's distinction between these two forms of consensus might be favorably compared with Steven Lukes's concern to generate a radical conception of power and interest (*Power: A Radical View* [London, 1977], pp. 24–5, 32–5, 46–50). Lukes speaks of the problem of latent conflicts of

interest that arise from contradictions between the interests of those exercising power and the real interests of those excluded or shaped by this power. It is suggested (through rather empiricist and insufficiently developed arguments) that the category of real interests must be connected with an empirically grounded theory (based on adduced evidence) of the preconditions for autonomous political action. Habermas's theory of validity claims deepens this thesis, but through less positivist arguments.

83 *CES*, p. 14; *TP*, p. 17. The positivist claim that an actually existing agreement must always be final is defended in the well-known work of Peter Bachrach and Morton Baratz on "non-decisionmaking" (*Power and Poverty, Theory and Practice* [New York, 1970], p. 49). In the absence of observable (overt or covert) political conflict, Bachrach and Baratz claim, "the presumption must be that there is consensus on the prevailing allocation of values, in which case non-decisionmaking is impossible."

84 Jürgen Habermas, "Consciousness-Raising or Redemptive Criticism – The Contemporaneity of Walter Benjamin," *New German Critique*, no. 17 (Spring 1979), p. 59, quoting Walter Benjamin's 1929 essay *Der Sürrealismus*, translated in *Reflections* (New York, 1978), p. 191. Cf. also the explicitly political and uncharacteristically metaphoric rendition of this same point in "SR," p. 127: "Reason in the sense of the principle of rational discourse is the rock on which hitherto factual authorities are smashed rather than the rock on which they are founded."

85 "TTCC," pp. 117ff.

86 Ibid., p. 117; cf. "SR," pp. 125–6; and *CES*, p. 210, note 2.

87 Cf. H. Arendt, *The Origins of Totalitarianism* (New York, 1973), chs. 11–13.

88 *TP*, pp. 32–7. Habermas's rejection parallels Maurice Merleau-Ponty's dismissal of a "politics of reason" in favor of a "politics of understanding" (*Adventures of the Dialectic* [Evanston, Ill., 1973], pp. 3–7).

89 *TP*, pp. 36–7 (translation altered). Somewhat uncharacteristically, Habermas here adds that under certain political conditions (the opposition to war? the subjection of a woman to a wife-beating husband?) such strictures on the need for cautious prudence are simply scurrilous or ridiculous. This point will be pursued further in the section entitled "Public life as consensual communication?."

90 G. Lukács, "Towards a Methodology of the Problem of Organization," in *History and Class Consciousness* (Cambridge, Mass., 1971), p. 304.

91 *KK*, pp. 112–17.

92 This conception of the analysis of processes of drive dynamics as linguistic analysis draws explicitly upon Alfred Lorenzer's *Kritik des psychoanalytischen Symbolbegriffs* (Frankfurt am Main, 1970) and *Sprachzerstörung und Rekonstruktion* (Frankfurt am Main, 1970). Compare also K-O. Apel's interpretation of psychoanalysis as a critical emancipatory inquiry that dialectically mediates communicative understanding with the quasi-naturalistic objectification and explanation of action, in "Analytic Philosophy and the 'Geisteswissenschaften,'" in *Foundations of Language*, suppl. series, vol. 5 (Dordrecht, 1967), pp. 25ff., 55ff.; and in "The a Priori of Communication and the Foundation of the Humanities," in Fred Dallmayr and Thomas A. McCarthy (eds.), *Understanding and Social Inquiry* (Notre Dame, Ind., 1977), pp. 310–12. Habermas's appropriation of psychoanalysis (and his corresponding attempt to differentiate two forms of interpretation and communication) is evident in "TTCC," pp. 116–30; *KHI*, chs. 10–12; *KK*, pp. 264ff.; and *TP*, pp. 22ff.

93 *KHI*, p. 218; *CES*, pp. 68, 70; *KK*, 264–30.

94 *KHI*, ch. 11. Habermas's criticism of Freud's "self-misunderstanding" of the epistemological status of the psychoanalytic project parallels that of Michel Foucault (*Madness and Civilization: A History of Insanity in the Age of Reason* [New York, 1973]).

According to Foucault, Freudian psychoanalysis counters contemporary positivist accounts of madness by engaging unreason at the level of its language. Freud established the possibility of a *dialogue* with unreason (ibid., p. 198). On the other hand, this dialogue is premised upon the interrogating authority of the analyst. Freud "did deliver the patient from the existence of the asylum within which his 'liberators' had alienated him; but he did not deliver him from what was essential in this existence; he regrouped its powers, extended them to the maximum by uniting them in the doctor's hands" (ibid., 278).

95 *TP*, pp. 24, 29.

96 Ibid., p. 39.

97 Ibid., p. 23.

98 H. J. Geigel, "Reflexion und Emanzipation," in Apel et al., *Hermeneutik und Ideologiekritik*, pp. 278ff.; cf. the reply to Habermas by H. G. Gadamer in Apel et al., *Hermeneutik und Ideologiekritik*, pp. 307ff.; and Albrecht Wellmer, *Critical Theory of Society* (New York, 1971).

99 *TP*, pp. 16, 29ff.

100 *TGOS*, p. 120. Cf. the attempt by Claus Mueller (*The Politics of Communication* [New York, 1973]) to deploy the theory of ideologically distorted communication.

101 *TGOS*, p. 120; cf. "TTCC," p. 117; and Jürgen Habermas, "Hannah Arendt's Communications Concept of Power," *Social Research*, vol. 44, no. 1 (1977), pp. 21–2.

102 See *TRS*, esp. pp. 98–100, 111–12; *LC*, pp. 22–3; and Jürgen Habermas, *Strukturwandel der Öffentlichkeit: Untersuchungen zu einer Kategorie der bürgerlichen Gesellschaft* (Neuwied, 1975), 65–6, 110–11. Habermas's concern with these ideologies is unfortunately ignored in Paul Ricoeur's discussion of Gadamer and Habermas in *Hermeneutics and the Human Sciences*, ed. John B. Thompson (Cambridge, 1981), essay 2.

103 *LC*, p. 22; *TRS*, p. 99.

104 *LC*, p. 22; *TRS*, pp. 98–9. Of course, Habermas acknowledged that bourgeois, ideological forms of communication also displayed an "evident contradiction between idea and reality" (*LC*, p. 23). They were thus plagued by internal contradictions and therefore condemned to successive internal erosions and immanent criticisms. Bourgeois ideologies typically repressed, invited, and provoked their opposite: criticisms of ideology addressed to the exploited victims of the new bourgeois order. "Ideologies are coeval with the critique of ideology. In this sense there can be no prebourgeois 'ideologies' " (*TRS*, p. 99). In respect of their "utopian" or "illusory" qualities (which also functioned as a substitute gratification among the dominated, as Marx stressed with reference to Christianity in his polemic against Feuerbach), bourgeois ideologies were indeed false, even though they were not simply "false consciousness" (Engels). As the young Habermas noted with reference to the growth of public argumentation in the seventeenth and eighteenth centuries, ideologies "are not exclusively defined by their being the pure and simple falseness of a necessary social consciousness... [They] also display a moment whose truth consists in a utopian impulse which points beyond the present by bringing its justification into question" (*Strukturwandel der Öffentlichkeit*, p. 111); cf. ibid., p. 278. In this earlier formulation, Habermas is closer to Theodor Adorno, according to whom ideology is an objective and necessarily illusory form of consciousness, marked by the "coalescence of the true and false" ("Beitrag zur Ideologienlehre," *Kölner Zeitschrift für Soziologie*, vol. 6 [1953–4], p. 366).

105 Frankfurt Institute for Social Research, *Aspects of Sociology* (London, 1973), p. 183.

106 *KK*, p. 79; cf., *TRS*, p. 111; and Herbert Marcuse, *One Dimensional Man* (London, 1968), p. 26: "This absorption of ideology by reality does not, however, signify the 'end of ideology.' "

107 *CES*, p. 169; cf. *LC*, p. 19.
108 *TP*, pp. 237–42. Habermas here pointed to a few subsequent (and, in his view, less than satisfactory) attempts to reconstruct historical materialism as a critique of ideology: Ernst Bloch's concern with the critical utopian moments of ideological consciousness, Benjamin's theory of the allegorical, and Adorno's defense of the critical potential of modern art through the categories of negative-dialectical thought. Habermas's own project can be placed within this failed tradition.
109 *KHI*, p. 45.
110 Scientistic Marxism enjoyed a powerful reputation throughout the whole of the Second and Third Internationals, as has been shown by Russell Jacoby, "Towards a Critique of Automatic Marxism: The Politics of Philosophy from Lukács to the Frankfurt School," *Telos*, no. 10 (Winter 1971), pp. 119–46. This scientism culminates in contemporary Soviet Marxism. Against those ideologists who dare to speak and act rebelliously, this Marxism confidently asserts the unquestionable dualism between science and ideology; it therefore also insists upon its role as the privileged bearer of scientific insight into the laws of both nature and history. Another recent instance of this scientism is to be found in the Althusserian account of those universal and indispensable processes through which ideology functions "to shape men, to transform them and enable them to respond to the exigencies of existence" (Louis Althusser, *For Marx* [London, 1969], p. 235 [translation altered]). Althusser claims that scientific knowledge of social formations consists in an autonomous discourse that both speaks in ideology and tries to break with ideology (*Lenin and Philosophy and Other Essays* [London, 1971], p. 162). This kind of formulation, as critics of Althusser have pointed out, obscures the logic of the mediations between scientific discourse and its ideological referent. Scientific inquiry, it is said, must proceed from the most abstract concepts (which are seen as related to "formal abstract objects") to the most concrete concepts (which are supposedly related to "real-concrete singular objects"). It is as if these categories were detached, spontaneous thoughts, independent of actual social and political relations of power, and attributable only to some ill-conceived movement of pure scientific reason. According to this potentially bureaucratic formulation, the dualism between science and ideology cannot be questioned. The object of thought is represented as virtually internal to thought. In addition, knowledge itself is dehistoricized. It is to be preserved (for eternity?) as valid against a ubiquitous ideology that tends – by virtue of the allegedly indisputable claims of science itself – to become synonymous with "false consciousness" (as has been pointed out by Anthony Giddens, *Central Problems in Social Theory* [London, 1979], p. 181). The maxim that "there is no practice except by and in an ideology" (Althusser, *Lenin and Philosophy*, p. 159) is not extended to science itself.
111 Althusser, *Lenin and Philosophy*, p. 151: "Ideology...is for Marx an imaginary assemblage (*bricolage*), a pure dream, empty and vain, constituted by the 'day's residues' from the only full and positive reality, that of the concrete history of concrete material individuals producing their existence. It is on this basis that ideology has no history in *The German Ideology*, since its history is outside it, where the only existing history is, the history of concrete individuals, etc."
112 See Francis Bacon, "Novum Organum," in *Works*, ed. James Spedding et al. (London, 1883), pp. 54ff.; Theodor Geiger, *Ideologie und Wahrheit* (Stuttgart, 1953); and, concerning Bacon and de Tracy, Hans Barth, *Truth and Ideology* (Berkeley, Calif., 1976), chs. 1, 2.
113 Karl Marx, *Theories of Surplus Value*, vol. 3 (Moscow, 1971), p. 536. Commenting on this myth (appropriated from Luther's own rendition), Marx notes: "An excellent

picture, it fits the capitalist in general, who pretends that what he has taken from others and brought into his den emanates from him, and by causing it to go backwards he gives it the semblance of having come from his den." Cf. Marx's note attached to "The German Ideology" in *Writings of the Young Marx on Philosophy and Society*, ed. L. D. Easton and K. H. Guddat (New York, 1967), p. 472: "Ideologists turn everything upside down."

114 See Marx, "The German Ideology," pp. 413–14

115 "A Review of Gadamer's *Truth and Method*," in Dallmayr and McCarthy, *Understanding and Social Inquiry*, pp. 335–63; cf. Gadamer's pointed response in the later supplement to *Truth and Method* (New York, 1975), pp. 495–6.

116 "Review of Gadamer's *Truth and Method*," p. 360; cf. *TP*, p. 158, where work as purposive-rational action is seen as always endowed with meaning or significance by virtue of its embeddedness within a framework of communicatively generated rules.

117 Habermas, "Review of Gadamer's *Truth and Method*," pp. 360–1.

118 Alfred Schmidt, *The Concept of Nature in Marx* (London, 1973), p. 30. See also Adam Schaff, *Marxism and the Human Individual* (New York, 1970), p. 75; and Marshall Sahlins, *Culture and Practical Reason* (Chicago, 1976), esp. ch. 3.

119 *CES*, p. 3.

120 *KK*, pp. 118–94, 195–231; *CES*, pp. 69–94; Jürgen Habermas, "Zur Einführing," in Habermas et al., *Entwicklung des Ichs* (Köln, 1977), pp. 9–30.

121 According to Habermas's more recent (and somewhat hyper-analytic) formulations (see *CES*, pp. 209–10, note 2), consensual action, in which interacting speakers explicitly and agreeably acknowledge the structuring of their communications by the four validity claims, is only one form of social action, which also includes (1) communicative action that is explicitly oriented to reaching understanding (*verständigungsorientierten Handelns*); (2) *discourse*, in which such agreement is temporarily suspended, even though participants retain their cooperative disposition toward each other; (3) *strategic action*, in which actors openly and explicitly adopt an uncooperative, instrumental orientation toward others; (4) *manipulative action*, through which the manipulators *deliberately* deceive others about their apparently communicative conduct; and (5) *systematically distorted communication*, in which participants typically deceive each other about their interactions.

122 Ibid., pp. 4, 35–41, 208, note 1.

123 Ibid., pp. 24–5.

124 Of great relevance here are Walter Benjamin's allegation about the threatened art of embodied storytelling in "The Storyteller," in *Illuminations* (London, 1973), p. 108, and his references (with Asja Lacis) to the "fastidiously specialized eroticism" of the Neapolitans in "Naples," in *Reflections*, p. 173.

125 "TTCC," pp. 121–2; cf. *CES*, pp. 1 and 38 (a reference to propositionally differentiated gestures).

126 *KHI*, p. 146 and, more generally, chs. 7–8.

127 Ibid., pp. 163ff.

128 Ibid., p. 168; cf. also his discussions of Wittgenstein in *ZL*, pp. 220ff.; and in *Philosophisch-politisch Profile*, pp. 141–6.

129 *KHI*, p. 168; cf. *KHI*, pp. 171, 172; and "TTCC," p. 121. A similar point has been stressed by Erving Goffman, *The Presentation of Self in Everyday Life* (Garden City, N.Y., 1959), p. 2.

130 See esp. Klaus Doerner, *Madmen and the Bourgeoisie* (Oxford, 1981); Michel Foucault, *The History of Sexuality* (New York, 1978); Michel Foucault, *Discipline and Punish: The Birth of the Prison* (London, 1977); Michel Foucault, *Power/Knowledge* (Brighton, 1980);

Michel Foucault, "Governmentality," *I and C*, no. 6 (Autumn 1979), pp. 5–21; Michel Foucault, "War in the Filigree of Peace," *Oxford Literary Review*, vol. 4, no. 2 (1980), pp. 15–19; and Jacques Donzelot, *The Policing of Families* (New York, 1979).
131 *CES*, p. 41.
132 Searle, *Speech Acts*, pp. 17–18; *CES*, pp. 5-6, 30–1, 46.
133 *ZL*, p. 220; cf. *CES*, pp. 67–8; and *KHI*, p. 157.
134 Ferdinand de Saussure, *Course in General Linguistics* (New York, 1966). According to Saussure, particular speakers produce utterances or messages (*parole*), but only because they are already embedded within a primordial linguistic code or set of codes (*langue*). Especially when extended to entities larger than the sentence, this dualism has the effect (among others) of bracketing speech act events in favor of a concern with synchronically coordinated systems of linguistic structures. By no means conceived as coterminous with "forms of life" (Wittgenstein), language is analyzed as if it were a self-sufficient ensemble of inner relationships between signs.
135 *CES*, pp. 5, 67–8.
136 Ibid., p. 40; cf. Searle, *Speech Acts*, pp. 19–21, 68, 87–8.
137 Aristotle, *De Poetica*, in *The Basic Works of Aristotle*, ed. Richard McKeon (New York, 1968), sect. 21. The movement to transform radically the classical tradition of theories of metonymy and rhetoric can be dated from I. A. Richards, *The Philosophy of Rhetoric* (Oxford, 1936). Subsequent works include those of Max Black, *Models and Metaphors* (Ithaca, N.Y., 1962); Monroe Beardsley, "Metaphor," in *Encyclopedia of Philosophy* (New York, 1967), vol. 5, pp. 284–9; and Colin Turbayne, *The Myth of Metaphor* (Columbia, S.C., 1970). I have drawn especially upon the "tension" theory of metaphor proposed by Paul Ricoeur in *Interpretation Theory: Discourse and the Surplus of Meaning* (Fort Worth, Tex., 1976), ch. 3, and in *The Rule of Metaphor: Multi-Disciplinary Studies of the Creation of Meaning in Language* (London, 1978).
138 *CES*, p. 93; "A Reply to My Critics," p. 270.
139 See Herbert Marcuse, "On Hedonism," in *Negations: Essays in Critical Theory* (Boston, 1968); Herbert Marcuse, *Eros and Civilization* (Boston, 1955); Silvia Bovenschen et al., *Gespräche mit Herbert Marcuse* (Frankfurt am Main, 1978), pp. 9–62; and Herbert Marcuse, *An Essay on Liberation* (Boston, 1969), ch. 2; cf. Habermas's commentaries in "Psychic Thermidor and the Rebirth of Rebellious Subjectivity," *Berkeley Journal of Sociology*, vol. 25 (1980), pp. 1–12; and in "Zum Geleit," in Jürgen Habermas (ed.), *Antworten auf Herbert Marcuse* (Frankfurt am Main, 1968), pp. 9–16.
140 "Some Social Implications of Modern Technology," *Studies in Philosophy and Social Science*, vol. 9 (1941), p. 438; cf. Marcuse, *An Essay on Liberation*, ch. 2.
141 *Eros and Civilization*, p. 205.
142 Herbert Marcuse, "Preface," *Reason and Revolution* (Boston, 1960), p. x. This thesis first appears in his earliest work (on novels whose favored protagonists are rebellious artists), *Der Deutsche Künstlerroman* (1922), in *Schriften*, vol. 1 (Frankfurt am Main, 1978). It is repeated in many others, including *Eros and Civilization*; *Counterrevolution and Revolt* (Boston, 1972), ch. 3; and *The Aesthetic Dimension* (Boston, 1978). In these works, Marcuse radicalizes the thesis presented by Freud in "Formulations regarding the Two Principles in Mental Functioning [1911]," in *A General Selection from the Works of Sigmund Freud*, ed. J. Rickman (Garden City, N.Y., 1957), pp. 38-45. According to Freud, there exists a biological and psychological tie among the repressed instinctual energies, the pleasure principle (which, in the face of the dominant reality principle, continues to rule the repressed instincts), fantasy (the wish for immediate gratification), and art (which allows for the full play of erotic fantasies).

143 This is the (somewhat exceptional) theme of "The Affirmative Character of Culture," in Marcuse, *Negations*, pp. 88–103.

144 Cf. Marcuse, *Counterrevolution and Revolt*, p. 132; and Herbert Marcuse, "Theorie und Praxis," in *Zeit-Messungen* (Frankfurt, 1975), pp. 32–3: "When ideology itself, reason itself become means of domination which are reproduced by the individuals themselves, then the necessity exists for a *counter*-psychology, a *counter*-sociology, a *counter*-rationality, a *counter*-education."

145 This allegation informs the amusing exchange with Marcuse on the problem of environmental pollution in Bovenschen et al., *Gespräche mit Herbert Marcuse*, pp. 32–3, and underpins Habermas's more critical assessment of the student movement (and its alleged inclination to "free political activism from the painful hesitations of moral-practical reasoning" ["Psychic Thermidor," pp. 10–11]); cf. also Jürgen Habermas, *Protestbewegung und Hochschulreform* (Frankfurt am Main, 1969); and the student response to Habermas's allegations about student "left-fascist" tendencies in Oskar Negt (ed.), *Die Linke antwortet Jürgen Habermas* (Frankfurt am Main, 1968).

146 Habermas, "Psychic Thermidor," p. 9. This chiliasm is evident in "Art as a Form of Reality," *New Left Review*, no. 74 (1972), pp. 51–8, where Marcuse defends the Kantian concept of *interesseloses Wohlgefallen* (i.e., delight or pleasure divorced from all interest, desire, inclination).

147 *One Dimensional Man*, p. 235.

148 Cf. "Habermas Talking: An Interview," *Theory and Society*, vol. 1 (1974), p. 53; and Habermas, "Psychic Thermidor," p. 10: "If rebellious subjectivity had to owe its rebirth to something that is beyond – a too deeply corrupted – reason, it is hard to explain why some of us should at all be in a position to recognize this fact and to give reasons in defence of it." The trajectory of this argument parallels Michel Foucault's critique of the "repressive hypothesis" in *The History of Sexuality*.

149 "Theorien des deutschen Faschismus" (1930), in Walter Benjamin, *Gesammelte Schriften*, vol. 3 (Frankfurt am Main, 1972), pp. 238–250.

150 Walter Benjamin, "Epilogue: The Work of Art in the Age of Mechanical Reproduction," in *Illuminations*, pp. 243–4. Cf. Brecht's analysis of the theatrical aspects of the relationship between Hitler and the masses ("Über die Theatralik des Faschismus," in *Gesammelte Werke*, vol. 16 [Frankfurt am Main, 1967], pp. 558–68); and, more recently, Martin Jürgens, "Der Staat als Kunstwerk: Bemerkungen zur Ästhetisierung der Politik," *Kursbuch*, no. 20 (1970), pp. 119–39; and Rainer Stollmann, "Fascist Politics as a Total Work of Art: Tendencies of the Aesthetization of Political Life in National Socialism," *New German Critique*, no. 14 (Spring 1978), pp. 41–60.

151 *CES*, p. 1.

152 Ibid., pp. 78ff.; *LC*, p. 95.

153 Karl-Otto Apel, "Types of Rationality Today: The Continuum of Reason between Science and Ethics," in Geraets, *Rationality Today*, pp. 336ff.

154 *From Max Weber*, p. 123.

155 Ibid., p. 121. Cf. Bertolt Brecht's well-known advice on the political complexities of the means–end relationship ("To Those Born Later," *Brecht: Poems 1929–38* [London, 1976], p. 318):

You who will emerge from the flood
To which we have gone under
Remember
When you speak of our failings
The dark time too
Which you have escaped

For we went, changing countries oftener than our shoes
Through the wars of classes, despairing
When there was injustice only, and no rebellion.

And yet we know:
Hatred, even of meanness
Contorts the features.
Anger, even against injustice
Makes the voice hoarse. Oh we
Who wanted to prepare the ground for friendliness
Could not ourselves be friendly.

156 Hannah Arendt, *On Revolution* (Harmondsworth, 1973), chs. 3, 6; Hannah Arendt, *Crises of the Republic* (New York, 1972), p. 203; Negt and Kluge, *Öffentlichkeit und Erfahrung*, ch. 1. This theme of "public joy" is also emphasized in Rousseau's classic account of public festivals in *Politics and the Arts: Letter to M. D'Alembert on the Theatre* (Ithaca, N.Y., 1973), sect. 11. Free publics – Rousseau here offered his own Geneva as a paragon – could flourish only in a truly festive atmosphere. The people would assemble often, forming among themselves sweet, communicative bonds of pleasure. Public carnivals would thereby resemble the gathering of a big family (replete with the patriarchalism that Rousseau continually defended, thereby contradicting his claims on behalf of this public's universal accessibility). Before the eyes of the public, the young could fall in love and all could enter into cordial and passionate dalliances. Authentic joy, Rousseau urged, could be achieved only as public joy: "Plant a stake crowned with flowers in the middle of a square; gather the people together there, and you will have a festival. Do better yet; let the spectators become an entertainment to themselves; make them actors themselves; do it so that each sees and loves himself in the others so that all will be better united" (ibid., p. 126). Stripped of its patriarchalism and romantic identitarianism, this old Rousseauean insight remains crucial: Genuine public action frequently assumes a carnival-like form.

157 Arendt, *Crises of the Republic*, pp. 49–102.

158 Cf. John Rawls, *A Theory of Justice* (Cambridge, Mass., 1971), secs. 55, 57, 59; for Rawls civil disobedience, unlike "organized forcible resistance," serves merely to "warn and admonish" the sense of justice of the majority, which nevertheless retains the powers of inflicting legal/penal consequences upon those who dissent. For criticisms of contemporary liberalism as a self-contradictory discourse that analyzes disobedience as both justified and punishable, see Pateman, *The Problem of Political Obligation*, esp. pp. 55–60, 161–2; Brian Barry, *The Liberal Theory of Justice* (Oxford, 1973), pp. 151–3; and G. J. Schochet, "The Morality of Resisting the Penalty," in V. Held et al. (eds.), *Philosophy and Political Action* (Oxford, 1972).

159 See the especially pertinent comments of David Held in "Crisis Tendencies, Legitimation and the State," in Thompson and Held, *Habermas*, pp. 181–95.

160 This strategy explicitly draws upon the account of explicative discourse presented by H. Schnädelbach, *Reflexion und Diskurs* (Frankfurt am Main, 1977), pp. 277–336.

161 Cf. Habermas, "A Postscript to *Knowledge and Human Interests*," pp. 182–5; and *CES*, pp. 24, 12, and 16, where rational reconstructions are said to "correspond precisely to the rules that are operatively effective in the object domain [of communication] – that is, to the rules that actually determine the production of surface structures."

162 *CES*, p. 15.

163 Cf. ibid., pp. 13, 19, 213, note 41; and Habermas, "A Reply to My Critics," p. 235. Habermas's adoption of the "clear case" principle draws upon D. Wunderlich, *Grun-*

dlagen der Linguistik (Hamburg, 1974), p. 209, and upon Searle, *Speech Acts*, pp. 55–6. K-O. Apel's reservations about this principle are expressed in "The *a priori* of the Communication Community and the Foundations of Ethics," in *Towards a Transformation of Philosophy*, trans. Glyn Adey and David Frisby (London, 1980), pp. 274–5, 296-7. Mary Hesse has similarly argued that the theory of universal pragmatics cannot generalize its propositions beyond its highly restricted and normatively chosen "clear case" examples, in *Revolutions and Reconstructions in the Philosophy of Science* (Brighton, 1980), ch. 9.

164 Habermas indirectly acknowledges these difficulties in "Neue soziale Bewegungen: Ein Exkurs," *Aesthetik und Kommunikation*, vol. 45–6, no. 12 (1981), pp. 158–61.

165 *TP*, p. 32; *CES*, p. 209, note 2.

166 "SR," p. 128; cf. Habermas, "Der Universalitätsanspruch der Hermeneutik," p. 158; and *TP*, p. 40: "In a process of enlightenment there can only be participants."

6. Capitalism and creative destruction

1 Rudolf Bahro, *Elemente einer neuen Politik: Zum Verhältnis von Ökologie und Sozialismus* (Berlin, 1980).

2 Joseph A. Schumpeter, *Capitalism, Socialism, and Democracy* (New York, 1942), pt. 2, ch. 7.

3 Karl Marx, *Capital*, vol. 1 (Moscow, 1970), pp. 394-412.

4 See esp. Herbert Marcuse's critique of Weber, "Industrialization and Capitalism in the Work of Max Weber," in *Negations: Essays in Critical Theory* (Boston, 1968), pp. 201–26; and Jürgen Habermas, *Toward a Rational Society: Student Protest, Science, and Politics* (London, 1971), pp. 81–122 (hereafter cited as *TRS*).

5 It should be noted that Marcuse is not always consistent on this point. As Habermas correctly observes (*TRS*, pp. 88–9), Marcuse sometimes speaks of late capitalism's forces of production in terms almost identical with the original Marxian theses on the "fettered" potential of the forces of production.

6 *TRS*, p. 57; cf. Habermas's early quip against those who have only contempt for contemporary scientific-technical development: "Is it not the case that an epoch can be rescued only with its productive achievements, and not in opposition to them?" ("Die Dialektik der Rationalisierung: Vom Pauperismus im Produktion und Konsum," *Merkur*, vol. 8 [1954], p. 701.

7 See, for example, two influential works by Theodore Roszak: *The Making of a Counter Culture: Reflections on the Technocratic Society and Its Youthful Opposition* (London, 1970); and *Where the Wasteland Ends: Politics and Transcendence in Postindustrial Society* (Garden City, N.Y., 1972).

8 See Henri de Saint-Simon, "Introduction to the Scientific Studies of the Nineteenth Century (1808)," in *Social Organization: The Science of Man and Other Writings*, trans. Felix Markham (New York, 1964), pp. 12–20.

9 There were many instances of this expectation: for example, Galileo's anticipation that science would bring humans closer to God by "reading off " mathematical Nature – God's "Second Book"; Kepler's belief (cited in A. Koestler, *The Sleepwalkers* [Harmondsworth, 1964], p. 264) that "Geometry existed before the Creation, is co-eternal with the mind of God, *is God Himself*...; Geometry provided God with a model for the creation and was implanted into man, together with God's own likeness and not conveyed to his mind through the eyes"; and Newton's conviction that planetary order was indisputable proof of the existence of God.

10 Friedrich Nietzsche, *Human, All-Too-Human*, in *Collected Works*, trans. O. Levy (Edinburgh, 1915), vol. 6, pt. 1, bk. 3, sec. 111. This section ("The Origins of the Religious Cult") contains an extended discussion of the relationship between traditional cultures, their emphasis on religious interpretations of outer nature, and the notion of natural causality, discussed later in this essay.

11 Ibid.

12 Ibid.

13 Friedrich Nietzsche, *The Will to Power*, in *Collected Works*, vol. 15, bk. 3, sec. 610.

14 *TRS*, pp. 99–100. Habermas's discussion of the "positivization" of natural law is found in *Theory and Practice* (Boston, 1973), pp. 82–120 (hereafter cited as *TP*). Cf. his arguments on this general point with the classic account of E. J. Dijksterhuis, *The Mechanization of the World Picture*, trans. C. Dikshoorn (London, 1961), p. 491: "The mechanisation of the world-picture led with irresistible consistency to the conception of God as a retired engineer, and from this to his complete elimination was only a step."

15 René Descartes, "Discourse on Method (1637)," in *Philosophical Works*, trans. E. Haldane and G. Ross (New York, 1955), vol. 1, p. 119.

16 *TP*, p. 61; cf. *TP*, pp. 25–6; and Jürgen Habermas, *Legitimation Crisis* (Boston, 1975), p. 119.

17 Silvia Bovenschen et al., *Gespräche mit Herbert Marcuse* (Frankfurt am Main, 1978), p. 471.

18 *TRS*, p. 96; cf. Habermas, *Legitimation Crisis*, p. 21.

19 At least, this was the thesis of Edgar Zilsel, "The Genesis of the Idea of Scientific Progress," *Journal of the History of Ideas*, vol. 6 (1945), pp. 663–86. A similar argument was made earlier by Franz Borkenau, *Der Übergang vom feudalen zum bürgerlichen Weltbild: Studien zur Geschichte der Manufakturperiode* (Paris, 1934); cf. Georg Simmel's thesis that the notion of a mathematically ordered cosmos was expressive of an emerging market society mediated by money, in *The Philosophy of Money* (London, 1978), pp. 508–10.

20 This is well documented (via industrial records and evidence of science classes in industrial areas) for the period of the first Industrial Revolution by A. E. Musson and E. Robinson, *Science and the Industrial Revolution* (Manchester, 1970).

21 Cf. the excellent treatment of Bacon by William Leiss, *The Domination of Nature* (New York, 1972), ch. 2; and Christopher Hill, *The World Turned Upside Down* (London, 1972), ch. 14.

22 Habermas's thesis here owes much to Marx, who noted (in the famous passages on fixed capital in the *Grundrisse* [1857; Harmondsworth, 1973], pp. 690–711) the unprecedented "scientization" of the capitalist accumulation process. In the present phase of capitalist production, Marx there pointed out, science becomes a productive force distinct from labor and is pressed increasingly into the service of capital. "Pure" science becomes directly "technological" in character: "Invention becomes a business" (p. 704). The capitalist drive to dominate both outer nature and the labor process is not only stepped up as a consequence. To the extent that science-fueled, fixed capital begins to replace direct, living labor power in the production process, the latter also becomes relatively less crucial, even if no less alienated and at odds with itself. At least in large-scale industry, the generation of real wealth becomes less dependent on labor time and on the quantity of labor power employed. The "powerful effectiveness" of direct labor time comes to depend rather on the general state of scientific development and on the progress of technology, or the application of this science to production (ibid., pp. 704–5). See also Marx's commentary on W. Thompson's *An*

Inquiry into the Principles of the Distribution of Wealth (London, 1824) in *Capital*, vol. 1, p. 341. Marx quotes approvingly from Thompson: "The man of knowledge and the productive labourer come to be widely divided from each other, and knowledge, instead of remaining the handmaid of labour in the hand of the labourer to increase his productive powers...has almost everywhere arrayed itself against labour...systematically deluding and leading them (the labourers) astray in order to render their muscular powers entirely mechanical and obedient."

23 In support of Habermas's theses on the industrialized commodification of science during this period, see Nathan Rosenberg, *Technology and American Economic Growth* (New York, 1972); Jerome R. Ravetz, *Scientific Knowledge and Its Social Problems* (Harmondsworth, 1973), esp. ch. 2; Derek J. De Solla Price, *Little Science, Big Science* (New York, 1965); and Leslie Sklair, *Organised Knowledge* (Bungay, 1973).

24 According to this intellectual tendency (represented by Robert Lane, Lipset, Duverger, etc.) the logic of late capitalist society is identical with the expanded production of goods and services *and* social quiescence and technocratic politics. According to Lane, for example, this happy utopia signals the triumph of a "politics of consensus," the "lessening of hostility between parties and religious groups, and a rapprochement between men and their government" ("The Politics of Consensus in an Age of Affluence," *American Political Science Review*, vol. 59 [1965], p. 877). In Lipset's early view, the industrial world has entered a phase of "post-politics": "There is relatively little difference between the democratic left and right, the socialists are moderates and the conservatives accept the welfare state...[the chief issue becomes] the division of the total product within the framework of the Keynesian welfare state, and such issues do not require or precipitate extremism on either side" (*Political Man: The Social Bases of Politics* [New York, 1960], pp. 92-3). Maurice Duverger (*The Idea of Politics* [Indianapolis, 1966] pp. 208–9) succinctly summarizes these increasingly implausible arguments: "As technology develops political conflict decreases and social integration increases...politics replaces violence."

25 This ideology of technological determinism has been discussed earlier (see Essay 3). Habermas's concern is articulated with reference to Arnold Gehlen, "Über kulturelle Kristallisation," in *Studien zur Anthropologie und Soziologie* (Berlin, 1963); Arnold Gehlen, "Über kulturelle Evolution," in M. Hahn and F. Wiedmann (eds.), *Die Philosophie und die Frage nach dem Fortschritt* (Munich, 1964); Helmut Schelsky, *Der Mensch in der wissenschaftlichen Zivilisation* (Cologne–Oplsaden, 1961); and Jacques Ellul, *The Technological Society* (New York, 1964). In addition (and these are just representative examples of a still burgeoning literature) see William G. Carleton, *Technology and Humanism: Some Exploratory Essays for Our Time* (Nashville, Tenn., 1970), p. 255: "The overriding contribution of the twentieth century to history is technocracy: the technicalized, cybernetic, computerized society increasingly run by scientists, engineers and technicians. This society is drastically changing man's institutions and transforming his behavior and basic values"; R. J. Forbes, *The Conquest of Nature: Technology and Its Consequences* (Harmondsworth, 1971), p. 7: "Technology can no longer be viewed as only one of the many threads that form the texture of our civilization; with a rush, in less than half a century, it has become the prime source of material change and so *determines* the pattern of the total social fabric" (emphasis mine); and Emmanuel Mesthene, *Technological Change: Its Impact on Man and Society* (Cambridge, Mass., 1970). On "futurology" see the stimulating critique by Robert Nisbet, "Has Futurology a Future?" *Encounter*, vol. 37, no. 5 (1971), pp. 19–28.

26 *TRS*, p. 105; cf. *TRS*, p. 64, where Habermas castigates the thesis of technological determinism for its assumption of "an immanent necessity of technical progress which

owes its appearance of being an independent, self-regulating process only to the way in which social interests operate in it – namely through continuity with unreflected, unplanned, passively adaptive natural history." This same theme appears in Jürgen Habermas, "Praktische Folgen des wissenschaftlich-technischen Fortschritts," in *Theorie und Praxis* (Frankfurt am Main, 1974), pp. 336–58; and in *TRS*, pp. 50–61.

27 The concern to develop a "social technology" or techniques of technology assessment is a more recent reaction to what has been labeled (misleadingly) the "negative externalities" of scientific-technical progress under late capitalist conditions (e.g., ecological damage, the invasion of privacy, fears about genetic research, etc.). For two examples of this line of metabureaucratic reasoning see the Organisation for Economic Cooperation and Development's *Science, Growth and Society* (Paris, 1971); and Alvin Toffler, *Future Shock* (New York, 1972) p. 457: "A sensitive system of indicators geared to measuring the achievement of social and cultural goals, and indicated with economic indicators, is part of the technical equipment that any society needs before it can successfully reach the next stage of eco-technological development. It is an absolute precondition for post-technocratic planning and change management."

28 *TRS*, p. 59.

29 Ibid., p. 52; Jürgen Habermas, "Neue soziale Bewegungen: Ein Exkurs," *Ästhetik und Kommunikation*, vol. 45–6, no. 12 (1981) pp. 158–61; Jürgen Habermas, "A Reply to My Critics," in John B. Thompson and David Held (eds.), *Habermas: Critical Debates* (London, 1982), p. 276.

30 *The Joyful Wisdom*, in *Collected Works*, vol. 10, bk. 1, sec. 37.

31 Friedrich Nietzsche, *The Dawn of Day*, in *Collected Works*, vol. 9, sec. 10; cf. Nietzsche, *The Dawn of Day*, sec. 7.

32 *Notes to Zarathustra*, in *Collected Works*, vol. 16, sec. 3; cf. Nietzsche, *Human, All-Too-Human*, sec. 5, aph. 256; and Friedrich Nietzsche, *The Genealogy of Morals*, in *Collected Works*, vol. 13, essay 3, sec. 25.

33 Nietzsche, *The Will to Power*, vol. 2, bk. 3, sec. 608.

34 Ibid.; cf. Nietzsche, *The Joyful Wisdom*, bk. 5, sec. 373: "An essentially mechanical world would be an essentially *meaningless* world! Supposing we valued the *worth* of music with reference to how much it could be counted, calculated, or formulated – how absurd such a 'scientific' estimate of music would be! What would one have apprehended, understood, or discerned in it! Nothing, absolutely nothing of what is really 'music' in it!"

35 Nietzsche, *The Genealogy of Morals*, essay 3, sec. 24; cf. Nietzsche, *The Genealogy of Morals*, essay 3, sec. 25: "In every department science needs an ideal value, a power which creates values, and in whose *service it can believe* itself."

36 *The Joyful Wisdom*, bk. 5, sec. 373.

37 Ibid., bk. 3, aph. 125.

38 Friedrich Nietzsche, *Thus Spake Zarathustra*, in *Collected Works*, prologue, vol. 11, pt. 1.

39 *TRS*, p. 61.

40 Ibid.

41 Jürgen Habermas, *Zur Rekonstruktion des Historischen Materialismus* (Frankfurt am Main, 1976), pp. 162–3.

42 *Communication and the Evolution of Society* (Boston, 1979), p. 105.

43 See my earlier theses (which remained too heavily under the influence of Marcuse's ontology) in "On Tools and Language: Habermas on Work and Interaction," *New German Critique*, no. 6 (Fall 1975), pp. 82–100; and "On Turning Theory against Itself," *Theory and Society*, vol. 4 (1977), pp. 561–72.

44 *CES*, p. 120.

45 Ibid., p. 118.

46 Franco Ferrarotti, "Preliminary Remarks on the Interaction between American and European Social Science," *Social Research*, vol. 43, no. 1 (1976), pp. 25–45.

47 Jürgen Habermas, "The Place of Philosophy in Marxism," *Insurgent Sociologist*, vol. 5, no. 2 (1975), p. 48.

48 Habermas's thesis that the augmentation of the production forces is synonymous with late capitalist modes of technical rationalization can be compared with that of Marcuse, who has rightly raised the possibility of peripheral capitalist countries' "skipping the stage of repressive capitalist industrialization, an industrialization that has led to increasingly more powerful domination of the productive and distributive apparatus over the underlying population. Instead the backward countries may have the chance for a technological development which keeps the industrial apparatus in line with the vital needs and freely developing faculties of human beings" ("The Obsolescence of Marxism," in N. Lobkowicz [ed.], *Marx and the Western World* [Notre Dame, Ind., 1967], p. 415).

49 Jürgen Habermas, *Knowledge and Human Interests* (London, 1972), p. 133 (hereafter cited as *KHL*); Jürgen Habermas, "Conservatism and Capitalist Crisis," *New Left Review*, no. 115 (1979), pp. 81–2.

50 Hannah Arendt, *The Human Condition* (Chicago, 1974), esp. pts. 3–4.

51 *TP*, p. 8; Habermas, "A Reply to My Critics," pp. 223–6, 274.

52 This point underpins the occasional remark by Habermas that the achievement of democratic socialism "would...not lead to the abolition of poverty but assume it" (*Kultur und Kritik* [Frankfurt am Main, 1973], p. 84); cf. his earlier formulation of a theory of "consumption asceticism" appropriate to late capitalist conditions, in "Soziologisch Notizen zum Verhältnis von Arbeit und Freizeit," in G. Funke (ed.), *Konkrete Vernunft: Festschrift für E. Rothacker* (Bonn, 1958), p. 231.

53 Habermas, *Kultur und Kritik*, p. 86; Jürgen Habermas, *Philosophisch-politisch Profile* (Frankfurt am Main, 1971), p. 217; *TRS*, pp. 49 and 119: "The growth of the productive forces is not the same as the ultimate goal of the 'good life'. It can at best serve it."

54 *TRS*, pp. 92, 93.

55 Elements of this now questionable view – which can be traced to random notes within Marx, e.g., "Machinery, gifted with the wonderful power of shortening and fructifying human labour, we behold starving and overworking it. The new-fangled sources of wealth, by some strange weird spell, are turned into sources of want" ("Speech at the Anniversary of the *People's Paper*," in Karl Marx and Frederick Engels, *Selected Works*, vol. 1 [Moscow, 1969], p. 500), – reach their apogee in the tradition of technological Marxism. This tradition bestowed mystique upon the productive efficiency of bourgeois modernity by thinking in terms of a use–abuse continuum: While restructuring relations outside the factories and offices (and thus abolishing the profit imperative), revolution was to leave untouched the hierarchic divisions and instrumental domination within the realm of work itself. Such factory and office discipline was seen as the price to be paid for the technological superiority of the forces of production bequeathed to the postcapitalist epoch. An early expression of this technological Marxism is to be found in Engels's discussion of the problem of authority in large-scale industry: "If man, by dint of his knowledge and inventive genius, has subdued the forces of nature, the latter avenge themselves upon him by subjecting him in so far as he employs them, to a veritable despotism, independent of all social organization. Wanting to abolish authority in large-scale industry is tantamount to wanting

to abolish industry itself, to destroy the power loom in order to return to the spinning wheel" ("On Authority," in Karl Marx and Frederick Engels, *Basic Writings in Politics and Philosophy*, ed. L. Feuer [Garden City, N.Y., 1959], p. 483). In a different context, this was also Lenin's view; see his " 'Left-Wing' Childishness and the Petty Bourgeois Mentality," in *Selected Works*, vol. 2 (Moscow, 1970), esp. p. 702; and his "The Taylor System – Man's Enslavement by the Machine," in *On Workers' Control and Nationalization of Industry* (Moscow, 1970), pp. 15–17. These arguments on behalf of the technological superiority of the capitalist division of labor can be traced at least to Adam Smith and are commonplace in many mainstream historians' discussions of the introduction of the factory system. See, for example, P. Mantoux, *The Industrial Revolution in the Eighteenth Century* (New York, 1962), p. 246; "The factory system... was the necessary outcome of the use of machinery"; and D. S. Landes,, *The Unbound Prometheus* (Cambridge, 1976), p. 81: "[The first Industrial Revolution] required machines which not only replaced hand labour but *compelled* the concentration of production in factories – in other words, machines whose appetite for energy was too large for domestic sources of power *and whose mechanical superiority was sufficient to break down the resistance of the older forms of hand production*" (emphasis mine).

56 In opposition to the thesis that modern industry developed under pressure from the objective necessities of new and more efficient technologies, see Stephen Marglin's argument in "What Do Bosses Do?" (Harvard University, mimeo, 1971), published subsequently in the *Review of Radical Political Economics*, vol. 6, no. 2 (1974), pp. 60–112; cf. David Dickson, *Alternative Technology and the Politics of Technical Change* (Glasgow, 1974), ch. 3; and Dan Clawson, *Bureaucracy and the Labor Process* (New York, 1980). The thesis that the development of the factory system was tied to the perceived need to discipline wage labor through direct means of surveillance is defended by Anthony Giddens, *A Contemporary Critique of Historical Materialism* (London, 1982), ch. 6.

57 Cf. Maurice Dobb, *Studies in the Development of Capitalism* (New York, 1975), pp. 266–7; Dobb has stressed that these putting-out and craft relations persisted well into the nineteenth century in outwork trades such as saddling and ironmongering, in factory trades such as bridge stocking and stocktaking in the coal mines (the "butty" system), and in the rolling mills of the iron industries.

58 Marx, *Capital*, vol. 1, pp. 398–99.

59 Cf. A. Honneth, "Arbeit und instrumentales Handeln," in A. Honneth and U. Jaeggi (eds.), *Arbeit, Handlung, Normativität* (Frankfurt, 1980); and Jean Rousselet, *L'Allergie au travail* (Paris, 1974).

60 Stuart Hall et al., *Resistance through Rituals* (London, 1976).

61 This dialectic of resistance and administrative incorporation is commonly at work in employers' attempts to coax workers into reproducing their own bureaucratic servitude. The success of these capital-directed strategies of incorporation seems to depend very much on (1) the degree to which individual units of capital can secure their power vis-à-vis the state and other units of capital and (2) the degree to which the direct producers have been politicized by their own autonomous public spheres. Especially when introduced at the discretion of oligopoly capital, programs for job enrichment, participation in target setting, and so on can, in the short run at least, ensure both profit and labor discipline.

62 Cf. André Gorz, *Abschied vom Proletariat: Jenseit des Sozialismus* (Frankfurt am Main, 1980); and André Gorz, "Nine Theses for a Future Left," *Telos*, no. 48 (Summer 1981), p. 95: "The socialization of production necessarily implies that the microprocessors or the ball bearings, the sheet iron or the motor fuels be interchangeable no

matter where they were produced, and thus that work as well as machines have interchangeable characteristics everywhere."

63 Ivan Illich has argued persuasively, although from an overly naturalistic perspective, that a "convivial" society – one that sought to maximize autonomous and creative intercourse among persons and their natural environment – would necessitate a considerable reduction of the bureaucratic rationality of late capitalism. According to Illich, conviviality would imply a balance between those *programmed* tools which themselves create or structure demands they are supposed to satisfy and those *convivial* tools which directly foster autonomous relations among social actors. See especially his *Tools for Conviviality* (New York, 1973), whose arguments were at one time taken up by André Gorz in his contributions to *The Division of Labour* (Hassocks, 1978). Also relevant here is Pierre Rosanvallon's *L'Age de l'autogestion* (Paris, 1976).

64 *TRS*, p. 88; Jürgen Habermas, "Ernst Bloch – A Marxist Romantic," *Salmagundi*, no. 10–11 (1960–70), p. 320.

65 As several historians have recently emphasized, the growth of legitimacy of the new sciences in the seventeenth century was by no means unchallenged. In contrast to the more sober, bureaucratic discourses of the new mechanical philosophy, herme-ticism, for example, depicted the world of nature as sentient and alive, as bound together by stellar influences and secret ties of antipathy and sympathy. The natural magical mastery of this nature was accordingly to proceed through the deployment of incantations, amulets, music, numerologies, etc. Above all, this mastery was seen as conditional upon the species' self-understanding as a magus, as a facilitator guided by (no longer) secret traditions of knowledge of the essential forces in the universe. See, for example, Walter Pagel, *Paracelsus* (Basle, 1958); and Frances A. Yates, *Giordano Bruno and the Hermetic Tradition* (London, 1964).

66 *KHI*, chs. 5–6. Habermas here refers especially to Peirce's essays "Questions concerning Faculties Claimed for Man," "Fixation of Belief," and "How to Make Our Ideas Clear," which are assembled in C. S. Peirce, *Collected Papers*, ed. Charles Harts-horne and Paul Weiss (Cambridge, Mass., 1960).

67 *KHI*, p. 336, note 30; cf. *KHI*, pp. 137, 139.

68 Ibid., p. 124.

69 At least this is Karl-Otto Apel's argument in "Der philosophische Hintergrund der Entstehung des Pragmatismus bei Ch. S. Peirce," in *Charles Sanders Peirce: Schriften*, ed. K-O. Apel, vol. 1 (Frankfurt am Main, 1967), pp. 13-153.

70 K. R. Popper, *The Open Society and Its Enemies* (London, 1966), vol. 2, p. 224.

71 H. Putnam, "What Is 'Realism'?" *Proceedings of the Aristotelean Society*, vol. 76 (1976), p. 177.

72 K. R. Popper, *The Logic of Scientific Discovery* (London, 1965), p. 279; cf. K. R. Popper, *Conjectures and Refutations* (London, 1963), 113: "It is only in searching for refutations that science can hope to learn and to advance."

73 *KHI*, p. 121.

74 Ibid., p. 98. On "nature-in-itself" as a postulate or limit concept of Habermas's theory of the natural sciences, see his "A Reply to My Critics," pp. 241–2, 247; and Thomas McCarthy, *The Critical Theory of Jürgen Habermas* (Cambridge, Mass., 1978), pp. 113–25.

75 Jürgen Habermas, "Rationalism Divided in Two," in Anthony Giddens (ed.), *Positivism and Sociology* (London, 1974), p. 206.

76 In Habermas's view, Peirce wrongly affirmed the possibility that science could generate universally true propositions that are the correlates of natural reality. This mistake, which produced "hidden but unyielding" positivist effects, was a consequence

of Peirce's adoption of a circular, Scholastic realist understanding of the necessary relation of particular and universal: "The fact of scientific progress induces Peirce to define universal propositions exclusively in relation to the anticipated end of the process of inquiry as a whole and yet to assume at the same time that, in increasing measure, we objectively arrive at true statements even *before* the consummation of this process – despite subjective uncertainty about the truth value of every single one of these statements. If this is so, however, then we must be able *per se* to infer a universal matter of fact from a given, finite number of singular cases, although *for us* the validity of this procedure cannot be compelling, but at best probable" (*KHI*, p. 110).

77 *The Logic of Scientific Discovery*, p. 276.

78 Habermas, *Communication and the Evolution of Society*, p. 104.

79 Cf. the remarks of Dijksterhuis, *Mechanization of the World Picture*, p. 30: "Classical mechanics, with its principles of inertia and its proportionality of force and acceleration, makes assertions which not only are never confirmed by everyday experience, but whose direct experimental verification is fundamentally impossible: one cannot indeed introduce a material point all by itself into an indefinite void and then cause a force that is constant in direction and magnitude to act on it; it is not even possible to attach any rational meaning to this formulation."

80 This suggestion can be extrapolated from the well-known writings of Thomas Kuhn on scientific paradigms. These writings analyze scientific paradigms as "disciplinary matrices," i.e., as discourses marked by strong networks of commitments – conceptual, methodological, and instrumental – that serve to sustain these discourses' appearance as progressive and slowly maturing. According to Kuhn, scientific revolutions – for example, Einstein's inversion and replacement of the Newtonian view that time is absolute and that velocities add in a Galilean way – are discontinuous, *noncumulative* episodes in which a scientific paradigm is replaced in whole or in part by a seemingly more comprehensive, but nevertheless incommensurable, paradigm. (For Galileo, for example, a swinging stone was interpreted as a pendulum; for Aristotle, it was an example of retarded fall.) According to Kuhn, a recently triumphed scientific paradigm is not necessarily of a higher, more comprehensive generality. He emphasizes that this process of paradigm rupture and replacement is enormously complex: "Paradigm debates are not really about relative problem-solving ability, though for good reasons they are usually couched in these terms. Instead, the issue is which paradigm should in the future guide research on problems many of which neither competitor can yet claim to resolve completely" (*The Structure of Scientific Revolutions* [Chicago, 1962], p. 157. This thesis has a close affinity with the work of Gaston Bachelard, Foucault, and others; cf. also Michael Polanyi's *Personal Knowledge: Towards a Post-Critical Philosophy* (New York, 1964), p. 138, which speaks of scientists' "frameworks of commitment," as a consequence of which "it is the normal practice of scientists to ignore evidence which appears incompatible with the accepted system of scientific knowledge, in the hope that it will eventually prove false or irrelevant." Even Popper tends to admit this thesis, serving an injunction against those who would seek to criticize the totality of beliefs that constitute an already established scientific paradigm: "Almost all the vast amount of background knowledge...will, for practical reasons, necessarily remain unquestioned;...the misguided attempt to question it all – that is to say, *to start from scratch* – can easily lead to the breakdown of critical debate...Thus all criticism must be piecemeal...we should stick to our problem...and try to solve no more than one problem at a time" (*Conjectures and Refutations*, p. 238).

81 Mary Hesse, *The Structure of Scientific Inference* (London, 1974), pp. 51ff. and ch. 5.

Her theses on this point are crucial, despite her highly implausible, and certainly undemonstrable, suggestion (ibid., p. 132) that at least some of the more powerful coherence conditions that attend scientific inference result from genetic inheritance.

82 P. K. Feyerabend, "Problems of Empiricism," in R. G. Colodny (ed.), *University of Pittsburgh Series in Philosophy of Science*, vols. 2 (1965) and 4 (1970); cf. Barry Barnes's discussion of the weaknesses of attempts to establish definitively the necessary and sufficient conditions of what is to count as "science," in *Scientific Knowledge and Sociological Theory* (London, 1974), ch. 3.

83 *KHI*, pp. 161–4, 191–3.

84 These and other assertions are discussed in M. Teich and R. M. Young (eds.), *Changing Perspectives in the History of Science* (London, 1973); David Bloor, *Knowledge and Social Imagery* (London, 1976); and Barnes, *Scientific Knowledge and Sociological Theory*; see also Gaston Bachelard's very interesting account of the irrational illusions deployed in defense of eighteenth-century theories of heat in *The Psychoanalysis of Fire* (Boston, 1968).

85 Feyerabend has considerably extended this point, contending that scientific argumentation, in respect of its propagandizing strategies, is closely analogous to the dogmatism of religious and political movements. See Paul K. Feyerabend, *Against Method* (London, 1975), p. 17; and Paul K. Feyerabend, "Classical Empiricism," in R. E. Butts and J. W. Davis (eds.), *The Methodological Heritage of Newton* (Oxford, 1970), p. 150. This claim is in one respect misleading, because it does not pursue its theses radically enough: Their nihilistic implications are premature consequences of a failure to analyze more deeply the counterfactual conditions or "transcendental" rules that make possible the proliferation of imaginative scientific discourses in the first place (cf. Essay 2).

86 Wolf Schäfer, "Normative Finalisierung: Eine Perspektive," in Gernot Böhme et al., *Starnberger Studien 1: Die gesellschaftliche Orientierung des wissenschaftlichen Fortschritts* (Frankfurt am Main, 1978), pp. 377–415.

87 For some recent discussions of this concern, first raised in the 1930s radical science movement, see Ravetz, *Scientific Knowledge and Its Social Problems*, p. 3; Jeremy Ravetz, "Ideological Crisis in Science," *New Scientist and Science Journal*, 1 July 1971, pp. 35–6; and Jeremy Ravetz, *Science in Crisis* (Eastern Green, 1975). Cf. also Feyerabend, *Against Method*, sec. 18; and Paul K. Feyerabend, "How to Defend Society against Science," *Radical Philosophy*, no. 11 (Summer 1975), pp. 3–8.

88 The possibility of a world transformed into a "planetary hospital" directed by spiritual engineers bent on fabricating subjects adapted to these conditions is discussed and criticized by Ivan Illich, *Medical Nemesis: The Expropriation of Health* (London, 1975).

89 M. Foucault, *The Birth of the Clinic* (New York, 1975); M. Foucault, *The Archaeology of Knowledge* (London, 1972), pp. 163–5; Ian Hacking, "How Should We Do the History of Statistics?" *I and C*, no. 8 (Spring 1981), pp. 15–26.

90 See, for example, Hesse's discussion of the complementarity and constancy of accounts of "low-level laws of behaviour" of electricity in Maxwell's interpretation of atomic electric charges and the later field interpretation of charges, in *The Structure of Scientific Inference*, ch. 11.

91 Cf. Barry Commoner, *The Closing Circle* (New York, 1972.)

92 Cf. Commoner's criticism of molecular history in *Science and Survival* (New York, 1967), esp. ch. 3; and Ronald Munson (ed.), *Man and Nature: Philosophical Issues in Biology* (New York, 1975).

93 Cf. Hans Jonas, "Technology and Responsibility: Reflections on the New Tasks of Ethics," in *Philosophical Essays: From Ancient Creed to Technological Man* (Englewood

Cliffs, N.J., 1974); and I. Prigogine and I. Stengers, *Dialog mit der Natur: Neue Wege naturwissenschaftlichen Denkens* (Munich, 1981). From a different perspective, this thesis was earlier raised by Ernst Bloch and Herbert Marcuse. See, for example, Bloch's classic proposal for the replacement of "abstract-bourgeois technique" by "concrete-alliance technique" (the preservation and development of productive forces that facilitate the recuperation of outer nature and autonomous social labor) in *Das Prinzip Hoffnung* (Berlin, 1955), vol. 2, p. 259; cf. Herbert Marcuse, *One Dimensional Man* (London, 1968), pp. 135–6: "Science, *by virtue of its own method* and concepts, has projected and promoted a universe in which the domination of nature has remained linked to the domination of man – a link which tends to be fatal to this universe as a whole. Nature, scientifically comprehended and mastered, reappears in the technical apparatus of production and destruction which sustains and improves the life of the individuals while subordinating them to the masters of the apparatus. If this is the case, then the change in the direction of progress, which might sever this fatal link, would also affect the very structure of science – the scientific project. Its hypotheses, without losing their rational character, would develop in an essentially different experimental context (that of a pacified world); consequently, science would arrive at essentially different concepts of nature and establish essentially different facts." Habermas's discussion of Bloch is found in *Theorie und Praxis*, pp. 418–21, and in "Ernst Bloch"; his brief responses to Herbert Marcuse are launched in *TRS*, esp. pp. 81–90.

94 Lynn White, Jr., "The Historical Roots of Our Ecologic Crisis," in Paul Shepard and Daniel McKinley (eds.), *The Subversive Science: Essays toward an Ecology of Man* (Boston, 1969), p. 349.

95 This has been argued by, for example, Theodore Roszak, "Ecology and Mysticism," *Humanist*, vol. 86, no. 5 (1971), p. 136.

96 Herbert Marcuse, *Counterrevolution and Revolt* (Boston, 1972), p. 62; cf. Ernst Bloch, *Subjekt-Objekt: Erläuterungen zu Hegel* (Berlin, 1952), p. 195: "Just as in the commodity only the price is important, so in nature only quantifiability and not its qualitative content is crucial." Marx also pursued this theme in the *Grundrisse*, p. 410: "For the first time, nature in bourgeois modernity becomes purely an object for humankind, purely a matter of utility; ceases to be recognized as a power for itself; and the theoretical discovery of its autonomous laws appears merely as a ruse so as to subjugate it under human needs, whether as an object of consumption or as a means of production."

97 Of considerable relevance here is Edmund Husserl's thesis (in *The Crisis of European Sciences and Transcendental Phenomenology* [New York, 1965]) that the modern sciences have forgotten their "embeddedness" within the preconceptual dimension of practical life activity, that they have fallen victim to a certain "natural attitude," viz., a contemplative standpoint that represents the world dogmatically through naïvely accepted concepts that become synonymous with the "things themselves."

98 Jacques Monod, *Chance and Necessity* (London, 1972).

99 See Max Horkheimer, "Materialismus und Moral," *Zeitschrift für Sozialforschung*, vol. 2, pt. 2 (1933), p. 184, for some early discussion of the possible configuration of relations between humans and nature in a socialist society. This matter is taken up by Ernst Bloch in "Über Freiheit und objektive Gesetzlichkeit, politisch gefasst," *Deutsche Zeitschrift für Philosophie*, vol. 2, pt. 4 (1954), p. 818: "With regard to nature, in socialist society there is neither an aimless exploitation (with the profit-Subject in command), a naive paternalism towards nature, nor a worshipping of the existing natural realm." More recently, on the question of the needs of outer nature, see

William Leiss, *The Limits to Satisfaction* (Toronto, 1976), esp. pp. 113–24; and John Passmore, *Man's Responsibility for Nature* (London, 1974), pt. 4.

100 Thus it is forgotten (to take one example) that hunting and gathering societies were largely responsible for the extermination of many of the large mammals, e.g. the woolly mammoth in North America, the New Zealand moa bird, the giant kangaroo in Australia; similarly, these societies' use of fire resulted in the radical transformation of the face of the earth; see O. C. Stewart, "Fire as the First Great Force Employed by Man," in W. L. Thomas, Jr. (ed.), *Man's Role in Changing the Face of the Earth* (Chicago, 1956), pp. 115–33.

101 "Goethe, in an arrogant yet profound phase, showed how all Nature's attempts only have value in so far as the artist interprets her stammering words, meets her half-way, and speaks aloud what she really means" (*Schopenhauer as Educator*, in *Collected Works*, vol. 9, sec. 5). The origins of this (originally patriarchal) metaphor can be traced to the German tradition of Nature Philosophy generated by Leibniz, Boehme, Goethe, Schelling, Oken, Kielmeyer, and others. Their themes indirectly exerted considerable influence on the earlier members of the Frankfurt tradition (as Habermas himself notes in *TRS*, pp. 85–6). Theodor Adorno's proposal that the eyes of nature be opened in order that it might become "on the poor earth what perhaps it would like to be" (*Aesthetische Theorie* [Frankfurt am Main, 1970], p. 107) is repeated by others within this tradition. See, for example, Marcuse, *Counterrevolution and Revolt*, p. 66; Max Horkheimer, *The Eclipse of Reason* (New York, 1974), ch. 3; and Walter Benjamin: "Nature is sad because it is mute. However, the inverse formulation is more profoundly close to the essence of nature: the sadness of nature renders it mute" (cited in Russell Jacoby, "Towards a Critique of Automatic Marxism: The Politics of Philosophy from Lukács to the Frankfurt School," *Telos*, no. 10 [Winter 1971], p. 141). Note that the Frankfurt critics of contemporary scientific-technical progress were at the same time hostile to the private fad of sentimental animal and nature loving; see, for example, Max Horkheimer, "Egoismus und Freiheitsbewegung," in *Traditionelle und kritische Theorie* (Frankfurt am Main, 1970), p. 157.

102 Brian Easlea (*Liberation and the Aims of Science* [London, 1973], p. 279) has suggested that less reductionist, "anti-physicalist" perspectives – those which represent the world of nature (including the human species) as a multiplicity of interacting levels, higher levels being irreducible to the lower and vice versa – have appeared as a central theme within twentieth-century relativity theory and quantum mechanics. In his view, this development is sustained by the sciences' heightened awareness of two crucial themes: first, the recognition that the objects of investigation and the investigative apparatus itself must be analytically distinguished and secondly, the insistence that not all macroproperties of matter can be explained in terms of microproperties.

103 Bahro, *Elemente einer neuen Politik*; A. Touraine et al., *La Prophétie anti-nucléaire* (Paris, 1980); André Gorz, *Ecology as Politics* (Boston, 1980), pp. 3–9; cf. the transcript of a stimulating public discussion of this and other questions pertaining to the problem of ecological destruction in Cornelius Castoriadis et al., *De l'écologie à l'autonomie* (Paris, 1981). A revealing overview of state strategies of co-optation is provided by K. G. Nichols, *Technology on Trial: Public Participation in Decision-Making Related to Science and Technology* (Paris, 1979).

104 *TRS*, p. 74; Habermas, "A Reply to My Critics," pp. 243–4.

7. Liberalism under siege

1 "Of the First Principles of Government," in *Political Essays*, ed. Charles W. Hendel (Indianapolis, 1953), pp. 24–7. Hume, it should be noted, was unwilling to reduce

the legitimacy of political power wholly to this "sense" (as much contemporary political science has effectively done), recognizing tradition and rights to property as additional standards from which government draws its strength and authority.

2 Max Weber, *Economy and Society*, ed. Guenther Roth and Claus Wittich (Berkeley, Calif., 1978), vol. 1, ch. 1, sec. 5–7 (where actors' ascription of legitimacy to a social order is discussed through the concepts of tradition, affectual faith, value rationality, and legality); cf. Weber, *Economy and Society*, vol. 1, ch. 3, secs. 1–4, where legal, traditional, and charismatic authority are considered more precisely as pure types of legitimate domination.

3 Ibid., vol. 1, p. 37.

4 These controversies date from the time of Carl Schmitt's *Legalität und Legitimität* (Munich, 1932). Schmitt sought to complement the original Weberian theory of legitimacy with another: the unfettering of the plebiscite as the fundamental means of establishing the legitimacy of government and constitution. This proposal did not break with the uncritical and potentially authoritarian Weberian account; see the critical review of Schmitt by O. Kirchheimer and N. Leites, "Bemerkungen zu Carl Schmitts *Legalität und Legitimität*," *Archiv für Sozialwissenschaft und Sozialpolitik*, no. 68 (1932–3), pp. 457–87. Later discussions of the Weberian account include J. Winckelmann, *Legitimität und Legalität in Max Webers Herrschaftssoziologie* (Tübingen, 1952); Wolfgang J. Mommsen, *Max Weber und die deutsche Politik, 1880–1920* (Tübingen, 1959), pp. 414–9; A. Karsten, *Das Problem der Legitimität in Max Webers Idealtypus der rationalen Herrschaft* (Hamburg, 1960); and Fritz Loos, *Zur Wert- und Rechts-lehre Max Webers* (Tübingen, 1970). Some important discussion around the theme of "Legitimation Problems of Modern States" was initiated at the 1975 Kongress der Deutschen Vereinigung für Politische Wissenschaft, a portion of whose proceedings is published in Rolf Ebbighausen et al, *Bürgerlicher Staat und politische Legitimation* (Frankfurt am Main, 1976). This discussion was heavily indebted to the earlier controversy between Luhmann and Habermas; see N. Luhmann, *Legitimation durch Verfahren* (Neuwied, 1969); Jürgen Habermas and Niklas Luhmann, *Theorie der Gesellschaft oder Sozialtechnologie – Was leistet die Systemforschung?* (Frankfurt am Main, 1975); and Habermas's rendition of several Starnberg projects in *Legitimation Crisis* (Boston, 1975), and *Communication and the Evolution of Society* (Boston, 1979), pp. 178–205.

5 Robert MacIver, *The Web of Government* (New York, 1947), esp. pp. 225–6.

6 Luhmann, *Legitimation durch Verfahrung*.

7 Talcott Parsons, "Authority, Legitimation, and Political Action," in *Structure and Process in Modern Societies* (Glencoe, Ill., 1960).

8 S. M. Lipset, *Political Man: The Social Bases of Politics* (New York, 1960), p. 46. Compare Richard Löwenthal's contention ("Political Legitimacy and Cultural Change in West and East," *Social Research*, vol. 46, no. 3 [1979], p. 406) that "the legitimacy of a political order requires, in addition to the clarity, consistency, and effective functioning of the legally established procedures,...a value consensus between the governing...and the governed, and a confidence of the governed, rooted in their experience, that this procedure will normally promote successful action in the direction of those common values." This neo-Weberian formulation is repeated by Robert E. Lane, "The Legitimacy Bias: Conservative Man in Market and State," in Bogdan Denitch (ed.), *Legitimation of Regimes* (London, 1979), pp. 55–79.

9 *Legitimation Crisis*, p. 97.

10 Alan Wolfe, *The Limits of Legitimacy* (New York, 1977); James O'Connor, *The Fiscal Crisis of the State* (New York, 1973), pp. 4–7, 69–70; James O'Connor, "*The Fiscal Crisis of the State* Revisited: Economic Crisis and Reagan's Budget Policy," *Kapitalistate*, no.

9 (1981), pp. 45–6; Ralph Miliband, *The State in Capitalist Society* (London, 1973), chs. 7, 8.

11 Hannah Arendt, "What Was Authority?" in Carl J. Friedrich (ed.), *Authority* (Cambridge, Mass., 1958); Manfred Riedel, "Transcendental Politics? Political Legitimacy and the Concept of Civil Society in Kant," *Social Research*, Autumn 1981, pp. 588–613; cf. also John Schaar's "Legitimacy in the Modern State," in Philip Green and Sanford Levinson (eds.) *Power and Community* (New York, 1970; republished in John Schaar, *Legitimacy in the Modern State* [London, 1981]), behind whose preliminary questions most contemporary discussions of the legitimacy problems of late capitalism have fallen. The best critical treatment of the early modern (liberal) theories of legitimacy, obligation, and obedience is that of Carole Pateman, *The Problem of Political Obligation* (Chichester, 1979).

12 Weber, *Economy and Society*, p. 214; Anthony Giddens, *A Contemporary Critique of Historical Materialism* (London, 1982), pp. 64–8.

13 Cf. Harold Laski's classic account of European liberal individualism between the Reformation and the French Revolution in *The Rise of European Liberalism* (London, 1962). This interpretation is clarified and elaborated in C. B. Macpherson, *The Political Theory of Possessive Individualism* (Oxford, 1962), and considerably (and very productively) amended by Pateman, *The Problem of Political Obligation*.

14 *Democracy in America* (New York, 1945), vol. 2, bk. 2, ch. 2, p. 105. Note that the term *bodily individual* refers throughout to the "biological" individual, which, so to speak, is not yet endowed with a particular self-understanding of its body (as *egoistic individual, social individual, narcissist, public citizen*, etc.) in relation to others. This analytic distinction is difficult to render in English. The German language, however, makes it more plausible. For example, Hegel and Marx utilize (to be sure, not always consistently) the term *das Individuum* as the biological individual, whether human or not, in contradistinction to the ethical individual – *das einzelne Individuum* or *der Einzelne (Mensch)* – as a single body whose particular self-understanding and action embody certain universal qualities of the political or social totality. This distinction forms the standpoint from which Marx (*Grundisse* [Harmondsworth, 1973], p. 265) historicized eighteenth-century theories of the bourgeois individual: "Society does not consist of individuals (*Individuen*), but expresses the sum of interrelations, the relations within which these individuals stand . . . To be a slave, to be a citizen, are social characteristics."

15 Cf. J. Huizinga, *The Waning of the Middle Ages* (New York, 1954), ch. 3, an important study of the forms of social interaction in the Netherlands and France during the fourteenth and fifteenth centuries; W. Ullmann, *The Individual and Society in the Middle Ages* (London, 1967), lectures 1, 2; and Marc Bloch, *Feudal Society* (London, 1962), pts. 3–7.

16 Cf. de Tocqueville, *Democracy in America*, vol. 2, bk. 3, ch. 18; and Montesquieu, *The Spirit of the Laws* (New York, 1949), vol. 1, bk. 3, chs. 6–7.

17 Jacob Burckhardt, *The Civilisation of the Renaissance* (London, 1944), p. 81; cf. Colin Morris, *The Discovery of the Individual, 1050–1200* (New York, 1972).

18 The problems of analyzing the complex genealogy of Renaissance individualism can be elided here. It suffices to note that, insofar as the origins of Renaissance discourse were not exclusively within the Renaissance movements themselves, Burckhardt's classic thesis stands in need of considerable reinterpretation. Ernst Troeltsch (*The Social Teaching of the Christian Churches* [New York, 1931], vol. 1, ch. 1) has, for example, suggested that a nascent emphasis on the bodily individual was already present within primitive Christian discourse. According to his account, even the soul of the poorest and most humble individual was of supreme worth under the eye of an omniscient,

omnipotent, and universal God (for whose son, as we know, there was "neither Greek nor Jew, circumcision nor uncircumcision, Barbarian, Scythian, bond nor free...Christ is all and in all," [Col. 3:11], etc.). Analogously, Agnes Heller (*Renaissance Man* [London, 1978]) reappraises the Renaissance notions of individuated humanity, tracing their development from antiquity through (for example) the Judaeo-Christian tradition, Stoicism, and Epicureanism. Consistent with these interpretations, Louis Dumont (in *From Mandeville to Marx: The Genesis and Triumph of Economic Ideology* [Chicago, 1977], p. 15) has correctly modified his earlier exaggerations about the abstractly holistic character of medieval everyday life (in "The Modern Conception of the Individual: Notes on Its Genesis," *Contributions to Indian Sociology*, vol. 8 [1965], pp. 13–61). Each of these interpretations suggests that, against the organicism of the medieval world, the various Renaissance movements effected a transformation – and qualitative expansion – of an other-worldly individualism into more this-worldly forms.

19 Cf. Ernst Cassirer, *The Individual and the Cosmos in Renaissance Philosophy* (New York, 1963); and Ernst Cassirer, *The Philosophy of the Enlightenment* (Princeton, N.J., 1951), pp. 137–40. On the growth of civic humanism or classical republicanism during this period, see Hans Baron, *The Crisis of the Early Italian Renaissance* (Princeton, N.J., 1966); J. G. A. Pocock, *The Machiavellian Moment* (Princeton, N.J., 1975), pt. 2; Quentin Skinner, *The Foundations of Modern Political Thought* (Cambridge, 1978), vol. 1; and Richard C. Trexler, *Public Life in Renaissance Florence* (London, 1981).

20 Cf. Julian H. Franklin (ed.), *Constitutionalism and Resistance in the Sixteenth Century* (London, 1969); J. W. Allen, *A History of Political Thought in the Sixteenth Century* (London, 1961); and Skinner, *Foundations of Modern Political Thought*, vol. 2, chs. 7–9.

21 (Herborn, 1603), trans. and ed. by Frederick S. Carney as *The Politics of Johannes Althusius* (London, 1965); cf. Otto von Gierke, *Natural Law and the Theory of Society, 1500–1800* (Cambridge, 1934), vol. 1, pp. 70–6.

22 Max Weber, *The Protestant Ethic and the Spirit of Capitalism* (New York, 1958); R. H. Tawney, *Religion and the Rise of Capitalism* (New York, 1974).

23 Thomas Hobbes, *Leviathan*, ed. C. B. Macpherson (Harmondsworth, 1972), ch. 8, p. 139.

24 Heller, *Renaissance Man*, ch. 7; Pocock, *The Machiavellian Moment*, pt. 3; *The Political Works of James Harrington* (Cambridge, 1977).

25 Cf. Laski, *The Rise of European Liberalism*, pp. 19–20, 43–4, 54–8, 94ff., which insists that, even in the seventeenth century, this marketeering was by no means only an English phenomenon. The drive to unfetter zones of commodified exchange that were to be protected by state control was powerful among Swiss merchants and had a continuous pedigree in the Low Countries from the sixteenth century; in France, during the last years of Louis XIV, there were the beginnings of a powerful reaction against Colbertism. On these various developments working against statism and mercantilism, see E. Lipson, *The Economic History of England* (London, 1931), vol. 3, chs. 4–5; cf. the debate between Eli F. Heckscher, *Mercantilism*, rev. ed., 2 vols. (London, 1955), and Jacob Viner, "Power versus Plenty in the Seventeenth and Eighteenth Centuries," in his *The Long View and the Short* (Glencoe, Ill., 1958), pp. 287–305. This controversy is surveyed in D. C. Coleman (ed.), *Revisions in Mercantilism* (London, 1969).

26 John Locke, *Two Treatises of Civil Government* (New York, 1963), bk. 2, sec. 202.

27 Robert Paul Wolff, *The Poverty of Liberalism* (Boston, 1968), p. 124.

28 *Leviathan*, chs. 13, 21. Cf. Howard Warrender, *The Political Philosophy of Hobbes: His Theory of Obligation* (Oxford, 1957), whose claim that Hobbes's theory of obligation

crucially depends upon objective natural laws that are binding upon individuals seriously underestimates the importance of Hobbes's notion of (hypothetically) self-assumed obligation.

29 Locke, *Two Treatises*, bk. 2, sec. 22; cf. Locke, *Two Treatises*, sec. 106.

30 *Leviathan*, ch. 21. Here it is argued that subjects are obligated to obey the sovereign only so long as it is capable of monopolizing the means of violence *qua* sovereign. In the case of a legitimate sovereign defeated in war, individual subjects may withdraw their powers of consent, but they must bequeath their obedience to the victorious sovereign. Cf. Locke, *Two Treatises*, bk. 2, secs. 221–2, 240; for Locke the majority of individuals' political obligations to obedience to the government of the day are dissolved whenever these governments act illegitimately, that is, contrary to their "trust."

31 *Leviathan*, chs. 17, 29; cf. Thomas Hobbes, *De Cive*, in *The English Works of Thomas Hobbes*, ed. William Molesworth (London, 1839–44), vol. 2, chs. 5–7.

32 Locke, *Two Treatises*, bk. 2, secs. 22, 87, 89. Cf. Peter Laslett's contention that, for Locke, the relation between government and governed is not contractual but one of trust ("Introduction," in Locke, *Two Treatises*, pp. 126–30). This claim is misleading, precisely because the concept of trust is central only in the second phase of Locke's contractarianism.

33 On the growth of demands for "protective democracy," see C. B. Macpherson, *The Life and Times of Liberal Democracy* (Oxford, 1977), ch. 2. Concerning the emergence of the liberal public sphere as that space mediating the state apparatus and the private affairs of individuals in civil society, see Jürgen Habermas, *Strukturwandel der Öffentlichkeit: Untersuchungen zu einer Kategorie der bürgerlichen Gesellschaft* (Neuwied, 1975); Richard Sennett, *The Fall of Public Man* (New York, 1978), pt. 2; and Nannerl O. Keohane, *Philosophy and the State in France* (Princeton, N.J., 1980), chs. 11, 15, and pp. 454–7. Classical liberal arguments for public discussion, "democratical government," and the inalienable rights of individuals to rescind their contracts include John Millar, *Origin of the Distinction of Ranks*, ed. W. C. Lehmann (Cambridge, 1960), ch. 5; Immanuel Kant, "What Is Enlightenment?" in *On History*, ed. L. W. Beck (Indianapolis, 1975); *The Political Writings of Thomas Jefferson*, ed. E. Dumbauld (Indianapolis, 1976); chs. 2–3; and J. G. Fichte, *Beiträge zur Berichtigung der Urteile des Publicums über die französische Revolution* (1793), in *Sämmtliche Werke* (Berlin, 1845), vol. 6, p. 159. The slow eighteenth-century emergence of liberal demands for protective democracy of course carried with it a great and unforeseen danger for the male propertied classes. Their defense of the principles of public freedoms and free periodic elections against tyranny no doubt fostered the growth of complaints by women, artisans, and the laboring classes that this remained an age of tyranny. This dialectic is evident in, for example, Mary Wollstonecraft's *Vindication of the Rights of Woman* (Harmondsworth, 1978), and in the growth of English Jacobinism, whose remarkable attempts to establish autonomous, plebeian publics are best analyzed by Günther Lottes, *Politisches Aufklärung und plebejisches Publikum: Zur Theorie und Praxis des englischen Radikalismus im späten 18. Jahrhundert* (Munich, 1979).

34 Among the best recent accounts of the emergence of the primacy of the economic view in the modern world are Dumont, *From Mandeville to Marx*; Albert Hirschman, *The Passions and the Interests* (Princeton, N.J., 1977); Macpherson, *Political Theory of Possessive Individualism*; Jean Baudrillard, *The Mirror of Production* (St. Louis, 1975); Marshall Sahlins, *Culture and Practical Reason* (Chicago, 1976); and, on the Scottish Enlightenment, Ronald Meek, *Social Science and the Ignoble Savage* (Cambridge, 1976).

35 Isaiah Berlin, *Four Essays on Liberty* (Oxford, 1969), esp. pp. 127–9; cf. Gierke, *Natural*

Law, according to which the modern natural law theorists (from Hobbes to Kant) posited the sovereign individual as the fundamental source of "Group-authority."

36 *De Cive,* p. 109. In opposition to all others, each individual (to paraphrase Bentham on Locke) emerged fully armed, just like the fruit that sprang from the serpents' teeth planted by Cadmus in the corner of his cucumber plot. See also Bernard Mandeville's comments on "Savage Man" and the origins of the state in *The Fable of the Bees,* ed. F. B. Kaye (Oxford, 1957), vol. 1, pp. 41ff., and the first contractarian attempt – by Rousseau – to historicize civil society through a reinterpretation of the savage's movements from the state of nature into modernity: J. J. Rousseau, *The Social Contract and Discourses* (New York, 1967).

37 Cf. note 24 to this essay; Locke, *Two Treatises,* bk. 2, sec. 19 (on the state of nature as a governed, but not yet politically constituted, community of Christian believers, whose condition is that of "peace, goodwill, mutual assistance, and preservation"); S. Pufendorf, *The Law of Nature and Nations,* ed. J. Barbeyrac (London, 1749), vol. 2, bk. 3, sec. 15; Mandeville, *The Fable of the Bees,* vol. 1, p. 10; Adam Smith, *Wealth of Nations* (New York, 1937), bk. 3, ch. 4, bk. 4, ch. 2; Thomas Paine, *The Rights of Man* (New York, 1942), pt. 2, ch. 1; and Immanuel Kant's metaphor of trees in a forest, according to which the legally secured unfettering of individuals' unsocial sociability (*ungesellige Geselligkeit*) is desirable, because people "by seeking to deprive each other of air and sunlight, compel each other to find these by upward growth, so that they grow beautiful and straight – whereas those which put out branches at will, in freedom and in isolation from others, grow stunted, bent and twisted" ("Idea for a Universal History with a Cosmopolitan Purpose," in *Kant's Political Writings,* ed. Hans Reiss [Cambridge, 1970], p. 46).

38 Elie Halévy, *The Growth of Philosophic Radicalism* (London, 1972), p. 15.

39 I. Kant, "On the Common Saying: 'This May Be True in Theory, but It Does Not Apply in Practice,'" in *Kant's Political Writings,* ed. Hans Reiss (Cambridge, 1970), pp. 73–9.

40 Lawrence Stone, "The Rise of the Nuclear Family in Early Modern England: The Patriarchal Stage," in Charles E. Rosenberg (ed.), *The Family in History* (Pittsburgh, 1975), pp. 13–57; Philippe Ariès, *Centuries of Childhood: A Social History of Family Life* (New York, 1962), pp. 365–415. Stone's conclusion that this increased patriarchal authoritarianism was but a transitional stage to the "more individualistic" and "compassionate and egalitarian nuclear family of the eighteenth century" ("Rise of the Nuclear Family," pp. 14, 57) is evidently misleading; it is precisely during this period that a new phase of "government" of household life commenced, as has been suggested by Jacques Donzelot, *The Policing of Families* (New York, 1979). This criticism is also applicable to Edward Shorter's apologetic account of the emergence of the bourgeois family form as synonymous with the unfettering of the individual's naturalistic "wish to be free" and with a "surge of sentiment," romantic love, and mutuality (*The Making of the Modern Family* [New York, 1975]).

41 Ariès, *Centuries of Childhood,* pp. 257–8; Stone, "Rise of the Nuclear Family," pp. 36–49; Norbert Elias, *The Civilizing Process* (New York, 1978).

42 Ariès, *Centuries of Childhood,* pp. 365ff.; cf. Mark Poster, *Critical Theory of the Family* (New York, 1978), ch. 7, where the bourgeois family form is analyzed and compared with that of the aristocracy, peasantry, and working class.

43 See, for example, Sir Robert Filmer, *Patriarcha and Other Political Works,* ed. Peter Laslett (Oxford, 1949); cf., more generally, Gordon Schochet, *Patriarchalism in Political Thought* (Oxford, 1975).

44 Locke, *Two Treatises,* bk. 1, sec. 47.

45 Hobbes, *Leviathan*, pp. 253–4; cf. Teresa Brennan and Carole Pateman, " 'Mere Aux-iliaries to the Commonwealth': Women and the Origins of Liberalism," *Political Studies*, vol. 27, no. 2 (1979), pp. 183–200; and Jean Bethke Elshtain, *Public Man, Private Woman* (Princeton, N.J., 1981), ch. 3.

46 Hobbes, *Leviathan*, p. 254; Thomas Hobbes, "Philosophical Rudiments concerning Government and Society," in *The English Works*, vol. 2, pp. 114–125.

47 Hobbes, *Leviathan*, p. 285.

48 "Philosophical Rudiments," pp. 118, 121–2; *Leviathan*, pp. 250, 253.

49 Locke, *Two Treatises*, bk. 1, sec. 48; cf. his *Essays on the Law of Nature*, ed. W. von Leyden (Oxford, 1958), essay 5, p. 173.

50 *Law of Nature and Nations*, bk. 7, ch. 2, sec. 20.

51 As Gierke (*Natural Law*) pointed out, this historically informed critique of contrac-tarianism dates at least from the time of the Dutch jurist Horn (1620–70?). Cf. also J. W. Gough, *The Social Contract* (Oxford, 1957), ch. 12.

52 "Of the First Principles of Government"; cf. David Hume, "Of the Original Contract," in *Political Essays*, pp. 43–61; and his earliest discussion of the original contract in *A Treatise of Human Nature* (London, 1960), vol. 2, pp. 235–9. Cf. also Jeremy Bentham's *A Fragment of Government* (Oxford, 1891), ch. 1, secs. 36–48. According to Bentham, the doctrine of the original contract must be rejected as a mere fiction with sandy foundations, the principle of utility being a sufficient explanation of political duty.

53 *Hegel's Philosophy of Right*, ed. T. M. Knox (Oxford, 1973), p. 59.

54 Edmund Burke, *Reflections on the Revolution in France*, ed. Conor Cruise O'Brien (Harmondsworth, 1969), p. 194.

55 William Paley, *Moral and Political Philosophy* (London, 1785), bk. 6, ch. 3.

56 See Steven Lukes's analysis of early French critiques of *individualisme* in his *Individ-ualism* (Oxford, 1973), ch. 1.

57 Henri de Saint-Simon, *The Doctrine of Saint-Simon: An Exposition, First Year, 1828–9*, trans. G. Iggers (Boston, 1958), pp. 174–200 and passim.

58 This is one reason why the widespread twentieth-century concern about the bureau-cratically secured decline of the individual is overdrawn. This concern has its roots in a warning of Friedrich Nietzsche, "The Use and Abuse of History," in *Collected Works*, trans. O. Levy (Edinburgh, 1915), vol. 5, pt. 2, p. 41: "While there has never been such a full-throated chatter about 'free personality', personalities can be seen no more (to say nothing of free ones); but merely men in uniform, with their coats anxiously pulled over their ears." Individuals were seen by Nietzsche as increasingly fashioned to the needs of organized bureaucratic machines and their masters' ad-monitions to fall into line. All individuality is shaken to its foundations by this de-velopment; according to Nietzsche, the bodily individual, no longer sure of itself, begins to suffer from a weakened personality and sinks into its own disordered fantasies. This forewarning was repeated by many nineteenth-century thinkers (cf. Marx and Engels on the militarism of the factory system, J. S. Mill's concern that individuality would be lost among the "industrious sheep" effected by the "despotism of custom," etc.). It was taken up by the Frankfurt circle (whose unsubstantiated and exaggerated theses on the "liquidation of the individual" are here considerably rein-terpreted through the problematic of legitimacy) in numerous well-known works: Herbert Marcuse, "The Struggle against Liberalism in the Totalitarian View of the State," in *Negations: Essays in Critical Theory* (Boston, 1968); Herbert Marcuse, *Eros and Civilization* (New York, 1962), epilogue; Herbert Marcuse, "The Obsolescence of the Freudian Concept of Man," in *Five Lectures* (Boston, 1970); Theodor Adorno,

"Über den Fetischcharakter in der Musik und die Regression des Hörens," *Zeitschrift für Sozialforschung*, vol. 7 (1938), pp. 321–55; Theodor Adorno, *Minima Moralia* (London, 1974); Max Horkheimer, *The Eclipse of Reason* (New York, 1974); and Max Horkheimer and Theodor Adorno, *Dialectic of Enlightenment* (London, 1973). The theses of Horkheimer and Adorno in particular posit an altered personality type, formed no longer in accordance with the logic of the process of the internalization of patriarchal authority but, rather, through a complete conformity to a seamless web of external standards. This conformity is seen as induced by the unfettering of "primary instinctual wishes" upon which bureaucratic, capitalist totalitarianism in turn feeds. Aside from its latent patriarchalism (the emancipatory potential of the identification of the child with strong mothers is ignored), this argument leads to a self-contradictory theorem: The formation of the ego of "domination, command and organisation" (Horkheimer) through the internalization of patriarchal authority is posited as the only ground from which the maturing (boy) child's subsequent but ultimately *futile* rejection of this authority as illegitimate is possible (cf. Freud's allegory of the primary horde).

59 This distinction is outlined in Weber, *Economy and Society*, vol. 1, ch. 2, pp. 85–6 (see Essay 1).

60 Cf. the early suggestion of Paul A. Baran and Paul M. Sweezy, *Monopoly Capital* (Harmondsworth, 1969), p. 21: "The two parts of the economy – the world of the few hundred technically dynamic, massively capitalized and highly organized corporations on the one hand and of the thousands of small and traditional proprietors on the other – are very different. It is not a difference of degree but a difference which invades every aspect of economic organization and behaviour, including the motivation to effort itself." The absence of the state sector in this formulation is corrected by O'Connor, *The Fiscal Crisis of the State*, esp. ch. 1.

61 J. K. Galbraith, *The New Industrial State* (Harmondsworth, 1969).

62 See the respective discussions of the formation of stock companies in K. Marx, *Capital*, vol. 3 (Moscow, 1970), pp. 435–41, and of the thrust toward rational calculability in Max Weber, *General Economic History* (New York, 1966), esp. chs. 17, 22–30; cf. Weber, *The Protestant Ethic*, p. 76. The insights of both Marx and Weber upend the contemporary new liberal view that, by contrast with the bureaucratic collectivism of state activity, which cannot be checked through criteria of economic calculation, capitalist free enterprise ensures that each individual, freed from ties of personal dependence, will become the architect of his own fortune. Fictitious claims about the emergent "great historical conflict between individualism and collectivism" resulting from the spread of rigid state-initiated bureaucratic "meddling" with business are central in Ludwig von Mises, *Bureaucracy* (New Haven, 1962); and Frederick Hayek, *The Road to Serfdom* (London, 1944).

63 As a sample, see Gordon Wills, *Technological Forecasting* (Harmondsworth, 1972); and James Morrell, *Management Decisions and the Role of Forecasting* (Harmondsworth, 1972). The direct links between uncertainty and patterns of capital outlay were first emphasized by Keynes against Say's orthodoxy; more recently, see Galbraith, *The New Industrial State*, chs. 3–4.

64 Henri Lefebvre, *Everyday Life in the Modern World* (New York, 1971), ch. 2; cf. Stuart Ewen, *Captains of Consciousness: Advertising and the Social Roots of the Consumer Culture* (New York, 1976); William Leiss, *The Limits to Satisfaction: An Essay on the Problem of Needs and Commodities* (Toronto, 1976); and Michael B. Miller, *The Bon Marché: Bourgeois Culture and the Department Store, 1869–1920* (London, 1981).

65 J. S. Mill, "On Liberty," in *Essential Works of John Stuart Mill*, ed. Max Lerner (New York, 1961), p. 265.

66 Rudolf Hilferding, *Finance Capital: A Study of the Latest Phase of Capitalist Development*, ed. Tom Bottomore (London, 1981), pp. 360–1. The transition from a market-steered wages system to a "political" wage structure dependent upon trade union–corporate bargaining is a central theme of M. Kalecki, *Selected Essays on the Dynamics of the Capitalist Economy, 1933–1970* (Cambridge, 1971).

67 See Richard Edwards, *Contested Terrain* (London, 1979): and Claus Offe, *Industry and Inequality* (London, 1976); cf. Stanley Aronowitz, *False Promises* (New York, 1974), pp. 148–9, for some discussion of the famous 1892 Homestead Strike and the significance of employers' attempts to disrupt the functions of skilled workers; also important here is the argument of John Alt, "Beyond Class: The Decline of Industrial Labor and Leisure," *Telos*, no. 28 (Summer 1976), pp. 55—80.

68 Cf. Harry Braverman, *Labor and Monopoly Capital: The Degradation of Work in the Twentieth Century* (New York, 1974), pp. 124–5.

69 Neither the genealogy nor the difficulties of this expanded role of the state can be treated here. See Essay 3, and also Claus Offe, *Strukturprobleme des Kapitalistischen Staates* (Frankfurt am Main, 1972); Henri Lefebvre, *L'Etat dans le monde moderne* (Paris, 1976); and Gianfranco Poggi, *The Development of the Modern State* (Stanford, 1978), chs. 5–6.

70 O'Connor, *The Fiscal Crisis of the State*, ch. 6.

71 Hobbes, *Leviathan*, ch. 30, p. 386.

72 The following discussion relies heavily on C. B. Macpherson's theses on the transition from "market" to "quasi-market" society (*Democratic Theory: Essays in Retrieval* [Oxford, 1973], essay 6) and on Offe, *Strukturprobleme*, pp. 27–63.

73 *Two Treatises*, bk. 2, sec. 119. Equally enigmatic is Locke's contention (*Two Treatises*, bk. 2, secs. 73, 121–2) that sons are deemed to have given their political consent by virtue of their inheritance of their fathers' property, an inheritance that is guaranteed by civil law.

74 Most contemporary theorists of political consent and obligation continue to ignore the antinomies of this development. For example, and quite typically, Joseph Tussman (*Obligation and the Body Politic* [New York, 1960]) has insisted that liberal democracy is best understood as a system of voluntary association and obligation among autonomous citizens, at least some of whom ("child-bride citizens"), however, are necessarily governed without their consent.

75 Hannah Arendt, "Lying in Politics," in *Crises of the Republic* (New York, 1972).

76 Cf. Habermas, *Strukturwandel der Öffentlichkeit*, chs. 5–7; Alvin W. Gouldner, *The Dialectic of Ideology and Technology* (New York, 1976); Hans Magnus Enzensberger, *The Consciousness Industry* (New York, 1974); Hans Magnus Enzensberger, "Constituents of a Theory of the Media," in *Raids and Reconstructions* (London, 1976), pp. 20–53; and the candor of Joseph A. Schumpeter, *Capitalism, Socialism, and Democracy* (New York, 1942), p. 283: "The psycho-technics of party management and party advertising, slogans and marching tunes, are not accessories. They are the essence of politics. So is the political boss."

77 Although the enigmatic "benefits equal consent" argument is disavowed by Hobbes, it is early expressed by Locke in his discussion of inheritance (see note 73 to this essay). Antedating modernity, such *noblesse oblige* arguments resurfaced within the utilitarian and late nineteenth-century welfare liberal traditions. More recently, a version of the *noblesse oblige* thesis has been resurrected by John Rawls's *A Theory of Justice* (Cambridge, Mass., 1971), pp. 114–16, 344. His conclusion that the benefit-

receiving, "better-placed members of society" are obligated to the liberal democratic state relies upon the supplementary, but equally cryptic, proposition that the remainder of the constituents have a "natural duty" to obey, an obligation that "requires no voluntary acts in order to apply."

78 Concerning the emergence of forms of power that pride themselves on their life-enhancing capacities, see Michel Foucault, *The History of Sexuality* (New York, 1978), esp. pt. 5; and Michel Foucault, "Governmentality," *I and C*, no. 6 (Autumn 1979), pp. 5–21.

79 Several of the important interpretations of this corporatist development include Hilferding, *Finance Capital*; F. Pollock, "State Capitalism: Its Possibilities and Limitations," *Studies in Philosophy and Social Science*, vol. 9 (1941), pp. 200–25. Max Horkheimer, "The Authoritarian State," *Telos*, no. 15 (Spring 1973), pp. 3–20; Marcuse, *Negations*, pp. 3–42, Karl Korsch, "Capitalism and Planning," *Council Correspondence*, no. 4 (January 1935); Keith Middlemas, *Politics in Industrial Society* (London, 1979); Theda Skocpol, "Political Response to Capitalist Crisis: Neo-Marxist Theories of the State and the Case of the New Deal," *Politics and Society*, vol. 10, no. 2 (1980), pp. 155–202; and Charles S. Maier, *Recasting Bourgeois Europe* (Princeton, N.J., 1975). Rightist corporatism during this era of transition is discussed in Matthew Elbow, *French Corporative Theory, 1789–1948* (New York, 1953); and Ralph Bowen, *German Theories of the Corporative State, with Special Reference to the Period 1870–1919* (New York, 1947); its leftist versions are sketched in M. Beer, *A History of British Socialism* (London, 1953).

80 Cf. J. T. Winkler, "Corporatism," *European Journal of Sociology*, vol. 17 (1976), pp. 100–36; P. C. Schmitter, "Models of Interest Intermediation and Models of Societal Change in Western Europe," in P. C. Schmitter and G. Lehmbruch (eds.), *Trends toward Corporatism Intermediation* (Beverly Hills, Calif., 1979); and Theodore Lowi, *The End of Liberalism: Ideology, Policy, and the Crisis of Public Authority* (New York, 1969).

81 Winkler, "Corporatism," pp. 103–9.

82 The enforcement of "non-decisions" (Bachrach and Baratz) through processes of selectivity is analyzed in Claus Offe, "Structural Problems of the Capitalist State," *German Political Studies*, vol. 1 (1974), pp. 36ff.

83 Roberto Unger, *Law in Modern Society* (New York, 1976); Franz Neumann, "The Change in the Function of Law in Modern Society," in *The Democratic and the Authoritarian State*, ed. Herbert Marcuse (London, 1957); P. S. Atiyah, *The Rise and Fall of Freedom of Contract* (Oxford, 1979), esp. chs. 17–22.

84 The following discussion of the decay of family life pertains only to the fate of the *bourgeois* family form. Processes of development and decay of other household forms evidently display a different logic. On the subversion of the bourgeois patriarchal household, see Max Horkheimer, "Authority and the Family," in *Critical Theory* (New York, 1972), pp. 47–128; Frankfurt Institute for Social Research, *Aspects of Sociology* (London, 1973), ch. 9; Max Horkheimer, "Authoritarianism and the Family Today," in Ruth Nanda Anshen (ed.), *The Family: Its Function and Destiny* (New York, 1949); Alexander Mitscherlich, *Society without the Father* (London, 1969); and John Seeley's early but important discussion of the professional, bureaucratic appropriation of child rearing in "Parents – The Last Proletariat?" in *The Americanization of the Unconscious* (New York, 1967). This theme reappears in Donzelot, *The Policing of Families*; Jeffrey Weeks, *Sex, Politics and Society: The Regulation of Sexuality since 1800* (London, 1981); and a study of the "parental malaise" of the American family ("the sense of having no guidelines or supports for raising children, the feeling of not being in control as parents and the widespread sense of personal guilt for what seems to be going awry")

in Kenneth Keniston et al., *All Our Children: The American Family under Pressure* (New York, 1977).

85 Cf. Anthony Platt, *The Child Savers: The Invention of Delinquency* (Chicago, 1969); and Ivan Illich, *Medical Nemesis: The Expropriation of Health* (London, 1975). On the emergence of modern forms of punishment entangled within a corpus of regulatory techniques and normalizing legal and scientific discourse, see Michel Foucault, *Discipline and Punish: The Birth of the Prison* (London, 1977); and Michel Foucault, "About the Concept of the 'Dangerous Individual' in 19th Century Legal Psychiatry," *International Journal of Law and Psychiatry*, vol. 1, no. 1 (1978), pp. 1–16.

86 Christopher Lasch, *Haven in a Heartless World* (New York, 1977), esp. pp. 123–5, 167–89; Christopher Lasch, *The Culture of Narcissism* (New York, 1978); Christopher Lasch, "The Freudian Left and Cultural Revolution," *New Left Review*, no. 129 (1981), pp. 23–34. Cf. the somewhat different interpretations of this development by Sennett, *The Fall of Public Man*; and Daniel Bell, *The Cultural Contradictions of Capitalism* (New York, 1978). The reliance here upon Lasch's preliminary interpretation of the symptoms/pathological narcissistic personality type – an interpretation drawn in turn from the work of Kohut and Kernberg – should not be construed as a reliance upon the syncretism that is a consequence of Lasch's eclectic premises. His nostalgic (Freudian) theory of the indispensability of the classic bourgeois family form (its facilitation of that intense emotional involvement necessary for the reproduction of autonomous adults) severely underestimates the bourgeois household's historical specificity and unfreedom. The analytic subtlety of the original psychoanalytic insights tends to be lost; the argument also slips behind Horkheimer's uncompromising criticism of the thwarting of sisterly sensuousness and its *promesse de bonheur* by the *patriarchal* form of the bourgeois family (cf. "Authoritarianism and the Family Today"). Moreover, Lasch's argument displays an unthinking and nostalgic reliance on certain categories of orthodox historical materialism: Pathological narcissism is sometimes seen to "originate in changing modes of production," the state subversion of the old family form is usually interpreted as a *capitalist* strategy to commodify thoroughly the "worker's private life," etc. Structured by a considerable degree of theoretical ambivalence, the resulting analysis leads to political prescriptions marked by the sour melancholia that Lasch so despises. The "new ideas of sexual liberation" (oral sex, masturbation, homosexuality, feminism) are said to "spring from the prevailing fear of heterosexual passion, even of sexual intercourse itself," and the criticism of the bourgeois family by Keniston, Slater, Laing, Reich, and other "cultural revolutionaries" is said to be a blind affirmation of the strongest tendencies in late capitalist society. Notwithstanding this theoretical syncretism, Lasch's problematic interpretation remains a crucial starting point for grasping the significance of the decline of patriarchal authority and problems of ego development within middle-class households.

87 Lasch characteristically fails to distinguish the differential impact of these processes upon the anatomical sexes, a weakness that would need to be overcome in any plausible interpretation of what he calls the "narcissistic personality of our time."

88 Sigmund Freud, "Mourning and Melancholia," in *The Standard Edition of the Complete Psychological Works of Sigmund Freud*, ed. James Strachey (London, 1978), vol. 14, pp. 237–58.

89 Some discussions of this movement include Peter Steinfels, *The New Conservatives* (New York, 1977); M. M. Goldsmith and Michael Hawkins, "The New American Conservatism," *Political Studies*, vol. 20, no. 1 (1972), pp. 60–78; Philip Green, *The Pursuit of Inequality* (New York, 1981); James O'Connor, "Individualism" (Santa Cruz, unpub-

lished ms., 1981); and in the West German context, Claus Offe, "Neukonservative Klimakunde," *Merkur*, vol. 32 (1978), pp. 209–25.

90 Von Mises, *Bureaucracy*; Hayek, *The Road to Serfdom*; Milton Friedman, *Capitalism and Freedom* (Chicago, 1962).

91 Georg Simmel, " 'Individual' and Society in Eighteenth and Nineteenth Century Views on Life: An Example of Philosophical Sociology," in K. H. Wolff (ed.), *The Sociology of Georg Simmel* (Glencoe, Ill., 1950), pp. 78–83. More generally, see E. Durkheim, " 'Individualism' and the Intellectuals (1898)," *Political Studies*, vol. 17, no. 1 (1969), pp. 19–30; K. W. Swart, " 'Individualism' in the Mid-Nineteenth Century (1826–1860)," *Journal of the History of Ideas*, vol. 23 (1962), pp. 77–90; and Lukes, *Individualism*, pp. 11–12.

92 *Julie, ou la Nouvelle Héloise* (Paris, 1960), bk. 5, letter 2, p. 22; cf. J. J. Rousseau, *The Confessions* (Harmondsworth, 1971), p. 17: "I am made unlike anyone I have ever met; I will even venture to say that I am like no one in the whole world. I may be no better, but at least I am different." Reinterpreted through the category of social labor, this theory of cooperative individualism reappeared in the Marxian distinction between abstract, undifferentiated, bourgeois labor and the concrete labor of future communist society. Marx was adamant that bourgeois individualism was marked by a deep and enslaving irony: Individuality was impaired and liquidated when each Robinsonade individual greedily decided to shift for itself under social conditions that assumed the form of objective powers independent of interacting bodily individuals. The detail worker who has been reduced to a mere thinglike fragment under the capitalist mode of production was therefore to be replaced with "the fully-developed individual, fit for a variety of labors," a genuinely social individual whose "different social functions he performs are but so many modes of giving free scope to his own natural and acquired powers." In short, Marx envisaged free, social individuality, the appearance of universally developed individuals whose many-sided productive and consumptive capacities were to be secured and developed through the collective mastery of their social productive powers. See Marx, *Capital*, vol. 1, ch. 15, sec. 9; and Marx, *Grundrisse*, pp. 157–8 (where he distinguishes three historical periods, whose final and culminating stage was expected to emancipate "free individuality"), 161–2, 172–3, 325, 487–8, 540–2, 611, 652, 706–8, 712, 749, 831–2.

93 *The Social Contract and Discourses*, p. 16.

94 Letter 8, in J. J. Rousseau, *Oeuvres Complètes de J. J. Rousseau* (Paris, 1911), vol. 3, p. 227; in letter 6 Rousseau asks, "What more certain foundation can obligation among men have, than the free agreement of him who obliges himself?" Misunderstanding of this pathbreaking notion of free, moral individuality explains the continuing (and highly misleading) interpretations of Rousseau's political theory as "romantic collectivism" (Popper, Talmon, Crocker), as Lockean individualism (Bonald, Sée), or as simply confused (Morley, Barker). Particularly misleading is the insistence that Rousseau should be "given special responsibility for the emergence of totalitarianism" (J. W. Chapman, *Rousseau – Totalitarian or Liberal?* [New York, 1956], p. vii). Clearly, Rousseau is adamant that no individual is to be sacrificed physically by any government on behalf of the general will. Such an act, he says, would be "one of the most execrable rules tyranny ever invented, the greatest falsehood that can be advanced, the most dangerous admission that can be made, and a direct contradiction of the fundamental laws of society" (*The Social Contract and Discourses*, p. 248; cf. ibid., pp. 247–8). Rousseau is also convinced that when citizens either are forced or even promise to obey masters unconditionally, "the body politic has ceased to exist" (ibid., p. 20), and bodily individuals thereupon recover their right of natural liberty. Furthermore, Rousseau insists

upon a radical version of the liberal principle of the rule of law. Law must always be authorized by all and be equally applicable to all (ibid., pp. 25, 26, 85); the bureaucratic proliferation of law is seen as highly undesirable, reflecting the growth of the "corporate wills" of irresponsible states. Thus "the laws should be few in number. They should be well digested. They should, above all, be scrupulously obeyed" (*Political Writings*, ed. F. Watkins [Edinburgh, 1953], p. 223 [translation altered]). Finally, as Rousseau insists (in his self-defense against the Magistrates of Geneva) in letter 1 of the "Lettres écrites de la Montagne," the act of forcing individuals to live politically and in accordance with the principles of self-imposed obligation is synonymous with their being convinced through the force not of weapons but of good argument. Thus "an accuser must convince the accused before the judge. To be treated as a wrongdoer, it is necessary that I be convinced of being one."

95 *Emile* (London, 1972), p. 56. Compare his quip (in *The Social Contract and Discourses*, p. 241): "The first of all laws is to respect the laws."

96 *The Social Contract and Discourses*, p. 16; cf. also his critique of representation in ibid., bk. 3, ch. 15.

97 David Hume, "Of the Liberty of the Press," in *Political Essays*, p. 3.

98 Consider his typical insistence that "man should be strong and active; the woman should be weak and passive; the one must have both the power and the will; it is enough that the other should offer little resistance" (*Emile*, p. 322).

99 *The Social Contract and Discourses*, p. 17; cf. *The Social Contract and Discourses*, p. 254. This property clause is repeated in Rousseau's glowing description of the independence of small property holders in Switzerland in *Political Writings*, p. 295. It should also be noted that his practical proposals often seriously dilute this maxim – see, for example, ibid., p. 324.

100 *The Social Contract and Discourses*, bk. 4, ch. 1, pp. 108–9. As Jean Starobinski (*Jean-Jacques Rousseau: la transparence et l'obstacle* [Paris, 1957], pp. 1–10) has pointed out, Rousseau seeks to reassert "la transparence réciproque des consciences, la communication totale et confiante."

Index

331

Index

McCarthy, T., 136, 286n, 293n, 297–8n, 314n
Machiavelli, N., 113, 121–2, 132, 168, 287n
MacIver, R.M., 225, 296–7n, 319n
Mackinnon, W.A., 295n
Macpherson, C.B., 1, 270n, 283n, 287n, 295n, 320n, 322n, 326n
Maier, C.S., 277n, 295n, 327n
majority rule, 186–7, 257–8, *see also* disobedience
Mandel, E., 282n
Mandelbaum, K., 277n
Mandeville, B., 238, 323n
Mann, T., 182–3
Mannheim, K., 139–40, 285n, 293n
Mantoux, P., 313n
March, J.G., 270n
Marcuse, H., 8, 72, 83, 180–2, 193–4, 272n, 275n, 282–3n, 285n, 287n, 293n, 302n, 305–6n, 308n, 312n, 317–18n, 324n, 327n
marginality, 86–9, 98
Marglin, S., 313n
Mariana, 232
market relations, *see* commodification
Markus, G., 288n
Marramao, G., 260n
Marshall, A., 243
Marshall, G., 267n
Marshall, T.H., 260n
Marsilius of Padua, 78
Marx (Marxism), 28, 101, 180, 243, 273n, 278n, 290n, 291n
  abolition of distinction between state and civil society, 257
  analysis of value and commodity fetishism, 72–3, 86, 273n
  "barrack discipline," 207–8
  bureaucratic administration, 62, 63
  class-structured patterns of commodification, 80, 278n
  concept of social labor, 136, 139–40, 193
  critique of Hegel's theory of state, 97
  dialectic of forces and relations of production, 112–13, 126–33, 308n
  on freedom and necessity, 288–9n
  ideas of ruling class as ruling ideas, 226
  individualism, 229–30, 320n, 324n, 325n, 329n
  laboring activity, 245
  latent positivism, 291n
  on liberal capitalism, 280n
  mode of production, 120, 193, 273n

  modern bourgeois state, 38–9, 265n
  rate of profit, 81
  role of exploitation, 88
  scientization of capitalist accumulation, 309n
  technological Marxism, 312–13n
  theory of ideology, 168–72, 302n, 303n
mass media, *see* communications industry
Mayakovsky, 184
Mead, G.H., 299n
medical sciences, 217
Meek, R., 276n, 322n
Mehring, F., 259n
Mendelson, J., 294n
Menger, K., 51
Merleau-Ponty, M., 301n
Merton, R.K., 271n
Mesthene, E., 199, 310n
Meyer, G., 277n
Michels, R., 272n
Middlemas, K., 28, 261n, 295n, 327n
Milde, U., 281n
Miliband, R., 25, 226, 320n
militarism, 40–2, 83, 88, 109, 182–3, 185, 257, 264n
Mill, J.S., 3, 92, 94, 271n, 324n, 326n
Millar, J., 322n
Millar, M.B., 325n
Mills, C.W., 93, 281n, 294n
Mises, L. von, 325n, 329n
Misgeld, D., 294n
Mitscherlich, A., 166, 327n
modernization, 77–80, 104–5, 111–12, 118–20, 139–45, 148–9, 191–3, 221, 224–5, 275n
modern state, 38–42, 55–6, 78–9, 96–100, 111–12, 122, 234–7, 265n, 267n, 275–6n
Mommsen, W., 264n, 269–70n, 319n
Monod, J., 221, 317n
Morris, C., 300n, 320n
Mosely, J., 295n
Mueller, C., 302n
Müller, G., 277–8n
Müller, W., 84, 260n, 278n
Musson, A.E., 309n
Myrdal, G., 260n

Nagel, E., 26–7, 211
narcissism, 251–2, 328n
Narr, W.-D., 279n, 282n
nation state, *see* modern state
nationalism, 110, 182, 233, 284n
natural law, 122, 196, 237, 275–6n, 283n